PRESARGONIC PERIOD

(2700–2350 BC)

Volumes Published

ASSYRIAN PERIODS

1 Assyrian Rulers of the Third and Second Millennia BC (TO 1115 BC)
A. KIRK GRAYSON

2 Assyrian Rulers of the Early First Millennium BC I (1114–859 BC)
A. KIRK GRAYSON

3 Assyrian Rulers of the Early First Millennium BC II (858–745 BC)
A. KIRK GRAYSON

BABYLONIAN PERIODS

2 Rulers of Babylonia: From the Second Dynasty of Isin to the End of Assyrian Domination (1157–612 BC)
GRANT FRAME

EARLY PERIODS

1 Presargonic Period (2700–2350 BC)
DOUGLAS FRAYNE

2 Sargonic and Gutian Periods (2334–2113 BC)
DOUGLAS FRAYNE

3/1 Gudea and His Dynasty
DIETZ O. EDZARD

3/2 Ur III Period (2112–2004 BC)
DOUGLAS FRAYNE

4 Old Babylonian Period (2003–1595 BC)
DOUGLAS FRAYNE

SUPPLEMENTS

1 Royal Inscriptions on Clay Cones from Ashur Now in Istanbul
V. DONBAZ and A. KIRK GRAYSON

THE ROYAL INSCRIPTIONS OF MESOPOTAMIA

EARLY PERIODS / VOLUME 1

Presargonic Period

(2700–2350 BC)

DOUGLAS R. FRAYNE

UNIVERSITY OF TORONTO PRESS

Toronto Buffalo London

Toronto Buffalo London
utorontopress.com

Reprinted in paperback 2021

ISBN 978-0-8020-3586-8 (cloth)
ISBN 978-1-4875-4513-0 (paper)

Cataloguing in Publication information available from
Library and Archives Canada

The research and publication of this volume have been supported by the Social Sciences and Humanities Research Council of Canada and the University of Toronto.

University of Toronto Press acknowledges the financial assistance to its publishing program of the Canada Council for the Arts and the Ontario Arts Council, an agency of the Government of Ontario.

Funded by the Government of Canada
Financé par le gouvernement du Canada

In Memory of My Father
Ralph Waldo Frayne
1919–2003

Contents

Preface

This volume completes (with the exception of the indexes and additions and corrections), the Early Periods section of the Royal Inscriptions of Mesopotamia Project.

I have been aided in this work by numerous individuals and institutions; I would like to acknowledge their assistance here and give a brief work history of this volume.

First, I must thank Kirk Grayson, who first conceived and then procured funding for the RIM project; Kirk offered me my first (and only) job in Assyriology at the University of Toronto for which I will be eternally grateful. Indeed, Kirk and I started up the project on July 1, 1979 with one typewriter, one book, and with the uncertain promise of future funding.

I must thank the Social Science Humanities Council of Canada's for their support of this project over the numerous years I would also like to acknowledge the support of Lawrence Schiff who helped us out with very considerable financial assistance during a period of funding shortfall.

Funding problems to some extent delayed the appearance of this volume. For the anticipated readers who have patiently waited for this volume I express my apologies.

Research for this volume was carried out in various institutions around the world. An effort was made to collate every object where possible. Unfortunately, logistical problems prevented collation work in Turkey and Iraq.

Starting with my European colleagues, I would like to thank Christopher Walker for full access to materials in the British Museum and for his kind hospitality in London at the Student's Room (in August 1997). Béatrice Andre-Salvini was unstinting in her assistance at the Départment des Antiquités Orientales at the Louvre (during August 1997). Horst and Evelyn Klengel and Joachim Marzahn were very hospitable and helpful to me during my stay in Berlin (in July 1997) for collations at the Vorderasiatisches Museum.

Various institutions in North America have also opened their doors to me. Piotr Steinkeller and James Armstrong of the Harvard Semitic Museum enabled me to collate objects there (in October 1997). William Hallo and Ulla Kasten made the treasures of the Yale Babylonian collection available for my studies (in September 1997). Åke Sjöberg and Steven Tinney made the tablet room of the University Museum in Philadelphia a kind of second home to me (during October 1997). John Brinkman and Ray Tindel made it possible for me to examine objects in the Oriental Institute of the University of Chicago (in February 1997).

I must express my sincere thanks to Piotr Steinkeller (readers' report July 30, 1999), Miguel Civil (readers' report July 10, 1999) and Gebhard Selz (readers' report August 24, 1999) who served as readers for this volume. In addition, Jerold Cooper (in an e-mail dated February 4, 2001) kindly sent me a number of corrections, suggestions and added bibliography.

My first draft, which was written in great haste in 1998 after my collation trips, was able to carefully include all the collations from my various trips but unfortunately not all the relevant bibliographical material, especially the extensive notes found in Selz, Untersuchungen zur Götterwelt des altsumerischen Stadtstaates von Lagaš nor (because of staff shortfalls) was the volume adequately proofread. It had to be submitted to reach an unavoidable funding deadline in our RIM production schedule. Civil's frank assessment — "a through revision is absolutely essential before publication" was valid, and heeded, and work recommenced in late 1999 and 2000 on a new draft. I regret that the complete rewriting of the manuscript has delayed the appearance of the volume but it was thoroughly necessary. I have tried in this second version to incorporate and harmonize all the comments of the various readers as best I could; this has often been a difficult task because of divergent view of the reviewers. In particular, the understanding of the rulers names of the Presargonic rulers of Lagaš has been particularly problematic; in general I have followed the conclusions of Selz in this regard.

Furthermore, during the course of the production of this manuscript, on the advice and encouragement of our department chairman, funding was obtained by the author from the Social Sciences and Humanities Research Council of Canada to begin work on the Toronto Atlas of the Ancient Near East in 2003, and this considerable work necessarily slowed the completion of RIME 1. However, on a more positive note, the results of the research of that project have, in many cases been incorporated into this volume. It is hoped that the suggestions for the locations of the place names offered in this volume will stimulate further discussion of this important topic. I was not able to incorporate Giovanni Pettinato's recent *I re di Sumer* I in the bibliography of this volume.

Other scholars have kindly offered new or unpublished material; I would to single out Michael Müller-Karpe for some articles on inscriptions from Ur and Dominique Beyer for articles dealing with seal inscriptions from Mari. Also G. Marchesi kindly sent me an article on the kings of Ur and offered other valuable suggestions. Others who helped me but who are inadvertently unacknowledged here are thanked.

It goes without saying that all errors and omissions in this volume are the responsibility of the author alone.

The preparation of a manuscript as camera-ready copy can be an arduous experience and I can honestly say without the constant assistance and support of my computer savy assistant Tom Smyth this volume would not have appeared.

To Barbara Porter of the University of Toronto Press, the editor who carefully proofread the manuscript and who had to deal with my numerous publication delays I express my sincere thanks for her patience.

My friend Johanna Stuckey, Professor Emerita of York University, Toronto proofread the manuscript. Her constant encouragement kept the project alive for me and I cannot thank her enough for her unstinting support.

This volume is dedicated to the memory of my father whose constant unflagging support of myself and my younger sister (throughout her medical woes) cannot begin to be expressed here. His support of family, church and community was truly inspirational to me. May he rest in well deserved Toronto

April 13, 2007 D.R.F.

Bibliographical Abbreviations

AANL	Atti dell' Accademia Nazionale dei Lincei. GN, YY-
AfK	Archiv für Keilschriftforschung, vols. 1-2. Berlin, 1923-25
AfO	Archiv für Orientforschung, vol. 3- (vol. 1-2 = AfK). Berlin, Graz, and Horn, 1926-
AJ	The Antiquaries Journal, Being the Journal of the Society of Antiquaries of London. London, 1921-
AJA	American Journal of Archaeology. Boston, Concord, and Princeton, 1885-
AJSL	American Journal of Semitic Languages and Literatures. Chicago, 1884-1941
Allotte de la Füye, DP	F.-M. Allotte de la Füye, Documents présargoniques. Paris, 1908-1920
Amiet, Art	P. Amiet, Art of the Ancient Near East. New York, 1980
Amiet, Glyptique	P. Amiet, La Glyptique Mésopotamienne archaïque, Paris, 1980
Amiet, L'art d'Agadé	P. Amiet, L'art d'Agadé au Musée du Louvre. Paris, 1976
Amtl. Ber.	Amtliche Berichte. ?
André-Leicknam, Naissance de l'écriture	B. André-Leicknam, Naissance de l'écriture cunéiformes et hiéroglyphes, 4e édition. Paris, 1982
AnOr	Analecta Orientalia. Rome, 1931-
AO	Alte Orient, vols. 1-16. Leipzig, 1925-43
AOAT	Alter Orient und Altes Testament. Neukirchen-Vluyn, 1968-
AOS	American Oriental Series. New Haven, 1935-
Archi, ARES 1	A. Archi, Eblaite Personal Names and Semitic Name-Giving. Papers of a Symposium held in Rome, July 15-17, 1985 (=ARES 1). Rome, 1988
Archi, ARET 7	A. Archi, Testi Amministrativi: Registrazioni di metalli e tessuti (Archivio L. 2769) (=ARET 7). Rome, 1988
ARES	Archivi Reali di Ebla Studi . Rome, 1988-
ARET	Archivi Reali di Ebla Testi . Rome, 1985-
ARM	Archives royales de Mari. Paris, 1946-
ARMT	Archives royales de Mari, textes transcrits et traduits. Paris, 1950-
ArOr	Archiv Orientální. Prague, 1930-
ARRIM	Annual Review of the Royal Inscriptions of Mesopotamia Project. Toronto, 1983-91
AS	Assyriological Studies. Chicago, 1931-
ASJ	Acta Sumerologica. Hiroshima, 1979-
Babelon, Manuel	E. Babelon, Manuel d'archéologie orientale. London, 1888
Bagh. For.	Baghdader Forschungen. Mainz am Rhein, 1979-
Bagh. Mitt.	Baghdader Mitteilungen. Berlin, 1960-
Banks, Bismya	E.J. Banks, Bismya, or the Lost City of Adab. New York and London, 1912
Barton, RISA	G.A. Barton, The Royal Inscriptions of Sumer and Akkad (=Library of Ancient Semitic Inscriptions 1). New Haven, 1929
BASOR	Bulletin of the American Schools of Oriental Research. New Haven, 1919-
BE	Babylonian Expedition of the University of Pennsylvania, Series A: Cuneiform Texts, vols. 1-14. Philadephia, 1893-1914
Beek, Atlas	M.A. Beek, Atlas of Mesopotamia. London and Edinburgh, 1962
Beek, Bildatlas	M.A. Beek, Bildatlas der assyrisch-babylonischen Kultur. Gütersloh, 1961
BibMes	Bibliotheca Mesopotamica. Primary sources and interpretive analyses for the study of Mesopotamia civilization and its influences from late prehistory to the end of the cuneiform tradition. Malibu, 1975-
Biggs, Abu¢ Ùala¢b®kh	R.D. Biggs, Inscriptions from Tell Abu¢ Íala¢b®kh (=OIP 99). Chicago, 1974
Biggs, Al-Hiba	R.D. Biggs, Inscriptions from Al-Hiba-Lagash: The First and Second Seasons (=BibMes 3). Malibu, 1976
BIN	Babylonian Inscriptions in the Collection of J.B. Nies. New Haven, 1917-
BiOr	Bibliotheca Orientalis. Leiden, 1943-

Birot, ARMT 16/1	M. Birot, J.-R. Kupper, and O. Rounault, Répertoire analytique (2e volume) des tomes I-XIV, XVIII et textes divers Hors-collection: Première Partie Nomes propres (=ARMT 16/1). Paris, 1979
BJVF	Berliner Jahrbuch für Vor-und Frühgeschichte. Berlin, 1961-
BMAH	Bulletin des Musée Royaux d'Art et d'Histoire. Brussels, 1901-
BM Guide 1922	British Museum. A Guide o the Babylonian and Assyrian Antiquities, 2nd edition. London, 1922
BMQ	British Museum Quarterly, vols. 1-37. London, 1926-73
BNYPL	Bulletin of the New York Public Library. New York, 1897-
Börker-Klähn, Bildstelen	J. Börker-Klähn, Altvorderasiatische Bildstelen und Vergleichbare Felsreliefs (=Bagh. For. 4). Mainz am Rhein, 1982
Boese, Weihplatten	J. Boese, Altmesopotamische Weihplatten, Eine sumerische Denkmalsgattung des 3. Jahrtausends v. Chr. (=Untersuchungen zur Assyriologie und Vorderasiatischen Archäologie 6). Berlin and New York, 1971
Borger, HKL	R. Borger, Handbuch der Keilschriftliteratur, 3 vols. Berlin, 1967-75
Braun-Holzinger, Beterstatuetten	E.A. Braun-Holzinger, Frühdynastische Beterstatuetten (=Abhandlungen der Deutschen Orient-Gesellschaft 19). Berlin, 1977
Braun-Holzinger, Weihgaben	E.A. Braun-Holzinger, Mesopotamische Weihgaben der frühdynastischen bis altbabylonischen Zeit (=HSAO 3). Heidelberg, 1991
BRM	Babylonian Records in the Library of J. Pierpont Morgan, 4 vols. New Haven, New York, 1912-23
Buccellati and Biggs, AS 17	G. Buccellati and R.D. Biggs, Cuneiform Texts from Nippur, the Eighth and Ninth Seasons (= AS 17). Chicago, 1969
van Buren, Foundation Figurines	E.D. van Buren, Foundation Figurines and Offerings. Berlin, 1931
CAH	I.E.S. Edwards, C.J. Gadd, N.G.L. Hammond, et al. (eds.), The Cambridge Ancient History, 2nd and 3rd editions. Cambridge, 1970-
CAH 1/1	I.E.S. Edwards, C.J. Gadd, and N.G.L. Hammond (eds.), Prolegomena and Prehistory, 3rd edition (=CAH 1/1). Cambridge, 1970
CAH 1/2	I.E.S. Edwards, C.J. Gadd, and N.G.L. Hammond (eds.), Early History of the Middle East, 3rd edition (=CAH 1/2). Cambridge, 1971
Cavigneaux, Zeichenlisten	
Christian, Altertumskunde	V. Christian, Altertumskunde des Zweitromslandes von der Vorzeit bis zum Ende der Achämenidenherrschaft 1. Leipzig, 1940
Clay, BRM 4	A. Clay, Epics, Hymns, Omens, and Other Texts (=BRM 4). New Haven, 1923
Clay, YOS 1	A. Clay, Miscellaneous Inscriptions in the Yale Babylonian Collection. New Haven, 1915
de Clercq, Collection	H.F.X. de Clercq and J. Ménant, Collection de Clercq, catalogue méthodique et raisonné, antiquités assyriennes, cylinders orientaux, cachets, briques, bronzes, bas-reliefs etc., 2 vols. Paris, 1888/1903
Contenau, Manuel	G. Contenau, Manuel d'archéologie orientale depuis les origines jusqu'à l'époque d'Alexandre, 4 vols. Paris, 1927-47
Contenau, Monuments	G. Contenau, Monuments mésopotamiens nouvellement acquis ou peu connus. Paris, 1934
Cooper, Curse	J.S. Cooper, The Curse of Agade. Baltimore and London, 1983
Cooper, SANE 2/1	J.S. Cooper, Reconstructing History from Ancient Inscriptions: The Lagash-Umma Border Conflict (=SANE 2/1). Malibu, 1983
Cooper, SARI 1	J.S. Cooper, Sumerian and Akkadian Royal Inscriptions I: Presargonic Inscriptions (=The American Oriental Society Translation Series 1). New Haven, 1986
CRAIB	Comptes-rendus des séances de l'académie des inscriptions et belles-lettres. Paris, 1857-
Cros, Tello	G. Cros, Nouvelles fouilles de Tello, Mission française de Chaldée. Paris, 1910
CRRA	Compte Rendu de la Rencontre Assyriologique Internationale. [various locations], 1950-
CRRA 15	J.-R. Kupper (ed.), La civilisation de Mari, Liège, 1966 (=Les Congrès et colloques de l'Université de Liège 42, =Bibliothèque de la Faculté de Philosophie et Lettres de l'Université de Liège 172). Paris, 1967
CT	Cuneiform Texts from Babylonian Tablets in the British Museum. London, 1896-
Deimel, AnOr 2	P.A. Deimel, ſumerische Tempelwirtschaft zur Zeit Urkaginas und seiner Vorgänger (=AnOr 2). Rome, 1931
Delougaz, Temple Oval	P. Delougaz and T. Jacobsen, The Temple Oval at Khafa¢jah (= OIP 53). Chicago, 1940
Delougaz, Pre-Sargonid Temples	P. Delougaz, S. Lloyd, H. Frankfort, and T. Jacobsen, Pre-Sargonid Temples in the Diyala Region (=OIP 58). Chicago, 1942
Durand (ed.), Amurru 1	J.-M Durand (ed.), Mari, E¿bla et les Hourrites dix ans de travaux. Première parte, Actes du colloque international (Paris, mai 1993) (=Amurru 1). Paris, 1996

DV	Drevnosti Vosto√nyja, Trudy Vosto√noj Kommissii Imperatorskago Moskovskogo Archeologi√eskago Obß√estva. Moscow, 1889-
Edzard, Rechtsurkunden	D.O. Edzard, Sumerische Rechtsurkunden des III. Jahrtausends aus der Zeit vor der III. Dynastie von Ur. Munich, 1968
Eilers Festschrift	G. Wiessner, Festschrift für Wilhelm Eilers. Ein Dokument der internationalen Forschung zum 27. Sept. 1966. Wiesbaden Harrassowitz, 1967.
Ellis, Foundation Deposits	R.S. Ellis, Foundation Deposits in Ancient Mesopotamia (=YNER 2). New Haven and London, 1968
Falkenstein, Inschriften Gudeas	A. Falkenstein, Die Inschriften Gudeas von Lagaß 1. Einleitung (=AnOr 30). Rome, 1966
FAOS	Freiburger altorientalische Studien. Wiesbanden and Stuttgart, 1975-
Frankfort, Art and Architecture	H. Frankfort, The Art and Architecture of the Ancient Orient. Harmondsworth and Middlesex (paperback edition), 1970
Frayne, Early Dynastic List	D.R. Frayne, The Early Dynastic List of Geographical Names (=AOS 74). New Haven, 1992
Frayne, RIME 2	D.R. Frayne, Sargonic and Gutian Periods (2334-2113 BC) (=RIME 2). Toronto, 1993
Frayne, RIME 3/2	D.R. Frayne, Ur III Period (2112-2004 BC) (=RIME 3/2). Toronto, 1997
Gadd, Reading-book	C.J. Gadd, A Sumerian Reading-book. Oxford, 1924
Gadd, UET 1	C.J. Gadd, L. Legrain, and S. Smith, Royal Inscriptions. London (=UET 1), 1928
Garbini, Statuaria	G. Garbini, Le origini della statuaria sumerica (=Serie Archeologica 3). Rome, 1962
Gelb, Land Tenure	I.J. Gelb, P. Steinkeller and R.M. Whiting Jr., Earliest Land Tenue Systems in the Near East: Ancient Kudurrus (=OIP 104). Chicago, 1991
Gelb and Kienast, Königinschriften	I.J. Gelb and B. Kienast, Die Altakkadischen Königinschriften des dritten Jahrtausends v. Chr. (=FAOS 7). Stuttgart, 1990
Gelb, MAD 2^{2}	I.J. Gelb, Old Akkadian Writing and Grammar, 2nd edition (=MAD 2^{2}). Chicago, 1961
Gelb, MAD 3	I.J. Gelb, Glossary of Old Akkadian (=MAD 3). Chicago, 1957
de Genouillac, FT	H. de Genouillac, Fouilles de Telloh, 2 vols. Paris, 1934-36
de Genouillac, TCL 15	H. de Genouillac, Textes religeiux sumériens du Louvre (= TCL 15). Paris, 1930
George, House Most High	A.R. George, House Most High: The Temples of Ancient Mesopotamia (=Mesopotamian Civilizations 5). Winona Lake, Indiana, 1993
Gordon, Eblailica 2	C.H. Gordon and G.A. Rendsburg (eds.), Eblaitica: Essays on the Ebla Archives and the Eblaite Language, vol. 3. Winona Lake, Indian, 1990
Gordon, Eblailica 3	C.H. Gordon and G.A. Rendsburg (eds.), Eblaitica: Essays on the Ebla Archives and the Eblaite Language, vol. 3. Winona Lake, Indiana, 1992
Grégoire, Lagash	J.-P. Grégoire, La province méridionale de l'état de Lagash. Luxemburg, 1962
Grégoire, MVN 10	J.-P. Grégoire, Inscriptions et archives administrative cunéiformes, 1e partie (=MVN 10). Rome, 1981
Gressmann (ed.), ABAT^{2}	H. Gressmann (ed.), Altorientalische Bilder zum Alten Testament, 2nd edition. Berlin and Leipzig, 1926
Hackman, BIN 8	G.G. Hackman, Sumerian and Akkadian Administrative Texts from Predynastic Times to the End of the Akkad Dynasty (=BIN 8). New Haven, 1958
Hall, UE 1	H.R. Hall, C.L. Woolley, C.J. Gadd, and A. Keith, Al-^{a}Ubaid. A Report on the Work Carried Out at Al-^{a}Ubaid for the British Museum in 1919 and for the Joint Expedition in 1922-3 (=UE 1). Oxford, 1927
Hallo, Royal Titles	W.W. Hallo, Early Mesopotamian Royal Titles: a Philologic and Historical Analysis (=AOS 43). New Haven, 1957
Heuzey, Villa royale	L. Heuzey, Une villa royale chaldéenne vers l'an 4000 avant notre ère d'apres les levés et les notes M. de Sarzec. Paris, 1900
Heuzey, Catalogue Louvre	L. Heuzey, Cataolgue des antiquités chaldéennes, sculpture et gravure à la pointe. Paris, 1902
Heuzey, Armoires	L. Heuzey, ???
Heuzey and Thureau-Dagin, Restitution	L. Heuzey and F. Thureau-Dagin, La restitution metérielle de la Stèle des Voutours. Paris, 1909.
Hilprecht, BE 1	H.V. Hilprecht, Old Babylonian Inscriptions Chiefly from Nippur (=BE 1), 2 vols. Philadelphia, 1893/96
Hommel, Geschichte	F. Hommel, Geschichte Babyloniens und Assyriens. Berlin, (1885-) 1888
Hrouda, Vorderasien 1	B. Hrouda, Vorderasien 1: Mesopotamien, Babylonien, Iran und Anatolien. Handbuch der Archäologie. Munich, 1971
HSAO	Heidelberger Studien zum Alten Orient. Heidelberg, 1986-
IEJ	Israel Exploration Journal.. Jerusalem, 1950/51-
ILN	Illustrated London News. London, 1842-
Iraq Museum Guide	Anonymous, A Guide to the Iraq Museum Collections. Baghdad, 1942
Iraq Museum Guide	Anonymous, Guide-Book to the Iraq Museum. Baghdad, 1966

JAC	Journal of Ancient Civilizations. Changchun, 1986-
Jacobsen, SKL	T. Jacobsen, The Sumerian King List (=AS 11). Chicago, 1939
JAOS	Journal of the American Oriental Society. New Haven, 1893-
JCS	Journal of Cuneiform Studies. New Haven and Cambridge, Mass., 1947-
JEOL	Jaarbericht van het Vooraziatisch-Egyptisch Genootschap "Ex Oriente Lux", vols. 1-25. Leiden, 1933-78
Jeremias, HAOG^2	A. Jeremias, Handbuch der altorientalischen Geisteskultur, 2nd edition. Berlin and Leipzig, 1929
JESHO	Journal of the Economic and Social History of the Orient. Leiden, 1957-
Jestin, TSÍ	R. Jestin, Tablettes sumériennes de Íuruppak conservèes au Musée de Stamboul. Paris, 1937
JHS	Journal of Hellenic Studies. London, 1880-
JNES	Journal of Near Eastern Studies. Chicago, 1942-
JRAS	Journal of the Royal Asiatic Society. London, 1834-
JSOR	Journal of the Society of Oriental Research, vols. 1-16. Chicago and Toronto, 1917-32
JSS	Journal of Semitic Studies. Manchester, 1956-
Keiser, BIN 2	C.E. Keiser and J.B. Nies, Historical, Religious and Economic Texts and Antiquities (=BIN 2). New Haven, 1920
Keiser, BRM 3	C.E. Keiser, Cuneiform Bullae of the Third Millennium B.C. (=BRM 3). New York, 1914
King, Early History	L.W. King, A History of Sumer and Akkad: An Account of the Early Races of Babylonia from Prehistoric Times to the Foundation of the Babylonian Monarchy. London, 1910
King, History	L.W. King, A History of Babylon from the Foundation of the Monarchy to the Persian Conquest. London, 1915
Kramer Anniversary	B.L. Eichler (ed.), Kramer Anniversary Volume: Cuneiform Studies in Honor of Samuel Noah Kramer (=AOAT 25). Neukirchen-Vluyn, 1976
Kramer, FTS	S.N. Kramer, From the Tablets of Sumer. Twenty-five Firsts in Man's Recorded History. Indian Hills, 1956
Kramer, Sumerians	S.N. Kramer, The Sumerians: Their History, Culture and Character. Chicago and London, 1963
Langdon, Kish	S. Langdon and L. Watelin, Excavations at Kish, the Hebert Weld and Field Museum of Natural History Expedition to Mesopotamia, 4 vols. Paris, 1924-34
Larsen (ed.), Power	M.T. Larsen (ed.), Power and Propaganda: A symposium on Ancient Empires (=Mesopotamia 7). Copenhagen, 1979
Legrain, PBS 15	L. Legrain, Royal Inscriptions and Fragments from Nippur and Babylon (=PBS 15). Philadelphia, 1926
Legrain, UE 3	L. Legrain, Archaic Seal-impressions. London and Philadelphia, 1936
Lehmann, BAFSL	G. Lehmann, Bibliographie der archäologischen Fundstellen und Surveys in Syrien und Libanon (=Orient-Archäologie / Deutsches Archäologisches Institut, Orient-Abteilung; Bd. 9). Rahden, Germany, 2002.
Lenzen, UVB 16	H. Lenzen, H. Schmid, U. Schaefer, A.N. Haller, and J. van Dijk, Vorläufiger Bericht über die von dem Deutschen Archäologischen Institut und der Deutschen Orient-Gesellschaft aus Mitteln der Deutschen Forschungsgemeinschaft unternommenen Ausgrabungen in Uruk-Warka (=UVB 16). Berlin, 1960
Lich√ev, DBPÍ	N. Licha√ev, Drevneyßiya bully i pe√aty Íirpurly (= Mém. de la section class. de la. Soc. imp. russe d'archéologie 4). St. Petersberg, 1907
Liverani (ed.), Akkad	M. Liverani, Akkad the First World Empire:Structure, Ideology, Traditions. Padova, 1993
Longman, Autobiography	T. Longman III, Fictional Akkadian Autobiography: A Generic and Comparative Study. Winona Lake, Indiana, 1991
Luckenbill, Adab	D.D. Luckenbill, Inscriptions from Adab (=OIP 14). Chicago, 1930
MacKay, Kish	E. MacKay Report on the excavation of the "A" cemetery at Kish, Mesopotamia 1 (=Field Museum of Natural History, Anthropology, Memoirs). Chicago, 1925
MAD	Materials for the Assyrian Dictionary. Chicago, 1952-
MAM	Mission Archéologique de Mari
MAOG	Mitteilungen der Alterorientalischen Gesellschaft, vols. 1-43. Leipzig, 1901-45
MARI	Mari, Annales de Recherches Interdisciplinaires. Paris, 1982-
Maspero, Histoire	G. Maspero, Histoire ancienne des peoples de l'Orient classique, 3 vols. Paris, 1895-99
MEE	Materiali Epigrafici di Ebla, vols. 1-4. Naples, 1979-82
Messerschmidt, VAS 1	L. Messerschmidt and A. Ungnad, Vorderasiatische Schriftdenkmäler der königlichen Museen zu Berlin 1 (=VAS 1). Leipzig, 1907
G.R. Meyer, Altorientalische Denkmäler	G.R. Meyer, Altorientalische Denkmäler im Vorderasiatischen Museum zu Berlin. Leipzig, 1965

de Meyer, Tell ed-De¢r 3	L. de Meyer (ed.), Tell ed-De¢r: Soundings at Abu¢ Habbah (Sippar). Louvain, 1980
MJ	Museum Journal of the University Museum, University of Pennsylvania, vols. 1-24. Philadelphia, 1910-35
Moorey, Kish Excavations	P.R.S. Moorey, Kish Excavations 1923-33 with a Microfiche Cataoluge of the Objects in Oxford Excavated by the Oxford-Field Museum, Chicago, Expedition to Kish in Iraq. Oxford, 1978
Moortgat Festschrift	K. Bittel, E. Heinrich, B. Hrouda, and W. Nagel (eds.), Vorderasiatische Archäologie. Studien und Aufsätze Anton Moortgat zum fünfundsechzigsten Geburtstag gewidmet von Kollegen, Freunden und Schülern. Berlin, 1964
Moortgat, Kunst	A. Moortgat, Die Kunst der alten Mesopotamien. Die klassische Kunst Vorderasiens. Cologne, 1967
MSL	B. Landsberger, et al. (eds.), Materials for the Sumerian Lexicon. Rome, 1937-
MVAG	Mitteilungen der Vorderasiatisch-Aegyptischen Gesellschaft, vols. 1-44. Berlin and Leipzig, 1896-1939
MVN	Materiali per il vocabolario neosumerico. Rome, 1974-
NABU	Nouvelles assyriologiques brèves et utilitaires. Paris, 1987-
Nissen, Königsfriedhofes	H.J. Nissen, Zur Datierung des Königsfriedhofes von Ur, unter besonderer Berücksichtgung der Stratigraphie der Privatgräber (= Beiträge zur Ur- und Frühgeschlichlichen archäologie des Mittelmeer-Kulturraumes 3). Bonn, 1966
OIP	Oriental Institute Publications. Chicago, 1924-
OLZ	Orientalistische Literaturzeitung. Berlin and Leipzig, 1898-
OrAnt	Oriens Antiquus, Rivista del Centro per le Antichità e la Storia dell'Arte del Vicino Oriente. Rome, 1962-
Orthmann (ed.), Der alte Orient	W. Orthmann (ed.), Der alte Orient (=Propyläen Kunstgeschichte 14). Berlin, 1975
Parrot, MAM 1	A. Parrot, Le temple d'Ishtar (=MAM 1). Paris, 1956
Parrot, MAM 3	A. Parrot, Les temples d'Ishtarat et de Ninni-zaza (=MAM 3). Paris 1967
Parrot, MAM 4	A. Parrot, Le «Trésor» d'Ur (=MAM 4). Paris, 1968
Parrot, Mari	A. Parrot, Mari, capitale fabulese. Paris, 1974
Parrot, Tello	A. Parrot, Tello, vingt campagnes de fouilles (1877-1933). Paris, 1948
PBS	Publications of the Babylonian Section, University Museum, University of Pennsylvania, 15 vols. Philadelphia, 1911-26
Perrot and Chipiez, Chaldée et Assyrie	G. Perrot and C. Chipiez, Histoire de l'art dans l'antiquité, tome 2: Chaldée et Assyrie. Paris, 1884
Pettinato, Ebla	G. Pettinato, The Archives of Ebla: An Empire Inscribed in Clay. Garden City, 1981
Pettinato, MEE 1	G. Pettinato, Catalogo del Testi Cuneiform di Tell Mardikh-Ebla (=MEE 1). Naples, 1979
Pettinato, MEE 3	G. Pettinato, Testi lessicali monolingui della biblioteca L. 2769 (=MEE 3). Naples, 1981
PICO	?
Poebel, BE 6/2	A. Poebel, Babylonian Legal and Business Documents from the Time of the First Dynasty of Babylon, Chiefly from Nippur (=BE 6/2). Philadelphia, 1909
Poebel, PBS 4/1	A. Poebel, Historical Texts (=PBS 4/1). Philadelphia, 1914
Poebel, PBS 5	A. Poebel, Historical and Grammatical Texts (=PBS 5). Philadelphia, 1914
Pomponio, EDTS	F. Pomponio and G. Viscicato, Early Dynastic Adminstrative Tablets of Íurupal. Naples, 1994
Pomponio, Prosopografia	F. Pomponio, La Prosopografia dei testi presargonici di Fara. Rome, 1987
Potratz, Kunst	?. Potratz, Die Kunst des Alten Orient, ?, 1961
Pritchard, ANEP[2]	J.B. Pritchard, The Ancient Near East in Pictures Relating to the Old Testament, 2nd edition. Princeton, 1969
PSBA	Proceedings of the Society of Biblical Archaeology, vols. 1-40. London, 1878-1918
RA	Revue d'assyriologie et d'archéologie orientale. Paris, 1886-
Radau, EBH	H. Radau, Early Babylonian History down to the End of the Fourth Dynasty of Ur. London, 1900
RAI	Recontre Assyriologique Internationale. [various locations], 1954-
RAI 19	P. Garelli (ed.), Le Palais et la royauté (Archéologie et Civilisation) (= RAI 19). Paris, 1974
Rashid, Gründungsfiguren	S.A. Rashid, Gründungsfiguren im Iraq (=Prähistorische Bronzefunde 1/2). Munich, 1983
Reiner, MSL 11	E. Reiner and M. Civil, The Series ÓAR-ra = *'ubullu* (=MSL 11). Rome, 1974
RHR	Revue de l'historie des religions. Annales du Musée Guimet. Paris, 1880-
RIME	Royal Inscriptions of Mesopotamia, Early Periods. Toronto, 1990-
RLA	Reallexikon der Assyriologie. Berlin, 1932-
RLV	Reallexikon der Vorgeschichte, vols. 1-15. Berlin, 1924-32
RO	Rocznik Orientalistyczny. Kraków, Lwów, Warszawa, 1914-

RP NS	A.H. Sayce (ed.), Records of the Past, Being English Translations of the Ancient Monuments of Egypt and Western Asia, New Series, 6 vols. London, 1888-92
RSO	Rivista degli studi orientali. Rome, 1907-
RT	Receuil de travaux relatifs à la philologie et à l'archéologie égyptiennes et assyriennes, vols. 1-40. Paris, 1870-1923
SANE	Sources and Monographs of the Ancient Near East, vols. 1-2. Malibu, 1978-85
de Sarzec, Découvertes	E. de Sarzec, Découvertes en Chaldée par Ernest de Sarzec, ouvrage acompagné de planches, publié par les soins de Léon Heuzey, avec le concurs de Arthur Amiaud et François Thureau-Dagin pour la partie épigraphique, 2 vols. Paris, 1884/1912
Schäfer and Andrae, Kunst	H. Schäfer and W. Andae, Die Kunst des alten Orients (=Propyläen Kunstgeschichte 1-2). Berlin, 1925-30
Schmökel, Funde	H. Schmökel, Funde in Zweistromland. GN?, 1963
Schmökel, Ur, Assur und Babylon	H. Schmökel, Ur, Assur und Babylon, drei Jahrausende in Zweigtromsland. Stuttgart, 1955
Schott, Eanna	A. Schott, Die inschriftlichen Quellen zur Geschichte Eannas (=UVB 1). Berlin, 1930
SEb	Studi Eblaiti, vols. 1-7. Rome, 1979-84
Shileiko, VN	V.K. Shileiko, Votivnie nadpisi ßumerijskich pravitelej. St. Petersburg, 1915
Sollberger, ARET 8	E. Sollberger, Administrative Texts Chiefly Concerning Textiles (L. 2752) (=ARET 8). Rome, 1986
Sollberger, CIRPL	E. Sollberger, Corpus des inscriptions "royales" présargoniques de Lagaß. Genève, 1956
Sollberger, Système verbal	E. Sollberger, Le système verbal dans les inscriptions "royales" présargoniques de Lagaß. Genève, 1983
Sollberger, UET 8	E. Sollberger, Royal Inscriptions Part 2 (=UET 8). London, 1965
Sollberger and Kupper, IRSA	E. Sollberger and J.R. Kupper, Inscriptions royales sumériennes et akkadiennes. Paris, 1971
Solyman, Götterwaffen	T. Solyman, Die Entstehung und Entwicklung der Götterwaffen in alten Mesopotamia und ihre Bedeutung. Beirut, 1968
Speleers, Receuil	L. Speleers, Recueil des inscriptions de l'Asie antérieure des Musées Royaux du Cinquantenaire à Bruxelles. Textes sumériens, babyloniens et assyriens. Brussels, 1925
Spycket, Statuaire	A. Spycket, La statuaire du Proche-Orient ancien (=Hanbuch der Orientalistik 7/1/2/B 2). Leiden and Cologne, 1981
Spycket, Statues	A. Spycket, Les statues de culte dans les textes mesopotamiens des origines à la 1re dynastie de Babylone (=Cahiers de la Revue Biblique 9). Paris, 1968
Steible, ASBW	H. Steible, Die altsumerischen Bau- und Weihinschriften. Teil 1: Inschriften aus "Lagaß." Teil II: Kommentar zu den Inschriften aus "Lagaß". Inschriften ausserhalb von "Lagaß" (=FOAS 5/1-2). Wiesbaden, 1982
Stephens, YOS 9	F. J. Stephens, Votive and Historical Texts from Babylonia and Assyria (=YOS 9). New Haven, 1937
Stol, Studies	M. Stol, Studies in Old Babylonian History. Leiden, 1976
Strommenger and Hirmer, Mesopotamien	E. Strommenger and M. Hirmer, Fünf Jahrtausende Mesopotamien: Die Kunst von den Anfüngen um 5000 v. Chr. bis zu Alexander dem Grossen. Munich, 1962
Studies Deimel	Miscellanea Orientalis Dedicata A. Deimel Annos LXX Complenti (=AnOr 12). Rome, 1935
Studies Haupt	C. Adler and A. Ember (eds.), Oriental Studies Published in Commemoration of the fourtieth anniversary (1883-1923) of Paul Haupt as director of the Oriental Seminary of the John Hopkins University, Baltimore MD. Baltimore and Leipzig, 1926
Studies Jacobsen	S.J. Lieberman (ed.), Sumerological Studies in Honor of Thorkild Jacobsen on his Sevenieth Birthday June 7, 1974 (=AS 20). Chicago and London, 1976
Studies Jones	M.A. Powell and R.H. Sack (eds.), Studies in Honor of Tom. B. Jones (=AOAT 203). Neukirchen Vluyn, 1979
Tallon, Pierres	F. Tallon, Les pierres précieuses de lorient ancien des Sumériens aux Sassanides (= Exposition-dossier du départment des Antiqutés orientales 49). Paris, 1995
TCL	Textes cunéiformes du Musée du Louvre, Départment des Antiquités Orientales. Paris, 1910-
Thureau-Dangin, SAK	F. Thureau-Dangin, Die sumerischen und akkadischen Königschriften (=VAB 1). Leipzig, 1907
TUAT	O. Keiser (ed.), Texte aus der Umwelt des Alten Testaments. Gütersloh, 1982-
TUAT 1	O. Keiser (ed.), Rechts- und Wirschafturkunden Historisch-chonologishe Texte (=TUAT 1), Gütersloh, 1982-85
UE	Ur Excavations. Oxford, London, and Philadelphia, 1926-
UET	Ur Excavation, Texts. London, 1928-
Unger, SuAK	E. Unger, Sumerische und akkadische Kunst. Breslau, 1926

UVB	Vorläufiger Bericht über die von (dem Deutschen Archäologischen Institut und der Deutschen Orient-Gesellschaft aus Mitteln) der Deutschen Forschungsgemeinschaft unternommenen Ausgrabungen in Uruk-Warka. Berlin, 1930-
VAB	Vorderasiatische Bibliotek, vols. 1-7. Leipzig, 1907-16
VAS	Vorderasiatische Schriftdenkmäler der Königlichen Museen zu Berlin. Leipzig and Berlin, 1907-
VDI	Vestnik Drevnei Istorii. Moscow, 1937-
Walker, CBI	C.B.F. Walker, Cuneiform Brick Inscriptions in the British Museum, the Ashmolean Museum, Oxford, the City of Birmingham Museums and Art Gallery, the City of Bristol Museum and Art Gallery. London, 1981
Waterman, Tel Umar 1	L. Waterman, Preliminary Report upon the Excavations at Tel Umar Conducted by the University of Michigan and the Toledo Museum of Art. Ann Arbor, 1931
Westenholz, BibMes 1	A. Westenholz, Old Sumerian and Old Akkadian Texts in Philadephia Chiefly from Nippur. Part One. Literary and Lexical Texts and the Earliest Administrative Documents from Nippur (=BibMes 1). Malibu, 1975
WF	A. Deimel, Die Inscripten von Fara III. Wirtschaftstexte aus Fara (=WVDOG 45). Leipzig, 1924
WGE	H. Waetzoldt, and H. Hauptmann (eds.), Wirtschaft und Gesellschaft von Ebla: Akten der Internationalen Tagung Heidelberg, 4.-7. November 1986. Heidelberg: Heidelberger Orientverlag, 1988.
Wilcke, Lugalbanda	C. Wilcke, Das Lugalbandaepos. Wiesbaden, 1969
Winkler, AoF	H. Winkler, Altorientalische Forschungen, 3 vols. Leipzig, 1893-1905
WO	Die Welt des Orients. Wuppertal, Stuttgart, and Göttingen, 1947-
Woolley, UE 2	C.L. Woolley, E.R. Burrows, A. Keith, L. Legrain, and H.J. Plenderleith, The Royal Cemetery: A Report on the Predynastic aand Sargonid Graves Excavated Between 1926 and 1931 (=UE 2). London and Philadelphia, 1934
Woolley, UE 4	C.L. Woolley, The Early Periods: A Report on the Sites and Objects Prior in Date to the Third Dynasity of Ur Discovered in thr Course of the Excavations (=UE 4). London and Philadelphia, 1955
Woolley, UE 6	C.L. Woolley, The Buildings of the Third Dynasty (=UE 6). London and Philadelphia, 1974
WVDOG	Wissenschaftliche Veröffentlichungen der Deutschen Orient-Gesellschaft. Leipzig and Berlin, 1901-
WZJ	Wissenschaftiche Zeitschrift der Friedrich Schiller Universität Jena. Jena, 1951/2-
Yang, Sargonic Archive	Z. Yang, A Study of the Sargonic Archive from Adab, 2 vols. Ph.D. disseration, University of Chicago, 1986
Yang, Sargonic Inscriptions	Z. Yang, Sargonic Inscriptions from Adab (=Institute for the History of Ancient Civilizations, Periodic Publications on Ancient Civilizations 1). Changchun, 1989
YNER	Yale Near Eastern Researches. New Haven and London, 1967-
YOS	Yale Oriental Series, Babylonian Texts. New Haven, 1915-
Young (ed.), Mari	G.W. Young (ed.), Mari in Retrospect. Winona Lake, Indiana, 1988
ZA	Zeitschrift für Assyriologie und verwandte Gebiete. Berlin, 1886-
ZDMG	Zeitschrift der Deutschen Morgenländischen Gesellschaft. Leipzig and Wiesbaden, 1879-
Zervos, Encyclopédie	C. Zervos, ?
Zervos, L'art	C. Zervos, L'art de la Mésopotamie de la fin du quatrième millénaire au XVe siècle avant notre ère. Paris, 1935

Other Abbreviations

c	collated
cm	centimetre(s)
col(s).	column(s)
CTL	Cannonical Temple List
dia.	diameter
DN	divine name
dupl.	duplicate
E	east
Ea	lexical series ea A = *nâqu*
ED	Early Dynastic
ed(s).	editor(s)
ex(s).	exemplar(s)
fig(s).	figure(s)
frgm(s).	fragment(s)
GN	geographical name
km(s)	kilometer(s)
LGN	List of Geographic Names
MB	Middle Babylonian
n	not collated
N	north
NA	Neo-Assyrian
n(n).	note(s)
NB	Neo-Babylonian
no(s).	number(s)
NS	New Series
OAkk.	Old Akkadian
OB	Old Babylonian
obv.	obverse
OS	Old Series
p	collated from photo
p(p).	page(s)
pl(s).	plate(s)
PN	personal name
reg.	registration
rev.	reverse
RN	royal name
S	south
SKL	Sumerian King List
W	west
var(s).	variant(s)
vol(s).	volume(s)

+	Between object numbers indicates physical join
(+)	Indicates fragments from same object but no physical join

Object Signatures

A	Asiatic collection of the Oriental Institute, Chicago
Ag	Prefix of field numbers from the American excavations at Tell Agrab, Iraq
AO	Collection of Antiquités Orientales of the Musée du Louvre, Paris
As	Excavation numbers of the Chicago excavations at Tell Asmar, Iraq
Ash	Collection of the Ashmolean Museum, Oxford
B	Collection of the Allard Pierson Museum, Amsterdam
BM	British Museum, London
CBS	Babylonian Section of the University Museum, Philadelphia
D	Collection of the Royal Ontario Museum of Archaeology, Toronto
E˜	E^ki ˜ark Eserleri Müzesi of the Arkeoloji Müzeleri, Istanbul
F	Prefix of field numbers from the British excavations at Tell Brak
H	Prefix of field numbers from the American excavations at al-Hiba
HS	Hilprecht collection of Babylonian Antiquities of Fr. Schiller University, Jena
HSM	Collection of the Semitic Museum of Harvard University, Cambridge, Mass.
H-T	Prefix of field numbers from the second season of American excavations at al-Hiba
IM	Iraq Museum, Baghdad
Kh	Prefix of field numbers from the American excavations at Khafajah
LB	Tablets in the Liagre Böhl collection
M	Prefix of excavation numbers from the French excavations at Mari, Syria
MLC	J. Pierpont Morgan collection of the Yale University Library, New Haven
MNB	Collection of the Musées Nationaux of the Musée du Louvre, Paris
N	Prefix of field numbers from the American excavations at Nippur
NBC	James B. Nies collection of the Yale University Library, New Haven
NMS	Collection of the National Museum Stockholm
N-T	Excavation numbers of inscribed objects from the American excavations at Nippur
O	Objects in the Section du Proche Orient of the Musées Royaux du Cinquantenaire, Brussels
ROM	Royal Ontario Museum, Toronto
RR	Collection of the New York Public Libray, New York
Sn	Collection of the J. Mariaud de Serre, Paris
Í	Collection of the Damascus NationalMuseum, Damascus
TG	Prefix of field numbers from H. de Genouillac's excavations at Tello
TM	Prefix of field numbers from the Itialian excavations at Tell Mardikh
TO	Prefix of field numbers from the British excavations at Tell al-ªUbaid
U	Prefix of excavation numbers from the British-American excavations at Ur, Iraq
UCLM	Collection of the University of California R.H. Lowie Museum of Anthropology, Berkeley
UM	University Museum, Philadelphia
VA	Vorderasiatische Museum, Berlin
VAT	Tablets in the collection of the Vorderasiatische Museum, Berlin
W	Excavation numbers of the German excavations at Uruk/Warka
YBC	Babylonian collection of the Yale University Library, New Haven

Table I: List of Deities

Deity Name:	Appears in:	RIM #:	Text Reference:
Ama-geštin-ana	En-anatum I	E1.9.4	**2**: v 8
	En-anatum I	E1.9.4	**8**: iv 8
	En-anatum I	E1.9.4	**10**: ii 9
	En-anatum I	E1.9.4	**12**: ii′ 4′
	URU-KA-gina	E1.9.9	**5**: vii 1, 3
Ama-ušumgal-ana	En-anatum I	E1.9.4	**15**: i 2
	En-metena	E1.9.5	**23**: 2
An	Mes-kigala	E1.1.9	**2001**: i 2
	Mes-Ane-pada	E1.13.5	**1**: 1
	Lugal-SILA-si	E1.14.13	**1**: 1
	Lugal-kigine-dudu	E1.14.14	**2**: 1
	Lugal-KISAL-si	E1.14.15	**2**: 2
	Lugal-zage-si	E1.14.20	**20.1**: i 6, 14, iii 16
Asum	An(u)bu	E1.10.5	**2**: 1
Aštarat See Innana-NITA.	Ikū(n)-Šamagan	E1.10.11	**2002**: 9
Baba	Ur-Nanše	E1.9.1	**27**: 1
	Ur-Nanše	E1.9.1	**28**: 1
	En-anatum I	E1.9.4	**11**: i 0, iii 2′, iv 2′
	En-metena	E1.9.5	**24**: 1
	Lugal-Anda	E1.9.8	**2**: i′ 7′
	URU-KA-gina	E1.9.9	**1**: i 10, ix 14
	URU-KA-gina	E1.9.9	**2**: i 10, v 9″
	URU-KA-gina	E1.9.9	**3**: v 8
	URU-KA-gina	E1.9.9	**6**: iii 5
	URU-KA-gina	E1.9.9	**9**: 6′
	URU-KA-gina	E1.9.9	**11**: 1
Bau See Baba.	-	-	-
Dumuzi-Abzu	E-anatum	E1.9.3	**1**: rev. vi 3
	E-anatum	E1.9.3	**5**: ii 9
	E-anatum	E1.9.3	**6**: ii 12
Enki	E-anatum	E1.9.3	**1**: xviii 25, 33 xix 3, 13, 21, 31 rev. v 52
	E-anatum	E1.9.3	**5**: ii 7
	E-anatum	E1.9.3	**6**: ii 10
	En-anatum I	E1.9.4	**9**: ii 3
	En-metena	E1.9.5	**1**: v 25
	En-metena	E1.9.5	**12**: iv 5
	En-metena	E1.9.5	**15**: ii 6
	En-metena	E1.9.5	**16**: 34
	En-metena	E1.9.5	**17**: ii 9
	En-metena	E1.9.5	**25**: i′ 4′
	URU-KA-gina	E1.9.9	**1**: vi 15
	URU-KA-gina	E1.9.9	**9**: 35
	G̃iša-kidu	E1.12.6	**2**: 12
	Elili	E1.13.9	**1**: 1
	Lugal-zage-si	E1.14.20	**1**: i 18
	Lugal-zage-si	E1.14.20	**2**: ii 4
Enkigal	Ur-LUM-ma	E1.12.4	**1**: 1
Enlil	E-anatum	E1.9.3	**1**: obv. iv 5, xvi 15, 21, 36, xvii 1, 6, 17, xx 3, 12, xxi 8, xxii 10 rev. v 46
	E-anatum	E1.9.3	**2**: i 4, iv 6

Deity Name:	Appears in:	RIM #:	Text Reference:
Enlil (continued)	E-anatum	E1.9.3	**3:** i 3′, iii′ 4
	E-anatum	E1.9.3	**4:** i 2
	E-anatum	E1.9.3	**5:** i 6, ii 7
	E-anatum	E1.9.3	**6:** i 11
	E-anatum	E1.9.3	**8:** i 6
	E-anatum	E1.9.3	**9:** i 5
	E-anatum	E1.9.3	**10:** i 3
	E-anatum	E1.9.3	**11:** side 1 v 8
	E-anatum	E1.9.3	**12:** 5′
	En-anatum I	E1.9.4	**2:** i 7, vii 1
	En-anatum I	E1.9.4	**4:** 2
	En-anatum I	E1.9.4	**9:** i 5
	En-metena	E1.9.5	**1:** i 1, 23, 28, ii 14, iv 34, v 6, 23, vi 19
	En-metena	E1.9.5	**2:** i 2, ii 5
	En-metena	E1.9.5	**7:** 2
	En-metena	E1.9.5	**8:** i 2
	En-metena	E1.9.5	**9:** 2
	En-metena	E1.9.5	**11:** i 2
	En-metena	E1.9.5	**12:** i 2, vi 4
	En-metena	E1.9.5	**13:** i 2
	En-metena	E1.9.5	**14:** 2
	En-metena	E1.9.5	**15:** i 2
	En-metena	E1.9.5	**16:** 2, 21
	En-metena	E1.9.5	**17:** i 1, iii 5, 13, iv 9, v 5, vi 5,
	En-metena	E1.9.5	**18:** i 1′, 6′, 5″, ii 2′, 1″
	En-metena	E1.9.5	**26:** i 27
	En-metena	E1.9.5	**27:** i 2
	En-anatum II	E1.9.6	**1:** 2
	URU-KA-gina	E1.9.9	**1:** i 2, vii 30
	URU-KA-gina	E1.9.9	**2:** i 2, iii 1′, iv 2
	URU-KA-gina	E1.9.9	**5:** i 12
	URU-KA-gina	E1.9.9	**6:** i 2, ii 7
	URU-KA-gina	E1.9.9	**7:** ii 34
	URU-KA-gina	E1.9.9	**8:** i 2
	URU-KA-gina	E1.9.9	**10:** iii′ 0
	Unnamed, Lagaš	E1.9.10	**1:** 2′, 3′
	Ikū(n)-Šamaš	E1.10.7	**1:** 4
	Išgi-Mari	E1.10.17	**1:** 4
	Išgi-Mari	E1.10.17	**3:** 5
	Ur-Enlil	E1.11.2	**2:** 1
	Pa-bilga ...	E1.12.1	**1:** 1
	Ĝiša-kidu	E1.12.6	**2:** 2
	Lugal-kiĝine-dudu	E1.14.14	**1:** 1, 4, 17
	Lugal-kiĝine-dudu	E1.14.14	**3a:** 1
	Lugal-kiĝine-dudu	E1.14.14	**3b:** 1
	Lugal-kiĝine-dudu	E1.14.14	**4:** i 1, ii 1′
	Lugal-KISAL-si	E1.14.15	**1:** 1, 12
	Ur-zage	E1.14.16	**1:** 1, 6
	En-šakuš-Ana	E1.14.17	**1:** 1, 6′
	En-šakuš-Ana	E1.14.17	**2:** 1
	Lugal-zage-si	E1.14.20	**1:** i 1, 16, 36, ii 14, iii 7, 14, 38
Ĝatumdu	Ur-Nanše	E1.9.1	**6:** obv. iv 6
	Ur-Nanše	E1.9.1	**10:** iv 5, 7
	Ur-Nanše	E1.9.1	**11:** iv 5, 7
	Ur-Nanše	E1.9.1	**13:** iii 5

Deity Name:	Appears in:	RIM #:	Text Reference:
Ĝatumdu (continued)	Ur-Nanše	E1.9.1	**15:** iii 5
	Ur-Nanše	E1.9.1	**16:** ii 5
	Ur-Nanše	E1.9.1	**20:** iii 3
	Ur-Nanše	E1.9.1	**21:** 19
	Ur-Nanše	E1.9.1	**22:** 10
	E-anatum	E1.9.3	**11:** side 1 iv 2
	En-metena	E1.9.5	**12:** vi 8
	En-metena	E1.9.5	**16:** 25
	En-metena	E1.9.5	**17:** ii 22
	En-metena	E1.9.5	**21:** 1, 6
	En-metena	E1.9.5	**22:** 1, 10
DUG×KASKAL (dLAK 566)	Ur-Pabilsaĝ	E1.13.1	**1:** 1
GAN-gir	URU-KA-gina	E1.9.9	**3:** v 16′
Gušudu	Ur-Nanše	E1.9.1	**6b:** obv. vi 13
	Ur-Nanše	E1.9.1	**9:** ii 5
Ḫendursaĝ	E-anatum	E1.9.3	**1:** rev. vi 5
	E-anatum	E1.9.3	**5:** ii 11
	E-anatum	E1.9.3	**6:** ii 14
	En-anatum I	E1.9.4	**2:** i 1, ii 6, iv 2, xi 8, xiii 3
	En-anatum I	E1.9.4	**10:** ii 4
Igalima	URU-KA-gina	E1.9.9	**2:** ii 1
	URU-KA-gina	E1.9.9	**4:** v 10′
	URU-KA-gina	E1.9.9	**6:** ii 2
	URU-KA-gina	E1.9.9	**7:** 12
Inanna	Enna-il	E1.8.3	**1:** 1
	Enna-il	E1.8.3	**2:** ii 7
	E-anatum	E1.9.3	**1:** obv. iv 18, v 24, rev. v 50, vi 9
	E-anatum	E1.9.3	**5:** ii 5, v 26
	E-anatum	E1.9.3	**6:** ii 8
	E-anatum	E1.9.3	**8:** ii 5
	En-anatum I	E1.9.4	**2:** ii 4, iii 5
	En-anatum I	E1.9.4	**5:** i 1, 11, ii 9, iii 8, iv 6
	En-anatum I	E1.9.4	**6:** i 1
	En-anatum I	E1.9.4	**8:** iii 3
	En-anatum I	E1.9.4	**9:** ii 1, iii 10
	En-anatum I	E1.9.4	**10:** i 9
	En-anatum I	E1.9.4	**14:** i 5
	En-anatum I	E1.9.4	**15:** ii 2
	En-anatum I	E1.9.4	**17:** i 11
	En-anatum I	E1.9.4	**18:** i 5
	En-metena	E1.9.5	**3:** i 1
	En-metena	E1.9.5	**4:** v 9, vi, 9
	En-metena	E1.9.5	**5:** i 1, iv 1
	En-metena	E1.9.5	**5a:** obv. i 1, ii 6, rev. i 8, lower edge iii 2
	URU-KA-gina	E1.9.9	**5:** iv 5
	Abzu-kidu	E1.11.3	**1:** 1
	Aka	E1.12.2	**1:** 1
	Aka	E1.12.6	**2:** 15
	Lugal-SILA-si	E1.14.13	**1:** 2
	Lugal-kiĝine-dudu	E1.14.14	**2:** 2, 5, 15, 20
	Lugal-zage-si	E1.14.20	**1:** i 25
	Lugal-zage-si	E1.14.20	**2:** i′ 2′, ii′ 2′
Inanna-GIŠ.TIR See also Inanna.	Gullā	E1.10.19	**1:** 7

Deity Name:	Appears in:	RIM #:	Text Reference:
Inanna-NITA See also Inanna.	Išgi-Mari	E1.10.17	**1**: 7
Inanna-ZA.ZA	Ikū(n)-Šamagan	E1.10.11	**2001**: 6
	IB-LUL-il	E1.10.12	**1**: 10
	IB-LUL-il	E1.10.12	**2**: 6
	IB-LUL-il	E1.10.12	**3**: 5
	IB-LUL-il	E1.10.12	**4**: 4
Ištarān	En-metena	E1.9.5	**1**: i 10
	G̃iša-kidu	E1.12.6	**2**: 14, 81
Kindazi	Ur-Nanše	E1.9.1	**6**: obv. vi 11
	Ur-Nanše	E1.9.1	**9**: ii 7
dLAK 566 (DUG×KASKAL)	Ur-Pabilsağ	E1.13.1	**1**: 1
Lammasaga	URU-KA-gina	E1.9.9	**2**: ii 7
	URU-KA-gina	E1.9.9	**3**: v 20′
Lamma-šita-e	Ur-Nanše	E1.9.1	**6**: obv. vii 2-3
	Ur-Nanše	E1.9.1	**9**: iii 4-5.
Lugal-emuš	En-metena	E1.9.5	**3**: i 2
	En-metena	E1.9.5	**4**: i 1, iv 7, vi 4
	En-metena	E1.9.5	**5a**: i 2
	En-metena	E1.9.5	**5b**: obv. i 2, lower edge ii 1
Lugal-urtur	Ur-Nanše	E1.9.1	**6**: obv. vii 5
	Ur-Nanše	E1.9.1	**11**: iii 2
Lugal-urub	Ur-Nanše	E1.9.1	**11**: iii 4
(URU×KAR)	Ur-Nanše	E1.9.1	**17**: v 1
	E-anatum	E1.9.3	**1**: rev. vi 7
	E-anatum	E1.9.3	**5**: ii 13
	En-anatum I	E1.9.4	**2**: ii 8, v 3
	En-anatum I	E1.9.4	**5**: ii 1
	En-anatum I	E1.9.4	**8**: i 9, ii 8
	En-anatum I	E1.9.4	**9**: ii 5, 13, iv 2, v 7
	En-anatum I	E1.9.4	**10**: i 1, ii 6, iii 8
	En-anatum I	E1.9.4	**12**: ii′ 1′
	En-anatum I	E1.9.4	**15**: i 1, 15, ii 7, 14
	En-anatum I	E1.9.4	**17**: i 7
	En-metena	E1.9.5	**4**: iii 3
	En-metena	E1.9.5	**5b**: obv. iii 1
	En-metena	E1.9.5	**12**: iii 5
	En-metena	E1.9.5	**16**: 31
	En-metena	E1.9.5	**17**: ii 3
	En-metena	E1.9.5	**23**: 1, 21, 29, 32
	En-metena	E1.9.5	**26**: ii 7
	URU-KA-gina	E1.9.9	**5**: vi 2
Mes-sağ-unug	Lugal-zage-si	E1.14.20	**1**: i 30
	Lugal-zage-si	E1.14.20	**2**: i′ 3′
Nagar-paʾe	Ur-LUM-ma	E1.12.4	**2**: 1
Nammu	Lugal-KISAL-si	E1.14.15	**2**: 1, 6
Nanna	Lugal-kiğine-dudu	E1.14.14	**6**: 1
Nanše	Ur-Nanše	E1.9.1	**2**: a 9
	Ur-Nanše	E1.9.1	**4**: a 7
	Ur-Nanše	E1.9.1	**5**: b ii 1
	Ur-Nanše	E1.9.1	**6b**: obv. iii 9
	Ur-Nanše	E1.9.1	**10**: ii 4
	Ur-Nanše	E1.9.1	**11**: i 6, ii 2
	Ur-Nanše	E1.9.1	**12**: ii 2

Deity Name:	**Appears in:**	**RIM #:**	**Text Reference:**
Nanše (continued)	Ur-Nanše	E1.9.1	**13**: ii 2
	Ur-Nanše	E1.9.1	**14**: ii 2
	Ur-Nanše	E1.9.1	**15**: ii 2
	Ur-Nanše	E1.9.1	**16**: ii 1
	Ur-Nanše	E1.9.1	**17**: i 6, ii 1, 5, iii 5
	Ur-Nanše	E1.9.1	**20**: i 9, v 1
	Ur-Nanše	E1.9.1	**21**: 9
	Ur-Nanše	E1.9.1	**22**: 8
	Ur-Nanše	E1.9.1	**23**: 8
	E-anatum	E1.9.3	**1**: rev. v 54
	E-anatum	E1.9.3	**2**: iv 10
	E-anatum	E1.9.3	**4**: i 7
	E-anatum	E1.9.3	**5**: ii 1, iii 9
	E-anatum	E1.9.3	**6**: i 1, ii 4, iii 8
	E-anatum	E1.9.3	**8**: ii 1, iii 2
	E-anatum	E1.9.3	**9**: i 11
	E-anatum	E1.9.3	**11**: side 1 iv 6, v 2, side 4 i 1′, 6′, 10′, ii 2′, iii 5′, 7′, v 4′
	En-anatum I	E1.9.4	**2**: i 11
	En-anatum I	E1.9.4	**5**: i 7
	En-anatum I	E1.9.4	**8**: i 5
	En-anatum I	E1.9.4	**9**: i 7
	En-anatum I	E1.9.4	**15**: i 11
	En-anatum I	E1.9.4	**17**: i 5
	En-metena	E1.9.5	**1**: ii 19, 34, iv 3, 27, v 8, 17, 27, vi 7, 13
	En-metena	E1.9.5	**2**: ii 1
	En-metena	E1.9.5	**4**: i 6, iii 6
	En-metena	E1.9.5	**5b**: obv. ii 2
	En-metena	E1.9.5	**7**: 7
	En-metena	E1.9.5	**8**: ii 2
	En-metena	E1.9.5	**11**: ii 1
	En-metena	E1.9.5	**12**: iv 2, vii 2, 5
	En-metena	E1.9.5	**15**: ii 2
	En-metena	E1.9.5	**16**: 14
	En-metena	E1.9.5	**17**: i 7, ii 6, iii 1
	En-metena	E1.9.5	**19**: i 1, 7, ii 3
	En-metena	E1.9.5	**20**: 1, 7
	En-metena	E1.9.5	**22**: 6
	En-metena	E1.9.5	**23**: 7, 13
	En-metena	E1.9.5	**25**: i 1′
	En-metena	E1.9.5	**26**: ii 3, iii 7
	En-anatum II	E1.9.6	**1**: 7
	Lugal-Anda	E1.9.8	**2**: i′, 3′
	URU-KA-gina	E1.9.9	**1**: ii 7, xii 43
	URU-KA-gina	E1.9.9	**2**: iii 4′
	URU-KA-gina	E1.9.9	**4**: i′ 0′
	URU-KA-gina	E1.9.9	**5**: vi 7
	URU-KA-gina	E1.9.9	**8**: ii 5
	Unnamed, Lagaš	E1.9.10	**1**: iii′ 6′
ᵈNE.DAG!	Lugal-KISAL-si	E1.14.15	**3**: 1
Ninazu	Mes-KALAM-du	E1.13.6	**6**: 1
Nin-DAR	En-anatum I	E1.9.4	**2**: iv 7
(Nindara)	En-anatum I	E1.9.4	**10**: i 11
	En-metena	E1.9.5	**20**: 11
	URU-KA-gina	E1.9.9	**5**: v 4

Deity Name:	Appears in:	RIM #:	Text Reference:
Nin-eš-REC 107	Ur-Nanše	E1.9.1	**6b**: obv. vi 5
	Ur-Nanše	E1.9.1	**11**: iv 1
Nin-PA	Ur-Nanše	E1.9.1	**6b**: obv. vi 7
(Nin-gidru, Sud)	Ur-Nanše	E1.9.1	**11**: iv 3
Ningirim	Lugal-zage-si	E1.14.20	**1**: i 32
	Lugal-zage-si	E1.14.20	**2**: ii′ 5′
Ningirsu	Me-silim	E1.8.1	**1**: 4, 5
	Ur-Nanše	E1.9.1	**2**: a 5
	Ur-Nanše	E1.9.1	**3**: a 5
	Ur-Nanše	E1.9.1	**4**: a 5
	Ur-Nanše	E1.9.1	**5**: a 4
	Ur-Nanše	E1.9.1	**19**: 5
	Ur-Nanše	E1.9.1	**20**: I 5, iii 7
	Ur-Nanše	E1.9.1	**21**: 1
	Ur-Nanše	E1.9.1	**22**: 6
	Ur-Nanše	E1.9.1	**23**: 6
	Ur-Nanše	E1.9.1	**24a**: 1
	Ur-Nanše	E1.9.1	**26a**: 1
	A-kurgal	E1.9.2	**1**: 1
	E-anatum	E1.9.3	**1**: obv. iii 25, iv 4, 9, v 3 , 6, 13, vi 3, 31, xi 22, xii 1, 13, xiii 1, 13, 16, xvi 10, 28, xvii 36, xviii 40, xix 15, xx 18, rev. i 18, iv 6, vi 1, xi 20, 21, xii 26, 35, Cartouche A 3, B 3; **2**:i 1, 3, iii 5, iv 12, 13
	E-anatum	E1.9.3	**3**: i 1, ii 1, 9, iii 2
	E-anatum	E1.9.3	**4**: i 1, 10, ii 3, 9
	E-anatum	E1.9.3	**5**: i 1, 8, iii 4, iv 2, 22, v 1, 3, 15, 22, vi 16, vii 1, 3, 9, 16
	E-anatum	E1.9.3	**6**: i 6, ii 2, iii 3, iv 6, v 7, 14, vi 2, vii 2
	E-anatum	E1.9.3	**7**: i 1, ii 1, iii 1, 3
	E-anatum	E1.9.3	**8**: i 1, 8, ii 9, iv 10, vi 2, 7
	E-anatum	E1.9.3	**9**: i 9, iii 1, 8
	E-anatum	E1.9.3	**10**: i 1, 8, 9, ii 5, 9, iii 8
	E-anatum	E1.9.3	**11**: side 1 v 5
	E-anatum	E1.9.3	**13**: i 4′;
	E-anatum	E1.9.3	**14**: i′ 2′;
	E-anatum	E1.9.3	**16**: ii′
	E-anatum	E1.9.3	**17**: obv. 1;
	En-anatum I	E1.9.4	**2**: ii 2, iv 9, vi 6, vii 2, viii 3, ix 2, xi 1
	En-anatum I	E1.9.4	**3**: i 7, iii 5
	En-anatum I	E1.9.4	**4**: 1, 7, 11, 15
	En-anatum I	E1.9.4	**5**: i 9
	En-anatum I	E1.9.4	**8**: i 7
	En-anatum I	E1.9.4	**9**: i 9
	En-anatum I	E1.9.4	**11**: ii 2′;
	En-anatum I	E1.9.4	**15**: i 13;
	En-anatum I	E1.9.4	**19**: 1
	En-metena	E1.9.5	**1**: i 5, 22, ii 3, 12, 16, 20, 32, iii 3, iv 1, 5, 25, v 5, 7, 15, 29, vi 6, 11, 21
	En-metena	E1.9.5	**2**: i 1, ii 3, 6, iii 4, iv 5, v 3
	En-metena	E1.9.5	**4**: i 7, ii 1, 8;
	En-metena	E1.9.5	**5a**: obv. ii 4
	En-metena	E1.9.5	**6**: i 1
	En-metena	E1.9.5	**7**: 1, 9, 14, 15, 18, 22
	En-metena	E1.9.5	**8**: i 1, ii 4, iv 1

Deity Name:	**Appears in:**	**RIM #:**	**Text Reference:**
Ningirsu (continued)	En-metena	E1.9.5	**9**: 1, 10
	En-metena	E1.9.5	**10**: 5
	En-metena	E1.9.5	**11**: i 1, ii 3, iii 2, iv 2
	En-metena	E1.9.5	**12**: i 1, ii 6, v 6, viii 2, ix 2
	En-metena	E1.9.5	**13**: i 1, iii 1
	En-metena	E1.9.5	**14**: 1
	En-metena	E1.9.5	**15**: i 1, ii 4, iv 1
	En-metena	E1.9.5	**16**: i, 38
	En-metena	E1.9.5	**17**: i 9, 17, ii 17
	En-metena	E1.9.5	**19**: i 9
	En-metena	E1.9.5	**20**: 9
	En-metena	E1.9.5	**20a**: 9
	En-metena	E1.9.5	**22**: 8
	En-metena	E1.9.5	**23**: 9, 17
	En-metena	E1.9.5	**26**: i 1; ii 5, iii 1, iv 1, 7, 9, vi 8, vii 2, 8, viii 5, 8
	En-metena	E1.9.5	**27**: i 1, ii 1, iii 3, iv 7
	En-metena	E1.9.5	**28**: 1, 4, Caption 3
	En-anatum II	E1.9.6	**1**: 1, 9, 13, 18
	En-entarzi	E1.9.7	**1**: 3
	Lugal-Anda	E1.9.8	**2**: i′, 5′, ii′ 3′
	URU-KA-gina	E1.9.9	**1**: i 1, vii 13, 29, viii 11, ix 9, 23, xii 26, 32
	URU-KA-gina	E1.9.9	**2**: i 1, ii 16, iii 12′, iv 1, v 4″
	URU-KA-gina	E1.9.9	**4**: iv 15′, 16′, v 18′, 23
	URU-KA-gina	E1.9.9	**5**: vii 7, viii 2
	URU-KA-gina	E1.9.9	**6**: i 1, v 4
	URU-KA-gina	E1.9.9	**7**: 1, 23, 28, 38, 43, 47
	URU-KA-gina	E1.9.9	**8**: i 1, iii 5, v 2
	URU-KA-gina	E1.9.9	**9**: 1′, 11′, 15′
	URU-KA-gina	E1.9.9	**10**: iii′ 3′
	URU-KA-gina	E1.9.9	**13**: 2
	URU-KA-gina	E1.9.9	**14**
	URU-KA-gina	E1.9.9	**14a**: 1
	URU-KA-gina	E1.9.9	**14b**: 1
	URU-KA-gina	E1.9.9	**14e**: 1
	URU-KA-gina	E1.9.9	**14f**: 1
	URU-KA-gina	E1.9.9	**14g**: 1
	Unnamed, Lagaš	E1.9.10	**1**: iii′ 4′; 59, viii 4, 14, 24, 32, 49, ix 28; 24, xxvii 22, xxx 14, 15; 16, xvi 1, 8, 12, 16, xvii 2, xviii 4, xix 17, xxiv 1, 12, 15, 16
Ninḫursaĝ	Me-silim	E1.8.1	**3**: 4
	E-anatum	E1.9.3	**1**: obv. iv 24, 27, xvii 23, 30, 44, xviii 5, 9, 19, rev. v 48
	E-anatum	E1.9.3	**2**: iv 8
	E-anatum	E1.9.3	**5**: ii 3
	E-anatum	E1.9.3	**6**: ii 6
	E-anatum	E1.9.3	**8**: ii 3
	E-anatum	E1.9.3	**9**: i 7
	En-anatum I	E1.9.4	**2**: i 9
	En-anatum I	E1.9.4	**9**: v 9
	En-metena	E1.9.5	**1**: ii 15, iv 9, 35
	En-metena	E1.9.5	**12**: v 2
	En-metena	E1.9.5	**17**: ii 13
	En-metena	E1.9.5	**18**: i 8′

Deity Name:	Appears in:	RIM #:	Text Reference:
Ninḫursaĝ	En-metena	E1.9.5	**25**: i 8′
	En-metena	E1.9.5	**26**: ii 1
	Mes-Ana-pada	E1.13.4	**3**: 1, 6
	Mes-Ana-pada	E1.13.6	**4**: 1, 5
	Mes-Ana-pada	E1.13.6	**5**: 1, 5
	Lugal-zage-si	E1.14.20	**1**: i 29
Ninki	E-anatum	E1.9.3	**1**: rev. iii 6, 11, v 7, 15, 23, 32
Ninlil	Ur-Enlil	E1.11.2	**1**: 1
	Ur-zage	E1.14.16	**1**: 3
Ninmaḫ	En-metena	E1.9.5	**16**: 27
	URU-KA-gina	E1.9.9	**5**: ii 11
NinMAR.KI	Ur-Nanše	E1.9.1	**6**: obv. v 1, vi 3
	Ur-Nanše	E1.9.1	**9**: iii 2
	Ur-Nanše	E1.9.1	**13**: iv 2
	Ur-Nanše	E1.9.1	**15**: iv 4
	Ur-Nanše	E1.9.1	**22**: 14
NinSAR	URU-KA-gina	E1.9.9	**2**: ii 15
	URU-KA-gina	E1.9.9	**3**: v 22′
Ninšubur	Mes-kigala	E1.1.9	**2001**: i 1, 6′
	URU-KA-gina	E1.9.9	**6**: v 1
	URU-KA-gina	E1.9.9	**8**: iv 7
Nin-ur	Ĝiša-kidu	E1.12.6	**2**: 11
NIN.ZI	Ikūn-Mari	E1.10.10	**1**: 5
Nin[...]	Lugal-kiĝine-dudu	E1.14.14	**5**: 4′
Nipa᾿e	URU-KA-gina	E1.9.9	**2**: ii 12
Nis(s)aba	URU-KA-gina	E1.9.9	**5**: ix 1
	Lugal-zage-si	E1.14.20	**1**: i 8, 12, 27
	Lugal-zage-si	E1.14.20	**2**: i′ 5′
Pisan-saĝ-unug See Mes-saĝ-unug.	-	-	-
REC 290-KU-ra	En-šakuš-Ana	E1.14.17	**3**: 1
RU-kalama	Nammaḫ	E1.11.1	**1**: 1
Su᾿en	E-anatum	E1.9.3	**1**: obv. xx 1, 10, xxi 6, xxii 5, 8, xxiii 5
	Mes-KALAM-du	E1.13.3	**2**: 1
	Lugal-zage-si	E1.14.20	**1**: i 22
Šamaš	Ikū(n)-Šamaš	E1.10.7	**1**: 8
Šara	E-anatum	E1.9.3	**3**: i′ 2′
	En-metena	E1.9.5	**1**: i 6
	Ĝiša-kidu	E1.12.6	**1**: 1, 6, 9
	Ĝiša-kidu	E1.12.6	**2**: i 1, 26, 30, 34, 38, 43, 48, 52, 56, 60, 64, 68
	Lugal-zage-si	E1.14.20	**1**: ii 40
ŠU.KAL	E-anatum	E1.9.3	**3**: iii′ 7
Šulšag(ana)	Ur-Nanše	E1.9.1	**6b**: obv. vi 9
	Ur-Nanše	E1.9.1	**9**: ii 3
	Ur-Nanše	E1.9.1	**11**: ii 5
	URU-KA-gina	E1.9.9	**1**: ix 19
	URU-KA-gina	E1.9.9	**2**: ii 4, vi 3
	URU-KA-gina	E1.9.9	**3**: v 13′
	URU-KA-gina	E1.9.9	**6**: ii 8
	URU-KA-gina	E1.9.9	**7**: 15
	URU-KA-gina	E1.9.9	**10**: ii′ 1′
Šul-MUŠ×PA	E-anatum	E1.9.3	**1**: obv. xi 18, xiii 17
	E-anatum	E1.9.3	**5**: vii 18

Deity Name:	Appears in:	RIM #:	Text Reference:
Šul-MUŠ×PA (con′t)	E-anatum	E1.9.3	**6**: vii 4
	E-anatum	E1.9.3	**8**: vi 9
	E-anatum	E1.9.3	**9**: iii 6
	E-anatum	E1.9.3	**10**: iii 10
	E-anatum	E1.9.3	**11**: side 1 iv 4
	En-anatum I	E1.9.4	**2**: xi 10, xiii 5
	En-anatum I	E1.9.4	**5**: iii 10
	En-metena	E1.9.5	**1**: vi 2
	En-metena	E1.9.5	**2**: v 6
	En-metena	E1.9.5	**3**: ii 3
	En-metena	E1.9.5	**4**: vi 11
	En-metena	E1.9.5	**5a**: iv 4
	En-metena	E1.9.5	**5b**: rev. ii 6, iii 5
	En-metena	E1.9.5	**8**: iv 3
	En-metena	E1.9.5	**9**: 12
	En-metena	E1.9.5	**10**: 7
	En-metena	E1.9.5	**11**: iii 5
	En-metena	E1.9.5	**12**: ix 4
	En-metena	E1.9.5	**13**: iii 3
	En-metena	E1.9.5	**14**: 11
	En-metena	E1.9.5	**16**: 45
	En-metena	E1.9.5	**17**: iv 5
	En-metena	E1.9.5	**18**: ii 5′
	En-metena	E1.9.5	**21**: 8
	En-metena	E1.9.5	**23**: 34
	En-metena	E1.9.5	**27**: iv 5
	En-anatum II	E1.9.6	**1**: 21
	URU-KA-gina	E1.9.9	**9**: 13′
TAG.NUN	Il	E1.12.5	**1**: 1
Urnuntaʾe	URU-KA-gina	E1.9.9	**2**: ii 13
Utu	E-anatum	E1.9.3	**1**: obv. vii 7, rev. i 3, 11, 26, 36, ii 1
	En-metena	E1.9.5	**1**: ii 17
	En-metena	E1.9.5	**4**: vi 1
	URU-KA-gina	E1.9.9	**5**: i 13
	An(u)bu	E1.10.5	**2**: 1
	Lugal-zage-si	E1.14.20	**1**: i 20, 24, ii 35
Zababa	Utuk/Uḫub	E1.7.42	**1**: 1
Zazaru	URU-KA-gina	E1.9.9	**2**: ii 11
⌈x⌉-si	En-šakuš-Ana	E1.14.17	**4**: 1

Table II: List of Royal And Personal Names

Name:	Appears in:	RIM no.:	Text Reference:
A-Ane-pada: (king of the city Ur)	-	E1.13.6	**1-6**
A-Anzu: (father of Enna-il)	Enna-il	E1.8.3	**1**:4
A-Anzu (ruler? of the city Ur)	-	E1.13.1	**1**:1
Aba-Enlil (son of Lugal-ni-BE-du)	Ur-Enlil	E1.11.2	**1**:2
Abi(šu) (king of the city Kiš)	-	E1.7.42	-
Abur-Līm: (king of the city Ebla)	-	E1.4.16	-
Abzu-kidu: (ruler of the city Nippur)	-	E1.11.3	**1-2**
Addatur: (son of Ur-Nanše)	Ur-Nanše	E1.9.1	**2**: d ii 4
Addub-Dāmu (king of the city Ebla)	-	E1.4.23	-
Agur-Līm: (king of the city Ebla)	-	E1.4.17	-
A-kalam: (wife of Abzu-kidu)	Abzu-kidu	E1.11.3	**1**: 2
A-KALAM-du: (king of the city Ur)	-	E1.13.4	-
Aka: (king of the city Kiš)	-	E1.7.23	-
Aka: (king of G̃iša and Umma)	-	E1.12.2	-
A-kurgal: (son of Ur-Nanše)	-	E1.9.2	-
	Ur-Nanše	E1.9.1	**2**: b ii 2
	Ur-Nanše	E1.9.1	**3**: c 2
	Ur-Nanše	E1.9.1	**4**: lower registers, 3
	Ur-Nanše	E1.9.1	**5**: upper register, 4
	E-anatum	E1.9.3	**1**: obv. ii 30
	E-anatum	E1.9.3	**5**: iii 1, viii 1
	E-anatum	E1.9.3	**6**: ii 15, vii 8
	E-anatum	E1.9.3	**8**: ii 6
	E-anatum	E1.9.3	**9**: ii 1
	E-anatum	E1.9.3	**10**: ii 6
	En-anatum I	E1.9.4	**2**: ii 9
	En-anatum I	E1.9.4	**3**: i 4
	En-anatum I	E1.9.4	**4**: 8
	En-anatum I	E1.9.4	**5**: ii 2
	En-anatum I	E1.9.4	**8**: ii 1
	En-anatum I	E1.9.4	**9**: ii 6
	En-anatum I	E1.9.4	**10**: i 6
	En-anatum I	E1.9.4	**13**: 1′
	En-anatum I	E1.9.4	**15**: i 16
	En-anatum I	E1.9.4	**17**: i 8
Alma: (wife of Ikūn-Mar)	Ikūn-Mari	E1.10.10	**1**: 1

Name:	Appears in:	RIM no.:	Text Reference:
Ama-barasi: (lieutenant of the city Ur)	Ur-Nanše	E1.9.1	**6b**: rev. ii 6
Amar-Iškur: (father of A-kalam)	Abzu-kidu	E1.11.3	**2**: 2′
An(u)bu: (= Anbu, king of the city Mari)	-	E1.10.1	-
Anba: (king of the city Mari)	-	E1.10.2	-
Anikura: (son of Ur-Nanše)	Ur-Nanše	E1.9.1	**5**: upper register, 2
Anita: (cupbearer of Ur-Nanše)	Ur-Nanše	E1.9.1	**2**: b i 1
	Ur-Nanše	E1.9.1	**3**: c 1
	Ur-Nanše	E1.9.1	**4**: lower register, 1
Anunpad: (son of Ur-Nanše)	Ur-Nanše	E1.9.1	**2**: d ii 2
	Ur-Nanše	E1.9.1	**5**: lower register, 2
Anuzu: (commercial agent)	Lugal-kiĝine-dudu	E1.14.14	**6**: 2
Arbum: (king of the city Kiš)	-	E1.7.12	-
Ar-gandea (king of the city Uruk)	-	E1.14.19	-
Arra-ilum: (courtier of Ikūn-Šamaš)	Ikūn-Šamaš	E1.10.7	**1**:5
Ašumeʾeren: (wife of En-anatum I)	En-anatum I	E1.9.4	**15**: ii 12
	En-anatum I	E1.9.4	**16**: 2′
A-šu-sikil-àm: (wife of A-KALAM-du)	A-KALAM-du	E1.13.4	**1**: 4
Aššanu (king of the city Ebla)	-	E1.4.2	-
Atabba (king of the city Kiš)	-	E1.7.11	-
Awīl-kīnātim (son of Ur-Nanše?)	Ur-Nanše	E1.9.1	**4**: upper registers, 1′
Bābum: (king of the city Kiš)	-	E1.7.5	-
Baka-Damu: (king of the city Ebla)	-	E1.4.19	-
Baliḫ: (king of the city Kiš)	-	E1.7.14	-
Balul: (chief snake-charmer of Ur-Nanše)	Ur-Nanše	E1.9.1	**2**: d ii 1
	Ur-Nanše	E1.9.1	**4**: lower registers, 2
Balulu (king of the city of Ur)	-	E1.13.9	-
Bara-ḫeNIdu: (ruler of the city Adab)	-	E1.1.3	-
Bara-irnun: (wife of G̃iša-kidu of Giša	G̃iša-kidu	E1.12.6	**1**: 2
Bara-ki-TIL: (emissary of En-anatum I)	En-anatum I	E1.9.4	**19**: 7
Bara-namtara: (wife of Lugal-anda of Lagaš)	Lugal-Anda	E1.9.8	**3**: 1

Name:	Appears in:	RIM no.:	Text Reference:
Bara-sag-nudi (son of Ur-Nanše of Lagaš)	Ur-Nanše	E1.9.1	**3**: c 3
Barsal-nuna (king of the city Kiš)	-	E1.7.17	-
Bazi (king of the city Mari)	-	E1.10.3	-
Bilala (lieutenant of the city Umma)	Ur-Nanše	E1.9.1	**6b**: rev. iv 2
Būr-ilum (son of IB-LUL-il)	IB-LUL-il	E1.10.13	**1**: 5
Da-[x]-⌈x⌉ (king of the city Ebla)	-	E1.4.7	-
Dadasig (king of the city Kiš)	-	E1.7.25	-
Da-NE-nu (king of the city Ebla)	-	E1.4.9	-
Di-Utu (son of Lu-bara-si)	Lugal-KISAL-si	E1.14.15	**4**: 1
Dumu-zi (divine king of the city Uruk)	-	E1.14.4	-
E-abzu (king of G̃iša and Umma)	-	E1.12.3	-
E-anda-mua (father of Il)	Il	E1.12.5	**1**: 3
E-anna-Inanna-Ibgalkaka-tum (= E-anatum)	-	E1.9.3	**1**: obv. iv 20-22, v 26-28
E-anatum (king of the city Lagaš)	-	E1.9.3	-
	En-anatum I	E1.9.4	**2**: iii 2
	En-anatum I	E1.9.4	**5**: ii 6
	En-anatum I	E1.9.4	**8**: ii 5
	En-anatum I	E1.9.4	**9**: ii 10
	En-anatum I	E1.9.4	**15**: i 20
	En-metena	E1.9.5	**1**: i 32
E-IGI.NIM-paʾe (ruler of the city Adab)	-	E1.1.7	-
Elili (king of the city Ur)	-	E1.13.9	-
Elili (father of En-Šakuš-Ana)	En-Šakuš-Ana	E1.14.17	**3**: 5
Ibbini-Līm (king of the city Ebla)	-	E1.4.10	-
En-ʾar-Dāmu (king of the city of Ebla)	-	E1.4.20	-
Enakale (king of the city Umma)	En-metena	E1.9.5	**1**: i 39
	Ur-LUM-ma	E1.12.4	**1**: 4
	Ur-LUM-ma	E1.12.4	**2**: 4
	Il	E1.12.5	**1**: 5
	G̃iša-kidu	E1.12.6	**1**: 4
En-anatum I (king of the city Lagaš)	-	E1.9.4	-
	En-metena	E1.9.5	**1**: iii 5, 13
	En-metena	E1.9.5	**4**: i 8
	En-metena	E1.9.5	**5**: ii 2
	En-metena	E1.9.5	**5a**: obv. iii 2

Name:	Appears in:	RIM no.:	Text Reference:
	En-metena	E1.9.5	**6**: i 6
	En-metena	E1.9.5	**7**: 10
	En-metena	E1.9.5	**8**: ii 5
	En-metena	E1.9.5	**9**: 6
	En-metena	E1.9.5	**11**: ii 4
	En-metena	E1.9.5	**12**: i 6
	En-metena	E1.9.5	**13**: ii 1
	En-metena	E1.9.5	**15**: iii 1
	En-metena	E1.9.5	**16**: 6
	En-metena	E1.9.5	**17**: i 10
	En-metena	E1.9.5	**19**: i 10
	En-metena	E1.9.5	**20**: 13
	En-metena	E1.9.5	**23**: 10
	En-metena	E1.9.5	**26**: i 8
	En-metena	E1.9.5	**27**: i 6
En-anatum II (king of the city Lagaš)	-	E1.9.6	-
Enbi-Ištar (king of the city Kiš)	En-Šakuš-Ana	E1.14.17	**1**: 10
EN.DÁRA-AN-NA (king of the city Kiš)	-	E1.7.4	-
En-entarzi (king of the city Lagaš)	-	E1.9.7	-
EN.ME-barage-si (= Me-bara-si, king of the city Kiš)	-	E.1.7.22	-
EN.ME-nuna (king of the city Kiš)	-	E1.7.15	-
En-mer-kar (king of the city Uruk)	-	E1.14.2	-
En-metena (king of the city Lagaš)	-	E1.9.5	-
	En-anatum II	E1.9.6	**1**: 10
Enna-Dagān (king of the city Mari)	-	E1.10.14	-
Enna-il (king of the city Kiš)	-	E1.8.3	-
En-nun-dara-Ana (king of the city Uruk)	-	E1.14.9	-
En-šakuš-Ana (king of the city Uruk)	-	E1.14.17	-
Etana (king of the city Kiš)	-	E1.7.13	-
Gan-kuĝ-sig (Ereš-diĝir priestess of Ur-Pabilsaĝ)	Ur-Pabilsaĝ	E1.13.2.1001	-
Geme-Baba (daughter of En-entarzi)	En-entarzi	E1.9.7	**1**: 1
Gilgameš (king of the city Uruk)	-	E1.14.5	-
GIN.AK (king of the city Edina)	-	E1.5.1	-
Girimsi (governor of the city Uruk)	Lugal-KISAL-si	E1.14.15	**4**: 9
Giša-kidu (king of G̃iša and Umma)	-	E1.12.6	-

Name:	Appears in:	RIM no.:	Text Reference:
ĜIŠ.ÙR (king of the city Kiš)	-	E1.7.1	-
Gula (son of Ur-Nanše)	Ur-Nanše	E1.9.1	**3**: b 2
	Ur-Nanše	E1.9.1	**5**: lower register, 3
Gullā (son of Kūn-dūrī)	Unnamed, Mari	E1.10.18	**1**: 1
Gunidu (father of Ur-Nanše)	Ur-Nanše	E1.9.1	**2**: a 3
	Ur-Nanše	E1.9.1	**3**: a 4
	Ur-Nanše	E1.9.1	**5**: inscription beneath the feet of the king, i 4
	Ur-Nanše	E1.9.1	**6a**: obv. i 3
	Ur-Nanše	E1.9.1	**6b:** i 2
	Ur-Nanše	E1.9.1	**7**: 4
	Ur-Nanše	E1.9.1	**8**: i 4
	Ur-Nanše	E1.9.1	**9**: i 4
	Ur-Nanše	E1.9.1	**10**: i 4
	Ur-Nanše	E1.9.1	**11**: i 4
	Ur-Nanše	E1.9.1	**12**: i 4
	Ur-Nanše	E1.9.1	**13**: i 4
	Ur-Nanše	E1.9.1	**14**: i 4
	Ur-Nanše	E1.9.1	**15**: i 4
	Ur-Nanše	E1.9.1	**16**: i 4
	Ur-Nanše	E1.9.1	**17**: i 4
	Ur-Nanše	E1.9.1	**18**: i 4
	Ur-Nanše	E1.9.1	**19**: 4
	Ur-Nanše	E1.9.1	**20**: i 4
	Ur-Nanše	E1.9.1	**21**: 5
	Ur-Nanše	E1.9.1	**22**: 4
	Ur-Nanše	E1.9.1	**23**: 4
	Ur-Nanše	E1.9.1	**24a**: 5
	Ur-Nanše	E1.9.1	**24b**: 4
	Ur-Nanše	E1.9.1	**26**: 5
	Ur-Nanše	E1.9.1	**27**: 5
	Ur-Nanše	E1.9.1	**29**: i 4
	Ur-Nanše	E1.9.1	**30a**: i 4
	Ur-Nanše	E1.9.1	**30b**: i 4
	Ur-Nanše	E1.9.1	**31**: i 4
Ḫataniš (king of the city Ḫamazi)	-	E1.6.1	-
Ḫesamnu (wife of Mes-kiaĝ-nun)	Mes-kiaĝ-nun	E1.13.8	**1**: 3′
ḪI-daʾar (king of the city Mari)	-	E1.10.16	-
Ḫīšur (king of the city Awan)	-	E1.3.4	-
Ḫursagšemaḫ (chief merchant of Umma)	Ur-Nanše	E1.9.1	**4**: figures in upper registers from right to left 4′
	Ur-Nanše	E1.9.1	**6b**: rev. v 1
Ibbini-Dāmu (king of the city Ebla)	-	E1.4.18	-
Ibbi-[Ištar(?)] (king of the city Kiš)	-	E1.7.31	-

Name:	**Appears in:**	**RIM no.:**	**Text Reference:**
Ibbini-Līm (king of the city Ebla)	-	E1.4.10	-
IB-LUL-il (king of the city Mari)	-	E1.10.12	-
Igriš-Ḫalab (king of the city Ebla)	-	E1.4.24	-
Ikśud (king of the city Ebla)	-	E1.4.14	
Ikūn-Mari (king of the city Mari)	-	E1.10.10	-
Ikū(n)-Šamagan (king of the city Mari)	-	E1.10.11	-
Ikū(n)-Šamaš (king of the city Mari)	-	E1.10.7	-
Ikū(n)-išar (king of the city Mari)	-	E1.10.15	-
Il (king of G̃iša and Umma)	-	E1.12.5	-
	En-metena	E1.9.5	**1**: iii 28, iv 17, 19
	G̃iša-kidu	E1.12.6	**1**: 5
Ilkû (king of the city Kiš)	-	E1.7.20	-
I-lu-sikil (servant of En-anatum I)	En-anatum I	E1.9.4	**17**: ii 4
Ilta-śadûm (king of the city Kiš)	-	E1.7.21	-
Inimzi: (?)	A-Ane-pada	E1.13.6	**4:** 10
Iš/Uškun-Nūnu (son of RN of the city Kiš)	-	E1.7	p. 52.
Irkab-Dāmu (king of the city Ebla)	-	E1.4.25	-
Isidu (king of the city Ebla)	-	E1.4.12	-
Išu-il (king of the city Akšak)	-	E1.2.5	-
Išʾar-Dāmu (king of the city Ebla)	-	E1.4.26	-
Išʾar-Malik (king of the city Ebla)	-	E1.4.21	-
Išme-Šamaš (king of the city Kiš)	-	E1.7.38	-
Išqi-Mari (king of the city Mari)	-	E1.10.17	-
Išruṭ-Damu (king of the city Ebla)	-	E1.4.11	-
Išruṭ-Ḫalam (king of the city Ebla)	-	E1.4.13	-
Ištar-mūtī (king of the city Kiš)	-	E1.7.37	-
Išṭup-Šar (king of the city Mari)	-	E1.10.9	-
Kalbum (king of the city Kiš)	-	E1.7.27	-
Kalibum (king of the city Kiš)	-	E1.7.7	-

Name:	**Appears in:**	**RIM no.:**	**Text Reference:**
Kikkusiwetemti (king of the city Awan)	-	E1.3.7	-
Ku-Baba (queen of the city Kiš)	-	E1.7.32	-
Kulassina-ibēl (king of the city Kiš)	-	E1.7.2	-
Kūn-Dāmu (king of the city Ebla)	-	E1.4.22	-
Kūn-dūrī (brother of a king of Mari)	-	E1.10.19	**1**: 3
KUL-banu (king of the city Ebla)	-	E1.4.1	-
Labaḫ (king of the city Uruk)	-	E1.14.8	-
Līm-ēr (king of the city Mari)	-	E1.10.5	-
Lu-bara-si (son of Lugal-KISAL-si)	Lugal-KISAL-si	E1.14.15	**4**: 3
Lugal-Anda (king of the city of Lagaš)	-	E1.9.8	-
Lugal-Anda-nuḫunga (= Lugal-Anda)	Lugal-Anda	E1.9.8	**2**:iii' 3'
Lugal-Ane-mundu (king of the city Adab)	-	E1.1.8	-
Lugal-banda (king of the city Uruk)	-	E1.14.3	-
Lugalda-lu (king of the city Adab)	-	E1.1.4	-
Lugal-ezen (son of Ur-Nanše)	Ur-Nanše	E1.9.1	**2**: b ii 3
	Ur-Nanše	E1.9.1	**3**: b 1
	Ur-Nanše	E1.9.1	**4**: upper registers, 2′
	Ur-Nanše	E1.9.1	**5**: upper register ,1
Lugal-kiĝine-dudu (king of the city Uruk)	-	E1.14.14	-
	-	E1.14.15	**1**: 5
Lugal-kineš-dudu (king of the city Uruk)	En-metena	E1.9.5	**3**: ii 7
Lugal-KISAL-si (king of the city Uruk)	-	E1.14.15	-
	Lugal-kiĝine-dudu	E1.14.14	**6**:10
Lugal-ki-tun (?) (king of the city Uruk)	-	E1.14.12	-
Lugal-mu (king of the city Kiš)	-	E1.7.30	-
Lugal-namnir-sum (king of the city Kiš)	-	E1.8.2	-
Lugal-SILA-si (king of the city Uruk)	-	E1.14.13	-
Lugal-[SILA] (king of the city Uruk)	-	E1.14.21	-
Lugal-ša-ENGUR (ruler of the city Lagaš)	Me-silim	E1.8.1	**1**: 7
Lugal-TAR (king of the city Uruk)	Unnamed, Lagaš	E1.9.10	**2**: ii′ 8′

Name:	Appears in:	RIM no.:	Text Reference:
Lugal-ure (king of the city Uruk)	-	E1.14.18	-
LUGAL-UD (king of the city Kiš)	-	E1.7.41	-
Lugal-zage-si (king of Ĝiša and Umma)	-	E1.12.7	-
	URU-KA-gina	E1.9.9	**5**: viii 11
Lugal-zage-si (king of the city Uruk)	-	E1.14.20	-
LUM-ma (ruler of the city Adab)	-	E1.1.5	-
Luma (Tidnum name of E-anatum)	E-anatum	E1.9.3	**1**: rev. x 27
	E-anatum	E1.9.3	**5**: v 14
Lupa (lieutenant of the city Umma)	Ur-Nanše	E1.9.1	**6a**: rev. iv 1
Mamagala (king of the city Kiš)	-	E1.7.26	-
Meanesi (son of En-anatum I)	En-anatum I	E1.9.4	**15**: i 3
Me-bara-si See EN.ME-barage-si	-	-	-
Me-ba-LAK 551 (king of the city Adab)	-	E1.1.2	-
Me-girimta (daughter of Lugal-KISAL-si)	Lugal-KISAL-si	E1.14.15	**3**: 2
Melam-Ana (king of the city Uruk)	-	E1.14.11	-
Melam-Kiš (king of the city Kiš)	-	E1.7.16	-
Men-nuna (king of the city Kiš)	-	E1.7.29	-
Menusu (son of Ur-Nanše)	Ur-Nanše	E1.9.1	**2**: d ii 3
Me-silim (king of the city Kiš)	-	E1.8.1	-
	E-anatum	E1.9.3	**2**: i 6, iv 16
	E-anatum	E1.9.3	**3**: ii′ 6
	En-metena	E1.9.5	**1**: i 8, ii 7
Mes-Ane-pada (king of the city Ur)	-	E1.13.5	-
	A-Ane-pada	E1.13.6	**3**: 4
	A-Ane-pada	E1.13.6	**4**: 4
	A-Ane-pada	E1.13.6	**5**: 4
Mes-ḫe (king of the city Uruk)	-	E1.14.10	-
Mes-kiaĝ-gašer (king of the city Uruk)	-	E1.14.1	-
Mes-kiaĝ-nun (king of the city Ur)	-	E1.13.8	-
Mes-kigal(a) (ruler of the city Adab)	-	E1.1.9	-
Mes-KALAM-du (king of the city Ur)	-	E1.13.3	-
	Mes-Ane-pada	E1.13.5	**1**: 5

Name:	**Appears in:**	**RIM no.:**	**Text Reference:**
Mes-KALAM-du (prince of Ur)	-	E1.13.7	-
MUG-si (ruler of Adab)	-	E1.1.6	-
Muni-ḫursag (husband of Me-girimta)	Lugal-KISAL-si	E1.14.15	**3**: 6
[PN] DUMU MUNUS-UŠUMGAL (father of RN, king of Kiš)	-	E1.7.40	-
Namanu (king of the city Ebla)	-	E1.4.6	-
Namazu (scribe of Ur-Nanše)	Ur-Nanše	E1.9.1	**4**: lower registers, 4
Nam-maḫ (ruler of the city Nippur)	-	E1.11.1	-
na(?) ^{d}*is le-e* KU_5.DA (king of the city Kiš)	-	E1.7.3	-
Nanna-ursağ	A-Ane-pada	E1.13.6	**4**: 10
	A-Ane-pada	E1.13.6	**5**: 9
Nannia (king of the city Kiš)	-	E1.7.39	-
Napilḫuš (king of the city Awan)	-	E1.3.6	-
Nin-TUR (wife of Mes-ane-pada)	Mes-ane-pada	E1.13.5	**3**: 1
	Mes-ane-pada	E1.13.5	**4**: 1
Nin-TUR (wife of Lugal-kiğine-dudu)	Lugal-kiğine-dudu	E1.14.14	**6**: 8
Ningirsu-lumu (emissary of URU-KA-gina)	URU-KA-gina	E1.9.9	**11**: 3
Nin-KISAL-si (ruler of the city Adab)	-	E1.1.1	-
	Me-Silim	E1.8.1	**2**: 5
Nin-mete-bare (daughter of An(u)bu)	An(u)bu	E1.10.5	**2**: 2
NIzi (king of the city Mari)	-	E1.10.13	-
Pa-bilga … (king of G̃iša and Umma)	-	E1.12.1	-
Pabilgatuku (governor of the city Umma)	Ur-Nanše	E1.9.1	**6b**: rev. iv 5
PAP.GÁ (wife of IB-LUL-il)	IB-LUL-il	E1.10.12	**1**: 3
Pa-UN (wife of Nam-maḫ)	Nam-maḫ	E1.11.1	**1**: 2
Pelli (king of the city Awan)	-	E1.3.1	-
Pū-abum (queen of the city Ur)	Mes-KALAM-du	E1.13.3	**3**: 1
Puʾannaʾum See Ušum-anna.	-	-	-
Pussussu (unknown dynasty)	Unknown "Vanquisher of Ḫamazi"	E1.15.1	-

Name:	Appears in:	RIM no.:	Text Reference:
Puzur-Niraḫ (king of the city Akšak)	-	E1.2.4	-
Puzur-Sîn (king of the city Kiš)	-	E1.7.33	-
Qalumu (king of the city Kiš)	-	E1.7.9	-
Rumanu (king of the city Ebla)	-	E1.4.5	-
Saʾumu (king of the city Mari)	-	E1.10.8	-
Sag̃-dig̃ir-tuku (cup-bearer of Ur-Nanše)	Ur-Nanše	E1.9.1	**2**: d i 1
Samiʾu (king of the city Ebla)	-	E1.4.3	-
Samug$_5$ (king of the city Kiš)	-	E1.7.18	-
Simudara (king of the city Kiš)	-	E1.7.35	-
Sipa-sura (king of the city Kiš):	-	E1.7.24	-
Šagišu (king of the city Ebla)	-	E1.4.8	-
Šarrum-īter (king of the city Mari)	-	E1.10.6	-
Šuni-aldugud (chief barber of En-anatum I)	En-anatum I	E1.9.4	**18**: ii 3
Sur-Nanše	En-metena	E1.9.5	**17**: v 1
Šū-Sîn (king of the city Akšak)	-	E1.2.6	-
Šušuntaran (king of the city Awan)	-	E1.3.5	-
Talda-Līm (king of the city Ebla)	-	E1.4.15	-
Tatta (king of the city Awan)	-	E1.3.2	-
TI$_8$.MUŠEN (king of the city Kiš)	-	E1.7.8	-
Tizqā (king of the city Kiš)	-	E1.7.19	-
TÚG-e (king of the city Kiš)	-	E1.7.28	-
Ukkutaḫeš (king of the city Awan)	-	E1.3.3	-
Ug̃dalulu (king of the city Akšak)	-	E1.2.2	-
Ug̃zi (king of the city Akšak)	-	E1.2.1	-
Unnamed ruler of Lagaš (king of the city Lagaš)	-	E1.9.10	-
Ur-Enlil (ruler of the city Nippur)	-	E1.11.2	-
Ur-Ešlila (city elder of the city Adab)	Bara-ḫeNIdu	E1.1.3	**2001**: 6

Name:	Appears in:	RIM no.:	Text Reference:
Ur-LUM-ma (king of G̃iša and Umma)	-	E1.12.4	-
	En-anatum I	E1.9.4	**2**: vii 7, ix 5, x 6
	En-metena	E1.9.5	**1**: ii 28, iii 15
	URU-KA-gina	E1.9.9	**3**: iv 20′
	G̃iša-kidu	E1.12.6	**1**: 3
Ur-Nanše (king of the city Lagaš)	-	E1.9.1	-
	A-kurgal	E1.9.2	**1**: 5
	E-anatum	E1.9.3	**1**: obv. ii 33
	E-anatum	E1.9.3	**5**: viii 5
	E-anatum	E1.9.3	**6**: vii 12
	En-metena	E1.9.5	**5b**: obv. iii 6
	En-metena	E1.9.5	**12**: ii 3
	En-metena	E1.9.5	**17**: i 14
Ur-Nanše (master-musician of IB-LUL-il)	IB-LUL-il	E1.10.13	**3**: 3
	IB-LUL-il	E1.10.13	**4**: 2
Ur-nimin (man chosen to be the spouse of the goddess Nanše)	Ur-Nanše	E1.9.1	**17**: iii 3
Ur-Nungal (king of the city Uruk)	-	E1.14.6	-
Ur-pabilsag̃ (king of the city Ur)	-	E1.13.2	-
Ur-pusag (lieutenant of the city Umma)	Ur-Nanše	E1.9.1	**6b**: rev. iv 9
Ur-Šamša (father of Būr-ilum)	IB-LUL-il	E1.10.13	**1**: 6
URU-KA-gina (king of the city Lagaš)	-	E1.9.9	-
Urur (king of the city Akšak)	-	E1.2.3	-
Ur-Zababa (king of the city Kiš)	-	E1.7.34	-
Ur-zage (king of the city Uruk)	-	E1.14.16	-
Ušum-anna (king of the city Kiš)	-	E1.7.6	-
Ūṣi-watar (king of the city Kiš)	-	E1.7.36	-
UŠ (king of the city Umma)	En-metena	E1.9.5	**1**: i 13
Ušum-Ana (king of the city Kiš)	-	E1.7.6	-
Utuk/Uḫub (king of the city Kiš)	-	E1.7.42	-
Utul-kalam (king of the city Uruk)	-	E1.14.7	-
U-U (ruler of the city Umma)	Lugal-zage-si Lugal-zage-si	E1.12.7 E1.14.20	**1**: obv. i 6 **1**: i 9
Uʾuʾu (father of Papursag)	Ur-Nanše	E1.9.1	**6b**: rev. iii 3
Yaʿdub-Damu (king of the city Ebla)	=Adub-Damu	E1.4.23	-

Name:	**Appears in:**	**RIM no.:**	**Text Reference:**
Yigriš-Ḫalam (king of the city Ebla)	=Igriš-ḫalab	E1.4.24	-
Yinḥar-Damu (king of the city Ebla)	=En-ʾḪAR-da-mu	E1.4.20	-
Yirkab-Damu (king of the city Ebla)	=Irkab-Damu	E1.4.25	-
Yišʾar-Damu (king of the city Ebla)	=Išar-Damu	E1.4.26	-
Yišruṭ-Damu (king of the city Ebla)	=Išruṭ-Damu	E1.4.11	-
Zi-alu (king of the city Ebla)	-	E1.4.4	-
Zizi (king of Mari)	-	E1.10.4	-
Zuqaqīp (king of the city Kiš)	-	E1.7.10	-
Zuzu (king of the city Akšak)	E-anatum	E1.9.3	**5**: v 4
Yaʿdub-Damu (king of the city Ebla)	=Adub-Damu	E1.4.23	-
Yibbiʾ-Damu (king of the city Ebla)	=Ibi-Damu	E1.4.18	-
Yigriš-Ḫalam (king of the city Ebla)	=Igriš-ḫalab	E1.4.24	-
Yinḥar-Damu (king of the city Ebla)	=En-ʾḪAR-da-mu	E1.4.20	-
Yirkab-Damu (king of the city Ebla)	=Irkab-Damu	E1.4.25	-
Yišʾar-Damu (king of the city Ebla)	=Išar-Damu	E1.4.26	-
Yišruṭ-Damu (king of the city Ebla)	=Išruṭ-Damu	E1.4.11	-

Table III: List of Geographical Names

Toponym:	Appears in:	RIM no.:	Text Reference:
(A)-a-suḫur See id_5(A)-a-suḫur.	-	-	-
	Ur-Nanše	E1.9.1	**9**: iii 7
	E-anatum	E1.9.3	**5**: vi 19
Abarsal (city)	IB-LUL-il	E1.10.12	**5**: obv. vi 9
Aburu (city)	An(u)bu	E1.10.1	**1**: obv. i 8
	IB-LUL-il	E1.10.12	**9**: rev. iii 5
Adab (city)	Me-ba-LAK 551	E1.1.2	**1**: 3
	Bara-ḫeNidu	E1.1.3	**2001**: 5
	Lugalda-lu	E1.1.4	**1**: 3
	E-IGI.NIM-paʾe	E1.1.7	**1**: 4
	E-IGI.NIM-paʾe	E1.1.7	**2**: 4
	Mes-kigala	E1.1.9	**2001**: i 6
	Me-silim	E1.8.1	**2**: 5
	Me-silim	E1.8.1	**3**: 3′
Addani (city/land)	IB-LUL-il	E1.10.12	**6**: obv. vii 8
Akšak (city)	E-anatum	E1.9.3	**5**: iv 25, v 5, 6, vi 10, 21
	E-anatum	E1.9.3	**6**: v 10, vi 3
	En-šakuš-Ana	E1.14.17	**1**: 13
AL-[x] (canal)	G̃iša-kidu	E1.12.6	**2**: 27
Ambar (city)	URU-KA-gina	E1.9.9	**1**: iii 16
	URU-KA-gina	E1.9.9	**2**: iv 20
	URU-KA-gina	E1.9.9	**3**: i 6′, 9′
Angaʾi (land)	Saʾumu	E1.10.8	**1**: obv. iii 6
Anzagar (town)	G̃iša-kidu	E1.12.6	**2**: 66, 69
Arisum (city)	IB-LUL-il	E1.10.12	**6**: obv. vii 10
Arua (city)	E-anatum	E1.9.3	**1**: rev. viii 2′
	E-anatum	E1.9.3	**5**: iv 18
	E-anatum	E1.9.3	**6**: v 3
	E-anatum	E1.9.3	**8**: vi 10
A-sanga-(REC 107) (canal in the vicinity of G̃irsu)	Ur-Nanše	E1.9.1	**17**: ii 3
	Ur-Nanše	E1.9.1	**20**: v 3, 5
Ašaldu (city)	Saʾumu	E1.10.8	**1**: obv. iii 14
Baʾul (city)	Saʾumu	E1.10.8	**1**: obv. iv 1
babára (field)	E-anatum	E1.9.3	**1**: obv. xiv 1
Bad-tibira See Pa_5-tibira.	-	-	-

Toponym:	Appears in:	RIM no.:	Text Reference:
Barāma (city)	IB-LUL-il	E1.10.12	**9**: rev. iii 3
Belan (city)	An(u)bu	E1.10.1	**3**: obv. i 12
	IB-LUL-il	E1.10.12	**9**: rev. iii 9
Burman (city)	IB-LUL-il	E1.10.12	**6**: obv. vii 12
Dammiʾum (city)	IB-LUL-il	E1.10.12	**7**: obv. viii 8
Dasala (canal in the vicinity of Ur)	Ur-Nanše	E1.9.1	**31**: ii 1
Dilmun (island)	Ur-Nanše	E1.9.1	**2**: c 4
	Ur-Nanše	E1.9.1	**5**: b ii 5
	Ur-Nanše	E1.9.1	**17**: v 3
	Ur-Nanše	E1.9.1	**20**: iv 1
	Ur-Nanše	E1.9.1	**22**: 16
	Ur-Nanše	E1.9.1	**23**: 16
	Ur-Nanše	E1.9.1	**25**: 1′
Dua (canal)	G̃iša-kidu	E1.12.6	**2**: 28, 31
Duʾašri (field)	E-anatum	E1.9.3	**2**: ii 13
Duʾurgiga (city)	En-anatum I	E1.9.4	**2**: viii 8
Ebla (town near Emar)	Išṭup-Šar	E1.10.9	**1**: obv. v 2
Ebla (famous Syrian city)	IB-LUL-il	E1.10.12	**7**: obv. ix 13
Edimgalabzu (town)	G̃iša-kidu	E1.12.6	**2**: 54, 57
EʾEDIN (city)	Aga-ak	E1.5.1	**1**: 3
Elam (land)	Enna-il	E1.8.3	**1**: obv. 5
	E-anatum	E1.9.3	**1**: rev. vi 10
	E-anatum	E1.9.3	**5**: iii 13, vi 7, 8, 17
	E-anatum	E1.9.3	**6**: iii 12
	E-anatum	E1.9.3	**7**: ii 2
	E-anatum	E1.9.3	**8**: iii 6
	E-anatum	E1.9.3	**9**: ii 4
Eluḫa (field)	E-anatum	E1.9.3	**2**: ii 11
Enlilpadaušgal (canal in the vicinity of G̃irsu)	Ur-Nanše	E1.9.1	**9**: iv 3-4.
En-zišagal (quay wall of the G̃irsu ferry)	En-metena	E1.9.5	**27**: iv 2
Eridu (city)	En-metena	E1.9.5	**4**: ii 8
	En-metena	E1.9.5	**12**: iv 6
	En-metena	E1.9.5	**16**: 35
	En-metena	E1.9.5	**17**: ii 10
	En-metena	E1.9.5	**25**: i 5′
	Elili	E1.13.9	**1**: 3
Eša (garden in the city G̃irsu)	En-metena	E1.9.5	**15**: iv 2

Toponym:	Appears in:	RIM no.:	Text Reference:
Eša (continued) (garden in the city G̃irsu)	En-metena	E1.9.5	**27**: ii 5
Euphrates (Sum. Buranun, Akk. *Purattu*, river)	Lugal-zage-si	E1.14.20	**1**: ii 7
GalalaNEi (city)	IB-LUL-il	E1.10.12	**5**: obv. v 15
Gasur (city)	IB-LUL-il	E1.10.12	**8**: rev. ii 5
Gibil (canal)	G̃iša-kidu	E1.12.6	**2**: 50, 53
G̃irsu (city)	Ur-Nanše	E1.9.1	**6b**: obv. iv 2
	Ur-Nanše	E1.9.1	**7**: 5
	Ur-Nanše	E1.9.1	**8**: i 5
	Ur-Nanše	E1.9.1	**9**: ii 1
	Ur-Nanše	E1.9.1	**10**: ii 4
	Ur-Nanše	E1.9.1	**11**: ii 4
	Ur-Nanše	E1.9.1	**12**: 4
	Ur-Nanše	E1.9.1	**13**: 4
	Ur-Nanše	E1.9.1	**14**: ii 4
	Ur-Nanše	E1.9.1	**15**: ii 4
	Ur-Nanše	E1.9.1	**16**: ii 3
	Ur-Nanše	E1.9.1	**21**: 5
	E-anatum	E1.9.3	**4**: ii 8
	E-anatum	E1.9.3	**5**: iii 5
	E-anatum	E1.9.3	**6**
	E-anatum	E1.9.3	**8**: ii 10
	E-anatum	E1.9.3	**16**: i′ 3′
	En-metena	E1.9.5	**1**: iii 30, iv 7
	En-metena	E1.9.5	**27**: iii 10
	URU-KA-gina	E1.9.9	**1**: ii 14, x 23
	URU-KA-gina	E1.9.9	**2**: i 5, vi 21
	URU-KA-gina	E1.9.9	**4**: iii′ 2′
	URU-KA-gina	E1.9.9	**5**: viii 9
	URU-KA-gina	E1.9.9	**10**: ii′ 6′
	URU-KA-gina	E1.9.9	**13**: 4
G̃iša (g̃išKÚŠU.KI) (city)	Ur-Nanše	E1.9.1	**6b**: rev. i 3, iii 10, iv 7, vi 1
	E-anatum	E1.9.3	**1**: obv. ii 24, iii 16, 28, vi 9, vii 1, 23, viii 2, x 2, 15, xi 2, 5, 12, xvi 12, 18, 39, xvii 10, 19, 24, 27, 46, xviii 12, 21, 27, 30, xix 6, 24, 33, xx 4, 7, xxi 10, xxii 13, xxiii 7, rev. i 5, 8, 29, ii 5, 14, iii 4, 8, v 9, 12, 26, 34, 37
	E-anatum	E1.9.3	**2**: iii 7, 11, 14, 17
	E-anatum	E1.9.3	**3**: ii′ 4,′ 18′
	E-anatum	E1.9.3	**4**: i 19
	E-anatum	E1.9.3	**5**: iii 23
	E-anatum	E1.9.3	**6**: iv 2
	E-anatum	E1.9.3	**8**: iv 6
	E-anatum	E1.9.3	**9**: ii 8

Toponym:	Appears in:	RIM no.:	Text Reference:
G̃iša (g̃išKÚŠU.KI) (con′t) (city)	En-anatum I	E1.9.4	**2**: vii 3, 9, ix 7, x 8
	En-metena	E1.9.5	**1**: i 15, 25, 41, ii 3, 9, 22, 30, iii 17, 31, 36, iv 21, vi 9, 17
	URU-KA-gina	E1.9.9	**3**: iv 10′, 17′, 22′
	URU-KA-gina	E1.9.9	**5**: i 1, vii 10, viii 13
	Unnamed, Lagaš	E1.9.10	**1**: iii′ 3′;
	Aka	E1.12.2	**1**: 4
	E-abzu	E1.12.3	**1**: 3
	Lugal-zage-si	E1.12.7	**1**: i 4, 7, ii 17
	Lugal-zage-si	E1.14.20	**1**: i 10, ii 38
GIŠ.PIRIG.GÁ (field)	E-anatum	E1.9.3	**1**: obv. xv 11
Guʾedina (field)	E-anatum	E1.9.3	**1**: obv. iv 1, vi 12, xii 3; rev. x 20, xii 31
	E-anatum	E1.9.3	**4**: i 20, ii 5
	E-anatum	E1.9.3	**5**: iv 4
	E-anatum	E1.9.3	**6**: iv 8
	E-anatum	E1.9.3	**8**: v 1
	E-anatum	E1.9.3	**10**: ii 1
	E-anatum	E1.9.3	**16**: ii′ 2′
	En-metena	E1.9.5	**1**: ii 2
	En-metena	E1.9.5	**17**: vi 4
	En-metena	E1.9.5	**26**: vi 4
	En-metena	E1.9.5	**27**: iii 5
Gursar (GN or grandfather of Ur-Nanše?)	Ur-Nanše	E1.9.1	**2**: a 4
	Ur-Nanše	E1.9.1	**5**: inscription beneath the feet of the king i 5
	Ur-Nanše	E1.9.1	**6b**: obv. ii 1
	Ur-Nanše	E1.9.1	**9**: i 5
	Ur-Nanše	E1.9.1	**10**: ii 1
	Ur-Nanše	E1.9.1	**11**: i 5
	Ur-Nanše	E1.9.1	**12**: ii 1
	Ur-Nanše	E1.9.1	**13**: ii 1
	Ur-Nanše	E1.9.1	**14**: ii 1
	Ur-Nanše	E1.9.1	**15**: ii 1
	Ur-Nanše	E1.9.1	**16**: i 5
	Ur-Nanše	E1.9.1	**17**: i 5
	Ur-Nanše	E1.9.1	**18**: ii 1
	Ur-Nanše	E1.9.1	**22**: 5
	Ur-Nanše	E1.9.1	**23**: 5
	Ur-Nanše	E1.9.1	**31**: i 5
Ḫaral (town)	G̃iša-kidu	E1.12.6	**2**: 36, 39
Ḫazuwan (city)	IB-LUL-il	E1.10.12	**5**: obv. ix 6
Ḫenda (city)	URU-KA-gina	E1.9.9	**5**: v 1
Holy Canal (pa_5-kù, canal in the vicinity of the city G̃irsu)	En-metena	E1.9.5	**17**: v 5

Toponym:	Appears in:	RIM no.:	Text Reference:
id$_5$(A)-a-suḫur (canal in the vicinity of G̃irsu)	Ur-Nanše	E1.9.1	**6b**: obv. vi 1
Idigna (=Tigris, Akk. *Idiglat*, river)	En-metena	E1.9.5	**1**: iv 6, v 9
	Lugal-zage-si	E1.14.20	**1**: ii 6
Ilgi (city)	An(u)bu	E1.10.1	**1**: obv. i 10
Ilwi (city)	Saʾumu	E1.10.8	**1**: obv. ii 12
Imar (=Emar, city)	Išṭup-Šar	E1.10.9	**1**: obv. iv 14, v 8
	IB-LUL-il	E1.10.12	**7**: rev. i 5
Imsagga (city)	En-metena	E1.9.5	**12**: vi 6
	En-metena	E1.9.5	**16**: 23
	En-metena	E1.9.5	**17**: iii 6
	URU-KA-gina	E1.9.9	**2**: iii 2′
	URU-KA-gina	E1.9.9	**6**: iii 9
	URU-KA-gina	E1.9.9	**7**: 36
	URU-KA-gina	E1.9.9	**10**: iii′ 1′
i$_7$-pa$_5$-^{d}saman-KAS$_4$.DU (canal in the vicinity of G̃irsu)	URU-KA-gina	E1.9.9	**3**: iii 14′
	URU-KA-gina	E1.9.9	**10**: iii′ 5′
Ganane (city)	IB-LUL-il	E1.10.12	**8**: rev. ii 8
Kiʾan (city)	Lugal-zage-si	E1.14.20	**1**: ii 46
Ki-en-gi$_4$ (Sumer, Akk. *Šumeri*, land, = southern Babylonia)	E-anatum	E1.9.3	**1**: rev. viii 5′
	En-šakuš-Ana	E1.14.17	**1**: 4
	En-šakuš-Ana	E1.14.17	**3**: 3
	Lugal-zage-si	E1.14.20	**1**: ii 21
Kiʾeš (city)	URU-KA-gina	E1.9.9	**5**: v 3
Kiḫara (city)	E-anatum	E1.9.3	**1**: obv. xii 12
Kimari (field)	E-anatum	E1.9.3	**2**:ii 12
KinuNIR (city)	URU-KA-gina	E1.9.9	**5**: v 8
Kiš (city)	EN.ME-barage-si	E1.7.22	**2**: 3
	[RN] Offspring of "Lady Dragon"	E1.7.40	**1**: 2′
	Utuk/Uḫub	E1.7.42	**1**: 4
	Me-silim	E1.8.1	**1**: 3
	Me-silim	E1.8.1	**2**: 2
	Me-silim	E1.8.1	**3**: 2
	Lugal-namnir-sum	E1.8.2	**1**: 4
	Enna-il	E1.8.3	**2**: ii 2
	E-anatum	E1.9.3	**1**: obv. vii 2
	E-anatum	E1.9.3	**3**: i 7
	E-anatum	E1.9.3	**5**: vi 4; vi 9, 21
	E-anatum	E1.9.3	**11**: side 4 iii 3′

Toponym:	Appears in:	RIM no.:	Text Reference:
Kiš (continued) (city)	Mes-Ane-pada	E1.13.5	**1**: 6
	Mes-Ane-pada	E1.13.5	**2**: 2
	Lugal-SILA-si	E1.14.13	**1**: 5
	Lugal-kiğine-dudu	E1.14.14	**2**: 4
	Lugal-kiğine-dudu	E1.14.14	**6**: 6
	Ur-zage	E1.14.16	**1**: 8
	En-šakuš-Ana	E1.14.17	**1**: 8, 11, 14
	En-šakuš-Ana	E1.14.17	**2**: 3
Kiutu (city)	E-anatum	E1.9.3	**5**: iv 10
	E-anatum	E1.9.3	**6**: iv 14
Labnan (city)	An(u)bu	E1.10.1	**1**: obv. ii 7
Lagaš (city)	Me-silim	E1.8.1	**1**: 9
	Ur-Nanše	E1.9.1	**1**: 3
	Ur-Nanše	E1.9.1	**2**: a 2, c 3
	Ur-Nanše	E1.9.1	**3**: a 3
	Ur-Nanše	E1.9.1	**4**: a 3
	Ur-Nanše	E1.9.1	**5**: a 3, b i 3
	Ur-Nanše	E1.9.1	**6**: obv. i 3, v 8, rev. i 1, 6
	Ur-Nanše	E1.9.1	**7**: 3
	Ur-Nanše	E1.9.1	**8**: i 3
	Ur-Nanše	E1.9.1	**9**: i 3
	Ur-Nanše	E1.9.1	**10**: i 3
	Ur-Nanše	E1.9.1	**11**: i 3
	Ur-Nanše	E1.9.1	**12**: i 3
	Ur-Nanše	E1.9.1	**13**: i 3
	Ur-Nanše	E1.9.1	**14**: i 3
	Ur-Nanše	E1.9.1	**15**: i 3
	Ur-Nanše	E1.9.1	**16**: i 3
	Ur-Nanše	E1.9.1	**17**: i 3, iv 5
	Ur-Nanše	E1.9.1	**18**: i 3
	Ur-Nanše	E1.9.1	**19**: 3
	Ur-Nanše	E1.9.1	**20**: i 3, iv 4
	Ur-Nanše	E1.9.1	**21**: 4
	Ur-Nanše	E1.9.1	**22**: 3
	Ur-Nanše	E1.9.1	**23**: 3
	Ur-Nanše	E1.9.1	**24a**: 4
	Ur-Nanše	E1.9.1	**24b**: 3
	Ur-Nanše	E1.9.1	**26a**: 4
	Ur-Nanše	E1.9.1	**27**: 4
	Ur-Nanše	E1.9.1	**29**: i 3
	Ur-Nanše	E1.9.1	**30**: i 3
	A-kurgal	E1.9.2	**1**: 4, 6
	A-kurgal	E1.9.2	**3**: 3′
	E-anatum	E1.9.3	**1**: obv. i 26, ii 27, 32, iii 2, 19, iv 2, v 16, rev. v 44, Cartouche C 2
	E-anatum	E1.9.3	**2**: ii 7, iv 4
	E-anatum	E1.9.3	**3**: i 14
	E-anatum	E1.9.3	**4**: i 5, 13
	E-anatum	E1.9.3	**5**: i 4, iii 3, v 25, vi 3; 14, viii 3, 7

Toponym:	Appears in:	RIM no.:	Text Reference:
Lagaš (continued) (city)	E-anatum	E1.9.3	**6**: i 3, 9, iii 2, vii 7, 10, 14
	E-anatum	E1.9.3	**7**: i 5
	E-anatum	E1.9.3	**8**:i 4, ii 8
	E-anatum	E1.9.3	**9**:i 3, ii 3
	E-anatum	E1.9.3	**10**:i 6, ii 8
	E-anatum	E1.9.3	**11**:side 4 iii 10′;
	E-anatum	E1.9.3	**12**:3′;
	En-anatum I	E1.9.4	**1**:3
	En-anatum I	E1.9.4	**2**:i 5, ii 11, iii 4
	En-anatum I	E1.9.4	**3**:i 3, 6
	En-anatum I	E1.9.4	**4**:5, 10
	En-anatum I	E1.9.4	**5**:i 5, ii 4, 8, iv 4
	En-anatum I	E1.9.4	**6**:i 5
	En-anatum I	E1.9.4	**7**:3
	En-anatum I	E1.9.4	**8**:i 3, ii 3, 7, 11
	En-anatum I	E1.9.4	**9**:i 3, ii 8, 12, iii 3
	En-anatum I	E1.9.4	**10**:i 5, 8
	En-anatum I	E1.9.4	**11**:i 0, 1′, 4′, ii 0, 1′
	En-anatum I	E1.9.4	**13**: 3′
	En-anatum I	E1.9.4	**14**:i 3, ii 4
	En-anatum I	E1.9.4	**15**:i 6, 9, 18, ii 1
	En-anatum I	E1.9.4	**16**: 5
	En-anatum I	E1.9.4	**17**:i 3, 10
	En-anatum I	E1.9.4	**18**:i 3
	En-anatum I	E1.9.4	**19**: 5
	En-anatum I	E1.9.4	**20**: ii′ 2′
	En-metena	E1.9.5	**1**:i 9, 20, 34, 38, iii 7, iv 15, v 3, 21
	En-metena	E1.9.5	**2**:i 5
	En-metena	E1.9.5	**3**:i 5, ii 6
	En-metena	E1.9.5	**4**:i 4, 10; iii 10
	En-metena	E1.9.5	**5**:ii 1, 4
	En-metena	E1.9.5	**5a**:obv. i 5, iii 4, iv 1, lower edge col. iii 1
	En-metena	E1.9.5	**6**: i 5, ii 1
	En-metena	E1.9.5	**7**: 5, 12
	En-metena	E1.9.5	**8**: i 5, iii 2
	En-metena	E1.9.5	**9**: 5, 8
	En-metena	E1.9.5	**10**: 3
	En-metena	E1.9.5	**11**:i 5, ii 6
	En-metena	E1.9.5	**12**:i 5, ii 1, 5
	En-metena	E1.9.5	**13**:i 5, ii 3
	En-metena	E1.9.5	**14**:5
	En-metena	E1.9.5	**15**:i 5, iii 3
	En-metena	E1.9.5	**16**:5, 8
	En-metena	E1.9.5	**17**:i 5, 12, 16, vi 4
	En-metena	E1.9.5	**18**:i 4 , ii 6″
	En-metena	E1.9.5	**19**:i 5, ii 2
	En-metena	E1.9.5	**20**:5, 15
	En-metena	E1.9.5	**20a**:5, 15
	En-metena	E1.9.5	**21**:2, 5
	En-metena	E1.9.5	**22**:4
	En-metena	E1.9.5	**23**:5, 12, 15
	En-metena	E1.9.5	**26**:i 5, ii 10, v 3

Toponym:	Appears in:	RIM no.:	Text Reference:
Lagaš (continued) (city)	En-metena	E1.9.5	**27**:i 5, 8
	En-anatum II	E1.9.6	**1**: 5, 12
	Saʾumu	E1.9.8	**1**: 3
	Saʾumu	E1.9.8	**2**:i′ 1′, ii′ 1′
	URU-KA-gina	E1.9.9	**1**: i 5, viii 3, xii 13
	URU-KA-gina	E1.9.9	**2**: vi 27
	URU-KA-gina	E1.9.9	**5**: vii 11
	URU-KA-gina	E1.9.9	**6**: i 5, iv 7
	URU-KA-gina	E1.9.9	**7**: 4
	URU-KA-gina	E1.9.9	**8**: i 4, iii 4;
	URU-KA-gina	E1.9.9	**10**: iv′ 3′
	URU-KA-gina	E1.9.9	**11**: 7
	URU-KA-gina	E1.9.9	**12**: 3
	Unnamed, Lagaš	E1.9.10	**3**: 2′
LA.LA-bum (city)	Išṭup-Šar	E1.10.9	**1**: obv. iv 16, v 11
Larsa (city)	E-anatum	E1.9.3	**1**: rev. i 38
	En-metena	E1.9.5	**4**: v 5
	Lugal-zage-si	E1.14.20	**1**: ii 33
LUM-ma-g̃im-du (canal in the vicinity of G̃irsu)	E-anatum	E1.9.3	**5**: vii 4, 11
	En-metena	E1.9.5	**26**: vii 6
LUM-ma-(x) (canal, see LUM-ma-g̃im-du)	En-metena	E1.9.5	**26:** vi 3
Lumagirnunta (canal)	En-anatum I	E1.9.4	**2**: xi 3
	En-metena	E1.9.5	**1**: iii 20
Lumagirnunta-šakugepada (field)	E-anatum	E1.9.3	**4**: ii 11
Mane (city)	IB-LUL-il	E1.10.12	**7**: rev. i 2
Mari (city)	E-anatum	E1.9.3	**5**: vi 22
	An(u)bu	E1.10.1	**1**: obv. ii 2
	Ikūn-Šamaš	E1.10.7	**1:** 2
	Saʾumu	E1.10.8	**1:** obv. iii 2
	Saʾumu	E1.10.8	**2**: iv 4
	Išṭup-Šar	E1.10.9	**1**: obv. v 5
	Ikūn-Mari	E1.10.10	**1:** 4
	Ikū(n)-Šamagan	E1.10.11	**2001:** 2
	Ikū(n)-Šamagan	E1.10.11	**2002:** 2
	IB-LUL-il	E1.10.12	**1:** 2
	IB-LUL-il	E1.10.12	**2:** 2
	IB-LUL-il	E1.10.12	**3:** 2
	IB-LUL-il	E1.10.12	**5:** obv vi 7
	IB-LUL-il	E1.10.12	**6:** obv vii 4
	IB-LUL-il	E1.10.12	**7:** obv viii 10, ix 10
	IB-LUL-il	E1.10.12	**8:** rev. i 11
	IB-LUL-il	E1.10.12	**9:** rev. iii 1
	Enna-Dagān	E1.10.14	**1:** rev. iii 13
	Ikū(n)-išar	E1.10.15	**1:** 2
	Išgi-mari	E1.10.17	**1:** 2
	Išgi-mari	E1.10.17	**1:** 2

Toponym:	Appears in:	RIM no.:	Text Reference:
Me (gate in the city of G̃irsu)	Ur-Nanše	E1.9.1	**6b**: obv. v 4
Mešime (city)	E-anatum	E1.9.3	**5**: iv 16
	E-anatum	E1.9.3	**6**: v 1
	E-anatum	E1.9.3	**8**: v 7
Mubikurra (city)	En-metena	E1.9.5	**2**: iv 1
Murgu-Šara (town)	G̃iša-kidu	E1.12.6	**2**: 58, 61
Nag-Nanše (town)	G̃iša-kidu	E1.12.6	**2**: 46, 49.
Naḫal (city)	Saʾumu	E1.10.8	**2**: obv. iv 10
	IB-LUL-il	E1.10.12	**8**: rev. i 13
Namnunkigara (boundary-levee)	En-metena	E1.9.5	**1**: ii 13, 40, iv 8, v 12
Nanga (city)	E-anatum	E1.9.3	**1**: obv. viii 4
Nerat (city)	IB-LUL-il	E1.10.12	**7**: obv. ix 2
NÍG.BA.DU.DAR.KUR (field)	E-anatum	E1.9.3	**2**: iii 12
Nig̃in (city)	E-anatum	E1.9.3	**5**: iii 10
	E-anatum	E1.9.3	**6**: iii 9
	E-anatum	E1.9.3	**8**: iii 3
	En-metena	E1.9.5	**17**: v 3
	URU-KA-gina	E1.9.9	**1**: viii 37
	URU-KA-gina	E1.9.9	**2**: vi 36
Ninadua (canal in the vicinity of G̃irsu)	URU-KA-gina	E1.9.9	**1**: ii 8, xii 39
	URU-KA-gina	E1.9.9	**2**: iii 6′
	URU-KA-gina	E1.9.9	**4**: i′ 1′
	URU-KA-gina	E1.9.9	**8**: ii 6, iv 1
Nin-sanga$_x$(RÉC 107) (canal in the vicinity of G̃irsu)	Ur-Nanše	E1.9.1	**9**: v 3
Ning̃irsu Nibri.KI-ta nir-gál ("Ningirsu is Proudly Confident in Nippur = Turgirsuʾituka, canal in the vicinity of G̃irsu)	URU-KA-gina	E1.9.9	**1**: xii 36
Ning̃irsu-pada-LAK 500-ma-ni (canal in the vicinity of G̃irsu)	Ur-Nanše	E1.9.1	**12**: iii 2-3
Nippur (city)	E-anatum	E1.9.3	**1**: obv. xvii 3
	E-anatum	E1.9.3	**11**: side 1 v 9
	En-metena	E1.9.5	**18**: i 6″
	Lugal-Anda	E1.9.8	**2**: ii′ 6′
	Nammaḫ	E1.11.1	**1: 6**
	Ur-Enlil	E1.11.2	**1**: 7
	Ur-Enlil	E1.11.2	**2**: 3
	Abzu-kidu	E1.11.3	**1**: 5
	En-šakuš-Ana	E1.14.17	**1**: 7′
	Lugal-zage-si	E1.14.20	**1**: iii 38
NIrum (city)	Saʾumu	E1.10.8	**2**: obv. iii 12

Toponym:	Appears in:	RIM no.:	Text Reference:
Nubat (city)	IB-LUL-il	E1.10.12	**8**: rev. ii 1
Pa$_5$-tibira (=Bad-tibira, city)	En-metena	E1.9.5	**4**: iv 8, v 6
Pirigedena (canal)	E-anatum	E1.9.3	**1**: rev. xii 29
Pirig̃-ZÀ-[(x)]-g̃ir⌈nun⌉-šage (place? Near Lagaš)	E-anatum	E1.9.3	**1**: obv. iii 23-24.
Raʾak (city)	Saʾumu	E1.10.8	**1**: obv. iii 10
RÉC 107 (canal in the vicinity of G̃irsu)	Ur-Nanše	E1.9.1	**17**: ii 6
	Ur-Nanše	E1.9.1	**20**: v 5
Sag-⌈ub$_x$⌉ (EZEN×BAD) (city)	URU-KA-gina	E1.9.9	**5**: vi 11
Sala (canal in the vicinity of G̃irsu)	En-metena	E1.9.5	**27**: iii 4
Saman (Pa$_5$-saman) (canal in the vicinity of G̃irsu)	Ur-Nanše	E1.9.1	**6b**: obv. v 10
Sea, Lower (Sum. a-ab-ba-sig-sig, Akk. *tiʾāmtum šapiltum*)	Lugal-zage-si	E1.14.20	**1**: ii 4-5
Sea, Upper (Sum. a-ab-ba-IGI.NIM, Akk. *tiʾāmtum alītum*)	Lugal-zage-si	E1.14.20	**1**: ii 8-9
Sirara (city)	En-metena	E1.9.5	**26**: iii 8
Šubar (=Subartu, land)	E-anatum	E1.9.3	**1**: rev. vi 10
	E-anatum	E1.9.3	**5**: vi 17
	E-anatum	E1.9.3	**7**: ii 2
Sugurum (land)	IB-LUL-il	E1.10.12	**6**: obv. vii 14
Sulum (city)	En-metena	E1.9.5	**4**: iii 7
	En-metena	E1.9.5	**16**: 15
	En-metena	E1.9.5	**17**: ii 7
	En-metena	E1.9.5	**19**: ii 5
Sumtultul (field)	E-anatum	E1.9.3	**2**: ii 10
Surgindu (canal in the vicinity of G̃irsu)	Ur-Nanše	E1.9.1	**9**: iv 6
Susan (= Susa, city)	E-anatum	E1.9.3	**1**: rev. vii 3′
Šada (city)	IB-LUL-il	E1.10.12	**5**: obv. vii 6, rev. ii 3
Šaran (city)	IB-LUL-il	E1.10.12	**5**: obv. viii 6
Tibilat (city)	Saʾumu	E1.10.8	**1**: obv. ii 10
	IB-LUL-il	E1.10.12	**5**: rev. iii 7
Tidnum (people)	E-anatum	E1.9.3	**5**: v 13
Tirsig (canal in the vicinity of G̃irsu)	Ur-Nanše	E1.9.1	**9**: iv 1

Toponym:	Appears in:	RIM no.:	Text Reference:
Turgirsu'ituka (Also see Ningirsu Nibri.KI-ta nir-gál, "Ningirsu is Proudly Confident in Nippur," canal in the vicinity of G̃irsu)	En-metena	E1.9.5	**4**: iv 8, v 6
Ugigga (field)	En-metena	E1.9.5	**1**: iii 8
	URU-KA-gina	E1.9.9	**3**: iv 13′
Umma (ŠÁR×DIŠ)	Pa-bilga ...	E1.12.1	**1**: 2
	Ur-LUM-ma	E1.12.4	**1**: 3, 5
	Ur-LUM-ma	E1.12.4	**2**: 3, 5
	Il	E1.12.5	**1**: 2, 6
	G̃iša-kidu	E1.12.6	**1**: 2, 3, 4, 5
Ur (city)	Ur-Nanše	E1.9.1	**6b**: rev. i 2, ii 1
	E-anatum	E1.9.3	**1**: obv. xxi 17, rev. ix 2′
	E-anatum	E1.9.3	**5**: iv 8
	E-anatum	E1.9.3	**6**: iv 12
	E-anatum	E1.9.3	**9**: ii 10
	E-anatum	E1.9.3	**11**: side 1 iii 4
	A-KALAM-du	E1.13.4	**1**: 3
	Mes-Ane-pada	E1.13.5	**1**: 3
	A-Ane-pada	E1.13.6	**1**: 2
	A-Ane-pada	E1.13.6	**2**: 3
	A-Ane-pada	E1.13.6	**3**: 3, 5
	A-Ane-pada	E1.13.6	**4**: 3
	A-Ane-pada	E1.13.6	**5**: 3
	Mes-kiağ-nun	E1.13.8	**1**: 2′
	Elili	E1.13.9	**1**: 5
	Lugal-kiğine-dudu	E1.14.14	**1**: 12
	Lugal-kiğine-dudu	E1.14.14	**2**: 12
	Lugal-KISAL-si	E1.14.15	**1**: 7, 10
	Lugal-KISAL-si	E1.14.15	**2**: 5
	Lugal-zage-si	E1.14.20	**1**: ii 30
Ursa (city)	Enna-il	E1.8.3	**2**: i 3′
Urua (city)	E-anatum	E1.9.3	**1**: rev. vii 5′;
	E-anatum	E1.9.3	**5**: iii 17, vi 18
	E-anatum	E1.9.3	**6b**: iii 16
	E-anatum	E1.9.3	**8**: iii 10
	E-anatum	E1.9.3	**9**: ii 6
	En-metena	E1.9.5	**28**: 5
Uruaz (city)	E-anatum	E1.9.3	**5**: iv 12
	E-anatum	E1.9.3	**6b**: iv 16
	E-anatum	E1.9.3	**8**: v 5
Urub (URU×KAR) (temple district in G̃irsu?)	En-anatum I	E1.9.4	**10**: iii 5
Uruk (city)	E-anatum	E1.9.3	**5**: iv 6
	E-anatum	E1.9.3	**6**: iv 10
	E-anatum	E1.9.3	**8**: v 3
	E-anatum	E1.9.3	**11**: side 1 iii 2′
	En-metena	E1.9.5	**3**: ii 9

Toponym:	Appears in:	RIM no.:	Text Reference:
Uruk (continued) (city)	En-metena	E1.9.5	**4**: v 4, 10
	Unamed, Lagaš	E1.9.10	**2**: ii′ 10′
	Lugal-kiğine-dudu	E1.14.14	**1**: 9
	Lugal-kiğine-dudu	E1.14.14	**3**: 10
	Lugal-KISAL-si	E1.14.15	**1**: 6, 9
	Lugal-KISAL-si	E1.14.15	**2**: 4
	Ur-zage	E1.14.16	**1**: 9
	Lugal-zage-si	E1.14.20	**1**: i 4, 33, ii 23, iii 4
	Lugal-zage-si	E1.14.20	**2**: i′ 1′;
Uruku (Also Iriku, temple district in the city G̃irsu)	E-anatum	E1.9.3	**5**: iii 7
	E-anatum	E1.9.3	**6**: iii 6
	URU-KA-gina	E1.9.9	**1**: ii 5
Usardaʾu (field)	E-anatum	E1.9.3	**2**: ii 9
Warane (city)	Ikūn-Mari	E1.10.10	**1**: 5
Zabala(m) (city)	En-metena	E1.9.5	**1**: iii 29
	Lugal-zage-si	E1.14.20	**1**: ii 43
Zaḫiran (land)	IB-LUL-il	E1.10.12	**5**: obv. vi 12
x (field)	E-anatum	E1.9.3	**1**: obv. xv 10
x-AN (land)	Saʾumu	E1.10.8	**2**: obv. iv 8
x-gal-x (field	E-anatum	E1.9.3	**1**: obv. xv 17
x-GUR$_8$-x (field)	E-anatum	E1.9.3	**1**: obv. xv 15
x-lam-x (field)	E-anatum	E1.9.3	**1**: obv. xv 13, 14
x-tum-ma-al (field)	E-anatum	E1.9.3	**1**: obv. xv 12
x-x-x (field)	E-anatum	E1.9.3	**1**: obv. xv 16, 18
[...]-Ištaran (town)	G̃iša-kidu	E1.12.6	**2**: 62, 65

PRESARGONIC PERIOD

(2700–2350 BC)

Introduction

The texts edited in this volume date from the earliest known royal inscriptions in Mesopotamia down to the advent of the reign of Sargon of Akkad. Consequently, this period is designated in historical and philological works as the Presargonic period. The corresponding label used by archaeologists is the Early Dynastic (hereafter ED) period. S. Lloyd (Lloyd, Archaeology of Mesopotamia [1978], p. 91) notes:

> This so-called Pre-Sargonid era (preceding the unification of Mesopotamia under Sargon of Akkad), has come conventionally to be divided into three phases. 'Early Dynastic I' (ED I), following directly upon the end of the Protoliterate, is approximately dated to the years between 2900 and 2750 BC; 'Early Dynastic II' (ED II) lasted until 2650 BC; while 'Early Dynastic III' (ED III), divided into two sub-phases, 'a' and 'b', is taken to account for the greater part of three further centuries. This system of chronology was constructed largely from evidence obtained in the 1930s during excavations by the Oriental Institute of the University of Chicago at sites in the Diyala region, east of Baghdad. It was based ... on progressive variations in the architecture, sculpture, pottery, seal-cylinders and other small objects associated with several temples, founded in most cases at the end of the Protoliterate period and repeatedly rebuilt in Early Dynastic times. Its validity has been confirmed, with only minor reservations, by subsequent soundings of the same sort ...

According to another overview of ED times by D. Edzard (see Edzard, in Bottéro, Cassin and Vercoutter, The Near East: The Ancient Civilizations pp. 52–53):

> We divide the Early Dynastic Period into three stages, on the basis of archaeological finds; since their first application, to discoveries in the Diyala region, they have proved of practical use. Early Dynastic I extends from the Protoliterate period to the time of the archaic tablets of Ur. Early Dynastic II begins with the appearance of city walls in Sumer. Early Dynastic III has as its starting point the period of the archive of Shuruppak. In other words these divisions have nothing to do with turning points in political history, of which we know little enough in any case.

The periodization of the different phases of the ED times has been a matter of considerable scholarly debate. For example, in a recent assessment by Porada, Hansen, Dunham, and Babcock in Ehrich (ed.), Chronologies 3 p. 108, the authors write:

> In sum, the materials from level VIII of the Inanna temple [at Nippur] do not allow for the definition of a distinct period in the south of Mesopotamia that equates with the Early Dynastic II of the Diyala. At best, it is a transitional phase between Early Dynastic I and III of Nippur ...

Much scholarly attention has been focused on the periodization of the very end of the ED period, generally designated the "ED III period." For studies touching on this topic see H. Frankfort, Stratified Cylinders Seals from the Diyala Region, OIP 72 pp. 28–31; Porada, The Relative Chronology of Mesopotamia. Part I. Seals and Trade (6000–1600 B.C.) in E. Ehrich, Chronologies 2 pp. 161–65; B. Buchanan, Catalogue of Ancient Near Eastern Seals in the Ashmolean Museum I. Cylinder Seals I. pp. 33–50; M. Mallowan, The Early Dynastic Period in Mesopotamia, CAH I/2 pp. 244–72; R. Boehmer, "Zur Glyptik zwischen Mesilim- und Akkad Zeit (Early Dynastic III)," ZA 59 (1969) pp. 261–92; S. Pollock, "Chronology of the Royal Cemetery of

Ur," Iraq 47 (1985) pp. 129–58; Vértesalji and S. Kolbus, "Review of Protodynastic Development in Babylonia," Mesopotamia 20 (1985) pp. 53–109. Also of considerable interest has been the transitional period from the ED IIIb to the Akkadian periods; important articles on this subject are M. Gibson and A. McMahon, "Investigation of the Early Dynastic—Akkadian Transition: Report of the 18th and 19th Seasons of Excavation in Area WF, Nippur," Iraq 57 (1995) pp. 1–39; D. Matthews, "The Early Dynastic-Akkadian Transition Part 1: When Did the Akkadian Period Begin?" Iraq 59 (1997) pp. 1–7; and M. Gibson and A. McMahon, "The Early Dynastic-Akkadian Transition Part II: The Authors' Response," Iraq 59 (1997) pp. 9–14.

In general terms, a recent assessment of the archaeological data for the ED period by Porada, Hansen, Dunham and Babcock in Ehrich, Chronologies 3 p. 100 concludes that the ED I period started c. 2900 BCE, Late ED I about c. 2750 BCE, ED IIIa about c. 2600 BC, and ED IIIb about c. 2500 BCE.

The above figures are general dates; despite much scholarly effort, the absolute chronology of Mesopotamia has yet to be determined. The most recent bibliography of the technical discussion in this connection is found in F. Zeeb, Die Palastwirtschaft in Altsyrien nach den spätbabylonischen Getreidelieferlisten aus Alalaḫ, AOAT 282, pp. 73–89. Traditionally, the so-called Venus Tablets of Ammī-ṣaduqa served as a basis for Mesopotamian chronology establishing the possibilities of a "Low," "Middle" or "High" chronology. P.J. Huber, in his Astronomical Dating of Babylon I and Ur III, has argued for a "High" chronology. On the other hand, two recent studies have suggested an "Ultra-Low" chronology, namely H. Gasche, J. Armstrong, S. Cole, and V. Gurzadyan, Dating the Fall of Babylon: A Reappraisal of Second-Millennium Chronology. Mesopotamian History and Environment, Series II, Memoirs IV, University of Ghent, and H. Gasche, J. Armstrong, S. Cole, and V. Gurzadyan, "A Correction to Dating the Fall of Babylon. A Reappraisal of Second-Millennium Chronology (=MHEM 4), Ghent and Chicago, 1998," Akkadica 108 (1998) pp. 1–4. To these we can now add the further discussion (most of which favours the "Ultra-Low" chronology) in the publication Just in Time: Proceedings of the International Colloquium on Ancient Near Eastern Chronology (2nd Millennium BC) Ghent 7–9 July 2000, published in Akkadica 119–20 Sept.–Dec. 2000. Subsequently C. Michel and P. Rocher, in an article entitled "La chronologie du IIè millenaire revue à l'ombre d'une éclipse de soleil," JEOL 35/36 (1997/2000) pp. 111–26, have used the evidence of an eclipse recorded in the Mari eponym chronicle and dendrochronological data to suggest that the Middle chronology should be lowered 51 years. About the time of the appearance of the article of Michel and Rocher, Manning Newton as reported in http:www.science.org / 6 March 2001 have determined that the earlier conclusions published by Kuniholm et al., in Nature 381, 780 (1996) concerning the dendrochronological evidence from Gordion and other sites is to be modified as follows:

> We may note the following key revisions to synchronisms discussed previously. The dates for the construction of the Sarikaya Palace at Acemhöyük and the Warama Palace at Kültepe (= Karum Kaneš Ib) may now be dated c. 1774 +4/-7BC and c. 1832 +41-7 BC respectively. The latter palace was in use for at least 61 years due to the presence of later dated repair timbers. Prosopographical references on clay bullae found in these buildings allow us to resolve more than a century of debate over a problematic 300-year range in Assyrian-Mesopotamian chronology between Ultra-High, High, Middle, Low and Ultra-Low options. Sealings of Samši-Adad I, the Old Assyrian king, and of his officials, are found in an archive collection from the Sarikaya Palace at Acemhöyük, and must post-date its construction c. 1774 +41-7 BC. Some of the earliest documents from Kültepe Ib are also associated with Šamši-Adad I, and officials from the later part of his reign are subsequently attested in the Karum Kaneš-Aššur correspondence. The implication is that the beginning of Kültepe Ib was around, or a little before, the accession of Samši-Adad I, and that at least the later part of his reign was contemporary with a post-c. 1774 +41-7 BC date at Acemhöyük. Samši-Adad I was a king for a minimum for 57 years, the latter 33 of these as king of Assyria. With the revised Anatolian tree-ring dating, only a chronological solution close to the classic Middle chronology, which places the reign of Šamši-Adad I between c. 1832 +7/-1 BC and 1776+7/-I BC, is viable. The so-called Low-Middle chronology is also plausible. The High chronology, some 56 years earlier, is ruled out, and the Low chronology, some 64 years lower, or recent Ultra-Low proposals, some 89 years lower, are rendered respectively unlikely and very unlikely, as these options would require long pre-Šamši-Adad I phases for both contexts, but there is no pre-Šamši-Adad I documentation in either context, despite much epigraphical and glyptic evidence.

This revision of the dendrochronological data led C. Michel in "Nouvelles données pour la chronologie du IIè millénaire" in NABU 2002 no. 20 to suggest a different date for the eclipse noted in the Mari chronicle, namely 1833 BCE. Her conclusions were rejected by D. Warburton in his article "Eclipses, Venus-Cycles and Chronology" which appeared in Akkadica 123 (2002) pp. 108–14; Warburton argued for "Ultra-Low" chronology, with a date for the fall of Babylon in 1499 BCE.

(a) Royal Inscriptions: The Sources

While cuneiform writing in Sumerian is attested in economic and lexical texts dating back to the Uruk IV (c. 3400 BC) and Uruk III periods (c. 3000 BC) the earliest known royal inscriptions are label inscriptions naming King EN.ME-barage-si of Kiš; they date to c. 2600 BC in what was likely the ED II period. It is possible that inscriptions of city rulers existed before this time, but, as yet, none have been found. Indeed, apart from the sizable corpus of inscriptions from ancient G̃irsu (modern Telloh), relatively few ED royal inscriptions have survived.

(b) Problems in Evaluating the Royal Inscriptions

A number of factors complicate our understanding of historical documents of the Presargonic period. Cooper (in SANE 2 pp. 18–21), for example, has summarized the geographical, chronological, and philological difficulties inherent in our understanding of the texts dealing with the border dispute between Lagaš and G̃iša (Umma). Further complicating the historical picture in ED times is the fact, as Nissen (Königsfriedhof p. 134) points out, that the title lugal kiš "king of Kiš" of ED royal inscriptions, while clearly referring in some cases to actual kings of Kiš (such as EN.ME-barage-si), seems, at other times, to be an honorific epithet meaning something like "king of the world." It appears, in the titulary of Me-silim (for the dynastic affiliation of this ruler, see the discussion to E1.8.1 below), Enna-il, E-anatum of Lagaš, Mes-Ane-pada of Ur, En-šakuš-Ana of Uruk, and Lugal-kig̃ine-dudu of Ur and Uruk. It is uncertain whether any of these last three named rulers actually controlled Kiš. A further complication of our understanding of ED history is the practice of some city rulers to adopt a second name in addition to their personal name. The best known example of this practice is found in an inscription of E-anatum of Lagaš, who informs us (in E1.9.3.5 col. v lines 9–14): u_4-ba é-an-na-túm-ma é-an-na-túm mu-ú-rum-m[a]-ni mu-tidnum(=GÌR.GÌR)-ni L[U]M-ma-a "At that time, E-anatum, whose personal name is E-anatum and whose battle(?) (or Tidnum[?]) name is L[U]M-ma..."

Further, E. Gordon (BASOR 132 [1953] pp. 27–30) has argued on the basis of the comparative evidence of two proverbs that Me-silim may have been a second name of King Mes-Ane-pada of Ur. Certainly, the three cities linked to Me-silim and Mes-Ane-pada: Ur (Mes-Ane-pada), Lagaš (Me-silim), and Larsa (Me-silim) — if the omen tradition be correct — lie quite close together. Further, both Me-silim and Mes-Ane-pada adopted the title "king of Kiš" in their own inscriptions. However, the script of the Me-silim and Mes-Ane-pada inscriptions is sufficiently different to make an equation of the two highly unlikely.

(c) Historiographic and Literary Texts as Sources for ED History

The gap in our information of ED history due to the lack of royal inscriptions can be filled to a modest degree by later historiographic and literary documents. The most important of these is the Sumerian King List (hereafter cited in this monograph as SKL), a literary text whose original date of composition is still a matter of debate among scholars. It is known for the most part from (later) Old Babylonian period tablet copies. For the ground-breaking (but now outdated) editio princeps of this priceless document, see Th. Jacobsen, SKL. For additional studies and reviews, see F. Kraus, "Zur List der älteren Könige von Babylonien," ZA 50 (1952) pp. 29–60; M. Civil, "Texts and Fragments," JCS 15 (1961) pp. 79–80; J. Finkelstein, "The Antediluvian Kings: A University of California Tablet," JCS 17 (1963) pp. 39–51; W. Hallo, "Beginning and End of the Sumerian King List in the Nippur Recension," JCS 17 (1963) pp. 52–57 and pp. 112–18; A. Westenholz, "Early Nippur Year Dates and the Sumerian King List," JCS 26 (1974) pp. 154–56; B. Lukács and L. Vésgö, "The Chronology of the Sumerian King List," AoF 2 (1975) pp. 25–45; A. Kammenhuber, "Eine verkannte Überlieferungslücke in der sumerischen Königslisten," Orientalia NS 48 (1979) pp. 1–25; D. Edzard, "Die Sumerische Königsliste," RLA 6, pp. 77–84; P. Michalowski, "History as Charter: Some Observations on the Sumerian King List," JAOS 103 (1983) pp. 237–48; G. Steiner, "Der 'reale' Kern in den 'legendären' Zahlen von Regierungsjahren der ältesten Herrscher Mesopotamiens," ASJ 10 (1988) pp. 129–52; C. Wilcke, "Inschriftenfunde der 7. und 8. Kampagnen," in B. Hrouda, Isin III pp. 80–93; *idem*, "Die Sumerische Königsliste und erzählte Vergangenheit," in J. von Unger-Sternberg and H. Reinau (eds.), Colloquium Ruricum 1: Vergangenheit in mündlicher Überlieferung, pp. 113–140; idem, "Genealogical Thought in the Sumerian Kinglist", Studies Sjöberg pp. 557–71; C. Vincente, "Tell Leilan Recension of the Sumerian Kinglist," NABU 1990 pp. 8–9 no. 11; idem, "The Tell Leilān Recension of the Sumerian King List, ZA 85 (1995) pp. 234–70; J. Klein, "A New Nippur Duplicate of the Sumerian King List in the Brockmon Collection, University of Haifa," AuOr 9 (1991) pp. 123–29. A further addition to the manuscript list is a tablet in the Schøyen Collection (MS 2855) consisting of a fragment of the beginning of the King List; it may be viewed at the website www.nb.no/baser/schoyen/. An

Ur III copy of the King List from a private collection has been published by P. Steinkeller in "An Ur III Manuscript of the Sumerian King List," Studies Wilcke pp. 267–92. A re-edition of the SKL by G. Manchesis as a Harvard PhD dissertation has been announced by Steinkeller in the previously cited work on p. 267. Until this re-edition we may avail ourselves of the resources of the ETCSL project; a composite text of the King List may be consulted at the website: www-etcsl.orient.ox.ac.uk.

The SKL listed the city rulers of various states starting with the first dynasty of Kiš (in one recension), and an antediluvian series of kings followed by the first dynasty of Kiš (in a second recension). The text concludes with the names of the kings of the first dynasty of Isin. The SKL is structured on the premise that at any given time kingship (nam-lugal), apparently meaning hegemony over the land of Sumer, was exercised by the ruler of only one city-state. The particular phraseology utilized by the SKL can be exemplified by the model found in the Weld Blundell MS of the SKL. It gives: (a) a list of rulers and lengths of reigns for one city: GN_1 RN_1 mu N_1 ì-ak, RN_2 mu N_2 ì-ak, etc. "In GN_1 RN_1 reigned N_1 years, RN_2 reigned N_2 years," etc.; (b) a dynastic total: N_3 lugal mu-bi N_4 "N_3 kings reigned (a total) of N_4 years"; and (c) a change of dynasty statement: GN_1 GIŠ.tukul ba-an-sìg GN_2-šè nam-lugal-bi ba-túm "GN_1 was smitten with weapons, its kingship was transferred to GN_2." While the sequence of successively dominant powers in the SKL appears in general terms to be correct, the fact that the SKL gives a seemingly complete list of the kings of a particular city dynasty, whether or not they actually exercised hegemony in Sumer, paints on first examination a misleading picture. For example, it would seem that the SKL indicates that the hegemony of Aka of the Kiš I dynasty was followed by the hegemony of Mes-kiag̃-gašer, the first king of the Uruk I dynasty. But the evidence of the literary composition "Gilgameš and Aka" tells us that Gilgameš and Aka were, in fact, contemporaries, and we know from the SKL that Gilgameš was the fifth, not first, king of the Uruk I dynasty. Further, a new exemplar of the SKL discussed by J. Klein (in Aula Orientalis 9 [1991] pp. 123–29) relates that the second predecessor of Gilgameš at Uruk, King Dumuzi, captured King EN.ME-barage-si of Kiš, Aka's father. Bearing in mind the SKL's convention of listing whole dynasties as indivisible units, we can reconstruct the general outline of ED II and III history using the additional data provided by contemporary royal inscriptions and later literary texts.

Another important source of ED royal names is an apparent "Bilingual" King List edited as Chronicle 18 in Grayson, Chronicles pp. 139–44, and now supplemented by additional tablet fragments published by Lambert in Studies Böhl pp. 271–75 and Finkel in JCS 32 (1980) pp. 65–72.

A third important source for the names of Presargonic rulers is the so-called Tummal Chronicle (see Ali, Sumerian Letters pp. 99–104 letter B 9, Sollberger, JCS 16 [1962] pp. 40–47, and now the edition posted by the ETCSL at its website www-etcsl.orient.ox.ac.uk/). This text was possibly composed in Ur III times to commemorate a religious festival held in the city of Tummal (possibly modern Tell Dlihim c. 21 km SE of Nippur; see M. Yoshikawa, ASJ 11 [1989] pp. 285–91 for the location). Five episodes in the text recount how a particular king built a shrine for the god Enlil in Nippur and how the same king's son subsequently had a statue(?) of the goddess Ninlil brought into the goddess's temple in Tummal. The four episodes of the Tummal Chronicle relevant to ED history are: (a) EN.ME-barage-si (of Kiš) and his son Aka, (b) Mes-Ane-pada (of Ur) and his son Mes-kiag̃-nuna, (c) Bilgameš (= Gilgameš) (of Uruk) and his son Ur-lugal, and (d) Nanne (of Ur?) and his son Mes-kiag̃-Nanna. Entry (d) would appear to be a simple variant of entry (b), although this is not entirely certain. The Chronicle provides us with the historical sequence: EN.ME-barage-si, Gilgameš, and Mes-Ane-pada and agrees with the evidence of the SKL and other literary texts. It also suggests that EN.ME-barage-si, Gilgameš, and Mes-Ane-pada, for at least part of their reigns, had close links with Nippur, the exact nature of which is hard to ascertain from our meager sources — control over the city is conceivable.

(d) The Dominant Mesopotamian Powers in ED II–ED III Times

Five dominant heartland powers are named in the SKL: Kiš, Uruk, Ur, Adab, and Akšak. This list, however, does not provide a complete picture of the players on the stage of Presargonic history. For reasons that are not entirely clear to us, city-states such as G̃iša (Umma) and Lagaš, which were clearly preeminent powers at various times in the ED III period and which have left us large numbers of royal inscriptions, are totally ignored by the SKL. This apparent snub seems to have inspired a later Lagaš author to compose a separate king list for Lagaš; the text gives all appearances of being a parody of the SKL (see E. Sollberger, "The Rulers of Lagaš," JCS 21 [1967] pp. 279–91) posted at www-etcsl.orient.ox.ac.uk.

Among the five dominant core powers named in the SKL two most commonly vied for hegemony over Sumer and Akkad, Kiš and Uruk.

(e) Political Structures of Sumer and Akkad in ED Times

As to the respective forms of government of the land of Sumer and Kiš, Steinkeller (in a seminal study in D.N. Freedman [ed.], Anchor Bible volume 4 p. 725) notes:

> The key characteristic feature of the S[outhern] system was the institution of city-states. Although it is clear that the origin of the city-state must have

> been exceedingly ancient, certainly going back to the Uruk period, the lack of pertinent information makes it impossible to tell exactly how this institution came about.
>
> In its classic form, the southern city-state was a clearly demarcated territorial unit, comprising a major city, the state's capital, and the surrounding countryside, with its towns and villages. The city-states bordered contiguously on one another, and there was little, if any, neutral space between them.
>
> According to the official ideology, the city-state was the private property of an extended divine family. The main god, the head of the family, was the de facto proprietor of the whole state. At the same time, he — together with his spouse and children — owned as his exclusive domain the capital city and its surroundings. Junior deities owned smaller domains, centered upon towns and villages.
>
> The divine families of all the city-states were united into one very large extended family, with Enlil, god of Nippur, occupying the position of the *paterfamilias*. Because of his rank, Enlil exercised lordship over the whole S[outh]. In this role, he served as an arbitrator in conflicts, especially border disputes, between individual city-states.
>
> The single most important point about the city-state ideology is that the S[outh] was viewed as a closed political system, with the assumed existence of permanent, divinely sanctioned borders between the individual city-states. Obviously, this tenet made any form of territorial expansion within the system exceedingly difficult, rendering any notion of unification theoretically unthinkable.

The rulers of Kiš, on the other hand, seem to have ruled through a different concept of government. Steinkeller (in D.N. Freedman [ed.], Anchor Bible volume 4 pp. 725–26) writes:

> To begin with the question of the N[orthern] government, the most striking fact is that the N[orth] seems never to have developed a system of independent city-states even remotely comparable to that of the S[outh]. On the contrary, there are strong reasons to believe that during the ED II and III periods (ca. 2700-2300) N[orthern] Babylonia formed, for most of the time, a single territorial state, whose gravity point usually remained at Kish. The qualification "usually" that was just applied to the role of Kish is necessary, for we know that the political landscape of the N[orth] involved two other major powers, Mari and Akshak, which actively competed with Kish for the control of N Babylonia. And, if we can trust the testimony of the "Sumerian King List" (henceforth SKL), on at least two occasions first Mari and then Akshak actually achieved ascendancy over Kish (Jacobsen 1939: 103–7).
>
> The reason why the N[orth] followed this particular path of development finds explanation in the distinctive character of its kingship, which was strong, authoritarian, and predominantly secular. As such, it sharply contrasted with the S[outhern] kingship, which, as noted earlier, was generally weak and had an unmistakable religious character.

In addition to the cited paragraphs one may add the remarks of Steinkeller in "Early Political Development in Mesopotamia and the Origins of the Sargonic Empire," in M. Liverani, (ed.), Akkad: The First World Empire pp. 107–29, and Visicato, in Visicato, Bureaucracy pp. 147–48. Admittedly, because of the lack of data, Steinkeller's conclusions are somewhat conjectural, and not necessarily shared by all Assyriologists. One may cite, for example, the difference of opinion given by Cooper in his article "Sumerian and Semitic Writing in Ancient Syro-Mesopotamia" in CRRA 42 p. 62 n. 3. Further, G. Selz (in RIM readers' notes) suggests that the structuring of the pantheon as an "extended family" seems to be a relatively late development at Lagaš (during the reigns of Lugal-Anda and URU-KA-gina).

(f) The Kienĝir League

The largely autonomous city states of southern Mesopotamia, facing the military threat of a large, seemingly more centralized northern opponent (according to Steinkeller's hypothesis), sought a way that they could work in concert against their common foe without sacrificing their ancient independence. Their solution to the problem seems (in the opinion of many scholars) to have been the institution of an amphictyony, the so-called "Kienĝir League." The existence of the league was first postulated by Jacobsen in two ground-breaking studies ("Primitive Democracy in Ancient Mesopotamia," JNES 2 [1954] pp. 159–72 and "Early Political Development in Mesopotamia," ZA 52 [1957] pp. 91–140). The nature of the league has been described in more detail in subsequent studies, most recently by G. Selz (Selz, "Enlil und Nippur nach präsargonischen Quellen," CRRA 35 pp. 189–225) and G. Visicato ("The Hexapolis of Šuruppak, Political and Economic Relationship Between the Towns of Central and Southern Mesopotamia," in Pomponio and Visicato, Early Dynastic Administrative Tablets of Šuruppak, pp. 10–20). The following brief notes are heavily indebted to these last two important studies.

At the heart of the amphictyony was the institution of the assembly (Sumerian uĝkin, Akkadian *puḫrum*). It was led (in the divine sphere) by the god Enlil of Nippur, the effective head of the Sumerian pantheon. Evidence of Enlil's role as leader of the assembly is indicated by PNs of ED IIIa period tablets from Fāra that contain the element ^{d}en-líl-uĝkina "Enlil of the assembly." The assembly's secular head was the "leader of the assembly" (Sumerian uĝkin-gal [commonly written GAL:uĝkin], Akkadian *muʾerrum*). His symbol of authority seems to have been an august sceptre, to judge from the DN ^{d}nin-ĝidru-uĝkin-gal "Divine Lady of the sceptre of the leader of the assembly."

The place where the assembly is thought to have met is Nippur. Possible evidence for an actual meeting of Sumerian city governors in Nippur in very late ED III times comes from an inscription of Lugal-zage-si of Uruk. Numerous fragments of stone vessels inscribed with a text celebrating the reign of peace and prosperity brought about by Lugal-zage-si were found by Hilprecht in the area southeast of the Enlil ziqqurrat in Nippur (see E1.14.17.1). Westenholz (RLA 7 pp. 155–56) notes:

> The occasion for the dedication of such a large number of cups or vases is likely to have been the coronation in Nippur of L[ugalzagesi] as "king of the land." Each cup could then represent one of the ensis who acknowledged his suzerainty; cf. Sargon's remark about the 50 ensis allied with L[ugalzagesi].

This event may be connected with a broken year name of Lugal-zage-si found on a Nippur tablet (see Westenholz, BibMes 1 p. 115 no. 4); it is likely to be restored: mu lugal-z[à]-g[e-si] na[m-lugal] šu ba-ti "The year Lugal-za]g[e-si] received ki[ngship]" and it may be that the recognition of Lugal-zage-si's hegemony over the land of Sumer was ratified by the meeting of a city governors in Nippur.

An idea of the territory comprising the Kienĝir league can be gained by studying the toponyms named in the ED IIIa period archival texts from Šuruppak (modern Fāra). In the chart below we have listed only the major cities; there WF = A. Deimel, Wirtschaftstexte aus Fara, Die Inschriften von Fara III; TSŠ = R. Jestin, Tablettes sumériennes de Šuruppak conserveés au Musée de Stamboul; EDTS = Pomponio and Visicato, Early Dynastic Administrative Tablets of Šuruppak.

Major Sumerian Cities Named in the Fāra Texts

City	WF 67 EDTS 23	WF 68 EDTS 24	WF 69 EDTS 25	WF 70 EDTS 4	WF 72 EDTS 12	WF 73 EDTS 5	WF 75 EDTS 13	WF 107 EDTS 35	TSŠ 150 EDTS 10
Uruk	x	x	x	x	—	x	x	x	x
Lagaš (BUR.NU$_{11}$.LA .KI)	—	—	—	x	x	—	—	—	—
Ĝiša (Umma) (^{giš}KÚŠU.KI)	x	x	x	—	x	—	—	x	x
Adab	x	x	x	x	x	x	x	x	x
Nippur	—	—	—	x	x	x	x	x	—

Of particular interest is the inclusion of Ĝiša (Umma) (^{ĝiš}KÚŠU.KI) and Lagaš (BUR.NU$_{11}$.LA.KI) in the texts; as noted earlier, they were not recognized as being important powers in the SKL. Of considerable interest is the fact (pointed out by Visicato in Pomponio and Visicato, Early Dynastic Administrative Tablets of Šuruppak, p. 13) that the very same city names appear in two literary tablets of ED III date, one from Abū Ṣalābīḫ (no. 463) and the other from ancient Ebla (MEE 3 no. 44); they are listed below in order according to the Abū Ṣalābīḫ tablet.

Biggs, Abū Ṣalābīkh no. 463	**Pettinato, MEE 3 no. 44**
(1) [Uruk]	(1) Uruk
(2) Adab	(4) Adab
Biggs, Abū Ṣalābīkh no. 463	**Pettinato, MEE 3 no. 44**
(3) Nippur	(3) Nippur
(4) Lagaš(NU$_{11}$.BUR.LA.KI)	(2) Lagaš(BUR.NU$_{11}$.LA.KI)
(5) Šuruppak	(5) Šuruppak
(6) G̃iša (Umma) (g̃išKÚŠU.KI)	(6) G̃iša (Umma) (g̃išKÚŠU.KI)

The Ebla tablet continues with the names of Elam, Dilmun, and various GNs which are as yet unidentified; the Abū Ṣalābīḫ tablet is broken away in the corresponding section. The fact that this particular series of cities appears in the lexical tradition may suggest the premise that they shared some common bond.

Possible evidence for the active role that the Kieng̃ir league played in the defence of the land of Sumer is found in Fāra tablets; they list "able-bodied men" (Sumerian g̃uruš — in this case most likely to be translated as "militia-men" as their duties extended beyond warfare) who were assigned service to Kieng̃ir. The tablets in question have been discussed by H. Martin (Martin, Fara: A Reconstruction of the Ancient City of Shuruppak pp. 98–99). In the following chart WF = A. Deimel, Wirtschaftstexte aus Fara, Die Inschriften von Fara. The listing of Uruk at the beginning of the lists suggests that this city may have headed the league.

Guruš Lists from Šuruppak

WF 92		**WF 94**	
Obv. i	Obv. i	Obv. i	
1) 182 g̃uruš	1) 182 "militia-men"	1) 140 g̃uruš	1) 140 "militia-men"
2) unu.KI	2) of Uruk.	2) unu.KI	2) of Uruk.
		3) lú-dab$_5$	3) drafted men.
3) 192 adab.KI	3) 192 ["militia-men"] of Adab.	4) 215 adab.KI	4) 215 ["militia-men"] of Adab.
		5) 74	5) 74
		Obv. ii	Obv. ii
4) 94 nibru	4) 94 ["militia-men"] of Nippur.	1) nibru.KI	1) ["militia-men"] of Nippur.
Obv. ii	Obv. ii		
1) 60 lagaš(NU$_{11}$.BUR. LA).MUŠEN.KI	1) 60 ["militia-men"] of Lagaš	2) 110 lagašx(NU$_{11}$.BUR) MUŠEN.KI	2) 110 ["militia-men"] of Lagaš
2) 56 šuruppak.KI	2) 56 ["militia-men"] of Šuruppak.	3) 66 šuruppak.KI	3) 66 ["militia-men"] of Šuruppak.
		Rev. i	
3) 86 g̃iša (umma) (gišKÚŠU).KI)	3) 86 ["militia-men"] of G̃iša (Umma).	1) 128 (g̃išKÚŠU).KI	1) 128 ["militia-men"] of G̃iša (Umma).
		Rev. ii	
4) lú dab$_5$-	4–5) Men drafted (and)	1) an-šè-gú 650 guruš	1) Total of 650 "militia-men"
5) dab$_5$:ba		2) lú-dab$_5$	2) drafted men.

Guruš Lists from Šuruppak (continued)

Obv. iii	Obv. iii		
1) ki:en-g̃i	1–2) going to/standing for Kieng̃ir.	3) ki:en-gi	3) To/for Kieng̃ir.
2) DU.DU			
3) šu-sum	3) Handed over.		

Also noteworthy is a Fāra tablet (WF 103) which mentions "overseers" (maškim) of the cities of Adab, Keš, and IM (the last appears without KI [collation J. Marzahn]; it almost certainly refers to the city of Karkar). Of particular interest is a tablet (WF 101) that mentions: "611 g̃uruš mè-šè DU" "611 'soldiers' going to battle." The same tablet mentions: 1612 g̃uruš ki-ug̃kin "1612 'militia-men' of the assembly place." Even more remarkable are the texts TSŠ 671 and TSŠ 50 that mention 164,100 and 164,571 g̃uruš respectively. According to Martin (Fara: A Reconstruction of the Ancient City of Shuruppak p. 128) these figures are six to ten times the total estimated population of Šuruppak. However, Civil (in RIM readers' notes) provided a cautionary note in connection with the interpretation of these two last texts. He notes that studies by G. Guitel, M. Powell, and J. Friberg have pointed out that these tablets are not real-life accounts, but simply mathematical exercises of no demographic significance calculating how many individual rations of 7 sila one can theoretically obtain from one gur_7 (=1,152,000 sila) of barley. The statement that Šuruppak texts list very large groups of men would stem from this fact. In contrast to the afore-mentioned texts, WF 94 lists a very reasonable number of 650 men, and WF 92 only 470. The g̃uruš would not need to be "soldiers," but simply may have been needed for non-military activities, such as flood control or harvesting. Evidence from the Ur III period (de Genouillac TCL 5 6041 discussed by Goetze JCS 17 [1961] p. 1 ff.) shows, for instance, no fewer than 21,799 workers, from several provinces, conscripted for the harvest season.

Even if these two texts do not conform to reality, Martin's comments are still relevant; she notes (Fara: A Reconstruction of the Ancient City of Shuruppak p. 98):

> The fact that texts of this type were found together in one archive is undoubtedly significant ...
>
> These texts seem to come from the archives of a powerful administrative center which was concerned with the organization of very large groups of men and not merely the distribution of work and rations among the members of a private "household." Two texts, Jestin, 1937, 554 and 613, mention guruš šà é-gal and šà uru (men of the palace and of the city), which suggests that the texts came from the archives of the palace of Shuruppak. Certain of these texts are not confined to the internal management of the palace, land and city of Shuruppak, however, but apparently refer to the guruš of Kengi (men of Sumer?), including men from Uruk, Adab, Nippur, Lagash, Shuruppak, and Umma. The inclusion of Shuruppak with the other cities implies that these texts belonged to a higher administrative unit than the government of Shuruppak. Although many other texts do not state directly whether the men listed belonged to the palace of Shuruppak or to a larger organization, the large numbers of men referred to suggest the latter.
>
> One of the primary purposes of such a league could have been mutual defense. Deimel 1925, 95 and 101 indicates that at least some of the guruš involved were soldiers. Jestin, 1937, 782, notes [TSŠ 782 ii 7 – iii 1 [GIŠ].gigir [...] mè DU] "(repairs made) on chariots going to battle." [The same text later lists people coming back from battle (rev. i 9 mè-ta DU)].

Also relevant to the conception of the Kieng̃ir league are the earlier Jemdat Naṣr period city seals; for the latest discussion of these, see R. Matthews, Cities, Seals and Writing, and the literature cited there. See also P. Steinkeller

(g) The Land of Sumer in ED Sources

The place where the troops were stationed (or, in an alternative understanding, being sent to) is named as ki-en-g̃i in the Fāra tablets. It is very likely that this ki-en-g̃i is to be related to the term ki-en-g̃i "land of Sumer" found in the later (Ur III) royal epithet (Sumerian) lugal ki-en-g̃i ki-uri (Akkadian) *šar māt šumerim u akkadîm* "king of the land of Sumer and Uri/Akkad." The genitive form (ki-en-g̃i-ra-[ak]) tells us that the full writing of Kieng̃i was Kieng̃ir. While some scholars have maintained that kieng̃ir corresponds to *šumerum*, this is technically incorrect; in the Akkadian translation *māt* corresponds to Sumerian ki, and *šumerim* corresponds to en(e)g̃i(r). Bearing in mind that the emeSAL dialect š corresponds in many cases to emegir dialect n, and emeSAL dialect m corresponds to emegir dialect g̃, we may postulate the evolution: /eneg̃ir/ > */ešumer/ > /šumer/. The ancient city of Enegir which we have suggested gave rise to the term ki-en-g̃i "Land (around) Kieng̃i(r)" is possibly located at modern Mašar about 25 km north-northwest of modern Al- Muqayyir, ancient Ur (see Frayne, in a forthcoming study).

The various ED period references to ki-en-g̃i have been collected by Wilcke (Wilcke CRRA 19 pp. 203–204):

a) Keš Temple Hymn lines 29–30:

Version		Translation
ED	[...]	
OB	é šà-bi-ta 1 ŠÀ.ÁB kalam-ma	"House — from its centre (comes) the life for the land"
ED	[...][zi ki]-en-[g̃i]	
OB	a-ga-bi-ta zi-ki-en-g̃i-ra	"From its back-room(? — the meaning of a-ga is debated among scholars) comes the life for the land of Sumer"

Admittedly, so little is left of the ED version of these two lines that we cannot be absolutely certain that it was a duplicate of the OB version.

(b) The evidence of the archival texts WF 92 and 94 were noted in our discussion above.

(c) E-anatum "Stele of the Vultures" E1.9.3.1 col. viii 4′ – 5′) šu-è ki-en-g̃i "... of the land of Sumer."

(d) Biggs, Abū Ṣalābīkh no. 3 col. ii lines 8–9: ⌜UD⌝ SA_6-me (an UD.GAL.NUN writing for ^{d}inanna-me) nin ki-en-g̃i "The goddess Inanna, lady of the land of Sumer" (an addition to Wilcke's list).

(e) En-šakuš-Ana (E1.14.7.1 lines 3–5): en-šà-kúš-an-n[a] en ki-en-⌜g̃i⌝ lugal ka[lam-ma ...] "En-šakuš-Ana, lord of the land of Sumer and king of the land."

(f) Lugal-zage-si E1.14.19.1 col ii lines 21–24: bára-bára-ki-en-g̃i énsi-kur-kur-ra ki-unu.KI-ge me nam-NUN-šè mu-na-TAR-e-ne "The suzerains of the land of Sumer and city rulers of other lands at the land of Uruk determine for him the princely *mes*."

(g) G̃iša-kidu E1.7.5.2 lines 9–10: nir-gál-sag-ḫuš-ki-en-g̃i-ke_4 gaba-gál-nu-gi_4-kur-kur-ra-ke_4 "fierce-headed noble of the land of Sumer, who is irresistible in all the lands."

(h) The Kingdom of Kiš in ED Times

Due to a lack of documentation, very little is known about the kingdom of Kiš in ED times. As argued by the present author in his study of the ED List of Geographical Names (LGN), (see Frayne, Early Dynastic List p. 87; for a review of the monograph see R. Englund, OLZ 90 [1995] cols. 162–69), an idea of the extent of the territory either controlled by Kiš or with which it conducted trade in ED III times can be gained from a study of the city names which appear in the LGN; of note is the fact that no cities south of Isin and Šarrākum appear. This view is concordant with Steinkeller's assessment that the LGN "may actually be a gazetteer of the Kišite kingdom" (Steinkeller, in Liverani [ed.], Akkad: The First World Empire p. 120).

An even more concrete idea of the intercity connections of cities belonging to the Kišite state may be gained by a study of the toponyms found in the ED IIIa period economic texts from Abū Ṣalābiḫ. The correlations between these toponyms from Abū Ṣalābiḫ and those in the LGN have been studied by the author in Frayne, Early Dynastic List pp. 90–93. In the present context we may note the following:

City Name	Abū ṢalābīḫText No.	LGN
Ṣarbat in the Sippar region	511 obv. col. vi line 4	263–64
Lallat (likely modern Hilal, see Gibson, Kish p. 135 no. 75)	511 obv. col. vi line 2	136
Kun-Kulab (likely modern Tell Abū Gulub, see Adams in Gibson, Kish p. 195 no. 122)	504 rev.	123

City Name	Abū Ṣalābīḫ Text No.	LGN
Urum (possibly modern Tell Imām Ibrāḥīm, see Adams in Gibson, Kish p. 196 no. 140)	508 rev.! col. ii line 3′, col. iv line 2′	44

Two facts emerge from these data: (a) apparently all the GNs mentioned in the Abū Ṣalābīḫ tablets are located in the area of (later) Babylonia as far south as the city of Isin — no cities of the southern part of Sumer appear — and (b) many of the Abū Ṣalābīḫ GNs also appear in the LGN. These facts would seem to indicate that at the time of the Abū Ṣalābīḫ archive, the city, whose ancient name in unknown, was part of the kingdom of Kiš.

The evidence of the LGN suggests that Kiš controlled a huge territory. As far as the findspots of actual Kišite royal inscriptions are concerned, we note that a label inscription of EN.ME-barage-si (see E1.7.22.1) was found in the temple oval at Ḫāfāji (ancient Tutub) and likely attests to Kiš's control over that city. City names of the Diyālā region (but not Tutub itself) appear in the LGN. A broken stela of a ruler who styled himself as "king of Kiš," but whose name is unfortunately broken away from the monument, was found at Ḫāfāji (see E1.7.43.1). He may have been an actual king of Kiš, but we can not be absolutely certain of the fact since it is not inconceivable that a southern king could have campaigned in the Diyālā region. If we can believe the evidence of a later proverb, King Nanne — possibly a reference to King A-Ane-pada of Ur — mounted an unsuccessful campaign against the eastern city of Simurrum.

If, in a comparative study, we plot on a map the cities of the (postulated) Kiengir League in the south (as attested in the economic tablets from Fāra) and of the (presumed) Kišite domains in north as attested in the economic tablets from Abū Ṣalabīḫ and the GNs in the LGN, we see a clear division of Mesopotamia into two separate (political?) regions.

(i) The Border Region between the Kiengir League and the Kingdom of Kiš in Late ED times.

As noted, no identifiable cities in the LGN lie south of Isin or Šarrākum, and a line connecting points just south of those two cities appears to give the southern border of the Kišite domains. The city of Kisura lies on this postulated southern boundary line, and the fact that the name Kisura itself means border in Sumerian may be significant. As for the archaeological evidence, J. Moon points out (in Iraq 44 [1982] p. 68):

> ... it is possible to draw a tentative line south of Abū Ṣalābīkh and place Semitic literary traditions and upright ladled jars to the north of it, and "proper" Sumerians to the south, with Šuruppak and Adab as border regions.

(j) The Major Political Powers of Late ED IIIb Times in Greater Mesopotamia as Attested in the Ebla Archives.

With the discovery and publication of the extensive late ED IIIb royal archives of Ebla, a flood of light has been shed on the histories of the kingdoms that lay to the northwest of the land of Sumer and Akkad, namely Mari (modern Tell Ḥarīrī), Nagar (almost certainly modern Tell Brāk), and Ebla (modern Tell Mardīḫ). A comprehensive overview of this material is clearly beyond the scope of the present volume, but a few words may be in order.

The Ebla documents give us a general idea of the predominate states that competed for power in Greater Mesopotamia at the end of the Early Dynastic period. Of particular relevance are the so-called annual accounts of metals of the Ebla kingdom; these have been discussed by A. Archi in an article entitled "Les comptes rendues annuels de métaux (CAM)," in Durand (ed.), Amurru 1 pp. 73–99. Of particular note are entries that refer to the ceremony(?) called NÍG.DIĜIR.DIĜIR.DIĜIR.DIĜIR, which is named in connection with major states lying to the east of Ebla. Unfortunately, the meaning of the term NÍG.DIĜIR.DIĜIR.DIĜIR.DIĜIR is not clear (see Fronzaroli in Fronzaroli [ed.], Literature and Literary Language at Ebla p. 171 for one possible interpretation). The data concerning the NÍG.MUL ceremony can be summarized thanks to the cited article of Archi:

(i) NÍG.MUL GÍN.ŠÈ ***ma-rí*.KI** *wa* UG_7 *wa-ru*$_{12}$*-tum* (connection with **Mari**).

(ii) Ibrium 3: obv. XIII Ur-na *ma-rí*.KI NÍG.MUL ***kiš*.KI** TIL.

(iii) Ibrium 4: obv. VII NÍG.BA ab-NI *ma-rí*.KI NÍG.DIĜIR.MUL ***ag-sa-gú*.KI** ŠU BA_4.TI

(iv) Ibrium 5: obv. XII NÍG.BA *ip-ḫur*-ÚR ... NÍG.BA *sa*-NI-*gú* MAŠKIM NÍG.MUL ***ʾà-du*.KI** GÍN.ŠE (connection with the town **Addu**).

(v) Ibrium 5: rev. VI ... *ba-da-lum ma-rí*.KI NÍG.DIĞIR.MUL ***na-ĝàr*.KI** GÍN.ŠÈ (connection with **Nağar**).

(vi) Ibrium 10: obv. III [NÍG.BA] ur-na ***ma-rí*.KI** NÍG.MUL ***kiš*.KI** TIL.

(vii) Ibbi-Zikir 4: rev. III NÍG.BA *šu-ga-du ma-rí*.KI NÍG.MUL ***adab*.KI** ŠU BA_4.TI (connection with **Adab**).

Three city states can be unequivocally identified in this selection of references: (1) Addu (a city likely located on the Upper Euphrates at or near ancient Till Barsip [modern Tell Aḥmar] possibly corresponding to OB Dūr-Addu; for the location of the latter, see Joannès in Durand [ed.], Amurru 1 p. 325 [map]); this identification is supported by the recent find of a stele of the god Adad in the Euphrates near Tell Aḥmar, (2) Mari, (3) Nağar (almost certainly Tell Brāk).

Subsequent to Archi's article in Amurru 1 Archi and Biga have re-examined the pertinent material in an article "A Victory over Mari and the Fall of Ebla," JCS 55 (2003) pp. 1–44. In this article they repeat the assertion of the earlier Amurrru article that ***kiš*.KI** and ***ag-sa-gú*.KI** refer to the cities of Kiš and Akšak in Mesopotamia. However, a very detailed examination by the author of the modern toponyms in the area of the western Ḫabur region coupled with a study of the toponyms found in text 2 in Archi and Biga's article has led the author to conclude that the Kiš referred to in text 2 is not Kiš in Mesopotamia but rather a homophonous locality in the western Ḫabur region likely to be identified with modern Tell Kashashok III. The mound in question, which was partially excavated by a mission of the Directorate of General of Antiquities of Syria under the direction of A. Suleiman (see Anastasio, Lebeau, and Sauvage [eds.], Subartu XIII p. 202), shows levels dating to the Early Dynastic period and a destruction level dating to the same period. If the Kiš mentioned in this text of the Archi and Biga article refers to a Kiš in the Ḫabur region then this would indicate that the Ebla archive does not document contacts between Ebla and Kish in Mesopotamia. If this is true than it may well be that the place name ***ag-sa-gú*.KI** similarly does not refer to Akšak in Mesopotamia. It would seem likely, however, that Adab of the texts described by Archi does indeed refer to ancient Adab in Mesopotamia.

(k) Chronological Questions

In view of the meager sources at our disposal, the chronology of the ED II–III period is only sketchily known. In general, our documentation increases towards the end of the ED IIIb period, with very large numbers of economic texts coming from the cities of Lagaš and Ebla. The SKL, which in theory ought to give us a chronology of the period, is virtually useless for this purpose; it gives impossibly long reigns to many rulers and seems in other cases to give only approximate and rounded off figures. Consequently in the brief discussion of chronology that follows we have restricted our comments to the evidence provided by economic texts.

(i) Lagaš

(i) En-metena reigned at least 19 years (Cooper SANE 2 p. 30)

(ii) E-anatum I reigned 5 years according to Cooper SANE 2 p. 33; this seems to be too short in the view of the present author.

(iii) En-entarzi reigned 6 years(?) (Cooper SANE 2 p. 33)

(iv) Lugal-Anda reigned 7 years (Cooper SANE 2 p. 33)

(v) URU-KA-gina reigned 11(?) years (Cooper SANE 2 p. 33)

(ii) Zabala

A small archive of economic texts of late Presargonic date (probably coming from the city of ancient Zabala) has been studied by M. Powell (Powell, "Texts from the Time of Lugalzagesi: Problems and Perspectives in Their Interpretation," HUCA 49 [1978] pp. 1–58). The tablets come from the period of the reign of Lugal-zage-si; they are sometimes dated with the notation: lugal-zà-ge-si énsi mu N, where N is most commonly the number 6 or 7. Other similar tablets from Zabala have been found in the Nies Babylon Collection at Yale by B. Foster (see Powell, HUCA 49 [1978] n. *). Some of the Yale tablets, seemingly part of the same archive, are dated with the mu dates 29 and 30. The Zabala archive could conceivably span the period of transition from the reign of Lugal-zage-si to the reign of Sargon. The lower numbered dates could come from the time of Lugal-zage-si who, according to our understanding, was able to hold Zabala for about 7 years, and the higher dates from the reign of Sargon, assuming that Sargon conquered Zabala around the 29th year of his reign.

(iii) Mari

According to Charpin (MARI 5 p. 66), five locations at Mari have yielded Presargonic tablets: (a) the Sanctuary P25, (texts with no dates); (b) the "Red House" (texts with no dates); (c) the "Commons" west of the esplanade (texts dated from years 6–8); (d) the Presargonic palace (text dated to years 4–8); and (e) "Trench B" (texts dated to years 20–35). Some of these tablets likely date to the time of the destruction of Mari, almost certainly by Sargon. They show a disparity in the sequence of dates similar to that which was found in the archive studied by Powell. Charpin MARI 5 p. 96 notes:

> On est en particulier frappé par le fait que les dates des tablettes du chantier MB soient des années 20 à 35 alors que celles de P. 1 et des "communs" ne dépassent par l'an 8.

Whether these Mari tablets might again date to the transition from the reign of a local king (in this case possibly Ḫida᾿ar, the last king of Mari mentioned in the Ebla archives) to the reign of Sargon is conceivable, albeit uncertain.

(iv) Ebla

The following data are available for the kings of Ebla:

(i) Igriš-Ḫalab reigned at least 12 years (Archi, in Durand (ed.), Amurru 1 p. 27).

(ii) Irkab-Dāmu reigned during the time period corresponding to the last years of the viziers Darmia and Tir, the three or four years of the vizier Arrugum, and the two(?) early years of the vizier, that is 5+ or 6+ years (Archi, in Durand (ed.), Amurru 1 p. 27).

(iii) Išar-Dāmu reigned in years corresponding to 15 or 16 years of the vizier Ibrium, the 17 years of the vizier Ibbi-Zikir, plus the months before the destruction of Ebla, that is, 32+ or 33+ years altogether (Archi, in Durand (ed.), Amurru 1 p. 27).

(l) Connecting the Various Sequences of ED Kings Known from Non-Literary Sources

While a reasonably secure list of rulers is available from actual historical inscriptions and economic texts for the city states of Lagaš, G̃iša (Umma), Mari, and Ebla — a source of data that importantly stands independently from the literary tradition — the question of linking these series of kings with other rulers known from Ur, Nippur, and Kiš remains. A list of synchronisms connected with this question is presented in chart on p. N.

(m) The Use of Palaeography

A tool that might conceivably elucidate the chronological relationships of the various rulers of the city-states in late ED times is the study of the script of the royal inscriptions and dated economic texts. Unfortunately, this is an area which has received relatively little scholarly attention. The most recent study of the palaeography of the texts from Fāra and Tell Abū Ṣalābīḫ is a very important study by Krebernik in Bauer, Englund and Krebernik (eds.), Mesopotamien pp. 272–83. In addition, a useful recent contribution relevant for dating purposes is W. Sallaberger's article "Ein Synchronism der Urkunden von Tell Beydar mit Mari and Ebla?" in Lebeau (ed.), About Subartu: Studies Devoted to Upper Mesopotamia, Subartu IV/2 pp. 23–39. Sallaberger compares various texts from the ED III-Old Akkadian periods from the sites of Ebla, Mari, Tell Beydar, Abū Ṣalābīḫ, Nippur, Isin, Adab, and Girsu, comparing 10 index signs. In this work he was anticipated by Alberti and Pomponio's study in their Pre-Sargonic and Sargonic Texts from Ur Edited in UET 2, Supplement pp. 9–17, in which 11 index signs were used. Other palaeographic studies of the Presargonic and Sargonic periods have included R.D. Biggs, "The Abū Ṣalābīkh Tablets," JCS 20 (1966) pp. 77-78, note 37 (concerning the "KU" signs); idem, "On Regional Cuneiform Handwritings in Third Millennium Mesopotamia," Orientalia 42 (1973) pp. 39–46 (the signs ZI, NAM, UD, and KA); P. Steinkeller, "Studies in Third Millennium Paleography, 1: Signs TIL and BAD," ZA 71 (1982) pp. 19-28; idem, "Studies in Third Millennium Paleography. 2: Signs ŠEN and ALAL," Or Ant. 20 (1981) pp. 243–49; I.J. Gelb, "Terms for Slaves in Ancient Mesopotamia," in Studies Diakonoff pp. 96-98 (the signs NITA and GÉME); A. Englund, "Dilmun in the Archaic Uruk Corpus" in D.T. Potts (ed.), New Studies in the Archaeology and Early History of Bahrain pp. 35-36 (the sign DILMUN). One may also consult with profit the chart of the various forms of the lugal sign during Presargonic times provided by Nissen in Königsfriedhof pl. 23 and Figure 1 found in Braun-Holzinger's Beterstauetten p. 23.

(n) The State of Knowledge of the Political History of the Presargonic Period.

Despite the various sources listed here, some scholars rightfully point out the woefully inadequate picture they paint of the history of Presargonic times. A particularly pessimistic view is given by Steinkeller in "Lugalzagesi's origins," in Selz (ed.), Studies Kienast p.621:

> It will not be an exaggeration to say that our knowledge of the political history of the Pre-Sargonic period is still virtually non-existent. All that we have is a smattering of accidentally preserved royal names and events that, in most cases, cannot be synchronized chronologically, let alone be made into a coherent historical narrative.

(o) Notes on the Transliterations in This Volume.

Because of the syllabic component of the mixed (syllabic and logographic) Sumerian writing system, strings such as /eanak/ "house of heaven," are written é-an-na in Sumerian with a seeming double consonant. In this volume we have rendered these with a single consonant following the practice now standard among Sumerologists. Two exceptions to this rule have been made, namely, the proper names Inanna and Eanna; the writings given here are conventional.

Another question concerning the transliteration of texts concerns the question of the so-called overhanging vowels of Sumerian writing. On this question, we may compare the various remarks of Falkenstein, Sprache Gudeas 1 pp. 12–20; Kärki, Sprache pp. 4–11; Klein, TAPS 71 p. 28 and n. 144; and Attinger, Eléments p. 143. In virtually all cases the so-called overhanging vowels occur after a phoneme that is a sonant, that is, a non-occlusive consonant, such as (using IPA values) m, b n, r (the "trilled" r or so-called dr phoneme of Sumerian), S (transliterated š), l, N (transliterated g̃ in this volume), and x (transliterated ḫ). A writing lugal-ni, then, may underlie a reading in which l, for example, served as a semi-vowel such as we find with the Czech l.

For a different interpretation of the phenomenon of so-called overhanging vowels see Yoshikawa, ASJ 2 (1980) pp. 188–95 and idem, ZA 78 (1988) pp. 71–75.

While Sumerian divine names such as /ninḫursag̃a/ "Lady of the mountain range" and /ninsuna/ "Lady of the wild cow" are clearly genitival constructions, we have rendered them as Ninḫursag̃ and Ninsun in this volume.

The Sumerian phoneme commonly transliterated g̃, has been indicated following the lists given in Krecher, Studies Matouš Part 2 pp. 7–73, and Schretter, Emesal-Sudien pp. 32–51, 284–87.

For notes on the complicated question of the sibilants /š/ /ś/ /ṣ/ /z/ and /s/ in Sumerian which are evidenced in part by various writings such as lagaŠ-sa, ŠeŠ-sa-né, ti-ra-áŠ-sa and úŠ-sa, see Landsberger, MSL II pp. 28–29; Falkenstein, Das Sumerische p. 24 note b; Bauer, AWL p. 66; Selz, Untersuchungen p. 184 n. 844; Schretter, Emesal Studien pp. 66–68; and C.P. Boisson, "Contraintes typologiques sur le système phonologique du sumérien," Bulletin de la Société de Linguistique de Paris 84 (1989) pp. 221–26. A detailed study of this question is clearly beyond the scope of the present volume.

It may be useful to highlight at the beginning of this monograph one difference from Steible's transliterations found in the previous edition of the Sumerian inscriptions of the ED period. The common Sumerian phrase "to defeat in battle" is rendered here as GÍN.ŠÈ ... sè correcting Steible's TÙN.SÈ ... sè. GÍN = LAK 666 has several vertical wedges in the right side of the sign; TÙN = LAK 667, on the other hand, has none of these verticals. For the clear distinction between the two one may consult the remarks of Krebernik in Bauer, Englund and Krebernik (eds.), Mesopotamien p. 277 where he contrasts ⌈DÙN⌉ in ZLE (Ebla Sign List) 22 = [*du*]-*wu-tum* (see Archi, in Gordon, Rendsburg and Winter,Eblaitica 1 p. 94 entry 22) and ZLE 41 = *a-ga-um* (p. 94 entry 41) For TÚN = tùn in inscriptions of Gudea, see Selz, NABU 1997 no. 36. The complex GÍN.ŠÈ ... sè may be related to the expression GÍN.KÁR ... sè for which see Gordon, Sumerian Proverbs p. 92 note 5 to 1.99. GÍN here could conceivably be read aga_x. If so the expression aga_x(GÍN)-kár might be related to the expression an-kára found in Gudea Cylinder A col. vi line 21 (and other passages cited by Sjöberg in Nanna-Suen p. 113), an apparent variant spelling of the of á-an-kára weapon, for which see Falkenstein, Götterlieder pp. 138–39 commentary to line 49 and Wilcke, Lugalbanda p. 217.

(p) A Note on the Translation of the Sumerian Term énsi

In ED period inscriptions from Lagaš the Sumerian term énsi was likely a "generic royal title" (Suter, Gudea's Temple Building p. 26) and was not, as in Ur III times, an indication of subservience to a suzerain. Steinkeller (in K. Watanabe [ed.], Priests and Officials in the Ancient Near East: Papers of the Second Colloquium on the Ancient Near East — the City and Its Life, held at the Middle Eastern Cultural Center in Japan [Mitaka, Tokyo], March 22–23, 1996 p. 112 notes:

> ... in my opinion, ensik and lugal are complementary titles, which describe the same form of kingship. The sole difference between them is that each emphasizes a different dimension of royal power. The title ensik, which has clear religious overtones, defines the status of a ruler in his rapport with the divine owner of the city-state. To use the case of Lagash as an example, a ruler like Eanatum ranks vis-à-vis Ningirsu as an ensik, that is, Ningirsu's steward or vicar, whereas, conversely, Ningirsu is the master (lugal) of Eanatum and of the whole city-state of Lagash. In contrast, the title lugal, when applied to humans, is free of any religious connotations. It describes the position of a ruler in relation to his subjects as their chief political and military leader. In this way Eanatum, though an ensik of Lagash vis-à-vis Ningirsu, is a lugal of Lagash on the level of socio-political relationships.

It would appear, then, that the commonly used Ur III translation "governor" is not appropriate in the ED context of this volume as a translation for énsi, and a translation "ruler," following Cooper, is given instead.

ADAB

E1.1

(a) Location

Ancient Adab is identified with the modern mound of Bismāya (NLat 31°57′ and ELong 45°37′).

(b) Excavation History

Adab was excavated in 1904 and 1905 by an expedition sponsored by the Babylonian and Assyrian Section of the Oriental Exploration of the University of Chicago under the direction of E.J. Banks. For a brief sketch of his excavations see Banks, Bismya, and Yang Zhi "The Excavation of Adab," JAC 3 (1988) pp. 1–21.

(c) Writing of the City Name

The most common writing of the city name Adab (particularly in post ED texts) is UD.NUN.KI. It occasionally occurs in early texts with the MUŠEN "bird" determinative, indicating that the city name was apparently derived from the city's totem, the adab bird. The lexical and literary sources give several writings for the city and bird name: /udubu/, /usab/, /adab/, and /arab/ (see Zhi Yang, JAC 2 [1987] pp. 121–25). The middle consonant would appear to be the /dr/ phoneme posited by Bauer, WO 8 (1975) pp. 1–9; Thomsen, Sumerian Language p. 44 § 23; Boison, Bulletin de la Société de Linguistique de Paris pp. 212–14; Cavigneaux, Zeichenlisten pp. 56 ff.; Steinkeller, JNES 46 (1987) pp. 56–57 and n. 5. Its existence was questioned by Yoshikawa, BiOr 45 (1988) col. 501 and Black RA 84 (1990) pp. 111, 115–16.

The "NUN" component in the later compound toponym UD.NUN.KI appears in the archaic seal impressions from Ur, the ED tablets from Abū Ṣalābīḫ (see Biggs, JCS 20 [1966] p. 83 n. 75, and the ED tablets from Adab (see Zhi Yang, JAC 2 [1987] p. 122) in a form with two separate strokes arranged in a > shape at the end; it is identical with the end of the kalam and un signs (see Edzard, RLA 5 p. 553 fig. 25). Thus it differs from the real NUN sign which has one upright final wedge; consequently the sign in the city name Adab should be distinguished from the NUN sign. The logogram UD.NUN as a whole could have developed from a depiction of an adab bird on a standard; such bird standards are found on the so-called Stele of the Vultures; see E1.9.3.1. The upraised wings of the bird could have developed into an UD sign.

(d) Patron Deities

The patron deity of Adab was the mother goddess Nintu/Ninmaḫ/Ninḫursag/Belēt-ilī; her consort was the god Ašgi (for the reading of the latter DN see Biggs, JCS 24 [1971–72] pp. 1–2). Nintu's main shrine was the E-maḫ temple (see E1.1.7.1–2 and George, House Most High no. 714) whose small ziqqurrat was excavated by Banks (see Yang Zhi, JAC 3 [1988] pp. 16–19). A second shrine named E-namzu is also attested for Belēt-ilī (see George, House Most High no. 855 and E1.1.8.1). Another temple attested at Adab is the E-SAR shrine of Inanna (see E1.1.2.1, E1.1.3.1, E1.1.4.1, E1.1.5.1, and George, House Most High no. 978).

(e) Appearance in the Sumerian King List

The SKL assigns one king, a certain Lugal-Ane-mundu, to whom a fantastic reign of ninety years is credited (see Jacobsen, SKL p. 102) to its (one) dynasty of Adab. Lugal-Ane-mundu has been assigned the number E1.1.1.8 in this volume.

(f) Early Dynastic Period Rulers

Other Early Dynastic period rulers of Adab are known from their own inscriptions, but, unfortunately, their chronological order is unknown.

Evidence for the importance of Adab in late Early Dynastic times is attested by the mention of Adab (in addition to Kiš and Akšak) in the archives from ancient Ebla (see Archi, MARI 4 p. 76 document 62 and p. 77 document 110). The precise significance of this mention is unclear.

King	RIM number
Nin-KISAL-si	E1.1.1
Me-ba-LAK 551	E1.1.2
Bara-ḫeNIdu	E1.1.3
Lugalda-lu	E1.1.4
LUM-ma	E1.1.5
MUG-si	E1.1.6
E-IGI.NIM-pa'e	E1.1.7
Lugal-Ane-mundu	E1.1.8
Mes-kigala	E1.1.9

A large clay cone in a private collection in Rome of a ruler of Adab has been published by M. Biga in her article "A Sargonic Foundation Cone," in Y. Sefati (et al., eds), An Enlightened Scribe Who Neglects Nothing: Ancient Near Eastern Studies in Honor of Jacob Klein, Bethseda, Maryland: CDL Press 2005 pp. 29–38. One might have been tempted to date this cone to the Presargonic period. However, Biga points out that the name of the ruler mentioned in the cone, a certain, Ur-LAGAB×SIG$_7$+ME, can be shown from other tablets now in the Banca d'Italia and the Real Academia de Historia de Madrid to date to the reign of Narām-Sîn. A duplicate of this cone is in the Schøyen Collection; transliteration of the piece was kindly communicated to the author by P. Steinkeller in RIM readers' notes. Since the piece is Sargonic, it is not edited here.

Nin-KISAL-si

E1.1.1

1

An inscription found on a vase fragment from Adab mentions Nin-KISAL-si (perhaps to be read nin-g̃ipar-si) serving as ruler at Adab under Me-Silim, "king of Kiš." For the text, see E1.8.1.2 below.

Me-ba-LAK 551

E1.1.2

1

Fragments of a vase and bowl bear an inscription of Me-ba-LAK 551, king (lugal) of Adab.

CATALOGUE

Ex.	Museum number	Object	Dimensions (cm)	Provenance	Lines preserved	cpn
1	A 212 (Chicago)	Frgm. of a conical creamy (yellow-white) alabaster (Banks), or limestone (Braun-Holzinger) vessel	9 cm high; original diameter 25	Mound V, trench NW of ziqqurrat	1–3	c
2	A 1164 (Chicago)	Limestone vessel	—	Mound V, trench NW of ziqqurrat	1–3	c

COMMENTARY

To judge from the inscription, the vase and bowl apparently (originally) came from the E-SAR temple, the shrine of the goddess Inanna at Adab. The discovery of these vessels is described on p. 259 of Banks, Bismya where he writes:

> One of the most interesting of the discoveries at Bismya was that of the ancient temple dump-heap, where the priests threw away their broken and discarded vases and other objects no longer required for the temple service.

For a discussion of the E-SAR temple at Adab, see George, House Most High p. 140 citing Reiner, MSL XI p. 142 vii 17 and CTL (Canonical Temple List) no. 342. For a plan of the temple of Mound V showing the trench which yielded the E-SAR inscriptions, see Banks, Bismya, p. 235.

The reading of the royal name of line 2 is uncertain. Jacobsen (ZA 52 [1957] p. 125 n. 74) suggested me-dur-ba. M. Lambert (Sumer 8 [1952] p. 211), followed by Borger (HKL 3 p. 7), read me-ba-dé. The third sign would appear to be the sign listed by Deimel as LAK 551. It appears in King, CT 32 pl. 7 Right Side line 7′ = Gelb, Land Tenure p. DAM ^{d}ur-LAK 551, LAK 551 (the vertical in the first sign after the DIĜIR (as copied by Deimel) is revealed by the published photo in Gelb, Land Tenure pl. 63 no. 37 bottom to be a flaw in the stone. The line was read in Gelb, Land Tenure as DAM ^{d}ur-gú-gú, but the last two signs do not appear to be gú signs. The reading of the sign LAK 551 is unknown to me.

In ex. 1 the lugal sign of line 3 appears below the city name Adab. In both texts Adab appears without the KI determinative.

BIBLIOGRAPHY

1912 Banks, Bismya p. 259 (provenance); p. 264 (ex. 2, copy, drawing)
1930 Luckenbill, Adab nos. 8–9 (exs. 1–2, copy)
1952 Lambert, Sumer 8 p. 211 n. 76 (exs. 1–2, study)
1957 Jacobsen, ZA 52 p. 125 n. 74 (exs. 1–2, study)
1966 Nissen, Königsfriedhof p. 141 n. 509 (exs. 1–2, study)
1971 Sollberger and Kupper, IRSA IF2a (exs. 1–2, translation)
1982 Steible, ASBW 2 p. 187 Medurba 1 (exs. 1–2, edition)
1986 Cooper, SARI 1 p. 15 Ad 1 (exs. 1–2, translation)
1989 Yang, Sargonic Inscriptions p. 11 § 1.1.1.1 nos. 4–5 (exs. 1–2, study)
1991 Braun-Holzinger, Weihgaben p. 121 G 32 (ex. 1, edition, study); G 33 (ex. 2, edition, study)

TEXT

1) ⸢é⸣-SAR(SAR:⸢é⸣)
2) me-ba-x
3) lugal-adab

1) (Property of) the E-SAR.
2–3) Me-ba-LAK 551 (is) king of Adab.

Bara-ḫeNIdu

E1.1.3

1

An inscription on a rim fragment of an alabaster bowl indicates it was property of the E-SAR temple during the reign of Ba[ra-ḫeNIdu].

COMMENTARY

The bowl fragment, which measures 4.1×6 cm, was found in the rubble-dump in the trench NW of the ziqqurrat at Mound V at Adab. It now bears the museum number A 227 (Chicago). The inscription was not collated.

The restoration of line 2 as the name of a ruler of Adab follows Cooper, and is not entirely certain. The inscription was listed as an anonymous Adab inscription by Steible (ASBW 2 p. 197 AnAdab 9; cf. Bauer, BiOr 46 [1989] col. 638).

BIBLIOGRAPHY

1930 Luckenbill, Adab no. 16 (copy)
1982 Steible, ASBW 2 p. 197 AnAdab 9 (edition)
1986 Cooper, SARI 1 p. 16 Ad 4.1 (translation)
19086 Sargonic Archive p. 29 §2.1.1.1.1 no. 16 (study)
1989 Bauer, BiOr 46 col. 638 (study)
1989 Yang, Sargonic Inscriptions p. 12 § 1.1.1.1 no. 16 (study)
1991 Braun-Holzinger, Weihgaben p. 123 G 46 (transliteration, study)

TEXT

1) é-[SAR]
2) bá[ra-ḫé-NI-du_{10}]
Lacuna

1) (Property of) the E-[SAR].
2) Ba[ra-ḫeNIdu]
Lacuna

2001

A headless stone statuette was dedicated by a certain Ur-Ešlila for the life of Bara-ḫeNIdu, ensi-G̃AR of Adab.

COMMENTARY

The limestone statuette, a headless male figure with a preserved height of 29.5 cm, was acquired through purchase; it probably came from Adab. It now bears the museum number A 7447 (Chicago). The inscription was not collated.

For the title énsi-G̃AR in Presargonic inscriptions, see Hallo, Royal Titles pp. 35–39; Edzard, JSS 4 (1959) pp. 378ff.; idem, Rechtsurkunden p. 60; idem., RLA 4 (1973) p. 337; and Pomponio and Visicato, Šuruppak pp. 18–19. The precise meaning of the term is unclear.

As noted by Hallo (Royal Titles p. 108 and n. 1) the Adab city elder Ur-Ešlila named in line 6 appears in two other ED inscriptions: (a) a limestone plaque published by Scheil in RA 25 (1928) p. 38 (see also Boese, Weihplatten pp. 213–14 K 11, and pl. XLI K 11 and Steible, ASBW 2 pp. 187–89) and (b) a limestone tablet published by Mercer in JSOR 12 (1928) p. 149 no. 32.

BIBLIOGRAPHY

1957 Hallo, Royal Titles pp. 38, 107 and 108 nn. 1–2 (study)
1982 Steible, ASBW 2 pp. 187–188 Baraḫe-NI-du 1 (edition)
1986 Cooper, SARI 1 pp. 16–17 Ad 4.2 (translation)
1988 Römer, Orientalia NS 57 p. 224 Ad 4.2 (study)
1989 Yang, Sargonic Inscriptions p. 12 § 1.1.1.1 no. 15 (study)
1991 Braun-Holzinger, Weihgaben p. 242 St 9 (edition, study)

TEXT

1) ^{d}nin-šubur	1) For the god Ninšubur,
2) nam-ti-	2–5) for the life of Bara-ḫeNIdu, ensi-G̃AR of Adab,
3) bára-ḫé-NI-du$_{10}$	
4) énsi:G̃AR(G̃AR-énsi)	
5) adab.KI-da	
6) ur-èš-líl-lá	6–8) Ur-Ešlila, city elder, dedicated (this statuette).
7) ab-ba-uru	
8) a mu-ru	

Lugalda-lu

E1.1.4

1

A stone statuette names King Lugalda-lu "(Things) flourish beside the king," and the E-SAR temple.

COMMENTARY

The statuette, which measures 78 cm in height, was found at the west corner of the ziqqurrat on Mound V at Adab (see Banks, Bismya p. 188); it bears the museum number EŞ 3235. The inscription was collated from the published photo.

BIBLIOGRAPHY

1904–1905 Banks, AJSL 21 pp. 57–59 (photo, copy, edition, study)
1907 Thureau-Dangin, SAK pp. 152–53 V. E-sar, König von Adab (edition)
1912 Banks, Bismya p. 188 (findspot); pp. 191–93 (photos, study); p. 196 (copy)
1926 Unger, SuAk pp. 29 and 70 no. 2 (photo, study)
1929 Barton, RISA pp. 90–91 2. Lugaldalu (edition)
1931 Contenau, Manuel 2 pp. 554–556 fig, 361 (photo, study)
1935 Zervos, L'art pl. 101 (photo)
1940 Christian, Altertumskunde pl. 257 (photo)
1960 Strommenger, Bagh. Mitt. 1 p. 31 (study)
1971 Sollberger and Kupper, IRSA IF3a (translation)
1977 Braun-Holzinger, Beterstatuetten pp. 61 and 68 and pl. 26 e–f (photo, edition, study)
1981 Spycket, Statuaire p. 85 and n. 207 (study); pl. 55a–b (photo)
1982 Steible, ASBW 2 p. 191 Lugaldalu 1 (edition)
1986 Cooper, SARI 1 p. 17 Ad 5 (translation)
1986 Yang, Sargonic Archive p. 29 no. 14 (study)
1987 Edzard and Calmeyer, RLA 7 p. 132 (study)
1989 Yang, Sargonic Inscriptions p. 12 § 1.1.1.1 no. 14 (study)
1991 Braun-Holzinger, Weihgaben p. 242 St 10 (edition, study)

TEXT

1) é-SAR(SAR:é)
2) lugal-da-lu
3) lugal-adab.KI

1) (Property of) the E-SAR,
2) Lugalda-lu (is) king of Adab.

LUM-ma

E1.1.5

Two vessels from Adab bear inscriptions of a certain LUM-ma; one of these names him as being ensi-G̃AR of Adab.

L. Curchin (RA 71 [1977] pp. 94-95) has suggested that this LUM-ma, is to be identified with E-anatum of Lagaš, whose "battle" (or "Tidnum") name was LUM-ma (see E1.9.3.5 col. v lines 11–14). At present there seems to be no clear evidence either to confirm or refute the hypothesis. However, we should bear in mind that LUM-ma is a very common Presargonic PN; see Pomponio, Prosopografia pp. 162–63 for the references from Šuruppak, and Bauer, RLA 7 3/4 (1988) pp. 168–71 for the references in general. See further Selz, Untersuchungen pp. 171–75, for an exhaustive survey of the divine and personal name LUM-ma in Presargonic sources.

Selz (in RIM readers' notes) suggests that the PN Lummānum cited in Gelb, Amorite p. 315, argues strongly that the reading of the name should be lum-ma. However, I find it strange that a ruler of a Sumerian city-state would adopt an Amorite name.

1

A fragment of a stone vessel bears an inscription naming LUM-ma and the E-SAR temple.

COMMENTARY

The text is incised on a vase of hornfels which measures 6.3×3.4 cm. It was found on Mound V, in the trench NW of the ziqqurrat containing the dump heap, and was given the museum number A 217 (Chicago). The inscription was collated.

Since LUM-ma's title is not preserved, it is not certain that this inscription belongs to a ruler of Adab; it could simply be a dedication of a private citizen.

BIBLIOGRAPHY

1930 Luckenbill, Adab no. 25 (copy)
1982 Steible, ASBW 2 pp. 191–92 Lumma 1 (edition)
1986 Cooper, SARI 1 p. 15 Ad 2 (translation [conflated with E3.1.1.3.2])
1989 Yang, Sargonic Inscriptions p. 12 § 1.1.1.1 no. 6 (study)
1991 Braun-Holzinger, Weihgaben p. 121 G 34 (transliteration, study)

TEXT

1) ⸢é-SAR⸣(⸢SAR:é⸣)
2) LUM-m[a]
Lacuna

1) (Property of) the E-SAR.
2) LUM-m[a]
Lacuna

2

A steatite cup mentions LUM-ma as ensi-G̃AR of Adab.

COMMENTARY

The cup, which measures 15.5×8.8 cm, was found on Mound V, in the trench NW of the ziqqurrat containing the dump heap, and was given the museum number A 208 (Chicago). The inscription was not collated.

Although the title ensi-G̃AR is written above the PN, the title is clearly to be translated after the PN.

BIBLIOGRAPHY

1930 Luckenbill, Adab no. 26 (copy)
1982 Steible, ASBW 2 pp. 192–93 Lumma 2 (edition)
1986 Cooper, SARI 1 p. 15 Ad 2 (translation [conflated with E1.1.3.13.1.1.1a])
1989 Yang, Sargonic Inscriptions p. 12 § 1.1.1.1 no. 7 (study)
1991 Braun-Holzinger, Weihgaben p. 121 G 35 (transliteration, study)

TEXT

Lacuna(?)
1′–2′) ensi$_x$(PA.SI)-G̃AR
LUM-ma

Lacuna(?)
1′–2′) LUM-ma (is) the ensi-G̃AR.

MUG-si

E1.1.6

A certain MUG-si is attested as ensi-G̃AR of Adab in an economic text from Adab (Luckenbill, Adab no. 52). To date no inscriptions of this ruler are known. As for the date of MUG-si, we may note the comments of Yang, Sargonic Inscriptions p. 18):

> Among the legal and administrative tablets from Adab of the Early Dynastic period, we can separate out two groups. The first consists of A 1118, A 1130, A 1131, and A 732+1023. The first two of these are land-sale documents. Their relation to UCLM 9-1798 has been discussed by Foxvog. [Foxvog in Alster (ed.), Death pp. 67–75]. UCLM9-1798 was written in the reign of E-igi-nim-pa-e. It mentions the deceased Bil-lal-la (the *sanga* "priest" of Keš) and some of his family and followers. A 1118 and A 1130 mention many of the same persons, including Bil-lal-la as a living person. Thus A 1118 and A 1130 were written earlier than UCLM 9-1798, i.e., in the reign of Muk-si or in the early part of the reign of E-igi-nim-pa-e. A 1131 is a broken tablet with less than half preserved. It records the weight of various metal objects and other merchandise. It ends with *Muk-si GAR.énsi adab*^{ki}. A 732-1023 is a field measurement record which is also only partially preserved; the traces close to the end of the tablet allow the restorations: [*ada*]*b*^{ki} and [*mu*]*k-si*. These four texts can tentatively be dated to Muk-si's *ensi*dom.

E-IGI.NIM-pa'e

E1.1.7

MUG-si, ensi-G̃AR of Adab, was succeeded by E-IGI.NIM-pa'e, ensi-G̃AR of Adab. For a land sale document dating to the time of E-IGI.NIM-pa'e, see Foxvog, in Alster (ed.), Death pp. 67–75 and Gelb, Land Tenure pp. 99–103.

1

A stone ram figurine was dedicated to the goddess Diğirmaḫ by E-IGI.NIM-pa'e, likely ensi of Adab.

COMMENTARY

The ram figurine, of unknown provenance but almost certainly from Adab, bears the museum number CBS 9222. The inscription was collated.

The spacing of the text suggests that there was no G̃AR sign before the title ensi in line 3, although this cannot absolutely be ruled out. If this be correct it would suggest a change in title of E-IGI.NIM-pa'e.

BIBLIOGRAPHY

1914 Poebel, PBS 5 no. 31 (photo, copy)
1982 Steible, ASBW 2 pp. 190–91 E'iginimpa'e 2 (edition)
1986 Cooper, SARI 1 p. 16 Ad 3.1 (translation)
1986 Yang, Sargonic Archive p. 29 § 2.1.1.1.1 no. 13 (study)
1989 Sargonic Inscriptions p. 12 § 1.1.1.1 no. 13 (study)

TEXT

1) diğir-maḫ
2) é-IGI.NIM-pa-è
3) [P]A.TE.SI-
4) [ad]ab.KI
5) [...] ⌈x⌉ x
6) [é]-maḫ dù-a

1) For the goddess Diğirmaḫ.
2–4) E-IGI.NIM-pa'e, [e]nsi of [Ad]ab ..., who built the [E]-maḫ.

2

Foundation deposits from Mound V at Adab yielded bronze and stone foundation tablets, as well as bronze plates fixed with pegs, that were incised with a seven-line inscription commemorating E-IGI.NIM-pa'e's construction of Ninmaḫ's temple.

CATALOGUE

Ex.	Museum number	Object	Material	Dimensions (cm)	Luckenbill, Adab no.	Lines preserved	cpn
Perforated bronze plates (a) with spikes (b)							
1a	A 541b	Plate	Bronze	14.4×4.8×0.8	—	1–7	n
1b	A 541a	Spike	Bronze	9.4×2.6	—	Uninscribed	n
2a	A 543	Plate	Bronze	14.5×5.2×0.9	18	1–7	n
2b	A 542	Spike	Bronze	17×2.3	—	Uninscribed	n
3a	EŞ	Plate	Bronze	—	—	1–7	n
3b	EŞ	Spike	Bronze	—	—	Uninscribed	n
Foundation tablets							
4	A 1159	Tablet	Marble	6.5×4.6×1.9	22	1–7	n
5	A 1160	Tablet	Bronze	6.4×4.4×1.7	20	1–7	n
6	A 1161	Tablet	Bronze	6.5×4.6×1.6	21	1–7	n
7	A 1162	Tablet	Bronze	7.3×4.9×1.4	19	1–7	n
8	Hermitage	Tablet	Marble	—	—	1–7	p

COMMENTARY

For a drawing showing a reconstruction of the original layout of a bronze plate and spike, see Ellis, Foundation Deposits pl. 3 no. 9. For the term temen ... si, see Dunham RA 80 (1986) pp. 40–54.

BIBLIOGRAPHY

1912 Banks, Bismya p. 200 (ex. 5, copy); p. 275 (exs. 2a–2b, photo)
1913 Hommel, OLZ 16 cols 349–50 (ex. 5, edition, study)
1915 Shileiko, VN p. 8 and pl. 3 no. 2 (ex. 8, photo, copy, edition)
1930 Luckenbill, Adab nos. 18–22 (exs. 2a, 4–7, copy)
1968 Ellis, Foundation Deposits p. 55 and nn. 66–67 (exs. 1a, 1b, 2a, 2b, 4–7 study); pl. 3 no. 9 (drawing)
1971 Sollberger and Kupper, IRSA, 1F4a (translation)
1982 Steible, ASBW 2 pp. 189–90 E'iginimpa'e 1 (exs. 2a, 4–8, edition)
1983 Rashid, Gründungsfiguren p. 13 (exs. 1a, 1b, 2a, 2b, study); pl. 10 e (drawing)
1986 Cooper, SARI 1 p. 16 Ad 3.2 (exs. 1–8, translation)
1986 Dunham, RA 80 p. 40 (edition)
1986 Yang, Sargonic Archive p. 29 § 2.1.1.1.1 no. 8–12 (study)
1989 Yang, Sargonic Inscriptions p. 12 § 1.1.1.1 nos. 8–12 (study)

TEXT

1) diĝir-maḫ
2) é-IGI.NIM-pa-è
3) énsi:G̃AR(G̃AR-énsi)
4) adab.KI
5) é-maḫ mu-na-dù
6) úr-bi ki-šè
7) temen ba-si

1) For the goddess Diĝirmaḫ,
2–4) E-IGI.NIM-pa'e, ensi-G̃AR, of Adab,
5) built the E-maḫ for her
6–7) (and) buried foundation deposits below its base.

Lugal-Ane-mundu

E1.1.8

1

A composition belonging to the genre of pseudoautobiographical literature (for this type of text, see Longman, Autobiography) and known from three Old Babylonian tablet copies, CBS 474, CBS 1217, and CBS 342 (see Civil, RA 73 [1979] p. 93), said to belong to the "Khabaza collection," deals with Lugal-Ane-mundu's campaign against the enemy forces of Marḫaši and his construction of the E-namzu, temple of the goddess Nintu/Diğirmaḫ in Adab. For the temple see George, House Most High p. 131 no. 855.

Although there may be a kernel of historicity in this text, it seems unlikely that it originated in an ED inscription. In a discussion of the evidence Zhi Yang (JAC 4 [1989] pp. 55–60) concludes (p. 60): "... it appears that the Lugal-ane-mundu inscription should probably be considered either as a literary fiction or as the inscription of an early Old Babylonian king aspiring to fame," and it has not been edited in this volume.

BIBLIOGRAPHY

1909 Poebel, BE 6/2 no. 130 (ex. 2, copy); pp. 123–24 (ex. 2, edition)
1914 Poebel, PBS 5 no. 75 (ex. 1, copy); pls. 105–106 nos. 75A (ex. 1, photo); pl. 107 no. 75B (ex. 2, photo)
1934 Güterbock, ZA 42 pp. 40–47 (exs. 1–2, edition, study)
1939 Jacobsen, SKL p. 102 n. 183 (study)
1977 Curchin, RA 71 pp. 94–95 (study)
1979 Civil, RA 73 p. 93 (study)
1983 Cooper, Curse p. 19 n. 32 (study)
1987 Edzard, RLA 7 p. 114 (study)
1991 Longman, Autobiography pp. 92–93 (study)
1989 Yang, JIHAC 4 pp. 55–60 (study)

Mes-kigala

E1.1.9

One inscription of Mes-kigala, a late Presargonic governor of Adab, is known. Some scholars have identified him with the Mes-kigala named in a royal inscription of the Sargonic period king Rīmuš (the inscription was edited by the author in RIME 2 pp. 41–42 E2.1.2.1). Powell (in Studies Hirsch p. 311) writes:

> While the individuals named Irikagina and Meskigala who appear in the inscriptions of Maništušu and Rimuš respectively remain somewhat enigmatic, most who have discussed this problem seem to assume that the Meskigala ensi of Adab who appears in *BIN* 8 26 together with Lugalzagesi lugal is the same Meskigala ensi of Adab who appears in the OB copy of Rimuš's inscription describing the war with Adab and Zabala. D.O. Edzard, in his article "Mes-kigala," has adopted a cautious approach, saying only that if the Meskigala who appears in *BIN 8 26* is identical with the Meskigala who was defeated by Rimuš, then he must have been ensi for "mehrere Jahrzehnte". However, even this is not necessarily so, because we do not know the absolute dates for *BIN 8 26,* for Sargon's defeat of Lugalzagesi, nor for Rimuš's defeat of Meskigala, and, moreover, we have no independent evidence to substantiate the number of years assigned to Lugalzagesi and Sargon by the Sumerian King List.

2001

A statue fragment, probably from Adab, is incised with a dedicatory inscription for the life of Mes-kigala, governor of Adab.

COMMENTARY

The broken alabaster statue consists of three joined pieces that together measure 88 cm in height; they bear the museum number IM 5572. The statue was purchased from I. Géjou and is said to have come from Bismāya.

On the basis of its stylistic features, Strommenger and Nagel date the statue to the Fara/Ur I period, that is, to ED III times. Since we previously used a source (Nagel and Strommenger, BJVF 8 p. 177) in RIME 2 p. 253 (E2.9.1.2001) that contained only part of the inscription we have given the text anew here in full.

BIBLIOGRAPHY

1934 Meissner, MAOG 8 1/2 pp. 28–31 and fig. 19 (photo of statue [inscription not visible], study)
1942 Iraq Museum Guide p. 65 fig. 30 (photo)
1966 Iraq Museum Guide p. 22 no. 26 (study)
1968 Nagel and Strommenger, BJVF 8 p. 177 ([partial] transliteration [by Sollberger], study)
1970 Rowton, CAH 1/1 p. 220 and n. 1 (study)
1977 Braun-Holzinger, Beterstatuetten pp. 63, 73–74 and pl. 29c–29d (photo, transliteration, study)
1981 Spycket, Statuaire p. 85 n. 209 (study)
1986 Cooper, SARI 1 p. 17 Ad 6 (translation)
1986 Yang, Sargonic Archive pp. 51–52 § 2.2.2 no. 1and n. 55 ([partial] transliteration, study)
1991 Braun-Holzinger, Weihgaben p. 255 St 88 (study)
1993 Edzard, RLA 8 p. 93 (study)
1993 Frayne, RIME 2 p. 253 (edition)

TEXT

Col. i
1) ^{d}nin-šubur
2) sukkal-an-ra
3) nam-ti-
4) [mes]-ki-gal
5) [én]si-
6) [adab.KI]
Lacuna
1′) [...] GAR(?)
2′) ba(?)-[...]-ke$_4$-ne
3′) kur-GIŠ.erin-ta
4′) ŠU [... G]I-ŠÈ
5′) n[am-ti]-dam-dumu-ne-ne-šè
6′) ⌈d⌉nin-šubur
7′) [diğir]-ra-ni
8′) [a-m]u-na-ru
Col. ii
1′) x-KA×ŠU-[d]è arḫuš-tuku
2′) mu-bi

I 1–2) For the god Ninšubur, vizier of the god An,

i 3–6) for the life of [Mes]-kigala, [ru]ler of [Adab],

i 1′–4′) ... from the cedar mountains he ...

i 5′–8′) For the lives of his wife and children, he dedicated this to the god Ninšubur, his [go]d.

ii 1′–2′) Its [the statue's] name is, "Have mercy through (my) prayers!"

AKŠAK

E1.2

The Sumerian King List assigns the six kings of the single dynasty at Akšak a total reign of 99 years.

(a) Location

The location of ancient Akšak is unknown; for a possible location of the city at the large mound named Tell Sinker on the ancient Tigris bed northwest of Baghdad (site no. 016 in Adams, in Gibson, Kish, p. 189 with coordinates NLat 56° 24′ and ELat 44° 14′). See Frayne, Early Dynastic List pp. 47–48.

(b) Excavation History

As noted, the site has not been identified. Although Waterman (Tell Umar p. 6 and BASOR 32 [1928] p. 18) claims to have found inscriptions of Kings Urur and Unda-lulu of Akšak at Tell ʿUmar, this assertion was later withdrawn (see Barnett, JHS 83 [1963] p. 19 n. 90).

(c) Writing of the City Name

The city name Akšak is written ^{u_4}kúšu.KI in Presargonic inscriptions; cf. the Ur III writing ^{a}kúšu.KI cited in Edzard, Rép. Géog. 2 p. 6. A phonetic writing ak-šu-wa-ak occurs in the ED list of Geographical Names (Pettinato, Orientalia 47 [1978] p. 67, LGN no. 99). The meaning of the toponym is unknown.

(d) Patron Deities

The patron deity of the city of Akšak was the god Sîn (see Jacobsen, in Delougaz, Pre-sargonid Temples p. 291 no. 4 lines, and cf. Biggs, Abū Ṣalābīkh no. 106 col. viii line 3, and Thureau-Dangin, TCL 1 no. 179 line 3).

For various literary and historical references to the city of Akšak, see Gragg, AfO 24 (1973) pp. 70–71.

(e) Akšak in Historical and Literary texts

As for the history of Akšak in ED times, we note that an inscription of E-anatum of Lagaš (E1.9.3.5 line iv 26) relates that Zuzu, a king of Akšak (who is not mentioned in the Sumerian King List), made an unsuccessful raid on Lagaš. Later, En-šakuš-Ana of Uruk attacked Akšak (see E1.14.17.1 line 13); unfortunately, the name of the Uruk king's adversary is not given in the text. The importance of Akšak in late ED times is underscored by the fact, as noted, that Akšak is one of only three cities of Sumer and Akkad (the others being Kiš and Adab) that are mentioned in the Ebla archives (for the references see Archi, MARI 4 p. 77 document 100).

(f) Appearance in the Sumerian King List

Six ED rulers are named for Akšak in the SKL:

Early Dynastic Rulers of Akšak

King	No. of years assigned in SKL	RIM number
Uğzi	30	E1.2.1
Uğda-lulu	12	E1.2.2
Urur	6	E1.2.3
Puzur-Niraḫ	20	E1.2.4
Išu-il	24	E1.2.5
Šū-Sîn	7	E1.2.6

AWAN

E1.3

(a) Location of Awan

The precise location of the city of Awan is unknown. One clue to its location is the name of year 14 of Ibbi-Sîn (see Frayne RIME 3/2 p. 364) which mentions the land of Awan together with the cities of Susa and Adamšaḫ (for the reading Adamšaḫ, instead of the previously read Adamdun, see Civil, "'Adamdum' the Hippopotamus, and the Crocodile," JCS 50 [1998] pp. 11–14). Adamšah is likely to be located at the modern town of Andimishk not far NW of Dizful.

Further clues to Awan's location are found in three inscriptions of the Sargonic king Rīmuš (Frayne, RIME 2 pp. 51–58 E2.1.2.6–8 = Gelb and Kienast, Königsinschriften pp. 213ff. Rīmuš C 8, C 10, and C12). All the texts refer to a battle fought by the Qablītum River between the cities of Awan and Susa. Normally, the Sargonic inscriptions describe battle sites with some precision, so that we would expect that Awan lay not too far from Susa. The Qablītum River of the Rīmuš inscriptions may possibly equate with the Greek river name Coprates; the Coprates, in turn, is generally identified as the modern Diz (see Hansman, Iranica Antiqua 7 [1967] p. 32). All the evidence, then, points to a location for ancient Awan somewhere near the modern Dizful not far from Susa.

(b) Writing of the City Name

Awan, as far as can be determined, is always written a-wa-an.KI in cuneiform sources. A full discussion of the data for the city and state is given by M. Stolper in Encyclopaedia Iranica 3/5 pp. 113–14.

(c) Contacts Between Awan and Mesopotamia in Early Dynastic Times — Historical Sources

Relatively little is known of the political struggle between Mesopotamia and Elam in ED times. The SKL mentions King EN.ME-barage-si of Kiš as one "who carried off (as spoil) the weapons of Elam," a probable reference to campaigns of the Kišite king in the east. The fact that eastern (Elamite) cities such as Arawa, Karāna (GEŠTIN.KI, possibly to be connected with the modern hydronym Kārūn), and Uruʾaz (likely modern Aḫwāz, see Frayne in a forthcoming study) appear in the LGN supports the idea that Kiš, for at least a short period of time, may have controlled cities in Elam.

The royal inscriptions of the ED period concerning Elam have been collected and discussed by G. Selz in his article "'Elam' and 'Sumer' — Skizze einer Nachbarschaft nach inschriftlichen Quellen der vorsargonischen Zeit," in CRRA 36 pp. 27–44 and Potts, The Archaeology of Elam pp. 85–91. Several inscriptions of E-anatum of Lagaš allude to victories over the eastern cities of Elam, including Arawa, Uruʾaz, Mišime (the last likely Choga Mish, see Frayne in a forthcoming study), and a-dù-a (for the references see Potts, The Archaeology of Elam p. 89 Table 4.1).

Another defeat of Elam in ED times can be deduced from the title "who vanquished Elam" found in an Ur III copy of an inscription from Nippur of the ruler Enna-il named in the text as the "king of Kiš"; unfortunately, we do not know Enna-il's dynastic home.

Two sources attest to probable Elamite raids into Mesopotamia ED times. One is a famous letter from G̃irsu, once thought to date to the reign of En-entarzi of Lagaš but now dated by some scholars to year five of URU-KA-gina (see Volk, FAOS 19 pp. 25–29 for an edition and the complete bibliography on the text). The translation given here is from Michalowski, LEM pp. 11–12:

> To Enetarzi, the temple administrator of (the god) Ningirsu, speak: Thus says Lu-enna, the temple administrator of (the goddess) Ninmar:
>
> 600 Elamites carried off (plundered) goods from Lagaš toward Elam. Lu-enna, the temple administrator of (the goddess) Ninmar did battle in [x] and defeated the Elamites. He [captured/killed] 540 Elamites. Ur-Baʾu, the subordinate of Nig-lunutum, the chief of the smiths ... in ... he captured in the temple of Ninmarki. He [r*etriev*]*ed* five mirrors of washed silver, 20 ..., ... , five royal garments, (and) 16 fleeces from *sheep that had been eaten (by the enemy).*
>
> As long as the ruler of Lagaš is alive, as long as Enanatum-sipa-zi, the steward is alive ... shall bring ... to (the goddess) Ninmar. Year 5.

A second source possibly alluding to an Elamite raid on Sumer (this time on the territory of Keš and Adab) is found a land sale document dated to the time of E-IGI.NIM-paʾe of Adab; it was originally published by Foxvog (in Alster [ed.], Death pp. 67–75) and later discussed by Steinkeller (in Gelb, Land Tenure pp. 99–103) and Wilcke (in ZA 86 [1996] p. 17). According to Steinkeller, this interesting (but difficult text) is open to several interpretations. One of these is given by Steinkeller in the following words:

> In yet another scenario, the purpose of the sale was to obtain capital to ransom Làl-la from her captivity in Urua. Assuming that Bìl-làl-la was already dead at the time of the transaction, one could speculate that Làl-la's capture and Bìl-làl-la's death were connected with the same event, perhaps a raid of the army of Urua on Keš.

This text suggests that a major raid of Elamites on the territory of Keš took place shortly before or at the beginning of the reign of E-IGI.NIM-paʾe of Adab. Further, if the Lugal-Ane-mundu inscription (introduction to E1.1.8.1 above) has a kernel of historicity, it could conceivably be connected with the response of Lugal-Ane-mundu to an attack of eastern invaders, in this case, a coalition of enemy forces headed by the king of Marḫaši.

It may be that the hegemony of the kings of Awan acknowledged in the SKL may refer to a time when an Elamite king was briefly able to achieve a toehold in the land of Sumer.

(d) Appearance in the Sumerian King List

The Sumerian King list assigns 356 years as the total length of rule of the three kings of the dynasty of Awan. Unfortunately, the names of the Awanite kings are largely broken away, and a meaningful transcription of the traces is not possible.

Another source for the names of the (presumably) Presargonic kings of Awan is a clay tablet from Susa that can be dated on the basis of its script to the period c. 1800–1600 BC (see Scheil, RA 28 [1931] p. 2 = Scheil MDP 23 [1932] pp. iii–v). The first part of the tablet gives a list of twelve personal names (without regnal years or genealogy) which are summarized by the rubric "twelve kings of Awan" (12 LUGAL.MEŠ *šà a-wa-an*.K[I]) (see Carter and Stolper, Elam p. 12). The eighth PN, *lu-uḫ-ḫi-iš-šà-an* is almost certainly a variant spelling of the royal name *lu-uḫ-iš-an* found in a royal inscription of Sargon (Frayne, RIME 2 p. 23 E2.1.1.8 = Gelb and Kienast, Königsinschriften pp. 178–81 Sargon C 7, caption 5 line 1). We have assumed (following the general scholarly consensus) that the PNs in the Susa tablet preceding *lu-uḫ-ḫi-iš-šà-an* are the names of the Presargonic rulers of Awan (see table below). Unfortunately, although the names of the kings are complete, they are otherwise unattested.

(e) Contacts Between Awan and Mesopotamia in Early Dynastic Times — Literary Sources

There are tantalizing allusions in ED literary texts to campaigns directed by Mesopotamian rulers in the east. A mythic(?) text from Abū Ṣalābīkh written in UD.GAL.NUN orthography (IAS no. 32) mentions (col. ii line 8′–9′) the goddess Inanna (UD.SAG$_6$ in UD.GAL.NUN writing) "lady of Sumer" (nin ki-en-gi) taking up residence in the Elamite city of Uruaz (col ii line 2′) presumably as a result of a military conquest or a divine journey of the goddess. Another literary text from Abū Ṣalābīkh (IAS no. 327) describes how the Uruk king Lugalbanda brought back to Uruk a bride (the goddess Ninsuna) from the Elamite city of Uruaz.

Later Sumerian literature also deals with campaigns of the ED kings of Uruk in the east. The epic tale "Enmerkar and the Lord of Aratta" (edited by S. Cohen in Enmerkar and the Lord of Aratta, Ph. D. dissertation University of Pennsylvania 1973) describes long journeys taken by the royal ambassadors of Uruk and Aratta between their respective cities; the motive was apparently to establish long-distant trade between the cities. The epic tale "Enmerkar and En-suḫkešda-ana"(edited by A. Berlin in Enmerkar and Ensuḫkešdanna, A Sumerian Narrative Poem, OPBF 2, 1979) recounts a series of contests between the rulers of Uruk and Aratta. The "Lugalbanda Epic," (edited by C. Wilcke in Das Lugalbanda Epos, Weisbaden, 1969) in turn opens with the Uruk king campaigning in the eastern mountain land of Sabu'a, an Elamite GN attested in ED economic texts and thought by some scholars to have been situated near modern Agha Jari in western Iran (J. Duchene, in Studies Steve p. 69). A location of Elamite Sabu'a at modern Tappe Mūsīān will be suggested by the author in a forthcoming study. Later in the text a siege of the far-off city of Aratta is described. A passage in the Gilgameš Epic (Neo-Assyrian recension, see Parpola, Epic of Gilgamesh, p. 99 Tablet 8 line 18) alludes to Gilgameš and Enkidu's proud march along the bank of the Ulaya River (the Ulai River of the Bible and the Eulaiois River of Greek sources, it is identified with the modern Karkhah or a branch of this river in Susiana). The passage possibly refers to a campaign of Gilgameš in Elam. Further, some scholars have suggested a connection between the PN Ḫuwawa of the epic tale "Gilgameš and Ḫuwawa" and the Elamite DN Ḫumban, and have posited that the Gilgameš story may ultimately derive from a campaign of Gilgameš against Elam (J. Hansman, Iraq 38 (1976) pp. 23–35).

Table of Early Kings of Awan from the "Scheil" Tablet

RIM number	Royal Name
E1.3.1	*pe-el-li*
E1.3.2	*ta-at-ta*
E1.3.3	*uk-ku-ta-he-eš*
E1.3.4	*ḫi-i-šu-ur*
E1.3.5	*šu-šu-un-ta-ra-an*
E1.3.6	*na-pi-il-ḫu-uš*
E1.3.7	*ki-ik-ku-si-we-te-em-ti*

EBLA

E1.4

(a) Location

Ancient Ebla is identified with the large mound named Tell Mardīḫ (NLat 35° 48′ and ELat 36° 47′) located in western Syria.

(b) Excavation History

The site has been excavated since 1964 by a team from the University of Rome headed by P. Matthiae. For accounts of the excavations one may refer to the items listed in section O Archeologia/Archeology in the bibliographies of F. B. Guardata, M. Baldacci, and F. Pomponio cited in section (e) below.

The site was made famous by the uncovering of a huge ED IIIb royal archive during 1975. For early accounts (in English) of the discovery, see P. Matthiae, "Ebla in the Late Early Syrian Period: The Royal Palace Archives and the State Archives," BA 39 (1976) pp. 94–113; idem, "Preliminary Remarks on the Royal Palace of Ebla," SMS 2/2 (1978) pp. 1–40; idem, "Ebla in the Period of the Amorite Dynasties and the Dynasty of Akkad: Recent Archaeological Discoveries at Tell Mardikh (1975)," MANE 1 pp. 112–39.

(c) Writing of the City Name

The city name appears in the late ED archive as *eb-la*.KI. While the first sign of the name could theoretically could be read ib or eb or ip or ep comparative evidence indicates the correct reading of the toponym is Ebla.

(d) Patron Deity

The patron deity of the city was the god Kura; cf. Pomponio and Xella, Les dieux d'Ebla p. 245:

> L'ensemble de la documentation éblaite indique, sur la base de la quantité et de la qualité des attestations, que Kura était sans aucun doute le plus grand dieu poliade ... .

(e) General Studies on Ebla

The scholarly literature on Ebla is enormous; for extremely useful bibliographies one may consult M. Baldacci, F. Pomponio, Bibliografia Eblaita, in L. Cagni (ed.), Ebla 1975-1985 Dieci anni di studi linguistici e filologici, Napoli 1987, pp. 429–56; F. B. Guardata, M. Baldacci, and F. Pomponio, Bibliografia Eblaita II, SEL 6 (1989), pp. 145–58; idem, Eblaite Bibliography III, SEL 10 (1993) pp. 93–110; and idem, Eblaite Bibliography IV, SEL 14 (1997) pp. 109–24.

Beautiful illustrated volumes (in Italian) dealing with the Ebla discoveries include P. Matthiae, I tesori di Ebla (1985); idem, Ebla: Alle origini della civilità urbana (1995); and idem, Ebla. La città rivelata (1995).

(f) General Studies on the Ebla Archive

For general surveys of scholarship on the tablet archive, see B. Kienast, "Zwölf Jahre Ebla: Versuch einer Bestandsaufnahme," in Gordon and

Rendsberg (eds.), Eblaitica 3 pp. 31–77 and A. Archi, "Fifteen Years of Studies on Ebla, A Summary," OLZ 8 (1993) cols. 461–74. An extremely useful index of the Ebla texts has been provided by G. Conti, Index of Eblaic Texts (published or cited), Florence, 1992. It supercedes the now out of date S. Beld, W. Hallo and P. Michalowski, The Tablets of Ebla: Concordance and Bibliography.

For the Ebla toponyms one may consult Archi, Luogo and Bonechi, Rép. Géogr. 12/1. A convenient list of cities attested as having kings (EN) is found in Bonechi, AuOr 8 (1990) pp. 157–69.

For the personal names at Ebla we may consult M. Krebernik, Personennamen, A. Archi (ed.), Eblaite Personal Names and Semitic Name-Giving (=ARES 1) and J. Pagan, A Morphological and Lexical Study of Personal Names in the Ebla Texts (=ARES 3).

(g) The History of Ebla

For a very preliminary history of Ebla, see M. Astour, "An Outline of the History of Ebla (Part 1)" in Gordon and Rendsburg (eds.), Eblaitica 3 pp. 3–82. One may also refer to the articles in section G. Storia/History cited in the bibliographies listed in section (e) above.

(h) Early Dynastic Period Rulers

Apparently no copies of royal inscriptions of Eblaite kings are found among the 112 chancery texts from Tell Mardīḫ listed by Pettinato (in MEE 1, passim) and summarized by Kienast (in Gordon and Rendsberg [eds.], Eblaitica 2 pp. 58–66). Archi (in OLZ 88 [1993] col. 461) states in connection with these chancery texts that "the definition of these texts as 'historical texts' in MEE I (pp. XXVII–XXIX) is in no way justified by their contents ..."

They do, however, include important texts such as the treaty between Ebla and the city of Abarsal, the letter of King Enna-Dagān of Mari (edited under various rubrics in the Mari section of this volume), and the "donation of the vizier Ibrium to his sons."

As for the order of the Eblaite kings, we are most fortunate in Archi's discovery of the tablet TM.74.G.120 (and similar tablets) that enable us to determine the order of the kings of Ebla. For the relevant material, see Archi, ZA 76 (1986) pp. 213–17; Biga and Pomponio, NABU 1987 pp. 60–61 no. 106; Archi ARES 1 pp. 205–21; Archi, ARET 7 no. 150; Astour, in Gordon and Rendsberg (eds.); Eblaitica 3 pp. 19–26; Archi, in Durand (ed.), Amurru 1 pp. 13–15; and Archi, CRRA 45/1 pp. 1–13.

The evidence of the offering texts giving the royal names is present in chart form below. The interpretation of the royal names follows that given in J. Pagan, A Morphological and Lexical Study of the Personal Names in the Ebla Texts, ARES 3. Of interest is the fact that so many royal names are composed with the theophoric elements Dāmu, Ḫalab, and Līm paralleling the fact that the most frequent theophoric elements in the Ebla onomastica in general are Dāmu, Malik, Il(um), Līm, Baʿal, Kura and Zikir (see Pomponio and Xella, Les dieux d'Ebla p. 454).

Kings of Ebla
(those attested in the archive are shown in bold font)

RIM number	**King' Name**	**Translation of Name**
E1.4.1	KUL-ba-nu	"Blessed"(?))
E1.4.2	aš-ša-nu	—
E1.4.3	[sa]-mi-ù	"Listener"(?)
E1.4.4	zi-a-lu	"The city is Protection"(?)
E1.4.5	EN-ma-nu	"(Have) mercy, Beloved"
E1.4.6	na-ma-nu	"Gracious"
E1.4.7	da-[x]-⸢x⸣	—
E1.4.8	sa-[gi]-su	"Slayer"

E1.4.9	d[a-NE-n[u]	"God is strong"
E1.4.10	i-bí-ni-li-im	"Līm has called me"
E1.4.11	$iš_{11}$-ru_{12}-uṭ-da-nu	"The god Dāmu is just"
E1.4.12	⌜i⌝-si-du	"Support"
E1.4.13	iš-ru_{12}-uṭ-ḫa-lab_x(LAM)	"The god Ḫalab is just"
E1.4.14	ik-su-ud	"He (the child) has arrived"
E1.4.15	tal-da-li-im	"The god Līm has led"
E1.4.16	a-bur-li-im	"May I prosper, oh god Līm"
E1.4.17	a-gur-li-im	"The god Līm sojourned"
E1.4.18	i-bí-da-mu	"The god Dāmu has called (me)"
E1.4.19	ba-kà-da-mu	"The god Dāmu has wept"
E1.4.20	En-ḪAR-da-mu	"The god Dāmu has slain"
E1.4.21	i-šar-ma-lik	" The god Malik was victorious"
E1.4.22	**kùn-da-mu**	**"Be true, oh god Dāmu"**
E1.4.23	a-dub-da-mu	"The god Dāmu gave (generously)"
E1.4.24	**`ig-ri-iš-ḫa-lab_x(LAM)**	**"The god Ḫalab has approached"**
E1.4.25	**`ìr-kab-da-mu-**	**"The god Dāmu has mounted"**
E1.4.26	**$iš_{11}$-ar-da-mu**	**"The god Dāmu was victorious"**

The first of the kings in the table above to be mentioned in the Ebla archive is Kūn-Dāmu. His successor, Addub-Dāmu, does not appear and apparently his reign was quite short. His successor, Igriš-Ḫalab, reigned at least 12 years (see Archi, in Durand [ed.], Amurru I p. 27). His successor, Irkab-Dāmu, reigned during the time period corresponding to the last years of the viziers Darmia and Tir, the three or four years of the vizier Arrukum, and the two (?) first years of the vizier Ibrium, that is, 5+ or 6+ years in total (Archi, in Durand [ed.], Amurru I p. 27), and finally Irkab-Dāmu's successor, Išar-Dāmu, during the years corresponding to 15 or 16 years of the vizier Ibrium, the 17 years of the vizier Ibbi-Zikir plus the months before the destruction of Ebla, that is 32+ or 33+ years altogether (Archi, in Durand [ed.], Amurru I p. 27).

E'EDIN

E1.5

(a) Writing of the City Name and Its Location

The city of E'edin appears in the writing edin with a variant din as entry 171 in the Early Dynastic List of City Names (Pettinato, Orientalia 47 [1978] p. 69 = idem, MEE 3 p. 235). The city probably occurs in the writing x-edin.KI just before the city of Ašnak in the Early Dynastic period "Dar-a-a Tablet" (see Gelb, Land Tenure pp. 113–15 no. 38 obv. i line 13). According to Matthews (Cities pp. 41–42), the city name also appears in the archaic Ur city sealings.

Cities in the vicinity of E'edin in the area southeast of Nippur have been studied recently by Steinkeller (ZA 91 [2001] pp. 83–84); there he mentions the settlements Ašgi-pada, Ummud, E-tena, Šarrākum, Kiri-g̃eštin, and Šešdu'a. According to research of the author, E'edin is likely to be located at modern Tell al Hayyād (Adams, Heartland of Cities site no. 1306). The city apparently lay at the junction of the ancient Tigris canal (which flowed through modern Tell el-Wilayah) and a canal flowing east from Nippur.

(b) Inscriptions

The name of one of the ruler of E'edin appears in an Early Dynastic period statue inscription.

Aga-ak

E1.5.1

1

A statuette bears the inscription of Aga-ak (reading uncertain), ruler of the city E'edin.

COMMENTARY

The limestone statue of a standing male figure is of unknown provenance; it came from a private collection and was sold at the Hôtel Druout at Paris on 12 April 1951. The piece was presented by the "Amis du Louvre" in 1951. The statue bears the museum number AO 20146. The inscription was collated from the published photo.

For the reading of the PN of line 1, see Bauer, AoN 21 (1985) p. 12.

BIBLIOGRAPHY

1952 Parrot, Iraq 14 pp. 73–74 and pl. XXIV (photo, copy, transliteration, study)
1957 Parrot, Syria 34 pp. 224–26 (photo, copy, transliteration)
1977 Braun-Holzinger, Beterstatuetten pp. 43 and 75 and pl. 13a–b (photo, transliteration, study)
1977 Edzard, Rép. Géogr. 1 p. 40 (study)
1980 Amiet, Art fig. 261 (photo)
1981 Spycket, Statuaire p. 71 and n. 137 (study); pl. 45 fig. 45 (photo)
1982 Steible, ASBW 1 p. 364 AnLag. 12 (edition)
1986 Cooper SARI 1 pp. 17–18 Ee 1 (translation)
1991 Braun-Holzinger, Weihgaben p. 241 St 6 (edition, study)
1992 Frayne, Early Dynastic List p. 33 (study)

TEXT

1) àga(GÍN)-ak
2) énsi-
3) é-edin

1–3) Aga-ak, ruler of E'edin

ḪAMAZI

E1.6

(a) Location

The state of Ḫamazi, located in the Zagros Mountain region somewhere between the Upper Zāb and Diyālā Rivers (see provisionally Edzard, RLA 4 pp. 70–71), seems to have been a major political power in ED times. An important text shedding light on its location is an Ur III text dating to year 8 of Amar-Suena (Sigrist, JCS 31 [1979] pp. 166–70). According to the research of the present author based on a study of the text published by Sigrist and modern toponyms, the city of Ḫamazi was likely located at the site of Kani Jowez about 10 kms SE of modern Halabjah.

(b) Writing of the City Name

The city and state name of Ḫamazi is written ḫa-ma-zi.KI in ED sources.

(c) ED Ruler of Ḫamazi

The SKL assigns one ruler, a certain Ḫataniš, to the single dynasty of Ḫamazi (Jacobsen, SKL pp. 96–99 and nn. 166–68). The Weld Blundell prism exemplar credits him a reign of 360 years (6 šu-ši).

While we have, as yet, no inscriptions of Ḫataniš, the proper name does appear in an Old Babylonian god list (de Genouillac, TCL 15 no. 10 line 54), and as a "shade" ($gidim_4$) of the E-kur in An: *Anum* I no. 189 (Litke, Reconstruction p. 42). He appears in the latter source after another shade, LUM-ma; cf. An: *Anum* I no. 188 (Litke, Reconstruction p. 42). Selz (Untersuchungen p. 139) has pointed out the existence of a PN ur-^{d}ḫa-ma-zi-da in a Presargonic tablet from Lagaš (Sollberger, CT 50 no. 26 col. ii line 3) which leads him to posit the full name of the GN to be Ḫamazid. However, since it is not entirely certain that this PN is connected to the state of Ḫamazi, we have retained the conventional spelling of the GN.

(d) Ḫamazi in ED History

An allusion to the defeat of Ḫamazi is found in the vessel inscription edited as E1.15.1.1 in this volume. While the extant text does not give the name of the ruler responsible for the victory over Ḫamazi, his probable filiation (son of) [P]ussussu is preserved; for the name type, see Römer Orientalia NS 57 (1988) pp. 224–25, note to Ki 6. Hilprecht thought that the fragment with the name [P]ussussu (BE 1/2 no. 109) belonged to the same vessel that named Utuk/Uḫub, ruler of Kiš (BE 1/2 no. 108); see E1.7.42.1. However, as Cooper (Iraq 46 [1984] p. 42) points out, an autopsy of the two vessel fragments clearly reveals that they do not belong to the same vessel.

A letter from Tell Mardīḫ, TM.75.G.2342, (Pettinato Rivista Biblica Italiana 25 [1977] pp. 238–40; idem, The Archives of Ebla, pp. 96–99; Shea, OrAnt 23 [1984] pp. 143–58; Chiera, OrAnt 25 [1986] pp. 81–86), apparently formed part of the diplomatic correspondence between the states of Ebla and Ḫamazi. The letter's sender was a certain Ibubu, superintendent of the palace at Ebla; his correspondent appears to have been a messenger of the king of Ḫamazi. It is extremely unlikely that the Ḫamazi of the Ebla tablet refers to the eastern Ḫamazi. A study of the Ebla toponyms undertaken by this author reveals that most of them (with the exceptions of major southern cities of Kiš, Akšak, and Adab) lay in Syria, the Upper Euphrates region, and the Ḫābūr basin. It is probable that the Ḫamazi of the Ebla texts refers to the ancient Ḫamazi that lay at modern Qalʿah Ḥomṣ, the "citadel hill" of modern Ḥomṣ. According to M. Moussli ("Tell Ḥomṣ [Qalʿat Ḥomṣ]," Zeitschrift des Deutschen Palästina-Vereins [100] pp. 9–11) the site exhibits ceramics dating from the Early Bronze Period; I am thankful to M. Astour for the reference. This identification of the Ebla Ḫamazi was rejected by P. Steinkeller in his RIM readers' notes.

KIŠ

E1.7

(a) Location

Twenty-odd mounds make up the area we now know to be ancient Kiš (see Gibson, Kish pp. 67–92; idem, RLA 5 pp. 613–20). The most prominent of these are Tell Uḥaimir in the west (NLat 32° 33′ ELong 44° 35′) and Tell Ingharra in the east; the latter is located about 2 km east of Tell Uḥaimir.

(b) Excavation History

The mounds of Kiš were excavated in large part by two archaeological expeditions. One by de Genouillac in 1912 examined the ziqqurrat at Tell Uḥaimir and an area of Old Babylonian houses around it. A section of the Neo-Babylonian temple at Ingharra was also unearthed.

A second series of excavations, funded by the Ashmolean Museum (Oxford) and the Field Museum of Natural History (Chicago) under the general direction of S. Langdon, was carried out during the years 1923–33. Field directors for the expedition were E. MacKay (1923–26) and L.C. Watelin (1927–33). Among the important finds was a series of ED burials (including spectacular "chariot burials"), two ziqqurrats made of plano-convex bricks, an ED III period palace from Mound A, and a large ED administrative building made of plano-convex bricks found at Mound P.

According to an article in the journal Science (no. 293 6 July 2001 p. 36) archaeological work has started up again at Kiš directed by a Japanese expedition.

(c) Patron Deities

Tell Uḥaimir marks the site of the temple E-mete-ursag "House Befitting the Champion" shrine of the warrior god Zababa, patron deity of Kiš. His ziqqurrat, attested archaeologically in structures dating to the times of Ḫammu-rāpi and Samsu-ilūna of Babylon I, Adad-apla-iddina, and Nebuchadnezzar II was known as E-unir-kituš-maḫ "Ziqqurrat, Lofty Abode" (with a variant name E-anur-kituš-maḫ "Temple (of) the Horizon, Lofty Abode)." Remains of an ED structure likely lie buried (and thus inaccessible) at the core of the Uḥaimir ziqqurrat.

Ingharra marks the site of ancient (E)-ḫursag̃-kalama "(Temple) Mountain of the Land." Its tutelary deity was known from OB royal inscriptions to have been the goddess Inanna; she appears earlier in ED economic tablets from Ingharra (Grégoire, Contribution, Ashm 1928-16, Ashm 1928-428, Ashm 1928-429, Ashm 1928-432) in the writing INANNA.G̃AR. The certain reading of the complex is unknown. Her consort in ED times (to judge from the economic texts) would appear to be the god Enki. The two ziqqurrats made of plano-convex bricks found at Ingharra were likely dedicated to this divine pair. Later, in OB times, the deities Zababa and Eštar were the patron city gods of Kiš (see Frayne RIME 4 p. 385).

(d) Writing of the City Name

The city name Kiš is written with the sign LAK 248, which according to

Deimel (Šumerisches Lexikon p. 825 note to sign no. 425) depicts the head of a hoofed animal; see also Steinkeller, ZA 77 (1987) pp. 162–63. It could conceivably be regarded as a city totem. Related signs to LAK 248 are alim (with lim phonetic complement added) "aurochs," lulim (with lu and lim phonetic complements added) "stag," i.e., "male red deer," and anše (with *šeššig* added) "donkey." The precise nature of the Kiš animal is not known. It may possibly be linked to the figure of an equine shown as a symbol of Zababa on a thirteenth century BCE kudurru stone; see Black and Green Gods p. 16.

The Sumerian King List assigns four dynasties to the city of Kiš.

Early Kings of Kiš
Kings Whose Names are Otherwise Attested Appear in Bold Font

The names of most of the first twelve kings of Kiš can be connected with ancient constellation names.

Kiš I Section 1: Kings after the Flood: Kings 1–612 (Constellation Names)

No.	Name in Sumerian King List and no. of years of reign	Other Attestations	Mesopotamian Constellation	Entry in MUL: APIN col. and line no.	Greek Transcription in Berossus	Modern Con-stellation	RIM no.
1	GIŠ.ÙR "Beam" 1,200	Kassite period omen *gu-šu-ur* = *gušūru* "Beam"	GIŠ.GANA. ÙR (= *maš-kakātu*) "(Wooden) Harrow"	I ii 23	Ἐυηχοις (apparently for en-gišur) "Lord Beam"	Eastern Part of Vela	E1.7.1
2	*Kullasina-bēl* "(Of) all of them (i.e., "the people") (he is) lord" or *Kullasina-ibēl* "He rules all of them " 900	^{d}EN.ME-ŠÁR.RA "Lord of all"	^{d}EN.ME-ŠÁR.RA "Lord of all"	I i 3	*Χωλλας-βηλοψ (apparently for *Kullasina-bēl*) (*Preserved text has: Χωμας-βηλοψ	Pleiades	E1.7.2
3	NA(?) ^{d}*is le-e* KU$_5$.DA"... (Divine) Severed Jaw of the Bull ..." 670	See von Soden AHw p. 389	^{d}*is le-e* "(Divine) Jaw of the Bull" MUL *is le-e* "Jaw of the Bull Star"	I ii 1 I ii 39	—	a Tauri and Hyades	E1.7.3
4	EN-DÁRA-AN-NA "Lord, ibex of heaven"	—	—	—	—	Monocerus	E1.7.4
5	*ba-bu-um* "gate (of heaven)" 300	Cf. Sumerian ká-an-na "Gate of Heaven"	—	—	—	Likely the constellati on Auriga	E1.7.5

6	ušum-an-na “Snake of Heaven” ⌜240⌝	ušumgal-an-na “Dragon of Heaven”	—	—	—	Cetus(?)	E1.7.6
7	*kà-lí-bu-um* “dog” 960	—	MUL UR.GIR$_7$ “Dog Star”	I i 25 I iii 2, 25 I iv 4, 29	—	Southern Part of Hercules	E1.7.7
8	TI$_8$.MUŠEN	“Eagle”	MUL. TI$_8$.MUŠEN	I ii 12 I iii 5, 8, 29	—	Most of Aquila	E1.7.8
9	*qà-lu-mu* “Lamb” 840	—	—	—	—	—	E1.7.9
10	*zú-qá-qi$_4$-ip* “Scorpion” 900	—	MUL.GÍR.TA B	I ii 28–31 III 3ff. 25ff. iv 35	—	Scorpio	E1.7.10
11	á-tab-ba “Adapa” 600	“Adapa” as Keeper of the Gate of Heaven	—	—	—	Near the point of the Vernal Equinox beside Taurus. Likely the eastern side of the “Gate of Heaven”	E1.7.11
12	*ar-bu-um* “Raven” 720	—	MUL.UGA. MUŠEN	I ii 9 I iii 20 II B 3	—	Corvus	E1.7.12

Kiš I Section II Kings 13–22

Number	**King**	**No. of years of reign**	**RIM number**
13	**Etana** “Ascender of Heaven”(?)	1,560	E1.7.13
14	Balīḫ “Balīḫ (River)”	400	E1.7.14
15	EN.ME-nuna “Noble Lord (EN.ME)”	660	E1.7.15
16	Melam-Kiš “Radiance of Kiš”	900	E1.7.16
17	bar-sal-nun-na “Noble Sheep.” For bar-sal = “sheep,” see PSD B pp. 125–26	1,200	E1.7.17
18	Sumug$_5$$^{\text{sà-mug}}$ “Mole (i.e., birthmark)”	140	E1.7.18
19	Tizqārum “Exalted one”	305	E1.7.19
20	Ilkû (?)	900	E1.7.20
21	Ilta-śadûm “The Goddess (is) a Mountain”	1,200	E1.7.21
22	**EN.ME-barage-si** “Lord who fills the dais”	900	E1.7.22
23	**Aka** “Product (of DN)”	625	E1.7.23

Kiš II			
1	Sipa-sura “Shepherd ...”	60	E1.7.24
2	Dadasig (?)	x	E1.7.25
3	Mamagala “Great Boats”(?)	420	E1.7.26
4	Kal(i)bum “Dog”	132	E1.7.27

5	TÚG-e "Fuller"(?)	360	E1.7.28
6	Men-nuna "Noble(?) Crown"	180	E1.7.29
7	Lugal-mu "My king"	420	E1.7.30
8	**Ibbi-[Ištar(?)]** "[Ištar(?)] has called (me)"	120	E1.7.31

Kiš III			
1	**Ku-Baba** "Radiant Baba"	100	E1.7.32

Kiš IV			
1	Puzur-Sîn "Protected by the god Sîn"	25	E1.7.33
2	**Ur-Zababa** "Servant of the god Zababa"	400	E1.7.34
3	Simudara "Simudara (City[?])"	30	E1.7.35
4	Ūṣi-watar "The Surpassing One has Come Forth"(?)	7	E1.7.36
5	Ištar-mūtī "Ištar is a warrior for me"	11	E1.7.37
6	Išme-Šamaš "The god Šamaš has heard"	11	E1.7.38
7	Nannia (?)	7	E1.7.39

Kings Not Mentioned in the Sumerian King List

1	**[PN] DUMU MUNUS.UŠUMGAL** **[PN] "Offspring of Lady Dragon"**	—	**E1.7.40**
2	**Lugal-UD**	—	**E1.7.41**
3	Abīšu "His father"; see Archi, SEb 4 p. 87 no. 45; idem, in Gordon (ed.), Eblaitica 1 p. 139 no. 28 and idem, MARI 5 p. 47 TM.75.G.10091 col. iv lines 1–4; cf. Steinkeller, Studies Hallo p. 242 and n.19; Archi and Biga, JCS 55 (2003) p. 32 and n. 91. If the Kiš mentioned in this tablet refers to a Kiš in the Ḫabur region then this would not be a king of Kiš in Mesopotamia; see the notes in the introduction to this book.	—	E1.7.42

Son of a King of Kiš

1	Iš/Uš-kun-Nūnu "The deity Nunu has established"; Archi, MARI 5 p. 46 n. 28; Steinkeller, Studies Hallo p. 243; Archi and Biga, JCS 55 (2003) p. 32 and n. 92. For the deity Nunu see Cavigneaux and Krebernik, RLA 6 pp. 619–20. If the Kiš mentioned in this tablet refers to a Kiš in the Khabur region then this would not be a king of Kiš in Mesopotamia; see notes in the introduction to this book.	—	—

City Ruler

1	**Utuk/Uḫub**	—	**E1.7.43**

For the early kings of Kiš see Hallo, JCS 17 (1963) pp. 52–53, Wilcke in Studies Sjöberg pp. 567–70, and Frayne (forthcoming).

The name of the first king of Kiš appears as GIŠ(?).⸢ÙR.RA⸣ in B(rockmon) T(ablet) 14 and GIŠ.ÙR in the Weld Blundell Prism (collation Hallo). It clearly corresponds to MUL GIŠ.GÁNA.ÙR of MUL APIN I ii 23. The latter means "Harrow Star." The asterism corresponds to the eastern part of the modern constellation of Vela.

Based on the constellation name Hallo suggested a reading *maškakātu*(*m*)

"Harrow" for the name of the first king of Kiš (JCS 17 [1963] pp. 52–53). However, the evidence of an omen collection known from two tablets, one dating from the Kassite period and one from Seleucid times (see Frayne and George, NABU 1990 no. 30,) suggests a different reading. The omen collection mentions a certain *gu-šu-ur* who is said to have ruled the land, an indication that he was an important ruler. He may well be identified with the first king of Kiš in the Sumerian King List.

A second datum arguing for a rendering /gušur/ or the like for the name of the first king of Kiš is the Greek transcription Ευηχοις given for the name of the first post-diluvian king in the Βαβυλονιακα of Berossus. Here the element Ευη- at the beginning of the RN is likely a Greek transcription of Sumerian EN.ME. Greek Ευη- is also comparable to the element Σευη- in the name Σευηχορος given by the Roman historian Aelian in his Greek account "On the Nature of Animals" as the name of Gilgameš's grandfather, that is, Enmerkar. Scholars have universally agreed that the initial Σ here results from a textual corruption. We may also note the comment of Edzard (RLA 7/-8 p. 614) that SB and Greek αμε, ευε corresponds to Sumerian EN.ME. Ευηχοισ, then, could interpreted as having arisen from *en-giš-ù(r), with the final r being lost. The appearances of χ for Sumerian g and σ for Sumerian š are totally concordant with the correspondences between Sumerian and Akkadian words expressed in Greek letters as has been discussed recently by Geller in ZA 87 (1997) pp. 64–68.

As for the second king of Kiš we may note Wilcke's observation (in Studies Sjöberg p. 567) that the second name in the Βαβυλονιακα of Berossus, Χωμας–βηλοψ, is likely a corruption of an original *Χωλλας–βηλοψ corresponding to Akkadian Kullassina-ibēl, for which see Hallo, JCS 17 (1963) pp. 52–53.

EN.ME-barage-si

E1.7.22

The first king of Kiš for whom we have any inscriptions is EN.ME-barage-si. Two contemporaneous inscriptions are known for the king; one was excavated from the temple oval at Ḫafāji and the other possibly came from the vicinity of modern Kūt on the lower Tigris.

The reign of EN.ME-barage-si seems to have marked a high point in the fortunes of the Kišite kingdom. The Tummal Chronicle relates that EN.ME-barage-si built the temple of Enlil named uru-na-nam in Nippur and connected his son Aka with the Tummal shrine.

Possible evidence of building activity by a ED king of Kiš for the god Enlil in Nippur is found in an ED literary text (Biggs, Abū Ṣalābīkh no. 142) written in UD.GAL.NUN orthography. Its five concluding lines read: UD.za-ba$_4$-ba$_4$ MUG:mì / UD UNU-šè GUG / UD.nissaba zà-mì / èš-UD.GAL.NUN / al-dù which in conventional orthography would be written: ^{d}za-ba$_4$-ba$_4$ zà:mì / DIG̃IR(?) ki-šè g̃ar / ^{d}nissaba zà:mì / èš ^{d}en-líl / al-dù "Praise to the god Zababa, the god(?) is set on earth, Praise to the god Nissaba, the shrine of the god Enlil has been built." The mention of the god Zababa in the hymn clearly provides a link to Kiš, since, as noted, Zababa was the tutelary deity of that city.

Further, EN.ME-barage-si's construction of the uru-na-nam temple in Nippur may possibly have been commemorated in another literary composition, namely "Enlil and Ninlil." The opening lines of the poem set the locale of the story in the place called uru.KI na-nam, apparently a precinct or temple quarter of Nippur. Its description of the banishment of the goddess Ninlil and her subsequent coupling with the disguised god Enlil outside the city is particularly reminiscent of the Tummal festival which is known from Ur III sources. During the festival Enlil and Ninlil travelled by boat from Nippur to Tummal (possibly modern Tell Dlēḥim, 12 km southeast of Nippur; see Yoshikawa, ASJ 11 [1989] p. 289) where a religious ceremony, possibly a sacred marriage rite, was performed.

Another literary text may be connected with an ED king of Kiš. This is the "Keš Temple Hymn" once known only from Old Babylonian tablet copies but now attested in ED manuscripts from Abū-Ṣalābīḫ and Adab. Commenting on line 107 of the text Biggs (ZA 61 [1971] p. 202) writes:

> The new text [the Abū Ṣalābīḫ MS] casts doubt on the correctness of the interpretation of é-e lugal-bur-ra àm-mi-gub as "the lugalburra-priest stepped up to the temple," [in the OB version] since there is an intervening line between lugal and bur. It appears that bur is the object of the gub "put in place," and that the archaic version should be translated "the king of Kish put a stone bowl in place in the temple," which implies composition of the text at a time when Kish controlled Sumer at least as far south as the region of Nippur and Adab, in the general area of which Kesh is to be located.

The same *burgi* rite is found in inscription E1.8.1.2 in this volume and has been discussed by Jacobsen in ZA 52 (1957) p. 135 n. 100; see also G. Selz, "ne-saĝ, bur-saĝ und gú-ne(-saĝ-ĝá): Zu zwei Gefäßbezeichnungen, ihren Bedeutungsentwicklungen und einem sumerischen Wort für (Gefäß) Schrank," SEL 13 (1996) pp. 3–8.

The GN Keš is known from a later literary text to be the name of the sacred precinct of the city of Šarrākum (see Wilcke, ZA 62 [1972] p. 55), and it is noteworthy that Šarrākum appears as entry 167 (written śar-ra-kum$_{x}$[LUM]) in the LGN.

Now, in our earlier discussion we suggested that the LGN listed cities "in territory either controlled by Kiš or with which it conducted trade in ED times." Of interest in the context of this study is the appearance in the LGN of cities in three geographical areas: Nippur (LGN 177), Šarrākum (i.e., Keš) (LGN 167) and the territory in Elam, the latter including the cities of Arawa (LGN 73), Gizinu (LGN 75), and Uruʾaz (LGN 78). The last group of cities recalls the statement in the SKL that EN.ME-barage-si "carried away as spoil the weapons of the land of Elam." If the LGN is indeed an ED list of Kišite dominated territory, then the mention of Nippur and Elam in the list would suggest a date of the text's creation to the time of King EN.ME-barage-si.

As for the reading of the ^{f}'s name, we may note the comments of Wilcke (in Lugalbandaepos p. 41, n. 96):

> Die Zeichengruppe EN.ME ist bereits in den Texten der archaischen Schicht IV aus Uruk belegt. S.A. Falkenstein, ATU S. 122; J. Renger, ZA NF XXIV 115. Doch bleibt unklar, wie sie dort zu deuten ist. Besonders häufig findet sie sich in Personennamen vorsintflutlicher Könige aus Badtibira und Sippar und bei Königen der ersten Dynastie von Kiš. S. die Zusammenstellung der Namen bei D.O. Edzard, ZA NF XIX 18. S. weiter J. van Dijk, UVB XVIII 47 zu en-me-ušumgal-an-na als Variante zu amaušum-gal-an-na. Die Namen der vorsintflutlichen Könige von Badtibira, en-me-(en)-lu-an-na, en-me-en)-gal-an-na und des Königs von Larak, en-sipa-zi-an-na, erscheinen in aB syllabisch schreibenden Texten als am-me-[lu-an-na] und am-me-gal-an-na (NFT 211, AO 4346 1–2; s. Th. Jacobsen, PAPS CVII, 477 Anm. 8) und als am-mi-lu-a-na und am-mi-gal-la-na (PRAK II C 51 Rs. 3-4) und in einem jungen Text (K. 5044) als am-me-lu-an-[na], ^{d}am-me-gal-an-[na] und ^{d}am-me-sipa-zi-an-na (S. Th. Jacobsen, a.a.O.; s. auch AS XI 72 Anm. 18); vgl. in dem seleukidischen Text W 20030, 7 (s. J. van Dijk, UVB XVIII 46) am-me-lu-an-na und am-me-gal-an-na.

1

An alabaster vessel fragment found in the "temple oval" at ancient Tutub (modern Ḫāfāji) is inscribed with the name ME-bara-si (without title); it probably refers to EN.ME-bara(ge)si named in the Sumerian King List.

COMMENTARY

The vessel fragment was found at Temple Oval I, C 46:4 and was given the excavation number Kh. III 35. Its Iraq Museum number is unknown. It is not known whether this inscription is in Akkadian or Sumerian.

BIBLIOGRAPHY

1940 Jacobsen, Temple Oval p. 147 no. 2 (copy, edition)
1958 Edzard, ZA 53 p. 10 and n. 2 (study)
1969 Wilcke, Lugalbandaepos p. 41 n. 96 (study)
1971 Sollberger and Kupper, IRSA IA1a n. 2 (study)
1982 Steible, ASBW 2 Mebarasi 1 p. 213 (edition)
1986 Cooper, SARI 1 p. 18 Ki 1 (translation [conflated with E1.3.1.2])
1990 Edzard, RLA 7 p. 614 (study)
1991 Braun-Holzinger, Weihgaben pp. 125 G 62 (edition, study)

TEXT

1) ME-bára-⌈si⌉	1) (EN).ME-barage-si
Lacuna	Lacuna

2

A fragment of an alabaster vessel of unknown provenance bears an inscription of ME-bara-si with the title "king of Kiš"; it almost certainly refers to the EN.ME-barage-si of the Sumerian King List.

COMMENTARY

The vessel fragment, which measures 12×12×1.4cm, was "confiscated at Kut," and bears the museum number IM 30590. The inscription was collated from the published photo. It is not known whether this inscription is in Akkadian or Sumerian.

BIBLIOGRAPHY

1958 Edzard, ZA 53 pp. 9–26 (photo, transliteration, study)
1959 Edzard, Sumer 15 p. 19 and pl. 1 (photo, edition, study)
1971 Sollberger and Kupper, IRSA IA1a (translation [conflated with E1.3.1.1])
1982 Steible, ASBW 2 p. 213 Mebarasi 2 (edition)
1986 Cooper, SARI 1 p. 18 Ki 1 (translation, [conflated with E1.3.1.1])
1991 Braun-Holzinger, Weihgaben p. 125 G 60 (edition, study)

TEXT

1) ME-bára-si	1) (EN).ME-barage-si,
2) LUGAL	2) king
3) [K]IŠ	3) of [K]iš.

[RN], Offspring of "Lady Dragon"

E1.7.40

1

A fragment of a stone vessel from Tell Agrab bears an inscription of an unnamed son or daughter of a king (or queen) of Kiš; he (or she) is said to be an offspring of a certain MUNUS.UŠUMGAL "Lady Dragon."

COMMENTARY

The inscription was given the excavation number Ag 35:777. Its Iraq Museum number is unknown. The inscription was collated from the published photo.

The find of this text at a northern site — Tell Agrab is about 102 kms north of Kiš — suggests that it belongs to an actual ruler of Kiš, not simply a potentate who bore the title "king of Kiš." The inscription is listed by Steible ASBW 2 as an anonymous Agrab inscription (AnAgr. 2; cf. Bauer, BiOr 46 p. 638), but the title "king of Kiš" clearly marks it as being royal. It is not known whether this inscription is to be read in Akkadian or Sumerian.

BIBLIOGRAPHY

1942 Jacobsen, Pre-Sargonid Temples pp. 291 and 296 no. 9 (copy, edition)
1982 Steible, ASBW 2 pp. 199–200 AnAgr. 2 (edition)
1986 Cooper, SARI 1 pp. 18–19 Ki 2 (translation)
1989 Bauer, BiOr 46 p. 638 (study)
1991 Braun-Holzinger, Weihgaben p. 123 G 50 (edition, study)

TEXT

Lacuna
1′) [RN]
2′) LUGAL KIŠ
3′) DUMU
4′) MUNUS.UŠUMGAL (GAL:MUNUS:UŠUM)
Lacuna (?)

Lacuna
1′–4′) [RN], king of Kiš, offspring of "Lady Dragon."

Lacuna (?)

LUGAL-UD

E1.7.41

1

A mother-of-pearl inlay fragment from Kiš is inscribed with the name LUGAL-UD; it may well refer to a king of Kiš.

COMMENTARY

The inlay fragment is one of a set that was numbered as Group 1531 by the excavator. They were found together, close to the NW corner of room 35 of Palace A at Kiš. Group 1531 was assigned to the Iraq Museum, but the IM numbers for the group are not known. We might expect that this apparent caption named a figure of an enemy ruler defeated by the king of Kiš (on the basis of its findspot in the palace at Kiš), but the fact that this caption is found beside a figure which is much larger than the other figures on the relief argues that this figure was, in fact, a depiction of the king of Kiš. It is not known whether this inscription is in Akkadian or Sumerian.

BIBLIOGRAPHY

1924 Langdon, Kish 1 p. 4 and pl. VI no. 1 (photo, study)
1925 MacKay, Kish p. 122 and pl. XXXN no. 1 (photo, study)
1982 Steible, ASBW 2 p. 220 Lugal-UD 1 (edition)
1986 Cooper, SARI 1 p. 20 Ki 5 (translation [conflated with 1b)]
1987 Edzard, RLA p. 153 (study)
1998 Tonietti, in Lebeau, Subartu 4/2 p. 95 (study)

TEXT

Lacuna
1′ LUGAL-UD
2′) LUGAL (...)
Lacuna (?)

Lacuna
1) LUGAL-UD
2) king (of ....).
Lacuna (?)

2

A second inscription naming a certain LUGAL-UD as king is found on a fragmentary mace-head from Mari.

COMMENTARY

The limestone mace-head, which measures 4.4 cm in height and 2.5 cm in width, was found in courtyard 20 of the Ištar temple in Mari and given the excavation number M 413. Its present location is unknown.

BIBLIOGRAPHY

1956 Parrot, MAM 1 p. 130 and pl. LIV no. 413 (photo, edition)
1990 Gelb and Kienast, Königinschriften p. 44 (edition)
1991 Braun-Holzinger, Weihgaben p. 44 (edition) K 10
1998 Tonietti, in Lebeau, Subartu 4/2 p. 95 (study)

TEXT

Lacuna
1′) ⌜LUGAL⌝-UD
2′) LUGAL
Lacuna (?)

Lacuna
1) LUGAL-UD
2) king (of ....).
Lacuna (?)

Utuk/Uḫub

E1.7.42

1

A stone vessel fragment from Nippur bears the inscription of a certain Utuk or Uḫub, ruler (énsi) of Kiš.

COMMENTARY

Although this is actually an inscription of a city ruler of Kiš, the text has been included in our corpus. It may have been written in Sumerian.

The vessel fragment, which measures 13.3×7.4×1.7 cm, was found by the Hilprecht Expedition to Nippur in the area southeast of the ziqqurrat and was given the museum number CBS 9572. The piece was subsequently transferred to the British Museum where it was assigned the museum number BM 129402. For the reasons for this transfer, see Cooper, Iraq 46 (1984) p. 92.

Hilprecht indicated that the fragment BE 1/2 no. 109 (CBS 9571+9577; see E1.15.1.1) was a second piece of this vessel, but Cooper (Iraq 46 [1984] pp. 92–93) points out that they come from separate objects. He notes (p. 93): "the fragments are of different thickness and curvature ..."

In line two the broken second sign could be the beginning of either túku (Deimel, LAK 473), or ḫúb (Deimel, LAK 474). Both could be PNs. For ú-tuku, see Pomponio, Prosopografia p. 240, sub ú-tuku. For ú-ḫúb, compare the Ur III PN Sukkukum "deaf," found in Rashid, TIM 6 no. 34 line 11.

BIBLIOGRAPHY

1896 Hilprecht, BE 1/2 no. 108 (copy)
1906 Thureau-Dangin, SAK pp. 160–61 VIII Patesis und Könige von Kiš 1. U-tug (edition [conflated with E1.15.1.1])
1929 Barton, RISA pp. 2–3 KISH 1. Utug (edition [conflated with E1.15.1.1]
1940 Gadd, BMQ p. 32 (study)
1961 Goetze, JCS 15 p. 108 n. 13 (study)
1972 Sollberger and Kupper, IRSA IA2a (translation [conflated with E1.15.1.1])
1982 Steible, ASBW 2 pp. 214–15 Uḫub 1 (edition [conflated with E1.15.1.1])
1984 Cooper, Iraq 46 pp. 92–93 and pl. V a (photo, study)
1986 Cooper, SARI 1 p. 21 Ki 6 (edition)
1991 Braun-Holzinger, Weihgaben p. 125 G 61 (edition, study)

TEXT

1) ^{d}za-[ba$_{4}$-ba$_{4}$]	1) To the god Zababa,
2) ú-t[uk]/ú-ḫ[úb]	2–4) Utuk/Uḫub, ruler of K[iš]
3) én[si]-	Lacuna
4) k[iš.KI]	
Lacuna	

Unnamed King of Kiš

E1.7.43

1

A stone fragment, one of fifteen pieces of an Early Dynastic victory stele found in the Temple Oval at Ḫāfāji, is incised with an apparent royal inscription. One line of the text contains the title "king of Kiš" (LU[GAL] KI[Š]), but too little of the preceding PN is preserved to propose a restoration.

COMMENTARY

The inscribed piece, fragment B, measures 22.5×14.5 cm. It was found in level III, locus J 44:1, near the northwest gateway of the Temple Oval, and was given the excavation number Kh II 51. It is now housed in the Iraq Museum; its museum number is not known.

BIBLIOGRAPHY

1939 Frankfort, Sculpture pp. 38, 48, 78–79 and pl. 113 no. 207 (photo, study)

1949 Delougaz, Temple Oval pp. 146–47 (edition, copy, study [by Jacobsen])

1943 Frankfort, More Sculpture p. 23 (study)

1982 Börler-Klähn, Bildstelen pp. 117–18 no. 8 (study, drawing)

1991 Braun-Holzinger, Weihgaben p. 336 Stele 8 (transliteration, study)

TEXT

Lacuna	Lacuna
1′) [...]	1′–4′) Too broken for translation
2′) Ḫ[É] / ⌈x⌉	
3′) KI[Š(?) ...]	
4′) ⌈x⌉ [...] / ⌈x⌉ [...] / GÁNA [...]	
5′) LU[GAL] / KI[Š]	5′) ki[ng] of Ki[š],
6′) ÉNSI ⌈x⌉/ ⌈x⌉ [...]	6′) ruler of ....
Lacuna	Lacuna

Rulers with the Title "King of Kiš" Whose Dynastic Affiliations Are Unknown

E1.8

The example of inscription E1.13.5.1, in which Mes-Ane-pada, king of Ur, refers to his father Mes-KALAM-du as "king of Kiš," reveals that the title "king of Kiš" could be adopted by Early Dynastic period rulers who did not have Kiš as their original dynastic capital.

A handful of inscriptions from cities in the Sumerian south name rulers who use the title "king of Kiš," but who are unattested in the Sumerian King List as being rulers of Kiš and whose dynastic home is not known from other sources.

The exact significance of the term "king of Kiš" in these inscriptions is unclear. Three possibilities come to mind (of which [a] and [b] were suggested to me by G. Selz in RIM readers' notes).

(a) It is conceivable, although far from certain, that the royal families of Uruk and Kiš were related. The only evidence for this known to me comes from later literary texts, namely: (i) "Gilgameš and Ḫuwawa A," in which Gilgameš refers to EN.ME-barage-si, otherwise known as the ruler of Kiš, as his sister, and (ii) "Gilgameš and Aka" in which Gilgameš seems to refer to some previous favour granted to him by King Aka of Kiš. Wilcke (in Studies Sjöberg p. 563) notes:

> Gilgameš refers there [in "Gilgamesh and Aka"] to the shelter he had found at Agga's, and, setting Agga free, he repays the good deed done to him by Agga. This seems to suggest that Gilgameš had found asylum in Kiš, that for some reason, which could well be the circumstances of his birth, he could not stay in Uruk.

(b) Perhaps the title "king of Kiš" was adopted because of a significant military victory of a southern ruler over Kiš.

(c) It is likely that the title LUGAL KIŠ was an honorific title, with the connotation "king of the world" corresponding to Akkadian *šar kiššatim*, indicating hegemony over the land of Sumer.

Since the particular dynastic affiliations of the kings edited below are not clearly known, I have grouped them under the rubric "Rulers with the Title 'king of Kiš' whose Dynastic Affiliations are Unknown."

For the supposed Lugal-[x], ruler of Kiš proposed by Gadd (UE 1 p. 126), see the of inscription Lugal-[SILA] edited as E1.14.21.1 in this volume under the rubric of Uruk kings.

Me-silim

E1.8.1

The reading of the royal name, always written Me-DI-(ma), has not been entirely clear. In inscription E1.9.5.1 line ii 7 the writing me-DI-ma made it certain that the second element ends in -m. Jacobsen, in ZA 52 (1957) p. 129 n. 87, citing the writing me-DI-lim in the Obelisk of Maništūsu (see now Gelb, Land Tenure p. 140 col. vi line 11: ME-sá-lim, cf. also Gelb, Land Tenure p. 147 col. iv′ line 24′: ME-sá-lim), indicated a reading Me-salim. However, Steinkeller (in Studies Hallo p. 239) notes the writings si-li-mu-du for the Presargonic PN DI-^{d}Utu, and argues (in RIM readers' notes) that the correct reading is Me-silim; this reading has been accepted here.

Pettinato's premature identification of Me-silim in the Ebla documents is to be rejected; see A. Archi, "A Mythologem in Eblaitology: Mesilim of Kish at Ebla," SEb 4 (1981), 227–30.

1

A stone mace-head from G̃irsu is incised with an inscription of Me-silim, "king of Kiš."

COMMENTARY

The mace-head, which measures 10.6 cm in height and 27 cm in breadth, with a thickness of 1.7-2.0 cm, was found at Tello about 11 metres SW of the Ur-Nanše construction, at a lower level than the base of that structure. It bears the museum number AO 2349. The inscription was collated.

The reading of the possible first sign of line nine is not entirely clear; indeed, it is not even clear that a sign is inscribed there at all. The area in question is carved with lines representing the lion's mane which obscures the reading of any possible sign. The NU_{11}(ŠIR) sign before the broken L[A] has two horizontal wedges at the beginning of the sign, an unexpected form.

BIBLIOGRAPHY

1884–1912 de Sarzec, Découvertes 2 p. XXXV and pl. 1ter no. 2 (photo, copy)
1893 Heuzey, RA 3 pp. 55–58 and pl. III (copy, study, photogravure)
1897 Heuzey, RA 4 p. 109 fig. 15 (copy, translation, drawing)
1902 Heuzey, CatalogueLouvre pp. 81–83 no. 4 (study, drawing)
1907 Thureau-Dangin, SAK pp. 160–61 2. Me-silim Streitkolben (edition)
1926 Unger, SuAK p. 69 no. 1 (drawing)
1929 Barton, RISA pp. 2–3 2. Mesilim (edition)
1935 Frankfort, AnOr 12 p. 116 fig. 12 (drawing)
1935 Zervos, L'art pl. 54 (photo)
1940 Christian, Altertumskunde 1 pl. 260 no. 3 (photo)
1948 Parrot, Tello pp. 54, 63, 72 and fig. 17b (study, drawing)
1960 Parrot, Sumer, figs. 160 a–b (photos) pp. 134–36 and fig. 32g (ex. 2, copy, translation)
1962 Strommenger and Hirmer, Mesopotamien pl. 43 (photo)

1967 Moortgat, Kunst pls. 35–36 (photo)
1968 Solyman, Götterwaffen pl. 32 no. 223 (drawing)
1971 Sollberger and Kupper, IRSA, IA3a (translation)
1980 Amiet, Art fig. 302 (photo)
1982 André-Leicknam, Naissance de l'écriture p. 85 no. 41 (photo, translation)
1982 Steible, ASBW 2 pp. 215–16 Mesalim 1 (edition)
1986 Cooper, SARI 1 p. 19 Ki 3.1 (translation)
1991 Braun-Holzinger, Weihgaben p. 44 K 9 (edition, study)

TEXT

1) me-silim(DI) 2) lugal- 3) kiš	1–3) Me-silim, king of Kiš,
4) é-dù-[d]nin-g̃ír-su 5) [d]nin-g̃ír-su 6) mu-DU	4) temple builder for the god Ning̃irsu, 5) set up(?) this mace for the god Ning̃irsu.
7) lugal-šà-ENGUR 8) énsi- 9) x?-NU_{11}.L[A.KI]	7–9) Lugal-ša-ENGUR (is) the ruler of La[gaš].

2

An inscription found on two bowl fragments from Adab mentions Me-silim, "king of Kiš."

CATALOGUE

Ex.	Museum number	Object	Dimensions (cm)	Lines preserved	cpn
1	A 211 (Chicago)	Stone bowl	Height: 10.6 Width: 27 Thickness: 1-7–2 Original diameter: c. 37	1–5	
2	A 228 (Chicago)	Alabaster bowl	Height: 3.5 Width: 3.5 Thickness: 0.95	2–3	

COMMENTARY

Both vessels were found on Mound V at Adab. The inscription apparently deals with Me-silim's performing of the *burgi*-rite in the E-SAR temple in Adab. For the *burgi*-rite, see Jacobsen ZA 52 (1957) p. 135 n. 100, CAD B p. 329 sub *burgû*, PSD p. 186, and Selz, Untersuchungen p. 27 n. 74. For the reading of the PN in line 5, see the comments to E1.1.1 above.

It is not absolutely certain that ex. 2 is a duplicate of this text; we have edited it here with ex. 1 following Cooper.

BIBLIOGRAPHY

1912 Banks, Bismya p. 201 (ex. 1, copy)
1930 Luckenbill, Adab nos. 5 and 7 (exs. 1 and 2, copy)
1971 Sollberger and Kupper, IRSA, IA3b (exs. 1–2, translation)
1982 Steible, ASBW 2 pp. 216–17 Mesalim 2 (edition)
1986 Cooper, SARI 1 p. 19 Ki 3.2 (exs. 1–2, translation)
1986 Yang, Sargonic Archive p. 22 § 1 b (ex. 1, study)
1989 Yang, Sargonic Inscriptions p. 11 § 1.1.1.1 nos. 2–3 (exs. 1–2, study)
1991 Braun-Holzinger, Weihgaben p. 125 G 62 (ex. 1, edition, study); G 63 (ex. 2, transliteration, study)

TEXT

1) me-silim(DI)
2) lugal-kiš
3) é-SAR(SAR:é)
4) bur mu-gi$_4$
5) nin-KISAL-si énsi:G̃AR(G̃AR-énsi) adab

1–2) Me-silim, king of Kiš,

3–4) performed the *burgi*-rite in the E-SAR.

5) Nin-KISAL-si is the ensi-G̃AR of Adab.

3

An inscription incised on a chlorite vase fragment from Adab mentions Me-silim, as "king of Kiš."

COMMENTARY

The vase fragment, which was found on Mound V at Adab, measures 12.8 cm in height. The original diameter of the vessel would have been about 21 cm. It bears the museum number A 192 (Chicago).

BIBLIOGRAPHY

1930 Luckenbill, Adab no. 1 (copy)
1960 Delougaz, Iraq 22 p. 93 and pl. 9 a (photo, study)
1971 Sollberger and Kupper, IRSA, IA3c (translation)
1982 Steible, ASBW 2 p. 217 Mesalim 3 (edition)
1986 Cooper, SARI 1 pp. 19–20 Ki 3.3 (translation)
1989 Yang, Sargonic Inscriptions p. 11 § 1.1.1.1 no. 1 (study)
1991 Braun-Holzinger, Weihgaben p. 126 G 64 (edition, study)

TEXT

1) me-silim(DI)
2) lugal-kiš
3) dumu-⸢ki⸣-ág̃-
4) ^{d}nin-ḫur-sag̃(nin:sag:ḫur:dig̃ir)
5) ⸢sag̃-rig$_7$⸣(?)
Fragment possibly belonging to this inscription
Lacuna
1′) ⸢x x⸣
2′) ⸢énsi⸣
3′) Lacuna

1–2) Me-silim, king of Kiš,

3–4) beloved son of Ninḫursag̃,

5) *dedicated* (this bowl).

Lacuna
1′–3′) PN, ruler (of Adab).

Lugal-namnir-sum

E1.8.2

1

The sleeve of a bronze sword from G̃irsu bears the inscription of a certain Lugal-namni[r]-sum, "king of Kiš." As far as can be determined, he is otherwise unattested.

COMMENTARY

The sword, which was found in excavations on Tell K at G̃irsu by de Sarzec, measures 84 cm long and 13.8 cm wide at its widest point; it was assigned the museum number AO 2675. The inscription was collated.

The PN in line 2 was formerly illegible because this area of the sword was covered with corrosion. With the cleaning of the sword (September 1994), the PN in line 2 is entirely clear. It is published here through the kind permission of Mme André-Salvini.

The shape of the lugal sign, with its pronounced curved bottom, most closely resembles the shape of the lugal signs in the EN.ME-barage-si and Lugalda-lu inscriptions tabled by Nissen in Königsfriedhofe Tafel 23. This suggests a date of this ruler to the ED II period.

BIBLIOGRAPHY

1884–1912 de Sarzec, Découvertes 2 p. LVI and pl. 5 ter 1 a–c (photo, copy)

1894 Heuzey, RA 3 pp. 52–54 (study, drawing)

1897 Heuzey, RA 4 p. 111 fig. 18 (drawing)

1907 Thureau-Dangin, SAK pp. 160–61 VIII. Patesis und Könige von Kiš 5. Lugal-[ ] (edition)

1939 Jacobsen, SKL p. 181 n. 34 (study)

1948 Parrot, Tello pp. 74–75 (study); p. 109 fig. 26 (drawing)

1982 Steible, ASBW 2 pp. 221–22 AnKiš 1 (edition)

1986 Cooper, SARI 1 p. 20 Ki 4.1 (translation)

TEXT

1) lugal-
2) nam-ni[r]-sum(SUM:NAM:NI[R])
3) lugal-
4) kiš

1–4) Lugal-namni[r]-sum (is) king of Kiš.

Enna-il

E1.8.3

1

A tablet from Nippur gives an Ur III period copy of an inscription of a certain Enna-il. While Enna-il appears in this text without the title "king" (lugal) or "ruler" (énsi), the epithet in lines 5–6 "who smote Elam with weapons" suggests that he was a ruler, since epithets of this kind are normally the prerogative of kings alone. Thus, this Enna-il is almost certainly the same figure who is named in inscription E1.5.4.2 as "king of Kiš" (lugal-kiš).

COMMENTARY

The tablet bearing this inscription was given the excavation number 6 NT 100. Lines 1–6 are found on the obverse of the tablet, line 7 on the reverse.

The inscription is almost certainly in Akkadian.

For recent literature on the reading of the element AM.IM.MI.MUŠEN in line 4, see Cooper, JCS 26 (1974) p. 121, Pettinato, JCS 31 (1971) pp. 116–17, Alster, RA 85 (1995) pp. 1–5.

BIBLIOGRAPHY

1961 Goetze, JCS 15 pp. 107–109 (photo, copy, edition)
1978 Moorey, Kish Excavations p. 168 (translation)
1982 Steible, ASBW 2 p. 218 Enna᾽il A1 (edition)
1986 Cooper, SARI 1 p. 21 Ki 7 (edition)

TEXT

Obv.	
1) ᵈINANNA	1) For the goddess Inanna,
2) *en-na-il*	2–4) Enna-il, son of A-Anzu,
3) DUMU-	
4) a-an[zú](AM.[IM].MI).MUŠEN	
5) NIM	5–6) who smote Elam with weapons.
6) GÍN.ŠÈ	
Rev.	
7) ur-GIŠGAL	7) Ur-GIŠGAL

2

A fragment of a limestone statuette of a male figure — only the right half of the upper torso is preserved — records Enna-il's setting up of a statue(?) for the goddess INANNA.

COMMENTARY

The statue fragment measures 10.2×10.7×8.8 cm. It was found "at SB 76 in fill of the Parthian platform under a temple, built over the Inanna temple below level II." See Gelb, Land Tenure p. 91. The piece was given the excavation number 6 N 271. It is now housed in the Iraq Museum, IM 61325.

The text is written in Akkadian, as is evidenced, among other things, by the prepositions *in* and *ašte* and the graphotactical sequence x MA.NA URUDU as noted by Steinkeller.

BIBLIOGRAPHY

1961 Goetze, JCS 15 p. 108 fig. 2 (photo)
1977 Braun-Holzinger, Beterstauetten p. 72 (transliteration, study)
1991 Braun-Holzinger, Weihgaben p. 250 St 56 (edition, study)
1991 Gelb, Land Tenure pp. 91–92 and pls. 49–50 no. 26 (photo, copy, edition)

TEXT

Col. i	
1′) [x]+4(BÙR) GÁN	1′–3′) [x]+4 *bur* of land ... in Ursa.
2′) É(?) ḪA(?) GUD(?) x	
3′) *in* ur-sa$_6$.KI(ur:KI:sa$_6$)	
4′) 6(BÙR) GÁN	4′–8′) 6 *bur* of land ...
5′) ⌜x x x⌝	
6′) GÁN [...]	
7′–8′) [...]	
9′) 2(BÙR) GÁN	9′–12′) 2 *bur* of land, the field purchased from Inimani-zi.
10′) GÁN ŠÁM	
11′) *áš-te$_4$*	
12′) inim-ma-ni(?)-⌜zi⌝(?)	
Lacuna	Lacuna
Col. ii	
1) *en-na-il*	1–2) Enna-il, king of Kiš
2) LUGAL KIŠ	
3) A[LAM-*šu*]	3–8) set up a s[tatue(?) of himself] ... before the goddess Aštar/Inanna.
4–6) [...]	
7) IGI ^{d}INANNA	
8) MU.GUB	

LAGAŠ

E1.9

(a) The Cities of Greater Lagaš

The GN Lagaš referred in ancient times to both a city, Lagaš proper (modern al-Hibā, NLat 31° 25′ ELong 46° 24′), and to a larger district (greater Lagaš) in the southeastern part of Sumer.

In more specific terms, greater Lagaš was divided (in Ur III times, when our most explicit descriptions of the province are found) into three tracts: (a) the G̃irsu district in the northwestern region, (b) the Ki-nu-NIR/Nig̃in district in the middle region, and (c) the Guʾaba district in the southeastern region. The name of the last, gú-ab-ba = Sumerian "shore of the sea," indicates it was readily accessible to the Gulf.

(i) The G̃irsu District

In region (a), the most northerly, the capital was ancient G̃irsu (modern Tello, NLat 31° 30′ ELong 46° 24′).

G̃irsu/Tello has been excavated in a long series of French archaeological campaigns, namely those in 1877–1900 (director E. de Sarzec), in 1903–09 (director G. Cros), in 1929–31 (director H. de Genouillac), and in 1931–33 (director A. Parrot).

The city name G̃irsu is written syllabically as g̃ír-su.KI in ED later texts; a reading *gir-ši-im* (genitive) is found as an Akkadian translation in an OB literary text (Sjöberg, JCS 26 [1974] p. 163 line 14). The Eme-SAL form is mer-si (see Bergman ZA 56 [1964] p. 36).

The etymology of the GN g̃ír-su is totally unclear. Jacobsen (JCS 21 [1967] p. 100) suggests a (not convincing) etymology "naked captive(s)." Suter (Gudea's Temple Building p. 107 n. 186) remarks:

> The reading G̃IR in G̃IR-su is not confirmed. If read *irsu (see Civil, BiOr 40 [1983] 562), nin-*irsu-a(k) and nin-urta would simply be two dialectal writings, both irsu and urt(a) being derived from Semitic ard/ṣ "earth." Ninigirsu/Ninurta would then mean "Lord of the Earth."

On the other hand, an etymology "(place) full of snakes" was suggested by G. Selz (in RIM readers' notes). In short no absolutely compelling etymology for the name is known.

G̃irsu's patron god was the deity Ning̃irsu (lit. "lord of G̃irsu"), apparently a local form of the god Ninurta at G̃irsu (see most recently Selz, Untersuchungen pp. 218ff.); his wife was the goddess conventionally read Baba (other readings such as Bawu, Bawa and Baʾu have been proposed; see Limet, L'anthroponymie pp. 356–57 and Falkenstein, Inschriften Gudeas p. 63 and n. 5. For Baba, see most recently Selz, Untersuchungen pp. 26ff. Ning̃irsu and Baba's temples lay on the "Tell du Palais" at G̃irsu. Ningirsu's temple was overlain by the "palace" of an Aramean-Hellenistic local potentate named Adad-nādin-aḫḫe.

(ii) Lagaš Proper

In tract (b), in Ur III times, the largest city was Lagaš. Lagaš (modern al-Hibā) was excavated in 1887 by an expedition from the Königliche Preussische Museen, Berlin (director R. Koldewey) and by an expedition funded by the Metropolitan Museum of Art and the Institute of Fine Arts of

New York University in 1968–69, 1970–71, and 1972–73, and 1975–76 (director V. Crawford), and 1990 (director D. Hansen).

The city name Lagaš was normally written logographically in Early Dynastic sources as NU_{11}(LAK 24):BUR:LA:KI. For the reading of the first element of the compound as NU_{11}, not ŠIR, see Biggs, JCS 24 (1971–72) p. 2. In the Fāra texts we find the writings BUR.NU_{11}.MUŠEN.KI (with no LA) (WF 94 col. ii line 2) and NU_{11}.BUR.LA.MUŠEN.KI (WF 92 col. ii line 2). The writing of the city name in these economic texts recalls the discussion of the city name Lagaš by Jacobsen in JCS 21 (1961) pp. 101–2. He cites there a passage from the later lexical list Diri IV 152–53:

152 bu-ur: ŠIR.BUR.MUŠEN: si-ir-bu-ur-mu-še-en-nu: *a*-[*ri-bu*]
153 la-ga-aš: ŠIR.BUR.LA.KI: si-ir-bu-ur-la-a-ki-ki: ŠU

In the first line, Sumerian $buru_4$ is equated with Akkadian *āribu*(*m*) "raven." Since the second line has the notation ŠU ("the same"), it seems likely that Lagaš originally had a bird as city totem. But the city name Lagaš itself was apparently not derived from this word.

How the lexical equation ŠIR.BUR.LA.KI = *nakkamtum* "storehouse" cited by Jacobsen (AfO 26 [1978–79] pp. 12–13 n. 48) relates to this question is unclear.

The appearance of the city name in the writing NU_{11}.BUR.LA.KI-sa (in En-metena E1.9.5.23 line 15) indicates a reading /lagas/ in Presargonic times. The exact significance of this writing is uncertain, and, as is noted in the introduction to this volume, the general question of sibilants in Sumerian is a very complex issue.

While it is clear that the goddess Inanna had a very large temple complex at Lagaš, the ib-gal "Great Oval" located in the southwest corner of the site and excavated in part by the American expedition to al-Hibā (see Hansen, RLA 6 pp. 423–25), the naming of the goddess G̃atumdu in the *zami* hymnal collection (see Biggs, Abū Ṣalābīḫ p. 49 lines 108–9) indicates that, at least at the time the *zami* hymns were redacted, G̃atumdu (Eme-SAL ^{d}ma-zé-zé-eb or ^{d}ma-zé-eb-zeb) was considered to be the chief deity of Lagaš. She appears with the epithet "mother of Lagaš" (ama-NU_{11}.BUR.LA.KI) in the En-metena inscription edited as E1.9.5.21 (lines 1–2) in this volume.

Another important deity at Lagaš was the god Ning̃irsu; part of his Bagara temple complex at Lagaš was uncovered by the American expedition to al-Hibā (see Hansen, RLA 6 pp. 426–30).

(iii) Nig̃in

The second largest city of the Ki-nu-NIR/Nig̃in district was ancient Nig̃in, written AB×ḪA.KI. It was located at modern Zūrghūl (NLat 31° 22′ ELong 46° 29′). Nig̃in/Zūrghūl was excavated in the year 1887 by the Königliche Preussische Museen, Berlin (director R. Koldewey). Its tutelary deities were the goddess Nanše (for which now see Heimpel, RLA 9 pp. 152–60 and Selz, Untersuchungen p. 181 ff.) and her spouse Nin-DAR (see Selz, Untersuchungen pp. 215–17).

The reading of the city name Nig̃in with its logogram AB×ḪA.KI has, until recently, been unclear. As a summary of the discussion of this question we may offer: Krecher, in Studies Matouš 2 p. 53; Civil, MSL XIV p. 43 (where the glosses: ni-mi-en, ni-ne-em, ni-èm-en, ni-mi-[x] for AB×ḪA.KI are noted); Heimpel, JCS 33 (1981) pp. 99–101; Black, Sumer 46 (1989–90) p. 71; Bauer (in Bauer, Englund and Krebernik [eds.], Mesopotamien p. 438). Finally, and most definitively, Steinkeller (in K. Watanabe [ed.], Priests and Officials in the Ancient Near East: Papers of the Second Colloquium on the Ancient Near East — the City and Its Life, held at the Middle Eastern Cultural Center in Japan [Mitaka, Tokyo], March 22–23, 1996 p. 188 n. 46) cites a passage from Ur-Nanše E1.9.1.17 col. iii lines 3–6:

ur-nig̃in(40) dam-^{d}nanše maš bi-pà "[Ur-Nanše] chose Ur-nig̃in by oracular means to be the spouse of the goddess Nanše" and notes: "In Ur-Nimin, -nimin appears to be a variant writing of the toponymn $Nimin_{x}$(NANŠE)^{ki}."

(iv) Other Cities in Lagaš Province

A forthcoming study by the present author will deal with other cities in Lagaš province.

Ur-Nanše

E1.9.1

The first king of Lagaš for whom we have a substantial number of royal inscriptions is Ur-Nanše. An earlier ruler, Lugal-ša-ENGUR, is attested in one inscription (see E1.8.1.1); he appears there as a ruler at Lagaš with Me-silim "king of Kiš" as his apparent overlord.

Relatively little is known about Ur-Nanše including his origins and the length of his reign. G. Selz has given compelling arguments that Ur-Nanše and the dynasty had its roots at the city of Niĝin or its vicinity. He writes (Untersuchungen p. 298):

> Für die Herkunft der Familie des Ur-Nanše aus NINA sprechen folgende Punkte: (a) Im Namen des Begründers der I. Dynastie von Lagaš, Ur-Nanše, ist ^{d}nanše theophores Element. Solche Namen deuten in aller Regel auf die Herkunft des Namensträgers aus oder seine Zugehörigkeit zu einem bestimmten Templebereich. (2) Der Familiengott der Ur-Nanše-Dynastie rechnet zum Götterkreiss der Nanše. (3) Eine Statue des Ur-Nanše wurde am Hauptfesttag der Nanše-Feste in NINA beopfert. (4) Auch Nanše konnte das Könïgtum von Lagaš verleihen. (5) Noch die Nanše-Hymne kennt die Berufung des Ur-Nanše durch Nanše und mag somit seine Herkunft reflektiert.

Concerning argument (5), I have suggested elsewhere that the Ur-Nanše referred to in the Nanše hymn could possibly be identified with the Ur-Nanše who apparently served as an independent ruler in the Lagaš region in late Ur III times (see Frayne, RIME 3/2 pp. 429–30 E3/2.2.2.2).

Although Ur-Nanše mentions his father Gu-NI.DU in many of his inscriptions, he does not name him as being king of Lagaš. Bauer (in Bauer, Englund, and Krebernik [eds.], Mesopotamien p. 447) suggests he might have been a temple official. Apparently Gu-NI.DU was an inhabitant of the city of Gursar; the PN is mentioned in one economic text (Allote de la Füye DP 159 col. ii 1). Perhaps it was a city quarter of Niĝin and finds a reflex in the modern GN Zūrghūl. Selz (Untersuchungen p. 105) notes that offerings to Gu-NI.DU and other dead notables at gú-^{d}bìl-ga-mes-ka "the shore of Gilgamesh" are noted in connection with the Baba festival in archival texts from G̃irsu. Selz also notes (Untersuchungen pp. 18–19) three economic texts that record offerings for the statue of (the deceased) Ur-Nanše.

According to E1.9.1.6a, Ur-Nanše's wife was Men-bara-abzu.

According to Ur-Nanše inscription E1.9.1.32 col. iv line 1, Ur-Nanše's personal deity was ^{d}šul-LAK 442 (MUŠ×PA). The reading of the DN is not entirely certain. It has conventionally been read šul-utul$_{12}$ following Landsberger (MSL II pp. 106–107). Recent evidence from Ebla (Pettinato, MEE 3 p. 198 line 50: LAK 442 la-ḫa-šu-um), suggests a reading of the GN as ^{d}šul-laḫšu$_{x}$ or ^{d}šul-laḫša, with the second element being a possible loan related to the Akkadian root *laḫāšu*(*m*) "to murmur prayers." One may compare

Akkadian *luḫšu(m)* (GUDU$_4$.U) "a member of the temple personnel concerned with the preparation of offerings (CAD)." For a discussion of this term, see Pettinato, MEE 3 p. 203 note to line 50; Mander, Pantheon p. 66; Selz, RA 83 (1989) pp. 7–12; Lambert, Orientalia 64 (1985) pp. 135–36; Krebernik, in Bauer, Englund, and Krebernik (eds.), Mesopotamien p. 279; and Selz, Untersuchungen pp. 279–81.

The majority of the extant Ur-Nanše inscriptions deal with building activities of the king in Lagaš and give us relatively little historical information. One text (E1.9.1.6b) mentions a campaign of Ur-Nanše against Ur and G̃iša (Umma). Another stele (E1.9.1.6a) records conflicts with Arawa (in Elam). A stele of Ur-Nanše was found at Ur, but whether this indicates that he held some control over the city or rather the piece was brought to Ur as booty is unclear. Other texts (E1.9.1.2, 5, 17, 20, 22, 23, 25) mention trade with Dilmun.

As for the orthography of the Ur-Nanše's inscriptions, his presumably earlier inscriptions have relatively crudely made signs arranged in a somewhat haphazard manner within the cases of the inscription. His likely later inscriptions show more carefully rendered signs in an order which, to a large degree, reflects (as best we can determine) the spoken order.

Ur-Nanše was responsible for the construction of a large number of temples in the greater state of Lagaš.

1

A mother-of-pearl figure bears a label inscription of Ur-Nanše.

COMMENTARY

The broken inlay figure, AO 4109, was unearthed in excavations of Cros at G̃irsu and measures 7 cm in height and 6.3 cm in width. It was found in the area of the two "bassins" NE of the "Maison des fruits"; the basins are indicated as nos. I and K on the plan published by Parrot in Tello fig. 15. Cros (Tello, p. 13) writes:

> A l'angle nord du plus petit des deux bassins, était un escalier de cinq marches faites en briques du même modèle. Du côté opposé, à 2m 90 au Sud-Est de ces deux bassins, fut dégagé un groupe de trois piliers, dont j'ai donné la description avec croquis dans le journal des fouilles. C'est au pied de l'un de ces piliers, celui du Nord, que j'ai découvert une petite figure decoupée, en coquille mate, portent écrits sur la poitrine: "Our-Nina, roi de Sirpourla."

The inscription is to be read from bottom to top. It was collated.

BIBLIOGRAPHY

1908 Toscanne, RT 30 p. 136 (drawing, copy in NA script)
1910 Cros, Tello pp. 13 and 111 (findspot, study); pl. II no. 1 (photo)
1929 Barton, RISA pp. 20–21 Ur-Nina 13 (edition)
1948 Parrot, Tello pp. 110–11 (Plaquette au nom, d'Ur-Nanshe), fig. 27a (study, drawing)
1956 Sollberger, CIRPL 1 p. vii Urn. 1 (study); p. 1 Urn. 1 (copy)
1982 Steible, ASBW 1 p. 79 Urnanše 1 (edition)
1986 Cooper, SARI 1 p. 22 La 1.1 (translation)

TEXT

1) ur-^{d}nanše
2) lugal-
3) lagaš(NU$_{11}$.BUR.LA)

1) Ur-Nanše,
2–3) king of Lagaš.

2

An inscription on a white limestone plaque records Ur-Nanše's construction of: (a) the temple of the god Niñirsu; (b) the Abzu-banda "Little Fountainhead"; and (c) the temple of Nanše. The reliefs depict various members of the royal family.

COMMENTARY

The limestone plaque, which measures 40×47×17 cm, was found by de Sarzec in 1888 on Tell K at G̃irsu about 5 m SW of the SW corner of "Chambre A" of the "Maison des fruits" (see no. 5 in the plan published as Parrot, Tello fig. 15). It, along with three other votive plaques (inscriptions E1.9.1.3–5), apparently came from a building dedicated to the god Niñirsu that is named in line 5 of this text as the é-^{d}nin-g̃ír-su (see Parrot, Tello p. 67). Unfortunately, its walls were not traced by de Sarzec. The plaque, which bears the museum number AO 2344, was collated. In addition to the family plaques, foundation deposits dealing with the èš-g̃ír-su (of Niñirsu) were found in the same general area.

According to Asher-Grève, Frauen p. 90, the hair style of the figure standing immediately in front of Ur-Nanše identifies her as being a woman, hence the translation "daughter" for dumu in this inscription. Sollberger and Kupper, IRSA, IC3c, apparently missing the dumu sign, identified the figure as the wife of Ur-Nanše. The reading of her name is uncertain; for a discussion of the evidence, see Steible, ASBW 2 p. 4. For the reading of the PN in line Caption b ii v as mu-kur-šuba$_{4}$-ta, see the comments of Bauer, BiOr 46 (1989) col. 640.

In this text, the E-Niñirsu of line 5 of the column next to the upper figure of the king refers to the chief temple of Niñirsu in G̃irsu. The name Abzu-banda in line 7 also appears in the URU-KA-gi-na text E1.9.9.5 mentioned between the towns of Tiraš and Bara-Enlila; it is not known if the two texts refer to the same place. The temple of Nanše named in line 9 is likely the main temple of the goddess in the city of Niñin.

BIBLIOGRAPHY

1884–1912 de Sarzec, Découvertes 2 pl. 2bis no. 1 (photo)
1897 Heuzey, RA 4 p. 103 fig. 8 (drawing)
1907 Thureau-Dangin, SAK pp. 8–9 Ur-ninâ m (edition)
1927 Contenau, Manuel 1 p. 452 fig. 348 (photo)
1929 Barton, RISA pp. 18–19 Ur-Nina 9 (edition)
1935 Zervos, L'art p. 83 (photo)
1940 Christian, Altertumskunde 1 pl. 261 no. 1 (photo)
1948 Parrot, Tello p. 61 no. 4 and fig 15 (top) no. 4 (study, findspot); pl. V a (photo); pp. 90–91 Relief a (study)
1956 Sollberger, CIRPL 1 p. viii Urn. 20 (study); p. 2 Urn. 20 (copy)
1960 Parrot, Sumer, figs. 159 a–b (photos)
1962 Strommenger and Hirmer, Mesopotamien pl. 73 (photo)
1967 Moortgat, Kunst pl. 109 (photo)
1971 Boese, Weihplatten pp. 197–98 T 4 and pl. XXIX no. 1 (study, drawing)
1971 Sollberger and Kupper, IRSA IC3c (partial translation)
1975 Orthmann (ed.), Der alte Orient fig. 85 (photo)
1977 Heimpel, ZA 77 p. 70 no. 1 (study)
1980 Amiet, Art figs. 44 and 324 (photos)
1982 Steible, ASBW 1 pp. 82–84 Urnanše 20 (edition); ASBW 2 pl. 1 (photo)
1986 Cooper, SARI 1 pp. 22–23 La 1.2 (translation)

TEXT

a) Inscription next to the upper figure of the king (read left to right, then down, then left to right)

1) ur:^{d}nanše(^{d}nanše-ur)	1–2) Ur-Nanše, king of Lagaš,
2) lugal-lagaš(NU$_{11}$.BUR.LA)	
3) dumu gu-NI.DU	3) son of Gu-NI.DU,
4) dumu-gur-sar	4) (Gu-NI.DU was) "son" of (the city of) Gursar,
5) é-^{d}nin-g̃ír-su	5–6) built the temple of the god Niñirsu;
6) mu-dù	
7) abzu(zu+ab)-bànda^{da}	7–8) built Abzu-banda
8) mu-dù	9–10) (and) built the temple of the goddess Nanše.

9) é-^{d}nanše	
10) mu-dù	
b) Captions in the upper register	
i) Cupbearer behind Ur-Nanše	
1) á-ni-ta	i 1) Anita.
ii) Row of people facing the king, from left to right	
1) ÁB-d[a](?)/ dumu (read left to right)	ii 1) ABd[a(?)], a daughter;
2) a-kur-gal/ dumu (read right to left as in all following captions)	ii 2) A-kurgal, a son;
3) lugal-ezem/ dumu	ii 3) Lugal-ezem, a son;
4) á-ni-kur-ra/ dumu	ii 4) Ani-kura, a son;
5) mu-kur-šuba$_4$(MÙŠ)-ta/ dumu	ii 5) Mu-kuršubata, a son.
c) Beside head of lower figure of the king shown seated and drinking, rows read left to right	
1) ur-^{d}nanše	1–3) Ur-Nanše, king of Lagaš
2) lugal-	
3) lagaš(NU$_{11}$.BUR.LA)	
In front of the skirt of the king reading right to left	
4) má-dilmun	4–6) had ships of Dilmun submit timber as tribute from the foreign lands (to Lagaš).
5) kur-ta	
6) gú-g̃iš mu-g̃ál	
d) Captions in the lower register of figures	
i) Person behind Ur-Nanše (as cupbearer)	
1) sag̃-dig̃ir-tuku	1) Sag̃-dig̃ir-tuku.
ii) People before Ur-Nanše	
1) ⌜ba⌝-lul/<muš>-laḫ$_5$-<gal> (read left to right)	1) Balul, <chief snake>-charmer;
2) a-nun-pà/ dumu (read right to left)	2) Anun-pa, a son;
3) men-u$_4$-sù/ dumu (read right to left)	3) Men-usu, a son;
4) ad-da-tur/ dumu (read right to left)	4) Adda-tur, a son.

3

A second plaque records Ur-Nanše's construction of the temple of the god Niñg̃irsu and depicts various members of the royal family.

COMMENTARY

The limestone plaque, which measures 23×30×7 cm, was unearthed by de Sarzec in 1888 on Tell K at G̃irsu in room 13 of a building that lay west of "Chambres A and B" of the "Maison des fruits" (see no. 4 on the plan published by Parrot, in Tello Fig. 15). It now bears the museum number AO 2345. The inscription was collated.

BIBLIOGRAPHY

1884–1912 de Sarzec, Découvertes 1 p. 171 (study); Découvertes 2 p. XXXVII (partial copy) and pl. 2bis no. 2 (photo)
1907 Thureau-Dangin, SAK pp. 8–9 Ur-ninâ n (edition)
1926 Unger, SuAK p. 74 no. 6 (photo)
1929 Barton, RISA pp. 18–19 Ur-Nina 10 (edition)
1935 Zervos, L'art p. 82 (photo)
1948 Parrot, Tello p. 61 no. 5 and fig 15 (top) no. 5 (study, findspot); pl. V b (photo); pp. 91–92 Relief b (study)
1956 Sollberger, CIRPL 1 p. 2 Urn. 21 (copy)
1967 Moortgat, Kunst pl. 112 (photo)
1971 Boese, Weihplatten pp. 198–99 T 6 and pl. XXX no. 1 (study, drawing)
1980 Amiet, Art fig. 326 (photo)
1982 Steible, ASBW 1 pp. 84–85 Urnanše 21 (edition); ASBW 2 pl. 3 (photo)
1986 Cooper, SARI 1 p. 23 La 1.3 (translation)
1991 Braun-Holzinger, Weihgaben p. 308 W 2 (edition, study)

TEXT

a) Inscription in front of the king (reading down)
1) ur:^{d}nanše(^{d}nanše-ur)
2) lugal-
3) lagaš(NU$_{11}$.BUR.⸢LA⸣)
Inscription behind the king (reading right to left)
4) dumu gu-NI.DU
5) é-^{d}nin-g̃ír-su
6) mu-dù
Figures behind the king in the upper register, from right to left
1) lugal-ezem
2) gu-la
c) Figures behind the king in the lower register
1) á-ni-ta
2) a-kur-gal / dumu
3) bára-^{sa}sag$_{7}$-nu-di

1–3) Ur-Nanše, king of Lagaš,
4) son of Gu-NI.DU,
5–6) built the temple of the god Ning̃irsu.
1–2) Lugal-ezem, Gula.
1–3) Anita; A-kurgal, a son; Bara-sag-nudi.

4

A third limestone plaque of Ur-Nanše is housed in Istanbul.

COMMENTARY

The plaque, which consists of the left portion of a relief plaque, measures 45×30×8 cm. It was found in 1889 by de Sarzec on Tell K at G̃irsu, in a building that lay west of "Chambres A and B" of the "Maison des fruits" (see no. 8 in Parrot, Tello, Fig. 15). It now bears the museum number EŞ 401. The inscription was collated from the published photo.

For the proper name Sešg̃ar, see Selz, Untersuchungen p. 185 §§7–8. For the PN Ḫursag̃še-maḫ of the lower register 4′, see Krebernik, BiOr 41 (1984) col. 642. The name reoccurs in rev. col. v line 1 of E1.9.1.6b; there he is mentioned as the "chief of the merchants" captured by Ur-Nanše.

BIBLIOGRAPHY

1884–1912 de Sarzec, Découvertes 2 p. XXXVII (partial copy) and pl. 2ter no. 1 (photo)
1907 Thureau-Dangin, SAK pp. 8–9 Ur-ninâ o (edition)
1927 Contenau, Manuel 1 p. 456 fig. 349 (photo)
1929 Barton, RISA pp. 20–21 Ur-Nina 11 (edition)
1948 Parrot, Tello p. 61 no. 6 and fig 15 (top) no. 56 (study, findspot); pl. V c (photo); p. 92 Relief c (study)
1956 Sollberger, CIRPL 1 p. viii Urn. 22 (study); p. 22 Urn. 22 (partial copy)
1967 Moortgat, Kunst pl. 110 (photo)
1971 Boese, Weihplatten pp. 199 T 7 and pl. XXX no. 2 (study, drawing)
1982 Steible, ASBW 1 pp. 85–86 Urnanše 22 (edition)
1986 Cooper, SARI 1 pp. 23– 24 La 1.4 (translation)
1991 Braun-Holzinger, Weihgaben p. 309 W 3 (edition, study)

TEXT

Between upper and lower rows of figures
1) ur:^{d}nanše(^{d}nanše-ur)
2) lugal-
3) lagaš(NU$_{11}$.BUR.LA)
4) dumu g[u]-⸢NI.DU⸣

1–3) Ur-Nanše, king of Lagaš,
4) son of Gu-NI.DU

5) é-^{d}nin-g̃ír-su
6) mu-dù
7) é-^{d}nanše
8) mu-dù
9) abzu(zu+ab)-bànda^{da}
10) mu-dù
11) šeš-g̃ar mu-dù
Figures in lower registers from right to left
1) á-ni-ta
2) ba-lul/ muš-laḫ$_5$-gal
3) a-kur-gal/ dumu
4) nam-azu(ZU$_5$[LAK 117]+A)/ lú-dub-sar
Figures in upper registers, from right to left
1′) [...] ⸢LÚ-*kí-na-tum*⸣
2′) lugal-ezem/ dumu
3′) mu-kur-šuba$_4$(MÙŠ)-ta/ dumu
4′) ḫur(Text: GUR$_8$)-sag̃-šè(Text: NÁM)-máḫ(AL)

5–6) built the temple of the god Niñgirsu,
7–8) built the temple of the god Nanše,
9–10) built Abzu-banda,
11) built Šešg̃ar.

1) Anita (cup-bearer);
2) Balul, the chief "snake charmer";
3) A-kurgal, a son;
4) Namazu, commissioner of the scribes.

1′) [...] Awīl-kīnātim;
2′) Lugal-ezem, a son;
3′) Mu-kuršubata, a son;
4′) Ḫursag̃še-maḫ.

5

A fourth limestone plaque of Ur-Nanše is also housed in Istanbul.

COMMENTARY

Since the limestone plaque, which measures 43×49.5×4 cm, was not published by Heuzey, its findspot is unknown. We expect that, like the other "family plaques," it came from the building that lay west of "Chambres A and B" of the "Maison des fruits." It bears the museum number EŞ 1633. The inscription was collated from the published photo.

BIBLIOGRAPHY

1926 Unger, SuAK p. 73 no. 5 (photo)
1948 Parrot, Tello pl. 5d (photo); p. 93 Relief d (study)
1956 Sollberger, CIRPL p. viii Urn. 23 (study); p. 2 Urn. 23 (copy)
1967 Moortgat, Kunst pl. 111 (photo)
1971 Boese, Weihplatten pp. 198 T 5 and pl. XXIX no. 2 (study, drawing)
1982 Steible, ASBW 1 pp. 87–88 Urnanše 23 (edition); ASBW 2 pl. 3 (photo)
1986 Cooper, SARI 1 pp. 24 La 1.5 (translation)
1991 Braun-Holzinger, Weihgaben p. 309 W 4 (edition, study)

TEXT

Inscription in front of figure of Ur-Nanše
Col. i (in front of basket, read from left to right)
1) ur:^{d}nanše(nanše-ur)
2) lugal-
3) lagaš(NU$_{11}$.BUR.LA)
Col. ii (in front of the arm of the king, read from right to left)
4) é-^{d}nin-g̃ír:su
5) mu-dù
Col. iii (in front of the skirt of the king, read from right to left)
6) abzu(zu+ab)-bànda^{da}
7) mu-dù

1–3) Ur-Nanše, king of Lagaš,
4–5) built the temple of the god Niñgirsu;
6–7) (and) built Abzu-banda.

Inscription beneath the feet of the king
col. i (read from right to left)
1 u[r]:^{d}nan[še])(^{d}nan[še]-u[r])
2 lu[gal]-
3) lagaš(NU$_{11}$.BUR.LA)
4) dumu gu-NI.DU
5) dumu-⌈gur⌉-sar
Col. ii (read from right to left)
1) ⌈é⌉:^{d}nanše(^{d}nanše-⌈é⌉
2) mu-dù
3) šeš-g̃ar
4) ⌈mu⌉-dù
5) [má-d]ilmun
6) gú-[giš] ⌈mu⌉-[gál]
Figures in the upper register, facing the king, from left to right
1) lugal-e[zem] / dumu
2) ⌈á⌉-ni-[kur-ra]/ dumu
3) mu-kur-šuba$_{4}$(MÙŠ)-ta/ dumu
4) ⌈a⌉-kur-gal/ dumu
Figures in the lower register, facing the king, from left to right.
1) [...]
2) ⌈a⌉-[nun-pà]/ [dumu]
3) gu-l[a] / dumu
4) x ⌈x⌉ [x]/ dumu

i 1–3) U[r]-Nan[še], ki[ng] of Lagaš,

i 4) son of Gu-NI.DU,
i 5) (Gu-NI.DU was) "son" of (the city of) Gursar,

ii 1–2) built the temple of the goddess Nanše;

ii 3–4) (and) built Šešg̃ar.

ii 5–6) He [had the ships of Dil]mun sub[mit] [timber] (to Lagaš) as tribute.

1) Lugal-ezem, a son;
2) Ani-k[ura], a son;
3) Mu-kuršubata, a son;
4) A-kurgal, a son.

1) ... (cupbearer)
2) A[nun-pa, a son];
3) Gul[a], a son;
4) ... , a son.

6a

A limestone stele found on the surface of al-Hibā depicts a seated deity on one side and the figures of Ur-Nanše, his cup-bearer, and family members on the other side.

The worn figure of the goddess on the reverse of the stele is strikingly similar in form to a goddess depicted on a large vessel with an inscription of En-metena (see E1.9.5.25) that was purchased by the Berlin Museum. On the basis of its iconography the figure on the Berlin piece can be confidently identified with the goddess Inanna. By extension, the goddess figure appearing on the stele in the Iraq Museum is almost certainly a representation of Inanna. The stele probably came from the area of the Ibgal temple at Lagaš (al-Hibā).

The text of this inscription is badly corroded and much of it is illegible; the following translation is a first attempt to gain an idea of the general content of the piece; most of the transliteration is very uncertain.

COMMENTARY

The limestone stele, which measures 91 cm in height, and has a base measuring 47×17 cm, bears the museum number IM 61404. The inscription apparently started on the side depicting the king and his family (six columns of text) and continued on the side showing the seated goddess Inanna (two columns of text).

BIBLIOGRAPHY

1959 Basmachi, Sumer 15 pp. 21–23 and pls. 1–2 (Arabic section) (photos, study)
1960 Basmachi, Sumer 16 pp. 45–47 and pl. 1 (photos, study [English translation by Al-Haik])
1960 Sollberger, Iraq 22 p. 84 and n. 16 (study)
1970 Spycket, JNES 29 pp. 236 no. d (drawing); p. 237 § [1.1.4] (study)
1975 Orthmann (ed.), Der alte Orient figs. 84a–c (photos)
1982 Börker-Klähn, Bildstelen p. 123 no. 16 (photos, study)
1985 Asher-Grève, Frauen pp. 86–87 and 205 no. 556 (study)
1986 Steible, ASBW 1 p. 112 Urnanše 50 (partial edition)
1991 Braun-Holzinger, Weihgaben p. 335 Stele 5 (partial t transliteration, study)

TEXT

Side of stela with depictions of Ur-Nanše and the royal family

Caption on figure of Ur-Nanše

Col. i

1) ur-^{d}nanše
2) dumu
3) gu-NI.DU

i 1–3) Ur-Nanše, son of Gu-NI.DU

Col. ii

1) énsi
2) lagaš(NU$_{11}$.BUR.LA)
3) ⸢ib:gal⸣(gal-ib)
4) mu-dù

ii 1–2) ruler of Lagaš.

ii 3–4) built the Ibgal ("Great Oval").

Caption on standing male figure holding a cup facing Ur-Nanše

Inscription illegible; because the figure holds a cup, Börker-Klähn (Bildstelen p. 123) suggests it is a depiction of Anita, known elsewhere to be the cup-bearer of Ur-Nanše.

Caption on seated figure with female hairstyle on the right side of stele facing figure on left of stele

1) ⸢men-bára-abzu⸣ ⸢dam⸣
2) ur-^{d}nanše
3) énsi-
4) lagaš(NU$_{11}$.BUR.LA)

1–4) Men-bara-abzu, wife of Ur-Nanše, ruler of Lagaš.

Caption on seated figure with female hair-style on the left side of stele facing the queen

1) nin-u$_{4}$-sù
2) dumu
3) ur-^{d}nanše
4) énsi-
5) lagaš(NU$_{11}$.BUR.LA)

1–5) Nin-usu, daughter of Ur-Nanše, ruler of Lagaš.

Main text on "family side" of stele running from right to left between the four royal figures

Col. i

1) ⸢ur-^{d}nanše⸣
2) ⸢dumu⸣
3) ⸢gu-NI.DU⸣
4) ⸢énsi⸣-
5) [lagaš(NU$_{11}$.BUR.LA)]
6) ⸢ib⸣:[gal]([gal]-⸢ib⸣
7) [mu]-⸢dù⸣

i 1–5) ⸢Ur-Nanše, son of Gu-NI.DU, ruler of⸣ [Lagaš]

i 6–7) ⸢built⸣ the ⸢Ib⸣-[gal ("Great Oval").

Col. ii

1–10) Illegible
11) má dilmun

Col. iii

1) [gú-g̃iš]
2) [mu-g̃ál]

ii 1–10) Illegible

ii 11 – iii 2) He had the ships of Dilmun [submit timber (to Lagaš) as tribute].

3–7) Illegible	iii 3 – 7) Illegible
8) [x.KI]	iii 8–9) He defeated [...].
9) mu-dab$_5$	
Col. iv	
1) [...]	iv 1) Illegible
2) [I$_7$.x]	iv 2–3) He dug the ... canal.
3) mu-dun	
Col. v	
1) [...]	v 1–3) Illegible
2) [...]	
3) [...]	
4) kínda-[zi]	v 4 – vi 1) [He formed a (statue of]) Kinda[zi].
Col. vi	
1) [mu-tu]	
Rest of column illegible	
Side of stela with depiction of Inanna	
The inscription is largely illegible; no coherent translation can be provided	

6b

A limestone slab found at al-Hibā/Lagaš commemorates Ur-Nanše's building of the Bagara temple in general, and its temple kitchen (the likely provenance of the slab) in particular. The inscription concludes with a catalogue of temples built by Ur-Nanše. Concerning the inscription Cooper (RA 74 [1978] pp. 104–5) notes:

> Along the upper edge (as we read it) of both sides, each column begins at a different level to match the contours of the breaks. The absence of any traces of case rulings either above or below what is preserved of each column, proves that nothing is missing from the text. ... We must remove the brackets indicating textual breaks from Crawford's preliminary edition and read the reverse not, as he did from right to left, as if on a tablet, but from left to right, as the obverse. ... The lone lú umma^{ki} in rev. vi can perhaps be explained by the fact that this is a practice piece. Either the inscription went on but was not finished, as in No. 4, or the lú umma^{ki} was intended as practice for a cartouche that on the actual monument would label the figure of the defeated ruler.

The Bagara temple was likely the main shrine of the god Ningirsu in the city of Lagaš/ al Hibā (Falkenstein, Inschriften Gudeas p. 81). For references to this temple in the Presargonic Lagaš royal inscriptions and economic texts, see Selz, Untersuchungen pp. 219–20 § 3–4, p. 233 § 62 and p. 241 § 104. For references to the temple in the time of Gudea, see Falkenstein, Inschriften Gudeas pp. 157–58 § 3.

COMMENTARY

The slab, which was found in locus 4 H 5 (findspot N549/W101) at al-Hibā in the area of the Bagara temple, was given the excavation number 4 H-T 1. Its IM number is unknown.

The slab was probably originally a stele; it was apparently later used as a door socket.

In obv. vi line 3' for the reading of the divine name see Whiting, ZA 75 (1985) pp. 1–3, and Frayne, RIME 3/2 p. 123.

In obv. col. iii lines 4–5 for the reading of the DN as ^{d}lamma-šita$_{4}$-è, see Selz, Untersuchungen p. 159 § 6.5 who notes:

> Während Urn. 28 iii 4-5 eine Lesung ^{d}lamma-šita$_{4}$(=U.KID)-e nahelegt, ist nach Urn. 51 vii 2–3 auch eine Lesung ^{d}lammau$_{6}$(=IGI!.KID)-e nicht auszuschliessen. Beide Lesungen hat bereits F. Thureau-Dangin erwogen. Während J.-P. Gregoire die letzte Auffassung vertritt, zieht H. Steible die erstere vor, der den Namen mit "Lam(m)a, (die) die Šita(-Waffe) herausgehen lässt" wiedergibt.

In obv. col. v 4′ the translation "battle gate" is a guess based on understanding me as a phonetic writing for mè "battle."

In obv. vi 5 for the divine name ^{d}nin-RÉC 107:èš, see Selz Untersuchungen p. 269 sub. ^{d}nin-RÉC 107-èš. For the reading of the proper name we may note the comment of Civil (in Cagni, Il bilinguismo p. 95):

> In text no. 51 the sign is LAGABxLAK 175 [= RÉC 107], a variant of the sign ancestor of sanga2-6, to be transliterated preferably as šangax (Diri VI ii 25f.; the form with s — is from Sb). This sign is known in Ur III in the title šangax ^{d}en-líl-lá (Owen, NATN 155 and unpubl. Nippur tablets) its form differs slightly from LAK 175. Its rare occurrences in OB texts are often misinterpreted, see Steible, *Haja,* ad UET 6,101:19′.

The proper name RÉC 107 probably refers to a toponymn whose chief deity was Nin-RÉC 107. According to Selz, the name RÉC 107:èš of line vi 5 of our text would be a form of the deity worshipped perhaps in the city of Niĝin. The town RÉC 107 was likely located along the id$_{5}$-(A)-RÉC 107 canal (see Selz, Untersuchungen, p. 269 and nn. 1313–14). A variant of the canal name seems to be the nin-RÉC 107 107-ba-DU "the (canal) which goes to (the city of) Nin-RÉC 107" found in col. v line 3 of E1.9.1.9.

In obv. col. v line 10, for the reading of the element sàman "lead-rope" in the canal name, see Sjöberg, Nanna-Suen pp. 20–21; Cooper AnOr 52 p. 158; Heimpel Tierbilder p. 99; Bauer, WO 6 (1970) p. 150; Steinkeller, Sale Documents p. 203; Cavigneaux and Al-Rawi, RA 87 (1993) p. 109, and Selz, Untersuchungen p. 234 § 17.

For the location of the Saman canal mentioned in v 10, see a forthcoming work by Frayne where a connection with modern Tell Duhaim, 34 km NNE of G̃irsu/Tello, is proposed. For an ancient map showing the location of the Suhur canal mentioned in vi 1, see André-Salvini, Geographia Antiqua 1 (1992) pp. 57–65. According to the research of the author, the town of Suḫur is likely to be located at modern Tell az Zarki, 39.3 km NE of G̃irsu/Tello.

The šul-šà "(statue of) Šulšag" mentioned in vi 9 also appears in E1.9.1.9 col. ii line 3 in the fuller form šul-ša-ga. For the divine name see Selz, Untersuchungen p. 46 n. 210 and p. 251 n. 1203. The gods Šulšaga and Ig-alim were likely connected with the cult of the children of the city ruler (Selz, Untersuchungen p. 46 n. 210). In the Gudea inscriptions Šulšagana and Igalim appear as two brothers, offspring of Ninĝirsu (Falkenstein, Inschriften Gudeas pp. 111–12).

In obv. col. vi 11 and 13 for the deities Kindazi and Gušudu, see Selz, Untersuchungen pp. 156–57 and 139 respectively.

As called to my attention by G. Selz (following Bauer, in Bauer, Englund and Krebernik [eds.], Mesopotamien p. 564), the references in rev. iii 8–9 and v 4–5 to tumuli are not to heaps of the enemy dead (as some scholars have previously translated) but rather to respectful burial mounds of Ur-Nanše's fallen soldiers.

In obv. col. iv line 9 for the reading pú-sag "pit," see Selz, Harvard Semitic Museum pp. 175–76 note to 3:12.

BIBLIOGRAPHY

1977 Crawford, JCS 29 pp. 193–97 and 211–14 (photo, copy, edition)
1982 Steible, ASBW 1 pp. 112–16 Urnanše 51 (edition)
1983 Cooper, SANE 2 pp. 13, 23 and 44–45 no. 1 (translation, study)
1984 Römer, in TUAT 1/4 pp. 289–92 (translation)
1985 Bauer, AoN 21 p. 4 (study)
1986 Cooper, SARI pp. 24–25 La 1.6 (translation)
1991 Braun-Holzinger, Weihgaben p. 335 Stele 6 (study)

TEXT

Obverse
Col. I
1) [ur-^{d}nan]še
2) [dumu gu-NI.DU]
Col. ii
1) dumu-gur-sar
2) ba-gára
3) sig$_4$-BÁḪAR(LAK 742)
4) [m]u-dù
5) [ba]-gára
6) [...]-SAR
7) [mu-d]un
Col. iii
1) é-muḫaldim
2) ba-gára
3) si-sá-šè sum-ma
4) ib-muḫaldim
5) ba-gára
6) si-sá-šè sum-ma
7) ib:gal(gal-ib)
8) mu-dù
9) é-^{d}nanše
Col. iv
1) mu-dù
2) èš-g̃ír-sú
3) mu-dù
4) ki-NIR
5) mu-dù
6) é-g̃á-tum-du$_{10}$
7) mu-dù
8) ti-ra-áš
9) mu-dù
10) nin-g̃ar
11) mu-dù
Col. v
1) é-nin-MAR.KI
2) mu-dù
3) é-dam mu-dù
4) ká-me
5) mu-dù
6) abzu(zu+ab)-e
7) mu-dù
8) bàd-lagaš(NU$_{11}$.BUR.LA)
9) mu-dù
10) pa$_5$(E.PAP.PAP)-saman(ŠE.NÁM.NUN.BU)
11) mu-dun
Col. vi
1) a-suḫur
2) mu-dun
3) ^{d}nin-MAR.KI
4) mu-tu
5) ^{d}nin-RÉC 107-èš
6) mu-tu
7) ^{d}nin-PA
8) mu-tu
9) šul-šà
10) mu-tu

Obverse
Col. i
i 1 [Ur-Nan]še,
i 2 [son of Gu-NI.DU]
Col. ii
ii 1) (Gu-NI.DU was "son") of (the city of) Gursar,
ii 2–4) built the Bagara of fired bricks;

ii 5–7) [d]ug the [Ba]gara ... (canal).

Col. iii
iii 1–3) Having set the temple kitchen of the Bagara in working order,

iii 4–6) having set the "oval" kitchen of Bagara in working order,

iii 7–8) he built the Ibgal ("Great Oval").

iii 9 – iv 1) (He built) the temple of the goddess Nanše;

iv 2–3) he built the "Shrine-G̃irsu;"

iv 4–5) he built Ki-NIR;

iv 6–7) he built the temple of the goddess G̃atumdu;

iv 8–9) he built Tiraš;

iv 10–11) he built Ning̃ar;

v 1–2) he built the temple of the god NinMAR.KI;

v 3) he built the Edam;
v 4–5) he built the battle(?)-gate;

v 6–7) he built Abzu-e;

v 8–9) he built the wall of Lagaš.

v 10′–11′) He dug the Saman canal.

vi 1–2) He dug the A-suḫur (canal).

vi 3–4) He formed a (statue of) the god NinMAR.KI;
vi 5–6) he formed a (statue of) the deity Nin-RÉC 107:eš;
vi 7–8) he formed a (statue of) Ningidru;

vi 9–10) he formed a (statue of) Šulšag;

11) kínda-zi
12) mu-tu
13) ^{d}gú-šu-du$_{8}$
Col. vii
Lacuna
1) m[u]-tu
2) ^{d}lamma-
3) u$_{6}$(DUL.KID)-è
4) mu-tu
5) ^{d}lugal-ur-tùr
6) mu-tu
Reverse
Col. i
Read from left to right
1) [ur-^{d}nanse]
2) [lugal]
3) lagaš(NU$_{11}$.BUR.LA)
4) lú-uri$_{5}$(ŠEŠ.AB)
5) lú-^{giš}KÚŠU.KI
6) ME+LAK 526
7) e-šè-DU
8) lú-lagaš(NU$_{11}$.BUR.LA)
Col. ii
1) lú-úri(ŠEŠ.AB)
2) GÍN.ŠÈ m[u]-⸢sè⸣
3) mu-[dab$_{5}$]
4) éns[i]-má-gur$_{8}$
5) mu-dab$_{5}$
6) ama-bára-si
7) kišib-gál
8) nu-bànda^{da}
Col. iii
1) mu-dab$_{5}$
2) pap-ur-sag
3) dumu-Ú.Ú.Ú
4) [mu-dab$_{5}$]
5) [PN]
6) [nu-bàn]da
7) mu-dab$_{5}$
8) SAḪAR.DU$_{6}$.TAG$_{4}$
9) m[u]-dub
10) lú-$^{g̃iš}$KÚŠU
11) GÍN.ŠÈ mu-sè
Col. iv
1) lú-pà
2) bìl-la-la
3) nu-bànda^{da}
4) mu-dab$_{5}$
5) pa-bìl(BÍL.GIŠ)-ga-tuku
6) [é]nsi-
7) [g̃]^{iš}KÚŠU.KI
8) mu-dab$_{5}$
9) ur-pú-sag-
10) nu-bànda
11) mu-dab$_{5}$
Col. v
1) ḫur-sag̃-šè-máḫ
2) dam-gàr-gal
3) mu-dab$_{5}$

vi 11 –12) he formed a (statue of) Kindazi;

vi 13 – vii 1) [he formed] (a statue of) Gušudu;

Lacuna
vii 1) he formed [a statue of [...];
vii 2–4) he formed a (statue of) Lamma-šita-e;

vii 5–6) he formed a (statue of) Lugal-urtur,

Reverse
Col. i

i 1–2) [Ur-Nanše, king]

i 3–7) of Lagaš went to war against the leader of Ur and the leader of G̃iša (Umma).

i 8 – ii 3) The leader of Lagaš ⸢defeated⸣ and [captured] the leader of Ur.

ii 4–5) He captured the admir[al].

ii 6 – iii 1) He captured Ama-barasi and Kišibgal, lieutenants.

iii 2–4) [He captured] Papursag, son of Uʾuʾu.

iii 5–7) He captured [PN, the lieut]enant

iii 8–9) (and) buried (his own casualties with honour) in tumuli.
iii 10–11) He defeated the leader of G̃iša (Umma).

iv 1–4) He captured Lupa and Bilala, the lieutenants.

iv 5–8) He captured Pabilgatuk, the [ru]er of G̃iša (Umma).

iv 9–11) He captured Ur-pusag, the lieutenant.

v 1–3) He captured Ḫursag̃šemaḫ, the chief of the merchants

4) SAḪAR.DU$_{6}$.TAG$_{4}$
5) mu-dub
Col. vi
1) lú-$^{\text{g̃iš}}$KÚŠU.KI

v 4–5) (and) buried (his own casualties with honour) in tumuli.

vi 1) The leader of G̃iša (Umma) ...

7

A six-line inscription deals with Ur-Nanše's construction of the "Shrine-G̃irsu." The text appears on: (a) a purchased alabaster foundation figurine of unknown provenance (but almost certainly from G̃irsu) (ex. 1); (b) sets of copper nails and copper plates excavated from foundation deposits from the area around the "Maison des fruits" (see Parrot, Tello fig. 15 nos. 9a–d) now housed in Paris and Istanbul (exs. 3–7); (c) sets of copper nails and copper plates now in Brussels, London, and Athens (exs. 2, 8, and 9) (clearly from G̃irsu); and (d) bricks excavated at G̃irsu and now housed in Istanbul (exs. 11–18). Accompanying the pegs and plates were various stone foundation tablets; Parrot (Tello p. 63) notes: "Quant aux tablettes, quatre mentionnaient le temple de Nanshe, huit l'Ab-G̃irsu [èš-g̃ír-su.KI]." The texts on the foundation tablets (here inscriptions E1.9.1.9–18) differ from the peg and plate inscription (although they are clearly related to it), and also from each other, the differences being minor variants. In his plan of the excavations Parrot indicates the findspots of four of these foundation tablets (p. 62 figs. 15 nos. 19a–d); unfortunately, we cannot link up these findspots with the different foundation tablets.

CATALOGUE

Ex.	Museum number	Object	Provenance	Dimensions (cm)	Sollberger, CIRPL no.	Lines preserved	cpn
Nails and Plates							
1	HSM 7495 = 1913.2.178	Alabaster foundation nail	Purchased	Length: 20 Width at shoulders: 5.5	Um. 2	1–6	c
2a	0.23 (Brussels)	Copper nail	Purchased	16.5×4.5	Um. 3	1–2	n
2b	0.23 (Brussels)	Copper plate	Purchased	11.5×7.5	Um. 3	3–6	n
3a	EŞ 493	Copper nail	Tello	14.5×3.2×2.6	Um. 4	—	n
3b	EŞ 493	Copper plate	Tello		Um. 4	1–6	n
4	EŞ 496	Copper plate	Tello	Height: 12.2 Dia.: 7.8	Um. 5	1–6	p
5a	AO 2351	Copper nail	Tello	Height:14.3	Um .5	—	n
5b	AO 2351	Copper plate	Tello	7×10	Um. 5	1–6	c
6a	AO 294	Copper nail	Tello	15	Um. 6	—	n
6b	AO 294	Copper plate	Tello	11.8×7	Um. 6	1–6	c
7a	AO 314	Copper nail	Tello	Height: 15	Um. 7	—	n
7b	AO 314	Copper plate	Tello	—	Um. 7	—	n
8a	BM 96565 (reg. no.) 1902-4-12, 677	Copper nail	Purchased	Length: 15.3 Width: 8	—	1–6	c
8b	BM 96565	Copper plate	Purchased	11.6×6.3 Hole dia. : 4.2	—	1–6	c
9	National Museum, Athens no. 14803	Copper nail	Found at Epirus	Length: 16.2	—	—	n
Bricks							
10	AO 350	Brick	Tello	35×20×7	Um. 9	1–5	p
11	EŞ 394	Brick	Tello	29×20×4.5	Um. 10	—	n
12	EŞ 395	Brick	Tello	29×19.5×6	Um. 11	—	n
13	EŞ 396	Brick	Tello	29×19.5×6	Um. 12	—	n
14	EŞ 397	Brick	Tello	29×20.5×6.5	Um. 13	—	n
15	EŞ 400	Brick	Tello	28×20×6	Um. 14	—	n
16	EŞ 8880	Brick	Tello	29×19.5×7.5	Um. 15	—	n
17	EŞ 8881	Brick	Tello	29×19.5×7.5	Um. 16	—	n
18	EŞ 8883	Brick	Tello	29×19.5×5.5	Um. 17	—	n

COMMENTARY

Ex. 5 was listed by Sollberger (CIRPL p. vii sub. Urn. 6) as AO 254. The nail actually bears the museum number AO 294. The bricks differ from the foundation pegs and tablets in having line 5 written above line 4, to the right of line 2.

BIBLIOGRAPHY

1884–1912 de Sarzec, Découvertes 1 p. 240 (study); Découvertes 2 pl. 2ter no. 3 (exs. 6a–b, photo); pl. 31 no. 1 (ex. 10, photo)
1897 Heuzey, RA 4 p. 113 fig. 20 (exs. 6a–b, drawing)
1902 Heuzey, Catalogue Louvre pp. 298–99 nos. 142–44 (exs. 5–7, study)
1907 Thureau-Dangin, SAK pp. 6–7 Ur-ninâ i (ex. 10, edition)
1922 BM Guide p. 83 no. 2 (exs. 8a–b, study)
1925 Speleers, Receuil p. 1 no. 2 (exs. 2a–b, copy)
1926 Unger, SuAK p. 85 no. 27 (exs. 3a–b, photo)
1927 Papaspiridi, Guide p. 185 no. 34 (ex. 9, study)
1927 Unger, RLV 8 pl. 138 (exs. 3a–b, 4, photo)
1929 Barton, RISA pp. 22–23 Ur-Nina 15 (ex. 10, edition)
1931 Hussey, RA 28 pp. 81–83 (ex. 1, photo, edition, study)
1931 van Buren, Foundation Figurines p. 7 (exs. 3–9, study); pl. II (exs. 8a–b, photo)
1940 Christian, Altertumskunde pl. 146 no. 1 (ex. 9, photo); pl. 153 no. 1 (ex. 5, photo)
1948 Parrot, Tello, p. 63 and fig. 15 nos. 19 a–d (study, findspots); p. 81 (ex. 1, study); p. 105 (exs. 5a, 7a, study)
1956 Sollberger, CIRPL 1 p. vii–viii Urn. 2–18 (study); p. 1 Urn. 2–7, 9–17 (exs. 1, 2, 10, copy)
1971 Sollberger and Kupper, IRSA IC3a (translation)
1982 André-Leicknam, Naissance p. 78 no. 32 (ex. 10, translation, photo)
1982 Steible, ASBW 1 pp. 79–80 Urnanše 2 (exs. 1–7, 10–18, edition)
1983 Rashid, Grundungsfiguren pp. 7–8 nos. 41–48 (exs. 1, 3–9, study); pls. 4–5 (exs. 1, 3–5, 8–9, drawing)
1986 Cooper, SARI 1 p. 25 La 1.7 (translation)

TEXT

1)	ur:^{d}nanše(^{d}nanše-ur)	1–3) Ur-Nanše, king of Lagaš,
2)	lugal-	
3)	lagaš(NU$_{11}$.BUR.LA)	
4)	dumu gu-NI.DU	4) son of Gu-NI.DU,
5)	èš-g̃ír-su	5–6) built the "Shrine-G̃irsu."
6)	mu-dù	

8

A stele from G̃irsu deals with Ur-Nanše's building of the "Shrine-G̃irsu."

COMMENTARY

The stele, which measures 58×28×5.5 cm, was found near the triangular plaque of inscription E1.9.1.20; the triangular plaque was given a find spot: "à une distance à peu près égale entre la face sud-est du palais [Tell A] et *le tell des piliers* [Tell I]" (de Sarzec, Découvertes 1 p. 92). It bears the museum number MNB 1415. The inscription was collated.

The inscription was clearly left unfinished.

BIBLIOGRAPHY

1884–1912 de Sarzec, Découvertes 1 pp. 92–93 (study, findspot); Découvertes 2 p. XXXVI Our-Nina 2 (copy); pl. 2 no. 2 (photo)
1907 Thureau-Dangin, SAK pp. 6–7 Ur-ninâ g (edition)
1929 Barton, RISA pp. 18–19 Ur-Nina 7 (edition)
1956 Sollberger, CIRPL 1 p. viii Urn. 39 (study); p. 6 Urn. 39 (copy)
1980 Cooper, RA 74 pp. 108–10 fig. no. 4 (photo, study)
1982 Steible, ASBW 1 p. 105 Urnanše 39 (edition)
1986 Cooper, SARI 1 p. 26 La 1.8 (translation)
1991 Braun-Holzinger, Weihgaben p. 334 Stele 3 (edition, study)

TEXT

Col. i	
1) ur:^{d}nanše(^{d}nanše-ur)	i 1–3) Ur-Nanše, king of Lagaš,
2) lugal-	
3) lagaš(NU$_{11}$.BUR.LA)	
4) dumu gu-NI.DU	i 4) son of Gu-NI.DU,
5) èš-g̃ír-su	i 5 – ii 1) built the "Shrine-G̃irsu."
Col. ii	
1) mu-dù	
2) temen-sig$_4$-tab	ii 2) (He built) the foundation with a double layer of bricks.

9

The stone foundation tablets bearing inscriptions 9–18, as noted, all came from foundation deposits in the area of the "Maison des fruits." They were presumably inscribed for the construction of "Shrine-G̃irsu" (èš-g̃ír-su.KI) in G̃irsu.

COMMENTARY

The first stone foundation tablet measures 19.5×12.6×4.8 cm and it bears the museum number AO 3177. The inscription was collated.

For the translation "reservoir(?)" in iv 4, see Selz, Untersuchungen p. 130 n. 512.

For the canal name in iv 6, see Bauer WO 6 (1970–71) pp. 149–50. For súr-dù.MUŠEN "falcon" see Heimpel, Tierbilder pp. 422–25. For depictions of falcons in ancient Mesopotamian art, see van Buren, AnOr 18 p. 85.

In this canal name Steible (ASBW 1 p. 92) gives a phonemic rendering of the equative postposition -GIM as gim. The actual reading of the sign in ED texts is not entirely certain; a rather wide number of writings of the postposition are attested. According to Falkenstein (Das Sumerisch p. 39): "für die älteren Sprachstufen ist -gim (oder -gin$_7$) > gi$_{18}$ und -gé anzusetzen." This is further evidenced now by Krebernik's edition of ED period incantations from Fāra and Ebla; in his monograph Beschwörung p. 8 Incantation 1 section b he notes a Fāra exemplar which gives -GIM, while the two Ebla exemplars give once -GIM and once -gi. Similarly, p. 65 of Krebernik's monograph Incantation 9 section f (from Ebla) exhibits the alternation gi, and gi-in in one text. For the immediate pre-Ur III period, Falkenstein, (Grammatik Gudeas p. 117 § 35) notes: "Da syllabische Schreibungen in den Gudea-Inschriften dafür nich vorkommen, ist hier als Behelf durchweg die Lesung -gim eingesetzt." In Ur III letter orders we find both -GIM and -gí or gé (KID) (see Sollberger, TCS 1 p. 120 no. 231 for the references). In OB EME-sal texts we generally find -GIM but also -ge-en (Messerschmidt, VS 2 no. 94 line 13), ge$_5$(KI) ibid., no. 95 line 12, -gi$_4$-in, ibid., no. 2 col. iii line 28, gi$_5$ (Langdon PBS 10/2 no. 3 rev. 9′-10′), -ge-en, King, CT 15 no. 15 line 21 (see most recently Cohen, Sumerian Hymnology p. 53 line 21), and gi$_5$(KI)-im, G. Farber, JNES 43 (1984) p. 315. In the Seleucid period texts from Babylon we invariably find -GIM (see Oberhuber Innsbrucker Sumerisches Lexikon pp. 184–88 no. 113); in the Eršaḫunga texts -GIM is normally found but -gin (DU) is also attested (Maul, 'Herzberuhigungsklagen' p. 414). Finally, in the "Graeco-Babyloniaca" text edited by Maul in ZA 81 (1991) pp. 87ff. we find a transcription -i in the version rendered in Greek script (see Maul pp. 95–96).

BIBLIOGRAPHY

1884–1912 de Sarzec, Découvertes 2 p. LIII OUR-NINA 12 (copy)

1907 Thureau-Dangin, SAK pp. 4–5 Ur-ninâ c (edition)

1929 Barton, RISA pp. 16–17 Ur-Nina 3 (edition)

1956 Sollberger, CIRPL 1 p. viii Urn. 26 (study); p. 3 Urn. 26 (partial copy)

1982 Steible, ASBW 1 pp. 91–92 Urnanše 26 (edition)

1986 Cooper, SARI 1 p. 26 La 1.9 (translation)

TEXT

Col. i
1) ur:^{d}nanše(^{d}nanše-ur)
2) lugal-
3) lagaš(NU$_{11}$.BUR.LA)
4) dumu gu-NI.DU
5) dumu-gur-sar
Col. ii
1) èš-g̃ír-su
2) mu-dù
3) ^{d}šul-šà-ga
4) mu-tu
5) gú-šu-du$_{8}$
6) mu-tu
7) ^{d}kínda-zi
Col. iii
1) mu-tu
2) é-^{d}nin-MAR.KI
3) mu-[dù]
4) ^{d}lamma
5) šita$_{4}$-è
6) mu-tu
7) id$_{5}$(A)-a-suḫur
8) mu-dun
Col. iv
1) ég-tir-sig
2) mu-dun
3) ^{d}en-líl-pà-da
4) uš-gal
5) mu-dun
6) súr-du$_{7}$-gin$_{7}$-DU
Col. v
1) GÁN[A-x (x)?]
2) mu-dun
3) nin-sanga$_{x}$(RÉC 107)-ba-DU
4) mu-dun
5) lú-inim-sì-
6) ^{d}nanše

i 1–3) Ur-Nanše, king of Lagaš,

4) son of Gu-NI.DU,
5) (Gu-NI.DU was) "son" of Gursar,

ii 1–2) built the "Shrine-G̃irsu,"

ii 3–4) formed (the statue) of Šulšaga,

ii 5–6) formed (the statue) of Gušudu,

ii 7 – iii 1) formed (the statue of) Kindazi,

iii 2–3) [built] the temple of NinMAR.KI,

iii 4–6) formed (a statue of) Lamma-šita-e,

iii 7–8) dug the Asuḫur canal,

iv 1–2) dug the "Ditch of the Southern Wood,"

iv 3–5) dug the "Great Reservoir(?)" at the Enlilpada (canal),

iv 6 – v 2) dug the "Canal Moving like a Falcon," the field ...,

v 3–4) dug the Nin-sanga-baDU (canal).

v 5–6) He is the one commissioned by the goddess Nanše.

10

A stone foundation tablet records various temple constructions of Ur-Nanše.

COMMENTARY

This stone foundation tablet bears the museum number AO 3867. The inscription was not collated.

BIBLIOGRAPHY

1884–1912 de Sarzec, Découvertes 2 p. LIII OUR-NINA 14 (copy)
1907 Thureau-Dangin, SAK pp. 4–5 Ur-ninâ e (edition)
1929 Barton, RISA pp. 16–17 Ur-Nina 5 (edition)
1956 Sollberger, CIRPL 1 p. viii Urn. 28 (study); Urn. 28 (partial copy)
1982 Steible, ASBW 1 pp. 93–94 Urnanše 28 (edition)
1986 Cooper, SARI 1 p. 26 La 1.10 (translation)

TEXT

Col. i
1) ^{d}ur:nanše(^{d}nanše-ur)
2) lugal
3) lagaš(NU$_{11}$.BUR.LA)
4) dumu gu-NI.DU
Col. ii
1) dumu-gur-sar
2) èš-g̃ír-su
3) mu-dù
4) é-^{d}nanše
5) mu-dù
Col. iii
1) ib:gal(gal-ib)
2) mu-dù
Hole in tablet
3) ki-NIR
4) mu-dù
Col. iv
1) é:^{d}:gá :tum:du$_{10}$(é-gá-^{d}tùm-du$_{10}$
2) mu-dù
3) abzu(zu+ab)-e
4) mu-d[ù]
5) ti-ra-áš
6) mu-dù
Col. v
1) èš-ba-gára
2) mu-dù
3) é-da[m]
4) ⌈mu-dù⌉
5) ká-ME
6) mu-dù

i 1–3) Ur-Nanše, king of Lagaš,
i 4) son of Gu-NI.DU,
ii 1) (Gu-NI.DU was) "son" of Gursar,
ii 2–3) built the temple "Shrine-G̃irsu,"
ii 4–5) built the temple of Nanše,
iii 1–2) built the Ibgal ("Great Oval"),
iii 3–4) built Ki-NIR,
iv 1–2) built the temple of the goddess Gatumdu,
iv 3–4) built Abzu-e,
iv 5–6) built Tiraš,
v 1–2) built "Shrine-Bagara,"
v 3–4) built the E-da[m] temple,
v 5–6) built the "*Battle Gate*."

11

A stone tablet from G̃irsu records Ur-Nanše's construction of various temples and fabrication of miscellaneous statues.

COMMENTARY

This stone foundation tablet, which measures 21.9×13.8×5.7 cm, bears the museum number AO 3179. The inscription was collated.

BIBLIOGRAPHY

1884–1912 de Sarzec, Découvertes 2 p. LIII OUR-NINA 11 (copy)
1907 Thureau-Dangin, SAK pp. 2–5 Ur-ninâ b (edition)
1929 Barton, RISA pp. 14–17 Ur-Nina 2 (edition)
1956 Sollberger, CIRPL 1 p. viii Urn. 25 (study): p. 3 Urn. 25 (partial copy)
1963 Kramer, Sumerians pp. 308–9 no. 7 (translation)
1982 Steible, ASBW 1 pp. 93–94 Urnanše 25 (edition)
1986 Cooper, SARI 1 pp. 26–27 La 1.11 (translation)

TEXT

Col. i	
1) ur:^{d}nanše(^{d}nanše-ur)	i 1–3) Ur-Nanše, king of Lagaš,
2) lugal-	
3) lagaš(NU$_{11}$.BUR.LA)	
4) dumu gu-NI.DU	i 4) son of Gu-NI.DU,
5) dumu-gur-sar	i 5) (Gu-NI.DU was "son" of) Gursar,
6) é-^{d}nanše	i 6 – ii 1) built the temple of the goddess Nanše.
Col. ii	
1) mu-dù	
2) ^{d}nanše nin-uru$_{16}$	ii 2–3) He formed (the statue) "the goddess Nanše is a mighty lady."
3) mu-tu	
4) èš-g̃ír-su mu-⌈dù⌉	ii 4) He built the "Shrine-G̃irsu."
5) ^{d}šul-šà-ga	ii 5–6) He formed (a statue of) Šulšaga.
6) mu-tu	
7) ib:gal(gal-ib)	ii 7 – iii 1) He bu[ilt] the Ibgal ("Great Oval").
Col. iii	
1) mu-d[ù]	
2) lu[gal]-ur-t[ùr]	iii 2–3) He formed (a statue of) Lu[gal]-urt[ur].
3) mu-tu	
4) lugal-URU×KÁR	iii 4–5) He formed (a statue of) the god Lugal-URU×KÁR,
5) mu-tu	
6) ⌈KI⌉-NI[R]	iii 6–7) He built Ki-NIR.
7) mu-dù	
Col. iv	
1) ^{d}nin-RÉC 107:èš(^{d}nin-èš-RÉC 107)	iv 1–2) He formed (a statue of) Nin-RÉC 107-èš.
2) mu-[t]u	
3) ^{d}nin-PA	iv 3–4) He formed (a statue of) Ningidru.
4) mu-tu	
5) é-^{d}g̃á-tùm-du$_{10}$	iv 5–6) He built the temple of the goddess G̃atumdu.
6) mu-dù	
7) é-^{d}gá:tùm:du$_{10}$(é-tum-^{d}gá-du$_{10}$)	iv 7 – v 1) He formed (a statue of) the goddess G̃atumdu.
Col. v	
1) mu-tu	
2) ba-gára	v 2–3) He built the Bagara,
3) mu-dù	
4) é-dam	v 4–5) built the E-dam,
5) mu-dù	
6) abzu(zu-ab)-e	6–7) built Abzu-e,
7) mu-dù	
8) ti-ra-áš	8–9) and bui[lt] Tiraš.
9) mu-d[ù]	

12

A stone foundation tablet from G̃irsu records Ur-Nanše's construction of various temples and the digging of a canal.

COMMENTARY

This stone tablet, which measures 14.2×8×4 cm, bears the museum number AO 3180. The inscription was collated.

BIBLIOGRAPHY

1884–1912 de Sarzec, Découvertes 2 p. LIII OUR-NINA 13 (copy)
1907 Thureau-Dangin, SAK pp. 4–5 Ur-ninâ d (edition)
1929 Barton, RISA pp. 16–17 Ur-Nina 4 (edition)
1956 Sollberger, CIRPL 1 p. viii Urn. 27 (study); p. 4 Urn. 27 (partial copy)
1982 Steible ASBW 1 p. 93 Urnanše 27 (edition)
1986 Cooper, SARI 1 p. 27 La 1.12 (translation)

TEXT

Col. i	
1) ur:^{d}nanše(^{d}nanše-ur)	i 1–3) Ur-Nanše, king of Lagaš,
2) lugal-	
3) lagaš(NU$_{11}$.BUR.LA)	
4) dumu gu-NI.DU	i 4) son of Gu-NI.DU,
Col. ii	
1) dumu-gur-sar	ii 1) (Gu-NI.DU) was "son" of Gursar,
2) é-^{d}nanše	ii 2–3) built the temple of the goddess Nanše,
3) mu-dù	
4) èš-g̃ír-su	ii 4 – iii 1) built the "Shrine-G̃irsu,"
Col. iii	
1) mu-dù	
2) ^{d}nin-g̃ír-su-pà-da	iii 2–4) dug the canal "Ning̃irsu-pada ... ."
3) NI IL(LAK500) MA or NI MA IL(LAK 500])	
4) mu-dun	
Col. iv	
1) abzu(zu+ab)	iv 1–2) built Abzu,
2) mu-dù	
3) é-dam	iv 3–4) built the E-dam.
4) mu-dù	

13

A stone foundation tablet from G̃irsu records Ur-Nanše's construction of various temples.

COMMENTARY

This stone foundation tablet bears the museum number AO 253. The inscription was not collated.

BIBLIOGRAPHY

1956 Sollberger, CIRPL 1 p. viii Urn. 29 (study); p. 4 Urn. 29 (partial copy)
1982 Steible, ASBW 1 p. 95 Urnanše 29 (edition)
1986 Cooper, SARI 1 p. 27 La 1.13 (translation)

TEXT

Col. i	
1) ur:^{d}nanše(^{d}nanše-ur)	i 1–3) Ur-Nanše, king of Lagaš,
2) lugal-	
3) lagaš(NU$_{11}$.BUR.LA)	
4) dumu gu-NI.DU	i 4) son of Gu-NI.DU,
Col. ii	
1) dumu gur-sar	ii 1) (Gu-NI.DU was) "son" of Gursar,
2) é-^{d}nanše	ii 2–3) built the temple of the goddess Nanše,
3) mu-dù	
4) èš-g̃ír-su	ii 4–5) built the "Shrine-G̃irsu,"
5) mu-dù	
Col. iii	
1) ib:gal(gal-ib)	iii 1–2) built the Ibgal ("Great Oval"),
2) mu-dù	
3) é-PA	iii 3–4) built the E-PA,
4) mu-dù	
5) é:^{d}g̃á:tùm:du$_{10}$(é-tùm-^{d}g̃á-du$_{10}$	iii 5 – iv 1) built the temple of the goddess G̃atumdu,
Col. iv	
1) mu-dù	
2) é-^{d}nin-MAR.KI	iv 2–3) built the temple of the god NinMAR.KI,
3) mu-dù	
4) é-dam	iv 4–5) built the E-dam.
5) mu-dù	

14

A stone foundation tablet from G̃irsu records Ur-Nanše's construction of various temples.

COMMENTARY

This stone foundation tablet, which measures 14.5×9.9×4.8 cm, bears the museum number AO 315. The inscription was collated.

BIBLIOGRAPHY

1956 Sollberger, CIRPL 1 p. viii Urn. 30 (study); p. 4 Urn. 30 (partial copy)
1982 Steible, ASBW 1 pp. 95–96 Urnanše 30 (edition)
1986 Cooper, SARI 1 p. 27 La 1.14 (translation)

TEXT

Col. i
1) ur:^{d}nanše(^{d}nanše-ur)
2) lugal-
3) lagaš(NU$_{11}$.BUR.LA)
4) dumu gu-NI.DU
Col. ii
1) dumu gur-sar
2) é-^{d}nanše
3) mu-dù
4) èš-g̃ír-su
Col. iii
1 mu-dù
2) ib:gal(gal-ib)
3) mu-dù
4) ki-NIR
5) mu-dù
6) é-dam
Col. iv
1) mu-dù
2) ba-gára
3) mu-dù
4) abzu(zu+ab)-e
5) mu-dù

i 1–3) Ur-Nanše, king of Lagaš,
i 4) son of Gu-NI.DU,
ii 1) (Gu-NI.DU was) "son" of Gursar,
ii 2–3) built the temple of the goddess Nanše,
ii 4 – iii 1) built the "Shrine-G̃irsu,"
iii 2–3) built the great Ibgal ("Great Oval"),
iii 4–5) built Ki-NIR,
iii 6 – iv 1) built the E-dam,
iv 2–3) built the Bagara,
iv 4–5) built Abzu-e.

15

A stone foundation tablet from G̃irsu records Ur-Nanše's construction of various temples.

COMMENTARY

This stone foundation tablet, which measures 14.3×8.2×5.7 cm, bears the museum number AO 2784. The inscription was collated.

BIBLIOGRAPHY

1956 Sollberger, CIRPL 1 p. viii Urn. 31 (study); p. 4 Urn. 31 (partial copy)
1982 Steible, ASBW 1 pp. 96–97 Urnanše 31 (edition)
1986 Cooper, SARI 1 pp. 27–28 La 1.15 (translation)

TEXT

Col. i
1) ur:^{d}nanše(^{d}nanše-ur)
2) lugal-
3) lagaš(NU$_{11}$.BUR.LA)
4) dumu gu-NI.DU
Col. ii
1) dumu-gur-sar
2) é-^{d}nanše

i 1–3) Ur-Nanše, king of Lagaš,
i 4) son of Gu-NI.DU,
ii 1) (Gu-NI.DU) was "son" of Gursar,
ii 2–3) built the temple of the goddess Nanše,

3) mu-dù
4) èš-g̃ír-su
5) mu-dù
Col. iii
1) ib:gal(gal-ib)
2) mu-dù
3) é-PA
4) mu-dù
5) é:^{d}gá:tùm:du$_{10}$(é-tùm-^{d}gá-du$_{10}$)
Col. iv
1) mu-dù
2) é-dam
3) mu-dù
4) é-^{d}nin-MAR.KI
5) mu-dù

ii 4–5) built the "Shrine-G̃irsu,"

iii 1–2) built the Ibgal ("Great Oval"),

iii 3–4) built the E-PA,

iii 5 – iv 1) built the temple of the goddess G̃atumdu,

iv 2–3) built the E-dam,

iv 4–5) built the temple of the god NinMAR.KI.

16

A stone foundation tablet from G̃irsu records Ur-Nanše's construction of various temples.

COMMENTARY

This stone foundation tablet bears the museum number EŞ 430. It was not collated.

BIBLIOGRAPHY

1956 Sollberger, CIRPL 1 p. viii Urn. 33 (study); p. 5 Urn. 33 (partial copy)
1982 Steible, ASBW 1 pp. 98–99 Urnanše 33 (edition)
1986 Cooper, SARI 1 p. 28 La 1.16 (translation)

TEXT

Col. i
1) ur:^{d}nanše(^{d}nanše-ur)
2) lugal-
3) lagaš(NU$_{11}$.BUR.LA)
4) dumu gu-NI.DU
5) dumu-gur-sar
Col. ii
1) é-^{d}nanše
2) mu-dù
3) èš-g̃ír-su
4) mu-dù
5) é:^{d}gá:tùm:du$_{10}$(é-tùm-^{d}gá-du$_{10}$)
6) mu-dù
Col. iii
1) é-PA
2) mu-dù
3) (line erased)
4) (line erased)

i 1–3) Ur-Nanše, king of Lagaš,

i 4) son of Gu-NI.DU,
i 5) (Gu-NI.DU was) "son" of Gursar,

ii 1–2) built the temple of the goddess Nanše,

ii 3–4) built the "Shrine-G̃irsu,"

ii 5–6) built the temple of the goddess G̃atumdu,

iii 1–2) built the E-PA,

iii 3–4) ...

5)	é-dam	iii 5–6) built the E-dam,
6)	mu-dù	
Col. iv		
1)	nin-g̃ar	iv 1–2) built Ning̃ar,
2)	mu-dù	
3)	ba-gára	iv 3–4) built the Bagara,
4)	mu-dù	
5)	ki-NIR	iv 5–6) built Ki-NIR.
6)	mu-dù	

17

A stone foundation tablet from G̃irsu records Ur-Nanše's construction of various temples, the fabrication of miscellaneous statues, and the digging of canals. Of particular note is the mention of the oracular designation of the "spouse" (dam) of the goddess Nanše (lines iii 3–6) and the construction of the wall of Lagaš (lines iv 5–6).

COMMENTARY

This stone foundation tablet, which measures 19.5×13×6 cm, bears the museum number EŞ 429. The inscription was collated from the published photo.

In line v 1, LUGAL-uru may possibly be a mistake for LUGAL-URU×KÁR, a divinity worshipped in a cult centre near G̃irsu (see Selz, Untersuchungen p. 163 and Frayne, forthcoming).

The A-edin of iii 7 is likely not to be identified with the é-edin of section E1.5 of this volume, but rather to a small settlement in the vicinity of G̃irsu; see Selz, Untersuchungen p. 184 n. 844 for the references. Selz notes that in an En-metena inscription the gú-edin (canal) is mentioned in connection with the [b]àd-da-sal$_4$ "Fortress along the Sala (canal)" and the é-igi-⌈íl-eden⌉-na "Building that Surveys the Plain"; see inscription E1.9.5.27 col. iii 4–8 in this volume. For a location of the toponyms in this text, see Frayne (forthcoming), where it is suggested that A-edin, Ning̃ar, and E-PA all lay along the same canal, presumably the A-edin.

BIBLIOGRAPHY

1884–1912 de Sarzec, Découvertes 2 p. XXXVI OUR-NINA 3 (copy); pl. 2ter no. 2 (photo)
1907 Thureau-Dangin, SAK pp. 2–3 Ur-ninâ a (edition)
1929 Barton, RISA pp. 14–15 Ur-Nina 1 (edition)
1956 Sollberger, CIRPL 1 p. viii Urn. 24 (study); p. 3 Urn. 24 (partial copy)
1971 Sollberger and Kupper, IRSA, IC3d (translation)
1982 Steible, ASBW 1 pp. 88–90 Urnanše 24 (edition)
1986 Cooper, SARI 1 p. 28 La 1.17 (translation)
1995 Selz, Untersuchungen p. 184 § 5 (study)

TEXT

Col. i		
1)	ur:^{d}nanše(^{d}nanše-ur)	i 1–3) Ur-Nanše, king of Lagaš,
2)	lugal	
3)	lagaš(NU$_{11}$.BUR.LA)	
4)	dumu gu-NI.DU	i 4) son of Gu-NI.DU,
5)	dumu-gur-sar	i 5) (Gu-NI.DU was) "son" of Gursar,
6)	é-^{d}nanše	i 6–7) built the temple of the goddess Nanše,
7)	mu-dù	

Transliteration	Translation
Col. ii	
1) ^{d}nanše	ii 1–2) formed (a statue of) the goddess Nanše,
2) mu-tu	
3) a-sanga$_{x}$(RÉC 107)	ii 3–4) dug the A-sanga$_{x}$(RÉC 107) canal,
4) mu-dun	
5) ^{d}nanše	ii 5–7) brought water into the sanga$_{x}$(RÉC 107) canal for the goddess Nanše,
6) sanga$_{x}$(RÉC 107)	
7) a mu-na-A+KU$_{4}$(= RÉC 558)	
Col. iii	
1) èš-ir	iii 1–2) formed (a statue of) EŠ-ir,
2) mu-tu	
3) ur-nimin	iii 3–6) chose Ur-nimin by oracular means to be the spouse of the goddess Nanše,
4) dam-	
5) ^{d}nanše	
6) maš bi-pà	
7) a-edin	iii 7–8) built A-edin,
8) mu-dù	
Col. iv	
1) nin-g̃ar	iv 1–2) built Ning̃ar,
2) mu-dù	
3) é-PA	iv 3–4) built the E-PA,
4) mu-dù	
5) bàd-lagaš	iv 5–6) built the wall of Lagaš,
6) mu-dù	
Col. v	
1) ^{d}lugal-URU×KÁR(Text: URU)	v 1–2) formed (a statue of) the god Lugal-URU×KÁR.
2) mu-tu	
3) má-dilmun	3–5) He had ships of Dilmun submit timber as tribute from the foreign lands (to Lagaš).
4) kur-ta	
5) gú-g̃iš mu-g̃ál	

18

A stone foundation tablet in Istanbul mentions Ur-Nanše's construction of several temples.

COMMENTARY

The stone foundation tablet, which measures 19×11 cm, bears the museum number EŞ 428. The inscription was not collated.

BIBLIOGRAPHY

1956 Sollberger, CIRPL 1p. viii Urn. 32 (study); p. 5 Urn. 32 (partial copy)
1982 Steible, ASBW 1 pp. 97–98 Urnanše 32 (edition)
1986 Cooper, SARI 1 pp, 28–29 La 1.18 (translation)

TEXT

Col. i	
1) ur:^{d}nanše(^{d}nanše-ur)	i 1–3) Ur-Nanše, king of Lagaš,
2) lugal-	
3) lagaš(NU$_{11}$.BUR.LA)	
4) dumu gu-NI.DU	i 4) son of Gu-NI.DU,
Col. ii	
1) dumu-gur-sar	ii 1) (Gu-NI.DU) was "son" of Gursar,
2) ib:gal(gal-ib)	ii 2–3) built the Ibgal ("Great Oval"),
3) mu-dù	
4) ki-NIR	ii 4–5) built Ki-NIR,
5) mu-dù	
6) nin-g̃ar	ii 6 – iii 1) built Ning̃ar,
Col. iii	
1) mu-dù	
2) ba-gára	iii 2–3) built the Bagara,
3) mu-dù	
4) é-dam	iii 4–5) built the E-dam,
5) mu-dù	
6) ti-ra-áš	iii 6 – iv 1) built Tiraš,
Col. iv	
1) mu-dù	
2) a-edin	iv 2–3) built A-edin,
3) mu-dù	
4) é-PA	iv 4–5) and built the E-PA.
5) mu-dù	

19

A brick inscription records Ur-Nanše's construction of Ning̃irsu's temple.

COMMENTARY

The brick, which measures 28×20×5.5 cm, was found in de Sarzec's excavations at G̃irsu. It bears the museum number EŞ 393.

BIBLIOGRAPHY

1956 Sollberger, CIRPL p. viii Urn. 8 (study); p. 1 Urn. 8 (copy)
1971 Sollberger and Kupper, IRSA IC3b (translation)
1982 Steible ASBW 1 p. 81 Urnanše 8 (edition)
1986 Cooper, SARI 1 p. 29 La 1.19 (translation)

TEXT

1) ur:^{d}nanše(^{d}nanše-ur)	1–3) Ur-Nanše, king of Lagaš,
2) lugal-	
3) lagaš(NU$_{11}$.BUR.LA)	
4) dumu gu-NI.DU	4) son of Gu-NI.DU,
5) é-^{d}nin-g̃ír-su	5–6) built the temple of Ning̃irsu.
6) mu-dù	

20

A triangular plate from G̃irsu mentions Ur-Nanše's construction first of the temple of Ning̃irsu (likely the main commemoration of this inscription) and secondly of various other shrines.

COMMENTARY

The plate was found in excavations of de Sarzec: "à une distance à peu près égale entre la face sud-est du palais et le tell des piliers [the latter is Tell I]; elle se trouvait enfouie sous un massif plein, d'environ un mètre cinquante de hauteur sur deux mètres et deux mètres cinquante de côté, construit en briques au nom de Goudéa" (de Sarzec, Découvertes 1 p. 92). The AO number of this plaque is not known; the inscription was collated from the published photo.

In col. iii lines 9–10 the 70 gur_7 mentioned is a huge amount of grain. According to Powell (RLA 7 p. 497 § IV.4) 1 gur_7 at Lagaš = 6×6×4×3,600 sìla = 518,400 sìla; 70 gur_7 then would be equal to 3,628,800 sìla). A sìla is thought to be roughly equivalent to a litre. The purpose of this large amount of grain has been disputed by scholars. Steible and Behrens in (ASBW 2 p. 12 n. 2) suggest it was an annual prebend for the temple, following M. Lambert (RA 53 [1959] p. 152) who considered it "un versement annuel de 7 greniers." On the other hand, Sollberger and Kupper, IRSA, IC3e, considered it to refer to a cultic meal ("un repas rituel"), which was offered to the construction workers and the population. However, because of the huge amount of grain Selz (Untersuchungen p. 220 n. 1049) suggests that the sum in col. iii 7 might refer not just to grain for the temple of the god Ning̃irsu but rather to all the temples named in this inscription.

BIBLIOGRAPHY

1884–1912 de Sarzec, Découvertes 1 p. 92 (findspot); Découvertes 2 pl. 2 no. 1 (photo)
1907 Thureau-Dangin, SAK pp. 4–7 Ur-ninâ f (edition)
1929 Barton, RISA pp. 20–21 Ur-Nina 14 (edition)
1956 Sollberger, CIRPL p. xviii Urn. 34 (study); p. 5 Urn. 34 (copy)
1959 Lambert, RA 53 pp. 152–53 (study)
1980 Cooper, RA 74 pp. 102–3 no. 1 (photo, study)
1982 Steible, ASBW 1 pp. 99–101 Urnanše 34 (edition)
1986 Cooper, SARI 1 p. 28 La 1.20 (translation)

TEXT

Col. i
1) ur:^{d}nanše(^{d}nanše-ur)
2) lugal-
3) lagaš(NU_{11}.BUR.LA)
4) dumu gu-NI.DU
5) é-^{d}nin-g̃ír-su
6) mu-dù
7) ib-gal
8) mu-dù
9) é-^{d}nanše
10) mu-dù
Col. ii
1) ki-NIR
2) mu-dù
3) ba-gára
4) mu-dù
5) é-dam
6) mu-dù

i 1–3) Ur-Nanše, king of Lagaš,
i 4) son of Gu-NI.DU,
i 5–6) built the temple of the god Ning̃irsu.
i 7–8) He built the Ibgal ("Great Oval"),
i 9–10) built the temple of the goddess Nanše,
ii 1–2) built Ki-NIR,
ii 3–4) built the Bagara,
ii 5–6) built the E-dam,

7)	é-PA	ii 7–8) built the E-PA,
8)	mu-dù	
9)	šeš-g̃ar	ii 9–10) built Šešgar,
10)	mu-dù	
Col. iii		
1)	ti-ra-áš	iii 1–2) built Tiraš,
2)	mu-dù	
3)	é:^{d}gá:tùm:du$_{10}$(é-du$_{10}$-^{d}gá-tùm)	iii 3–4) built the temple of the goddess G̃atumdu,
4)	mu-dù	
5)	abzu(zu+ab)-e	iii 5–6) built "Great Abzu-e."
6)	mu-dù	
7)	u$_4$ é-^{d}nin-g̃ír-su	iii 7–8) When he built the temple of the god Ning̃irsu,
8)	mu-dù	
9)	70 gur$_7$ še	iii 9–10) he had 70 gur$_7$ (c. 3,628,800 litres) of barley distributed (as a prebend?) to be consumed by the temple (or temples?).
10)	é bi-kú	
Col. iv		
1)	má-dilmun	iv 1–3)) He had ships of Dilmun submit timber as tribute from the foreign lands (to Lagaš).
2)	kur-ta	
3)	gú-g̃iš mu-g̃ál	
4)	bàd-lagaš	iv 4–5) He built the wall of Lagaš,
5)	mu-dù	
6)	abzu(zu+ab)-bànda^{da}	iv 6–7) built Abzu-banda,
7)	mu-dù	
Col. v		
1)	^{d}nanše nin-uru$_{16}$	v 1–2) He formed (a statue of) the goddess Nanše, the powerful lady,
2)	mu-tu	
3)	a-sanga$_{X}$RÉC 107	v 3–4) dug the canal sanga$_{X}$(RÉC 107),
4)	mu-dun	
5)	a-sanga$_{X}$(RÉC 107) a [...]	v 5) [brought] water into the sanga$_{X}$(RÉC 107) canal.

21

A door socket from G̃irsu commemorates Ur-Nanše's construction of various temples.

COMMENTARY

The door socket, which measures 37 cm in height, with a diameter of 20 cm at the base and 25 cm at the top, and which in shape resembles a jar rather than a door socket, was found by de Sarzec in the SE corner of "Chambre A" in the "Maison de fruits" (see Parrot, Tello fig. 15 top no. 1). It now bears the museum number AO 31136. The inscription was collated.

BIBLIOGRAPHY

1884–1912 de Sarzec, Découvertes 2 p. XXXVI OUR-NINA 4 (copy)
1897 de Sarzec and Heuzey, RA 4 p. 97 fig. 5 (study, drawing); p. 122 no. 1 (copy)
1907 Thureau-Dangin, SAK pp. 6–7 Ur-ninâ k (edition)
1929 Barton, RISA pp. 18–19 Ur-Nina 8 (edition)
1948 Parrot, Tello p. 61 and fig. 15 (top) no. 1 (study, findspot)
1956 Sollberger, CIRPL p. viii Urn. 35 (study); p. 6 Urn. 35 (copy)
1982 Steible, ASBW 1 pp. 101–2 Urnanše 35 (edition)
1986 Cooper, SARI 1 p. 29 La 1.21 (translation)

TEXT

1)	^{d}nin-g̃ír-su	1) For the god Ning̃irsu,
2)	ur:^{d}nanše(^{d}nanše-ur)	2–4) Ur-Nanše, king of Lagaš,
3)	lugal-	
4)	lagaš(NU$_{11}$.BUR.LA)	
5)	dumu gu-NI.DU	5) son of Gu-NI.DU,
6)	u$_{4}$ èš-g̃ír-su	6–7) when he built the "Shrine-G̃irsu,"
7)	mu-dù	
8)	a mu-ru	8) he dedicated (this door socket).
9)	é-^{d}nanše	9–10) He built the temple of the goddess Nanše,
10)	mu-dù	
11)	ib:gal(gal-ib)	11–12) built the great Ibgal ("Great Oval"),
12)	mu-dù	
13)	ki-NIR	13–14) built Ki-NIR,
14)	mu-dù	
15)	ba-gára	15–16) built Bagara,
16)	mu-dù	
17)	é-dam	17–18) built the E-dam,
18)	mu-dù	
19)	é-^{d}g̃á-tùm-du$_{10}$	19–20) built the temple of the goddess G̃atumdu,
20)	mu-dù	
21)	ti-ra-⌈áš⌉	21–22) and built Tiraš.
22)	⌈mu⌉-dù	

22

A door socket from G̃irsu commemorates Ur-Nanše's building of various temples.

COMMENTARY

The door socket, which measures 28 cm in diameter, came from the "Maison des fruits" (see Parrot, Tello fig. 15 top no. 2). It now bears the museum number AO 252. The inscription was collated.

BIBLIOGRAPHY

1884–1912 de Sarzec, Découvertes 2 pl. 2ter no. 4 (photo)
1897 de Sarzec and Heuzey, RA 4 p. 98 fig. 6 (study, drawing)
1907 Thureau-Dangin, SAK pp. 6–7 Ur-ninâ l (edition)
1929 Barton, RISA pp. 20–21 Ur-Nina 12 (edition)
1948 Parrot, Tello p. 61 and fig. 15 (top) no. 2 (study, findspot)
1956 Sollberger, CIRPL p. viii Urn. 35 (study); p. 6 Urn. 35 (copy)
1962 Grégoire, Lagash pp. 4–5 (translation)
1963 Kramer, Sumerians p. 308 no. 6 (translation)
1982 Steible, ASBW 1 pp. 102–3 Urnanše 36 (edition)
1986 Cooper, SARI 1 p. 30 La 1.22 (translation)

TEXT

1)	ur:^{d}nanše(^{d}nanše-ur)	1–3) Ur-Nanše, king of Lagaš,
2)	lugal-	

3) lagaš(NU$_{11}$.BUR.LA)	
4) dumu gu-NI.DU	4) son of Gu-NI.DU,
5) dumu-gur-sar	5) (Gu-NI.DU was) "son" of Gursar,
6) é-^{d}nin-g̃ír-su	6–7) built the temple of the god Ning̃irsu,
7) mu-dù	
8) é-^{d}nanše	8–9) built the temple of the goddess Nanše,
9) mu-dù	
10) é:^{d}g̃á:tùm:du$_{10}$(é-gá-^{d}tùm-du$_{10}$)	10–11) built the temple of the goddess G̃atumdu,
11) mu-dù	
12) é-dam	12–13) built the E-dam,
13) mu-dù	
14) é-^{d}nin-MAR.KI	14–15) (and) built the temple of the god NinMAR.KI.
15) mu-dù	
16) má-dilmun	16–18) He had ships of Dilmun submit timber as. tribute from the foreign lands (to Lagaš)
17) kur-ta	
18) gú-g̃iš mu-g̃ál	
19) ib-gal	19–20) He built the Ibgal ("Great Oval"),
20) mu-dù	
21) ki-NIR	21–22) built the Ki-NIR,
22) mu-dù	
23) é-PA	23–24) (and) built the E-PA.
24) mu-dù	

23

An inscription on a door socket in Istanbul records various temple constructions of Ur-Nanše in G̃irsu.

COMMENTARY

The door socket, which measures 17 cm in height and 27.5 cm in diameter, bears the museum number EŞ 1299.

Parrot (Tello p. 61) lists three door sockets coming from the area of the "Maison des fruits." The first two have been identified with door sockets in the Louvre (inscriptions E1.9.1.21 and 22). While Parrot (p. 61) does not identify the present-day location of the third door-socket, it is very likely the one in Istanbul. If so, the Istanbul door-socket would have come from a point about 8.5 m east of "Chambre A" of the "Maison des fruits."

BIBLIOGRAPHY

1956 Sollberger, CIRPL p. viii Urn. 37 (study); p. 6 Urn. 37 (copy)

1948 Parrot, Tello p. 61 and fig. 15 no. 3(?) (study, findspot)

1982 Steible, ASBW 1 p. 104 Urnanše 37 (edition)

1986 Cooper, SARI 1 p. 30 La 1.23 (translation)

TEXT

1) ur:^{d}nanše(^{d}nanše-ur)	1–3) Ur-Nanše, king of Lagaš,
2) lugal-	
3) lagaš(NU$_{11}$.BUR.LA)	
4) dumu gu-NI.[DU]	4) Son of Gu-NI.DU,
5) dumu gu[r]-sar	5) (Gu-NI.DU was) "son" of Gursar,
6) é-^{d}nin-g̃ír-su	6–7) built the temple of the god Ning̃irsu,

7) mu-dù	
8) é-^{d}nanše	8–9) built the temple of the goddess Nanše,
9) mu-[d]ù	
10) šeš:g̃ar(gar-šeš)	10–11) built Šešgar,
11) mu-dù	
12) abzu(zu+ab)-bànda	12–13) built Abzu-banda,
13) mu-dù	
14) ba-gára	14–15) built the Bagara.
15) mu-dù	
16) má-dilmun	16–18) He had ships of Dilmun submit timber as tribute.
17) kur-ta	
18) gú-g̃iš m[u]-g̃á[l]	

24a

An inscription of Ur-Nanše dedicated to the god Ning̃irsu is found on a fragmentary lion figurine.

COMMENTARY

The green onyx figurine, of which only the front half survives, measures 10 cm in length and 8 cm in height; it was found at Tell K at G̃irsu, 10 m northeast of the "construction d'Urnanše" (de Sarzec, Découvertes 1 p. 35) in a door socket of En-metena. It bears the museum number AO 3281. The inscription was collated.

The su sign is preserved at the end of the DN Ning̃irsu in line 1; it is written below the g̃ír sign (and does not appear in Sollberger's copy). The beginning of the sign after the DIG̃IR in line 2 does not appear to be the beginning of a NANŠE sign, since it contains at least five horizontal lines. However, [ur]-^{d}nanše seems to be the only conceivable restoration.

BIBLIOGRAPHY

1884–1912 de Sarzec, Découvertes 2 pl. 6ter nos. 3a–b (photo)
1931 Contenau, Manuel 2 p. 583 fig. 388 (photo)
1940 Christian, Altertumskunde 1 pl. 260 nos. 5a–b (photo?)
1956 Sollberger, CIRPL p. viii Urn. 44 (study); p. 7 Urn. 44 (copy)
1980 Amiet, Art fig. 339 (photo)
1982 Steible, ASBW 1 p. 108 Urnanše 44 (edition)
1986 Cooper, SARI 1 p. 30 La 1.24 (translation [conflated with E1.9.1.24b])
1991 Braun-Holzinger, Weihgaben p. 324 T 1 (edition, study)

TEXT

1) ^{d}nin-g̃ír-su	1) For the god Ning̃irsu,
2) [ur]:^{d}na[nše](^{d}na[nše]-[ur]	2–4)[Ur]-Na[nše], [king] of Lag[aš],
3) [lugal]-	
4) lag[aš](NU$_{11}$.[BUR].LA)	
5) dumu gu-NI.[DU]	5) son of Gu-NI.D[U]
Lacuna(?)	Lacuna(?)

24b

A limestone lion figurine from G̃irsu bears an inscription of Ur-Nanše.

COMMENTARY

The lion figurine, which measures 9 cm in height, was found in excavations of de Sarzec at G̃irsu, in room B, pavement F, in Tell K near the "Construction de Ur-Nanshe." It bears the museum number AO 233. Another similar lion likely from the same findspot (see Parrot, Tello p. 84 and fig. 24c) was given the museum number AO 231. It apparently was not inscribed.

BIBLIOGRAPHY

1884–1912 de Sarzec, Découvertes 2 pl. 25bis no. 4 (photo)
1897 de Sarzec and Heuzey, RA 4 p. 105, fig. 10a (translation, drawing)
1900 Heuzey, Villa royale fig. 10a (drawing)
1948 Parrot, Tello pp. 61, 84 and fig. 21 b (study, drawing)
1956 Sollberger, CIRPL p. viii Urn. 45 (study); p. 7 Urn. 45 (copy)
1982 Steible, ASBW 1 p. 188 Urnanše 45 (edition)
1986 Cooper, SARI 1 p. 30 La 1.24 (edition [conflated with E1.9.1.24b])
1991 Braun-Holzinger, Weihgaben p. 324 T 2 (transliteration, study)

TEXT

1) ur-^{d}nanše 2) luga[l]- 3) laga[š](NU$_{11}$.BUR.L[A]	1–3) Ur-Nanše, kin[g] of Laga[š],
4) dumu g[u]-NI.[DU]	4) son of G[u]-NI.[DU]
Lacuna(?)	Lacuna(?)

25

A limestone lion figurine from G̃irsu bears part of an inscription of Ur-Nanše.

COMMENTARY

The limestone lion figurine, which measures 15.2×11.5×5 cm, was found in excavations of de Sarzec at G̃irsu. It bears the museum number EŞ 456.

BIBLIOGRAPHY

1897 de Sarzec and Heuzey, RA 4 p. 105, fig. 10b (drawing)
1956 Sollberger, CIRPL p. viii Urn. 46 (study); p. 7 Urn. 46 (copy)
1982 Steible, ASBW 1 p. 109 Urnanše 46 (edition)
1986 Cooper, SARI 1 p. 30 La 1.25 (translation)
1991 Braun-Holzinger, Weihgaben p. 324 T 3 (edition, study)

TEXT

Lacuna
1′) má-dilmun
2′) kur-ta
3′) gú-g̃iš [mu-g̃ál]
Lacuna(?)

Lacuna
1′–3′) had ships of Dilmun [submit] timber as tribute from the foreign lands (to Lagaš).

Lacuna(?)

26

Three very similar wall plaques of Ur-Nanše from G̃irsu depict an Anzu bird standing on two lions. The inscription on the first of these plaques (ex. 1) relates that Ur-Nanše built Tiraš. While only part of the titulary of Ur-Nanše is preserved on the other two plaques, they very likely bore the same or a similar inscription.

COMMENTARY

The site of Tiraš is unknown; for a possible site for the city, see the forthcoming article of the author on the geography of Lagaš province where a location at modern Šaṭrah is proposed.

The find of these plaques at G̃irsu is not evidence (as it might appear at first glance) for the location of Tiraš at G̃irsu. The pieces may have been fabricated at G̃irsu to be transported to Tiraš, or may be strays from Tiraš itself.

The é-gal-ti-ra-aš "'palace' of Tiraš" is mentioned in col i line 8 of the URU-KA-gina inscription edited as E1.9.9.5 in this volume; it appears as one of the settlements plundered by Lugal-zagesi.

CATALOGUE

Ex.	Museum number	Provenance	Dimensions (cm)	Sollberger, CIRPL no.	Lines preserved	cpn
1	AO 2783	Purchased in Baghdad	15×21×2.5	Urn.41	1–7	c
2	AO 49	Reused in the "palace" of Adad-nādin-aḫḫē in Tell A	16×12	Urn.42	2–5	c
3	EŞ 420	—	21×18	Urn.43	2–5	p

BIBLIOGRAPHY

1884–1912 de Sarzec, Découvertes 1 pp. 87–88 (ex. 2, study); p. 203 (ex. 3, study); Découvertes 2 pl. 1 no. 2 (ex. 2, photo)
1902 Heuzey, Catalogue Louvre pp. 92–95 no. 7 (ex. 1, translation, study, drawing); pp. 91–92 no. 6 (ex. 2, study)
1926 Unger RLV 7 pl. 137b (ex. 3, photo)
1926 Unger, SuAK p. 75 no. 7 (ex. 3, photo)
1931–32 Contenau, Revue des arts asiatiques 7 pl. XXa (ex. 1, study)
1934 Contenau, Monuments pp. 8–9 and pl. IV a (ex. 1, photo, study); pl. 276 no. 2 (ex. 1. photo); pl. 276 no. 3 (ex. 2, photo)
1948 Parrot, Tello p. 87 no. 1 (ex. 1, study); p. 87 no. 2 and fig. 22 c (ex. 2, study, drawing); p. 87 no. 3 (study)
1956 Sollberger, CIRPL p. viii Urn. 41 (exs. 1–3, study); p. 7 Urn. 41 (ex. 1, copy)
1971 Boese, Weihplatten pp. 196–97 T 1 and pl. XXVIII no. 1 (ex. 1, study, drawing); p. 197 T 2 and pl. XXVIII no. 2 (ex. 2, study, drawing); p. 197 T 3 and pl. XXVII no. 3 (ex. 3, drawing)
1982 Steible, ASBW 1 p. 106 Urnanše 41 (ex. 1, edition); p. 107 Urnanše 42 (ex. 2, edition); p. 107 Urnanše 43 (ex. 3, edition)
1986 Cooper, SARI 1 p. 30 La 1.26 (exs. 1–3, translation)

TEXT

1) ^{d}nin-g̃ír-su(Text: BA)
2) ur:^{d}nanše(^{d}nanše-ur)

1) For the god Ning̃irsu,
2–4) Ur-Nanše, king of Lagaš,

3)	lugal-	
4)	lagaš(NU_{11}.BUR.LA)	
5)	dumu gu-NI.DU	5) son of Gu-NI.DU,
6)	é-ti-ra-áš	6–7) built the E-Tiraš.
7)	mu-dù	

27

An onyx cup was dedicated to the goddess Baba by Ur-Nanše.

COMMENTARY

The cup, which measures 7.5 cm in height, with a rim diameter of c. 21 cm, was found 8 m from the "construction d'Urnanše" at a level 1.25 m below "le niveau inférieur d'Ur-Nanše" in the excavations of de Sarzec on Tell K at G̃irsu; it is marked in Parrot's plan (Tello, p. 62 fig. 15 top as no. 8) It bears the museum number EŞ 427. Its findspot may possibly give us a clue as to the location of the Baba temple within the sacred precinct at G̃irsu.

BIBLIOGRAPHY

1884–1912 de Sarzec, Découvertes 2 p. XXXVII OUR-NINA 11 (copy)
1897 de Sarzec and Heuzey, RA 4 p. 106 fig. 11 (study, drawing)
1907 Thureau-Dangin, SAK pp. 8–9 Ur-ninâ p (edition)
1929 Barton, RISA pp. 18–19 Ur-Nina 6 (edition)
1940 Christian, Altertumskunde pl. 186 no. 6 (photo)
1948 Parrot, Tello p. 62 fig. 15 no. 8 (findspot); p. 67 (study)
1956 Sollberger, CIRPL p. viii Urn. 47 (study); p. 7 Urn. 47 (copy)
1971 Sollberger and Kupper, IRSA IC3f (translation)
1976 Hallo and Donbaz, OrAnt 15 p. 8 (copy)
1982 Steible, ASBW 1 p. 109 Urnanše 47 (edition)
1986 Cooper, SARI 1 p. 31 La 1.27 (translation)
1991 Braun-Holzinger, Weihgaben p. 115 G 1 (edition, study)

TEXT

1)	^{d}ba-ba$_{6}$	1) To the goddess Baba,
2)	ur:^{d}nanše(^{d}nanše-ur)	2–4) Ur-Nanše, king of Lagaš,
3)	lugal-	
4)	lagaš	
5)	dumu gu-NI.DU	5) son of Gu-NI.DU,
6)	a mu-ru	6) dedicated (this cup).

28

A second vase fragment from G̃irsu was dedicated to the goddess Baba.

COMMENTARY

The dark, blue-grey vase, which has a preserved height of 3.5 cm, a width of 3.4 cm, and a thickness of 0.5 cm, was found in excavations of de Sarzec at Tello; its findspot is unknown. It bears the museum number EŞ 4811.

BIBLIOGRAPHY

1956 Sollberger, CIRPL p. viii Urn. 48 (study); p. 7 Urn. 48 (transliteration)
1982 Steible, ASBW 1 p. 110 Urnanše 48 (edition)
1986 Cooper, SARI 1 p. 31 La 1.28 (translation)
1991 Braun-Holzinger, Weihgaben p. 115 G 2 (edition, study)

TEXT

1) [^{d}ba]-ba$_{6}$	1) To the goddess [Ba]ba,
2) ur-[^{d}n]anše	2) Ur-[N]anše
Lacuna	Lacuna

29

A six-line brick inscription of Ur-Nanše deals with the construction of the E-TAR.

COMMENTARY

The brick was found in excavations of de Sarzec at G̃irsu; unfortunately, its findspot is unknown. It bears the museum number EŞ 1538.

It is likely that the temple name in line ii 1 (é-TAR) is to be connected with the E-TARsirsir temple of the goddess Baba in the holy precinct (uru-kù) at G̃irsu. The references to its building have been catalogued by George, House Most High p. 148 no. 1085 where he cites constructions by Ur-Nanše, URU-KA-gi-na and Gudea. Selz (Untersuchungen p. 26 no. 73) suggests a reading of the TAR element as sila. George (op. cit., p. 148 no. 1085) points out the reading é-tàra(DAR)-sir-sir in a *lipšur*-litany.

BIBLIOGRAPHY

1956 Sollberger, CIRPL p. 1 Urn. 18 (partial copy)
1982 Steible, ASBW 1 pp. 81–82 Ur-Nanše 18 (edition)
1986 Cooper, SARI 1 p. 31 La 1.29 (translation)

TEXT

Col. i	
1) ur:nanše(^{d}nanše-ur)	i 1–3) Ur-Nanše, king of Lagaš,
2) lugal	
3) lagaš(NU$_{11}$.BUR.LA)	
4) dumu gu-NI.DU	i 4) son of Gu-NI.DU,
Col. ii	
1) é-TAR	ii 1–2) built the E-TAR.
2) mu-dù	

30a

A six-line brick inscription records Ur-Nanše's construction of the Šeš-g̃ar temple.

COMMENTARY

The brick bears the museum number EŞ 8882.

A temple of Nanše apparently by the name Šeš-g̃ar is known for Girsu; see Selz, Untersuchungen p. 184 § 5 and n. 841; p. 211 § 120 Falkenstein, Inschriften Gudeas pp. 130–31. For its building history, see George House Most High p. 146 no. 1044 who notes that it was built by Ur-Nanše, given new doors by En-metena and later rebuilt by Šulgi, in the last case, under the name é-šeš-šeš-gá-ra/é-šeš-šeš-g̃ar (see RIME 3/1 pp. 118–120 E3/2.1.2.9–10). Šulgi's temple was apparently located on Tell L′. De Genouillac, in his description of the "Chantier IX" of the 1929–1930 season (RA 27 [1930] pp. 181–82), writes:

> À 350 mètres environ à l'ouest de la maison de la Mission, se trouvent deux petits tells: L et L′. Il semble que ce soit dans le plus considérable (L) que Sarzec, dans des sondages rayonnants, avait rencontré des cachettes de fondation avec dieux de bronzes et de pierres à texte votif. ... Une large exploration de la région S.-O. fit rencontrer partout un massif de briques crues, qui doit correspondre à un bastion de l'ancienne enceinte signalée par Sarzec et Cros. ... En gagnant encore plus vers l'est, les équipes rencontrent les murs des trois petits temples, dont briques et clous nous disent les constructeurs et les bénéficiaires: temple de Šulgi à Ninâ [Nanše] temples de Gudéa à Nindara et à Meslamtaéa.

The original provenance of this brick is not entirely certain. For the location of a GN Šešgar not far G̃irsu, see the forthcoming study of the author.

BIBLIOGRAPHY

1956 Sollberger, CIRPL p. viii Urn. 19 (study); p. 1 Urn. 19 (partial copy)
1982 Steible, ASBW 1 p. 82 Ur-Nanše 19 (edition)
1986 Cooper, SARI 1 p. 31 La 1.30 (translation)

TEXT

Col. i	
1) ur:^{d}nanše(^{d}nanše-ur)	i 1–3) Ur-Nanše, king of Lagaš,
2) lugal-	
3) lagaš(NU$_{11}$.BUR.LA)	
4) dumu gu-NI.DU	i 4) son of Gu-NI.DU,
Col. ii	
1) šeš-g̃ar	ii 1–2) built the Šeš-gar.
2) mu-dù	

30b

A six-line brick inscription records Ur-Nanše's construction of the E-PA.

COMMENTARY

The brick, which measures 29.5×19.5×6.5 cm, is of unknown provenance; it may have come from G̃irsu. Its museum number is UM 84-26-1.

BIBLIOGRAPHY

1984 Behrens, JCS 36 p. 101 (copy, edition)

TEXT

Col. i	
1) ur:^{d}nanše(^{d}nanše-ur)	i 1–3) Ur-Nanše, king of Lagaš,
2) lugal-	
3) lagaš(NU$_{11}$.BUR.LA)	
4) dumu-gu-NI.DU	i 4) son of Gu-NI.DU,
Col. ii	
1) é-PA	ii 1–2) built the E-PA.
2) mu-dù	

31

A stele fragment found at Ur deals with Ur-Nanše's digging of an irrigation channel.

COMMENTARY

The mottled red, black, and white granite stele fragment, which measures 25×25×12 cm, was found at Ur in the west corner of the temenos area under the Nebuchadnezzar floor and was given the excavation number U 17829. It bears the museum number IM 13246.

In connection with col. ii lines 1–2 Cooper (SARI 1 p. 32 n. 1 notes):

> There are two problems in this line: 1) Why is the verb "to build" (dù) used with a canal rather than Urnanshe's usual "to dig" (dun), and 2) what does Martu, if it is really there, mean in this context? Poorly attested in Presargonic contexts, the term in later periods refers to the Amorites, the land of the Amorites, or can simply mean the direction "west."

Which translation is correct here is uncertain; the possible reference (see E1.9.3.1) to E-anatum's Tidnum name would mean that the translation "Channel at the side of Sala (against) the Amorites" is conceivable.

In connection with the broken temple name in col. ii line 4, Cooper (SARI 1 p. 32 n. 2) notes:

> [The DN was] restored S[in] by Sollberger, Iraq 22 83f. If so, this would suggest temporary hegemony of Urnanshe at Ur, where this inscription was found, possibly as a result of the hostilities described in La 1.6 rev. But since this small stela (25 cm. high) was not found in a Presargonic context, but under a Neo-Babylonian floor (Sollberger op. cit. 74; Woolley, UE 4 46 and 196), and the Dasal-channel is in the Lagash area, the stela is probably commemorating the building of the temple of Ning̃irsu, and was brought to Ur from Lagash in antiquity, as was the Enmetena statue La 5.17, likewise found in a Neo-Babylonian context.

BIBLIOGRAPHY

1951 Basmachi, Sumer 7 pp. 58–60 (Arabic section) and pl. IV no. 2 (photo, study)
1955 Woolley, UE 4 p. 46 and pl. 39d (photo [of squeeze], study)
1956 Sollberger, CIRPL p. 6 no. 40 (copy)

1960 Sollberger, Iraq 22 pp. 73–74 and 83–84 (transliteration, study)
1968 Spycket, Statues p. 24 (study)
1980 Barrelet, JNES 29 pp. 236–37 § 1.1.3 and fig. 5c (study, drawing)
1982 Börker-Klähn, Bildstelen no. 15 (photo, study)
1982 Steible, ASBW 1 pp. 105–106 Urnanše 40 (edition)
1986 Cooper, SARI 1 p. 32 La 1.31 (translation)
1991 Braun-Holzinger, Weihgaben pp. 334–35 Stele 4 (edition, study)

TEXT

Col. i	
1) [u]r:^{d}nan[še](^{d}nan[še]-[u]r)	i 1–3) [U]r-Nan[še], ki[ng] of L[aga]š,
2) lu[ga]l	
3) l[aga]š (N[U$_{11}$.BUR.L]A)	
4) du[mu gu-NI.DU]	i 4) so[n of Gu-NI.DU]
5) dumu-gur-sar	i 5) (Gu-NI.DU was) "son" of Gursar,
Col. ii	
1) e-da-sa[la$_4$]-	ii 1–3) built the wester[n] channel at the side of Sa[la]/ channel at the side of S[al] (against) the Amorites
2) mar-d[ú]	
3) mu-dù	
4) é!-^{d}⌈x⌉ [x(?)]	ii 4) The temple of the god [DN]
Lacuna	Lacuna

32

A diorite plaque found in de Sarzec's excavations at G̃irsu (exact findspot unknown) is inscribed in cols. i–iii with "an incantation to ensure the efficacy of reeds used in a dedication ceremony" (Cooper SARI 1 p. 3) and a royal inscription for the construction of a temple. The inscription possibly deals with a structure located in the same general area as the later èš-gi-gù-na of Enmetena mentioned in inscriptions E1.9.5.8–11 (see Selz, Untersuchungen p. 119 § 2). Their findspots indicate that they came from a specific building in the area west of the platform of the "Maison des Fruits" in the southern area of the sacred temenos (uru-kù) at G̃irsu.

COMMENTARY

The plaque bears the museum number AO 3866. It was collated from the photo published by Cooper. For the cultic personnel ŠEŠ.IB at Ebla, possibly connected to the "shining ŠEŠ.IB" of iii 4, see Pettinato, OrAnt 18 (1979) pp. 113 and 20 and ibid., MEE 2 p. 120. It may have designated a kind of standard (Selz in RIM reader's notes). The text is unusual in that it describes the god rather than the city ruler carrying the work basket; the plaques of Ur-Nanše normally show the city ruler performing this task. However, this plaque bears no picture and may have been a draft for a royal inscription, as Cooper, RA 74 (1980) p. 104 suggests. Cooper notes Jacobsen's comment that "evidence of a ruler's personal god participating alongside the ruler in the building of a temple" is found on Gudea Cylinder A col. xxx.

In iii 6 the GIŠ.BUR could refer either to a GIŠ.bu$_{10}$ = kippatu "loop" (Civil) or a giš-búr = *gišbúrru* "king of magicians wand" (Green).

BIBLIOGRAPHY

1884–1912 de Sarzec, Découvertes 2 p. XXXVII OUR-NINA 10 (copy)
1907 Thureau-Dangin, SAK pp. 6–7 Ur-ninâ h (edition)
1908 Toscanne, RT 30 pp. 124–28 (copy, edition)
1929 Barton, RISA pp. 22–23 Time of Ur-Nina 1 (edition)
1931–32 Witzel, AfO 7 pp. 33–36 (edition, study)
1932–33 Gustavs, AfO 8 pp. 58–59 (study)
1943 Jacobsen, JNES 2 pp. 117–18 no. II (study)
1951 Sollberger, RA 45 pp. 108–10 (edition, study)
1953 Lambert, RA 53 pp. 152 (edition, study)

1956 Sollberger, CIRPL 1 p. 7 Urn. 49 (copy)
1967 Civil, JNES 26 p. 211 (study)
1969 Jestin, RA 63 pp. 115–19 (study)
1976 Hruška, ArOr 44 pp. 353–60 (edition, study)
1980 Cooper, RA 74 pp. 103–104 no. 2 (photo, study)
1982 Steible, ASBW 1 pp. 110–11 Urnanše 49 (edition);
1986 Cooper, SARI 1 pp. 32–33 La 1.32 (translation)

TEXT

Col. i
1) gi-kù
2) gi giš:gi:engur(engur-giš-gi)
3) gi pa-zu$_5$
4) su$_4$-su$_4$
5) úr-zu$_5$
Col. ii
1) ^{d}en-ki
2) ki-buru$_5$ gál
3) pa-zu$_5$
4) u$_4$ šù[d](K[A]×ŠU) mu-⸢rá⸣
5) su$_6$(KA×KID-*tenû*)-zu$_5$
6) za:gìn(gìn-za)
7) gi kur:šùba(šùba-kur)-DU
8) gi en-ki nun-ki
9) du$_{10}$ ḫé-gá-gá
Col. iii
1) ^{d}en-ki
2) éš-bar-kin
3) ḫé-e
4) ŠEŠ(LAK 32).IB k[ù](?)-⸢ge⸣
5) zà-me-bi
6) ^{d}en-ki giš-bu$_{10}$
7) šè-šub
8) ^{d}nin-g̃ír-sú
9) zà-me
Col. iv
1) ^{d}šul-MUŠ×PA
2) dig̃ir-lugal
3) dusu-kù
4) e-íl
5) ur:^{d}nanše(^{d}nanše-ur)
6) lugal-
7) lagaš(NU$_{11}$.BUR.LA)
8) dumu gu-NI.DU
9) dumu-gur-sar
Col. v
1) èš-g̃ír-su
2) m[u]-dù

i 1) O shining reed!
i 2) O reed of the canebrake of the fresh water source!
i 3–4) O reed, you whose branches grow luxuriantly.
i 5–ii 2) After the god Enki set your roots in the (post) hole,
ii 3–4) your branches greet the day (or the sun god).
ii 5–6) Your "beard" (is made of) of lapis-lazuli.
ii 7) O reed that comes forth (from) the shining mountain,
ii 8–9) O reed, may the Earth lords and the Earth princes bow down (before you).
iii 1–3) May the god Enki pronounce a (favourable) omen (for your construction).
iii 4–5) Its shining renowned standard(?)
iii 6–7) The god Enki cast it (with?) his (magic) loop.
iii 8–9) Praise (be to) Nin̄girsu!
iv 1–4) Šul-MUŠ×PA, the personal god of the king, carried the shining work basket.
iv 5–v 2) Ur-Nanše, king of Lagaš, son of Gu-NI.DU, (Gu-NI.DU was) "son" of Gursar, built the "Shrine-G̃irsu."

33

A vase fragment from G̃irsu gives part of a dedicatory inscription of Ur-Nanše to the god Nin̄girsu.

COMMENTARY

The museum number was probably inscribed on a now missing fragment of this vase.

BIBLIOGRAPHY

1976 Donbaz and Hallo, OrAnt 15 p. 3 no. IV and p. 8 (copy, edition, study)

1982 Steible, ASBW 1 p. 117 Urnanše 52 (edition)

1991 Braun-Holzinger, Weihgaben p. 115 G 3 (edition, study)

TEXT

1) [^{d}ni]n-g̃ír:su
2) ur-[^{d}nanš]e
Lacuna

1) To the god Ning̃irsu,
2) Ur-[Nanš]e
Lacuna

A-kurgal

E1.9.2

One of Ur-Nanše's sons, A-kurgal, is mentioned in all four "family plaques" dated to the time of Ur-Nanše (see inscriptions E1.9.1.2–5). He apparently followed his father as city ruler of Lagaš. The scarcity of inscriptions from his reign suggests that he ruled for a short time. The name likely means "The father (is) the great mountain."

1

An eight-line inscription on a gypsum (or alabaster?) lion figurine records A-kurgal's construction of the Antasur.

COMMENTARY

The lion figurine, which measures 9×17 cm, was found in excavations of de Sarzec in 1900 on the "Tell-des-Tablettes." It bears the museum number AO 3295.

For the toponym an-ta-sur we may note the comments of Selz, Untersuchungen p. 227 n. 1103, who notes that the translation "descended from heaven" suggested by Falkenstein (Inschriften Gudeas p. 164) is unlikely. He notes that it may be related to sur "delimit a boundary" as an ellipsis for ki-sur, from which one might see an-ta-sur-ra as a temple name alluding its location on the border of Lagaš. He cites in this connection R. Englund, JESHO 31 (1988) 165 for sur with the meaning to "separate, divide." This agrees with the author's tentative location (in a forthcoming article) of an-ta-sur on the northern boundary of Lagaš province.

BIBLIOGRAPHY

1884–1912 de Sarzec, Découvertes 1 pp. 351–52 (translation, study); Découvertes 2 p. LIV AKOURGAL (copy)
1902 Heuzey, Catalogue Louvre p. 263 no. 115 (study)
1948 Parrot, Tello p. 86 (study)
1956 Sollberger, CIRPL p. ix Akg. 1 (study); p. 8 Akg. 1 (copy)
1971 Sollberger and Kupper, IRSA IC4a (translation)
1982 Steible, ASBW 1 p. 118 Akurgal 1 (edition)
1985 Bauer, AoN 21 p. 5 (study)
1986 Cooper, SARI 1 p. 33 La 2.1 (translation)
1991 Braun-Holzinger, Weihgaben p. 324 T 4 (edition, study)

TEXT

1) [^{d}n]in-g̃ír-su	1) For the god [N]ing̃irsu,
2) ⸢a-kur⸣-gal	2–4) A-kurgal, r[u]ler of Lagaš,
3) é[n]si-	
4) [la]gaš.[KI]	
5) du[m]u-ur-⸢^{d}⸣nanše	5) s[o]n of Ur-Nanše,
6) l[ugal-la]gaš.KI	6) k[ing of La]gaš,
7) [an]-ta-sur	7–8) [b]uilt the [An]tasur.
8) [m]u-dù	

2a

Another gypsum lion figure bears only the last line of a building inscription of A-kurgal. It may have been a duplicate of A-kurgal inscription 1.

COMMENTARY

The lion figurine was found in excavations of de Sarzec at Girsu. It bears the museum number EŞ 458.

BIBLIOGRAPHY

1926 Unger, SuAK p. 80 no. 15 (photo)
1956 Sollberger, CIRPL p. ix Akg. 2 (study); p. 8 Akg. 2 (transliteration)
1982 Steible, ASBW 1 p. 118 Akurgal 2 (edition)
1986 Cooper, SARI 1 p. 33 La 2.1 n. 1 (study)

TEXT

Lacuna
1′) mu-dù

Lacuna
1′) built the [...]

2b

Three gypsum lions from Girsu similar in shape to A-kurgal 1 and 2a bear no traces of their original inscription.

CATALOGUE

Ex	Museum number	CIRPL reference	cpn
1	EŞ 485	p. 8 Akg. 3	n
2	EŞ 486	p. 8 Akg. 4	n
3	EŞ 487	p. 8 Akg. 5	n

BIBLIOGRAPHY

1956 Sollberger, CIRPL p. 8 Akg. 3–6 (study)
1982 Steible, ASBW 1 p. 119 Akurgal 4–6 (study)

3

A brick found in excavations at al-Hibā mentions, in a restored text, the name and title of A-kurgal.

COMMENTARY

The brick was found on the surface of area B at al-Hibā during the third season of excavations (1972–73) and given the excavation number 3H–T13.

BIBLIOGRAPHY

1974 Crawford, Iraq 36 p. 34 fig. 14 and p. 35 n. 17 (copy, study)

1982 Steible, ASBW 1 p. 199 Akurgal 7 (edition)

TEXT

1′) [a-kur]-gal
2′) [é]nsi-
3′) lagaš.KI

1′–3′) [A-kur]gal, [r]uler of Lagaš.

E-anatum

E1.9.3

A-kurgal was succeeded by his son E-anatum. While the length of his reign is unknown, the relatively large number of his inscriptions suggests he reigned for a long time. Sollberger, Système verbal p. ix (followed by Nissen Königshof p. 122) suggests a reign of about 30 years. Unfortunately, we have no historical synchronisms for the ruler, nor does his name appear in the SKL.

Since the practice of dating by year names was not used by E-anatum (or the other Presargonic rulers of Lagaš) a chronological ordering of the events of his reign based on a date list is impossible; a history of his reign must be based on internal evidence alone. A sequence of the major events based on the military campaigns mentioned in the inscriptions was first given by Poebel in his article "The Events of Eannadu's Reign," PBS IV/1 pp. 159–69; cf. ibid., Studies Haupt p. 245 and Weissbach RLA 2 p. 261. Jacobsen, on the other hand (JNES 52 [1957] p. 130 n. 90), attempted to place the inscriptions in order based on the extant royal epithets. Further historical reconstructions have been given by Cooper in SANE 2/1 (1983) pp. 24–28 and Steiner in ASJ 8 (1986) pp. 241–42 § 4.5. Most recently, Selz has given an excellent overview of the chronology of the reign in CRRA 36 pp. 33–36 §§ 15–29.

E-anatum's inscriptions speak of a defeat of (a coalition of?) kings of the states of Kiš, Akšak, and Mari at a place named Antasur, likely on the northern border of G̃irsu province. One royal inscription mentions the king of Akšak by name, a certain Zuzu, who, unfortunately, is not mentioned in the extant section of the SKL dealing with Akšak.

Also recorded in the E-anatum's inscriptions are campaigns directed against Uruk and Ur, but in this case, the enemy kings are not specified by name.

Other texts speak of attacks on the Elamite cities of Uruaz, Mišime, Arawa and Arua; E-anatum's goal in these wars most likely was to secure the eastern trade routes in Elam. While E-anatum waged far-flung campaigns, we have no evidence that he actually expanded the territory of Lagaš as we know was the case for En-metena.

While he was not recognized as such in the SKL, the historical data suggest that E-anatum was a preeminent ruler in Sumer. A mark of his high status has been seen by some scholars (cf. Jacobsen, SKL p. 99 n. 168) in the appearance of a divine LUM-ma (for the equation LUM-ma = E-anatum, see the discussion below) in Tablet I entry 188 of the god list An:*Anum* (Litke Reconstruction p. 42; LUM-ma is found in the fragment assigned by Weidner to the Ur III or Isin period). However, the fact that the god LUM-ma appears already in the Fāra god lists would suggest that this deity predates the reign of E-anatum of Lagaš. In An:*Anum* LUM-ma is followed by the god Ḫataniš who, as Jacobsen (SKL p. 98) pointed out, is to be connected with the royal name Ḫataniš found in the SKL as an ED period king of Ḫamazi. LUM-ma appears in the "smaller An:Anum" King, CT 25 pl. 28 = Bu. 89-4-26, 77 line 3′ as ^{d}LUM-ba. A reading of the divine name as ^{d}ḫum-ba could conceivably be connected with the Elamite god Ḫumban; for the deity see Hinz and Koch, Wörterbuch p. 715 sub hu-um-ba.

E-anatum is noteworthy in having two names, his personal name (mu-ú-rum) E-anatum and his "battle name" (mu-GÌR.GÌR) or "Tidnum name" (mu-tidnu) LUM-ma. For the extensive bibliographical literature on the complex question of the two names see Bauer, RLA 7 3/4 (1988) p. 169, to which the article by Kobayashi entitled "Miscellaneous Notes on LUM-ma," BAOM 9 (1987) pp. 17–36 and Selz, Untersuchungen pp. 171–72 may be added. Further, one scholar, L. Curchin (RA 71 [1977] pp. 94–95), has argued that the LUM-ma who appears in Presargonic inscriptions from Adab may refer to the same ruler. A lengthy discussion of the question of the two names of E-anatum is beyond the scope of the present volume.

E-anatum's name has often been explained as a shortened form of the (ritual?) name ^{d}inanna-⌈ib-gal⌉-ka-ka-a-túm found in E1.9.3.1 iv 21–22. On this name see Steiner, WO 8 (1975–76) p. 19 and n. 43 where an extensive bibliography of the discussion of the question is given. However, Selz (in RIM reader's notes) suggests that the long name is likely only a scholarly elaboration and that E-anatum's name is probably simply to be understood as é-anatum with the element ana- to be taken as a verbal prefix chain. If he be correct, then the PN originally need not have had anything to do with the E-anna temple. There will likely be considerable scholarly debate on Selz's proposal; for the time being it has been adopted here (with reserve).

Without doubt the most impressive monument left by E-anatum is a huge limestone stele that he had erected in the sacred city quarter of G̃irsu to commemorate his victory over the ruler of the neighbouring city-state of G̃iša (Umma) (E1.9.5.1). The monolith is known today as the "Stele of the Vultures" because of its depiction of a flock of vultures devouring the corpses of his enemies slain in battle. While the preserved portion of the stele names E-anatum's foe simply as "the man of G̃iša (Umma)" a later inscription of En-metena, E-anatum's nephew, reveals his name to be Uš (or G̃iš).

1

A huge limestone stele from G̃irsu commemorates E-anatum's victory over the neighbouring city-state of G̃iša (Umma).

COMMENTARY

The extant portion of the monument measures 180 cm in height and 130 cm in width, with a thickness of 11 cm. The stele is reconstructed by the joining of several pieces; for the details see figure 1. Fragments A and C were found on Tell K in a trench between Tells I and I′. Fragment B had been re-used in the "palace" of Adad-nādin-aḫḫē. Fragments D, E, and F were found in the vicinity of the "construction inférieure." Fragment G was acquired by the British Museum in 1898 and accessioned under the museum number BM 23580; in 1932 it was ceded to the Louvre and given the museum number AO 16109.

For the reading of col. xiv line 1, see Bauer, BiOr 46 (1989) p. 639.

In col. i line 23, for še-gub-ba, "grain tax," see Grégoire, Archives p. 144 to no. 97; Maekawa, Zinbun 14 (1977) pp. 1–51; and Steinkeller, JESHO 26 (1981) pp. 115–45.

In col. ii line 25, šu-ur$_6$ is likely a syllabic writing for šúr = *ezzu* "angry"; see Bauer WO 8 (1975–76) p. 5 n. 29.

In col. ii lines 23–31, the complaint of the lion to Ning̃irsu about the abuses of the king of G̃iša (Umma) is reminiscent of the complaint of Šarur, the vizier and mace of the god Ninurta, about the attack of the Asakku demon found in the literary composition Lugal-e.

In col. iii line 23 the lion referred to could well be one of the beasts pulling the god Ningirsu's chariot (as suggested by Selz in RIM readers' notes); while the animals pulling the chariot are not preserved in the extant portion of the stele, a lion figure does appear on the rein ring of the chariot.

In col. iii line 24 the procession way (in G̃irsu) presumably ran through the town of G̃irnun, a settlement located not far to the east of G̃irsu (see Frayne, forthcoming); the highway is known from other texts to be the eastern road that led to Elam.

In col. iii line 27, for the reading KA.KID-a mu-NI-tak$_4$, see Cooper, SARI 1 p. 38 n. 3 who following Steible ASBW 1 p. 30 notes Sjöberg's equation with Akkadian *tēkītu(m)* "complaint."

In col. iii line 29, for ú-durun$_x$(DÚR.DÚR), see Bauer, AWL p. 281 note to no. 90 I 1.

In col. iv line 8, [na]-e is restored based on the apparent parallel in v 22 kur a-ne-šè na-e "the foreign land truly (belongs) to him"; see Steible, ASBW 2 p. 32 n. 17.

In col. iv lines 10–12 the restoration follows the apparent parallel in col. v lines 2–3 a-šà-ga-du$_{11}$-ga-^{d}nin-g̃ír-su-ka-da.

In col. v line 7, for zipaḫ(ŠU.BAD) "(open) hand span" see most recently Powell, RLA 7 pp. 461–62 § I.2.d. The passage would indicate that E-anatum was a towering man of c. 2.5 metres height. He paled in comparison with Ning̃irsu's gigantic height. On the interpretation of this passage see Jacobsen, in Kramer Anniversary p. 252 n. 19 and Powell RLA 7 p. 462 §I.2.d.

In col. v line 14, for the construction nam-gal-ḫúl-la-da see Edzard in Studies Falkenstein p. 51 § 6.1.

In col. vii line 4 for ze$_x$ (ÁB.ŠA)-ge, note the remark of Krecher in ASJ 9 (1987) p. 85 n. 4: "AB.ŠÀ.GI is but a curious syllabic sign to be read ze$_x$, as could have been concluded ever since from the variant ḫa-NI-gaz-e on the duplicate Ent. 28." The expression is also found in Biggs, BibMes 3 no. 26 obv. iii i$_7$-bi en-ze$_x$ (ÁB×ŠÀ)-⸢ge⸣ nu-DU; see Bauer, BiOr 36 (1979) p. 46.

For col. vii line 22, ul$_4$-ḫé, see Sjöberg TCS 3 p. 115 commentary to line 324, where he notes the variant ul-ḫé-a for ul$_4$-ḫé = *šupuk šamê,* establishing the value for ul$_4$ for GÍR in this compound, and the variant giš-he for giš-ḫé = *šupuk šamê* establishing the value ḫé for GAN. Sjöberg, op. cit. translates *šupuk šamê* as "vault of heaven"; von Soden (AHw p. 1280) gives "foundation of heaven" ("Himmelsgründung"). See also Steiner, ASJ 8 (1985–6) p. 62 n. 62 for this passage.

In col. viii line 4, for the reading of LÁL×NÍGIN see Powell, Orientalia NS 43 (1974) pp. 399–402 and Steinkeller, Sale Documents pp. 169 n, 4 and 242 n. 14. The sign following LÁL×NÍGIN is worn; it might be ki or du$_{10}$. Selz (in RIM readers' notes) suggests it might be a personal name.

In vii 10 the meaning of NE.⸢GI⸣.DU.ÚS is obscure. Jacobsen, in Kramer Anniversary p. 253 n. 28, guessed at a meaning "diadem." Sollberger, IRSA p. 49, gave "bandeau royal(?)." A comparison of NE.⸢GI⸣ with ^{d}BIL.GI = ^{d}girra "Fire (god)" or an understanding of it as a phonetic writing of g̃íbil = *qilûtu* "burning" has suggested our translation "blazing(?) ..."

In col. ix line 1, for giš-urbingu(UR.UR)-e e-da-lá, see Sjöberg ZA 63 (1973) p. 12 to line 59.

In col. xii line 21, Selz (in RIM readers' notes) points out that the é-maḫ as a proper name is attested so far only as sanctuary of Nanše in the Lagaš texts.

For the field names in col. xv, we may note Steible's remark (ASBW 2 p. 48 n. 65) that they likely belonged to the area of the Guʾeden named in both royal inscriptions and economic texts from Lagaš and G̃iša (Umma). Selz's particular restorations in Untersuchungen pp. 244–45 however are unlikely in view of the fact that the geographical names he compares them to can be shown by other texts to lie in an area SE of G̃irsu (as shown by the author in a forthcoming study).

For the reading of col. obv. xvi line 25, see Steinkeller, ZA 71 (1981) p. 24 n. 10.

We have followed Winter (ZA 76 [1986] pp. 205–12) in taking what was previously understood to be "Cartouche C" giving the name of a king of Kiš, rather as the end section of a curse formula in rev. col. xii.

BIBLIOGRAPHY

1884 Heuzey, Gazette archéologique pp. 164–80, 193–203 (study); pls. 24, 26

1884–1912 de Sarzec, Découvertes 1 pp. 36, 68, 94–103, 174–96, study), p. 195 (frgm. D, obv., photo); Découvertes 2 pls. 3, 3bis, 4, bis, 4ter, 48, 48bis (photo); pp. XXXVIII–XLII (copy)

1884 Perrot and Chipiez, Chaldée et Assyrie 2 pp. 590 ff. (study); figs. 283–85 (frgms. A, F rev., frgm. B obv., drawing)

1888 Babelon, Manuel pp. 35 ff. (study) and figs. 11–13 (frgms. A, F rev., frgm. B obv.)

1888 Hommel, Geschichte pp. 288–89 (study)

1892 Heuzey, CRAIB pp. 262–74 (study)

1895 Maspero, Histoire 1 pp. 606–67 (frgms. A, B, C, E, rev., drawing)

1897 Thureau-Dangin, CRAIB pp. 240 (study)

1899 King, CT 7 pls. 1–2 (frgm. G, photo, copy)

1902 Heuzey, Catalogue Louvre pp. 101–17 no. 10 (A, B, C, D, E, F obv., B, D, E obv., drawing, study)

1907 Thureau-Dangin, SAK pp. 10–21 E-an-na-tum a (edition)

1909 Pancritius, Memnon 2/3 pp. 155 ff. pl. 1 (D, E, rev., study), pl. 2 (F, rev. and edge, study)

1909 Heuzey and Thureau-Dangin, Restitution pls. I–II (photo); pls. III–IV (copy); pp. 42–63 (edition)

1910 Poebel, OLZ 13 cols. 197–99 (study [review of Thureau-Dangin and Heuzey, Restitution])

1915 Meissner, AO 15 figs. 18–21 (obv., A, D, E rev., photo)

1915 Weber, Amtl. Ber. 36/6 cols. 115, 117, 119 and fig. 46 B obv. (study)

1923 King, Early History p. 131 fig. 46 (frgms. D, E, rev., drawing); p. 140 fig. 47 (frgm. F rev., drawing); p. 141 fig. 48 (frgms. C, F, rev., drawing), pl. after p. 124 (frgms. D, E, obv., photo), pl. after p. 138 (frgm. F, obv., photo)

1925 Poebel, ZA 36 pp. 1–9 (study)

1926 Unger, SuAK pp. 31–32 (study), figs. 20–21 (obv., rev., photo) pl. 11, no. 32 (rev. and edge), pl. 12 no. 33 (frgms. D, E, obv.), pl. 12 no. 34 (frgms. C, G, F, rev.)

1927 Contenau, Manuel 1 p. 96 fig. 44 (D, E obv, photo); p. 465 fig. 351 (obv., photo); p. 469 fig. 352 (rev., photo)
1928–29 Meissner, AfO 5 pl. 2 no. 4 (D, E, rev., photo)
1929 Barton, RISA pp. 22–33 Eannatum 1 (edition)
1929 Jeremias, HAOG^2 pp. 66–67 (obv., rev., photo, study)
1935 Moortgat, MVAG 40/3 pp. 14–15 no. 14 (study); pl. 13 (D, rev., photo)
1935 Schäfer and Andrae, Kunst, pls. 456–57 (D, E, rev., photo)
1935 Zervos, L'art pp. 106–12 (excerpts, photo)
1935 Zervos, Encyclopédie 1 pls. 190–94 (obv., rev., edge; frgms. D, E, B, F, obv., frgms. D, E, C, G, F, A rev., photo)
1940 Christian, Altertumskunde 1 pls. 265–66 (obv., rev., photo)
1943 Jacobsen, JNES 2 pp. 119–21 (study)
1946 Jacobsen, JNES 5 p. 135 n. 12 (study)
1947 Contenau, Manuel 4 p. 1778 fig. 1006 (D, edge, photo)
1948 Parrot, Tello p. 62 fig. 15 nos. 9–11 (D, E, F, obv. and rev., drawing); pp. 95–101 (study); p. 98 fig. 23 (obv., rev., drawing)
1951 Groenewegen- Frankfort, Arrest and Movement pp. 154 and 164, n. 2 (study)
1951 Sollberger, RA 45 pp. 110–11 § III (partial edition [v 20–vi 7])
1952 Speiser, Vorderasiatische Kunst pl. 18 (rev., photo)
1953 Kramer, IEJ 3 p. 13 (D, E, rev., photo)
1954 Frankfort, Art and Architecture pp. 33–35 (study); pls. 34–35 (obv., side, and rev., photo)
1956 Sollberger, CIRPL p. ix Ean. 1 (study); pp. 9–16 Ean. 1 (copy)
1957 Perkins, AJA 61 pp. 57ff. and pl. 18 nos. 8–9 (obv., rev., edge, study, photo)
1961 Parrot, Sumer, pp. 134–37 (study); figs. 163–66 (photo [detail])
1961 Moscati, AA NL 358 p. 77 (xxx); pls. 14–15 (frgms. D, E, A, C, G, F rev., photo)
1961 Potratz, Kunst pp. 95ff. (study); pl. 18 (edge, photo)
1962 Strommenger and Hirmer, Mesopotamien pls. 66–69 (A, D, E, rev., photo)
1963 Kramer, Sumerians, pp. 310–13 § C 11 (partial translation)
1963 Schmökel, Funde pp. 81ff. (study); pl. 10 (A rev., photo)
1964 Falkner in RLA 3/3 p. 194 ([archaeological] study)
1964 Sollberger in RLA 3/3 pp. 194–95 ([historical] study)
1965 Lambert, RA 59 p. 136 (study)
1967 Moortgat, Kunst pp. 42–43, 52 (study); pls. 118–21 (obv. and rev. frgms. D, E, A, C, G photo)
1970 Barrelet, JNES 29 pp. 233–58 (study); pl. 14 (A, B, C obv and rev.), pl. 15 (D, E, F, G, obv. and rev., photo); pl. 16 (obv., rev., photo); figs. 10a, 10b, 12, 13, 15, drawing [reconstruction])
1971 Hrouda, Vorderasien I p. 123 (study); pls. 47a–b (rev., obv., photo)
1971 Sollberger and Kupper, IRSA IC5a (translation)
1973 Littauer and Crouwel, JNES 32 pp. 324–29 (study [of chariot designs])
1975 Orthmann (ed.), Der alte Orient figs. 89b (E, rev., photo); figs. 90–91 (obv., rev., photo)
1976 Edzar, in Studies Jacobsen pp. 64–68 (partial edition, study)
1976 Jacobse, in Kramer Anniversary pp. 247–59 (partial edition, study)
1980 Amiet, Art fig. 328 (D, E, rev., photo); figs. 329–30 (obv., rev., photo)
1982 Börker-Klähn, Bildstelen pp. 124–25 no. 17 (study); fig. 17a (arrangement of pieces); 17b–d (obv., rev., edge, photo)
1982 Steible, ASBW 1 pp. 120–45 E'annatum 1 (edition)
1983 Cooper, SANE 2 pp. 13–14, 25–27 and 45–47 no. 2 (translation, study)
1983 Krispijn, in Veenhof (ed.), Schrijvend verleden pp. 1–7 (translation [into Dutch])
1984 Römer, in Borger, et al., TUAT 1 pp. 297–308 (translation)
1986 Cooper, SARI 1 pp. 33–39 La 3.1 (translation)
1986 Steiner, ASJ 8 pp. 219–300 (passim) (study)
1986 Steiner, in CRRA 32 pp. 33–44 (study)
1986 Winter, ZA 76 pp. 205–212 (study); figs. 1–4 (photos)

TEXT

Col. i	
Lacuna of 20 lines	Lacuna of 20 lines
21) [...]-⌜ré⌝ [š]uku-bi	i 21–24) He would pay it as an (interest-bearing) [lo]an, and grain rent was imposed on it.
22) ⌜e⌝-lá	
23) [š]e-gub-ba-bi	
24) ba-DU	
25) lugal-	i 25–26) The king of Lagaš
26) lagaš(NU$_{11}$.BUR.LA).KI	
Lacuna	Lacuna
Col. ii	
Lacuna of 21 lines	Lacuna of 21 lines
22) [bar-...]	ii 22–23) ...
23) [... Ḫ]I-a-ka	
24) lú-^{ĝiš}KÚŠU.KI-ke$_4$	ii 24–29) The leader of G̃iša (Umma) acted *arrogantly* with him, and defied Lagaš.
25) šu-ur$_6$-rá	
26) e-ma-da-du$_{11}$	
27) lagaš(NU$_{11}$.BUR.LA).KI	
28) gaba-bé	
29) šu e-ma-ús	
30) a-kur-gal	ii 30–33) A-kurgal, king of Lagaš, son of Ur-Nanše,
32) lagaš(NU$_{11}$.BUR.LA).KI	
33) dumu-ur-^{d}nanše	

Col. iii
1) [lugal]
2) [lagaš(NU$_{11}$.BUR.LA).KI-ka-ke$_4$]

iii 1–2) [king of Lagaš]

Lacuna of 13 lines

Lacuna of 13 lines

16) [lú-$^{\tilde{g}iš}$KÚŠU.KI-ke$_4$]
17) [šu-ur$_6$-rá]
18) ⸢e⸣-m[a-da-du$_{11}$]
19) lagaš(NU$_{11}$.BUR.LA).KI
20) bar-nì-ní-ba-ka-ka
21) gaba-bé
22) šu e-ga-ma-ús

iii 16–22) [the leader of G̃iša (Umma) acted *arrogantly* with him] and defied Lagaš regarding its (Lagaš's) own property.

23) pirig̃-ZÀ(?)-[(x)]-
24) g̃ír-⸢nun⸣-šà-ga-ke$_4$
25) ^{d}nin-g̃ír-sú-⸢ke$_4$⸣
26) KA-na
27) KA.KID-a mu-ni-tak$_4$

iii 23–27) At/regarding Pirig̃-... g̃irnun-šage, the god Niñgirsu roared:

28) $^{g̃iš}$KÚŠU.KI
29) ⸢ú⸣-durun$_x$(DÚR.DÚR)-[n]a-mu
30) [n]ì-ní-gá
31) [a-š]àGÁNA

Col. iv
1) [g]ú-[ede]n-na-[k]a
2) [lag]aš([NU$_{11}$.BUR.L]A.)KI
3) [...]-⸢bi⸣ ⸢x⸣-[(x)]-le

iii 28 – iv 3) "G̃iša (Umma) has ... my forage, my own property, the fields of the G[u'ede]na ... [Lag]aš"

4) [e]n(?) ^{d}[ni]n-g̃ír-sú
5) [ur-s]ag̃-[^{d}en]-líl-lá]
6) [....-g]a
7) [...]
8) [na]-⸢e⸣

iv 4–8) [Lor]d(?) [Ni]ng̃irsu, [war]rior of [the god En]lil says ... .

9) [^{d}ni]n-[g̃ír]-sú-[k]e$_4$
10) [a]-⸢é⸣-[an]-na-túm-[ma]
11) [šà-g]a
12) [šu b]a-ni-du$_{11}$

iv 9–12) [The god Ni]n[g̃ir]su [imp]lanted the [semen] for E-[a]natum in the [wom]b

13) [...]
14) [...]

iv 13–14) [...]

15) [...]
16) [...] ⸢x⸣
17) mu-da-ḫúl

iv 15–17) [...] rejoiced over [E-anatum].

18) ^{d}inanna-ke$_4$
19) da mu-ni-díb

iv 18–19) The goddess Inanna accompanied him,

20) é-an-na-
21) ^{d}inanna-
22) ⸢ib-gal⸣-ka-ka a-túm
23) mu mu-ni-sa$_4$

iv 20–23) named him E-anna-Inanna-Ibgalakaka-tum ("Into[?]the E-anna of the goddess Inanna of the Great Oval I brought him),"

24) ^{d}nin-ḫur-sag̃-ra
25) du$_{10}$-zi-da-na
26) mu-ni-tuš

iv 24–26) and set him on the special knee of the goddess Ninḫursag̃.

27) ^{d}nin-ḫur-sag̃-ke$_4$
28) ubur-zi-da-né
29) ⸢mu⸣-[na-lá]

iv 27–29) The goddess Ninḫursag̃ [offered him] her wholesome breast.

Col. v
1) é-an-na-túm
2) a-šà-ga-šu-du$_{11}$-ga-
3) ^{d}nin-g̃ír-su-ka-da
4) ^{d}nin-g̃ír-su
5) mu-da-ḫúl

v 1–5) The god Niñgirsu rejoiced over E-anatum, semen implanted in the womb by the god Niñgirsu.

6) ^{d}nin-g̃ír-sú-ke$_4$
7) zapaḫ(ŠU.BAD)-ni

v 6–12) The god Niñgirsu laid his span upon him, for (a length of) five forearms he set his forearm upon

8) mu-ni-ra
9) [kù]š-⌈5⌉-am$_6$
10) kùš-a-ni
11) mu-ni-ra
12) kùš-5-zapaḫ(ŠU.BAD)-1

him: (he measured) five forearms (cubits), one span!

13) ^{d}nin-ĝír-sú-ke$_4$
14) nam-ga-ḫúl-da (copy has nam-gal)
15) [nam-lug]al-
16) [lagaš(NU$_{11}$.BUR.LA).KI]
17) [mu-na-sum]

v 13–17) The god Ninĝirsu, with great joy, [gave him] the kin[gship of Lagaš].

18) [...]
19) ^{d}[...]-ka-[...]

v 18–19) ...art quotes

20) é-an-na-túm
21) á(Text: DA)-tuku-e
22) kur a-ne-šè na-e

v 20–22) E-anatum, who has strength, declares, the foreign land belongs to him.

23) é-an-na-túm-ra
24) mu-^{d}inanna-ke$_4$
25) e-ni-sa$_4$-a-ni
26) é-an-na-
27) ^{d}inanna
28) ib-gal-ka-ka a-túm
29) mu mu-ni-[gar(?)]

v 23–29) For E-anatum, the name which the goddess Inanna gave him, E-anna-InannaIbgalakaka-tum "(Into[?]) the E-anna of Inanna of the Great Oval I I brought him)" I [have given(?)] him as a name.

30) mu-[(ni[?]) an]-⌈ki⌉(?)-[a(?)]
31) n[a(?)-...]

v 30–31) [His(?)] name [in(?) heaven and] earth ...

32) [é-an-na-túm-(me)]
Col. vi
1) á-tuku-e
2) mu-pà-da
3) ^{d}nin-ĝír-sú-ka-ke$_4$
4) é-an-na-túm-me
5) kur a-n[e]-šè g[á-gá-dè]
6) nì-ul-lí-a-d[a]
7) gù nam-mi-⌈dé⌉

v 32 – vi 7) [E-anatum], who has strength, ordained by the god Ninĝirsu, E-anatum, [who *declared*] "Now then, Oh enemy!" proclaimed for evermore:

8) énsi-
9) ^{ĝiš}KÚŠU.KI
10) me-an ì-ḫun

vi 8–10) The ruler of G̃iša (Umma) — where did he (ever) stay appeased?

11) lú-[x]-da ⌈x⌉-[(x)]
12) gú-eden-na
13) a-šàGÁNA-ki-ág-
14) ^{d}nin-ĝír-sú-ka
15) e-da-kú-e

vi 11–15) With other men ... he is able to exploit the Gu'edena, the beloved field of the god Ninĝirsu.

16) ḫé-šub-bé
17) an-né [x(?)] šár-ra

vi 16) May he (Ninĝirsu) strike him down!"
vi 17) ...

Lacuna of 3 lines

22) [...] ⌈x⌉ [...]
23) eger-[ra]-né
24) e-ma-ús

vi 22–24) he followed after him.

25) ná-a-ra
26) ná-a-ra
27) saĝ-ĝá mu-na-gub
28) é-an-na-túm
29) ná-a-ra
30) lug[al]-ki-[ág-ni]
31) [^{d}nin-gír-sú]
32) [saĝ-ĝá mu-na-gub]

vi 25–32) Him who lay (sleeping), him who lay (sleeping) — he approached his head. E-anatum who lay sleeping — [his] be[loved] ma[ster Ninĝirsu approached his head].

Lacuna of 3 lines

Col. vii
1) ^{ĝiš}KÚŠU.KI

vii 1–5) "Kiš itself must *abandon* G̃iša (Umma), and,

2) kiš.KI-am$_6$
3) šu šè-da[g]-g[e]
4) zex(ÁB.ŠA)-ge dab$_5$-ba-ta
5) nam-[m]a-da-DU
6) ⸢á⸣-zi-da-za
7) ^{d}utu
8) iri-è
9) sag̃-ki-za
10) NE.⸢GI⸣.DU.ÚS
11) iri-kéš
12) é-an-na-[tú]m
Lacuna of 7 lines
20) g̃iš mu-ni-ra
21) LÚ×ÚŠ-bi 3600
22) ul$_4$-ḫé bi-lá
23) g̃iš[KÙŠU](um[ma]).[KI]
Lacuna of 7 or 8 lines
Col. viii
1) šu e-na-zi
2) šà-$^{g̃iš}$KÚŠU.KI-ka
3) ì-gaz
4) ušùr-⸢ki(?)⸣
5) mu-ni-[...]
Lacuna of 18 lines
Col. ix
1) giš UR.UR-e e-da-lá
2) é-an-na-túm-ra
3) lú ti mu-ni-ra
4) ti-ta e-ta-si
5) mu-haš
6) ⸢igi-ba⸣ bí-mu$_7$(KA×LI)-mu$_7$(KA×LI)
7) lú-KID-e
Lacuna of 7 lines
15) [...] x
16) [...] NI
17) ⸢x⸣-LÍL(?)
18) [...]
19) [...] KI
Col. x
1) é-an-na-túm-me
2) $^{g̃iš}$KÚŠU.KI-a
3) im-ḫul-im-ma-gim
4) a-MAR mu-ni-tag$_4$
Lacuna of about 7 lines
12) é-an-na-túm
13) lú-inim-si-sá-kam
14) ki-sur-ra
15) [g̃išKÚŠU.KI-ta]
Col. xi
1) e-ta-ra
2) á-g̃išGÚŠU.KI-šè
3) mu-[t]ag$_4$
4) ki-ba na-[b]i-[r]ú
5) lú-g̃išKÚŠU.KI
Lacuna of 6 lines
12) [g̃išKÚŠU.KI]
13) G[ÍN].Š[Ě bi- sè
14) SA[ḪAR.DU$_6$.TAG$_4$-b]i 20

being angry, will not support it.

vii 6–11) The god Utu (the sun-god) will shine at your right and a ... will be afixed to your forehead.

vii 12) Oh E-anatum
Lacuna of 7 lines
vii 20) you will slay there.
vii 21–22) Their myriad corpses will reach the base of heaven."
vii 23 [In] G̃iš[a] (Um[ma])
Lacuna of 7 or 8 lines

viii 1) [his people] will raise a hand against him,
viii 2–3) and he will be killed within G̃iša (Umma) (itself).
viii 4–5) you will ...

Lacuna of 18 lines

ix 1) He fought with him.
ix 2–5) A person shot an arrow at E-anatum. He was shot through(?) by the arrow and *had difficulty moving*.

ix 6) He cried out in the face of it.
ix 7) The person ...
Lacuna of 7 lines
ix 15–19) ...

x 1–4) E-anatum provoked a windstorm, like the baneful rain of the storm he provoked a flood there in G̃iša (Umma).

Lacuna of about 7 lines
x 12 – xi 1) E-anatum, the man of just commands, measured off the boundary [from G̃iša (Umma)],

xi 2–4) [l]eft (some land) under the control of G̃iša (Umma) and erected a monument on that spot.

xi 5) The leader of G̃iša (Umma)
Lacuna of 6 lines
xi 12–15) [He] d[efe]at[ed G̃iša (Umma)] and made twenty b[urial tumuli (honouring his dead)] for it.

15) bí-dub	
16) é-an-na-túm 17) ér-du$_{10}$-ga-⸢pà⸣-a- 18) ^{d}šul-MUŠ×PA	xi 16–18) E-anatum, over whom the god Šul-MUŠ×PA cries sweet tears (of joy),
19) ⸢é⸣-[an-n]a-tú[m-(me[?])] 20) mu-[x]-ni-[x]	xi 19–20) ⸢E⸣-[an]atu[m]
21) é-[an-na-túm-me] 22) [^{d}nin-g̃ír-sú-ra] 23) kur-kur [e]-na-⸢ḫa⸣-lam	xi 21–23) E-[anatum] destroyed the foreign lands [for the god Ning̃irsu];
24) ⸢é-an⸣-[na-tú]m-[me] Col. xii 1) [^{d}nin]-g[ír-sú-ra] 2) a-[šàGÁNA-ki]-ág-[ni] 3) gú-eden-[na] 4) šu-na mu-ni-gi$_{4}$	xi 24 – xii 4) ⸢E-an⸣[atum⸣ restored to the god Ning̃irsu's control [his] belov[ed field], the Gu'eden[a].
Lacuna of 6 lines	Lacuna of 6 lines
11) a-šà da-n[a] 12) ki-ur$_{5}$-ra- 13) ^{d}nin-g̃ír-⸢sú-ka⸣	xii 11–13) The fields of his (Ning̃irsu's) side, the rent-bearing regions of Ning̃irsu
Lacuna of 2 lines	Lacuna of 2 lines
16) [...]-⸢x⸣-[...] 17) [...] 18) na(?) [...] 19) [...] 20) [e(?)]-na-DU	xii 16–20) ...
21) é-maḫ- Col. xiii 1) [...] 2) [na] ba-rú	xii 21 – xiii 2) [E-a]natum erected (this)[monument] in the lofty temple.
Lacuna of 8 lines	Lacuna of 8 lines
11) ⸢x⸣ [...] 12) ⸢x⸣ [...]-⸢x⸣-	xiii 11–12) ...
13) ^{d}nin-g̃ír-sú-ka 14) é-an-[na-túm] 15) [...] 16) ^{d}nin-g̃ír-sú-ka 17) dig̃ir-ra-ni <^{d}šul-MUŠ×PA(-am$_{6}$)>	xiii 13–17) ⸢of the god Ning̃irsu⸣, E-an[atum is the ...] of the god Ning̃irsu. His personal god <is Šul-MUŠ×PA>.
Col. xiv 1) a-šà-^{ba}bára	xiv 1) The fields Bara
Col. xv Lacuna of about 9 lines	Lacuna of about 9 lines
10) a-šà-⸢x(=NÁM[?])⸣.GAL.NIMGIR 11) a-šà-GI[Š].⸢PIRIG̃(?)⸣.G̃[Á(?)] 12) a-šà-[x]-tum-ma-[(x)] 13) a-šà-[x]-lam-[x(?)] 14) a-šà-[x]-lam-⸢x⸣ 15) a-šà-[x]-GUR$_{8}$-[(x)] 16) a-š[à]-⸢x⸣-[(x)] 17) a-šà-[x]-⸢gal⸣-[x(?)] 18) a-šà-⸢x x x⸣	xv 10–18) Too broken for coherent translation (various field names)
Lacuna of 24 lines	Lacuna of 24 lines
Col. xvi Lacuna of 7 lines	Lacuna of 7 lines
8) [é-an-na-túm] 9) [mu-pà]-⸢da⸣ 10) [^{d}n]in-g̃ír-[sú]-[k]a-ke$_{4}$ 11) [šu]-na mu-ni-gi$_{4}$	xvi 8–11) [E-anatum, nomi]nated by [the god Ni]ng̃irsu, restored to his (the god Ning̃irsu's) [control].
12) lú-g̃išKÚŠ[U.K]I-ra	xvi 12–17) E-anatum gave the great battle net of

13) é-an-na-túm-me
14) sa-šuš-gal-
15) ^{d}en-líl-lá
16) e-na-sum
17) nam e-na-ta-ku$_{5}$

the god Enlil to the leader of G̃iš[a] (Umm[a]), and made him swear to him by it.

18) lú-^{ğiš}KÚŠU.KI-ke$_{4}$
19) é-an-na-túm-ra
20) nam mu-na-ku$_{5}$-de$_{6}$

xvi 18–20) The leader of G̃iša (Umma) swore to E-anatum:

21) zi-^{d}en-líl
22) lugal-an-ki-ka
23) a-šà-^{d}nin-gír-sú-ka
24) ⸢GUR$_{8}$⸣ ì-kú

xvi 21–24) "By the life of the god Enlil, king of heaven and earth! I may exploit the field of the god Ning̃irsu as a(n interest-bearing) loan.

25) ⸢e⸣ idim-šè na-e

xvi 25) A dyke was dug (lit.: made) to spring.

26) d[a-rí-da-gal-la-šè]
27) [ki-sur-ra]-
28) [^{d}nin-ğír-sú-ka-ke$_{4}$]
29) [ba-ra-mu-bal-e]

xvi 26–29) F[orever and evermore, I shall not transgress the territory of the god Ning̃irsu!].

30) [e-pa$_{5}$-bi]
31) [šu-bal ba-ra-ak-ke$_{4}$]

xvi 30–31) I shall not shift (the course of) its irrigation channels and canals!

32) [na-rú-a-bi]
33) ba-ra-bux(PAD)-re$_{6}$]

xvi 32–33) [I shall not rip out its monuments!].

34) [u$_{4}$-da mu-bal-e]
35) [sa-šus-gal]-
36) [^{d}en-líl]-
37) [lugal-an-ki-ka]
38) [nam e-ta-ku$_{5}$-rá]
39) [^{ğiš}KÚŠU.KI-a]
40) [an-ta ḫé-šuš]

xvi 34–40) [Whenever I do transgress, may the great battle net of Enlil, king of heaven and earth, by which I have sworn, descend upon G̃iša (Umma)!"]

41) [é-an-na-túm-me]
42) [gal na-ga-mu-zu]

xvi 41–42) [E-anatum was very clever indeed and]

43) [tu.MUŠEN-2-nam]
44) [igi-ba šembi ba-ni-gar]
45) [eren sag-ba ì-mi-du$_{8}$]

xvi 43–45) [he made up the eyes of two doves with kohl, and anointed their heads with cedar (resin).

Col. xvii
1) [^{d}en-líl]
2) [lugal-an-ki-ra]
3) [nibru.KI-šè]
4) [é-kur-ra]
5) [šu e-ma-ni-ba]

xvii 1–5) [He released them to Enlil, king of heaven and earth, to the E-kur(?) in Nippur].

6) [^{d}en-líl]
7) [lugal-mu-ra]
8) [a-ba du$_{11}$-ga]-na
9) ⸢a⸣-ba šár-ra-na
10) lú ^{ğiš}KÚŠU.KI-a
11) inim-da gur-ra-da-am$_{6}$
12) u$_{4}$ an-dù
13) inim an-gál
14) u$_{4}$-d[a] inim-ba
15) šu ì-bal-e
16) sa-šuš-gal-
17) ^{d}en-líl-lá
18) nam e-ta-ku$_{5}$-rá
19) ^{ğiš}KÚŠU.KI-<a>
20) an-ta ḫé-šuš

xvii 6–20) ["After what he has declare]d and has reiterated [to my master the god Enlil], if any leader in G̃iša (Umma) reneges against the agreement, when he opposes or contests the agreement, whenever he violates this agreement, may the great battle net of Enlil, by which he has sworn, descend upon G̃iša (Umma)!"

21) é-an-na-tum-me
22) sa-šuš-gal-
23) ^{d}nin-ḫur-sağ-k[a]

xvii 21–26) E-anatum gave the great battle net of the goddess Ninḫursag to the leader of G̃iša (Umma), and made him swear to him by it.

24) lú-$^{ĝ[iš]}$KÚŠU.KI-r[a]
25) e-n[a]-sum
26) n[am] ⸢e⸣-na-ta-ku$_{5}$-rá
27) lú-^{ĝiš}KÚŠU.KI-ke$_{4}$
28) é-an-[n]a-túm-ra
29) [nam mu-na-ku$_{5}$-de$_{6}$]
30) [zi-^{d}nin-ḫur-saĝ-ka]
31) [a-šà-^{d}nin-ĝír-su-ka]
32) [ur ì-kú]
33) [e ÚŠ-šè na-e]
34) [da-rí-da-gal-la-šè]
35) [ki-sur-ra]-
36) [^{d}nin-ĝír-sú-ka-ke$_{4}$]
37) [ba-ra-mu-bal-e]
38) [e-pa$_{5}$-bi]
39) [šu-bal ba-ra-ak-ke$_{4}$]
40) [na-rú-a-bi]
41) [ba-ra-bux(PAD)-re$_{6}$]
42) [u$_{4}$-da mu-bal-e]
43) [sa-šus-gal]-
44) [^{d}nin-ḫur-saĝ-ka-ke$_{4}$]
45) [nam e-ta-ku$_{5}$-rá]
46) [^{ĝiš}KÚŠU.KI-a]
47) [an-ta ḫé-šuš]
48) [é-an-na-túm-me]
Col. xviii
1) gal ⸢na-ga⸣-mu-zu
2) tu.MUŠEN-2-nam
3) igi-ba šèmbi(BI×SIG$_{7}$) ba-ni-gar
4) ADKIN(LAK 668) saĝ-ba ì-mi-du$_{8}$
5) ^{d}nin-ḫur-saĝ-ra
6) kèš.KI-šè
7) š[u e-ma-ni-ba]
8) ama-mu
9) ^{d}nin-ḫur-saĝ-ra
10) a-ba du$_{11}$-ga-n[a]
11) a-ba šár-ra-[na]
12) lú $^{ĝi[š]}$K[ÚŠU.KI-a]
13) inim-[da gur]-ra-[da-am$_{6}$]
14) u$_{4}$ [an-dù]
15) ini[m an-gál]
16) u$_{4}$-[da inim-ba]
17) [šu ì-bal-e]
18) [sa-šuš]-⸢gal⸣-
19) ^{d}nin-ḫur-saĝ-ra
20) nam e-ta-ku$_{5}$-rá
21) ^{ĝiš}KÚŠU.KI-a
22) an-ta ḫé-šuš
23) é-na-na-túm-me
24) [sa-šuš-gal]-
25) [^{d}en-ki]
26) [lugal-abzu-ka]
27) [lú-^{ĝiš}KÚŠU.KI-r[a]
28) [e-na-sum]
29) [nam e-na-ta-ku$_{5}$-rá]
30) [lú-^{ĝiš}KÚŠU.KI-ke$_{4}$]
31) [é-an-na-túm-ra]

xvii 27–29) The leader of G̃iša (Umma) [swore] to E-anatum:

xvii 30–32) ["By the life of the goddess Ninḫursaĝ! I may exploit the field of the god Ninĝirsu as an (interest-bearing) loan].
xvii 33) [I shall not ... the irrigation channel!].
xvii 34–37) [Forever and evermore, I shall not transgress the territory of the god Ninĝirsu!]

xvii 38–39) [I shall not shift (the course of) its irrigation channels and canals!]
xvii 40–41) [I shall not rip out its monuments!]

xvii 42–47) [Whenever I do transgress, may the great battle net of the goddess Ninḫursaĝ, by which I have sworn, descend upon G̃iša (Umma)!"].

xvii 48 – xviii 1) [E-anatum] was very clever indeed and

xviii 2–4) he made up the eyes of two doves with kohl, and anointed their heads with cedar (resin).

xviii 5–7) He re[leased them] to the goddess Ninḫursaĝ in Keš:

xviii 8–22) "After what he has declared and has reiterated to [my] mother the goddess Ninḫursaĝ, if any leader [in] G̃iša (Umma) re[neg]es against the agreement, when [he violates this agreement], may the great [battle net] of the goddess Ninḫursaĝ, by which he has sworn, descend upon G̃iša (Umma)!"

xviii 23–29) E-anatum [gave the great battle net of the god Enki, king of the Abzu, to the leader of G̃iša (Umma), and made him swear to him by it]:

xvii 30–32) [The leader of G̃iša (Umma) (swore) to E-anatum:]

32) [nam mu-na-ku$_{5}$-de$_{6}$]
33) [zi-^{d}en-ki]
34) [lugal-abzu-ka]
35) [a-šà-^{d}nin-ĝír-sú-ka]
36) [GUR$_{8}$ ì-kú]
37) [e ÚŠ-šè na-e]
38) [da-rí-da-gal-la-šè]
39) [ki-sur-ra]-
40) [^{d}nin-ĝír-sú-ka-ke$_{4}$]
41) [ba-ra-mu-bal-e]
42) [e-pa$_{5}$-bi]
43) [šu-bal ba-ra-ak-ke$_{4}$]
44) [na-rú-a-bi]
45) [ba-ra-bu$_{X}$(PAD)-re$_{6}$]

Col. xix
1) ⸢u$_{4}$⸣-da mu-bal-e
2) sa-šus-gal-
3) ^{d}en-ki
4) lugal-abzu-ka
5) nam e-ta-ku$_{5}$-rá
6) ^{ĝiš}KÚŠU.KI-a
7) an-ta ḫé-šuš
8) ⸢é-an⸣-[na-túm-me]
9) [gal na-ga-mu-zu]
10) [tu.MUŠEN-2-nam]
11) [igi-ba šembi ba-ni-gar]
12) [ADKIN(LAK 668) sag̃-ba ì-mi-du$_{8}$]
13) [^{d}en-ki-ra]
14) [...]
15) [^{d}ni]n-ĝír-sú-ka-ka
16) šu e-ma-ni-ba
17) suḫur.KU$_{6}$ abzu-šè gub-gub-ba
18) é-an-na-túm-me
19) KA a-ku$_{5}$-de$_{6}$
20) lugal-mu
21) ^{d}en-ki-ra
22) a-ba du$_{11}$-ga-na
23) [a-ba šár-ra-na]
24) [lú ^{ĝiš}KÚŠU.KI-a]
25) [inim-da gur-ra-da-am$_{6}$]
26) [u$_{4}$ an-dù]
27) [inim an-gál]
28) [u$_{4}$-da inim-ba]
29) [šu ì-bal-e]
30) [sa-šuš]-gal-
31) [^{d}en-ki]
32) [nam e-ta-ku$_{5}$-rá]
33) [^{ĝiš}KÚŠU.KI-a]
34) [an-ta ḫé-šuš]
35) [é-na-na-túm-me]
36) [sa-šuš-gal]-

Col. xx
1) ^{d}EN.ZU
2) amar-bàn-da-
3) ^{d}en-líl-ka
4) lú-^{ĝiš}KÚŠU.KI-ra
5) e-na-sum

xviii 33–37) ["By the life of the god Enki, king of the Abzu! I may exploit the field of the god Ninĝirsu as an (interest-bearing) loan].

xviii 38) [I shall not ... the irrigation channel!].

xviii 39–41) [Forever and evermore, I shall not transgress the territory of the god Ninĝirsu!]

xviii 42–43) [I shall not shift (the course of) its irrigation channels and canals!]
xviii 44–45) [I shall not rip out its monuments!].

xix 1–7) Whenever I do transgress, may the great battle net of the god Enki, king of the Abzu, descend upon G̃iša (Umma)!"

xix 8–9) ⸢E-an⸣[natum was very clever indeed and]

xix) 10–12) [he made up the eyes of two doves with kohl, and anointed their heads with cedar (resin)]

xix 13–16) He released them [to the god *Enki* in the ...] of the god Ninĝirsu.

xix 17–19) E-anatum swore by the carp *set* toward the Abzu:

xix 20–34) "After what he has declared [and has reiterated] to my master the god Enki, [if any leader in G̃iša (Umma) reneges against the agreement, when he opposes or contests the agreement, whenever he violates this agreement, may the great battle net of the god Enki, by which he has sworn, descend upon G̃iša (Umma)!"].

xix 35–xx 6) [E-anatum] gave [the great battle net] of the god Sîn, the impetuous calf of the god Enlil, to the leader of G̃iša (Umma), and made him swear to him by it.

6) nam e-na-ta-ku$_5$-rá
7) lú-giš[KÚŠU.KI]-ke$_4$
8) [é-an-na-túm-ra]
9) [nam mu-na-ku$_5$-de$_6$]

xx 7–9) The leader of G̃iš[a (Um[ma]) swore to E-anatum]:

10) [zi-^{d}EN.ZU]
11) [amar-bàn-da]-
12) [^{d}en-líl-ka]
13) [a-šà-^{d}nin-g̃ír-sú-ka]
14) [GU]R$_8$ ì-kú

xx 10–14) ["By the life of the god Sîn, the impetuous calf of the god Enlil!] I may exploit [the field of the god Ning̃irsu as a(n interest-bearing) loan].

15) e ÚŠ-šè na-e

xx 15) [I will not ... the irrigation channel!]

16) da-rí-da-gal-la-šè
17) ki-sur-ra-
18) ^{d}nin-g̃ír-sú-ka-ke$_4$
19) ba-ra-mu-bal-e

xx 16–19) Forever and evermore, I shall not transgress the territory of the god Ning̃irsu!

20) e-pa$_5$-bi
Col. xxi
1) ⸢šu-bal ba-ra-ak-ke$_4$⸣

xx 20 – xxi 1) I shall not shift (the course of) its irrigation channels and canals!

2) ⸢na-rú-a-bi⸣
3) ba-ra-pad-re$_6$

xxi 2–3) I shall not rip out its monuments!

4) u$_4$-da mu-bal-e
5) sa-šus-gal-
6) ^{d}EN.ZU
7) amar-bàn-da-
8) [^{d}en-lí]l-ka
9) [nam e-ta-ku$_5$-rá]
10) [$^{\text{g̃iš}}$KÚŠU.KI-a]
11) [an-ta] ḫé-šuš

xxi 4–11) Whenever I do transgress, may the great battle net of the god Sîn, impetuous calf [of the god Enlil, by which I have sworn,] descend [upon G̃iša (Umma)]!

12) é-an-na-túm-me
13) gal na-ga-mu-zu

xxi 12–13) E-anatum was very clever indeed and

14) tu.MUŠEN-4
15) igi-ba šembi ba-ni-gar
16) eren! sag-ba ì-mi-du$_8$

xxi 14–16) he made up the eyes of four doves with kohl, and anointed their heads with cedar (resin).

17) 2-nam-uri$_5$.KI-šè
Col. xxii
1) [...]
2) [2-nam]
3) [... .KI-šè]
4) ki-[tuš-kù]
5) ^{d}E[N.ZU-ka]
6) [šu e-ma-ni-ba]

xxi 17 – xxii 6) [He released] two of them towards [*the Ekišnugal*] in Ur, [and he released two toward ... the *holy*] dwel[ling] of the god S[în].

7) lugal-mu
8) [^{d}EN.ZU]
9) ⸢amar⸣-⸢bàn⸣-da-
10) ^{d}en-líl-ra
11) a-ba du$_{11}$-ga-na
12) a-ba šár-ra-n[a]
13) lú $^{\text{g̃iš}}$KÚŠU.KI-<a>
14) inim-da gur-ra-da-am$_6$
15) u$_4$ an-dù
Col. xxiii
1) [inim an-gál]
2) [u$_4$-da inim-ba]
3) [šu ì-bal-e]
4) [sa-šuš-gal]-
5) [^{d}EN.ZU]
6) [nam e-ta-ku$_5$-rá]
7) [$^{\text{g̃iš}}$KÚŠU.KI-a]
8) [an-ta ḫé-šuš]

xxii 7–xxiii 8) "After what he has declared and has reiterated [to my master the god Sîn], impetuous calf of the god Enlil, if any leader in G̃iša (Umma) reneges against the agreement, when he opposes or [contests the agreement, whenever he violates this agreement, may the great battle net of the god Sîn, impetuous calf of the god Enlil, by which he has sworn, descend upon G̃iša (Umma)!"].

Rev. col. i

1) é-an-na-túm-me
2) sa-šuš-gal-
3) ^{d}utu
4) lugal-ni-sè-ga-ka
5) lú-^{ĝiš}KÚŠU.KI-ra
6) e-na-sum
7) nam e-na-ta-ku$_5$-rá

rev. i 1–7) E-anatum gave the great battle net of the god Utu, master *of vegetation*, to the leader of G̃iša (Umma), and ... made him swear to him by it.

8) lú- ^{ĝiš}KÚŠU.KI-ke$_4$
9) é-an-na-túm-ra
10) nam mu-na-ku$_5$-de$_6$

rev. i 8–10) The leader of G̃iša (Umma) swore to E-anatum:

11) zi-^{d}utu
12) [lugal-ni-sè-ga-ka]-
13) [a-šà-^{d}nin-ĝír-sú-ka]
14) [GUR$_8$ ì-kú]

rev. i 11–14) "By the life of the god Utu, [master *of vegetation*, I may exploit the field of the god Ninĝirsu as an (interest-bearing) loan].

15) [e ÚŠ-šè na-e]

rev. i 15) [I will not ... the irrigation channel!].

16) [da-rí-da-gal-la-šè]
17) [ki-s]ur-ra-
18) [^{d}n]in-ĝír-[s]ú-ka-ke$_4$
19) [b]a-ra-mu-bal-e

rev. i 16–19) [Forever and evermore], I shall [n]ot transgress the [terr]itory of the god [N]inĝir[s]u!

20) [e]-pa$_5$-bi
21) [šu]-bal ba-ra-ak-ke$_4$

rev. i 20–21) I shall not [sh]ift (the course of) its [irrigation channels] and canals!

22) na-rú-a-bi
23) ba-ra-bux(PAD)-re$_6$

rev. i 22–23) I shall not rip out its monuments!

24) ⸢u$_4$⸣-da mu-bal-e
25) sa-šus-gal-
26) ^{d}utu
27) lugal-ni-sè-ga-ka
28) [na]m e-ta-ku$_5$-rá
29) ^{ĝiš}KÚŠU.KI-a
30) an-ta ḫé-šuš

rev. i 24–30) Whenever I do transgress, may the great battle net of the god Utu, master of *vegetation*, by which I have sworn, descend upon G̃iša (Umma)!"

31) é-an-na-túm-me
32) gal na-ga-mu-zu

rev. i 31–32) E-anatum was very clever indeed and

33) tu.MUŠEN-2-nam
34) igi-ba šembi ba-ni-ĝar
35) eren saĝ-ba ì-mi-du$_8$

rev. i 33–35) he made up the eyes of two doves with kohl, and adorned their heads with cedar (resin).

36) ^{d}utu
37) lugal-ni-sè-ga-ra
38) larsa.KI
39) é-bábbar
40) nínda-gu$_4$-šè an-kú

rev. i 36–40) For the god Utu, master of *vegetation*, in the E-babbar at Larsa, he had them offered as *sacrificial* bulls.

Rev. col. ii

1) [^{d}utu]-
2) l[ugal]-m[u]-[ra]
3) a-ba [du$_{11}$]-ga-⸢na⸣
4) a-ba šár-ra-na
5) lú ĝ[^{iš}KÚŠU.KI-a]
6) inim-da gur-ra-da-am$_6$
7) u$_4$ a-dù
8) inim an-ĝál
9) u$_4$-da inim-ba šu ì-bal-e
10) sa-šuš-gal-
11) ^{d}utu
12) lugal-ni-sè-ga-ka
13) nam e-ta-ku$_5$-rá
14) ^{ĝiš}KÚŠU.KI-⸢a⸣

Rev. col. iii

1) [an-ta ḫé-šuš]

rev. ii 1 – iii 1) "After that which he has declared and reiterated to my m[aster the god Utu], if any leader in G̃i[ša] (U[mma]) reneges against the agreement, when he violates this agreement, opposes or contests the agreement, may the great battle net of the god Utu, master of *vegetation*, by which he has sworn, descend upon] G̃i[ša] (Um[ma])!"

2) [é-an-na-túm-me]
3) [...]
4) [lú-^{ĝiš}]KÚ[ŠU](um[ma]).KI-ra]
5) ⸢x⸣ [...]
6) mu-^{d}nin-ki-ka
7) mu-ni-pà-dè

rev. iii 2–7) [E-anatum ... to the leader of G̃iš]a [Um]ma ... and made him thereby invoke the name of the goddess Ninki.

8) lú-^{ĝiš}KÚŠU.KI-ke$_4$
9) é-an-na-túm-ra
10) nam mu-na-ku$_5$-de$_6$

rev. iii 8–10) The leader of G̃iša (Umma) swore to E-anatum:

11) zi-^{d}n[in]-ki-[ka]
Rev. col. iv
1) [a-šà-^{d}nin-ĝír-sú-ka]
2) GUR$_8$ ì-kú

rev. iii 11 – iv 2) "By the life of the goddess N[in]ki! I may exploit [the field of the god Nin̄girsu] as a(n interest-bearing) loan.

3) e ÚŠ-šè na-e

rev. iv 3) [I will not ... the irrigation channel!].

4) da-[rí]-d[a-gal-la-šè]
5) k[i-sur-ra]-
6) ^{d}[nin-gír-sú-ka-ke$_4$]
Rev. col. v
1) [ba-ra-mu-bal-e]

rev. iv 4 – rev. v 1) For[ever and] evermore, [I shall not transgress] the territory [of the god Nin̄girsu!]

2) e-pa$_5$-bi
3) šu-ba[l] ba-r[a]-ak-k[e$_4$]

rev. v 2–3) I shall not shift (the course of) its irrigation channels and canals!

4) na-r[ú]-a-bi
5) ba-r[a-bux(PAD)-re$_6$]

rev. v 4–5) I shall not [rip out] its monuments!

6) [u$_4$]-rá [mu]-bal-[e]
7) ^{d}nin-[ki]
8) m[u-ni] e-[pà]-d[a]
9) ⸢^{ĝiš}⸣KÚ[ŠU](um[ma].[KI]
10) m[uš ki-ta] gì[ri-ba]
11) z[ú ḫé]-m[i]-dù-dù-⸢e⸣

As for the goddess Nin[ki, whose] name I have [invoked] — may she have sn[akes from the ground] bite the feet of G̃iš[a] (Um[ma])!

12) ^{ĝiš}KÚ[ŠU](umm[a]).[KI]
13) e-[bi bal-e-da-bi]
14) [ĝìri-bi]
15) [^{d}nin-ki-ke$_4$]
16) [ki ḫé-da-kar-ré]

rev. v 12–16) When G̃iš[a] (Um[ma])[transgresses this] (boundary)-channel, [may the goddess Ninki ... their feet.]

17) [é-an-na-túm-me]
18) [gal na-ga-mu-zu]

rev. v 17–18) [E-anatum was very clever indeed and]

19) [...]
20) [...]
21) [...]
22) [...]

rev. v 19–22) Too broken for translation

23) [... ^{d}nin-ki-ra]
24) [a-ba du$_{11}$-ga-na]
25) [a-ba šár-ra-na]
26) [lú ^{ĝiš}KÚŠU.KI-a]
27) [inim-da gur]-ra-⸢da⸣-am$_6$
28) u$_4$ a-dù
29) inim a-ĝál
30) u$_4$-da inim-ba šu ì-bal-e
31) šu ì-bal-e
32) ^{d}nin-ki
33) nam-ni ma-ni-ku$_5$-rá
34) ^{ĝiš}KÚŠU.KI
35) muš ki-ta gìri-ba
36) zú ḫé-mi-dù-dù-e

rev. v 23–36) ["After that which he has declared and reiterated to the goddess Ninki ... , if any leader in G̃iša (Umma) rene]ges against the agreement, when he opposes or contests the agreement, whenever he violates this agreement, may the goddess Ninki, by whom he has sworn, have snakes from the ground bite the feet of G̃iša (Umma)!

37) ^{ĝiš}KÚŠU.KI
38) e-bi bal-e-da-bi
39) gìri-bi

rev. v 37–41) When G̃iša (Umma) transgresses this (boundary)-channel, may the goddess Ninki ... their feet.

40) nin-ki(Text:DI)-ke$_4$
41) ki ḫé-da-kar-ré
42) é-an-na-túm
43) lugal-
44) lagaš.KI
45) á-sum-ma-
46) ^{d}en-líl
47) ga-zi-kú-a
48) ^{d}nin-ḫur-sag̃
49) mu-du$_{10}$-sa$_4$-a-
50) ^{d}inanna
51) géštu-sum-ma-
52) ^{d}en-ki
53) šà-pà-da
54) ^{d}nanše
55) nin-uru$_{16}$
56) [kur-g]ú-[gar-gar]
Rev. col. vi
1) ^{d}n[in-g̃ír-sú-ka]
2) ki-ág̃-
3) ^{d}dumu-z[i]-abz[u]
4) mu-pà-da
5) ^{d}ḫendur-sa[g̃]
6) ku-[l]i-ki-ág̃-
7) ^{d}lugal-URU×KÁR
8) dam-ki-ág̃-
9) ^{d}inanna-ka-ke$_4$
10) NIM.KI ⸢ŠUBUR⸣.[KI]
11) kur GIŠ.⸢NÍG.GA⸣
12) [GÍN.ŠÈ bi-sè]
Lacuna
Rev. col. vii
1′) [...]
2′) G[ÍN.ŠÈ bi-sè]
3′) su-sín.[KI]-na
4′) GÍN.ŠÈ bi-sè
5′) šu-nir-URU×A.KI-ka
6′) énsi-bi
7′) sag̃ mu-gub-ba
Rev. col. viii
1) [GÍN.ŠÈ bi-sè]
Lacuna
1′) [GÍN.ŠÈ bi-sè]
2′) a-rú-a.[KI]
3′) mu-ḫa-lam
4′) šu-è
5′) ki-en-gi-
Rev. col. ix
1′) ur[i$_5$.KI]
2′) GÍN.ŠÈ bi-sè
Rev. col. x
Lacuna of about 19 lines
20) [gú-ede]n-[na]
21) [š]u-a gi$_4$-a
22) é-an-na-túm
Rev. col. xi
Lacuna of about 19 lines
20) [^{d}]ni[n-gír-s]u-ka-ke$_4$

rev. v 42–44) [E-anatum, king of Lagaš],

rev. v 45–46) granted strength by the god Enlil,

rev. v 47–48) nourished with wholesome milk by the goddess Ninḫursag̃,
rev. v 49–50) given a fine name by the goddess Inanna,
rev. v 51–52) granted wisdom by the god Enki,

rev. v 53–55) chosen in her heart by the goddess Nanše, the powerful mistress,

rev. v 56 – vi 1) who subj[ugates foreign lands for] the god N[ing̃irsu],

rev. vi 2–3) beloved of the god Dumuz[i]-abz[u],

rev. vi 4–5) nominated by the god Ḫendursag̃,

rev. vi 6–7) beloved friend of the god Lugal-URU×KAR,
rev. vi 8–9) beloved spouse of the goddess Inanna,

rev. vi 10–12) [defeate]d Elam and Subartu, mountainous lands of timber and treasure,

Lacuna

rev. vii 1′–2′) de[feated GN],

rev. vii 3′–4′) defeated Susa,

rev. vii 5′ – viii 1) [defeated] the ruler of Arawa, who stood with the (city's) emblem in the vanguard,

Lacuna
rev. viii 1′–3′) defeated [GN], and destroyed Arua.

rev. viii 4′–5′) ... the land of Sumer.

rev. ix 1′–2′) He defeated U[r].

Lacuna of about 19 lines
rev. x 20–22) who restored the Guʾedena to (Ning̃irsu's) [con]trol, E-anatum

Lacuna of about 19 lines
rev. xi 20–22) of N[ing̃irs]u who erected (this

21) ^{d}nin-gír-su-ra
22) mu-na-rú-a-e

monument) for Ningirsu.

Rev. col. xii
Lacuna
20) [g̃éštu-ni]
21) al [zu-a]
22) lug[al] kiš.[KI-(bi)]

Lacuna
rev. xii 20–22) [and it] is [brought to his attention], [may] (that) "kin[g] of Kiš" ...

Rev. col. xiii
Missing
Subscript
Rev. col. x
23) na-rú-a
24) mu-bi
25) lú-a nu mu-bi ši-e
26) ^{d}nin-g̃ír-sú
27) en men-LUM-ma
28) nam-ti-
29) I$_{7}$.pirig̃-eden-na
30) na-rú-a
31) gú-eden-na
32) a-šà-ki-ág̃-
33) ^{d}nin-g̃ír-su-ka
34) é-an-na-túm-me
35) ^{d}nin-g̃ír-su-ra
36) šu-na mu-ni-gi$_{4}$-a
37) ⸢mu⸣-[na-rú]

Missing
Subscript

rev. x 23–29) The name of the monument — it is not a man's (name)?— he proclaimed its name: "Ning̃irsu, the lord, crown of LUM-ma is the life of the Pirig̃-Edena-Canal!"

rev. xi 30–32) He [erected for him (the god Ning̃irsu)] the monument of the Guʾedena, the beloved field of the god Ning̃irsu, which E-anatum restored to the god Ning̃irsu's control

Caption on the reverse
Cartouche A (behind E-anatum in upper register)
1) é-an-na-túm
2) kur-gú-g̃ar-g̃ar-
3) ^{d}nin-g̃ír-su-ka

Cartouche A
1–3) E-anatum, who subjugates foreign lands for the god Ning̃irsu.

Cartouche B (in front of and behind E-anatum)
1) é-an-na-túm
2) kur-gú-g̃ar-g̃ar-
3) [^{d}]n[in]-g̃ír-su-[ka]

Cartouche B
1–3) E-anatum, who subjugates foreign lands for the god Ni[n]g̃irsu.

2

An inscription of E-anatum found on three boundary stones deals with a boundary dispute between G̃iša (Umma) and G̃irsu. One of these was found at G̃irsu.

CATALOGUE

Ex.	Museum number	Provenance	Lines preserved	cpn
1	EŞ 1715	G̃irsu	i 4–8; ii 5–13; iii 2, 5, 7–10, 12–14, 17–18; iv 1–17	n
2	HSM 7497	Antiquities trade	ii 14–17; iii 1–18	c
3	YBC 2408	No information on provenance	iv 1–21	c

COMMENTARY

The location of the fields in this inscription will be discussed in a forthcoming study of the author.

BIBLIOGRAPHY

1884–1912 de Sarzec, Découvertes 2 p. XLIV ÊANNADOU 6 (ex. 1, copy)
1907 Thureau-Dangin, SAK pp. 24–25 E-an-na-tum f (ex. 1, edition)
1918 Hussey, JAOS 38 pp. 264–66 (ex. 2, copy, edition)
1929 Barton, RISA pp. 38–41 Eannatum 6 (ex. 1, edition) and Eannatum 7 (ex. 2, edition)
1956 Sollberger, CIRPL p. ix Ean. 6 and 7 (study); pp. 21–22 Ean. 6 (ex. 1, copy) and Ean. 7 (ex. 2, copy)
1982 Steible, ASBW 1 pp. 158–60 E'annatum 6–7 (exs. 1–2, edition)
1983 Cooper, SANE 2 pp. 14, 24 and 48 no. 3 (translation, study)
1986 Cooper, SARI 1 pp. 39–40 La 3.2 (exs.1–2, translation; ex. 3 study)
1986 Steiner, ASJ 8 pp. 219–300 (passim) (study)

TEXT

Col. i
1) [^{d}nin-g̃ír-sú]
2) ⸢x⸣ [... -ra]
3) [(u$_4$?) ...]
4) [^{d}e]n-l[íl]-le
5) e-na-sur-ra
6) me-silim-e
7) na bí-rú-a
8) á-ág̃-g̃á-⸢né⸣
Lacuna of about 3 lines
Col. ii
Lacuna of about 4 lines
5) na-rú-a-⸢bi⸣
6) ì-bu$_x$(PAD)
7) eden-lagaš(NU$_{11}$.BUR.LA).KI-šè
8) ì-DU
9) a-šà usar-d[a]-ú
10) a-šà sum-túl-túl
11) a-šà é-luḫ-⸢ḫa!⸣
12) a-šà ki-ma-rí
13) a-šà du$_6$-áš-rí
14) [...] DU$_6$(?) [...] ⸢x⸣
15) [... -g]ír
16) [...] NÍGIN
17) [...] SUM.[M][U(?)
Col. iii
1) [...]
2) [...] ⸢x⸣ (=GIŠ[?]) [(...)] DÙ(?)-a
3) [... G]ÁNA [(...)] DAḪ(?)
4) [...]-ma
5) [^{d}ni]n-g̃ír-[sú]-ka
6) ⸢x⸣ [...] ⸢x⸣ [...] DÚR(?)
7) lú-$^{g̃iš}$KÚŠU.KI-ke$_4$
8) ba-ri-ri
9) na-rú-a
10) mu-bux(PAD)

i 1–2) [For the god Ning̃irsu ...]

i 3–5) [When the god E]nl[il] demarcated (the boundary between the gods Ning̃irsu and Šara),

i 6–7) Me-silim having erected a (boundary) monument there,
i 8) At his orders ...
Lacuna of about 3 lines

Lacuna of about 4 lines
ii 5–6) [the leader of G̃iša (Umma) ripped out that (boundary) monument,
ii 7–8) and proceeded to the plain of Lagaš.

ii 9–17) The field Usard[a]-u, the field Sum-tultul, the field Eluḫa, the field Kimari, the field Du'ašri, (other broken field names follow)

iii 1–6) Too broken for coherent translation

iii 7–8) The leader of G̃iša (Umma) amassed for himself
iii 9–10) and ripped out (their) (boundary) monument(s).

11) lú-^{giš}[KUŠÙ].KI-ke$_4$ 12) ⸢a-šà-NÍG.BA.DU.DAR.KUR⸣.[x]-⸢x⸣ 13) mu-šè ba-sa$_4$	iii 11–13) The leader of Giša (Umma) named the field ...
14) lú-^{giš}KÚŠU.KI-ke$_4$ 15) e-ma-DU 16) mu-šè ba-sa$_4$	iii 14–16) It was named "The Leader of Giša (Umma) Has Carried It Off."
17) lú-^{giš}KÚŠU.KI-ke$_4$ 18) e-ma-daḫ Col. iv 1) mu-šè ba-sa$_4$	iii 17 – iv 1) It was named "The Leader of G̃iša (Umma) Annexed It."
2) é-an-na-túm 3) énsi- 4) lagaš(NU$_{11}$.BUR.LA).KI	iv 2–4) E-anatum, ruler of Lagaš,
5) á-sum-ma- 6) ^{d}en-líl-ke$_4$	iv 5–6) granted strength by the god Enlil,
7) ga-zi-kú-a 8) ^{d}nin-ḫur-sag̃-ka-ke$_4$	iv 7–8) nourished with wholesome milk by the goddess Nin-ḫursag̃,
9) mu-du$_{10}$-sa$_4$-a- 10) ^{d}nanše-ke$_4$	iv 9–10) given a pleasant name by the goddess Nanše,
11) kur-gú-g̃ar-g̃ar 12) ^{d}nin-g̃ír-sú-ka-ke$_4$	iv 11–12) who subjugates foreign lands for the god Ning̃irsu,
13) ^{d}nin-g̃ír-sú-ra- 14) a-šàGÁNA-ki-ág̃-ni 15) šu-na mu-NI-gi$_4$	iv 13–15) restored to the god Ning̃irsu's control his beloved field(s).
16) ki me-silim-e 17) na bí-rú-a 18) é-an-na-túm 19) nu-bí-dib	iv 16–19) E-anatum did not pass beyond the point where Me-silim had erected the (boundary) monument,
20) na-rú-a-bi 21) ki-bé bí-gi$_4$	iv 20–21) and (even) restored that (boundary) monument.

3

An inscription found on two spheroid jars deals with a boundary dispute between G̃iša (Umma) and G̃irsu.

CATALOGUE

Ex.	Museum number	Excavation number	Provenance	Dimensions (cm)	Lines preserved	cpn
1	AO 4597 (frgm. 1) + AO 4442 (frgm. 2)	—	Girsu, "Tell-des-Tablettes" Trench G-G′, found beside a brick covered conduit	10.5×5.2	i′ 1′–3′ ii′ 2–8, 19 iii′ 1–8, 14–16	c
2	IM —	1 H 11	Lagaš (al-Hibā) surface in central area of tell	4.5×4.8	ii 16–19 iii 14–16	n

COMMENTARY

The inscription was restored by Cooper (RA 79 [1985] pp. 111–14), following (Steible) En-metena 1. However, since the restoration is not absolutely certain we have (conservatively) given an unrestored text here.

Ex. 1 was found in a trench (either trench G or G′) excavated by Cros in the "Tell-des-Tablettes." In his plan of Trenches G and G′ (Cros, Tello p. 229 Plan F) Cros indicates two small circles east of a covered conduit leading from a well, one in the area of trench G, and one in the area of trench G′. One of these likely marks the findspot of ex. 1.

In col. iii 7 the reading of the divine name ŠU.KAL is not entirely certain. It is probably to be read lirum "Wrestler(?)"; see Selz, Untersuchungen p. 277 n. 1376. Selz points out a second possibility, namely that the name is to be connected to the GN šu-gal attested in the Fāra period god lists.

BIBLIOGRAPHY

1910 Thureau-Dangin in Cross, Tello p. 216 (ex. 1 frgms. 1 and 2, copies); p. 217 (ex. 1 frgm. 2, edition); p. 251 [Cros] (ex. 1, frgm. 1, drawing)

1956 Sollberger, CIRPL p. x Ean. 63 (study); p. 26 Ean. 63 (ex. 1 frgm. 2, copy); p. 62 N 5 (ex. 1 frgm. 1, copy)

1976 Biggs, Al-Hiba no. 6 (ex. 2, copy)

1982 Steible, ASBW 1 pp. 175–78 E-annatum 63 (exs. 1–2, edition)

1985 Cooper, RA 79 pp. 111–14 (exs. 1–2, edition)

1983 Cooper, SANE 2 pp. 24 and 48 no. 4 (translation, study)

1986 Cooper, SARI 1 pp. 40–41 La 3.3 (exs. 1–2, translation)

1986 Steiner, ASJ 8 pp. 219–300 (passim) (study)

1989 Franke, Studies Sjöberg pp. 177–80 (study)

1990 Wilcke, in Studies Moran p. 491 (study)

TEXT

Col. i′

1′) [^{d}nin-ğír-s]u

2′) [šára-b]i

3′) [^{d}en-lí]l-[le]

Lacuna

Col. ii′

1) [^{d}nin-ğír-su-ke$_4$]

2) é-an-na-túm-ra

3) á e-na-áğ

4) ^{ğiš}KÚŠU.KI

5) e-ḫa-lam

6) [k]i! me-silim-e

7) [n]a bí-rú-a

8) ⸢é⸣-an-[na-t]úm-me

9) [inim]-⸢^{d}⸣[nin-ğír-su-ta]

Lacuna

17) [mu] ⸢e⸣-mi-[s]a$_4$

18) [lú]-^{ğiš}[KÚŠU].KI

19) [a-š]^{à}GÁNA [t]úm-šè

Col. iii′

1) ⸢x⸣ a mu-[(x)-ba]l-e-a

2) nin-ğír-su

3) ušumgal-ni ḫé

4) ^{d}en-l[íl]-le

5) àbsin-na-na

6) mun ḫa-bí-zi-zi

7) ^{d}ŠU.KAL

8) [...] ⸢x⸣

9) [(x) DA ...]

10) [ti na-na-sum-mu]

11) [a-ne]

12) [é diğir-šè na-dib-bé]

i′ 1′–3′) [The gods Ninğirs]u and [Šara], [Enl]i[l] ...

Lacuna

ii′ 1–3) [The god Ninğirsu] ordered E-anatum,

ii′ 4–5) and he destroyed G̃iša (Umma).

ii′ 6–7) At the [pl]ace where Me-silim had erected a (boundary) monument,

ii′ 8–11) E-a[nat]um, [at the god Ninğirsu's command]

Lacuna

ii′ 17) He [na]med [the (boundary) monument ...]

ii′ 18 – iii′ 1) [If a leader of G̃i[ša] (Um[ma]) [cros]ses the canal in order to [t]ake away fields,

iii 2–3) may the god Ninğirsu be a (hostile) dragon to him!

iii 4–6) May the god Enl[i]l make salt come up in his furrows!

iii 7–10) May the deity ŠU.KAL ("Wrestler[?]")[... not give him life!]

iii 11–12) [May he not enter the temple of (his) god!]

13) [...] x
14) [ti n]a-na-sum-mu
15) uru me:te(TE.ME)-na
16) šu ḫé-na-zi

iii 13–14) May [the god ...] not give him [life!]

iii 15–16) May (the people) rebel against him in his (very) own city!

4

A small stone pillar from G̃irsu was dedicated by E-anatum on the occasion of his restoration of the territory of Guʾedena to Ninĝirsu and to the state of G̃irsu.

COMMENTARY

The pillar, which measures 70 cm in height, with an upper diameter of 11.5 cm and a lower diameter of 27.5 cm, was found in excavations of de Sarzec at Girsu at a distance of c. 5 m south of the SW corner of the "Maison des Fruits" (see Parrot. Tello fig. 15 top no. 12). It now bears the museum number EŞ 385. The inscription was partially collated from the published photos.

BIBLIOGRAPHY

1884–1912 de Sarzec, Découvertes 2 pl. 2ter no. 5 (photo); p. XLIV ÊANNADOU 7 (copy)
1897 Heuzey, RA 4 p. 108 fig. 13 (study, drawing)
1907 Thureau- Dangin, SAK pp. 26–27 E-an-na-tum g (edition)
1929 Barton, RISA pp. 40–41 Eannatum 8 (edition)
1931 Contenau Manuel 2 fig. 443 (photo)
1956 Sollberger, CIRPL 1 pp. 24–25 Ean. 60 (copy)
1971 Sollberger and Kupper, IRSA IC5d (translation)
1982 Steible, ASBW 1 pp. 169-71 E-annatum 60 (edition)
1986 Cooper, SARI 1 p. 41 La 3.4 (translation)
1986 Steiner, ASJ 8 pp. 219–300 (passim) (study)

TEXT

Col. i
1) ^{d}nin-ĝír-sú
2) u[r]-saĝ-^{d}en-líl-ra

i 1–2) For the god Ninĝirsu, warrior of the god Enlil

3) é-an-na-túm
4) énsi-
5) lagaš(NU$_{11}$.BUR.LA).KI-ke$_{4}$

i 3–5) E-anatum, ruler of Lagaš,

6) šà-kù-ge-pà-da-
7) ^{d}nanše
8) nin-uru$_{16}$-na-ke$_{4}$

i 6–8) chosen in the pure heart by the goddess Nanše, the powerful mistress,

9) kur-gú-ĝar-ĝar
10) ^{d}nin-ĝír-sú-ka-ke$_{4}$

i 9–10) who subjugates the foreign lands for the god Ninĝirsu,

11) dumu-a-kur-gal
12) énsi-
13) lagaš(NU$_{11}$.BUR.LA).KI-ka-ke$_{4}$

i 11–13) son of A-kurgal, ruler of Lagaš,

Lacuna of about 4 lines
18) [énsi]-
19) ^{ĝiš} KÚŠU.KI
20) gú-⌜eden⌝-na-[šè(?)]
Col. ii
1) ba-DU-a

Lacuna of about 4 lines
i 18 – ii 2) [When] he crushed [the ruler] of G̃iša (Umma) who had marched on Guʾedena,

2) mu-ḫa-la[m-m]a-a
3) ^{d}nin-g̃ír-sú-ra
4) a-šàGÁNA-ki-ág-ni
5) gú-eden-na
6) šu-na mu-NI-gi$_4$

ii 3–6) he restored to Ning̃irsu's control his beloved field, the Guʾedena.

7) ki-sur-ra
8) gú-gú-g̃ír-sú.KI-ka
9) ^{d}nin-g̃ír-su-ra
10) šu-na mu-NI-[g]i$_4$-a

ii 7–10) The territory in the region of G̃irsu, which he restored to Ning̃irsu's control,

11) LUM-ma-g̃ír-nun-ta-šà-kù-ge-pà-da
12) mu mu-na-sa$_4$-a

ii 11–12) he named it LUM-ma-g̃irnunta-šakuge-pada "LUM-ma has been chosen from the 'Princely Way' by the pure heart."

13) [(x)] ⸢x⸣ ir$_{11}$
14) [...] ⸢x⸣ [(...)]

13–14) Too broken for translation

Lacuna of about 4 lines
19) a ⸢mu⸣-na-[ru]

Lacuna of about 4 lines
ii 19) He dedicated (this pillar) to him (the god Ning̃irsu).

5

Two boundary stones record various battles of E-anatum as well as his digging of the "New Canal" named LUM-ma-g̃im-du "Sweet Like LUM-ma." In all likelihood the canal lay in the same general area as the battle zone.

CATALOGUE

Ex.	Museum number	Excavation number	Provenance	Dimensions (cm)	Lines preserved	c
1	AO 2677	—	Girsu, excavations of de Sarzec	—	i 1–9 ii 1–13 iii 1–25 iv 1–28 v 1–26 vi 1–23 vii 1–20 viii 1–7	n
2	IM —	4 H-T 7	al-Hibā (excavations of Hansen). Findspot: N540-550/W90–100 Locus 29, SW corner, Level IIb	Max. width of flat side 11.29 Max. thickness (from flat side to top worn surface): 7.0 Max. length: 25.0	i 1–3 ii 4–9 iii 10–14, 16–17 iv 9–12, 17–19; v 6–10, 13–15 vii 8–10	n

Line numbers according to ex. 2.

Ex. 2	Ex. 1
col i	col. i 1–3, col. ii 4–6
col. ii	col. ii 7–9, iii 10–14
col. iii	col. iii 16–17, iv 9–13
col. iv	col. iv 16 –17, v 6–10
col. v	col. v 13–15, vi 5–9
col. vi	col. vii 8–10

COMMENTARY

The line count for this text comes from the master text, ex. 1. In the catalogue the lines preserved for ex. 2 are given according to the corresponding line numbers of ex. 1. The chart below the catalogue indicates the actual column arrangement of ex. 2.

For an ancient map fragment depicting the LUM-ma-g̃im-du canal mentioned in col. v line 18, see Thureau-Dangin, RA 4/1 (1897) p. 25 no. 3 (showing the Louvre tablet AOTb 345). Of interest is another map fragment (AOTb 370, see Thureau-Dangin, RA 4/1 [1897] pl. XXIV no. 66 no. 3) showing a toponym SAḪAR.DU$_6$-TAG$_4$.A "Tumulus Place," possibly to be connected to one of the SAḪAR.DU$_6$.TAG mentioned in this inscription. Perhaps the two canals and "tumulus place" lay in the same area The LUM-ma-g̃im-du canal is also mentioned in the En-metena inscription E1.9.5.26 col. iv line 3 and col. vii line 6.

BIBLIOGRAPHY

1884–1912 de Sarzec, Découvertes 2 p. XLIII ÊNNADOU 4 (ex. 1, copy)
1893 Oppert, RA 1 pl. V opposite p. 104 (ex. 1, copy)
1897 Heuzey, RA 5 pl. I opposite p. 34 (ex. 1, copy)
1907 Thureau-Dangin, SAK pp. 20–23 E-an-na-tum b (edition)
1929 Barton, RISA pp. 32–35 Eannatum 2 (ex. 1, edition)
1956 Sollberger, CIRPL p. ix Ean. 2 (study); pp. 17–18 Ean. 2 (ex. 1, copy)
1963 Kramer, Sumerians pp. 309–10 no. 10 (ex. 1, translation)
1971 Sollberger and Kupper, IRSA IC5b (ex. 1, translation)
1973–74 Bauer, WO 7 p. 10 (ex. 1, partial edition)
1975–76 Steiner, WO 8 pp. 10–21 (ex. 1, partial edition, study)
1977 Crawford, JCS 29 pp. 192 and 209–10 (ex. 2, photo, copy, study)
1982 Steible, ASBW 1 pp. 145–51 E'annatum 2 (exs. 1–2, edition)
1983 Cooper, SANE 2 p. 25 (partial translation, study)
1986 Cooper, SARI 1 pp. 41–42 La 3.5 (exs. 1–2, translation)
1986 Steiner, ASJ 8 pp. 219–300 (passim) (study)
1990 Wilcke, in Studies Moran p. 482 (study)

TEXT

Col. i
1) ^{d}nin-g̃ír-sú-ra
2) é-an-na-túm
3) énsi-
4) lagaš(NU$_{11}$.BUR.LA).KI
5) mu-pàd-da-
6) ^{d}en-líl-ke$_4$
7) á-sum-ma-
8) ^{d}nin-g̃ír-sú!-ka-ke$_4$
9) šà-pà-da-
Col. ii
1) ^{d}nanše-ke$_4$
2) ga-zi-kú-a
3) ^{d}[n]in-⸢ḫur⸣-[sag̃]-ka-⸢ke$_4$⸣
4) mu-⸢du$_{10}$⸣-sa$_4$-a-
5) ^{d}inanna-ka-ke$_4$
6) g̃éštu-sum-ma-
7) ^{d}en-⸢ki⸣-ka-ke$_4$
8) ki-ág-
9) ^{d}dumuz-abzu-ka-ke$_4$
10) giskim-ti-
11) ^{d}ḫendur-sag!-ka-ke$_4$
12) ku-li-ki-ág̃-
13) ^{d}lugal-URU×KÁR-ka-ke$_4$
Col. iii
1) dumu-a-kur-gal
2) énsi-

i 1) For the god Ning̃irsu,
i 2–4) E-anatum, ruler of Lagaš,
i 5–6) nominated by the god Enlil,
i 7–8) granted strength by the god Ning̃irsu,
i 9 – ii 1) chosen in the heart by the goddess Nanše,
ii 2–3) nourished with wholesome milk by the goddess Ninḫursag̃,
ii 4–5) given a pleasant name by the goddess Inanna,
ii 6–7) granted wisdom by the god Enki,
ii 8–9) beloved of the god Dumuzi-abzu,
ii 10–11) trusting in the god Ḫendursag̃,
ii 12–13) beloved friend of the god Lugal-URU×KAR,
iii 1–3) son of A-kurgal, ruler of Lagaš,

---

i 9.2 Omits -ka.

3) lagaš(NU$_{11}$.BUR.LA).[KI-ke$_{4}$]
4) [^{d}nin-g]ír-sú!-ra
5) gír-su.KI
6) [ki]-bé mu-[n]a-gi
7) bàd-uru-kù-ga
8) mu-na-dù
9) ^{d}nanše
10) AB×ḪA.KI
11) mu-na-dù
12) é-an-na-túm-e
13) NIM ḫur-sag̃-u$_{6}$-ga
14) GÍN.ŠÈ bi-sè
15) SAḪAR.DU$_{6}$.TAG$_{4}$-bi
16) mu-dub
17) šu-nir-URU×A.KI!-ka
18) énsi-bi
19) sag mu-gub-ba
20) GÍN.ŠÈ bi-sè
21) SAḪAR.DU$_{6}$.TAG$_{4}$-bi
22) mu-dub
23) ^{giš}KÚŠU.KI
24) GÍN.ŠÈ bi-sè
25) SAḪAR.DU$_{6}$.TAG$_{4}$-bi 20

Col. iv
1) [mu-d]ub
2) ⸢^{d}⸣nin-g̃ír-sú-ra
3) a-šà!-ki-ág̃-g̃[á]-ni
4) gú-eden-na
5) šu-na mu-NI-gi$_{4}$
6) unu.KI
7) GÍN.ŠÈ bi-sè
8) úri.KI
9) GÍN.ŠÈ bi-sè
10) ki-^{d}utu
11) GÍN.ŠÈ bi-sè
12) uru-az.KI
13) mu-ḫul
14) énsi-bi
15) mu-ug$_{7}$
16) mi-ši-me.KI
17) mu-ḫul
18) a-rú-a.KI
19) mu-ḫa-lam
20) é-an-na-túm
21) mu-pà!-da-
22) ^{d}nin-g̃ír-sú-ka-da
23) kur-kur-ré
24) sag e-da$_{5}$-sìg
25) mu lugal-akšak.KI-ka
26) ì-zi-ga-a
27) é-an-na-túm
28) mu-⸢pà⸣-da-

Col. v
1) ^{d}nin-g̃ír-su!-ka-ke$_{4}$
2) an-ta-sur-ra
3) ^{d}nin!-g̃ír-sú-ka-ta

iii 4–6) restored G̃irsu for the god Ning̃irsu,

iii 7–8) (and) built the wall of holy precinct for him.

iii 9–11) For the god Nanše, he built Nig̃in.

iii 12–16) E-anatum defeated Elam, the lofty mountain (land), and heaped up tumuli (honouring his own casualities).

iii 17–20) He defeated the ruler of Arawa who stood with the (city's) emblem in the vanguard,

iii 21–22) and heaped up tumuli (honouring his own casualties).

iii 23 – iv 1) He defeated G̃iša (Umma), and and [hea]ped up twenty tumuli (honouring his own casualties).

iv 2–5) He restored to the god Ning̃irsu's control his beloved field, the Guʾedena.

iv 6–7) He defeated Uruk,

iv 8–9) he defeated Ur,

iv 10–11) (and) he defeated Kiutu.

iv 12–15) He destroyed Uruaz and killed its ruler.

iv 16–17) He sacked Mišime,

iv 18–19) and destroyed Arua.

iv 20–24) All the foreign lands trembled before E-anatum, the nominee of the god Ning̃irsu.

iv 25–26) In the year of the offensive of Akšak

iv 27 v–v 8) E-anatum, nominee of the god Ning̃irsu, crushed Zuzu, king of Akšak, (all the way) from Antasur of Ning̃irsu to Akšak, and killed him.

---

v 12.2 Omits .KI.

4) zu-zu
5) lu[g]al-[a]kšak.KI
6) akšak.KI-šè!
7) mu-gaz
8) mu-ḫa-lam
9) u$_{4}$-ba
10) é-an-na-túm-ma
11) é-an-na-túm
12) mu-ú-rum-m[a]-ni
13) mu-GÌR.GÌR-ni
14) L[U]M-ma-a
15) ^{d}nin-g̃[ír]-sú-[r]a
16) a-gibil
17) mu-na-dun
18) LUM-ma-gim-du$_{10}$
19) mu mu-na-sa$_{4}$
20) é-an-na-túm
21) lú-inim-ma-sè-ga-
22) ^{d}nin-g̃ír-sú!-ka
23) é-an-na-túm
24) énsi-
25) [lag]aš.[KI]-ra
26) ^{d}inanna-ke$_{4}$
Col. vi
1) ki an-na-ág̃-g̃á-da
2) nam-énsi-
3) lagaš.KI-ta
4) na[m]-lugal-kiš.KI
5) mu-na-ta-sum
6) é-na-na-túm-da
7) NIM sag̃ e-da$_{5}$-sìg
8) NIM kur-ra-na bi-gi$_{4}$
9) kiš.KI ⸢sag̃⸣ e-d[a$_{4}$]-sìg
10) lugal-akšak.KI
11) kur-ra-na(Text: KI) bi-gi$_{4}$
12) é-na-na-túm
13) énsi-
14) lagaš.KI-ke$_{4}$
15) kur-gú-g̃ar-g̃ar-
16) ^{d}nin-g̃ír-su!-ka-ke$_{4}$
17) NIM ŠUBUR.KI
18) URU×A.KI
19) a-suḫur-ta
20) GÍN.ŠÈ bi-sè
21) kiš.KI akšak.KI
22) ma-rí!.KI
23) an-ta-sur-ra-
Col. vii
1) ^{d}nin-g̃ír-su-ka-ta
2) GÍN.Š[È] bi-s[è]
3) ^{d}nin-g̃ír-su-ra
4) LUM-ma-gim-du$_{10}$
5) mu-na-UŠ
6) sag̃-šè mu-NI-rig$_{8}$
7) é-an-na-túm
8) á(Text: DA)-sum-ma-
9) ^{d}nin-g̃ír-su-ka-ke$_{4}$
10) g̃iš-kéš-DU-

v 9–14) At that time E-anatum, whose personal name is E-anatum and whose battle(?) (or Tidnum[?]) name is LUM-ma

v 15–17) dug the "New Canal" for the god Ning̃irsu,

v 18–19) and named it LUM-ma-g̃im-du ("Sweet Like LUM-ma") for him.

v 20–22) (To) E-anatum, who is commissioned by the god Ning̃irsu,

v 23–vi 5) to E-anatum, the ruler of Lagaš, the goddess Inanna, because she loved him so, gave the kingship of Kiš to him in addition to the rulership of Lagaš.

vi 6–7) Elam trembled before E-anatum (and)

vi 8) he drove the Elamite back to his own land.

vi 9) Kiš trembled before E-anatum.

vi 10–11) He drove the king of Akšak back to his own land.

vi 12–14) E-anatum, ruler of Lagaš,

vi 15–16) who subjugates the foreign lands for the god Ning̃irsu,

vi 17–20) defeated Elam, Subartu, and Arawa at Asuḫur.

vi 21 – vii 2) He defeated Kiš, Akšak, and Mari at Antasur of the god Ning̃irsu.

vii 3–6) For the god Ning̃irsu, he joined up the LUM-ma-g̃im-du (canal) for him.

vii 8–13) E-anatum, granted strength by the god Ning̃irsu, built the reservoir of the LUM-ma-g̃im-du, (using) 3600 of 2 *ul* (each) (2592 hl.) of bitumen.

11) LUM-ma-gim-du$_{10}$
12) nígin 3600 gur-2-UL
13) mu-ni-dù
14) é-an-na-túm
15) lú-inim-sè-ga-
16) ^{d}nin-g̃ír-su-ka-ke$_{4}$
17) dig̃ir-ra-ni
18) ^{d}šul-MUŠ×PA

vii 14–18) E-anatum, who is commissioned by the god Ningirsu — his personal god is Šul-MUŠ×PA —

19) é-gal-ti-ra-áš.KI
20) mu-na-dù

vii 19–20) built the palace of Tiraš for him (Ning̃irsu).

Col. viii
1) dumu a-kur-gal
2) énsi-
3) lagaš.KI

viii 1–3) (He is) the son of A-kurgal, ruler of Lagaš.

4) pa-bìl-ga-ni
5) ur-^{d}nanše
6) énsi-
7) lagaš.KI-kam

viii 4–7) His grandfather was Ur-Nanše, ruler of Lagaš.

6

An inscription found on two boulders from G̃irsu gives a shorter version of the account found in E-anatum.

CATALOGUE

Ex	Museum number	Lines preserved	cpn
1	EŞ 1595	i 1–11 ii 1–15 iii 1–20 iv 1–19 v 1–14 vi 1–10 vii 2–6	n
2	AO 255	i 2, 5–6, 11 ii 5–7, 9–10, 15–iii 1 iii 8, 10 iv 5, 7–8 v 13–15 vii 8–10	n

Line numbers according to ex. 2

Ex. 2	Ex. 1
col. i	i 2, 5–6, 11
col. ii	ii 5–7, 9–10, 15
col. iii	iii 8, 10
col. iv	iv 5, 7–8
col. v	v 13–14
col. vii	vii 3
col. viii	?

COMMENTARY

The master text is ex. 1. Unfortunately, the findspot of neither boulder is known.

The translation of col. i line 5 is given (with due reserve) following Steible, ASBW 2 p. 69 note to E'anatum 3–4 (1). Steible follows Wilcke, Lugalbanda Epos pp. 195–97.

BIBLIOGRAPHY

1884–1912 de Sarzec, Découvertes 2 p. XLIV (ex. 1, partial copy); pl. 2ter no. 6 (ex. 2, photo)
1907 Thureau-Dangin, SAK pp. 22–25 E-an-na-tum c (ex. 1, edition); pp. 24–25 E-an-na-tum d and n. b (study)
1929 Barton, RISA pp. 34–37 Eannatum 3 (ex. 1, edition)
1956 Sollberger, CIRPL pp. 19–20 Ean. 3 (ex. 1, copy) Ean. c (ex. 2, partial transliteration)
1982 Steible, ASBW 1 pp. 152–56 E'annatum 3–4 (edition)
1986 Cooper, SARI 1 pp. 42–43 La 3.6 (exs. 1–2, translation)
1986 Steiner, ASJ 8 pp. 219–300 (passim) (study)

TEXT

Col. i	
1) ^{d}nanše	i 1–5) For the goddess Nanše, E-anatum built the wall of Lagaš and *contracted guards for her.*
2) é-an-na-túm-me	
3) bàd-lagaš.KI	
4) mu-na-dù	
5) ka mu-na(Text: KI)-kéš	
6) ^{d}nin-g̃ír-sú-ra	i 6) For the god Ningirsu,
7) é-an-na-túm	i 7–9) E-anatum, ruler of Lagaš,
8) énsi-	
9) lagaš.KI-ke$_4$	
10) mu-pà-da-	i 10–11) nominated by the god Enlil,
11) ^{d}en-líl-ke$_4$	
Col. ii	
1) á-sum-ma-	ii 1–2) granted strength by the god Ning̃irsu,
2) ^{d}nin-g̃ír-sú-ka-ke$_4$	
3) šà-pà-da-	ii 3–4) chosen in the heart by the goddess Nanše,
4) ^{d}nanše-ke$_4$	
5) ga-zi-kú-a	ii 5–6) nourished with wholesome milk by the goddess Ninḫursag̃,
6) ^{d}nin-ḫur-sag̃-ka-ke$_4$	
7) mu-du$_{10}$-sa$_4$-a-	ii 7–8) given a pleasant name by the goddess Inanna,
8) ^{d}inanna-ka-ke$_4$	
9) g̃éštu-sum-ma-	ii 9–10) granted wisdom by the god Enki,
10) ^{d}en-ki-ke$_4$	
11) ki-ág̃-	ii 11–12) beloved of the god Dumuzi-abzu,
12) ^{d}dumu-zi-abzu-ke$_4$	
13) giskim-ti-	ii 13–14) who trusts in the god Ḫendursag̃,
14) ^{d}ḫendur-sag̃-ka-ke$_4$	
15) dumu-a-kur-gal	ii 15 – iii 2) son of A-kurgal, ruler of Lagaš,
Col. iii	
1) énsi-	
2) lagaš(NU$_{11}$.BUR.LA).KI-ke$_4$	
3) ^{d}nin-g̃ír-⌈sú⌉-ra	iii 3–7) restored G̃irsu for the god Ning̃irsu and built the wall of the holy precinct for him.
4) g̃ír-sú!.KI	
5) ki-bé mu-na-gi$_4$	
6) bàd-u[r]u-kù-ga	
7) mu-na-dù	
8) ^{d}nanše	iii 8–10) For the goddess Nanše, he built Nig̃in.
9) AB×ḪA.KI	
10) mu-na(Text: KI)-dù	

11) é-an-na-túm-e
12) NIM ḫur-sag̃-u_6-ga
13) GÍN.ŠÈ bi-sè

iii 11–13) E-anatum defeated Elam, the lofty mountain (land),

14) SAḪAR.DU_6.TAG_4-[b]i
15) mu-dub

iii14–15) and heaped up tumuli (honouring his own casualities).

16) šu-nir-URU×A.KI-ka
18) énsi-bi sag̃ mu-gub-⸢ba⸣
19) GÍN-šè bi-sè

iii 16–19) He defeated the ruler of Urua, who stood with the (city's) emblem in the vanguard,

20) SAḪAR.DU_6.TAG_4-[b]i
Col. iv
1) mu-dub

iii 20 – iv 1) and heaped up tumuli (honouring his own casualities).

2) ^{giš}KÚŠU.KI
3) GÍN.ŠÈ bi-sè
4) SAḪAR.DU_6.TAG_4-bi 20
5) mu-dub

iv 2–5) He defeated G̃iša (Umma),and heaped up twenty tumuli (honouring his own casualities).

6) ^{d}nin-gír-sú!-ra
7) a-šà-ki-ág̃-ni
8) gú-eden-na
9) ⸢šu⸣-na m[u]-NI-gi_4

iv 6–9) He [r]estored to Niñgirsu's control his beloved field, the Guʾedena.

10) unu.KI
11) GÍN.ŠÈ bi-sè

iv 10–11) He defeated Uruk,

12) úri.KI
13) GÍN.ŠÈ bi-sè

iv 12–13) he defeated Ur,

14) ki-^{d}utu
15) GÍN.ŠÈ bi-sè

iv 14–15) (and) defeated Kiutu.

16) uru-az.KI
17) mu-ḫul
18) énsi-bi
19) mu-ug_7

iv 16–19) He sacked Uruaz and killed its ruler.

Col. v
1) mi-ši-me.KI
2) mu-ḫul

v 1–2) He sacked Mišime,

3) a-rú-a.KI
4) mu-ḫa-lam

v 3–4) and destroyed Arua.

5) é-an-an-túm
6) mu-pà-da-
7) ^{d}nin-g̃ír-sú-ka-da
8) kur-kur-ré
9) sag e-da_5-sìg

v 5–9) All the foreign lands trembled before E-anatum, the nominee of the god Niñgirsu.

10) mu lugal-akšak.[KI-ka]
11) ì-[zi-ga-a]

v 10– 11) In the year [of the offensive of] the king of Akšak

12) é-[an-na-túm]
13) m[u-pà-da]-
14) ^{d}[nin]-g̃ír-[sú]-ka-k[e_4]
Col. vi
1) an-t[a]-sur-[ra]
2) ^{d}[nin]-g̃ír-sú!-ka-ta
3) akšak.KI-šè(Text: TÚG)
4) mu-gaz
5) mu-ḫa-lam

v 12–vi 5) E-[anatum], no[minee of the god Nin]g̃ir[su,] crushed him from Ant[a]sur of the god [Nin]g̃irsu and killed him.

6) u_4-⸢ba⸣
7) é-an-na-túm-e
8) i_7-gibil
9) mu-na-dun

vi 6–9) At that time, E-anatum, dug the "New Canal" for him (the god Niñgirsu) ...

10) ⸢a⸣ [...]
Lacuna of 2 lines

10) ...
Lacuna of 2 lines

Col. vii
1) [...]

vii 1–4) [E-anatum, who is commissioned by]

2) ^{d}nin-g̃ír-sú!-ka
3) dig̃ir-ra-ni
4) ^{d}šu[l-MUŠ×PA]
5) é-[an]-na-[túm]
6) é[nsi]
7) [lagaš.KI]
8) [dumu-a]-kur-[gal]
9) [énsi]-
10) [lagaš.KI-ke$_4$]
11) [pa-bìl-ga-ni]
12) [ur-^{d}nanše]
13) [énsi]-
14) [lagaš.KI-kam]

the god Ning̃irsu — his personal god is the god Šu[l-MUŠ×PA]—

vii 5–7) E-[a]na[tum], r[uler of Lagaš],

vii 8–9) [son of A]-kur[gal, ruler of Lagaš]

vii 11–14) — [his grandfather was Ur-Nanše ruler of Lagaš].

7a

An inscription found on two boulders mentions E-anatum's construction of the E-Tiraš. For Ur-Nanše's construction of the same structure, see inscription E1.9.1.26.

CATALOGUE

Ex	Museum number	Provenance	Lines preserved	cpn
1	AO —	Under the pavement of the main court A of the "Palais" of Adad-nādin-aḫḫē (on Tell A) not far from the passageway MM′ (see de Sarzec, Découvertes 1 p. 105)	i 3–6; ii 1–8; iii 1–5	n
2	EŞ 1632	—	ii 6–8 iii 3–4	n

COMMENTARY

The text, following Cooper (SARI 1 p. 43 La 3.7), is a conflation of Steible's E᾽annatum 5 and E᾽annatum 8. Ex. 1 could not be located.

The construction of é-gals at both Tiraš and Antasur shows that these settlements had a special relationship to the ruler of Lagaš. Antasur was likely a fortress on the northern boundary of Lagaš province, and Tiraš likely served in a defensive role. In both cases a translation of "fortress" for é-gal may possibly be in order.

BIBLIOGRAPHY

1884–1912 de Sarzec, Découvertes 1 p. 105 (ex. 1, findspot); Découvertes 2 pl. 2 no. 3 (ex. 1, photo); p. LV ÊANNADOU 10 (ex. 1, copy)
1907 Thureau-Dangin, SAK pp. 24–25 E-an-na-tum d (ex. 1, edition)
1929 Barton, RISA pp. 36–39 Eannatum 4–5 (ex. 1, edition)
1956 Sollberger, CIRPL p. 9 Ean. 5 (ex. 1, study); p. 21 Ean. 5 (ex. 1, copy)
1957 Jacobsen, ZA 52 p. 130 n. 90 (exs. 1–2, study)
1982 Steible, ASBW 1 pp. 156–57 E᾽annatum 5 (ex. 1, edition [conflated with E1.9.3.7b]); p. 161 E᾽annatum 8 (ex. 2, edition)
1986 Cooper, SARI 1 p. 43 La 3.7 (exs. 1–2, translation)

TEXT

Col. i
1) [^{d}nin-gír-su-ra]
2) [é-an-na-tú]m
3) [én]si(PA.TE].SI-
4) [lag]aš.KI]([NU$_{11}$.BUR].LA).[KI]-ke$_4$
5) [kur-gú-g̃ar]-g̃ar-
Col. ii
1) ⸢^{d}⸣nin-[g̃í]r-sú-ke$_4$
2) [NIM] ŠUBUR
3) [g]ú mu-na-g̃ar
4) é-ti-ra-áš.KI(Text:DI)
5) mu-na-dù
6) pa m[u]-n[a]-è
7) ⸢é⸣-an-[na]-túm
8) lú-inim-ma-sè-ga-
Col. iii
1) ^{d}[nin]-g̃ír-[sú]-ka
2) kur-kur-šè
3) á-^{d}nin-g̃ír-sú-ka-ta
4) lú-ùlu gaba mu-ru-da
5) nu-tuk

i 1) [For the god Ning̃irsu]
i 2–4) [E-anatu]m [ru]ler of Lagaš

i 5 – ii 1) [who subjuga]tes [the foreign lands] for the god Nin[g̃i]rsu,

ii 2–3) [su]bjugated [Elam] and Subartu to him.

ii 4–6) He built the E-Tiraš for (the god Ning̃irsu) and made it splendid for him.

i 7 – iii 1) As for E-anatum who is commissioned (iii) by [the god Nin]g̃ir[su],

iii 2–5) because of the strength given by the god Ningirsu, (when he rages) against the foreign lands, nobody is able to resist him.

7b

An inscription on a vessel or mace-head fragment mentions the construction of the E-Tiraš; it may belong to E-anatum.

COMMENTARY

This vessel or mace-head fragment from Tello was found by J. Peters; it now bears the museum number CBS 9084.

BIBLIOGRAPHY

1926 Legrain, PBS 15 no. 8 (copy)
1982 Steible, ASBW 1 p. 156 E'annatum 5B (study)
1991 Braun-Holzinger, Weihgaben p. 115 G 4 (edition, study)

TEXT

Lacuna
1′) ⸢é-ti⸣-ra-áš.[KI]
2′) m[u-na-dù]
Lacuna

Lacuna
1′–2′) b[uilt] the E-Tiraš.
Lacuna

8

A 59-line brick inscription from G̃irsu mentions various military victories of E-anatum. The findspots of the bricks are not known.

CATALOGUE

Ex.	Museum number	Excavation number	Dimensions (cm)	CIRPL number	Lines preserved	cpn
1	AO 4644	—	—	Ean. 11	—	n
2	AO 351	—	—	Ean. 12	i 1–6 ii 1–7 iii 1–7 iv 1–8 v 3–8 vi missing	c
3	EŞ 1541	—	29×20×4.5	Ean. 13	—	n
4	VA 2599	—	20×16.5	Ean. 14	i 1–5 ii 1–8 iii 1–9 iv 4–9 v 6 – vi 2	c
5	Coll. Cros	—	—	Ean. 15	—	n
6	AO 4645	—	22×16×3.7	Ean. 16	i 1–3 ii 2–7 iii 5–7 iv 4–8 v 6–9 vi missing	c
7	AO 352	—	12×7.8×47	Ean. 17	iv 9–10 v 9 vi 8–11	c
8	AO —	—	—	Ean. 18	—	n
9	EŞ 8900	—	11×11×5.5	Ean. 19	—	n
10	—	TG 3131	—	Ean. 20	—	n
11	—	TG 4194	—	Ean. 21	—	n

BIBLIOGRAPHY

1884–1912 de Sarzec, Découvertes 2 p. XLV ÊANNADOU 8 (ex. 2, copy) and pl. 31 no. 2 (ex. 2, photo)
1907 Messerschmidt, VAS 1 no. 3 (ex. 4, copy)
1907 Thureau-Dangin, SAK pp. 26–27 E-an-na-tum h (ex. 2, edition)
1921 Unger, Babylonisches Schriftum pp. 11–12 no. 7 (photo)
1929 Barton, RISA pp. 40–41 Eannatum 9 (ex. 2, edition)
1936 de Genouillac, FT 2 p. 135 (exs. 10–11, study)
1956 Sollberger, CIRPL p. ix Ean. 11–21 (study); p. 23 Ean 11–21 (exs. 2–11, variants listed)
1982 ASBW 1 pp. 162–65 E'annatum 11 (exs. 1–11, edition)
1986 Cooper, SARI 1 pp. 43–44 La 3.8 (exs. 1–12, translation)
1987 Marzahn, WO 18 p. 169 (ex. 4, study)

TEXT

Col. i
1) ^{d}nin-g̃ír-su
2) é-an-na-túm
3) énsi-
4) lagaš(NU$_{11}$.BUR.LA).KI-ke$_{4}$

i 1) For the god Ning̃irsu,
i 2–4) E-anatum, ruler of Lagaš,

iv.4 NU$_{11}$.LA.KI-ke$_{4}$.

5) mu-pà-da-
6) ^{d}en-líl-ke$_4$
7) á-sum-ma-
8) ^{d}nin-g̃ír-sú-ke$_4$
9) šà-pà-da-
Col. ii
1) ^{d}nanše-ke$_4$
2) ga-zi-kú-a
3) ^{d}nin-ḫur-sag̃-ke$_4$
4) mu-du$_{10}$-sa$_4$-a-
5) ^{d}inanna-ke$_4$
6) dumu-a-kur-gal
7) énsi-
8) lagaš(NU$_{11}$.BUR.LA).KI-ke$_4$
9) ^{d}nin-g̃ír-su-ra
10) g̃ír-su.KI
Col. iii
1) mu-na-dù
2) ^{d}nanše
3) AB×ḪA.KI
4) mu-na-dù
5) é-an-na-túm-e
6) NIM ḫur-sag̃-u$_6$-ga
7) GÍN.ŠÈ bí-sè
8) SAḪAR.DU$_6$.TAG$_4$-bi
9) mu-dub
10) šu-nir-URU×A.KI-ka
Col. iv
1) énsi-bi
2) sag mu-gub-ba
3) GÍN.ŠÈ bí-sè
4) SAḪAR.DU$_6$.TAG$_4$-bi
5) mu-dub
6) ^{giš}KÚŠU.KI-a
7) GÍN.ŠÈ bí-sè
8) SAḪAR.DU$_6$.TAG$_4$-bi 20
9) mu-dub
10) ^{d}nin-g̃ír-su-ra
Col. v
1) GÁNA-gú-eden-na
2) šu-na mu-NI-gi$_4$
3) unu.KI
4) GÍN.ŠÈ ⌜bí⌝-sè
5) uru-az.KI
6) mu-ḫul
7) mi-ši-me.KI
8) mu-ḫul

i 5–6) nominated by the god Enlil,

i 7–8) granted strength by the god Ning̃irsu,

i 8 – ii 1) chosen in the heart by the goddess Nanše,

ii 2–3) nourished with wholesome milk by the goddess Ninḫursag̃,
ii 4–5) given a pleasant name by the goddess Inanna,

ii 6–8) son of A-kurgal, ruler of Lagaš,

ii 9 – iii 1) built G̃irsu for the god Ning̃irsu.

iii 2–4) For the goddess Nanše, he built Nig̃en.

iii 5–7) E-anatum defeated Elam, the lofty mountain,

iii 8–9) and heaped up tumuli (honouring his own casualties).
iii 10 – iv 3) He defeated the ruler of Arawa, who stood with the (city's) emblem in the vanguard

iv 4–5) and heaped up tumuli (honouring his own casualties).
iv 6–9) He defeated G̃iša (Umma), and heaped up twenty tumuli (honouring his own casualities).

iv 10 – v 2) He restored to the god Ning̃irsu's control his Gu᾿edena.

v 3–4) He defeated Uruk.

v 5–6) He sacked Uruaz.

v 7–8) He sacked Mišime.

---

ii 6.8 NIM.KI
iii 7.6–8 bi-sè.
v **3**.6–8 bi-sè.
v **6**.2–8 Omit-a.
v **7**.6–8 bi-sè.
v **8**.3, 4, 8 Omit 20.
iv 8–9.6 SAḪAR.DU$_6$.TAG$_4$-bi <<ŠE>> 20 20 mu-dub.
v **4**.6–8 bi-sè.
v **7**.2 mi-ši.KI.

9) é-an-an-tú[m]
Col. vi
1) mu-pà-da-
2) ^{d}nin-gír-su-ka-da
3) kur-kur-ré
4) sag e-da_5-sìg

v 9 – vi 4) All the foreign lands trembled before E-anatum, the nominee of the god Ningirsu.

5) é-an-an-túm
6) lú-inim-ma-sè-ga
7) ^{d}nin-g̃ír-su
8) dig̃ir-ra-ni
9) ^{d}šul-MUŠ×PA

vi 5–9) E-anatum is the one commisioned by the god Ning̃irsu — his personal god is the god Šul-MUŠ×PA.

10) a-rú-a.KI
11) mu-ḫa-lam

vi 10–11) He destroyed Arua.

9

About 25 m NW of the NW corner of the “Maison des fruits” E-anatum constructed a large well made of plano-convex bricks (for a photo of the well see de Sarzec, Découvertes 2 pl. 57 no. 2). The text inscribed on the bricks records E-anatum’s construction of a “brick-(lined) well” (pú-sig_4). Numerous examples of the bricks are now housed in various museum collections.

CATALOGUE

Ex.	Museum number	Excavation number	Dimensions (cm)	CIRPL number	Lines preserved	cpn
1	EŞ 1546	—	—	Ean. 22	—	n
2	BM 85977	—	—	Ean. 23	—	n
3	BM 85979	—	—	Ean. 24	—	n
4	BM 85980	—	—	Ean. 25	—	n
5	BM 88283	—	—	Ean. 26	—	n
6	BM 114404	—	—	Ean. 27	—	n
7	VA 3112	—	—	Ean. 28		c
8	Hermitage	—	—	Ean. 29	—	n
9	AO 353	—	—	Ean. 30	—	p
10	AO 354	—	32×20.5×4.5	Ean. 31	—	c
11	EŞ 1537	—	—	Ean. 32	—	n
12	EŞ 1542	—	—	Ean. 33	—	n
13	EŞ 1544	—	—	Ean. 34	—	n
14	EŞ 1545	—	—	Ean. 35	—	n
15	EŞ 1722	—	—	Ean. 36	—	n
16	EŞ 1723	—	—	Ean. 37	—	n
17	EŞ 1724	—	—	Ean. 38	—	n
18	EŞ 1725	—	—	Ean. 39	—	n
19	EŞ 2510	—	—	Ean. 40	—	n
20	EŞ 8890	—	—	Ean. 41	—	n
21	EŞ 8891	—	—	Ean. 42	—	n
22	EŞ 8892	—	—	Ean. 43	—	n
23	EŞ 8893	—	—	Ean. 44	—	n
24	EŞ 8896	—	—	Ean. 45	—	n
25	EŞ 1539	—	—	Ean. 46	—	n
26	EŞ 1543	—	—	Ean. 47	—	n
27	BM 85978	—	—	Ean. 48	—	n
28	A 1399	—	—	Ean. 49	—	n
29	EŞ 1540	—	—	Ean. 50	—	n
30	EŞ 2667	—	—	Ean. 51	—	n
31	EŞ 8894	—	—	Ean. 52	—	n
32	EŞ 8895	—	—	Ean. 53	—	n
33	EŞ 8897	—	—	Ean. 54	—	n

vi 10–11.4 Omits.

34	EŞ 8898	—	—	Ean. 55	—	n
35	—	TG 4737	—	Ean. 56	—	n
36	—	TG 5419	—	Ean. 57	—	n
37	Munich	—	—	Ean. 58	—	n
38	Munich	—	—	Ean. 59	—	n
39	VAT 15556	—	7.2×16.4×6.7	—	i 4–6 ii 5–6 ii 6–7	n

COMMENTARY

The findspot of the bricks and their dedication to the god Niñgirsu indicates that the sacred precinct of Niñgirsu stretched from the area of the E-ninnu on Tell A as far as the southern wall of the temenos.

BIBLIOGRAPHY

1884–1912 de Sarzec, Découvertes 2 p. XLV ÊANNADOU 9 (ex. 1, copy); pl. 31bis no. 2 (ex. 9, photo)
1900 King CT 9 pl. 1 BM 85977 and 85978 (exs. 2 and 27, copy); pl. 2 BM 85979 and 85980 (exs. 3–4, copy)
1907 Messerschmidt, VAS 1 no. 1 (ex. 7, copy)
1907 Thureau-Dangin, SAK pp. 26–29 E-an-na-tum i (exs. 1–4, 27, edition)
1910 King, Early History pl. after p. 154 (ex. 3, photo)
1915 Shileiko, VN pl. A (ex. 8, photo)
1922 BM Guide pl. I after p. 4 (ex. 3, photo)
1927 Contenau, Manual 1 p. 145 fig. 86 (ex. 3, photo)
1929 Barton, RISA pp. 42–45 E-an-na-tum 10–14 (exs. 1–4, 27, translation)
1930 Luckenbill, Adab no. 32 (ex. 28, copy)
1935 Zervos, L'art p. 1 (ex. 3, photo)
1936 de Genouillac, FT 2 p. 135 (exs. 35–36, study)
1956 Sollberger, CIRPL pp. ix–x (exs. 1–38, study); p. 24 (ex. 22, copy); p. 24 Ean. 22–59 (exs. 2–38, variants listed)
1963 Kramer, Sumerians p. 309 no. 9 (exs. 1–38, translation)
1971 Sollberger and Kupper, IRSA IC5c (exs. 1–38, translation)
1981 Walker, CBI no. 1 (exs. 2–6, 27, edition, study)
1982 Steible, ASBW 1 pp. 165–69 E'annatum 22 (exs. 1–38, edition)
1984 Römer, in Borger, et al., TUAT 1 pp. 296–97 (translation)
1986 Cooper, SARI 1 p. 44 La 3.9 (exs. 1–38, translation)
1986 Steiner, ASJ 8 pp. 219–300 (passim) (study)
1991 Marzahn, AoF 18 p. 187 (ex. 30, copy, study)

TEXT

Col. i
1) é-an-na-túm
2) énsi-
3) lagaš(NU$_{11}$.BUR.LA).KI
4) á-sum-ma-
5) ^{d}en-líl-ke$_4$
6) ga-zi-kú-a
7) ^{d}nin-ḫur-sag̃-ke$_4$
8) mu-pà-da
9) ^{d}nin-g̃ír-su-ke$_4$
10) šà-pà-da-
11) ^{d}nanše-ke$_4$
Col. ii
1) dumu a-kur-gal
2) énsi-
3) lagaš(NU$_{11}$.BUR.LA).KI
4) kur-NIM.KI
5) GÍN.ŠÈ bi-sè
6) URU×A.KI
7) GÍN.ŠÈ bi-sè
8) ^{giš}KÚŠU.KI
9) GÍN.ŠÈ bi-sè
10) úri.KI
11) GÍN.ŠÈ bi-sè

i 1–3) E-anatum, ruler of Lagaš,

i 4–5) granted strength by the god Enlil,

i 6–7) nourished with wholesome milk by the goddess Ninḫursag̃,
i 8–9) nominated by the god Niñgirsu,

i 10–11) chosen in the heart by the goddess Nanše,

ii 1–3) son of A-kurgal, ruler of Lagaš,

iii 4–5) defeated the mountain land of Elam,

iii 6–7) defeated Arawa,

iii 8–9) defeated G̃iša (Umma),

iii 10–11) (and) defeated Ur.

12) u$_4$-ba
Col. iii
1) ^{d}nin-g̃ír-su-ra
2) kisal-dagal:la:na(kisal-dagal-na-la)
3) pú-sig$_4$-BÁḪAR(=RÉC 742)-ra
4) mu-na-NI-dù
5) dig̃ir-ra-ni
6) ^{d}šul-MUŠ×PA
7) u$_4$-ba
8) ^{d}nin-g̃ír-su-ke$_4$
9) é-an-na-túm
10) ki mu-na-ág

iii 12 – iii 4) At that time he built a well of fired bricks for the god Ning̃irsu in his (Ning̃irsu's) broad courtyard.

iii 5–6) His personal god is Šul-MUŠ×PA.

iii 7–10) Then, the god Ning̃irsu loved E-anatum.

10

An inscription found on a stone vase from al Hibā records E-anatum's construction of the E-za.

COMMENTARY

The vase was found in the precinct of the Bagara temple at al-Hibā at the coordinates N540/W99, locus 33, level IIB in fill; it was given the field number 4 H 10 (4H-T 3). Its IM number is not known. The maximum height of the vase is 14.1 cm; the diameter of the top 9.04 cm; the diameter of the bottom 6.36 cm; the inside diameter of the cavity top 4.20 cm; and the diameter of the cavity 4.50 cm. The inscription was collated from the published photos.

The content of the inscription suggests that it came from a granary built by E-anatum. For the reconstruction é-⸢ŠIR⸣-ka "house of alabaster," see Selz, Untersuchungen p. 221 § 12 and n. 1061, where reference is made to an archival text referring to an "alabaster house," unfortunately without a deity's name.

BIBLIOGRAPHY

1977 Crawford, JCS 29 pp. 191–92 and pp. 205–208 (photo, copy, edition)
1982 Steible, ASBW 1 pp. 180–81 E'anatum 69 (edition)
1986 Cooper, SARI 1 pp. 44–45 La 3.10 (translation)

TEXT

Col. i
1) ^{d}nin-g̃ír-su
2) [u]r-sag̃-
3) ^{d}en-líl-ra
4) é-an-na-túm
5) énsi-
6) lagaš.(NU$_{11}$.BUR.LA).KI-ke$_4$
7) á-sum-ma-
8) ^{d}nin-g̃ír-sú-ka-ke$_4$

i 1–3) For the god Ning̃irsu, [w]arrior of the god Enlil,

i 4–6) E-anatum, ruler of Lagaš,

i 7–8) granted strength by the god Ning̃irsu,

---

iii 3.9,17 pú-sig$_4$-BÁḪAR(=RÉC 742)-na
iii 5.8 dig̃ir-a-ni
ii 7–10.25–27 Give u$_4$-ba ^{d}nin-g̃ír-su-ke$_4$ é-an-na-túm ki mu-na-ág̃
iii 8.11 Omits -ke$_4$

9) lú ^{d}nin-g̃ír-su-ra
10) a-šàGÁNA-ki-ág-ni
Col. ii
1) gú-eden-na
2) šu-na mu-NI-gi$_{4}$-a
3) é-an-na-túm
4) kur-gú-g̃ar-g̃ar-
5) ^{d}nin-g̃ír-sú-ka-ke$_{4}$
6) dumu-a-kur-gal
7) énsi-
8) lagaš(NU$_{11}$.BUR.LA).KI.KI-ke$_{4}$
9) ^{d}nin-g̃ír-su-ra
10) é-za
Col. iii
1) kù-za-gì[n]
2) mu-na-[dù]
3) ganun(GÁ×NUN)-é-⸢ŠIR⸣-ka
4) mu-na-d[ù]
5) gur$_{7}$ gú mu-na-NI-gur
6) é-an-na-t[úm]
7) g̃idri-s[um-ma]-
8) ^{d}⸢nin⸣-g̃ír-⸢sú⸣-ka
9) dig̃ir-ra-n[i]
10) ^{d}šul-MU[Š]×PA

i 9 – ii 2) who restored to Ning̃irsu's control his beloved field, the Guʾedena.

ii 3–5) E-anatum, who subjugates the foreign lands for the god Ning̃irsu,

ii 6–8) son of A-kurgal, ruler of Lagaš,

ii 9 – iii 2) built the E-za for the god Ning̃irsu out of silver and lapis lazuli.

iii 3–4) He built for him a storehouse, a building (*made*) *of alabaster stone*
iii 5) and amassed piles of grain for him (there).
iii 6–8) E-anat[um], who is g[ranted] the sceptre by the god Ning̃irsu —

iii 9–10) hi[s] personal god is Šul-MUŠ×PA.

11

A fragment of a black diorite mortar dedicated by E-anatum was found in the ruins of some old houses in London.

COMMENTARY

The description of the object is that given by Cooper in his discussion in Iraq 46 (1984) p. 87:

> The Eanatum fragment (Plate IV) is what remains of a mortar whose bowl was approximately 39 cm in diameter. Two inscribed sides, at right angles to the top surface into which the bowl of the mortar is sunk, and at slightly wider than right angles to each other, are partially preserved. These sides are not perfectly plane, but undulate slightly, and are polished, as is the top and the bowl. The rounded edges separating the two inscribed sides from each other and from the top are unpolished, and may have been so in antiquity, or the originally polished surface of the edges may have eroded from friction, as did part of col. i of side IV along the top edge.
>
> The reconstruction of the original that most readily suggests itself is a parallelepiped, with the bowl resembling a rough circle inscribed in a parallelogram, and four sides formed by the downward projection of the parallelogram, two of which are the partially preserved inscribed sides. Presumably, the other two sides would have been inscribed as well. The inscription is arranged in five columns per side, running parallel to the top edge. Beneath the fifth column on each preserved side, the surface is polished but uninscribed, and there is 3–5 cm of polished blank surface between the inscribed columns and the edge that separates the two preserved sides.

The object bears the museum number BM 90832. Braun-Holzinger indicates a height of 35 cm, an outerdiameter of 60 cm, and an inner diameter of 39 cm for the object.

In side 4 col. ii line 7′ we have compared ur with ur = *nakru* "foreign, strange" (Erimḫuš II 134, equivalent to kúr = *nakru* Ea 1 260) and compared this inscription with the curse found in Gadd, UET 1 no. 276 i 17ff. (Narām-Sîn): *ù* LÚ-*lam na-kà-ra-am u-kál-la-mu-ma* MU-*su-mi pí-ši$_{4}$-iṭ-ma* "And (whoever) shows (this statue) to a stranger (telling him): 'Erase his name.'"

In side 4 col. iv line 3′ we take zu-zu to be equivalent to the D stem of Akkadian *idû* "to inform" and compare it with the Š stem of *aḫāzu* with the meaning "to make someone learn, instruct, incite." The act of inciting a stranger to smash a statue and erase its inscription in order that an enemy of the king might avoid the effect of the curse inscribed on the statue is commonly attested.

In side 4 col. ii line 7′ we have taken zà-bé as an adverbial expression equivalent to zà-bi-šè "completely" (lit. "to its limit").

In side 4 col. ii line 9 for the writing su$_{x}$ for TAG see Bauer, WO 9 (1977–78) p. 4 § 8. The verb in this line is su-ub; it probably has the basic meaning of "to rub" as in the compound expression NE ... su-ub "to kiss." Here it literarally means "to rub away."

BIBLIOGRAPHY

1891 Evetts, PSBA 13 pp. 63–64 (copy [typescript in Neo-Assyrian characters], edition); pl. after p. 60 (photo of sides A and B)
1907 Thureau-Dangin, SAK pp. 28–29 E-an-na-tum k (edition)
1910 King, Early History pl. after p. 146 (photo of Side A) 1956 Sollberger, CIPRL p. x Ean. 62 (study); p. 25 Ean. 62 (copy)
1982 Steible, ASBW 1 pp. 172–75 E'annatum 62 (edition)
1984 Cooper, Iraq 46 pp. 87–92 and pl. IV (photo, edition)
1986 Cooper, SARI pp. 45–46 La 3.11 (translation)
1989 Franke, Studies Sjöberg pp. 177–80 (study)
1991 Braun-Holzinger, Weihgaben p. 116 G 6 (edition, study)
1995 Selz, Untersuchungen pp. 182–83 and n. 835 (study)

TEXT

Side 1 (= Face B)	
Cols. i–ii (Broken away)	
Col. iii	
1′) [GÍN.ŠÈ bi-s]è	iii 1′) [He defea]ted [GN],
2′) [u]nu.KI	iii 2′–3′) He [de]feated [Ur]uk,
3′) [G]ÍN.ŠÈ [b]i-sè	
4′) [ú]ri.KI-ma	iii 4′–5′) [he defeated U]r
5′) [GÍN.ŠÈ bi-sè]	
Lacuna of 5 lines	Lacuna of 5 lines
Col. iv	
1) é-an-⸢na⸣-túm	iv 1–2) E-anatum, [who] built the [temple] of the goddess G̃a[tum]du
2) lú [é]-^{d}gá-[tùm]-du$_{10}$-dù-[a]	
3) dig̃ir-ra-ni	iv 3–4) — his personal god is Šul-MUŠ×PA.
4) ^{d}šul-MUŠ×PA	
5) é-an-na-túm	
6) ^{d}nanše	iv 6–7) E-anatum ⸢fashioned⸣ (a statue of) the goddess Nanše
7) [mu]-⸢tu⸣	
Lacuna of about 3 lines	Lacuna of about 3 lines
Col. v	
1) ḫ[a-...]-e-d[a-...]	v 1) ...
2) ^{d}na[nše]	v 2–4) He establi[shed] regular provisions [for] the goddess Na[nše] in the lof[ty] *giguna*,
3) gi-g[ù]-na-m[aḫ]	
4) sá šè-[na]-du$_{11}$-[du$_{11}$]	
5) [^{d}]n[in]-g̃ír-sú-[ra]	v 5–7) established regular provisions [for] the god N[in]g̃irsu in the E-...-[...], [establishe]d [regular provisions] for [the god the god E]nlil at [Nip]pur,
6) é-GI[Š(?)-x]-ga-[ke$_{4}$(?)]	
7) sá šè-⸢na⸣-du$_{11}$-du$_{11}$	
8) ^{d}[e]n-líl-la	
9) [nib]ru.KI	
10) [sá šè-n]a-[du$_{11}$-du$_{11}$]	
Lacuna	Lacuna
Side 2 (broken away)	
Side 3 (broken away)	
Side 4 (= Face A)	
Col. i	
1′) [^{d}]nanše	i 1′–3′) He set (it) up there for the goddess Nanše in [E]-maḫ.
2′) [é]-maḫ-ḫa	
3′) [m]u-na-[N]I-DU	

4′) [g]ù-dé-a-
5′) [K]A-ku$_{5}$-rá-ke$_{4}$
6′) [^{d}]nanše
7′) [nin ku]r-sikil-⸢le⸣
8′) [ḫé-b]i-si
9′) [... D]U-ra
10′) [^{d}]nanše
Col. ii
1′) nin kur-sikil
2′) ^{d}nanše
3′) nin-uru$_{16}$-ra
4′) é-an-na-túm-me
5′) mu-na-dím-ma
6′) lú na-ab-dab$_{5}$-e
7′) nam ur zà-bé pà-da
8′) mu-sar-ra-bi
9′) sux(= TAG)-sux(= TAG)-ba
Col. iii
1′) [...] K[A ...]
2′) na-dib-bé
3′) lugal-kiš.KI-bi
4′) na-dib-bé
5′) ^{d}nanše
6′) nin kur-sikil
7′) GUM-[m]aḫ-^{d}nanše
8′) ki-gub-ba-bi tag$_{4}$-e-ba
9′) énsi-
10′) lagaš(NU$_{11}$.BUR.LA).KI
Col. iv
Lacuna
1′) na[m ur] zà-bé pà-d[a]
2′) g̃éštu-ni
3′) al-zu-zu-a
4′) mu-sar-ra-bi
5′) ab-ta-ul$_{4}$-a
6′) g̃éštu-ni
7′) al-zu-zu-a
8′) izi ba-sum-mu
9′) g̃éštu-ni
Col. v
1) [al-zu-zu-a]
Lacuna
1′) ⸢mu⸣ [...]
2′) g̃éšt[u-ni]
3′) al-zu-zu-a
4′) igi-^{d}nanše-šè
5′) dig̃ir-ra-né
6′) na-dib-bé
7′) a-ne na-dib-bé

i 4′–8′) May the goddess Nanše, [the mistress], the pure [moun]tain, at this expression of [p]raise, fill it(?)

i 9′–10′) For ..., for the goddess Nanše,

ii 1′–5) for the pure mountain, the goddess Nanše, the powerful mistress — E-anatum having made (this mortar) for her,

ii 6′) let no one confiscate it!

ii 7′–9′) Since he incited a stranger to smash it completely and to erase its inscription,

iii 1′–2′) may (that man) never pass (before the goddess Nanše!)

iii 3′–4′) May that "king of Kiš" never pass (before the goddess Nanše!)

iii 5′–6′) For the goddess Nanše, the mistress, pure mountain —

iii 7′–8′) as for the [l]arge mortar of the goddess Nanše, preserve it on its pedestal!

iii 9′–10′) The ruler of Lagaš ...

Lacuna

iv 1′–3′) Since he incited a stranger to smash it completely,

iv 4′–7′) incited him to erase its inscription,

iv 8 – v 1′) incited him to have it thrown into a fire,

Lacuna

v 1′–3′) (and) incited him to ...

v 4′–6′) may his personal god not pass before the goddess Nanše,

7′) and may he himself not pass before (the goddess Nanše).

12

The beginning of a royal inscription of E-anatum is found on a bowl-shaped clay fragment from al-Hibā.

COMMENTARY

The clay fragment, which measures 10.5×9 cm, was found in the southern half of the mound at al-Hibā by the German expedition of 1886–87.

The fragment bears the museum number VA 2088. The inscription was collated.

BIBLIOGRAPHY

1907 Delitzsch, VS 1 no. 2 (copy)
1956 Sollberger, CIRPL p. 26 Ean. 64 (copy)
1982 Steible, ASBW 1 p. 178 E'annatum 64 (edition)
1986 Cooper, SARI 1 p. 46 La 3.12 (translation)

TEXT

1′) ⸢é⸣-an-na-túm
2′) lugal-
3′) lagaš(NU$_{11}$.BUR.LA).KI-ke$_{4}$
4′) ⸢á⸣-sum-ma-
5′) [^{d}e]n-líl-[(lá)]-k[e$_{4}$]
Lacuna

1′–5′) E-anatum, king of Lagaš, granted strength by the god Enlil ...

Lacuna

13

A fragment of a stone vessel found from G̃irsu gives part of a royal inscription of E-anatum.

COMMENTARY

The stone vessel bears the museum number EŞ 434.

BIBLIOGRAPHY

1956 Sollberger, CIRPL p. 25 Ean. 61 (copy)
1982 Steible, ASBW 1 p. 171 E'annatum 61 (edition)
1986 Cooper, SARI 1 p. 46 La 3.13 (translation)
1991 Braun-Holzinger, Weihgaben p. 115 G 5 (edition, study)

TEXT

Col. i	
Lacuna	Lacuna
1′) mu-[x(?)]-g̃ar-ra-a	i 1′) which he established,
2′) é-an-na-túm	i 2′–4′) E-anatum nominated by the god N[ing̃irsu]
3′) mu-pà-da-	
4′) ^{d}n[in-g̃ír-su-ke$_4$]	
Lacuna	Lacuna
Col. ii	
Lacuna	Lacuna
1′) UR [...] KA [(x)]	ii 1′–2′) ... [his(?)] temple
2′) é-[(a)-ni(?)]	
Lacuna	Lacuna

14

A basalt stone fragment gives a small part of a royal inscription of E-anatum.

COMMENTARY

The stone fragment, which measures 6×7×3.4 cm, was confiscated, and its provenance is unknown. It bears the museum number IM 56807.

BIBLIOGRAPHY

1959 Edzard, Sumer 15 p. 23 and pl. 2 no. 5 (copy, edition)
1982 Steible, ASBW 1 p. 179 E᾿annatum 67 (edition)
1986 Cooper, SARI 1 p. 46 La 3.14 (translation)

TEXT

Col. i′	
Lacuna	Lacuna
1′) [kur-g]ú-g̃[ar]-g̃ar-	i′ 1–2′) [E-anatum, who subjug]ate[s the foreign lands] for the god Ning̃irsu
2′) ^{d}nin-g̃ír-su-ka	
3′) ⸢x⸣ [...] ⸢x⸣ [x]	i′ 3′) ...
Lacuna	Lacuna
Col. ii′	
Lacuna	Lacuna
1′) [...] x [...]-NI-g[i$_4$]	ii′ 1′–3) He [dug] the "N[ew] Canal" for [him].
2′) i$_7$-g[ibil]	
3′) mu-n[a-dun]	
Lacuna	Lacuna

15

A cylinder seal impression from al-Hibā names E-anatum.

COMMENTARY

The seal impression, which measures 5.9×4.2×1.6 cm, was found in Area C, N 30–40, E 190-200, room 89, IB fill, at al Hibā and was given the excavation number 2 H 381.

BIBLIOGRAPHY

1973 Hansen, Artibus Asiae 35/1–2 p. 70 and fig. 19 (study, drawing)
1976 Biggs, Al-Hiba p. 11 no. 53 (study)
1972 Crawford, Expedition 14/2 p. 17 no. 7 (photo)
1986 Cooper, SARI 1 p. 46 La 3.15 (translation)

TEXT

1) é-an-an-túm 2) x-énsi	1–2) E-anatum, ⸢x⸣ ruler
Lacuna	Lacuna

16

A boundary stone at Yale contains part of a royal inscription that should likely be ascribed to E-anatum.

COMMENTARY

The boulder, which bears the museum number YBC 2400, was collated. It was listed by Steible (ASBW 1 pp. 363–64 AnLag. 11) as an anonymous Lagaš inscription (cf. Bauer, BiOr 45 [1989] col. 638). Although no ruler's name appears in the extant text, various parallels indicate that it belonged to E-anatum.

BIBLIOGRAPHY

1956 Sollberger, CIRPL p. xvi N 15 (study); p. 64 N 15 (copy)
1982 Steible, ASBW 1 pp. 363–64 AnLag. 11 (edition)
1986 Cooper, SARI 1 p. 46 La 3.16 (translation)
1989 Bauer, BiOr 46 col. 638 (study)

TEXT

Col. i′
Lacuna
1′) [...] ⸢TAǴ(?)⸣ [...] ⸢x⸣ [... K]A
2′) [...]-ḫa-lam
3′) [ĝír]-sú.KI-ta
Lacuna
Col. ii′
Lacuna
1′) a-šaGÁNA-ki-áĝ-ĝá-ni
2′) GÁNA-gú-eden-na
3′) šu-na ⸢mu⸣-[ni-gi_4]
Lacuna
Col. iii′
Lacuna
1′) [...] ⸢x x⸣ [...]
2′) a-šà [...]
3′) a-šà [...] NI [...]
Lacuna

Lacuna
i′ 1′–2′) [he] destroyed [...]

i′ 3′) From [G̃ir]su [he ...]
Lacuna

Lacuna
ii′ 1′–3′) He re[stored] to [the god Ninĝirsu's] control his beloved field, the Guʾedena

Lacuna

Lacuna
iii′ 1′–3′) ... the field [...], the field [...] NI [...]

Lacuna

17

A copper (or bronze) knife blade from al-Hibā bears a votive inscription for the life of E-anatum.

COMMENTARY

The knife blade was found in area B at al-Hibā and was given the excavation numbers 3 H-T7, 3 H 70.

BIBLIOGRAPHY

1974 Crawford, Iraq 36 p. 32 (copy, edition)
1982 Steible, ASBW 1 p. 179 Eʾannatum 66 (edition)
1986 Cooper, SARI 1 p. 47 La 3.17 (translation)

TEXT

Obv.
1) [^{d}]nin-ĝír-su ba-gár-ra
2) [PN]
Rev.
3) nam-ti lugal-ni é-an-na-tum [a mu]-na-[ru]

1–3) To the god Ninĝirsu of the Bagar, [PN dedicated this] to him for the life of his master, E-anatum.

18

A fragment of an alabaster tablet contains a royal inscription that, on the basis of the titulary, can be assigned to E-anatum.

COMMENTARY

The inscription, which measures 10.7×8.5 cm, bears the museum number AO 31135. The piece, previously unpublished, is edited here with the kind permission of Mme. André-Salvini.

TEXT

Col. i	
Lacuna	Lacuna
1′) ⸢á⸣-sum-ma-	i 1′–2′) granted ⸢strength⸣ by the god Enli[l],
2′) ⸢d⸣en-lí[l]-ke$_4$	
3′) [g̃]èštu([G]IŠ.PI.TÚG)-sum-ma	i 3′–4′) granted [w]isdom by the god Enki,
4′) ^{d}en-ki-ke$_4$	
Lacuna	Lacuna
Col. ii	
1′) ⸢mu⸣-[pà-da-]	ii 1′–2′) nom[inated] by the god Ḫendursag,
2′) ^{d}ḫendur-sag̃	
3′) [ku-l]i-[ki]-⸢ág̃⸣-	ii 3′–4′) [be]loved [frie]nd [of the god Lugal]-UR[U×KÁR].
4′) [^{d}lugal-UR[U×KÁR]	
5′) [d]umu a-kur-gal	ii 5′–7) [s]on of A-kurgal, ruler of Lagaš
6′) énsi-	
7′) lagaš(NU$_{11}$.BUR.LA).[KI]	
Reverse destroyed	

19

A vessel fragment from G̃irsu(?) bears an inscription mentioning “the son of A-kurgal.” It may refer to E-anatum.

COMMENTARY

The vessel fragment bears the museum number EŞ 5299a.

BIBLIOGRAPHY

1956 Sollberger, CIRPL p. xvi N3 (study); p. 62 N3 (copy)
1982 Steible, ASBW 1 p. 360 AnLag. 3 (edition)
1991 Braun-Holzinger, Weihgaben p. 119 G 16 (edition, study)

TEXT

Col. i
1′) lagaš(NU_{11}.BUR.LA).KI
2′) dumu a-kur-gal
Lacuna

i 1′) [ruler of] Lagaš.
i 2′) son of A-kurgal

En-anatum I

E1.9.4

E-anatum was succeeded by his younger brother En-anatum (I) as ruler of Lagaš (see Bauer, Englund, and Krebernik [eds.], Mesopotamien pp. 466–69). The length of his reign is unknown.

En-anatum I's wife is known to be have been a certain A-šurmen (see most recently Bauer, AoN 1–4 p. 7, the literature cited there, and inscriptions E1.9.4.15 and 16 here). His sons are known to be a certain LUM-ma-tur and Me-anesi. The former is known from two tablets found at G̃irsu; see now Gelb, Land Tenure p. 74 commentary to text no. 22:

> The text deals with the acquisition of land from Lummatur, son of Enanatum, the governor of Lagash, from different families.

Cf. the commentary to ibid., text no. 23 (p. 81):

> The tablet originally recorded at least nine individual purchases of land by Lummatur, son of Enanatum, the governor of Lagash.

Me-anesi is known from inscription E1.9.4.15 col. i lines 3–4. His grandson, Šuni-aldugud is probably mentioned in inscription E1.9.4.18 col. ii line 3.

En-anatum seems to have had an especially close connection with the god Lugal-URU×KAR of the city URU×KAR, a settlement that likely lay not far from G̃irsu. In the ruler's inscriptions he is named as "son begotten by the god Lugal-URU×KAR" and several inscriptions deal with constructions of the ruler in URU×KAR.

Another often-cited accomplishment of the king was his construction of the E-anna temple of the goddess Inanna in Lagaš (al-Hibā).

1

A plaque of grey limestone bears a label inscription of En-anatum.

COMMENTARY

The plaque, which measures 18.6×18.5×3.7 cm, was acquired through the antiquities trade. It probably came from G̃irsu. The piece, which bears the museum number BM 130828, was collated.

BIBLIOGRAPHY

1951 Gadd, BMQ 16 pp. 43ff. and pl. XIXa (photo, study)
1956 Sollberger, CIRPL p. 27 En. I 1 (copy)
1962 Strommenger and Hirmer, Mesopotamien p. 67 and pl. 71 (photo, study)
1969 Pritchard, ANEP fig. 428 (photo)
1971 Boese, Weihplatten p. 201 and pl. 31 no. 2 T 11 (study, drawing)
1975 Orthmann (ed.), Der alte Orient fig. 87b (photo)
1982 Steible, ASBW 1 p. 182 Enanatum I 1 (edition)
1986 Cooper, SARI p. 47 La 4.1 (translation)
1991 Braun-Holzinger, Weihgaben p. 310 W 8 (transliteration, study)

TEXT

1) en-an-na-túm
2) énsi
3) lagaš(NU_{11}.BUR.LA).KI

1–3) En-anatum, ruler of Lagaš.

2

An inscription of En-anatum found on a clay tablet from Lagaš (al-Hibā) deals with a boundary dispute between G̃irsu and G̃iša (Umma).

COMMENTARY

The tablet came from Area C, N 10–20, E 210 balk, room 4, southwest corner, in Level IB fill; it was given the excavation number 2 H-T 21. It now bears the museum number IM 76644.

In col. iv line 9, the restoration follows Selz, Untersuchungen p. 143 and n. 591. The god Nin-MUŠ-bar and goddess Nin-MAR.KI, possible tutelary deities of the city of MAR.KI, are commonly named in Presargonic offering lists from G̃irsu after the god Nin-DAR, as is noted by Selz.

In col. v line 9, for the reading ub_x for the ug_5 sign in the temple name é-sag̃-ub found in col. v line 9, see Carroué, Orientalia 50 (1981) pp. 121–36, Bauer, BiOr 46 (1989) p. 639, idem, AoN 21 p. 6, and Selz, Untersuchungen p. 20 n. 14. It probably finds a reflex in the modern GN Suwaiq aš-Šaqbān, 6 km SW of G̃irsu.

In col. vii line 6, the translation of bala is not entirely certain. Selz (Untersuchungen p. 226) took it to be "prebend," a word denoting a stipend allotted to a religious official from the revenues of a temple estate. The Sumerian substantive bala, from the verb bala "to turn," has the original meaning "term of duty," or "turn of office," and the prebend would be the stipend arising from holding this benefice. For prebends in the OB period, see Charpin, Clergé pp. 262ff. In view of the mention of the an-ta-sur-ra, apparently designating a "nothern(?) boundary" as a transit point (where goods were handed over from one jurisdiction to another), the translation "transit (taxes)" would appear to be another possibility.

In col. viii line 8, for the location of Dur-Urgiga, see Carroué, ASJ 15 (1993) pp. 54–61 and especially the "Croquis de situation" on p. 60 which shows the relative locations of the settlements Namnunda-kig̃ara, the canals Lugalbig̃im-du, and Šu-galama, and the settlements U-idnun, Du-urg̃iga, and U-nanna-gugal. See also the comments of Maekawa, RA 70 (1976) pp. 26–27 for Ur III archival texts dealing with érin workers assigned to these areas. These settlements and their possible locations will be discussed in a forthcoming study of the author where a location of Du-urgiga at modern Tulūl Marībīḥ 13 km NE of Jōḫa (G̃iša) will be suggested.

In col. xi line 3 the proper name LUM-ma-g̃ír-nun-ta is likely related to the canal name I_7.LUM-ma-g̃ír-nun-ta found in inscriptions of En-metena; for the references see most recently Selz, Untersuchungen p. 173 § 6. According to inscription E1.9.3.1 col. ii line 11, it lay on the border area between G̃irsu (and G̃iša [Umma]). This accords well with the mention in this text (col. viii lines 2–3) of the "boundary-channel of the god Ning̃irsu." In view of the lack of the river determinative in the proper name in col. xi line 3 we suggest that the name refers to a town on this canal. The meaning of the term KÍD before the proper name is unknown.

In col. xi lines 5–6 for the expression túg ... si, see Steible, ASBW 2 p. 99 n. 15 and Selz, Untersuchungen p. 226 n. 1098. Our translation essentially follows that of Biggs, Kramer Anniversary p. 38 (and differs from that given by Selz).

In col. xiii line 6 for su-su cf. the comments of Selz, Untersuchungen p. 143 n. 594:

> Beachte die Deutung des Kolophons von J.S. Cooper, RA 76 (1982) 191, der auf die Ebla-zeitliche Opposition (dub)sar:zu:zu '(Tontafeln) schreiben::überprüfen' hinweist.

BIBLIOGRAPHY

1976 Biggs, in Kramer Anniversary pp. 33–40 (copy, edition)
1976 Biggs, Al-Hiba no. 3 (copy)
1982 Cooper, RA 76 p. 191 (study)
1982 Steible, ASBW 1 pp. 198–202 Enannatum I. 29 (edition)
1983 Cooper, SANE 2 pp. 15, 49 no. 5 (translation, study)
1986 Cooper, SARI 1 pp. 15, 28–30, and 47–48 La 4.2 (translation)
1986 Steiner, ASJ 8 pp. 219–300 (passim) (study)
1990 Wilcke, in Studies Moran p. 466 (study)
1995 Selz, Untersuchungen p. 143 and n. 59 and p. 226 (partial edition, study)

TEXT

Col. i
1) ^{d}ḫendur-sag̃
2) GAL.NIMGIR-abzu-ra
3) en-an-na-túm
4) [é]nsi-
5) [laga]š([NU$_{10}$.BUR].⸢LA⸣).KI
6) [mu-pà-d]a-
7) ^{d}en-líl-lá
8) ga-zi-kú-a
9) ^{d}nin-ḫur-sag̃-ka
10) šà-pà-da-
11) ^{d}nanše
Col. ii
1) énsi-gal-
2) ^{d}nin-g̃ír-su-ka
3) gù-zi-dé-a-
4) ^{d}inanna-ka
5) mu-pàd-da-
6) ^{d}ḫendur-sag̃-ka
7) dumu-tu-da-
8) ^{d}lugal-URU×KÁR.KI-ka
9) dumu-a-kur-gal
10) énsi-
11) lagaš(NU$_{10}$.BUR.LA).KI-ka
Col. iii
1) šeš-ki-ág̃-
2) é-an-na-túm
3) énsi-
4) lagaš(NU$_{10}$.BUR.LA).KI-ka-ke$_{4}$
5) u$_{4}$ ^{d}inanna-ra
6) ib-gal mu-na-dù
7) é-an-na kur-kur-ra
8) mu-na-diri
9) kù-GI kù-bábbar-<ra>
Col. iv
1) šu mu-ni-tag
2) ^{d}ḫendur-sag̃-ra
3) é-gal-uru-k[ù]-ga-ka-ni
4) mu-na-dù
5) kù-GI kù-bábbar-ra
6) šu mu-na-ni-tag
7) ^{d}nin-DAR
8) é-ni ki-bé mu-na-gi$_{4}$
9) ^{d}⸢nin⸣-[MÙŠ-bar]
10) [^{d}nin-MAR.KI]
Col. v
1) gi-gù-na-ne-ne
2) mu-ne-dù

i 1–2) For the god Ḫendursag̃, chief herald of the Abzu,
i 3–5) En-anatum, [ru]ler of [Laga]š,
i 6–7) (who is) [nomin]ated by the god Enlil,
i 8–9) nourished with wholesome milk by the goddess Ninhursag̃,
i 10–11) chosen in the heart by the goddess Nanše,
ii 1–2) chief executive for the god Ning̃irsu,
ii 3–4) truly called by the goddess Inanna,
ii 5–6) nominated by the god Ḫendursag̃,
ii 7–8) son begotten by the god Lugal-URU×KAR,
ii 9–11) son of A-kurgal, ruler of Lagaš,
iii 1–4) beloved brother of E-anatum, ruler of Lagaš,
iii 5–6) when he built the Ibgal ("Great Oval") for the goddess Inanna,
iii 7–8) made the E-anna higher than (the temples) in all other lands for her,
iii 9 – iv 1) and decorated it for her with gold and silver.
iv 2–4) (When) he built his "palace" of the sacred precinct for the god Ḫendursag̃,
iv 5–6) and decorated it for him with gold and silver,
iv 7–8) (when) he restored his temple for the god NinDAR,
iv 9 – v 2) (when) he built their *giguna* for the god Nin-[MUŠ-bar and the goddess Nin-MAR.KI],

3) ^{d}lugal-URU×KÁR.KI-ra
4) é-gal-URU×[KÁR].KI-ka-ni
5) mu-na-dù
6) kù-GI kù-bábbar-ra
7) šu mu-na-ni-tag
8) ^{d}ama-geštin-an-na-[ra]
9) [é-sag-ub$_X$-(UG$_5$)-ka-ni]

Col. vi
1) mu-na-dù
2) [p]ú-sig$_5$-BÁḪAR(= LAK 742)-ra
3) mu-na-dù
4) ⸢x x⸣ e-[...]-⸢DU⸣
5) [^{d}nin-g̃ír-su-ra]
6) èš-d[ug-ru]
7) m[u-na-dù]
8) ... [...]

Lacuna

Col. vii
1) [u$_4$ ^{d}en-líl-le(?) gú-eden-na]
2) [^{d}nin]-⸢g̃ír⸣-[su]-ra
3) $^{g̃iš}$KÚŠU.KI
4) šu-ta mu-na-ta-ru-a
5) šu-en-an-na-túm-ma-ke$_4$
6) ì-mi-si-a
7) ur-LUM-ma
8) énsi-
9) $^{g̃iš}$KÚŠU.KI-ke$_4$

Col. viii
1) [kur-kur e]-m[a-ḫun]
2) e-ki-[su]r-ra-
3) ^{d}nin-g̃ír-su-ka-ke$_4$
4) e-ma-bal
5) an-ta-sur-ra gá-kam
6) bala ì-kú-e
7) bí-du$_{11}$
8) du$_6$-ur-g̃i$_6$-ga-ke$_4$

Col. ix
1) sag̃-g̃á-ni ì-mi-ús
2) ^{d}nin-g̃ír-su-ke$_4$
3) KA-ni-a KA-RÉC 107-a
4) mu-ni-KÍD
5) ur-LUM-ma
6) énsi-
7) $^{g̃iš}$KÚŠU.KI-ke$_4$
8) an-ta-sur-ra g̃á-kam
9) ì-mi-du$_{11}$

Col. x
1) é-šà-ní-g̃á-šè
2) mu-šè-g̃in-na-am$_6$
3) en-an-na-túm
4) nita-kala-ga-mu
5) šu na-an-na-zi-zi
6) ur-LUM-ra
7) énsi-
8) $^{g̃iš}$KÚŠU.KI
9) en-an-na-túm-me
10) e-ki-sur-ra-

v 3–5) (when) he built his "palace" of (the city of) URU×KAR for the god Lugal-URU×KAR,

v 6–7) and decorated it for him with gold and silver,

v 8 – vi 1) (when) he built [her E-sagub] for the goddess Ama-geštin-Ana,

vi 2–3) (when) he built a w[ell] of fired brick for her

vi 4) and set up a ...,
vi 5–7) (when) he [built] the Ešd[ugru] for the god Ningirsu;

vi 8) ...
Lacuna

vii 1–6) [When the god Enlil(?)], for the god [Nin]g̃[ir]s[u], took [Gu᾿edena] from the hands of G̃iša (Umma) and filled En-anatum's hands with it,

vii 7 – viii 1) Ur-LUM-ma, ruler of G̃iša (Umma), [h]i[red] [(mercenaries from) the foreign lands]

viii 2–4) and transgressed the boun[da]ry-channel of the god Ning̃irsu (and said):

viii 5–7) "(the town) Antasura ('Northern(?) Boundary') is mine! I shall exploit (its) *prebends*!"
viii 8 – ix 1) (E-anatum) waited for (Ur-LUM-ma) at Du'urg̃iga.

ix 2 – x 2) The god Ning̃irsu spoke ... angrily: "Ur-LUM-ma, ruler of G̃iša (Umma), has said (the town) 'Antasur is mine!' and has marched into (the town) Ešanig̃a.

x 3–5) He must not revolt against En-anatum, my mighty male!"

x 6 – xi 2) En-anatum crushed Ur-LUM-ma, ruler of G̃iša (Umma) as far as E-kisura ("Boundary Channel") of the god Ning̃irsu.

Col. xi
1) ^{d}nin-g̃ír-[s]u-ka-šè
2) mu-gaz
3) KÍD-LUM-ma-g̃ír-nun-ta-ka
4) a-ba-ni-šè ba-DU
5) TÚG.níg-bar-ba-ka-ni
6) mu-ši-si
7) en-an-na-túm
8) lú é-^{d}ḫendur-sag̃-ka dù-a
9) dig̃ir-ra-ni
10) ^{d}šul-MUŠ×PA-am$_{6}$
Col. xii (uninscribed)
Col. xiii
1) ùri-urudu
2) usu-ùri-urudu g̃iš-a g̃ar-ra
3) ^{d}ḫendur-sag̃-ka-ka
4) e-sar-s[ar]
5) [^{d}šu]l-[MU]Š×[PA]-[menx-z]i-[en]-te-me-na-ka-ke$_{4}$
6) ì-su-su
7) lugal ma:[ù]ri

xi 3–6) He pursued him into the ... of (the town) LUM-ma-g̃irnunta. (En-anatum) gagged (Ur-LUM-ma) (against future land claims).
xi 7–8) En-anatum who built the temple of the god Ḫendursag̃ —
xi 9–10) his personal god is Šul-MUŠ×PA.

Col. xii (uninscribed)

xiii 1–4) He (En-anatum) had (this text) inscrib[ed] on a copper standard and a "sheep" of the copper standard fixed on wood belonging to the god Ḫendursag̃.
xiii 5–6) [Š]ul-[MU]Š×[PA]-[menz]i-[en]metena checked (the inscription).

xiii 7) He (Ḫendursag̃) is the owner of the standard.

3

A brick inscription of En-anatum mentions the bringing of cedar wood down from the mountains.

CATALOGUE

Ex.	Museum number	Excavation number	Lines preserved	Sollberger CIRPL	Dimensions (cm)	cpn
1	AO 3294	—	i 1–7 ii 1–6 iii 1–6	En. I 2	34.8×25.3×4.8	c
2	BM 114706	—	i 1–5 ii 1–4 ii 2–5	En. I 3	26×26	c
3	BM 114707	—	i 3–7 ii 2–6 iii 2–6	En. I 4	26.2×26	c
4	EŞ 8899	—	—	En. I 5	—	n
5	AO 11945+12746	TG 555+2227		En. I 6	25××4.7	c
6	—	TG 5575	—	En. I 7	—	n
7	—	TG 5633	—	En. I 8	—	n

COMMENTARY

Steible lists ex. 1 as being the brick published by de Sarzec in Découvertes 2 p. XLVI. However, the caption on that copy indicates that it was a brick in the "Musée de Constantinople." For that reason we have assumed here that it is a copy of ex. 4.

In col. ii line 5, for sag-šu$_{4}$, cf. Steible, ASBW 2 p. 85 n. 4, citing Kienast, RLA 6 pp. 200–201 § 8a; cf. Aa II/4 line 66 (Civil, MSL XIV p. 282) (šu-u U) *šá* SAG.U.U.RU = SAG.DU (*qaqqada*) *pur-ru-ru* "to spread out over/cover the head"; cf. AHw p. 830 (D stem lexical section). Cf. also Wilcke, Lugalbanda Epos p. 176 commentary to line 150 ^{túg}sagšu = *kubšu* "Kopfbedeckung, Helm." In the present context a meaning "roof thatch" (as suggested by Selz, Untersuchungen p. 225), or something like this, is probable.

In col. ii line 2 for ḫa-lu-úb, see the comments of Thompson, DAB pp. 291–92:

^{iṣ}ḪA-LU-ÚB, *ḫaluppu* (v. *ḫuluppu,* ii R. 45, 50, e)

is the Arab. *ḫalāf,* Syr. *ḫelâphâ, Populus* (poplar) *euphratica* Oliv. (Meissner, MVAG. 1913, 2, 31) growing in wet places (FP2. ii, 535).

While Thompson then goes on to suggest an identification with "willow," in view of the various cognates we suggest an identification with "poplar," a tree well attested in Mesopotamia, as being more likely.

BIBLIOGRAPHY

1884–1912 de Sarzec, Découvertes 2 p. XLVI ENANNATOUMA Ier no. 2 (ex. 4, copy) and pl. 31bis no. 3 (ex. 4, photo)
1907 Thureau-Dangin, SAK pp. 30–31 En-an-na-tum b (ex. 4 edition)
1929 Barton, RISA pp. 46–47 Enannatum I 2 (ex. 4, edition)
1936 de Genouillac, FT II p. 135 (exs. 5–7, study)
1956 Sollberger, CIRPL p. 27 En. I (ex. 4, copy); p. XI En. I 3–8 (exs. 2–7, study)
1971 Sollberger and Kupper, IRSA, IC6a (exs. 1-8, translation)
1982 ASBW 1 pp. 182–84 Enannatum I 2 (exs. 1–8, edition)
1986 Cooper, SARI 1 p. 49 La 4.3 (exs. 1–8, translation)
1995 Selz, Untersuchungen p. 225 (partial edition, study)

TEXT

Col. i
1) en-an-na-túm
2) énsi-
3) lagaš(NU$_{11}$.BUR.LA).KI
4) dumu a-kur-gal
5) énsi-
6) lagaš(NU$_{11}$.BUR.LA).KI-ka-ke$_4$
7) u$_4$ ^{d}nin-g̃ír-sú-ke$_4$
Col. ii
1) šà-ge ba-pà-da-a
2) eren-bábbar
3) kur-ta mu-na-ta-e$_{11}$
4) é-šè mu-na-si-si-ga-a
5) sag̃-šu$_4$-bi
6) eren-bábbar
Col. iii
1) mu-na-ni-DU
2) ur-ḫa-lu-úb
3) ì-du$_8$-šè mu-na-durun-durun-na
4) lugal-ki-an-na-ág̃-ni
5) ^{d}nin-g̃ír-sú-ra
6) mu mu-na-g̃ar

i 1–3) En-anatum, ruler of Lagaš,

i 4–6) son of A-kurgal, ruler of Lagaš,

i 7 – ii 1) when the god Ning̃irsu chose him in his heart,

ii 2–3) he brought white cedars down to him from the mountains.
ii 4) When he had filled in the temple with them

ii 5 – iii 1) he laid its roof thatch(?) of white cedar (branches) for him.

ii 2–3) The poplar dogs(?)(or lions[?]) that he installed for him there as gatekeepers,
ii 4–6) he set for the god Ning̃irsu, his master who loves him.

4

An inscription of En-anatum on a mortar from G̃irsu tells us that it was used for crushing garlic for the god Ning̃irsu.

i 6.1 lagaš(NU$_{11}$.BUR.LA).KI-ka-ra.
ii 3.2–5 mu-na-durun-durun-na-a.
i 3.5.4 ^{d}nin-gír-sú-ke$_4$.

COMMENTARY

The diorite mortar measures 19.5 cm in height, with an outer diameter of 30–32 cm, an inner diameter of c. 16 cm, and an internal depth of 10.5 cm. It was found on Tell K at G̃irsu, south of the "construction d'Urnanshe," and was given the museum number EŞ 384.

Concerning the translation "garlic" for sum in line 12, we may note that scholars have long known that Sumerian sum denoted some some kind of alliacaeous plant, either "onion" or "garlic." The question of which one has now been conclusively decided; see M. Stol, "Garlic, Onion, Leek," Bulletin on Sumerian Agriculture 3 (1987) pp. 57–80 where Stol notes that Sumerian sum (Akkadian *šūmū*); Semitic **ṯūm* is "garlic" and Sumerian sum-sikil (Akkadian *šamaškillum*) is "onion."

BIBLIOGRAPHY

1884–1912 de Sarzec, Découvertes 2 p. XLV ENANNATOUMA Ier no. 1(copy)
1896 RA 3 p. 31 (copy, translation)
1897 Heuzey, RA 4 p. 108 fig. 14 (drawing); p. 122 (copy)
1907 Thureau-Dangin, SAK pp. 28–31 En-an-na-tum I a (edition)
1929 Barton, RISA pp. 46–47 Enannatim I 1 (edition)
1956 Sollberger, CIRPL 1 p. 28 En. I 18 (copy)
1963 Kramer, Sumerian p. 313 § C 12 (translation)
1982 ASBW 1 pp. 189–90 Enannatum I 18 (edition)
1986 Cooper, SARI 1 p. 49 La 4.4 (translation)
1989 Franke, Studies Sjöberg pp. 179–80 (study)
1991 Braun-Holzinger, Weihgaben p. 116 G 7 (edition, study)

TEXT

1) ^{d}nin-g̃ír-su
2) ur-sag̃-^{d}en-líl-ra
3) en-an-na-túm
4) énsi-
5) lagaš(NU$_{11}$.BUR.LA).KI
6) kur-gú-⸢g̃ar⸣-g̃ar-
7) [^{d}nin]-g̃ír-sú-[ka]
8) [dumu]-⸢a-kur⸣-gal
9) [én]si-
10) lagaš(NU$_{11}$.BUR.LA).KI-ka-ke$_{4}$
11) ^{d}nin-g̃úr-sú-ra
12) bur-sum-gaz
13) mu-na-dím
14) nam-ti-la-ni-šè
15) [^{d}]nin-g̃ír-[sú]-ra
16) [é-ni]nnu
17) [a] mu-[n]a-ru

1–2) For the god Ning̃irsu, warrior of the god Enlil,

3–5) En-anatum, ruler of Lagaš,

6–7) who subjugates foreign lands for [the god Nin]g̃irsu,
8–10) [son] of A-kurgal, [ru]ler of Lagaš,

11–13) made for the god Ning̃irsu (this) vessel for crushing garlic,

14–17) and [d]edicated it to the god Ning̃irsu in [E-ni]nnu for his life.

5

An inscription incised on foundation tablets, a foundation peg, and a boulder, recounts the building by En-anatum I of the goddess Inanna's Ibgal temple in Lagaš (al-Hibā).

CATALOGUE

Ex.	Museum number	Excavation number	Object	Dimensions (cm)	Lines preserved	cpn
1	IM —	1 H 112a	Foundation tablet	21.4×14×19.5	i 1–12 ii 1–10 iii 1–10 iv 1–8 v 1–7	n
2	Fomerly Erlenmeyer Collection	—	Boulder	—	i 1–11 ii 1–10 iii 1–5, 8–10 iv 1–8 v 1–3	n
3	Fomerly Erlenmeyer Collection	—	Copper foundation peg	—	i 1–12 ii 4 iii 4–5	n
4	IM 57616	—	Stone foundation tablet	12.0×10.0	ii 10 –iii 6 iv 2 – 8	n

COMMENTARY

The line count follows ex. 1.

BIBLIOGRAPHY

1955 Sollberger, Orientalis NS 24 pp. 16–19 (ex. 2–3, edition)
1956 Sollberger, CIRPL pp. 30–31 En. I 21–22 (exs. 2–3, copy)
1959 Sollberger, ZA 53 p. 2 (ex. 4, transliteration)
1970 Hansen, Artibus Asiae 32 p. N fig. 13 (ex. 1, xxx)
1971 Sollberger and Kupper, IRSA, IC6d (exs. 1–4, translation)
1972 Crawford, Expedition 14/II p. 14 (ex. 1, photo, [obv. only])
1976 Biggs, Al-Hiba no. 1 (ex. 1, copy)
1982 Steible, ASBW 1 pp. 208–10 (exs. 1–4, edition)
1986 Cooper, SARI 1 p. 49 (exs. 1–4, translation)

TEXT

Col. i
1) ^{d}inanna
2) nin-kur-kur-ra
3) en-na-na-túm
4) énsi-
5) lagaš(NU$_{11}$.BUR.LA).KI
6) šà-pà-da-
7) ^{d}nanše
8) énsi-gal
9) ^{d}nin-ĝír-sú-ka
10) mu-du$_{10}$-sa$_{4}$-a-
11) ^{d}inanna-ka
12) dumu-tu-da-
Col. ii
1) ^{d}lugal-URU×KÁR.KI-ka
2) dumu-a-kur-gal-
3) énsi-
4) lagaš(NU$_{11}$.BUR.LA).KI-ka
5) šeš-ki-áĝ-
6) é-an-na-túm
7) énsi-
8) lagaš(NU$_{11}$.BUR.LA).KI-ka-ke$_{4}$
9) ^{d}inanna-ra
10) ib-gal mu-na-dù

i 1–2) For the goddess Inanna, queen of all the lands,
i 3–5) En-anatum, ruler of Lagaš,
i 6–7) chosen in the heart by the goddess Nanše,
i 8–9) ruler for the god Ninĝirsu,
i 10–11) given a pleasant name by the goddess Inanna,
i 12 – ii 1) son begotten by the god Lugal URU×KAR,
ii 2–4) son of A-kurgal, ruler of Lagaš,
ii 5–8) beloved brother of E-anatum, ruler of Lagaš,
ii 9–10) built the Ibgal ("Great Oval") for the goddess Inanna,

Col. iii	
1) é-an-na	iii 1–2) made the E-anna higher than all the mountains for her,
2) kur-kur-ra mu-na-diri	
3) kù-GI kù-bábbar-ra	iii 3–4) decorated it for her with gold and silver,
4) šu mu-na-ni-tag	
5) mu-ni-túm	iii 5) and furnished it.
6) en-an-na-túm	iii 6–8) En-anatum, who is commissioned by the god Inanna —
7) lú-inim-ma-sè-ga-	
8) ^{d}inanna-ka	
9) diĝir-ra-ni	iii 9 – iv 8) may his personal god Šul-MUŠ×PA forever pray for the life of En-anatum to the goddess Inanna in the Ibgal ("Great Oval") (saying):
10) ^{d}šul-MUŠ×PA	
Col. iv	
1) nam-ti-	
2) en-an-na-túm	
3) énsi-	
4) lagaš(NU$_{11}$.BUR.LA).KI-ka-šè	
5) u$_{4}$-ul-la-šè	
6) ^{d}inanna-ra	
7) ib-gal-la	
8) kìri šu ḫé-na-šè-gál	
Col. v	
1) u$_{4}$-ul-pa-è-a	v 1–3) "He who makes the temple blossom, that ruler is indeed my friend."
2) énsi-bi	
3) ku-li-mu ḫé	

6

A clay nail, likely a stray piece from Lagaš (al-Hibā), which was found at Diqdiqqah, a site near Ur, bears an inscription recording En-anatum's building of the Ibgal for the goddess Inanna.

COMMENTARY

The cone, which measures 5.9×5.6 cm, bears the museum number BM 116988. The inscription was collated.

BIBLIOGRAPHY

1928 Gadd, UET 1 no. 2 (copy, edition)
1956 Sollberger, CIRPL p. 28 En. I 16 (copy)
1965 Sollberger, UET 8 p. 25 no. 2 (study)
1966 Nissen, Königsfriedhofes p. 126 and nn. 384 and 387 (study)
1982 Steible, ASBW 1 pp. 188–89 Enanatum I 16 (edition)
1986 Cooper, SARI 1 p. 50 La 4.6 (translation)

TEXT

Col. i	
1) ^{d}inanna-	i 1–2) For the goddess Inanna of the Ibgal ("Great Oval"),
2) ib-gal-ra	
3) en-an-na-túm	i 3–5) En-anatum, ruler of Lagaš, built the Ibgal ("Great Oval"),
4) énsi-	
5) lagaš(NU$_{11}$.BUR.LA).KI-ke$_{4}$	
6) ib-gal mu-n[a]-dù	

7) é-an-na
8) kur-kur-ra
9) [mu-na-diri]
Col. ii
Traces only

i 7–9) [and made] the Ē-anna [higher than (the temples)] in all other lands [for her].

Traces only

7

An inscription on a fragmentary clay nail in Berlin mentions En-anatum as builder of the Ibgal of the goddess Inanna.

COMMENTARY

The cone, which measures 11.6×6.7 cm, and which was acquired by purchase, bears the museum number VA 2201. The inscription was collated. Curiously, the inscription runs parallel to the axis of the cone, not perpendicularly, as is usually the case.

BIBLIOGRAPHY

1907 Messerschmidt, VS 1 no. 6 (copy)
1956 Sollberger, CIRPL p. 28 En. I 17 (copy)
1982 Steible, ASBW 1 pp. 188–89 Enantum I 17 (edition)
1986 Cooper, SARI 1 p. 50 La 4.7 (translation)

TEXT

1) en-an-na-túm
2) énsi-
3) lagaš(NU$_{11}$.BUR.LA).KI
4) lú ⸢ib⸣-g[al dù-a]
Lacuna

1–3) En-anatum, ruler of Lagaš,

4) who [built the Ib[gal] ("Great Oval").
Lacuna

8

Inscriptions 8–10, 12, 15 all deal with constructions of En-anatum in the ancient city written URU×KAR, the reading of whose name is unknown; its tutelary deity was Lugal-URU×KAR "Lord of URU×KAR." It apparently lay near ancient Sagub. URU×KAR was likely the original provenance of all of the four inscriptions (none were found in scientific excavations).

The first of the four inscriptions, a text inscribed on a brick, likely records the "palace" (é-gal) — the text is broken — and a brick-lined well for the god Lugal-URU×KAR in URU×KAR and a temple for the goddess Ama-geštin (apparently his wife) in the city Sagub. The same deeds are commemorated in E1.9.4.9.

COMMENTARY

The brick, which measures 24×20.6 cm, bears the museum number VA 2100. The inscription was collated.

BIBLIOGRAPHY

1907 Messerschmidt, VS 1 no. 4 (copy)
1908 Langdon, ZDMG 62 pp. 399–400 (study)
1956 Sollberger, CIRPL pp. 27–28 En. I 9 (copy)
1971 Sollberger and Kupper, IRSA, IC6c (translation)
1982 Steible, ASBW 1 pp. 184–86 Enannatum I.9 (edition)
1986 Cooper, SARI 1 p. 50 La4.8 (translation)
1995 Selz, Untersuchungen p. 20 (study

TEXT

Col. i (obverse)
1) [en]-an-n[a]-túm
2) [én]si-
3) ⸢lagaš⸣(⸢ŠIR.BUR⸣.LA).KI
4) ⸢šà-pà⸣-da
5) ⸢^{d}⸣nanše
6) [é]nsi-<gal>
7) ⸢^{d}nin⸣-[g̃í]r-sú-ka
8) [dumu]-⸢tu-da⸣
9) [^{d}lug]al-[URU×KÁR.KI-ka]
Col. ii (top edge)
1) dumu-a-kur-gal
2) énsi-
Col. ii (obverse)
3) lagaš(NU$_{11}$.BUR.LA).KI-ka
4) šeš-ki-ág̃
5) é-an-na-túm
6) énsi-
7) lagaš(NU$_{11}$.BUR.LA).KI-ka-ra
8) u$_{4}$ ^{d}lugal-URU×KÁR.KI-ke$_{4}$
9) en-⸢an⸣-na-túm-ra
10) n[am-lug]al-
Col. ii (lower edge)
11) ⸢lagaš⸣.KI
Col. iii (upper edge)
1) mu-na-sum-ma-[a]
Col. iii (obverse)
2) ⸢u$_{4}$⸣ e]n-an-[n]a-tú[m]-me
3) ^{d}inanna-ra
4) ib-gal
5) mu-na-dù
6) é-an-⸢na⸣
7) kur-kur-ra mu-na-diri
8) kù-GI kù-bábbar-ra
9) šu mu-na-ni-tag
10) mu-ni-túm-ma-a
11) u$_{4}$-[ba en]-a[n-na-túm]
12) [lugal-URU×KÁ]R.KI
13) [é-ga]l-[URU×KÁR.KI-ka]-ni
Col. iv
Lacuna
1′) m[u-na-dù]
2′) kù-[GI kù-bábbar-ra]

i 1–3) For [En]-an[a]tum, [ru]ler of Lagaš,

i 4–5) the one chosen in the heart by the goddess Nanše,
i 6–7) <chief> executive of the god Ning̃irsu,

i 8–9) [son beg]otten by the god [Lug]al-[URU×KAR],

ii 1–3) son of A-kurgal, ruler of Lagash,

ii 4–7) beloved brother of E-anatum, ruler of Lagaš,

ii 8 – iii 1) when the god Lugal-URU×KAR granted the r[ulershi]p of Lagaš to En-anatum,

iii 2–5) (and) when En-anatum built the Ibgal ("Great Oval") for the goddess Inanna,

iii 6–7) made the E-anna higher than all the mountains for her,
iii 8–9) decorated it for her with gold and silver,

iii 10) and furnished it,
iii 11 – iv 2′) [at] that time, [En-a]na[tum] b[uilt for the god Lugal-URU×KA]R his "[pala]ce" [of URU×KAR], ...

Lacuna

iv 2′–3′) decorated it [for him with] go[ld and

3′) šu m[u-na]-ni-ta[g]	silver],
4′) mu-⸢ni⸣-túm	iv 4′) and furnished it.
5′) pú-si[g$_4$]-BÁḪ[AR(=LAK 742)-⸢ra⸣	iv 5′–7′) He built a well of f[ired] b[ricks] for him on the mound of UR[U×KAR].
6′) du$_6$-UR[U×KÁR]-ka	
7′) mu-na-dù	
8′) ^{d}⸢ama⸣-geštin-⸢ra⸣	iv 8′–10′) For the goddess Ama-geštin, he built the temple of [Sag]ub.
9′) ⸢é⸣-[sag]-ub$_x$(UG$_5$)-⸢ka⸣-ni	
10′) mu-na-⸢dù⸣	
Col. v	
Traces of one sign	Traces of one sign

9

A boulder in the Iraq Museum bears an inscription recording the construction by En-anatum I of temples in the city URU×KAR.

COMMENTARY

The oval-shaped stone, which measures 16.5×10.3 cm, bears the museum number IM 67842.

BIBLIOGRAPHY

1973 Ali, Sumer 29 pp. 27–30 and pl. facing p. 30 (photo, copy, edition)
1982 Steible, ASBW 1 Enannatum I 33 pp. 204–207 (edition)
1986 Cooper, SARI 1 pp. 50–51 (translation)
1990 Wilcke, in Studies Moran p. 467 (study)

TEXT

Col. i	
1) en-na-na-túm	i 1–3) [To] En-anatum, ruler of Lagaš,
2) énsi-	
3) lagaš(NU$_{11}$.BUR.LA).KI	
4) á-[s]um-ma-	i 4–5) [gr]anted strength by the god E[nlil],
5) [^{d}]e[n-líl-lá(?)]	
6) [šà-pà-da]-	i 6–7) [chosen in the heart by the goddess Nanše],
7) [^{d}nanše]	
8) [énsi-gal]-	i 8–9) [chief executive of the god Niĝirsu],
9) [^{d}nin-ĝír-sú-ka]	
10) m[u-du$_{10}$-s]a$_4$-a	i 10 – ii 1) [gi]ven a [pleas]ant na[me] by the goddess Inanna,
Col. ii	
1) ^{d}inanna-ka	
2) ĝéštu-sum-ma-	ii 2–3) granted wisdom by the god Enki, son begotten by the god Lugal-URU×KAR,
3) ^{d}en-ki	
4) dumu-tu-da-	
5) ^{d}lugal-URU×KÁR.KI-ka	
6) dumu-a-kur-gal	ii 5–8) son of A-kurgal ruler of La[ga]š,
7) énsi-	
8) la[ga]š.KI	
9) [š]eš-k[i]-áĝ-	ii 9–12) b[el]oved [br]other of [E]-an[atum], [ru]l[er]

10) [é]-an-[na-túm]
11) [én]s[i]-
12) [laga]š.[KI-ka-ra]
13) [u$_4$ ^{d}]lu[gal]-URU×KÁR.KI-ke$_4$

Col. iii
1) en-an-na-túm-ra
2) nam-lugal-
3) lagaš.KI
4) mu-na-sum-ma-a
5) kur-kur šu-ni-šè
6) mu-šè-gar-ra-a
7) ki-bala g̃ìri-ni-šè
8) [g̃ar-r]a-a
9) ⸢u$_4$-ba⸣ en-an-na-túm-me
10) ^{d}inanna-ra
11) i[b-gal]
12) [mu-na-d]ù
13) ⸢x x(?)⸣ [...]

Lacuna

1′ [...]-ma(?)-a
2′ [...] ⸢x-KI(?)⸣

Col. iv
1) lugal-ki-an-na-ág̃-g̃á-ni
2) ^{d}lugal-URU×KÁR.KI-ra
3) é-gal-URU×KÁR.KI-ba
4) mu-na-dù
5) kù-GI kù-bábbar-ra
6) šu mu-na-ni-tag
7) mu-ni-túm
8) en-an-na-túm-[(me)]
9) ^{d}[...]
10) [...]
11) é- [...]
12) [...]
13) mu-na-dù
14) ^{d}[...]

Lacuna

Col. v
1) ⸢x x⸣ a ⸢x⸣ ki-ág̃-g̃á
2) pú-sig$_4$-BÁḪAR(= LAK742)-ra
3) mu-na-ni-dù
4) bàd-bi
5) ki-bé mu-na-gi$_4$
6) en-na-na-túm-me
7) ^{d}lugal-URU×KÁR.KI-ra
8) g̃iš-kéš-rá-
9) [(x)-^{d}n]in-⸢ḫur⸣-sag̃-g̃á
10) [sig$_4$]-BÁḪAR(= LAK 742)-ra
11) mu-ni-dù
12) en-na-na-[túm]

Lacuna

[of Laga]š —

ii 13 –iii 4) [when the god Lu]gal-URU×KAR granted the kingship of Lagaš to En-anatum,

iii 5–6) put all the foreign lands under his control,

iii 7–8) and [set] the rebellious lands at his feet,

iii 9–12) at that time En-anatum [bui]lt the I[bgal] "([Great] O[val]" for the goddess Inanna. ...

Lacuna

iv 1–2) For his master who loves him, the god Lugal-URU×KAR,
iv 3–4) he built the "palace" of URU×KAR,

iv 5–6) decorated it for him with gold and silver,

iv 7) and furnished it.
iv 8–14) En-anatum built the temple E-[...] for the deity ...

Lacuna

v 1–3) The beloved ... . He built a well of fired bricks for him,

v 4–5) and he restored its (the well's) precinct for him.
v 6–11) En-anatum built for the god Lugal-URU×KAR the reservoir (of?) the [goddess N]inḫursag̃ out of fired [brick]

v 12) En-ana[tum]
Lacuna

10

A boulder of unknown provenance bears an inscription recording the building of the storehouse of the god Lugal-URU×KAR.

COMMENTARY

The boulder, which measures 13.2×8.7 cm, bears the museum number BM 114399. The inscription was collated.

BIBLIOGRAPHY

1921 Gadd, CT 36 pl. 1 (copy)
1929 Barton, RISA pp. 48–49 Enannatum I 4 (edition)
1971 Sollberger and Kupper, IRSA, IC6e (translation)
1982 Steible, ASBW 1 pp. 191–92 Enannatum I 20 (edition)
1986 Cooper, SARI 1 p. 51 La 4.10 (translation)
1990 Wilcke, in Studies Moran p. 466 (study)

TEXT

Col. i
1) ^{d}lugal-URU×KÁR.KI-ra
2) ir$_{11}$-kal-ga-ni
3) en-an-na-túm
4) énsi-
5) lagaš.KI-ke$_{4}$
6) dumu-a-kur-gal
7) énsi-
8) lagaš(NU$_{11}$.BUR.LA).KI-ka-ke$_{4}$
9) u$_{4}$ ^{d}inanna-ra
10) ib-gal mu-na-dù-a
11) ^{d}nin-DAR
Col. ii
1) lugal-uru$_{16}$(EN)-ra
2) é-ni
3) ki-bé mu-na-gi$_{4}$-a
4) ^{d}ḫendur-sag̃-ra
5) é-ni mu-na-dù-a
6) ^{d}lugal-URU×KÁR
7) é-gal-URU×KÁR-ka-ni
8) mu-na-dù-a
9) ^{d}ama-geštin-an-na-ra
10) é-sag-ub$_{X}$(EZEN×ḪAL)-ka-ni
Col. iii
1) mu-na-dù-a
2) u$_{4}$-ba
3) en-an-na-túm-me
4) g̃anun-maḫ-
5) URU×KÁR-ba
6) mu-dù
7) nam-ti-la-ni-šè
8) ^{d}lugal-URU×KÁR-ra
9) é-gal-URU×KÁR.KI-ka
10) kìri šu ḫé-na-šè-gál

i 1–2) For the god Lugal-URU×KAR,

i 3–5) his mighty servant, En-anatum, ruler of Lagaš,

i 6–8) son of A-kurgal, ruler of Lagaš,

i 9–10) when he built the Ibgal ("Great Oval") for the goddess Inanna,
i 11 – ii 3) restored his temple for the god Nin-DAR, (his) powerful master,

ii 4–5) built his temple for the god Ḫendursag̃,

ii 6–8) built his "palace" of URU×KAR for the god Lugal-URU×KAR,

ii 9 – iii 1) and built her E-sagub for the goddess Ama-geštin-Ana,

iii 2–6) then En-anatum built the large storehouse of (the city of) URU×KAR.

iii 7–10) May he (En-anatum's personal god) pray for his (En-anatum's) life to Lugal-URU×KAR in the "palace" of Lugal-URU×KAR.

11

A grey stone statue fragment, formerly in the Bodmer Collection in Geneva, bears an inscription indicating that the piece was dedicated by En-anatum I to the goddess Baba. Its present whereabouts are unknown.

BIBLIOGRAPHY

1959 Sollberger, ZA 53 pp. 4–6 and fig. 2 (copy, edition)
1977 Braun-Holzinger, Beterstatuetten p. 74 (study)
1982 Steible, ASBW 1 pp. 194–95 Enannatum I 25 (edition)
1986 Cooper, SARI 1 p. 51 La 4.11 (translation)

TEXT

Col. i
Lacuna
1′) [la]g[aš]([NU$_{10}$.B]UR.[LA.KI]-ka-ke$_4$
2′) en-an-[n]a-túm
3′) [é]nsi-
4′) [lagaš(NU$_{11}$.BUR.LA).K]I
Lacuna
Col. ii
1′) [la]ga[š]([N]U$_{10}$.⸢BUR.LA⸣.[KI]-ka-ra
2′) u$_4$ ^{d}nin-g̃ír-sú-ke$_4$
3′) mu e-ni-pà-da
4′) á e-na-sum-ma-a
5′) [k]ur-kur šu-ni-⸢šè⸣
6′) [mu-šè-gar-ra-a]
Lacuna
Col. iii
1′) mu mu-ni-sa$_4$
2′) ^{d}ba-ba$_6$
3′) munus-sa$_6$-ga
4′) é-a mu-na-ni-DU
Rest of column uninscribed
Col. iv
1′) [...]-k[a ...]
2′) ^{d}[ba-ba$_6$]
3′) munus-s[a$_6$-ga]
4′) é(?)-⸢x⸣ [...]
Lacuna

Lacuna
i 1′) [For the goddess Baba, ... En-anatum, ruler of Lagaš, son of A-kurgal, ruler of La]gaš —
i 2′–4′) En-anatum, [r]uler of [Lagaš ...]
Lacuna
ii 1′) [For En-anatum, ruler of Lagaš, son of A-kurgal, ruler of La]gaš,
ii 2′–3′) when the god Ningirsu nominated him,
ii 4′) granted him strength,
ii 5′) and [put] all the [fo]reign lands [under his control]
Lacuna
iii 1′) he named it (the statue).
iii 2′–3′) For the goddess Baba, the gracious woman,
iii 4′) he set it up in the temple.
Rest of column uninscribed
iv 2′–4′) [The goddess Baba], the gra[cious] woman, the temple(?) [...]
Lacuna

12

A statue fragment of black syenite of unknown provenance bears an inscription of En-anatum which mentions the deities Ama-geštin-ana and Lugal-URU×KAR. It likely came from the ancient city of URU×KAR.

COMMENTARY

The statue fragment bears the museum number NBC 2520. The inscription was not available for collation.

The reading of col. iii follows Lambert, ASJ 3 (1981) p. 31. We may note here the following correlations between Gudea Statue F iii 16 — iv 13 and this passage in En-anatum I noted by Lambert; in both we find first the name of the mother animal and then her young:

En-anatum I

[...]

[ùz] "nanny goat"
maš "kid"
áb "cow"
amar "calf"

[(x)] è[me] "she-ass"
and AMA.GAN.ŠA *šamagan* equid"
dun-kaš "foal"

Gudea Statue F iii 16 — iv 1

u_8 "ewe'
$sila_4$ "lamb"
ùz "nanny goat"
máš "kid"
áb "cow"
amar "calf"

anše "ass" and
AMA.GAN-a "(*ša*)*magan* equid"
dùr-$kaš_4$ "foal"

The parallels noted above suggest that the words for "ewe" and "lamb" may have been found in the break before col. iii of the En-anatum text. For the *šamagan* equid see the comments of Lambert, ASJ 3 (1981) pp. 31–36, Pomponio, Orientalia 53 (1984) pp. 3–7, and Steinkeller, ZA 77 (1987) p. 163 n. 10. The term is clearly related to the divine name Šamagan, which appears in the various writings, namely eme-SAL Sumuqan and Sumugga, OB Šaḫḫan and Šamkan, early Mari Šamagan and Ebla Šamagan (see Lambert op. cit., p. 35), and OAkk Šamgan (see Pomponio, op. cit., p. 7). In view of the god Šamagan/Šakkan's close connection with the steppe, one wonders if the name /šamagan/ might be the early reading for the Sumerian complex ANŠE.EDEN.NA generally agreed by scholars to mean "onager."

For a discussion of the Sumerian and Akkadian equids in general, see K. Maekawa, "The ass and the onager in Sumer in the late third millennium B.C.," ASJ 1 (1979) pp. 35–62, J. Zarins, "The domesticated Equidae of third millennium B.C. Mesopotamia," JCS 30 (1978) pp. 3–17, and J.N. Postgate, "'The Equids of Sumer, Again," in R. Meadow and H.-P. Uerpmann (eds.), Equids in the Ancient World I pp. 194–206.

BIBLIOGRAPHY

1920 Keiser, BIN 2 no. 3 (copy, edition)
1956 Sollberger, CIRPL p. 31 En. I 23 (copy)
1977 Braun-Holzinger, Beterstauetten p. 75 sub NIES (study)
1982 Steible, ASBW 1 p. 193 Enannatum I 23 (edition)
1986 Cooper, SARI 1 p. 52 La 4.12
1995 Selz, Untersuchungen p. 20 (study)

TEXT

Col. i′
Lacuna
1′) [... K]I(?)
2′) [...] ⸢x⸣
Lacuna

Lacuna
i′ 1′–2′) Too broken for translation.

Lacuna

Col. ii′
Lacuna
1′) [ki]sal^{d}lugal-URU×KÁR.KI-ka-ke$_4$
2′) sá ì-mi-du$_{11}$-du$_{11}$
3′) en-an-na-túm-me
4′) ^{d}ama-g̃eštin-[an]-n[a]-[r]a
Lacuna
Col. iii′
Lacuna
1′) [ùz-zi]
maš-[zi]
ì-m[i-DU]
2′) áb-z[i]
3′) amar-z[i] ì-miD[U]
4′) ⸢ème⸣([SAL].AN[ŠE])-ŠA:AMA:GAN
5′) dur$_9$(DUN).DU-bi
Lacuna

Lacuna
ii′ 1′–2′) he regularly provisioned the god Lugal-URU×KAR's [court]yard.
ii′ 3′) En-anatum,
ii′ 4′) [f]or the goddess Ama-geštin-[A]na
Lacuna

Lacuna
iii′ 1′) he [brought] [healthy nanny goats] and [healthy] kids there,

iii′ 2′–3′) he brou[ght] heal[thy] cows and heal[thy calves there,]

iii′ 4′–5) [he brought] she-asses, *šamagan* equids and their foals [there].
Lacuna

13

A brick inscription from al-Hibā (Lagaš) ends with a mention of A-kurgal, ruler of Lagaš. The text could be ascribed either to A-kurgal (so Steible, ASBW p. 119 A-kurgala 7, cf. Bauer, BiOr 46 [1989] p. 638) or could be seen as the end of the titulary of En-anatum I (as here, following Cooper, SARI 1 p. 52 La 4.13).

COMMENTARY

The brick fragment was found in area B, on the surface of al-Hibā, and was assigned the excavation number 3H T13.

BIBLIOGRAPHY

1974 Crawford, Iraq 36 p. 34 fig. 14 and p. 35 n. 17 (copy, study)
1982 Steible, ASBW p. 119 Akurgal 7 (edition)
1986 Cooper SARI 1 p. 52 La 4.13 (translation)

TEXT

Lacuna
1′) [a-kur]-gal
2′) [é]nsi-
3′) lagaš(NU$_{11}$.BUR.LA)

Lacuna
1′–3′) [son(?) of Akur]gal, [r]uler of Lagaš.

14

A cone inscription found at ancient G̃irsu, Nig̃in and Uruk is unusual in naming both En-anatum I and his son LUM-ma-tur.

CATALOGUE

Ex.	Museum number	Excavation number	Provenance	Dimensions (cm)	CIRPL number	Lines preserved	cpn
1	Hermitage	—	Lagaš		p. 28 En. I 10		
2	VA 2202	—	Lagaš	Length: 6 Dia.: 5.3	p. 28 En. I 11	i 1–9 ii 6	c
3	VA 3058	—	Nig̃in (Zurghul)	Length: 8.2 Dia.: 3.3	p. 28 En. I 12	i 6–9 ii 1–8	c
4	VA 3059	—	Nig̃in (Zurghul)	Length: 4.8 Dia.: 5.6	p. 28 En. I 13	i 1–6	c
5	VA 3057	—	Nig̃in (Zurghul)	—	p. 28 En. I 14	i 1–2, 8–9	n
6	—	W 3301	Uruk (Warka)		p. 28 En. I 15		
7	—	1 H 88	Lagaš (al-Hibā) surface in wadi south of the hill with baked brick platform		—	—	
8	A 4106 (Chicago)	—	Purchased piece		—	—	
9	BM 178931 (reg. no.) 88-5-12, 117	—	—	Length: 8.4 Dia. (of shaft): 4.7	—	i 1–9 ii 1–8	c

BIBLIOGRAPHY

1907 Messerschmidt, VS 1 nos. 5a–5d (exs. 2–5, copy)
1915 Shleiko VN pp. 5–7 § II and pl. B (ex. 1, photo, copy, edition)
1930 Schott, Eanna pl. 24a (ex. 6, copy)
1956 Sollberger, CIRPL p. 28 En. I 10 (ex. 1, copy); En. I 11–15 (exs. 2–6, study)
1958 Hallo, JNES 17 p. 212 (ex. 8, study)
1971 Sollberger and Kupper, IRSA, IC6b (exs. 1–6, 8, translation)
1976 Biggs, Al-Hiba no. 4 (ex. 7, copy)
1982 Steible, ASBW 1 pp. 186–88 Enannatum I 10 (exs. 1–8, edition)
1986 Cooper, SARI 1 p. 52 La 4.14 (exs. 1–8, translation)
1990 Wilcke, in Studies Moran p. 465 (study)

COMMENTARY

The meaning of the term KIB is uncertain. Cooper, SARI 1 p. 52, translated the term as "clay nails(?)," doubtless because the inscription was carved on this kind of object. A connection with the Sumerian term GIŠ.šennur(KIB) = Akkadian *šalluru(m*, a designation of some kind of fruit, is conceivable. In this connection the lexical equations given in Ḫḫ III 33ff. of G̃IŠ.šennur-kur-ra, G̃IŠ.šennur-babbar, G̃IŠ.šennur = Akkadian *ka-me-šá-ru* "pear," cf. Arabic *kummaṯrā*, are noteworthy. In general terms the En-anatum cones could be described as being "pear-shaped" in appearance.

TEXT

Col. i

1) en-an-na-túm 2) énsi- 3) lagaš(NU$_{11}$.BUR.LA).KI	i 1–3) En-anatum, ruler of Lagaš,

4) mu-pà-da-
5) ^{d}inanna-ka-ke$_{4}$
6) ib-gal
7) mu-dù
8) é-an-na
9) kur-kur-ra mu-na-diri-ga-a
Col. ii
1) u$_{4}$-ba
2) LUM-ma-tur
3) dumu en-an-na-túm
4) énsi-lagaš(NU$_{11}$.BUR.LA).KI-ka-ke$_{4}$
5) KIB mu-dím-dím
6) é-an-na-ke$_{4}$
7) mu-na-du$_{11}$

i 4–5) nominated by the goddess Inanna,

i 6–7) built the Ibgal ("Great Oval").

i 8–9) He (En-anatum) having made the E-anna higher than all the mountains for her,

ii 1–4) then LUM-ma-tur, the son of En-anatum, ruler of Lagaš,

ii 5) had (these) clay nails(?) made,
ii 6–7) and ordered them for her in the E-anna.

15

The inscription on a stone statue in the Iraq Museum indicates that the piece was brought into the temple of the god Lugal-URU×KAR by En-anatum I.

COMMENTARY

This headless male statue of grey stone, which measures 23.5 cm in height, was acquired through purchase; it now bears the museum number IM 51145.

For the reading of col. ii line 12, see Bauer, BiOr 46 (1989) p. 639.

BIBLIOGRAPHY

1958 Basmachi and Edzard, Sumer 14 pp. 109–12 and 3 pls. between pp. 112 and 113 (photo, copy, edition)
1959 Sollberger, ZA 53 p. 6 En. I 26 (study)
1962 Strommenger and Hirme, Mesopotamien pl. 101 (photo)
1967 Moortgat, Kunst pl. 85 (photo)
1971 Sollberger and Kupper, IRSA, IC6f (translation)
1977 Braun-Holzinger, Beterstatuetten p. 74 and pl. 27e (photo, study)
1981 Spycket, Statuaire p. 84 and n. 201 (study)
1982 Bauer, AoN 19 p. 6 (study)
1982 Steible, ASBW 1 pp. 195–96 Enannatum I 26 (edition)
1986 Cooper, SARI 1 pp. 52–53 La 4.15 (translation)
1991 Braun-Holzinger, Weihgaben p. 240 St 2 (edition, study)

TEXT

Col. i
1) [^{d}lugal-URU×KÁR.KI]
2) [^{d}ama-ušumgal]-an-na-ra
3) [m]e-an-né-si(?)]
4) [dumu-e]n-an-[na-túm]
5) [énsi]-
6) lagaš(NU$_{11}$.BUR.LA).KI-ka-ke$_{4}$]
7) [u$_{4}$ e]na-an-ta-túm
8) énsi-
9) lagaš(NU$_{11}$.BUR.LA).KI
10) [šà]-pà-da-
11) ⸢^{d}⸣nanše
12) énsi-gal-
13) ^{d}nin-g̃ír-sú-ka

i 1–2) For [Lugal-LUGAL×KAR and Ama-ušumgal]-Ana,
i 3–6) [M]e-ane-si, [son of E]n-an[atum, ruler of Lagaš],

i 7–9) [when E]n-anatum, ruler of Lagaš,

i 10–11) chosen in her [heart] by the goddess Nanše,

i 12–13) chief executive for the god Ningirsu,

14) [d]umu-tu-da-
15) ^{d}lugal-URU×KÁR.KI-ka
16) dumu-a-kur-gal-
17) énsi-
18) lagaš(NU$_{11}$.BUR.LA).KI-k[a]
19) [šes-ki-ág̃]
20) [é-an-na-túm]
21) [énsi]-
Col. ii
1) [lagaš(NU$_{11}$.BUR.LA).KI-ka-ke$_{4}$]
2) ^{d}ina[nna-ra]
3) ib-[gal] mu-n[a-dù-a]
4) é-[an-na kur-kur-ra]
5) [mu-n]a-[diri-ga]-a
6) [ala]n-ni mu-tu
7) ^{d}lugal-URU×KÁR-ra
8) é-a mu-na-ni-DU
9) nam-ti-ab-ba-ni
10) en-an-na-túm-ma-šè
11) nam-ti-ama-ni
12) a-[^{š}]$^{u.me}$.šurmenx(EREN)-šè
13) nam-t[i]-la-ni-š[è]
14) ^{d}lugal-URU×KÁR.KI-[ra]
15) [é-gal-URU×KÁR.KI-ka]
16) [kìri šu ḫé-na-šè-gál]

i 14–15) [s]on begotten by the god Lugal-URU×KAR

i 16–18) son of A-kurgal, ruler of Lagaš,

i 19 – ii 1) [beloved brother of E-anatum ruler of Lagaš],

ii 2–3) [built] the Ib[gal] ("[Great] Oval") [for] the goddess In[anna],
ii 4–5) [and made] the E-[anna higher than (the temples) in all other lands for he]r,
ii 6) he (Me-ane-si) fashioned his [stat]ue
ii 7–8) and set it up before Lugal-URU×KAR in his temple.
ii 9– 16) [May it pray to] the god Lugal-URU×KAR [in the "palace" of URU×KAR] for the life of his father En-anatum, for the life of his mother, for A-šurmen (his wife), and for his own life!

16

A clay cylinder fragment from Lagaš (al-Hibā) mentions A-šurmen, wife of En-anatum I.

COMMENTARY

The baked clay cylinder fragment was found in Area B, on the surface of Lagaš (al-Hibā).

BIBLIOGRAPHY

1974 Crawford, Iraq 36 pp. 34 and 35 n. 17 (copy, study)
1982 Steible, ASBW 1 p. 207 Enanatum I 34 (edition)
1986 Cooper, SARI 1 p. 53 La 4.16 (translation)

TEXT

Lacuna
1′) [...] ⸢x⸣
2′) [a]-$^{šu.me}$.šurmen$_{x}$(EREN)-šè
3′) dam-en-an-na-túm
4′) énsi-
5′) [l]agaš(NU$_{11}$.BUR.LA).KI!
Lacuna

Lacuna
1′–2′) [...] x [A]-šurmen,

3′–5′) wife of En-anatum, ruler of [L]agaš.

Lacuna

17

A clay nail of unknown provenance (but almost certainly from Lagaš [al-Hibā]) mentions En-anatum's servant I-lu-sikil.

COMMENTARY

The cone bears the museum number A 3604.

I-lu-sikil was a member of a very high class of personnel denoted in other Presargonic Lagaš texts as the lú-é-šà-ga, which apparently means "inner palace officials"; they figure (according to Yamamoto ASJ 3 [1981] p. 108) in the archival sources known as the "palace tablets" (šà-dub-é-gal). Personnel recorded on these tablets included court officials such as the "cup-bearer" (sìla-šu-du$_8$), "cook" (muḫaldim), "court messenger" (sukkal), "barber" (šu-i), and likely "coiffure" (kinda) (as Šuni-aldugud mentioned in inscription E1.9.4.18 col. ii line 3 line below). I-lu-sikil served as "private scribe" (dub-sar-é-šà-ga); according to Selz (in RIM readers' notes), he may have been a personal scribe of the ruler.

BIBLIOGRAPHY

1958 Hallo, JNES 17 pp. 214–15 (transliteration)
1982 Steible, ASBW 1 pp. 197–98 Enantum I 28 (edition)
1986 Cooper, SARI 1 p. 53 La 4.17 (translation)
1990 Wilcke, in Studies Moran p. 465 (study)

TEXT

Col. i
1) e[n-an]-na-túm
2) énsi-
3) lagaš(NU$_{11}$.BUR.LA),K[I]
4) šà-pà-d[a]-
5) ^{d}nanše
6) dumu-tu-da-
7) ^{d}lugal-URU×KÁR.KI-ka
8) dumu a-kur-gal
9) ⸢énsi⸣-
10) la[g]aš(NU$_{11}$.BUR.LA).KI-ka-ke$_4$
11) u$_4$ ^{d}inanna-ra
12) ib-gal mu-na-dù-a
13) é-an-na kur-kur-ra
14) mu-na-diri-ga-a

Col. ii
1) ⸢kù-GI⸣ [kù]-⸢bábbar!-ra⸣
2) [šu] ⸢mu⸣-na-ni-[ta]g-g[a]-a
3) KIB ir$_{11}$(?)-ra-ni
4) ⸢i$_7$⸣-lú-sikil
5) dub-sar-é-šà-ga-ka-né
6) e-ma-an-dím

i 1–3) E[n-an]atum, ruler of Lagaš,

i 4–5) chose[n] in the heart by the goddess Nanše,

i 6–7) son begotten by the god Lugal-URU×KAR,

i 8–10) son of A-kurgal, ruler of La[g]aš —

i 11–12) when he built the Ibgal ("Great Oval") for the goddess Inanna,

i 13–14) made the E-anna higher than (the temples) in all other lands for her,

ii 1–2) and dec[ora]ted it for her with gold and [sil]ver,

ii 3–6) then his (En-anatum's) servant, I-lu-sikil, his private palace(?) (or temple[?]) scribe, had (these) clay nails made for it.

18

A cone inscription from Lagaš (al-Hibā) mentions the chief (court?) barber Šuni-aldugud.

CATALOGUE

Ex.	Museum number	Excavation number	Provenance	Dimesions (cm)	Lines preserved	cpn
1	—	2H-T 28	Area C, 200 balk between N 10 and N 20, room 18, cut in Level 1A	—	i 1–9 ii 1–9	n
2	—	1 H 49	—	—	—	n

COMMENTARY

Concerning the identity of Šuni-aldugud, we may note the comments given in "Appendix to nos. 22–23 = no. 144 Bibl. Mes. III 10" in Gelb, Land Tenure p. 88:

> According to this passage, Shuni-aldugud was the son of Lummatur and therefore the grandson of Enanatum I. The same person occurs in another inscription from al-Hibā. published by Biggs in Bibl. Mes. 3 p. 18 no. 2 and briefly discussed on p. 3.

BIBLIOGRAPHY

1976 Biggs, Al-Hiba no. 2 (ex. 1, copy, ex. 2, study)

1982 Steible, ASBW 1 pp. 202–203 Enanatum I 30 (exs. 1–2, edition)

1986 Cooper, SARI 1 p. 53 La 4.18 (exs. 1–2, translation)

1990 Wilcke, in Studies Moran p. 466 (study)

TEXT

Col. i		
1)	en-na-na-túm	i 1–3) En-anatum, ruler of Lagaš,
2)	énsi-	
3)	lagaš(NU$_{11}$.BUR.LA).KI	
4)	mu-pà-da-	i 4–5) nominated by the goddess Inanna,
5)	^{d}inanna-ka-ke$_4$	
6)	ib-gal	i 6–7) built the Ibgal ("Great Oval").
7)	mu-dù	
8)	é-an-na	i 8–9) He (En-anatum) having made the E-anna higher than (the temples) in all other land s for her,
9)	kur-kur-ra mu-na-diri-ga-a	
Col. ii		
1)	u$_4$-[ba]	ii 1–4) then his servant, Šuni-aldugud, chief barber,
2)	ir$_{11}$!-ra-ni	
3)	šu-ni-al-dugud	
4)	GAL.KINDA	
5)	nam-nu-bànda-é-šà-ga	ii 5–6) to whom was given in addition (to his post) the inspectorship of the inner palace,
6)	an-na-daḫ-ḫa	
7)	KIB mu-dím-dím	ii 7) had (these) clay nails(?) made for it
8)	é-an-na-ke$_4$	ii 8–9) and ordered them for he[r] (the goddess Inanna) at the E-anna temple.
9)	mu-n[a]-du$_{11}$	

19

A limestone mace-head bears an inscription of Bara-kiTIL, in which he dedicates the piece for the life of his lord En-anatum I.

COMMENTARY

The mace-head, which measures 12.7 cm in height and 11 cm in diameter, was purchased; it probably came from G̃irsu. It now bears the museum number BM 23287, and the registration 97–5–14, 1. The inscription was collated.

BIBLIOGRAPHY

1898 King, CT 5 pl. 1 BM 23287 (copy)
1907 Thureau-Dangin, SAK pp. 30–32 En-an-na-tum I c (edition)
1929 Barton, RISA pp. 46–47 Enannatum I 3 (edition)
1935 Zervos, L'art pp. 120–122 (photos)
1956 Sollberger, CIRPL p. 29 En. I 19 (copy)
1960 Parrot, Sumer, figs. 159 a–b (photos)
1962 Strommenger and Hirmer, Mesopotamien pl. 70 (photos)
1963 Kramer, Sumerians p. 313 § C 13 (translation)
1975 Orthmann (ed.), Der alte Orient figs. 86a and b (photos)
1980 Amiet, Art fig. 333 (photo)
1982 Steible, ASBW 1 pp. 190–91 Enannatum I 19 (edition)
1986 Cooper, SARI 1 p. 54 La 4.19 (translation)
1991 Braun-Holzginger Weihgaben p. 42 K 1 (edition)

TEXT

1) ^{d}nin-g̃ír-sú
2) é-ninnu-ra
3) en-na-na-túm
4) énsi-
5) lagaš(NU$_{11}$.BUR.LA).KI-ka
6) guruš!-a-ni
7) bára-ki-TIL
8) sukkal-le
9) nam-ti-
10) lugal-ni
11) en-an-na-túm-ma-šè
12) a mu-na-šè-ru

1–2) For the god Niñgirsu of E-ninnu,

3–8) the workman of En-anatum, ruler of Lagaš, (named) BarakiTIL, (who was) an emissary,

9–12) dedicated this (mace-head) for the life of En-anatum, his master.

20

A clay cone fragment from Lagaš (al-Hibā) gives a few lines of an inscription (in a restored text) of En-anatum I.

COMMENTARY

The cone fragment was found in a wadi south of the hill with the baked brick platform, and was given the excavation number 1 H 3.

The fragment measures 6.6×4.4 cm.

BIBLIOGRAPHY

1976 Biggs, Al-Hiba no. 5 (copy)
1982 Steible, ASBW 1 p. 204 Enannatum I 32 (edition)
1986 Cooper, SARI 1 p. 54 La 4.20 (translation)

TEXT

Col. i′
Lacuna
1′) [...] BUR
2′) [...] KI-ta [x-n]a-[x]-a
3′) [...] ⌈x⌉ [...]
Lacuna
Col ii′
1′) [énsi]-
2′) lagaš(NU$_{11}$.BUR.LA).KI-ka-ke$_4$
3′) KIB m[u]-dím-dí[m]
Lacuna
Col. iii′
Broken away.

Lacuna
i′ 1′–3′) Too broken for translation.

Lacuna

ii′ 1′–3′) [En-anatum, ruler] of Lagaš, had (these) clay nails(?) mad[e].

Lacuna
Col. iii′
Broken away

En-metena

E1.9.5

En-anatum I was succeeded by his third son, En-metena (see Bauer in Bauer, Englund, and Krebernik [eds.], Mesopotamien p. 469). The evidence of an economic text (Cros, Tello p. 181 AO 4156) tells us that he reigned at least 19 years.

For the reading of the ruler's name as en-me:te-na, see the discussion of Alster, JCS 26 (1974) pp. 178–80 and Steible in ASBW 2 p. 106. Bauer (AoN 21 [1985] p. 7) notes the later writings en-me-te-na found in Thureau-Dangin ITT I no. 1081 rev. line 1 and no. 1467 line 2. See also the comments of Cooper in SARI 1 p. 54.

En-metena's wife, Nin-ḫili-su, is commonly attested in economic texts (see Selz, Untersuchungen p. 19).

The reign of En-metena was a period of territorial expansion for Lagaš. This is evidenced by the annexation of the city of Pa-tibira (variant writing Bad-tibira) located about 33 km SW of G̃irsu. There En-metena (re)built the temple of the city's chief gods Inanna and Lugalemuš (see inscriptions E1.9.5.3–6); the latter deity is likely a form of the god Dumuzi. Text E1.9.5.3 (uniquely) mentions the "brotherhood" pact established between En-metena of Lagaš and Lugal-kig̃ine-dudu of Uruk. The latter is known from his own inscriptions found at Nippur and Ur (see E1.14.14); unfortunately, none of his inscriptions have been found to date at Uruk itself. The nature of the "brotherhood" pact between the two rulers is uncertain. What confuses the picture is the statement in inscription E1.9.5.4 v 4–8 that En-metena "cancelled obligations for the citizens of Uruk, Larsa, and Pa-tibira." These actions normally follow a ruler's "liberation" of a city and suggest that, for at least a brief time, En-metena controlled Uruk, Larsa, and Pa-tibira. If the passage in E1.9.5.4 does in fact refer to a "liberation" (i.e., newly asserted control by Lagaš), it is not known whether En-metena reneged on his earlier "brotherhood" pact or possibly installed Lugal-kig̃ine-dudu as a dependent of Lagaš. Since Lugal-kig̃ine-dudu has left us votive inscriptions from Nippur without any mention of an overlord, the latter possibility is likely to be excluded. It may be noted in this context that inscriptions of En-metena were also found both at Uruk (E1.9.5.1 ex. 4; see Marzahn, MDOG 28 [1997] pp. 87–96) and at Ur (E1.9.5.17). The exact significance of these finds is hard to determine. The En-metena text from Ur mentions (iii 5–7) the construction of the E-ada-imsag̃a for Enlil. En-metena may have been the first Lagaš ruler to build an é-ad-da dedicated to Enlil, and Selz (Untersuchungen pp. 127–28 §8) has suggested that there was a promotion of the cult of Enlil in Lagaš at this time (see also Bauer, in Bauer, Englund, and Krebernik [eds.], Mesopotamien p. 470).

An unusual feature of the reign is the appearance of inscriptions dated by the phrase "at that time Dudu was the *sag̃a* priest of Nin̂girsu" (E1.9.5.7 lines 21–22 and E1.9.1.26 col. viii line 8); a similar phrase occurs in an economic text (Hallo, Orientalia NS 42 [1973] p. 28 lines 65–68). Further, Dudu has left us one dedicatory inscription of his own (E1.9.5.28 caption), a boundary stone (E1.9.5.27), and two weight stones (see Steible, ASBW 1 p. 267 Ent. 77–78).

1

An inscription found on a clay cone (ex. 1), a clay cylinder (ex. 2), and fragments of clay vessels (ex. 3–4) records a boundary dispute between En-metena of Lagaš and Il, ruler of G̃iša (Umma).

CATALOGUE

Ex.	Museum number	Object	Dimensions (cm)	Lines preserved	cpn
1	AO 3004	Clay cone	Length: 26.5 Dia.: 10.5	i 1–42 ii 1–42 iii 1–38 iv 1–36 v 1–30 vi 1–29	c
2	NBC 2501	Clay cylinder with a net design	Length: 21.5 Dia. 13.2	Omits lines corresponding to ex. 1 iv 6–7	c
3	AO 4443	Vessel fragment	8×7	vi 29–34	c
4	VAT 16438	Vessel fragment	Length: 10.1	iv 28–31 v 22–24 vi 23–29	n

COMMENTARY

For the original provenances of exs. 1–2, we may note the comments of Nies (BIN 2 p. 1):

> According to the dealer from whom this remarkable inscribed object [here ex. 2] was bought, it was found by an Arab belonging to a tribe located between Jokha and Tello. The claim is that the same man, Hassan of Qararul, in 1895, found the famous cone of Entemena published by Thureau-Dangin in 1898 [here ex. 1]. If this is accepted, neither the cone nor the net-cylinder was found at Tello, but between that site and Jokha ...

Ex. 4 was found in Uruk near the city wall; its excavation number is W 14983.

For a discussion of the particular shapes of exs. 1–3, see the comments of Cooper in RA 79 (1985) pp. 97–110.

In col. i line 19 for bu_x/bur_9 (PAD) = *nasāḫu(m)* "to tear out" see Sjöberg, PSD 2 p. 161. According to Selz (in RIM readers's notes), this reading is likely. Another possibility is to read the verb as padr = *kasāpu(m)* "to break into bits."

In ii 27 for the translation of "to repay" for sù-sù (taking sù-sù as a variant spelling for su-su), see Steinkeller, JESHO 24 (1981) p. 144.

In ii 39 for bára-RU-a-dingir-ré-ne, cf. the comments of Selz, Untersuchungen p. 109:

> Auf uns namentlich bekannte Gottheiten [dingir] bezieht sich der Plural dingir-réne in bará-ru-a-dingir-ré-ne "die errichteten Postament der Götter"

Cf. p. 109 n. 395:

> So mit J. Cooper, SARI 143 Anm. 2 zu La 3.7, der in ru in bará-ru und gaba-ru as Schreibungen für bará-ri (siehe W. Ph. Römer, SKIZ S. 92, 110; A. Sjöberg, TCS 3, 180) und gaba-ri erkannt hat. Auch für balag-RU-a in Fö 75 ii 5-iii 5 mag mit einem Ansatz ru = "errichten," d.h. "die errichteten Harfen," auszukommen sein.

Sjöberg, in PSD B p. 140 sub bara2 § 1, gives "he destroyed the votive daises of the gods" for this passage. See further, Selz, ASJ 17 (1995) pp. 273–74.

For iii 10, see the comments of Sjöberg, ZA 63 (1973) p. 12:

> I consider giš-UR-e-lá-lá of B a scribal error for *giš-UR.UR-e-lá-a; see E. Sollberger, CIRPL Ean. i IX I giš-UR.UR-e e-da-lá-a "he fought with him"; Ent. 28-29 A III 10 = B IV i giš-UR.UR-šè e-da-lá. UR.UR = *šitnunu*, cf. SAK 13 fn. g; for a possible reading UR.UR = urbingu (=*šitnunu*) see MSL 3, 132 Sb 11 7, signs: UR : UR cf. CBS 11319+ rev. 1 17′ (pronunciation:) ki še-eš-bi = UR UR *ašar ša-gaš-tim* "place of slaughter".

The translation of iii 19 is uncertain. Steinkeller, NABU 1990 no. 12 suggests the translation "team" for ÉREN in connection with anše "ass." Selz, Amerikansichen Sammlungen p. 129, translates sipa-anše-ÉREN-ka as "hirten der Gespannesel" with ÉREN denoting a type of ass. For asses yoked for ploughing purposes, see Salonen,

Agricultura pp. 396–97.

In iii 32 for gàr-dar = *sakāpu(m)*, cf. Angim line 139 (= 40, see Cooper, Return p. 80 [only line 139 was available to Cooper at the time of his edition]): gàr-da mè-ḫuš: *sa-kip ta-ḫa-zi* "the (mace) which destroys in fierce battle."

BIBLIOGRAPHY

1884–1912 de Sarzec, Découvertes 2 p. XLVII ENTÉMÉNA 6 (ex. 1, copy); pl. 32bis no. 3 (ex. 1, photo)
1897 Thureau-Dangin, RA 4 pp. 37–50 and pl. 2 (ex. 1, copy, edition)
1907 Thureau-Dangin, SAK pp. 36–41 En-te-me-na n (ex. 1, edition)
1910 Thureau-Dangin, in Cros, Tello pp. 216–17 (ex. 3, copy, study)
1914 Poebel, PBS 4/1 pp. 159–69 (exs. 1–2, study)
1920 Keiser, BIN 2 pp. 1–14 (ex. 2, edition); pls. 1–3 (ex. 2, copy); pls. 57–58 (ex. 2, photo)
1924 Gadd, Reading-book pp. 110–29 § XV (exs. 1–2, conflated copy, edition)
1926 Poebel, in Studies Haupt pp. 220–67 (exs. 1–2, partial edition, study)
1929 Barton, RISA pp. 56–61 Entemena 15 (ex. 1, edition)
1956 Kramer, FTS pp. 32ff. (exs. 1–3, translation)
1956 Lambert, RA 50 pp. 141–46 (exs. 1–2, edition)
1956 Sollberger, CIRPL p. xii Ent. 28–29 (exs. 1–2, study); pp. 37–39 Ent. 28–29 (exs. 1–2, conflated copy); p. 39 Ent. 31 (ex. 3, copy)
1963 Kramer, Sumerians pp. 313–15 § C 14 (exs. 1–3, translation)
1971 Sollberger and Kupper, IRSA IC7i (exs. 1–3, translation)
1981 Steinkeller, JESHO 24 pp. 143–45 (study)
1982 André-Leicknam, Naissance de l'écriture p. 198 no. 132 (photo, study)
1982 Steible, ASBW 1 pp. 230–45 Entemena 28–29 (exs. 1–2, edition); p. 247 Entemena 31 (ex. 3, study)
1983 Cooper, SANE 2 pp. 15, 28, 30–33, and 49–50 no. 6 (translation, study)
1984 Römer in TUAT 1/4 pp. 308–312 (exs. 1–3, translation)
1985 Cooper, RA 79 p. 98 (exs. 1–3, study); pp. 100–101 pls. I–II no. 1 (ex. 1, photos); pp. 102–103 pls. II–IV (ex. 2, photos)
1986 Cooper, SARI 1 pp. 54–57 La 5.1 (exs. 1–3, translation)
1986 Steiner, ASJ 8 pp. 219–300 (passim) (study)
1990 Lambert, ZA 80 pp. 42–43 (study)
1995 Selz, Untersuchungen p. 106
1997 Marzahn, MDOG 28 pp. 87–96 (ex. 4, copy, edition, study)

TEXT

Col. i

1) ^{d}en-líl
2) lugal-kur-kur-ra
3) ab-ba-dingir-dingir-ré-ne-ke$_4$

i 1–3) The god Enlil, king of the lands, father of the gods,

4) inim-gi-na-ni-ta
5) ^{d}nin-g̃ír-su
6) ^{d}šára-bi
7) ki e-ne-sur

i 4–7) by his authoritative command, demarcated the border between the gods Ning̃irsu and Šara.

8) me-silim
9) lugal-kiš.KI-ke$_4$

i 8) Me-silim, king of Kiš,

10) inim-^{d}ištaran(=KA.DI)-na-ta
11) éš GÁNA bi-ra
12) ki-ba na bí-rú

i 9–12) at the command of the god Ištaran stretched the measuring rope on the field and erected a monument there.

13) UŠ
14) ensí-
15) ^{giš}KÚŠU.KI-ke$_4$

i 13–15) UŠ, ruler of G̃iša (Umma),

16) nam-inim-ma diri-diri-šè
17) e-ak
18) na-rú-a-bi
19) ì-bux/bur$_9$(PAD)
20) eden-lagaš(NU$_{11}$.BUR.LA)KI-šè
21) ì-DU

i 16–21) acted arrogantly; he ripped out (or smashed) that monument and marched on the Eden district of Lagaš.

22) ^{d}nin-g̃ír-su
23) ur-sag̃-^{d}en-líl-lá-ke$_4$

i 22–23) The god Ning̃irsu, warrior of the god Enlil,

24) inim-si-sá-ni-ta
25) ^{giš}KÚŠU.KI-da
26) dam-ḫa-ra
27) e-da-ak

i 24–27) at his (Enlil's) just command, did battle with G̃iša (Umma).

28) inim-^{d}en-líl-lá-ta
29) sa-šuš-gal bí-šuš

i 28–29) At the god Enlil's command, he cast the great battle-net upon it,

30) SAḪAR.DU$_6$.TAG$_4$-bi

i 30–31) and set up its burial tumuli (honouring his

31) eden-na ki ba-ni-ús-ús

dead) in the Eden (district).

32) é-an-na-túm
33) énsi-
34) lagaš(NU$_{10}$BUR.LA).KI
35) pa-bìl-ga-
36) en-TE.ME-na
37) énsi-
38) lagaš.KI-ka-ke$_4$

i 32–38) E-anatum, ruler of Lagaš, uncle of En-metena, ruler of Lagaš,

39) en-á-kal-le
40) énsi-
41) $^{\tilde{g}iš}$KÚŠU.KI-da
42) ki e-da-sur

i 39–42) demarcated the border with En-akale, ruler of G̃iša (Umma).

Col. ii

1) ég-bi i$_7$-nun-ta
2) gú-eden-na-šè

ii 1–2) He led off the (boundary) channel from the Nun canal to the Guʾedena district,

3) íb-ta-ni-è
GÁNA-^{d}nin-g̃ír-su-ka
210 ÉŠE (1) BA$_7$ NINDA.DU
á-$^{g̃iš}$KÚŠU.KI-šè
mu-tag$_4$
GÁNA lugal nu-tuku

ii 3) leaving a 215 *nindan* (1290 m) (strip) of Ning̃irsu's land under the control of G̃iša (Umma) and establishing a no-man's land there.

4) ég-ba na-rú-a
5) e-me-sar-sar
6) na-rú-a-
7) me-silim-ma
8) ki-bé bí-gi$_4$
9) eden-$^{g̃iš}$KÚŠU.KI-šè
10) nu-díb

ii 4–10) He inscribed (and erected) monuments at that (boundary) dike and restored the monument of Me-silim, but did not cross into the Eden (district) of G̃iša (Umma).

11) im-dub-ba-
12) ^{d}nin-g̃ír-su-ka
13) nam-nun-da-ki-g̃ar-ra
14) bára-^{d}en-líl-lá
15) bára-^{d}nin-ḫur-sag̃-ka
16) bára-^{d}nin-g̃ír-su-ka
17) bára-^{d}utu
18) bí-dù

ii 11–18) On the boundary-levee of the god Ning̃irsu (called) Namnun-kig̃ara, he built a chapel of the god Enlil, a chapel of the goddess Ninḫursag̃, a chapel of the god Ning̃irsu, and a chapel of the god Utu.

19) še-^{d}nanše
20) še-^{d}nin-g̃ír-su-ka
21) 1 gur$_7$-am$_6$
22) lú-$^{g̃iš}$KÚŠU.KI-ke$_4$
23) ur$_5$-šè ì-kú

ii 19–23) The leader of G̃iša (Umma) could exploit 1 *gur* (5184 hl.) of the barley of the goddess Nanše and the barley of the god Ning̃irsu as an (interest-) bearing loan.

24) ku$_5$-DU ba-ús
25) 144,000 gur$_7$-gal
26) ba-ku$_4$

ii 24–26) It bore interest, and 8,640,000 *guru* (44,789,760,000 hl.) accrued.

27) bar še-bi nu-da-sù-sù-da-ka

ii 27) Since he was unable to *repay* that barley,

28) ur-LUM-ma
29) ensí-
30) $^{g̃iš}$KÚŠU.KI-ke$_4$
31) ég-ki-sur-ra-
32) ^{d}nin-g̃ír-su-ka
33) ég-ki-sur-ra-
34) ^{d}nanše
35) a-e ì-mi-è

ii 28–35) Ur-LUM-ma ruler of G̃iša (Umma), diverted water from the boundary dike of the god Ning̃irsu and the boundary dike of the goddess Nanše.

36) na-rú-a-bé
37) izi ba-sum
38) ì-bu$_x$-bu$_x$ (or bur$_9$-bur$_9$)

ii 36–38) He set fire to their monuments and ripped them out (or smashed them)

39) bára-RU-a-dingir-ré-ne
40) nam-nun-da-ki-g̃ar-ra
41) ab-dù-a

ii 39–42) and destroyed the dedicated(?) chapels of the gods that were built on the (boundary-levee called) Namnunda-kig̃ara.

42) ì-gul-gul

Col. iii

1) kur-kur e-ma-ḫun
2) ég-ki-sur-ra-
3) ^{d}nin-g̃ír-su-ka-ka
4) e-ma-ta-bal

iii 1–4) He hired the (people) of the foreign lands (as mercenaries) and transgressed the boundary dike of the god Ning̃irsu from above (i.e., from the north).

5) en-an-na-túm
6) ensí-
7) lagaš(NU$_{10}$.BUR.LA).KI-ke$_4$
8) GANÁ-ù-g̃ig-ga
9) $^{a\text{-}šà}$GANÁ-^{d}nin-g̃ír-su-ka-ka
10) giš UR.UR-šè e-da-lá

iii 5–10) En-anatum, ruler of Lagaš, fought with him in the Ugiga-field, the field of the god Ning̃irsu.

11) en-TE.ME-na
12) dumu-ki-ág̃-
13) en-an-na-túm-ma-ke$_4$
14) GÍN.ŠÈ ì-ni-sè

iii 11–14) En-metena, beloved son of En-anatum, defeated him.

15) ur-LUM-ma
16) ba-da-kar
17) šà-$^{g̃iš}$KÚŠU.KI-šè
18) e-gaz

iii 15–18) Ur-LUM-ma escaped, but was killed in G̃iša (Umma) itself.

19) anše-ni ÉREN-60-am$_6$
20) gú-i$_7$-LUM-ma-g̃ír-nun-ta-ka
21) e-šè-tag$_4$
22) nam-lú-ulù-ba
23) g̃irì-PAD.DU-bi
24) eden-da e-da-tag$_4$-tag$_4$

iii 19–24) His asses — there were sixty teams(?) of them — he abandoned on the bank of the LUM-ma-g̃irnunta canal, and left the bones of their personnel strewn over the Eden district.

25) SAḪAR.DU$_6$.TAG$_4$-bi
26) ki-5-a
27) ì-mi-dub

iii 25–27) He (En-metena) heaped up there tumuli (honouring his own casualities) in five places.

28) u$_4$-ba íl
29) sag̃a-zabalam.KI-kam
30) g̃ír-su.KI-ta
31) gišKÚŠU.KI-šè
32) g̃àr-dar-ra-a
33) e-DU

iii 28–33) At that time, Il, who was the temple-estate administrator at Zabala, marched in retreat from G̃irsu to G̃iša (Umma).

34) íl-le
35) nam-énsi
36) $^{g̃iš}$KÚŠU.KI-a
37) šu e-ma-ti

iii 34–37) He took the rulership of G̃iša (Umma) for himself.

38) ég-ki-sur-ra-

Col. iv

1) ^{d}nin-g̃ír-su-ka
2) ég-ki-sur-ra-
3) ^{d}nanše

iii 38 – iv 3) He diverted water from the boundary dike of the god Ning̃irsu and the boundary dike of Nanše

4) im-dub-ba-
5) ^{d}nin-g̃ír-su-ka
6) gú-I$_7$.idigna-šè g̃ál-la
7) gú-gú-g̃ír-su.KI-ka
8) nam-nun-da-ki-gar-ra-
9) ^{d}nin-ḫur-sag̃-ka
10) a-e ì-mi-è

iv 4–10) at the boundary levee of Ning̃irsu in the direction of the bank of the Tigris in the region of G̃irsu, the Namnunda-kig̃ara of Enlil, Enki, and Ninḫursag̃.

11) še-lagaš.KI 3600 gur$_7$-am$_6$
12) ì-su

iv 11–12) He repaid(?) (only) 3600 *guru* (IX,662,400 hl.) of Lagaš's barley.

13) en-TE.ME-me-na
14) énsi-
15) lagaš.KI-ke$_4$
16) bar-e-ba-ka
17) íl-šè

iv 13–18) When, because of those (boundary-) channels, En-metena, ruler of Lagaš, sent envoys to Il, ruler of G̃iša (Umma),

18) lú ḫé-šè-gi$_4$-gi$_4$
19) íl
20) ensí-
21) ^{giš}KÚŠU.KI-a
22) $^{a-šà}$GANÁ kar-kar
23) níg-NE.RU-du$_{11}$-du$_{11}$-ge

iv 19–23) Il, ruler of Ğiša (Umma), the field thief, speaking hostilely, said:

24) ég-ki-sur-ra-
25) ^{d}nin-ğír-su-ka
26) ég-ki-sur-ra-
27) ^{d}nanše
28) ğá-kam
29) ì-mi-du$_{11}$

iv 24–29) "The boundary dike of the god Ninğirsu and the boundary dike of the goddess Nanše are mine!

30) an-ta-sur-ra-ta
31) é-^{d}dimgal (=gal:dim)-abzu-ka-šè
32) im ba-ni-è-dè
33) ì-mi-du$_{11}$

iv 30–33) I will dry them up from (the town of) Antasur ('[Northern(?)] Boundary') (as far as) the temple of Dimgal-abzu ('Mast of the Sweet Water Source')," he said.

34) ^{d}en-líl-le
35) ^{d}nin-ḫur-sağ-ke$_4$
36) nu-na-sum

iv 34–36) But the god Enlil and the goddess Ninḫursağ did not allow him (to do) this.

Col. v
1) en-TE.ME-na
2) énsi-
3) lagaš.KI

v 1–3) En-metena, ruler of Lagaš,

4) mu-pà-da-
5) ^{d}nin-ğír-su-ka-ke$_4$

v 4–5) nominee of the god Ninğirsu,

6) inim-si-sá-^{d}en-líl-lá-ta
7) inim-si-sá-^{d}nin-ğír-su-ka-ta
8) inim-si-sá-^{d}nanše-ta

v 6–8) at the just command of the god Enlil, at the just command of the god Ninğirsu, and at the just command of the goddess Nanše,

9) ég-bi I$_7$.idigna-ta
10) i$_7$-nun-šè
11) e-ak

v 9–11) constructed that (boundary) dike from the Tigris River to the Nun canal.

12) nam-nun-da-ki-ğar-ra
13) úr-bi na$_4$-a mu-na-ni-dù

v 12–13) He built the foundations of the Namnunda-kiğara for him (the god Ninğirsu) out of stone,

14) lugal-ki-an-na-áğ-ğá-ni
15) ^{d}nin-ğír-su-ra
16) nin-ki-an-na-áğ-ğá-ni
17) ^{d}nanše
18) ki-bé mu-na-gi$_4$

v 14–18) restoring it for the master who loves him, the god Ninğirsu, and for the mistress who loves him, the goddess Nanše.

19) en-TE.ME-na
20) énsi-
21) lagaš(NU$_{10}$-BUR.LA).KI

v 19–21) En-metena, ruler of Lagaš,

22) ğidri-sum-ma-
23) ^{d}en-líl-lá

v 22–23) granted the sceptre by the god Enlil,

24) ğéštu-sum-ma-
25) ^{d}en-ki-ka

v 24–25) granted wisdom by the god Enki,

26) šà-pà-da-
27) ^{d}nanše
28) énsi-gal-
29) ^{d}nin-ğír-su-ka

v 26–29) chief ruler for the god Ninğirsu,

30) lú inim-dingir-ré-ne dab$_5$-ba

v 30) who realizes the commands of the gods —

Col. vi
1) diğir-ra-ni
2) ^{d}šul-MUŠ×PA
3) nam-ti-
4) en-TE.ME-na-ka-šè
5) u$_4$-ul-la-šè

vi 1–8) may his personal god, Šul-MUŠ×PA, forever stand (interceding) before the god Ninğirsu and the goddess Nanše for the life of En-metena!

---

vi 18.2 ḫé-šè-gi-gi-a.

6) ^{d}nin-ĝír-su-ra
7) ^{d}nanše
8) ḫé-na-ši-DU
9) lú-^{ĝiš}KÚŠU.KI-a
10) ég-ki-sur-ra-
11) ^{d}nin-ĝír-su-ka-ka
12) e-ki-sur-ra-
13) ^{d}nanše-ka
14) á-zi-šè
15) $^{\text{a-šà}}$GANÁ tùm-dè
16) an(am_6)-ta-bal-e-da
17) lú-^{ĝiš}KÚŠU.KI ḫé
18) lú-kur-ra ḫé
19) ^{d}en-líl-le
20) ḫé-ḫa-lam-me
21) ^{d}nin-ĝír-su-ke_4
22) sa-šuš-gal-ni
23) ù-ni-šuš
24) šu-maḫ gìr-maḫ-ni
25) an-ta ḫé-gá-gá
26) nam-lú-ùlu-uru-na
27) šu ù-na-zi
28) šà-uru-na-ka
29) ḫa-ni-gaz-ze_x(ÁB.ŠÀ.GE)

vi 9–16) If the leader of G̃iša (Umma) crosses over the boundary dike of the god Ninĝirsu and the boundary dike of the goddess Nanše, to take away fields by force,

vi 17–18) — whether he be the leader of G̃iša (Umma) or any other leader —
vi 19–20) may the god Enlil destroy him!

vi 21–25) May the god Ninĝirsu, after casting his great battle-net upon him, bring down upon him his giant hands and feet!

vi 26–29) May the people of his own city, after rising up against him, kill him there within his (own) city!

2

A brick inscription of En-metena records the digging of the "exalted boundary-channel" for the god Ninĝirsu.

COMMENTARY

The provenance of the brick (YBC 2184), which measures 30.8×22.7×7 cm, is unknown. Clay (YOS 1 p. 5) says it and the boulder inscription edited as inscription E1.9.5.27 in this volume "apparently were found at Tello ...," but the content of the brick does not exclude a findspot in the general region of Lagaš, perhaps from the same site that yielded the "Net Cylinder" of En-metena (E1.9.5.1). The content of inscription E1.9.5.27 suggests that the ancient name of the site was Antasur.

The inscription was collated.

BIBLIOGRAPHY

1915 Clay, YOS 1 pp. 5–7 no. 5 (copy, edition)
1956 Sollberger, CIRPL p. xii Ent. 41 (study); p. 41 Ent. 41 (copy)
1982 Steible, ASBW 1 pp. 256–57 (edition) Entemena 41 (edition)
1986 Cooper, SARI 1 p. 57 La 5.2 (translation)
1986 Steiner, ASJ 8 pp. 219–300 (passim) (study)

vi 8.2 ḫé-na-ši!(ME)-DU.
vi 29.2 ḫa-ni-GAZ-e.

TEXT

Col. i	
1) ^{d}nin-ĝír-sú	i 1–2) For the god Ninĝirsu, warrior of the god Enlil,
2) ur-sag-^{d}en-líl-ra	
3) en-TE.ME-na	i 3–5) En-metena, ruler of Lagaš,
4) énsi-	
5) lagaš(NU$_{10}$-BUR.LA).KI	
6) [ša-pà]-da-	i 6 – ii 1) chosen in the [heart] by the goddess Nanše,
Col. ii	
1) ^{d}nanše	
2) énsi-gal-	ii 2–3) chief executive for the god Ninĝirsu,
3) ^{d}nin-ĝír-sú-ka-ke$_{4}$	
4) ég-maḫ ki-sur-ra	ii 4– iii 1) constructed the exalted boundary dike which the god Enlil demarcated for the god Ninĝirsu.
5) ^{d}en-líl-le	
6) ^{d}nin-ĝír-sú-ra sur(Text: NI)-ra	
Col. iii	
1) mu-na-ak	
2) en-TE.ME-na-ke$_{4}$	iii 2–iv 2) En-metena extended it from the Nun canal to (the town) Mubikura for the god Ninĝirsu, his master who loves him,
3) lugal-ki-an-na-ág-gá-ni	
4) ^{d}nin-ĝír-sú-ra	
5) i$_{7}$-nun-ta	
Col. iv	
1) mu-bi-kur-ra	
2) e-na-ta-ni-è	
3) na-rú-a-	iv 3–6) and erected monuments for him in the fields on the god Ninĝirsu's boundary.
4) a-^{šà}GÁNA-ki-sur-ra-	
5) ^{d}nin-ĝír-sú-ka	
6) mu-na(Text: KI)-rú	
Col. v	
1) en-TE.⸢ME⸣-na	v 1–4) En-metena, who constructed the exalted boundary dike of the god Ninĝirsu —
2) lú e-maḫ-	
3) ^{d}nin-ĝír-sú-ka	
4) ak-ka	
5) dingir-ra-ni	v 5–6) his personal god is Šul-MUŠ×PA.
6) ^{d}šul-MUŠ×PA-am$_{6}$	

3

A cone inscription known from numerous exemplars from Tell al-Madā'in (ancient Pa-tibira located on the ancient Iturungal canal roughly midway between Larsa and G̃irsu) records En-metena's building of the E-muš temple for the goddess Inanna.

The En-metena text also mentions the "brotherhood" pact between En-metena, and Lugal-kiĝine-dudu of Uruk.

COMMENTARY

Carroué (ASJ 15 [1993] p. 32) notes that the temple at Pa-tibira is noted in various Presargonic texts from Lagaš as being an ib, likely a designation for a temple oval. We have understood mùš in é-mùš as Akkadian *zīmu(m)* "radiance, lustre" for which see CAD Z pp. 119–22. The fuller name of the temple known from other sources (see Sjöberg, TCS 3 p. 95 and George, House Most High p. 129 no. 829) is E-muš-kalama "House — Radiance of the Land."

CATALOGUE

Ex.	Museum number	CIRPL number	Dimensions (cm)	Lines preserved	cpn
1	BM 121208	Ent. 45	Length: 26.5 Dia. of head: 8.4 cm	i 1–9, ii 1–10	c
2	AO 12480	Ent. 46	Length: 24.3 Dia. of head: X	i 1–9 ii 1–10	c
3	AO 22934	Ent. 47	Length: 12.5 Dia. of head: 6.2	i 1–9 ii 1–10	c
4	—	Ent. 48	—	—	n
5	Baghdad, private possession	Ent. 49	Length: 26.5 Dia. of head: 8	i 1–9 ii 1–10	n
6	O 868	Ent. 50	—	—	n
7	Collection Banks	Ent. 51	—	—	n
8	Collection Banks	Ent. 52	—	—	n
9	IM 10701	Ent. 53	—	—	n
10	IM 20649	Ent. 54	—	—	n
11	IM 20869	Ent. 55	—	—	n
12	IM 21028	Ent. 56	—	—	n
13	Collection Samhery	Ent. 57	—	—	n
14	LB 970	Ent. 58	Length: 26.5 Dia. of head: 7.3	i 1–9 ii 1–10	n
15	YBC 2316	Ent. 59	Length: 19 Dia. of head: 6.5	i 1–8 ii 1–10	c
16	YBC 2317	Ent. 60	Length: 22.4 Dia. of head: 6.5	i 1–8 ii 1–10	c
17	YBC 2318	Ent. 61	Length: 24.4 Dia. of head: 5.1	i 1–8 ii 1–10	c
18	YBC 2319	Ent. 62	Length: 26.6 Dia. of head: 6.7	i 1–6	c
19	YBC 2320	Ent. 63	Length: 24.5 Dia. of head: 7.6	i 1–8 ii 1–10	c
20	YBC 2321	Ent. 64	Length: 23.5 Dia. of head: 7.3	i 1–8 ii 1–10	c
21	YBC 2322	Ent. 65	Length: 22.6 Dia. of head: 6.4	i 1–8 ii 1–10	c
22	YBC 2323	Ent. 66	Length: 21 Dia. of head: 7	i 1–8 ii 1–10	c
23	Collection Greene, Providence	Ent. 67	—	—	n
24	Collection Tournay	Ent. 68	—	—	n
25	NMS 2089	Ent. 69	25.7×8.2	—	n
26	Collection Haldar	Ent. 70	—	—	n
27	Collection Bodmer	Ent. 71	—	—	n
28	Allard Pierson Museum, Amsterdam B.1641	Ent. 72	—	—	n
29	Berlin	Ent. 73	—	—	n
30	UCLM 9-1972	Ent. 81	27.5×7.5	i 1–9 ii 1–10	n
31	4 Fragments	—	—	—	n
32	—	—	—	—	n
33	RR-3	—	16.7×6.6	—	n
34	Milwaukee Public Museum no. 38126	See p. XVI note	—	—	n
35	ROM no. D 1297 Museum	Ent. 94			c
36	New Brunswick House, St. John	—	13.5×6	i 1–9 ii 1–10	c
37	Ash 1967–1502	—	10.8×7.0	i 1–9 ii 1–10	n
38	BM 136843 (reg. no.) 1930-4-15	—	Length: 25 Dia. (of head): 7.5	i 1–9 ii 1–10	c
39	Seattle Art Museum 41.56	—	Length: 25,5 Dia. (of head): 7.8	—	n

BIBLIOGRAPHY

1930 Gadd, RA 27 pp. 125–26 (ex. 1, copy, edition)
1930 de Genouillac, RHR 101 pp. 216–20 (exs. 2–4, study)
1931 Barton, JAOS 51 pp. 262–65 (exs. 7–8, conflated copy, edition)
1931 Langdon, JRAS pp. 421–24 (ex. 1, study)
1935 Böhl, JEOL 3 pp. 124–25 (ex. 14, edition)
1935 Krückmann in Studies Deimel pp. 200–201 (ex. 5, copy, edition, exs. 9–13, study)
1936 Speleers, BMRAH 8 fig. 20 (ex. 6, photo)
1937 Stephens, YOS 9 nos. 87–94 (exs. 15–23, study)
1939 Jacobsen, SKL p. 172 n. 8 (study)
1940 Schwartz, BNYPL pp. 808–10 no. 26 (ex. 33, copy, edition)
1951–52 Lettinga, JEOL 12 p. 210 and pl. XLVII (ex. 28, photo, copy)
1952 Tournay, RA 46 p. 110 no. 1 (ex. 24, study)
1953 Haldar, BiOr 10 p. 13 (ex. 25, study)
1956 Sollberger, CIRPL pp. xii–xiii (exs. 1–29, study); p. 43 Ent. 45–73 (ex. 2, copy, exs. 1–29, variants listed)
1958 Price, Monuments p. 70 (ex. 32, study)
1960 Crawford, Iraq 22 p. 199 (ex. 31, copy)
1962 Beek, Atlas fig. 31 (ex. 14, photo)
1962 Grégoire, Lagash p. 7 (study)

1971 Sollberger and Kupper, IRSA IC7h (exs. 1–29, translation)
1978 Foxvog, RA 72 p. 41 ENTEMENA 2 (ex. 30, study)
1979 Snell, MVN 9 p. 21 (ex. 39, study)
1981 Grégoire, MVN 10 pl. 1 no. 2 (ex. 37, copy, study)
1982 Steible, ASBW 1 pp. 260–64 Entemena 2 (exs. 1–37, edition)
1983 Kobayashi, Orient 19 pp. 29–50 (study)
1986 Cooper, SARI 1 p. 58 La 5.3 (exs. 1–37, translation)
1987 George, ARRIM 5 p. 31 no. B1 44.311 (ex. 36, study)
1990 Kutscher in Studies Artzi pp. 30–31 (study)
1993 Carroué, ASJ 15 p. 32 (study)
1995 Selz, Untersuchungen p. 150 (partial edition, study)

TEXT

Col. i
1) ^{d}inanna-ra
2) ^{d}lugal-é-mùš-ra
3) en-TE.ME-na
4) énsi-
5) lagaš(NU$_{10}$.BUR.LA).KI-ke$_4$
6) é-mùš é-ki-áĝ-ne-ne
7) mu-ne-dù
8) KIB mu-na-du$_{11}$
9) en-TE.ME-na
Col. ii
1) lú é-mùš dù-a
2) dingir-ra-ni
3) ^{d}šul-MUŠ×PA-am$_6$
4) u$_4$-ba en-TE.ME-na
5) énsi-
6) lagaš(NU$_{10}$.BUR.LA).KI
7) lugal-ki-né-éš-du$_7$-du$_7$
8) énsi-
9) unu.KI-bi
10) nam-šeš e-ak

i 1–2) For the goddess Inanna and the god Lugal-emuš,
i 3–5) En-metena, ruler of Lagaš,

i 6–7) built the E-muš ("House — Radiance [of the Land]"), their beloved temple,
i 8) and ordered (these) clay nails(?) for them.
i 9–ii 1) En-metena, who built the E-muš temple —

ii 2–3) his personal god is the god Šul-MUŠ×PA.

ii 4–10) At that time En-metena, ruler of Lagaš, and Lugal-kiĝine-dudu, ruler of Uruk, established a brotherhood (pact) (between themselves).

4

An inscription on foundation tablets records En-metena's building of the E-muš temple in Pa-tibira. All exemplars, as far as is known, come from Tell al-Madāʾin.

i 6.10, 16, 19, 20, 25, 37 é-ki-áĝ-ĝá-ne-ne.
i 6.1 é-ki-áĝ.
i 7.10, 12, 14–16, 19–20, 28, 33 mu-na-dù.
i 8.1, 3, 8, 9, 17, 24, 26, 28 mu-ne-du$_{11}$.
ii 1.1 dù!(NI)-a.
ii 3.1, 6, 15, 16, 19 Omit -am$_6$.
ii 4. 8, 10, 12, 20, 25 Omit u$_4$-ba.
ii 6.9, 11 Add -ke$_4$.
ii 7.9, 28, 37 lugal-ki-né-du$_7$-du$_7$.
ii 10.6 Gives in one line unu.KI nam-ak.

CATALOGUE

Ex.	Museum number	Object	Dimensions (cm)	Lines preserved	cpn
1	AO 24414	Foundation tablet	25.7×13.7×7.2	i 1–10 ii 1–10 iii 1–10 iv 1–8 v 1–11 vi 1–11	p
2	A 7121 (Chicago)	Foundation tablet	—	—	p
3	A 7122 (Chicago)	Foundation peg	—	—	n
4	Supposedly in Brussels	Foundation tablet	—		n

COMMENTARY

In col. ii line 8: we have taken dub in the expression kur-dub to be equivalent to Akkadian *šapāku*(*m*) "to heap up." The end of the line is restored as gam$_{4}$(GAN).[gam-bi] "its *gamgammu*(*m*) (bird)," for which see CAD G p. 32 sub *gamgammu* and cf. Falkenstein, ZA 56 (1964) p. 71 note to line 185 and Heimpel, Tierbilder p. 409 § 65.1, both citing line 187 from "Enki and the World Order" (see now the Electronic Text Corpus of Sumerian Literature edition: gù ra-e-ne gam$_{4}$-gam.MUŠEN-an-na-gin$_{7}$ [...] "The stroke-callers, like heavenly *gamgam* birds ... .)" The *gamgam* bird apparently was part of En-metena's impressive decoration of Ningirsu's chariot; evidence of his concern for the proper furnishing and protection of the chariot is also attested in inscription E1.9.4.14 which deals with the construction of a coach-house for the vehicle. For a general idea of what Ningirsu's chariot may have looked like, we may observe the depiction of Gudea's chariot of Ningirsu (see conveniently now Suter, Gudea's Temple Building p. 388 ST.61); it shows a bird (possibly an *anzu* bird, one of Gudea's war trophies) standing in triumph on the very top of a heap of various other war trophies of Ningirsu. The chariot of Enlil built by Išme-Dagān of Isin had a "bat" (su-din) resting on its pole or yoke (see Civil, JAOS 88 [1968] p. 13).

In connection with col. iii line 1 for dùr(ANSE.NÍTA) "male donkey" cf. Landsberger, MSL 8/1 p. 52 (Urra = *ḫubullu*(*m*) 13 line 376: ANŠEdu-ur.NÍTA "male donkey"= Akkadian *mu-ú-ri* "(donkey) foal"); cf. Salonen, Hippologica p. 48 where the variant spellings anše-dur$_{9}$(ŠUL) and anše-dur$_{9}$(ŠUL)-ùr in Gudea Cylinders A and B are noted and Maekawa ASJ 1 (1979) p. 36. For zi-le see Falkenstein, Bag. Mit. 3 (1964) pp. 29–30 commentary to line 4 and Sjöberg, Orientalia Suecana 19–20 (1970–71) p. 171.

BIBLIOGRAPHY

1956 Sollberger, CIRPL p. xi Ent. 15 (ex. 2, study)
1968 Ellis, Foundation Deposits p. 54 and n. 53 (exs. 2–3, study)
1972 Lambert, RSO 47 pp. 1–22 (ex. 1, copy, edition, study)
1975 Biggs, RA 69 pp. 185–86 (exs. 2–3, study)
1977–78 Bauer, WO 9 pp. 5–6 (ex. 1, study)
1982 Steible, ASBW 1 pp. 267–70 Entemena 79 (exs. 1–2, edition)
1983 Rashid, Gründungsfiguren p. 10 no. 69 (ex. 3, study)
1983 Cooper, SANE 2 p. 31 (study)
1986 Cooper, SARI 1 pp. 58–59 La 5.4 (exs. 1–2, translation)
1995 Selz, Untersuchungen p. 229 (study)

TEXT

Col. i	
1) ^{d}lugal-é-mùš-ra	i 1) For the god Lugalemuš,
2) en-TE.ME-na	i 2–4) En-metena, ruler of Lagaš,
3) énsi-	
4) lagaš(NU$_{10}$.BUR.LA).KI	
5) šà-pà-da-	i 5–6) chosen in the heart by the goddess Nanše,
6) ^{d}nanše	
7) [é]nsi-gal-^{d}nin-ĝír-sú-ka	i 7) chief [ex]ecutive for the god Ninĝirsu,
8) dumu-en-an-na-túm	i 8–10) son of En-anatum, r[u]ler of Lagaš,
9) é[n]si-	
10) lagaš(NU$_{10}$.BUR.LA).KI-ka-ke$_{4}$	
Col. ii	
1) ^{d}nin-ĝí[r-s]ú-ra	ii 1–3) built the Eš-dugru ("Shrine [in which] Pots Are Arranged") for the god Ninĝi[rs]u,
2) èš-dug-ru	
3) mu-na-dù	

4) a-ḫuš	ii 4–7) built for him the Aḫuš ("Terrifying Water"), the temple where (Niñgirsu) looks approvingly upon (En-metena), and furnished it.
5) é-igi-zi-bar-ra	
6) mu-na-dù	
7) mu-ni-túm	
8) GIŠ.gígir kur-dub-^{d}nin-ĝír-sú-ka ^{ḫa}ḫar-ra-an-eridu.KI-ka GAM$_4$.GAM-bi	ii 8–10) He fashioned for him the chariot (called) "Heaper up of the foreign (enemy) lands of the god Niñgirsu on the road (to) Eridu, the radiance of whose *gam*[*gam*] bird reaches into the heart of the foreign (enemy) land(s)."
9) ní-bi kur-šà-ga	
10) mu-na-dím	
Col. iii	
1) é-[d]u$_{24}$-ùr-zi-le	iii 1–2) and built the E-durzile ("House— Princely Male Donkeys").
2) mu-na-dù	
3) ^{d}lugal-URU×KÁR.KI-r[a]	iii 3–5) He built his "palace" of (the town) URU×KAR for the god Lugal-URU×KAR.
4) é-gal-URU×KÁR.KI-ka-ni	
5) mu-na-dù	
6) ^{d}nanše	iii 6–9) He built the E-engur ("Temple of the Fountainhead") of (the town) Zulum for the goddess Nanše and furnished it.
7) é-engur-ra-zú-lum-ma	
8) mu-na-dù	
9) mu-ni-túm	
10) ama-gi$_4$-lagaš(NU$_{10}$.BUR.LA.KI).KI	iii 10 – iv 3) He cancelled obligations for Lagaš, restored child to mother and mother to child.
Col. iv	
1) ⌈e⌉-ĝar	
2) ama dumu ì-ni-gi$_4$	
3) dumu ama ì-ni-gi$_4$	
4) ama-gi$_4$!-še-ur$_5$-ka	iv 4–5) He cancelled obligations regarding interest-bearing grain loans.
5) e-ĝar	
6) u$_4$-ba en-TE.ME-na-ke$_4$	iv 6 – v 3) At that time, En-metena built for Lugalemuš, the E-muš ("House — Radiance [of the Land]") of Pa-tibira, his beloved temple, restoring it for him.
7) ^{d}lugal-é-mùš-ra	
8) é-mùš-pa$_5$-ti-bir$_5$-ra.KI-ka	
Col. v	
1) é-ki-áĝ-ĝá-ni	
2) mu-na-dù	
3) ki-bé mu-na-gi$_4$	
4) dumu-unu!(=AB).KI	v 4–8) He cancelled [oblig]ations for the citizens of Uruk, Larsa, and Pa-tibira.
5) dumu-larsa.KI	
6) dumu-pa$_5$-ti-bir$_5$-ra-ka	
7) [ama]-gi$_4$-bi	
8) e-ĝar	
9) ^{d}inanna-ra	v 9–11) He restored (the first) to the goddess Inanna's control in Uruk,
10) unu.KI-šè	
11) šu-na ì-ni-gi$_4$	
Col. vi	
1) ^{d}utu-[ra]	vi 1–3) he restored (the second) to the god Utu's control in Larsa,
2) larsa.KI-šè	
3) šu-na ì-ni-gi$_4$	
4) ^{d}lugal-é-mùš-r[a]	vi 4–6) he restored (the third) t[o] the god Lugal-emuš's control in the E-muš (in Pa-tibira).
5) é-mùš-šè	
6) šu-na ì-ni-gi$_4$	
7) en-TE.ME-na	v 7–9) En-metena, who is commissioned by the goddess Inanna —
8) lú-inim-ma-sè-ga-	
9) ^{d}inanna-ka	
10) dingir-ra-ni	v 10–11) his personal god is the god Šul-MUŠ×PA.
11) ^{d}šul-MUŠ×PA-am$_6$	

ii 10.6 Gives in one line unu.KI nam-ak.
v 6.2 pa$_5$-ti-bir$_5$-ra.KI-ka.

5a

A sixteen-line inscription found on foundation tablets and bricks records En-metena's construction of the E-muš temple.

CATALOGUE

Ex.	Museum number	Dimensions (cm)	Lines preserved	cpn
Foundation tablets				
1	HSM 8668	21.7×28.7×6.3	1–16	c
2	Private collection	14.5×10.7	1–16	n
Bricks				
3	UCLM 9-1766	20×28×6	1–16	n
4	UCLM 9-1767	20×28×6	1–16	n
5	Rosicrucian Egyptian Museum, San Jose no. RC 479	—	1–16	n
6	Dyke College Collection	27.5×19.5×6	1–16	n

BIBLIOGRAPHY

1935 Böhl, JEOL 3 p. 125 (ex. 2, edition)
1947 Pfeifer, Ancient Alphabets pl. I (ex. 1, study)
1956 Sollberger, CIRPL p. xiii Ent. 74–75 (study); p. 43 Ent. 75 (ex. 2, study); p. 43 Ent. 74 (ex. 1, copy)
1972 Lewis, Brochure "Mesopotamia" pp. 8 and [16] (ex. 5, photos)
1979 Hallo, in Studies Jones pp. 3–4 (ex. 5, study)
1982 Steible, ASBW 1 pp. 264–65 Entemena 74 (exs. 1–5, edition)
1983 (M.) Cooper, JCS 35 pp. 197–98 (ex. 6, copy, study)
1986 Cooper, SARI 1 p. 59 La 5.5 (exs. 1–5, translation)

TEXT

Col. i	
1) ᵈinanna-ra	i 1–2) For the goddess Inanna and the god Lugal-emuš,
2) ᵈlugal-é-mùš-ra	
3) en-te-me-na	i 3 – ii 1) En-metena, ruler of Lagaš,
4) énsi-	
Col. ii	
1) lagaš(NU_{10}.BUR.LA).KI	
2) dumu-en-an-na-túm	ii 2–4) son of En-anatum, ruler of Lagaš,
3) énsi-	
4) lagaš.KI-ka-ke_4	
Col. iii	
1) é-mùš é-ki-ág̃-ne-ne	iii 1–2) built the E-muš "(House — Radiance [of the Land])" their beloved temple.
2) mu-ne-dù	
3) en-te-me-na!	iii 3 – iv 1) En-metena, nominee of the goddess Inanna,
4) mu-pà-da-	
Col. iv	
1) ᵈinanna-ka	
2) lú é-mùš dù	iv 2) who built the E-muš temple,
3) dingir-ra-ni!	iv 3–4) his personal god is the god Šul-MUŠ×PA.
4) ᵈšul-MUŠ×PA-am_6	

v 2.2 dù-a.
iv 3.2 du!(NI).

5b

An alabaster foundation tablet in the Iraq Museum bears a dedicatory inscription for the deities Inanna and Lugalemuš (of Pa-tibira) and likely dealt with the construction of their temple.

COMMENTARY

The tablet, which was acquired by the Iraq Museum in 1933 through confiscation, measures 17×13×6 cm. The inscription was collated from the published photo.

BIBLIOGRAPHY

1981 Sollberger, Sumer 37 pp. 111–13 (photo, edition, study)

1986 Cooper, SARI 1 p. 59 La 5.5a (translation)

TEXT

Obv. col. i
1) [^{d}]i[nanna-r]a
2) [^{d}]lugal-é-mùš-ra
3) en-TE.ME-na
4) énsi-
5) lagaš(NU$_{10}$.BUR.LA).KI
Obv. col. ii
1) [šà-pà]-d[a]
2) [^{d}]nanše
3) [én]si-gal
4) [^{d}ni]n-g̃ír-[sú]-ka
5) gù-[zi]-dé-[a]
6) ^{d}inanna-[ka]
7) dumu-tu-da
Obv. col. iii
1) [^{d}lugal]-URU×[KÁR].KI-ka
2) dumu en-an-na-túm
3) énsi-
4) la[gaš(NU$_{10}$.[LA.BUR]).KI-ka]
5) [dumu]-KA
6) [ur-^{d}nanše]
7) lugal
Obv. col. iv
1) la[g]aš(=NU$_{10}$.[LA].BUR.[KI]-ka-[ke$_4$]
2) é-[gal]-URU×[KÁR.KI]
3) m[u-dù]
4) [...]
5) ^{d}[...]
6) [...]
7) [...]
8) m[u-...]
Lower edge col. i
1) [é]-[...]

Obv. i 1–2) [F]or the goddess I[nanna] and the god Lugalemuš,
Obv. i 3–5) En-metena, ruler of Lagaš,

Obv. ii 1–2) [chose]n [in the heart] by the goddess Nanše,
Obv. ii 3–4) chief [ex]ecutive for [the god Ni]ng̃ir[su],

Obv. ii 5–6) [specially] summoned [by] the goddess Inanna,
Obv. ii 7 – obv. iii 1) son begotten by [the god Lugal]-URU×[KAR],

Obv. iii 2–4) son of En-anatum, ruler [of] La[gaš],

Obv. iii 5 –obv. iv 1) [desce]ndant of [Ur-Nanše], king of La[ga]š,

Obv. iv 2–3) bu[il]t the "pa[lace]" of (the town) URU×[KAR].
Obv. iv 4–8) Too broken for translation.

Lower edge i 1–3) Too broken for translation.

2) KAK [...]
3) [...] ⸢x⸣ [...]
Rev. col. i
1) [...]
2) [...]
3) [...]
4) [...]
5) [...]
6) [...]
7) [...]
8) ^{d}[inanna]-ra
Lower edge col. ii
1) ^{d}lugal-é-mùš-ra
2) [...] ⸢x⸣ [...] ⸢x⸣
Rev. col. ii
1) [...]
2) Traces
3) [...]
4) [...]
5) [dingir-ra-ni]
6) [^{d}šul-MUŠ×PA]
7) [nam-ti-la-ni-šè]
8) [nam]-ti-
Lower edge col. iii
1) lagaš(NU$_{10}$.BUR.LA).KI-šè
2) ^{d}inanna-[ra]
3) [...]
Rev. col. iii
1) [ḫ]é-na-[x]-gub
2) [en-TE.ME-na]
3) [lú é-^{d}LUGAL-U RU×KÁR.KI dù-a]
4) [dingir-ra-ni]
5) [^{d}šul]-MUŠ×PA-am$_{6}$

Rev. col. i 1–7) Lacuna

Rev. col. i 8) — Lower edge ii 2) For the goddess [Inanna] and the god Lugalemuš [he ...].

Rev. col. ii 1–4) Too broken for translation.

Rev. col. ii 5 – Lower edge col. iii 1) [M]ay [his personal god,
the god Šul-MUŠ×PA]
[for his life] and for the [li]fe of Lagaš

Lower edge col iii 2 – rev. col. iii 1)
(And) [for} the goddess Inanna [...]
May he (the god Šul-MUŠ×PA]) stand.

Rev. iii col. 2–3) [En-metena, who built the "palace" of (the town) URU×KAR],
Rev. col. iii 4–5) his personal god] is [the god Šul]-MUŠ×PA.

6

A clay nail fragment found at Ur bears an inscription recording En-metena's building of Ninĝirsu's E-ninnu temple at G̃irsu.

COMMENTARY

The clay nail fragment was found loose during Season VIII and given the excavation number U 13606. It bears the museum number IM 92968.

This text may possibly refer to the main shrine of the Ninĝirsu temple at G̃irsu, which almost certainly lay beneath the E-ninnu temple built by Gudea on Mound A.

BIBLIOGRAPHY

1955 Woolley, UE 4 pp. 47 and 175 (findspot, study)
1960 Sollberger, Iraq 22 pp. 75–76 no. 75 (study)
1965 Sollberger, UET 8 no. 9 (copy, study)
1982 Steible, ASBW 1 p. 270 Entemena 80 (edition)
1986 Cooper, SARI 1 p. 60 La 5.6 (translation)

TEXT

Col. i
1) [^{d}nin-g̃ír-]sú-
2) [é-ninnu]-ra
3) [en-TE].ME-na
4) [én]si-
5) [lag]aš.KI
6) [du]mu-[en-a]n-[na]-t[ú]m
7) [éns]i-
Col. ii
1) la[g]aš.[KI]-ka-[ke$_4$]
2) é-ni [mu]-na-[dù]
3) kù-G[I]] kù-báb[bar-ra]
4) [š]u mu-[na]-ni-[tag]
5) KIB [mu]-na-d[u$_{11}$]

i 1–2) For [the god Niñgir]su [of E-ninnu],

i 3–5) [En-me]tena, [ru]ler of [Lag]aš,

i 6 – ii 1) [s]on of [En-a]n[a]tum, [rul]er of La[g]aš,

ii 2) [built] his temple,
ii 3–4) [decorated] it for him with gol[d] and silv[er],

ii 5) and o[rdered] (these) clay nails(?) for him.

7

A magnificent silver vase found in excavations of de Sarzec at G̃irsu bears an inscription of En-metena.

COMMENTARY

The vase was excavated by de Sarzec from a trench that ran from the area of the "Maison des Fruits" west to the area of the "Massif d'Entéména" (see de Sarzec, Découvertes 1 p. 219 and Parrot, Tello p. 65). The vase, which measures 35 cm in height and 18 cm in diameter, bears the museum number AO 2674. The inscription was collated.

BIBLIOGRAPHY

1884–1912 de Sarzec, Découvertes 2 pls. 43A–C and 44 (photos); p. XLVII ENTÉMÉNA 5 (copy)
1897 Heuzey, RA 4 p. 35 (edition)
1907 Thureau-Dangin, SAK pp. 34–35 En-te-me-na h (edition)
1910 King, Early History pl. after p. 168 (photo)
1911 Poebel, Babylonica 4 p. 194 (transcription, translation)
1926 Unger, SuAK p. 86 fig. 28 (photo)
1929 Barton, RISA pp. 52–53 Entemena 8 (edition)
1931 Contenau, Manuel 2 figs. 406–407 (photo, drawing [detail])
1931 Zervos, Encyclopédie p. 209 (photo)
1940 Christian, Altertumskunde 1 pl. 192 (photo)
1948 Parrot, Tello pp. 108–109 (study); pl 8a (photo)
1956 Sollberger, CIRPL 1 p. xii Ent. 34 (study); p. 40 Ent. 34 (copy)
1960 Beek, Bildatlas fig. 124 (photo)
1960 Parrot, Sumer, fig. 188 (photo)
1967 Moortgat, Kunst pl. 113 (photo)
1971 Sollberger and Kupper, IRSA IC7e (translation)
1972 Lambert, RSO 47 p. 19 n. 1 (study)
1975 Orthmann (ed.), Der alte Orient fig. 120 (photo)
1976 Steible, Freiburger Universitätsblätter 51 pp. 27–29 (photo, copy, edition)
1980 Amiet, Art fig. 335 (photo)
1980 Kienast, OrAnt 19 pp. 252–53 (edition)
1982 André-Leicknam, Naissance de l'écriture p. 86 no. 43 (photo, translation)
1982 Steible, ASBW 1 pp. 250–51 Entemena 34 (edition)
1985 Bauer, AoN 21 p. 7 note to 34, 15 (study)
1986 Cooper, SARI 1 p. 60 La 5.7 (translation)
1990 Powell, RLA 7 7/8 p. 506 § IVB.2e (study)
1991 Braun-Holzinger, Weihgaben pp. 117–18 G 11 (edition, study)
1993 Selz, AulOr 11 pp. 107–11 (study)

TEXT

1) ^{d}nin-g̃ír-sú
2) ur-sag-^{d}en-líl-ra

1–2) For the god Niñgirsu, warrior of the god Enlil,

3) en-TE.ME-na
4) énsi-
5) lagaš(NU$_{10}$.BUR.LA).KI
6) šà-pà-da-
7) ^{d}nanše
8) énsi-gal-
9) ^{d}nin-g̃ír-sú-ka
10) dumu-en-an-na-túm
11) énsi-
12) lagaš(NU$_{10}$.BUR.LA).KI-ka-ke$_{4}$
13) lugal-ki-an-na-ág̃-g̃á-ni
14) ^{d}nin-g̃ír-sú-ra
15) gur$_{4}$-gur$_{4}$-kù-luḫ-ḫa ì-itu-da ^{d}nin-g̃ír-sú-ke$_{4}$ ab-ta-kú-a
16) mu-na-dím
17) nam-ti-la-ni-šè
18) ^{d}nin-g̃ír-sú-
19) é-ninnu-ra
20) mu-na-DU
21) u$_{4}$-ba du-du
22) sag̃a-^{d}nin-g̃ír-sú-ka-kam

3–5) En-metena, ruler of Lagaš,

6–7) chosen in the heart by the goddess Nanše,

8–9) chief executive for the god Ning̃irsu,

10–12) son of En-anatum, ruler of Lagaš,

13–14) for his master who loves him, the god Ning̃irsu,
15–16) made (this) *gurgur* (= double *gur*?) vessel of refined silver, whose monthly fat (offering) the god Ning̃irsu consumes
17–20) and set it up for his own life for the god Ning̃irsu of E-ninnu.

21–22) At that time, Dudu was the temple administrator for the god Ning̃irsu.

8

Four inscriptions of En-metena — E1.9.5.8, a 17-line foundation tablet inscription; E1.9.5.9, a 12-line door-socket inscription; E1.9.5.10, a 7-line door-socket inscription known from four copies; and E1.9.5.11, a 22-line brick inscription known from five copies — deal with En-metena's construction of the "reed shrine" of Ning̃irsu's *giguna.*

COMMENTARY

A 17-line foundation tablet from G̃irsu commemorates En-metena's construction of the "reed shrine" of Ning̃irsu's *giguna*. The tablet bears the museum number EŞ 9577.

For a general discussion of *giguna* see K. Szarzynska ASJ 14 (1992) pp. 278–80. Szarzynska points out (following Falkenstein) that the *giguna*s were apparently artificial pleasure gardens, that is, groves planted with cedars and other aromatic trees and plants. Selz (in RIM readers' notes) points out that they apparently were also zoos where exotic animals were kept. According to CAD, the word *giguna* "seems originally to have denoted a reed structure erected on an artificial mound." The name may literally mean "multi-coloured reeds" (gi-gunu).

The bricks of En-metena connected with the *giguna* came from the so-called "Massif d'Entéména," a huge wall that was situated in the SW corner of the sacred precinct of Ning̃irsu about 15 m west of the "Maison des Fruits." The door-sockets connected with the *giguna* shrine came from points not far east of the "Massif d'Entéména." These data give us a general idea of the location of Ning̃irsu's "reed shrine" (èš-gi) at G̃irsu. It apparently lay within the area of Tell K.

BIBLIOGRAPHY

1956 Sollberger, CIRPL p. xii Ent. 43 (study); p. 42 Ent. 43 (copy)
1982 Steible, ASBW 1 pp. 258–59 Entemena 43 (edition)
1985 Bauer, AoN 21 p. 7 (study)
1986 Cooper, SARI 1 p. 60 La 5.8 (translation)

TEXT

Col. i
1) ^{d}nin-ĝír-sú
2) ur-sag-^{d}en-líl-ra
3) en-TE.ME-na
4) énsi-
5) lagaš(NU$_{10}$.BUR.LA).KI
Col. ii
1) šà-pà-da-
2) ^{d}nanše
3) énsí-gal-
4) ^{d}nin-ĝír-sú-ka
5) dumu-en-an-na-túm
Col. iii
1) énsi-
2) lagaš(NU$_{10}$.BUR.LA).KI-ka
3) lú èš-gi-
4) gi$^{!}$-gù-na-
Col. iv
1) ^{d}nin-ĝír-[sú]-ka dù-a
2) dingir-ra-ni
3) ^{d}su[l-MUŠ×PA-am$_{6}$]

i 1–2) For the god Ninĝirsu, warrior of the god Enlil,

i 3–5) En-metena, ruler of Lagaš

ii 1–2) chosen in the heart by the goddess Nanše,

ii 3–4) chief executive for the god Ninĝirsu,

ii 5 – iii 2) son of En-anatum, ruler of Lagaš,

iii 3 – iv 1) who built the "reed shrine" of Ninĝirsu's *giguna* ("Multi-coloured Reeds(?)")

iv 2–3) His personal god is Šu[l-MUŠ×PA].

9

A 12-line door-socket inscription records En-metena's construction of Ninĝirsu's "reed shrine" and *giguna*.

COMMENTARY

The door socket almost certainly came from Ĝirsu; it bears the museum number BM 90932 (old number BM 12061). The inscription was collated.

BIBLIOGRAPHY

1898 King, CT 5 pl. 1 BM 12061 (copy)
1907 Thureau-Dangin, SAK pp. 32–33 En-te-me-na e (edition)
1910 King, Early History pl after p. 162 (photo)
1952 Sollberger, ZA 50 p. 4 (study)
1956 Sollberger, CIRPL p. xii Ent. 17 (study); p. 34 Ent. 17 (copy)
1982 Steible, ASBW 1 pp. 220–21 Entemena 17 (edition)
1986 Cooper, SARI 1 pp. 60–61 La 5.9 (translation)

TEXT

1) ^{d}nin-ĝír-sú
2) ur-sag-^{d}en-líl-ra
3) en-TE.ME-na
4) énsi
5) lagaš(NU$_{10}$.BUR.LA).KI
6) dumu-en-an-na-túm
7) énsi-
8) lagaš(DU$_{10}$.BUR.LA).KI-ka

1–2) For the god Ninĝirsu, warrior of the god Enlil,

3–5) En-metena, ruler of Lagaš,

6–8) son of En-anatum, ruler of Lagaš,

9) lú èš-gi-gi-gù-n[a]-
10) ^{d}nin-⌈ĝír⌉-sú-⌈ka dù-a⌉
11) dingir-⌈ra⌉-ni
12) ⌈^{d}šul-MUŠ×PA⌉-am$_6$

9–10) who built the "reed shrine" of the god Ninĝirsu's *giguna* "(Multi-coloured Reeds),"
11–12) his personal god is the god Šul-MUŠ×PA.

10

A shorter version of the previous inscription is found on four door sockets.

CATALOGUE

Ex.	Museum number	Dimensions (cm)	Lines preserved	cpn
1	EŞ 388	Dia.: 33	1–7	n
2	EŞ 389	Height: 15 Dia.: 38	1–7	n
3	VA 3311	Dia.: 34×36.5 Height: 21	1–7	n
4	Art Museum, Princeton	—	1–7	n

COMMENTARY

Exs. 1–2 were found in excavations of de Sarzec at G̃irsu. One door-socket came from a point 4.7 m from the wells of the "Esplanade d'Entéména" and a second 1.4 m from the "Porte a." Exs. 1–2 are now housed in Istanbul. Exs. 3–4, presumably from the same general area, were purchased.

BIBLIOGRAPHY

1884–1912 Sarzec, Découvertes 2 p. XLVI ENTÉMÉNA 2 (ex. 1 [or 2], copy)
1888 Oppert, RA 2 pp. 87–88 (ex. 1, translation)
1907 Thureau-Dangin, SAK pp. 32–33 En-te-me-na b (edition)
1907 Messerschmidt, VAS 1 no. 7 (ex. 3, copy)
1952 Sollberger, ZA 50 p. 4 (exs. 1–3, study)
1956 Sollberger, CIRPL p. xvi Ent. 18–21 (exs. 1–4, study); p. 34 Ent. 18 (ex. 1, copy);
1982 Steible, ASBW 1 pp. 221–22 Enmetena 18 (exs. 1–4, edition)
1986 Cooper, SARI 1 p. 61 La 5.10 (exs. 1–4, translation)

TEXT

1) en-TE.ME-na
2) énsi-
3) lagaš(NU$_{10}$.BUR.LA).KI
4) lú èš-gi-gi-gù-na-
5) ^{d}nin-ĝír-sú-ka dù-a
6) dingir-ra-ni
7) ^{d}šul-MUŠ×PA

1–3) En-metena, ruler of Lagaš,

4–5) who built the "reed shrine" of the god Ninĝirsu's *giguna* "Multi-coloured reeds),"
6–7) his personal god is the god Šul-MUŠ×PA.

5.3 dù(NI)-a.
7.2–3 Adds -am$_6$.

11

The construction of Niñĝirsu's "reed shrine" is also commemorated in a 22-line brick inscription from Ĝirsu.

CATALOGUE

Ex.	Museum number	Excavation number	Dimensions (cm)	Lines preserved	cpn
1	EŞ 2507	—	31×22×6.5	i 1–6 ii 1–6 iii 1–6 iv 1–4	p
2	AO 355	—	31.7×22.4×4.2	i 1–6 ii 1–6 iii 1–6 iv 1–4	c
3	—	TG 464	—	—	n
4	—	TG 573	—	—	n
5	—	TG 575	—	—	n

COMMENTARY

The bricks with this inscription came from the so-called Massif d'Entéména, a huge wall that was situated in the SW corner of the sacred precinct of Ninĝirsu about 15 m west of the "Maison des Fruits." Ex. 1 was collated from two RIM photos.

BIBLIOGRAPHY

1884–1912 de Sarzec, Découvertes 2 pl. 31 no. 3 (ex. 2, photo)
1907 Thureau-Dangin, SAK pp. 36–37 en-te-me-na 1 (ex. 2, edition)
1936 de Genouillac, FT p. 135 (exs. 2–4, study)
1956 Sollberger, CIRPL p. xii Ent. 36–40 (exs. 1–5, study); p. 41 Ent. 36 (ex. 1, copy)
1982 Steible, ASBW 1 pp. 264–65 Entemena 36 (exs. 1–5, edition)
1986 Cooper, SARI 1 p. 61 La 5.11 (exs. 1–5, translation)

TEXT

Col. i
1) ᵈnin-ĝír-sú
2) ur-sag-ᵈen-líl-ra
3) en-TE.ME-na
4) énsi-
5) lagaš(NU$_{10}$.BUR.LA).KI
6) šà-pà-da-
Col. ii
1) ᵈnanše
2) énsi-gal-
3) ᵈnin-ĝír-sú-ka
4) dumu-en-an-na-túm
5) énsi-
6) lagaš(NU$_{10}$.BUR.LA).KI-ka
Col. iii
1) lú èš-gi-

i 1–2) For the god Ninĝirsu, warrior of the god Enlil,

i 3–5) En-metena, ruler of Lagaš,

i 6 – ii 1) chosen in the heart by the goddess Nanše,

ii 2–3) chief executive for the god Ninĝirsu,

ii 4–6) son of En-anatum, ruler of Lagaš,

iii 1–3) who built the "reed shrine" of the god

2) ^{d}nin-g̃ír-sú-ka
3) dù-a
4) dingir-ra-ni
5) ^{d}šul-MUŠ×PA
6) u_4-ul-la-šè
Col. iv
1) nam-ti-la-ni-šè
2) ^{d}nin-g̃ír-sú-ra
3) é-ninnu-a
4) ḫé-na-šè-DU

Ning̃irsu,

iii 4 – iv 4) may his personal god, the god Šul-MUŠ×PA, forever stand (interceding) before the god Ning̃irsu in E-ninnu for his life!

12

A 57-line inscription found on eight alabaster foundation tablets from Tell K at G̃irsu records En-metena's construction of a brewery for the god Ning̃irsu. The master text is ex. 1.

CATALOGUE

Ex.	Museum number	Dimensions (cm)	Lines preserved	cpn
1	AO 256	15×22×4.5	i 1–7 ii 1–7 iii 1–6 iv 1–7 v 1–6 vi 1–8 vii 1–7 viii 1–5 ix 1–4	p
2	AO 2353B	22.5×15×7.1	i 1–7 ii 1–7 iii 1–6 iv 1–7 v 1–6 vi 1–8 vii 1–7 viii 1–5 ix 1–4	p
3	VA 3095	23×15.7×5.1	i 1–7 ii 1–7 iii 1–6 iv 1–7 v 1–6 vi 1–8 vii 1–7 viii 1–5 ix 1–4	c
4	EŞ 1529	22×14×4.2	—	n
5	EŞ 1530	22×14×4.2	—	n
6	EŞ 1531	22×14×4.2	—	n
7	EŞ 1532	22×14×4.2	—	n
8	EŞ 1534	—	—	n

COMMENTARY

Concerning the findspots of the pegs which accompanied the foundation tablets, we may note the comments of Parrot (Tello, p. 66 and the map on p. 64):

> Plusieurs figurines de fondation en cuivre avaient été déposées sous le dallage de l'esplanade: deux vers le N.-O., une sur le côté de la porte, une non loin du bassin ovale; trois vers le S.-E., deux en dehors des petites réservoirs, une en deçà de la porte. Ces figurines diffèrent de toutes les

précédentes: elles répresentent des divinités ou mieux des genies divins dont la tête émerge des tablettes de pierre auxquelles ils sont associés [Fig. 25, b]. Le texte indique qu'Entéména construisit "pour son roi qui l'aime, pour Ningirsu, son E-kash-gar."

The location of a brewery in the "esplanade" area of Tell K may be related to the large number of wells unearthed by de Sarzec in this precinct.

Bauer, AoN 21 (1985) p. 7 points out that the reading of vi line 2 as me-lám is conventional; he notes a possible reading me-li$_{9}$(-m).

BIBLIOGRAPHY

1884–1912 de Sarzec, Découvertes 2 p. XLVI ENTÉMÉNA 1 (ex. 1, copy); pl. 5bis no. 1a (ex. 2, photo)
1888 Oppert apud de Sarzec, RA 2 pp. 148–49 (ex. 2, copy, translation)
1893 Oppert apud Heuzey RA 3 pp. 61–63 (exs. 1–7, translation)
1897 Heuzey, RA 4 p. 36 § 5 (study)
1900 Heuzey, Villa royale p. 89 (study)
1900 Radau, EBH pp. 112–15 (ex. 2, edition)
1907 Messerschmidt, VAS 1 no. 8 (ex. 3, copy)
1907 Thureau-Dangin, SAK pp. 30–33 En-te-me-na a (ex. 2, edition)
1926 Unger, SuAK p. 85 fig. 25 (ex. 6, photo)
1927 Unger, RLV VIII pl. 139b (ex. 6, photo)
1940 Christian, Altertumskunde 1 pl. 153 no. 3b (ex. 2, photo)
1956 Sollberger, CIRPL p. xi Ent. 8–14 (exs. 1–7, study); p. 33 Ent. 8 (ex. 1, copy); p. 33 Ent. 9–14 (variants listed)
1982 Steible, ASBW 1 pp. 215–18 Entemena 8 (exs. 1–7, edition)
1986 Cooper, SARI 1 pp. 61–62 La 5.12 (exs. 1–7, translation)

TEXT

Col. I	
1) ^{d}nin-g̃ír-sú	i 1–2) For the god Ning̃irsu, warrior of the god Enlil,
2) ur-sag̃-^{d}en-líl-ra	
3) en-TE.ME-na	i 3–5) En-metena, ruler of Lagaš,
4) énsi-	
5) lagaš(NU$_{10}$.BUR.LA).KI	
6) dumu en-an-na-túm	i 6 – ii 1) son of En-anatum, ruler of Lagaš,
7) énsi-	
Col. ii	
1) lagaš(NU$_{10}$.BUR.LA).KI-ka	
2) dumu-KA-	ii 2–5) descendant of Ur-Nanše, king of Lagaš,
3) ur-^{d}nanše	
4) lugal-	
5) lagaš(NU$_{10}$.BUR.LA).KI-ka-ke$_{4}$	
6) ^{d}nin-g̃ír-sú-ra	ii 6 – iii 1) built the Eš-dugru ("Shrine [in which] Pots Are Arranged") for the god Ning̃irsu,
7) èš-dug-ru	
Col. iii	
1) mu-na-dù	
2) a-ḫuš	iii 2–4) built for him the Aḫuš "Terrifying Water" the temple where (the god Ning̃irsu) looks approvingly upon (En-metena).
3) é-igi-zi-bar-ra	
4) mu-na-dù	
5) ^{d}lugal-URU×KÁR.KI-ra	iii 5 – iv 1) For Lugal-URU×KAR he built his "palace" of (the town of) URU×KAR,
6) é-gal-URU×KÁR.KI-ka-ni	
Col. iv	
1) mu-na-dù	
2) ^{d}nanše	iv 2–4) built the E-engur "Temple of the Fountainhead" of (the town) Zulum for the goddess Nanše
3) é-engur-ra-zú-lum-ma	
4) mu-na-dù	
5) ^{d}en-ki	iv 5 – v 1) built the Abzu-pasira "Fountainhead with

i 2.2–7 ur-sag̃-^{d}en-líl-lá-ra.
ii 5.7 NU$_{11}$.LA.KI-ka-ke$_{4}$.
ii 1. 7 mu-na-du!(NI).
iii 5.7 Omits KI.

6) lugal-eridu.KI-ra
7) abzu-sír-ra

Narrow Channels" for the god Enki, king of Eridu,

Col. v
1) mu-na-dù
2) ^{d}nin-ḫur-sag̃-g̃á-ra
3) gi-gù-na-
4) tir-kù-ga
5) mu-na-dù

v 2–5) built the *giguna* ("Multi-coloured Reeds") of the shining grove for the goddess Ninḫursag̃,

6) ^{d}nin-g̃ír-sú-ra
Col. vi
1) an-ta-sur-ra
2) é-me-lám-bi kur-kur-ra-a-dul$_{5}$
3) mu-na-dù

v 6 – vi 3) built for the god Ning̃irsu the (town) Antasur ("[Northern(?)] Boundary") (whose) temple's awesome splendour covers all the lands,

4) ^{d}en-líl-la
5) é-ad-da-
6) im-sag̃-g̃á
7) mu-na-dù

vi 4–7) built the E-ada ("House of the Father") of Imsag for the god Enlil,

8) é-^{d}g̃á-tùm-du$_{10}$
Col. vii
1) mu-dù

vi 8 – vii 1) built the temple of the goddess G̃atumdu,

2) ^{d}nanše
3) šà-pà-da
4) mu-na-dù
5) ^{d}nanše gi-gù-na-maḫ-ni
6) mu-na-dù

vii 2–6) built (the town) Šapada ("Chosen (in) the Heart") for the goddess Nanše.

7) u$_{4}$-ba en-TE.ME-na-ke$_{4}$
Col. viii
1) lugal-ki-an-na-ág̃-g̃á-ni
2) ^{d}nin-g̃ír-sú-ra
3) é-bappìr(KAŠ×GAR)-ka-ni
4) mu-na-dù

vii 7 – viii 4) At that time, En-metena built for the god Ning̃irsu, the master who loves him, his (Ning̃irsu's) brewery.

5) en-TE.ME-na
Col. ix
1) lú é-bappìr-
2) ^{d}nin-g̃ír-[sú]-ka dù-a

viii 5 – ix 2) En-metena, who built the brewery of the god Ning̃irsu —

3) dingir-ra-ni
4) ^{d}šul-MUŠ×PA-am$_{6}$

ix 3–4) his personal god is the god Šul-MUŠ×PA.

13

A twelve-line inscription found on six foundation pegs deals with En-metena's construction of a brewery for the god Ning̃irsu. For the findspots, see the commentary to the previous inscription.

---

iv 6.7 lugal-eridu.KI-ga-ra.
v 2. 2, 5–7 ^{d}nin-ḫur-sag̃-ra.
ii 1.7 mu-dù(!)NI
ii 3.3–4 Omit -da.
vii 5.2–3, 5–6 Omit ^{d}nanše.

CATALOGUE

Ex.	Museum number	Dimensions (cm)	CIRPL number	Rashid number	Lines preserved	cpn
1	EŞ 1523	25.5×5×3.5	Ent. 6(?)	63 (?)	—	n
2	EŞ 1522	Height: 25.5 Width at shoulders: 5.1	Ent. 3	60	—	n
3	EŞ 1520	26.5×5.1×3	Ent. 4	61	—	n
4	EŞ 1521	25.5×5.1×3.7	Ent. 5	59	—	n
5	EŞ 490	28×20×6	—	(?)	—	n
6	AO 2353A	Length: 24 Width: 5.15	Ent. 7	62	—	n
7	VA 3024	—	—	—	i 1–5 ii 1–4 iii 1–3	n

COMMENTARY

It is unclear whether Sollberger CIRPL Ent. 6 refers to ex. 1 or 5; the same is true of Rashid p. 9 no. 63.

BIBLIOGRAPHY

1926 Unger, SuAK p. 85 figs. 25–26 (ex. 4, photo)
1927 Unger, RLV 8 pl. 139a (ex. 4, photo)
1956 Sollberger, CIRPL p. xi Ent. 2–7 (exs. 1–6, study); p. 33 Ent. 2 (ex. 1, copy)
1971 Sollberger and Kupper, IRSA IC7c (exs. 1–6, translation)
1982 Steible, ASBW 1 Entemena 2 pp. 214–15 (exs. 1–6, edition)
1983 Rashid, Gründungsfiguren p. 9 (see catalogue) (study); pls. 6–7 (exs. 2, 4, and 6, drawing)
1986 Cooper, SARI 1 p. 62 La 5.13 (exs. 1–6, translation)

TEXT

Col. i
1) ᵈnin-g̃ír-sú
2) ur-sag̃-ᵈen-líl-[ra]
3) [en-T]E.ME-na
4) énsi-
5) lagaš(NU$_{10}$.BUR.LA).KI
Col. ii
1) dumu-en-an-na-túm
2) [é]nsi-
3) lagaš(NU$_{10}$.BIR.LA).KI-ka
4) lú é-bappìr(KAŠ×GAR)-
Col. iii
1) ᵈnin-g̃ír-sú-ka dù-a
2) dingir-ra-ni
3) ᵈšul-MUŠ×PA-am$_6$

i 1–2) [For] the god Niñgirsu, warrior of the god Enlil,

i 3–5) [En]-metena, ruler of Lagaš,

ii 1–3) son of En-anatum, [ru]ler of Lagaš,

ii 4 – iii 1) who built the brewery of the god Niñgirsu,

iii 2–3) his personal god is the god Šul-MUŠ×PA.

14

A door socket inscription from G̃irsu records En-metena's construction of a "coach-house" (é-GIŠ.gigir) for the god Niñgirsu.

COMMENTARY

The door socket with this inscription, which was found during de Sarzec's excavations at Tello on Tell K (see de Sarzec, Découvertes 2 pl. LVI no. 9), bears the museum number AO 3297. The inscription was collated.

The fact that inscriptions alluding to the construction of the brewery and coach-house were found in situ on Tell K at G̃irsu suggests that the two structures lay close to one another in that area. Recalling the common practice of Mesopotamian rulers to rebuild structures on top of pre-existing ruins, it may be that the Lagaš ruler Gudea rebuilt these two structures on Tell K. This is suggested by a passage in Gudea Cylinder A (col. xxviii 10–16, see now Edzard, RIME 3/1 p. 87) where mention is made of a nesag, perhaps "wine-cellar(?)" or "sacristry" (Heimpel, NABU 1994 no. 83), together with a brewery, store-house, and coach-house of the god Ning̃irsu. A correlation of the En-metena and Gudea texts would assume that the Gudea inscription contained a topographical description of the temple precinct of Ning̃irsu. It also coincides with the mention together in G̃irsu of a coach-house and brewery in an inscription of URU-KA-gi-na (E1.9.9.6 ii 3–7): "He built a coach-house for him, a building whose awesome splendour overwhelms all lands, and he built for him a winery, which provides (him with) great vats of wine from the mountains."

In lines 6 and 9 for the reading GIŠ.gígir, the reader is referred to the rather confusing evidence concerning the early signs consisting of LAGAB with inscribed element that were used for the separate words for "public fountain," "well," and "chariot," discussed by Powell in ZA 62 (1972) pp. 210–11 n. 128 and Orientalia NS 43 (1974) p. 27 n. 14 and by Steinkeller in ZA 71 (1981) pp. 26–28.

BIBLIOGRAPHY

1884–1912 de Sarzec, Découvertes 2 p. LVI ENTÉMÉNA 9 (copy)
1907 Thureau-Dangin, SAK pp. 32–33 En-te-me-na d (edition)
1929 Barton, RISA pp. 50–51 Entemena 4 (edition)
1956 Sollberger, CIRPL p. xii Ent. 35 (study); p. 35 Ent. 22 (copy)
1963 Kramer, Sumerians p. 315 § C 16 (translation)
1982 Steible, ASBW 1 pp. 222–23 Entemena 22 (edition)
1986 Cooper, SARI 1 p. 62 La 5.14 (translation)

TEXT

1) ᵈnin-g̃ír-sú 2) ur-sag̃-ᵈen-líl-lá-ra	1–2) For the god Ning̃irsu, warrior of the god Enlil,
3) en-TE.ME-na 4) énsi- 5) lagaš(NU$_{10}$.BUR.LA).KI-ke$_4$	3–5) En-metena, ruler of Lagaš,
6) é-GIŠ.gígir-ra 7) mu-na-dù	6–7) built a coach-house.
8) en-TE.ME-na 9) lú é-GIŠ.gígir-ra dù-a	8–9) En-metena, who built the coach-house —
10) dingir-ra-ni 11) ᵈšul-MUŠ×PA-am$_6$	10–11) his personal god is the god Šul-MUŠ×PA.

15

A brick inscription records En-metena's planting of a garden named [E]-ša.

COMMENTARY

The brick, which measures 26×22×4.5 cm, bears the museum number EŞ 8902. Its findspot at G̃irsu is not known. The inscription was not collated.

The "garden of E-ša" (kiri$_6$-⌈é⌉-šà-ga) figures together with the "palace of Antasur (é-gal-an-ta-sur-ra) in inscription E1.9.4.27. According to the understanding of the author Antasur and Ešaga were two neighbouring towns; Selz (Untersuchungen pp. 227–28 § 33) prefers to see Ešaga as part of the town of Antasur.

BIBLIOGRAPHY

1956 Sollberger, CIRPL p. xii Ent. 42 (study); p. 42 Ent. 42 (copy)
1982 Steible, ASBW 1 pp. 257–58 Entemena 42 (edition)
1986 Cooper, SARI 1 p. 62 La 5.15 (translation)

TEXT

Col. i	
1) ^{d}nin-g̃ír-sú$^{!}$	i 1–2) For the god Ning̃irsu, warrior of the god Enlil,
2) ur-sag̃-^{d}en-líl-ra	
3) en-TE.ME-na	i 3–5) En-metena, ruler of Lagaš,
4) énsi-	
5) lagaš(NU$_{10}$.BUR.LA).KI	
Col. ii	
1) š[à-pà]-da-	ii 1–2) chosen in the heart by the goddess Nanše,
2) ^{d}nanše	
3) énsi-gal-	ii 3–4) chief executive for the god Ning̃irsu,
4) ^{d}nin$^{!}$-g̃ír-sú$^{!}$-ka	
5) géštu-sum-ma-	ii 5–6) granted wisdom by the god Enki,
6) ^{d}en-ki-k[a]	
Col. iii	
1) dum[u]-e[n]-an-n[a]-t[úm]	iii 1–3) so[n] of E[n]-an[a]t[um], ruler of Lagaš,
2) énsi-	
3) lagaš(NU$_{10}$.BUR.LA).KI-ka-ke$_{4}$	
4) lugal-ki-an-na-ág̃-[g̃á-ni]	iii 4 – iv 1) for [his] master who loves him, [the god Ning̃irsu],
Col. iv	
1) [^{d}nin-g̃ír-sú-ra]	
2) [k]iri$_{6}$-[é]-šà-ga	iv 2–3) constructed the [g]arden of [E]-ša.
3) mu-na-dù	
4) [k]a-bé é-maš-⸢dà⸣-[...]	iv 4) At its [en]trance, the "House of *Gazelles*" ...
Col. v	
Traces	Traces

16

A stone door socket of unknown provenance gives an inscription recording various temple constructions of En-metena.

COMMENTARY

The door socket, which measures 55×40×21 cm, was given the museum number BM 86900. The inscription was collated.

BIBLIOGRAPHY

1910 King, CT 10 pl. 1 (copy)
1907 Thureau-Dangin, SAK 1 pp. 32–33 En-te-me-na f (edition)
1929 Barton, RISA pp. 50–53 Entemena 6 (edition)
1956 Sollberger, CIRPL p. xii Ent. 23 (study); p. 35 Ent. 23 (copy)
1982 Steible, ASBW 1 pp. 223–24 Entemena 23 (edition)
1986 Cooper, SARI 1 pp. 62–63 La 5.16 (translation)

TEXT

1) ^{d}nin-[g̃]ír-sú
2) [u]r-sag̃-^{d}en-líl-lá-ra
3) en-TE.ME-na
4) énsi-
5) lagaš(NU$_{10}$.BUR.LA).KI
6) dumu-en-an-na-túm
7) énsi-
8) lagaš(NU$_{10}$.BUR.LA).KI-ka-ke$_{4}$
9) èš-dug-ru
10) m[u]-n[a]-dù
11) a-ḫuš
12) é-igi-zi-bar-ra
13) mu-na-dù
14) ^{d}nanše
15) é-engur-ra-zú-lum-ma
16) mu-na-dù
17) ⌜gi-gù-na-ni⌝
18) mu-na-dù
19) é-šà-pà-da
20) mu-dù
21) ^{d}en-líl-la
22) é-ad-da-
23) im-sag̃-g̃á
24) mu-na-dù
25) é-^{d}g̃á-tùm-du$_{10}$
26) mu-dù
27) é-^{d}nin-ma[ḫ]
28) [gi-gù-na]-
29) tir-kù-ga
30) mu-dù
31) ^{d}lugal-URU×KÁR.KI-ra
32) é-gal-URU×KÁR.KI-ka-ni
33) mu-na-dù
34) ^{d}en-ki
35) lugal-eridu.KI-ra
36) abzu-pa$_{5}$-sír-ra
37) mu-na-dù
38) ^{d}nin-g̃ír-sú-ra
39) an-ta-sur-ra
40) é-me-lám-bi-kur-kur-ra-a-dul$_{5}$
41) mu-na-dù
42) en-TE.ME-na
43) l[ú an]-ta-sur-ra dù-a
44) dingir-ra-ni
45) ^{d}šul-MUŠ×PA

1–2) For the god Ning̃irsu, warrior of the god Enlil,

3–5) En-metena, ruler of Lagaš,

6–8) son of En-anatum, ruler of Lagaš,

9–10) built the Eš-dugru "Shrine (in which) Pots Are Arranged,"
11–13) built for him the Aḫuš "Terrifying Water" the temple where (Ning̃irsu) looks approvingly upon (En-metena).
14–16) He built the E-engur "Temple of the Fountainhead" of (the town) Zulum for the goddess Nanše,
17–18) and built her *giguna* "Multi-coloured Reeds(?)" for her,
19–20) he built the E–šapada ("House Chosen in the Heart"),
21–24) he built the E-ada ("House of the Father") of Imsag̃a for the god Enlil,

25–26) he built the temple of the goddess G̃atumdu,

27–30) he built the temple of the goddess Ninmaḫ, the [*giguna* ("Multi-coloured Reeds?")] of the sacred grove,

31–33) he built his "palace" of (the town of) URU×KAR for the god Lugal-URU×KAR,

34–37) he built the Abzu-pasira ("Fountainhead With Narrow Channels") for the god Enki, king of Eridu,

38–41) and for Ning̃irsu, he built the Antasur ("[Northern(?)] Boundary"), the temple whose awesome splendour covers all the lands.

42–43) En-metena, [w]ho built the [An]tasura ("[Northern(?)] Border") —
44–45) his personal god is the god Šul-MUŠ×PA.

17

A statuette found at Ur was dedicated by En-metena to the god Enlil.

COMMENTARY

The diorite statue, which measures 76 cm in height, was found in debris in a gateway in the southwest wall of the temenos leading into the ziqqurrat enclosure of Nabonidus at Ur and was given the excavation number U 805. It bears the museum number IM 5. The original provenance of the piece is unknown. It probably came from the Lagaš region.

Col. ii line 20 refers to a place named Šapada. Since a reference to a temple named Šapada dedicated to the goddess Ninḫursag (Selz, Untersuchungen p. 186 § 13) is known, Selz (Untersuchungen p. 228 § 40) suggests that the temple in ii 20 of our text should have been dedicated to the goddess Ninḫursag̃, and the text is in error in assigning it to the god Ning̃irsu. However, the author intends to show in a separate communication that there were two towns named Šapada in Lagaš province, one located south of G̃irsu near the town Giguna, dedicated to the goddess Ninḫursag̃, and another, north of G̃irsu, which is referred to in this text. According to E1.9.4.17 line 22, the latter was dedicated to the god Ning̃irsu.

In col. v line 2 for aški = *urbatu*(*m*) "reed" see AHw p. 1428 and Foxvog and Kilmer JCS 27 (1975) p. 94 (cited in Selz, Untersuchungen p. 128 n. 502).

In col. vi line 7 the tentative translation "cleared it (from stubble)?" follows Selz's "gerodet(?)" (Untersuchungen p. 128 § 8).

BIBLIOGRAPHY

1923 Woolley, AJ 3 pp. 317 and 331 (findspot); pl. XXXI (photo)
1926 Unger, SuAK p. 84 figs. 22–23 (photos)
1929 Barton, RISA pp. 64–67 Entemena 17 (edition)
1929 Gadd, UET 1 pls. A–B, pl. 1 and pp. 1–2 no. 1 (photo, copy, edition)
1931 Contenau, Manuel 2 fig. 371 (photo)
1940 Christian, Altertumskunde 1 pl. 256 (photo)
1948 Parrot, Tello pl. IV b (photo)
1956 Sollberger, CIRPL p. xi Ent. 1 (study); p. 32 Ent. 1 (copy)
1956 Woolley, UE 4 p. 47 (findspot); pl. 40 (photos)
1957 Jacobsen, ZA 52 p. 124 n. 72 (study)
1965 Sollberger, UET 8 p. 25 n. 1 (collations)
1967 Moortgat, Kunst pls. 87–88 (photos)
1968 Spycket, Statues p. 31 (partial edition)
1971 Sollberger and Kupper, IRSA IC7a (translation)
1975 Orthmann (ed.), Der alte Orient fig. 31 (photo)
1977 Braun-Holzinger, Beterstatuetten p. 56 and pl. 27d (study, photo)
1981 Spycket, Statuaire p. 84 and n. 202 (study)
1982 Steible, ASBW 1 pp. 211–12 Entemena 1 (edition)
1986 Cooper, SARI 1 pp. 63–64 La 5.17 (translation)
1988 Römer, TUAT 2/4 pp. 466–69 (translation)
1991 Braun-Holzinger, Weihgaben p. 2441 St 3 (edition, study)
1995 Selz, Untersuchungen pp. 127–28 § 8 (study), p. 228 § 40 (study)

TEXT

Transliteration	Translation
Col. i	
1) [^{d}e]n-líl-	i 1–2) For [the god E]nlil of [E]-a[da] ("House of the Father") —
2) [é-a]d-[da]-ka-ra	
3) en-TE.ME-na	i 3–5) En-metena, ruler of Lagaš,
4) énsi-	
5) lagaš(NU$_{10}$.BUR.LA).KI	
6) šà-pà-da-	i 6–7) chosen in the heart by the goddess Nanše,
7) ^{d}nanše	
8) énsi-gal-	i 8–9) chief executive for the god Ning̃irsu,
9) ^{d}nin-g̃ír-sú-ka	
10) [dumu-e]n-an-[na]-túm	i 10–12) [son of E]n-anatum, [ru]ler of Lagaš,
11) [én]si-	
12) lagaš(NU$_{10}$.BUR.LA).KI-ka	
13) dumu-KA-	i 13–16) descendant of Ur-Nanše, king of Lagaš,
14) ur-^{d}nanše	
15) lugal-	
16) lagaš.KI-ka-ke$_4$	
17) ^{d}nin-g̃ír-sú-ra	i 17–19) built the Eš-dugru ("Shrine [in which] Pots Are Arranged") for the god Ning̃irsu,
18) èš-dug-ru	
19) mu-na-dù	
20) a-ḫuš	i 20 — ii 12) built for him the Aḫuš ("Terrifying Water") the temple where (the god Ning̃irsu) looks approvingly upon (En-metena),
Col. ii	
1) é-igi-zi-bar-ra	
2) mu-na-dù	

3) ^{d}lugal-URU×KÁR.KI-ra
4) é-gal-URU×KÁR.KI-ka-ni
5) mu-na-dù
6) ^{d}nanše
7) é-engur-ra-zú-lum-ma
8) mu-na-dù
9) ^{d}en-ki
10) lugal-eridu.KI-ra
11) abzu-pa$_{5}$-sír-ra
12) mu-na-dù
13) ^{d}nin-ḫur-sag̃-g̃á
14) gi-gù-na-
15) tir-kù-ga
16) mu-na-dù
17) ^{d}nin-g̃ír-sú-ra
18) an-ta-sur-ra
19) mu-na-dù
20) šà-pà-da
21) mu-na-dù
22) é-^{d}g̃á-tùm-du$_{10}$
23) mu-dù

Col. iii
1) ^{d}nanše
2) gi-gù-na-maḫ-ni
3) mu-na-dù
4) é-ni ki-bé mu-na-gi$_{4}$
5) ^{d}en-líl-la
6) é-ad-da-im-sag̃-g̃á
7) mu-na-dù
8) u$_{4}$-ba en-TE.ME-na-ke$_{4}$
9) alan-na-ni
10) mu-tu
11) en-TE.ME-na ^{d}en-líl-le ki-ág
12) mu mu-ni-sa$_{4}$
13) ^{d}en-líl-la
14) é-a

Col. iv
1) mu-na-ni-DU
2) en-TE.ME-na
3) lú é-ad-da dù-a
4) dingir-ra-ni
5) ^{d}šul-MUŠ×PA
6) nam-ti-
7) en-TE.ME-na-ka-šè
8) u$_{4}$-ul-la-šè
9) ^{d}en-líl-la
10) kìri šu ḫé-na-g̃ál

Col. v
1) 25 (bùr) GÁNA en-an-na-túm sur-^{d}nanše e-ta-e$_{11}$
2) 11(bùr) GÁNA-IM.KA-aškix(=) $\frac{\text{ZI}}{\text{ZI}}$.ŠÈ
3) GANÁ-ambar-AB×ḪA.KI-ka
4) pa$_{5}$-kù-ge ús-sa
5) 60 (BUR) GÁNA ^{d}en-líl

Col. vi
1) GÁNA-gú-eden-na-ka
2) en-TE.ME-na
3) énsi-

ii 3–5) built his "palace" of (the town of) URU×KAR for the god Lugal-URU×KAR,

ii 6–8) built the E-engur ("Temple of the Fountainhead") of (the town) Zulum for the goddess Nanše,

ii 9–12) built Abzu-pasira ("Fountainhead With Narrow Channels") for the god Enki, king of Eridu,

ii 13–16) built the *giguna* ("Multi-coloured Reeds[?]") of the sacred grove for the goddess Ninḫursag̃,

ii 17–19) built Antasur ("[Northern(?)] Boundary") for the god Ning̃irsu,

ii 20–21) built Šapada ("Chosen in the Heart"),

ii 22–23) built the temple of the goddess G̃atumdu,

iii 1–3) he built her lofty *giguna* ("Coloured Reeds[?]") for the goddess Nanše,

iii 4) and restored her temple for her,

iii 5–7) and he built the E-ada ("House of the Father") of Imsag̃ for the god Enlil.

iii 8–10) At that time, En-metena fashioned a statue of himself,

iii 11–12) named it ("En-metena (is the) Beloved of the god Enlil")

iii 13 – iv 1) and set it up before the god Enlil in the temple.

iv 2–3) En-metena, who built the E-ada ("House of the Father") —

iv 4–5) may his personal god, the god Šul-MUŠ×PA,

iv 6–10) forever pray to the god Enlil for the life of En-metena.

v 1–3) E-anatum had ceded 25 *bur* (162.5 hectares) from Sur-Nanše, 11 bur (71.5 hectares) of ... rushes, lands in the marshes of Nig̃en, adjacent to the

v 4– vi 1) Holy Canal, and 60 *bur* (390 hectares) already belonging to) Enlil, land in the Guʾedena,

vi 2–7) En-metena, ruler of Lagaš, cleared it (from stubble)? for the god Enlil of E-ada ("House of the

4) lagaš.KI-ke$_4$
5) ^{d}en-líl-
6) é-ad-da-ka-ra
7) g̃ír e-na-dù

Father.")

18

An inscription found on a vase from Nippur relates that the vessel was dedicated by En-metena to the god Enlil.

COMMENTARY

The vase is formed by the join of several fragments: CBS 9463+9690+9328+9919+9920+9669+9672+9992+10122, which were given the all inclusive number CBS 14568. They apparently came from rooms of the Enlil temple SE of the ziqqurrat. The reconstructed vase measures 14 cm in height, with an inside diameter of 17 cm and an outside diameter of 23 cm. The inscription was collated.

The restoration of lines 0′–1′ follows the suggesion of Selz, Untersuchungen p. 127 n. 497.

BIBLIOGRAPHY

1896 Hilprecht, BE 1/2 nos. 115, 116 and 117 (copy of three fragments, two of which were formed by joins of smaller pieces)
1907 Thureau-Dangin, SAK pp. 34–35 En-me-te-na g (edition of then known fragments)
1926 Legrain, PBS 15 pl. 1 (photo of lower part of vase)
1929 Barton, RISA pp. 52–53 Entemena 9 (edition)
1956 Sollberger, CIRPL p. 39 Ent. 32 (composite copy)
1982 Steible, ASBW 1 pp. 247–48 Entemena 32 (edition)
1986 Cooper, SARI 1 p. 64 La 5.18 (translation)
1987 Westenholz, OSP 2 p. 21 n. 5 (study [of findspot])
1991 Braun-Holzinger, Weihgaben pp. 116–17 G 8 (edition, study)

TEXT

Col. i
Lacuna
0′) [^{d}en-líl]-
1′) [é-ad-da]-k[a]-ra
2′) en-TE.ME-na
3′) énsi-
4′) lagaš.KI
5′) á-sum-ma-
6′) ^{d}en-líl
7′) ga-zi-kú-a-
8′) ^{d}nin-ḫur-sag̃-ka
Lacuna
1″) [...] ⸢x x⸣
2″) [šà-l]ú-3600-ta
3″) [šu]-ni ba-ta-[dab$_5$]-ba-a
4″) [gidri]-maḫ-nam-tar-ra
5″) ^{d}en-líl-le
6″) nibru.KI-ta
7″) en-TE.ME-na-ra
8″) mu-n[a]-a[n-sum]

Lacuna
i 0′–2′) For [the god Enlil] of [E-ada ("House of the Father")],
i 2′–4′) En-metena, ruler of Lagaš,
i 5′–6′) granted strength by the god Enlil,
i 7′–8′) nourished with wholesome milk by the goddess Ninḫursag̃,
Lacuna
i 1″) [When ...] ...
i 2″–3″) he [select]ed him from [among] the myriad [pe]ople,
i 4″–8″) and in Nippur the god Enlil [granted] t[o] En-metena the lofty [sceptre] of destiny

Lacuna
Col. ii
Lacuna
1′) [...]-⌈x-da⌉-a
2′) a-ni ^{d}en-líl-la
3′) bur-maḫ
4′) kur-ta mu-na-ta-e$_{11}$
5′) ^{d}šul-MUŠ×PA
6′) dingir-en-TE.ME-[na-ka]
Lacuna
1″) [...]-⌈É(?)⌉-ke$_{4}$
2″) mu-na-dím
3″) kù-lu[ḫ-ḫa(?)] mu-na-ni-KÉŠ
4″) nam-ti-l[a]-ni-šè
5″) nam-ti-
6″) la[ga]š.KI-šè
7″) nam-ti-
8″) [...]
9″) [a mu-na-ru]

Lacuna

Lacuna
ii 1′–4′) ... (then) he (En-metena), for the god Enlil, had (this) huge vase brought down from the mountains.

ii 5′ – ii 6′) Šul-MUŠ×PA, the personal god of En-mete[na]
Lacuna
ii 1″–2″) he made for him in [the temple] of [Enli]l(?)
ii 3″) and amassed refi[ned] silver for him there.
ii 4″–9″) For his life, for Lagaš's life, [for ...] life, [he dedicated (this) to him].

19

An inscription known from two clay nails, records En-metena's building of Nanše's E-engur temple.

CATALOGUE

Ex.	Museum number	Excavation number	Findspot	Lines preserved	cpn
1	EŞ 1716	—	Tello, Tell K	i 1–10 ii 1–10	n
2	—	1 H 76	al-Hibā, surface area near C	ii 4–9	n

COMMENTARY

No precise findspot is known for ex. 1.

For the reading of the first sign in line 5, see Falkenstein, Inschriften Gudeas p. 163. The fact that the cones come from two different sites raises the possibility that they are stray pieces. For a location of the é-engur in question with modern Qalʿah Juranah 7 km northwest of Tello/G̃irsu and GÁNA(?)zú-lum at modern Qalʿat Muḥammad Salāmah 2 km northwest of Tello/G̃irsu, see a forthcoming study by Frayne. É-engur is also noted in En-metena's inscriptions E1.9.5.4 col. iv line 3, E1.9.5.12 col. iv line 3, and E1.9.5.17 col. ii line 7.

BIBLIOGRAPHY

1884–1912 de Sarzec, Découvertes 2 p. LVI ENTÉMÉNA 10 (ex. 1, copy)
1956 Sollberger, CIRPL p. xii Ent. 42 (study); p. 42 Ent. 44 (ex. 1, copy)
1976 Biggs, Al-Hiba p. 10 no. 48 (ex. 2, study)
1982 Steible, ASBW 1 pp. 259–60 Entemena 44 (ex. 1, edition)
1986 Cooper, SARI 1 pp. 64–65 La 5.19 (ex. 1, translation)

TEXT

Col. i
1) ^{d}nanše-

i 1–2) For the goddess Nanše of E-engur ("House of

2) é-engur-ra	the Fountainhead"),
3) en-ME.TE-na 4) énsi- 5) lagaš.KI	i 3–5) En-metena, ruler of Lagaš,
6) šà-pà-da- 7) ^{d}nanše	i 6–7) chosen in her heart by the goddess Nanše,
8) énsi-gal- 9) ^{d}nin-g̃ír-su$^{!}$-ka	i 8–9) chief executive for the god Ning̃irsu,
10) dumu-en-an-na-túm Col. ii 1) énsi- 2) lagaš(NU$_{10}$.BUR.LA).KI-ka-ke$_4$	i 10 – ii 2) son of En-anatum, ruler of Lagaš,
3) ^{d}nanše 4) é-engur-ra- 5) GÁNA(?)-zú-lum-ma 6) mu-na-dù	ii 3–6) built, for the goddess Nanše, the E-engur ("House of the Fountainhead") in the field of Zulum,
7) kù-GI kù-bábbar-ra 8) šu ⸢mu-na⸣-n[i]-⸢tag⸣	ii 7–8) decorated it for her with silver and gold,
9) mu-ni-túm	ii 9) and furnished it.
10) KIB mu-na-du$_{11}$	ii 10) He ordered (these) clay nails(?) for her.

20

An inscription found on a door socket from Tell L (located in the SW sector of G̃irsu) records En-metena's fashioning of a door for the Nanše temple named Šešgar ("[The Temple(?)] Established [by] the Brother") (i.e., Nanše's brother Ning̃irsu).

COMMENTARY

The door socket was found during de Genouillac's excavations in "Chantier IX" (Tell L) and given the excavation number TG 4070. Its IM number is not known.

There is some confusion as to the precise location of Šešgar (temple) at G̃irsu. De Genouillac (RA 27 [1930] p. 182) reports the finding of the En-metena door-socket dealing with the temple on Tell L. De Sarzec (Découvertes 1 p. 279), on the other hand, indicates that the tauriform foundation figurine inscribed with a text commemorating Šulgi's construction of Nanše's E-Šešegara temple (Frayne, RIME 3/2.1.2.9), very likely a later rebuilding of the same temple, was found on the neighbouring Tell M. While a change of location of the temple is conceivable, it is unexpected. Perhaps the En-metena door-socket was re-used.

BIBLIOGRAPHY

1930 de Genouillac, RA 27 (1930) pp. 181–82 [Chantier IX] (findspot)
1936 de Genouillac, FT II pl. XXXVIII (copy)
1956 Sollberger, CIRPL 1 p. xii Ent. 27 (study); p. 27 Ent. 27 (copy)
1971 Sollberger and Kupper, IRSA IC7f (translation)
1982 Steible, ASBW 1 pp. 227–28 Entemena 27 (edition)
1986 Cooper, SARI 1 p. 65 La 5.20 (translation)

TEXT

1) ^{d}nanše- 2) šeš-gar-ra	1–2) For the goddess Nanše of Šešgar ("[The temple(?)] Established [by] the Brother")

3) en-TE.ME-na
4) énsi-
5) lagaš.KI
6) šà-pà-da-
7) ^{d}nanše
8) énsi-gal-
9) ^{d}nin-g̃ír-sú-ka
10) šeš-pà-da-
11) ^{d}nin-dar
12) lugal-uru$_{16}$-na !(KI)
13) dumu-en-an-na-túm
14) énsi-
15) lagaš.KI-ka-ke$_{4}$
16) ig-eren-bábbar
17) mu-na-dím
18) nam-ti-la-ni-šè
19) é-a mu-na-DU

3–5) En-metena, ruler of Lagaš,

6–7) chosen in her heart by the goddess Nanše,

8–9) chief executive for the god Ning̃irsu,

10–12) chosen brother of the powerful master the god Nin-DAR-a,

13–15) son of En-anatum, ruler of Lagaš,

16–19) made a door of white cedar and set it up for her in the temple, for his life.

21

A stone door socket inscription from G̃irsu commemorates En-metena's construction of the temple of the goddess G̃atumdu.

COMMENTARY

The door socket, which measures 55 cm across, was found in excavations of de Sarzec at G̃irsu and given the museum number MNB 1418. The inscription was collated.

It is noteworthy that this piece comes from G̃irsu and not G̃atumdu's main cult city of Lagaš/al-Hibā.

BIBLIOGRAPHY

1884–1912 de Sarzec, Découvertes 2 pl. 5 no. 2 (photo)
1907 Thureau-Dangin, SAK pp. 32–33 En-me-te-na c (edition)
1929 Barton, RISA pp. 50–51 Entemena 3 (edition)
1956 Sollberger, CIRPL p. xii Ent. 24 (study); p. 35 Ent. 24 (copy)
1982 Steible, ASBW 1 p. 225 Entemena 24 (edition)
1986 Cooper, SARI 1 p. 65 La 5.21 (translation)

TEXT

1) ^{d}g̃á-tùm-du$_{10}$
2) ama-lagaš.KI-ra
3) en-TE.ME-na
4) énsi-
5) lagaš(NU$_{10}$.BUR.LA).KI
6) lú é-^{d}gá-tùm-du$_{10}$ dù-a
7) dingir-ra-ni
8) ^{d}šul-MUŠ×PA-am$_{6}$

1–2) For the goddess G̃atumdu, mother of Lagaš,

3–5) En-metena, ruler of Lagaš,

6) who built the temple of the goddess G̃atumdu —
7–8) his personal god is the god Šul-MUŠ×PA.

22

A black stone door socket of unknown provenance bears an inscription dedicated to the goddess G̃atumdug.

COMMENTARY

The door socket was acquired by the Iraq Museum in 1954. It bears the museum number IM 57010.

BIBLIOGRAPHY

1956 Sollberger, CIRPL p. xii Ent. 25 (study); p. 35 Ent. 25 (copy)
1957 Sollberger, Sumer 13 pp. 61–62 (edition)
1982 Steible, ASBW 1 pp. 225–26 Entemena 25 (edition)
1986 Cooper, SARI 1 p. 65 La 5.22 (translation)

TEXT

1) [^{d}g̃á-t]ù[m-du$_{10}$]
2) en-TE.ME-na
3) énsi-
4) lagaš(NU$_{10}$.BUR.LA).KI
5) šà-pà-da-
6) ^{d}nanše
7) énsi-gal-
8) ^{d}nin-g̃ír-sú-ka
9) dumu-tu-da-
10) ^{d}g̃á-[t]ùm-du$_{10}$
Lacuna

1) [For the goddess G̃at]um[du],
2–4) En-metena, ruler of Lagaš,
5–6) chosen in her heart by the goddess Nanše,
7–8) chief executive for the god Ning̃irsu,
9–10) son born by the goddess G̃a[t]umdu,
Lacuna

23

The inscription found on a black stone door socket of unknown provenance records En-metena's construction of the temple of Lugal-URU×KAR.

COMMENTARY

The door socket was acquired by the British Museum in 1923. The inscription forms a circle with an exterior diameter of 39 cm; the inscription has a width of 5 cm. The door socket itself measures 47.2×51×26 cm. The piece, which bears the museum number BM 115858, was collated.

For the the writing of the city name Lagaš in line 23 with an -sa Auslaut see Sollberger, ZA 50 [1952] p. 13 note to line 5. According to Selz (in RIM readers' notes) such writings with -sa are common.

BIBLIOGRAPHY

1952 Sollberger, ZA 50 pp. 4–22 (copy, edition)
1956 Sollberger, CIRPL p. xii Ent. 26 (study); p. 36 Ent. 26 (copy)
1971 Sollberger and Kupper, IRSA IC7g (translation)
1982 Steible, ASBW 1 pp. 226–27 Entemena 26 (edition)
1986 Cooper, SARI 1 pp. 65–66 La5.23 (translation)

TEXT

1) ^{d}lugal-URU×KÁR.KI
2) ^{d}ama-ušumgal-an-na-ra
3) en-TE.ME-na
4) énsi-
5) lagaš(NU$_{10}$.BUR.LA).KI
6) šà-pà-da-
7) ^{d}nanše
8) énsi-gal-
9) ^{d}nin-g̃ír-sú-ka
10) dumu-en-an-na-túm
11) énsi-
12) lagaš.KI-ka-ra
13) u$_4$ ^{d}nanše
14) nam-lugal-
15) lagaš(NU$_{10}$.BUR.LA).KI-sa
16) mu-na-sum-ma-a
17) ^{d}nin-g̃ír-sú-ke$_4$
18) mu e-ni-pà-da-a
19) u$_4$-ba
20) en-te-me-na-ke$_4$
21) ^{d}lugal-URU×KÁR.KI-ra
22) é-gal-URU×KÁR.KI-ka-ni
23) mu-na-dù
24) kù-GI kù-bábbar-ra
25) šu mu-na-ni-tag
26) kù-za-gìn
27) gu$_4$ 20(?)
28) udu 20(?)
29) kisal-^{d}lugal-URU×KÁR.KI-ka-ke$_4$
30) sá ì-mi-du$_{11}$-du$_{11}$
31) en-TE.ME-me-na
32) [l]ú é-^{d}lugal-URU×KÁR.KI-ka dù-a
33) dingir-ra-ni
34) ^{d}šul-MUŠ×PA-am$_6$

1–2) For the god Lugal-URU×KAR and Ama-ušumgal-Ana,
3–5) En-metena, ruler of Lagaš,
6–7) chosen in the heart by the goddess Nanše,
8–9) chief executive for the god Ning̃irsu,
10–12) son of En-anatum, ruler of Lagaš —
13–16) when the goddess Nanše gave to him the kingship of Lagaš,
17–18) and the god Ning̃irsu nominated him,
19–23) then En-metena built for Lugal-URU×KAR his "palace" of (the town of) URU×KAR,
24–25) decorated it for him with gold and silver,
26–30) and established regular offerings of precious metals, lapis lazuli, 20(?) bulls, and 207 sheep in (the town of) Lugal-URU×KAR's courtyard.
31–32) En-metena, who built the temple of Lugal-(the town of) URU×KAR —
33–34) his personal god is Šul-MUŠ×PA.

24

Two stone vase fragments, probably from G̃irsu, bear part of a dedicatory inscription of En-metena for the goddess Baba.

CATALOGUE

Ex.	Museum number	Dimensions (cm)	Lines preserved	cpn
1	EŞ 2496	Height: 8.5 Dia.:5.5	1–3	n
2	Collection Dr. Kuhs	8.1×5.4×0.9	1–6	n

BIBLIOGRAPHY

1976 Hallo and Donbaz, OrAnt 15 pp. 3 and 8 (ex. 1, copy, edition)
1982 Steible, ASBW 1 p. 272 Entemena 96 (ex. 1, edition)
1986 Cooper, SARI 1 p. 66 La 5.24 (ex. 1, translation)
1991 Englund, AoF 18 p. 188–89 (ex.2 copy, edition)
1991 Braun-Holzinger, Weihgaben p. 118 G 12 (ex. 2, edition, study)

TEXT

1) dba-ba6 2) munus-sa6-ga	1–2) For the goddess Baba, the gracious lady,
3) en-TE.ME-na 4) énsi- 5) lagaš(NU11.BUR.LA).KI 6) ⌜šà-pà-da⌝ 7) [dnanše]	3–7) En-metena, ruler of Lagaš, ⌜chosen in the heart⌝ [by the goddess Nanše]
Lacuna	Lacuna

25

A fragment of a stone vessel in Berlin, almost certainly a *bursag* vessel dedicated to the goddess Inanna, bears part of a dedicatory inscription of En-metena.

COMMENTARY

This purchased steatite or basalt vessel, which measures 25 cm in height, with an original diameter of 40 cm, and a thickness of 4 cm, bears the museum number VA 7248.

The relief on the vase depicts a seated goddess *en face* holding a date cluster(?) (or fly-wisk[?]) in her hand; she wears a single horned crown on her head. Various rays emanate from her shoulders. The iconography is utterly distinctive of the goddess Inanna (see Colbow, Ištar p. 96 and pl. 1 no. 3). The depiction of the goddess is strikingly similar to one found on a stele from al-Hibā (see E1.9.1.6a). For the bur-sag̃ vessel see Selz, "Ne-sag̃, bur-sag̃ und gú-ne-(sag̃-g̃á): zu zwei Gefässbezeichungen, ihren Bedeutungsentwicklungen und einem sumerischen Wort für (Gefäss)schrank," SEL 13 (1996) pp. 3–8.

BIBLIOGRAPHY

1914–15 Weber, Amtliche Berichte pp. 114ff. and figs. 44–45 (photo, edition, reconstruction)
1926 Unger, SuAK p. 84 fig. 24 (photo)
1927 Contenau, Manuel 1 fig. 108 (photo)
1935 Zervos, L'art pl. 99 (photo)
1940 Christian, Altertumskunde 1 pl. 268 (photo)
1948 Parrot, Tello p. 85 fig. 21 i (drawing); p. 102 (study)
1955 Schmökel, Ur, Assur und Babylon pl. 41 (photo)
1956 Sollberger, CIRPL 1 p. xi Ent. 33 (copy); p. 39 Ent. 33 (copy)
1959 Basmachi, Sumer 15 pl. 5 after p. 25 (photo)
1960 Parrot, Sumer, fig. 167B (photo)
1965 Meyer, Altorientalische Denkmäler im Vorderasiatische Museum zu Berlin pl. 28 (photo)

1967 Moortgat, Kunst pl. 115 (photo)
1975 Orthmann (ed.), Der alte Orient fig. 87a (photo)
1982 Steible, ASBW 1 p. 249 Entemena 33 (edition)
1983 Klengel-Brandt and Marzahn, Sumer p. 2 fig. 1 (photo)
1986 Cooper, SARI 1 p. 66 La 5.25 (translation)
1987 Rost, Vorderasiatische Museum p. 72 fig. 70 ([colour] photo)
1991 Braun-Holzinger, Weihgaben p. 117 G 10 (edition, study)
1991 Colbow, Ištar p. 96 and pl. 1 no. 3 (photo, study)

TEXT

Col. i
Lacuna
1′) [^{d}nanše]-⌈ra⌉
2′) é-engur-ra-zú-lum-ma
3′) mu-na-dù
4′) ^{d}en-ki
5′) lugal-eridu.KI-ra
6′) abzu-pa$_5$-sír-ra
7′) mu-na-dù
8′) ^{d}nin-ḫur-[sag̃-(ra)]

Lacuna
Col. ii
1′) [...]-sum-ma-a

2′) bur-sag̃ mu-na-DU

3′) ḫé-⌈x⌉ [...]
Lacuna

Lacuna
i 1′–3′) he built E-engur ("House of the Fountainhead") of Zulum for [the goddess Nanše];

i 4′–7′) he built Abzu-pasira ("Source With Narrow Channels") for the god Enki, king of Eridu;

i 8′ [he built the *giguna* ("Multi-coloured Reeds") of the sacred grove for] the goddess Ninḫur[sag̃].
Lacuna

ii 1′) [when she(?) (the goddess Inanna[?])] granted [...],
ii 2′) he (En-metena) set up (this) *bursag̃* vessel for her(?).
ii 3′) ...
Lacuna

26

A brick inscription of Enmetena records his building of the reservoir of the LUM-ma-g̃im-du canal.

COMMENTARY

The brick, which was found in excavations of de Sarzec at G̃irsu, is housed in the Museum of the Ancient Orient in Istanbul; its museum number is unknown.

As pointed out to me by Selz (in RIM readers' notes) col. iii apparently deals with events accompanying or preceding the ruler's inauguration; thus, in all likelihood, the inscription dates to a period very early in the reign. Of interest, then, is the mention in col. v line 2 — col. vi line 1 of the cancellation of (debt) obligations of the citizens of Lagaš and the manumission of slaves (Sumerian ama-ar-gi$_4$, literally "return to the mother" — for the various Ur III writings see Falkenstein, Gerichtsurkunden 1 p. 93 n. 1 = Akkadian *andurāram šakānum*) which van Dijk, ZA 55 (1962) p. 272 points out is the earliest occurrence in Sumerian texts of this phenomenon. If this inscription does in fact date to the early part of En-metena's reign, then it might be possibly seem as a very early forerunner of the Old Babylonian practice of periodic cancellation of debts early in the reign of a new ruler.

ii 2′ NA is written in mirror image.

BIBLIOGRAPHY

1884–1912 de Sarzec, Découvertes 2 p. XLVIII ENTÉMÉNA 7 (copy)
1907 Thureau-Dangin, SAK pp. 34–37 En-me-te-na k (edition)
1929 Barton, RISA pp. 54–55 Entemena 11 (edition)
1956 Sollberger, CIRPL p. xii Ent. 35 (study); p. 40 Ent. 35 (copy)
1963 van Dijk, ZA 55 p. 272 (study)
1971 Sollberger and Kupper, IRSA IC7d (translation)
1972 Lambert, RSO 47 p. 18 (study)
1973–74 Bauer, WO 7 pp. 10–11 (partial edition)
1982 Steible, ASBW 1 pp. 251–54 Entemena 35 (edition)
1986 Cooper, SARI 1 pp. 66–67 La 5.26 (translation)
1995 Selz. Untersuchungen p. 231 §§ 51–53 (study)

TEXT

Col. i	
1) [^{d}]⸢nin⸣-g̃ír-sú	i 1–2) For the god Niñirsu, warrior of the god Enlil,
2) ur-sag̃-^{d}[e]n-líl	
3) en-TE.ME-na	i 3–5) En-metena, [ru]ler of Lagaš,
4) [én]si-	
5) la[ga]š.(⸢NU$_{10}$.BUR⸣.LA.KI	
6) ⸢á-sum-ma⸣-	i 6–7) granted strength by the god Enlil,
7) ^{d}en-líl	
8) ⸢ga-zi-kú-a⸣-	i 8 – ii 1) nourished with wholesome milk by the goddess Ninḫursag̃,
Col. ii	
1) ^{d}nin-ḫur-sag̃-ka	
2) š[à]-pà-da	ii 2–3) chosen in her hea[rt] by the goddess Nanše,
3) ^{d}⸢nanše⸣	
4) ensí-<gal->	ii 4–5) <chief> executive for the god Niñirsu,
5) ^{d}nin-g̃ír-sú-ka-ke$_4$	
6) dumu-t[u]-da-	ii 6–7) son beg[ot]ten by the god Lugal-URU×KAR,
7) ⸢^{d}⸣[l]ugal-⸢URU×KÀR⸣.KI-⸢ka⸣	
8) dumu-en-an-na-túm	ii 8–10) son of En-anatum, ruler of Lagaš —
9) é[ns]i-	
10) ⸢lagaš⸣.(NU$_{10}$.BUR.⸢LA⸣).⸢KI⸣-ka-ke$_4$	
Col. iii	
1) ⸢u$_4$ ^{d}⸣nin-g̃ír-sú-ke$_4$	iii 1–4) When the god Niñirsu chose him in his pure heart from G̃irnun,
2) g̃ír-nun-ta	
3) š[à-k]ù$^{!}$-⸢ga-né⸣	
4) ba-⸢pà⸣-da-a	
5) é-ninnu-t[a]	iii 5–6) and determined his destiny from E-ninnu,
6) [n]am-n[i] mu-na-[ta]r-ra-[a]	
7) ^{d}nanše	iii 7–9) and Nanše looked approvingly at him from Sirara,
8) sìrara.KI-ta	
9) ⸢igi⸣-zi m[u-š]i-⸢bar⸣-r[a-a]	
10) e[n]-TE.ME-na-ke$_4$	iii 10 — iv 1) En-metena, for Niñirsu —
Col. iv	
1) ^{d}nin-g̃ír-s[ú]-ra	
2) giš-kéš-rá-	iv 2–8) En-metena built for Niñirsu the reservoir of the LUM-m[a]-g̃im-[du] (-canal), (out of) 648,000 fired bricks and 1840 standard *gur* (2649.6 hl.) (of bitumen).
3) LUM-[ma]-g̃im-[du$_{10}$]	
4) 3 šár-gal sig$_4$-BÀḪAR-ra	
5) 1840 gur-sag-gál	
6) en-TE.ME-na-ke$_4$	
7) ^{d}nin-g̃ír-sú-ra	
8) mu-⸢na-ni⸣-d[ù]	
9) [...]-⸢^{d}⸣[nin]-g̃í[r-sú-ka]	iv 9 – v 1) He made a ... [for Nin]g̃i[rsu].
Col. v	
1) ŠÁ(?) ⸢x x⸣(?) m[u]-na-dím	
2) am[a-g]i$_4$	v 2–4) He cancelled obligations for Lagaš,
3) laga[š.K]I	
4) e-d[a(?)]-⸢x⸣-gar$^{!}$	
5) a[ma du]mu mu-ni-[g]i$_4$	v 5) having mother restored to child,

6) du[mu am]a m[u-n]i-gi$_4$
7) [....K]I
8) [...]
Col. vi
1) mu-ni-gi$_4$
2) <giš->kéš-rá-
3) [LU]M-ma-
4) gú-eden-na-ka
5) mu-na-⸢ni⸣-dù
6) en-TE.ME-na-ka
7) mu-d[u$_{10}$-g]a-né
8) ⸢^{d}nin-g̃ír-sú-ke$_4$⸣
9) da-rí-šè
10) gé[š]tu na-gub
11) en-TE.ME-na
Col. vii
1) ⸢x⸣-[...]-⸢x⸣
2) ⸢^{d}⸣n[in]-g̃ír-sú-ka-ke$_4$
3) lugal-ki-an-na-ág̃-g̃á-ni
4) ^{d}nin-g̃ír-sú-ra
5) giš-kéš-rá-
6) LUM-ma-g̃im-du$_{10}$
7) mu-n[a]-dù
8) ^{d}nin-g̃ír-sú
Col. viii
1) [...](-)na-[...]
2) [mu mu]-na-s[a$_4$]
3) en-TE.ME-na
4) ⸢gis-kéš-rá-dù-a⸣-
5) ^{d}nin-g̃ír-sú-ka-ka
6) dingir-ra-ni
7) ^{d}šul-MUŠ×PA-am$_6$
8) u$_4$-⸢ba⸣ du-du [sag̃a-^{d}]ni[n-g̃ír]-s[ú]-ka-kam

v 6) chi[ld] restor[ed] to mother,
v 7 – vi 1) and ... restored ....

vi 2–5) He built the [re]servoi[r of the LU]M-ma-[g̃im-du] (-canal) of the Gu'edena district for him

vi 6–10) and (so) the god Ning̃irsu is forever mindful of En-metena's good name.

vi 11 – vii 2) En-metena, [nom]i[nee] of the god [N]ing̃irsu,

vii 3–7) built the reservoir of the LUM-ma-g̃im-du (canal) for the god Ning̃irsu, his master who loves him,

vii 8 – viii 2) and [he na]med it for him "Ning̃irsu ... ."

viii 3–4) En-metena, who built the reservoir for the god Ning̃irsu —

viii 6–7) his personal god is Šul-MUŠ×PA.

viii 8) [At that] time, Dudu was [the temple administrator] for the god Nin[g̃ir]su.

27

An inscription on a small boulder of unknown provenance records various construction works of both En-metena and his temple administrator Dudu.

COMMENTARY

The boulder, which measures 7.6×16.5×5.63 cm, bears the museum number YBC 2183. The inscription was collated.

BIBLIOGRAPHY

1915 Clay, YOS 1 pp. 5–6 and pl. 2 no. 4 (copy, edition)
1929 Barton, RISA pp. 52–53 Entemena 7 no. 4 (edition)
1956 Sollberger, CIRPL p. xii Ent. 16 (study); p. 34 Ent. 16 (copy)
1963 Kramer, Sumerians p. 316 § C 19 (translation)
1971 Sollberger and Kupper, IRSA IC7b (translation)
1982 Steible, ASBW 1 pp. 219–20 Entemena 16 (edition)
1986 Cooper, SARI 1 p. 67 La 5.27 (translation)

TEXT

Col. i
1) ^{d}nin-g̃ír-sú
2) ur-sag-^{d}en-líl-ra
3) en-TE.ME-na
4) énsi-
5) lagaš(NU$_{10}$.BUR.LA).KI-ke$_4$
6) dumu en-an(over erasure)-na-túm
7) énsi-
8) lagaš.KI-ka-ke$_4$
9) é-gal-an-ta(Text: bi)-sur-ra
Col. ii
1) ^{d}nin-g̃ír-sú-ra
2) mu-na-dù
3) kù-GI (break) kù-bábbar-ra
4) šu mu-na-ni-tag
5) ⸢kiri$_6$-é⸣-šà-ga mu-na-dù
6) pú-sig$_4$-BÁḪAR(=LAK 742)-ra
7) mu-na-ni-si-si
8) u$_4$-ba
Col. iii
1) ir$_{11}$-ra-ni
2) du-du
3) sag̃a-^{d}nin-g̃ír-sú-ka-ke$_4$
4) [b]àd-da-sala$_4$-
5) gú-eden-na-ka
6) mu-dù
7) é-igi-⸢íl-eden⸣-na
8) mu mu-na-sa$_4$
9) bàd-kar-má-addir$_x$ (=PAD.DUG.GIŠ.SI)-
10) g̃ír-sú.KI-ka
Col. iv
1) mu-dù
2) en-zi-šà-gál
3) mu mu-na-sa$_4$
4) dingir-ra-ni
5) ^{d}šul-MUŠ×PA
6) nam-ti-la-ni-šè
7) ^{d}nin-g̃ír-sú-ra
8) é-ninnu-a
9) kìri šu ḫé-na-šè-gál

i 1–2) For the god Ning̃irsu, warrior of the god Enlil,

i 3–5) En-metena, ruler of Lagaš,

i 6–8) son of En-anatum, ruler of Lagaš,

i 9 – ii 2) built the "palace" of Antasur ("[Northern(?)] Boundary") for the god Ning̃irsu,

ii 3–4) and decorated it for him with gold and silver.

ii 5–7) He planted the garden of (the town) E-ša for him and dug a well of fired bricks for him there.

ii 8 – iii 3) At that time, his servant Dudu, the temple administrator of the god Ning̃irsu,

iii 4–6) built a fortress along the Sala (canal), in the Guʾedena district

iii 7–8) and named it "Building that Surveys the Plain" for him.

iii 9 – iv 1) He built a wall for the G̃irsu ferry Terminal

iv 2–3) and named it "The Lord Provides Inspiration" for him.

iv 4–9) May his personal god, Šul-MUŠ×PA, pray for his life to Ning̃irsu in E-ninnu!

28

A bitumen stone (possibly slate) from G̃irsu records the temple administrator Dudu's fashioning of a plaque of stone brought from the Elamite city of URU×A.

COMMENTARY

The plaque, which measures 25×22×8 cm, was found in excavations of de Sarzec in the area of the "Massif d'Entéména" at Tell K at G̃irsu. It bears the museum number AO 2354. The inscription was collated.

As indicated by Hansen (JNES 22 [1963] pp. 146–47 the "Dudu plaque" finds parallels in various Early Dynastic stone plaques found at Nippur, various Diyala sites, Ur, Lagaš and Fara. He notes (p. 147):

> As an indication of how these slate plaques were used is provided by an unpublished plaque from Nippur ... from the "north" temple excavated in 1953–54. ... In the field records the substance of the plaque is recorded as being made of "bituminous limestone." ... The unique aspect of this plaque is that the central knob over the hole in the plaque is preserved in place (Plate I). Formed of two flat disks this knob is secured by bitumen. The central hole of the disk is only 1 cm. in diameter suggesting that the insert through the knob could only have been a metal or wooden peg.

The city of URU×A.KI mentioned in line 5 was probably pronounced. Arawa; cf. J. van Dijk, "Išbi-Erra. Kindattu, l'homme de l'ELAM, et la chute de la ville d'Ur," JCS 30 (1978) p. 193 line 24, which we would read and interpret with Steinkeller (ZA 72 [1982] p. 244) as: a-ra-wa.KI sag-kul -elam.[KI-ma ...] "Arawa, the bolt of Elam." It apparently lay at the western fringes of Elam. The city appears as entry 73 in the ED List of Cities names (Pettinato, Orientalia NS 47 [1978]) p. 66) written: *ar-ù*.KI/ URU×A.KI. The research of this author would strongly suggest that the city is to be placed at the archaeological site of Tell Farūhābād.

BIBLIOGRAPHY

1884–1912 de Sarzec, Découvertes 1 p. 205 (lithograph), Découvertes 2 p. XLVIII ÉPOQUE D'ENTÉMÉNA (copy); pl. 5bis no. 2 (ex. 1, photo)
1897 Heuzey, RA 4 p. 36 (edition)
1902 Heuzey, Catalogue Louvre pp. 121 and pl. following p. 122 (study, drawing)
1907 Thureau-Dangin, SAK pp. 34–35 En-te-me-na i (edition)
1927 Contenau Manuel 1 fig. 357 (photo)
1929 Barton, RISA pp. 54–55 Entemena 10 (edition)
1935 Zervos, L'art p. 151 (photo)
1935 Zervos, Encyclopédie pl. 208 (photo)
1940 Christian, Altertumskunde 1 pl. 275 no. 3 (photo)
1948 Parrot, Tello pp. 87–88, fig. 22e and pl. VII a (photo, study, drawing)
1956 Sollberger, CIRPL 1 p. xii Ent. 76 (study); p. 44 Ent. 76 (copy)
1960 Beek, Bildatlas fig. 128 (photo)
1960 Parrot, Sumer, fig. 167A (photo)
1963 Hansen, JNES 22 pp. 146–47 (study)
1963 Kramer, Sumerians p. 316§ C 21 (translation)
1967 Moortgat, Kunst pl. 117 (photo)
1969 Pritchard, ANEP^2 fig. 599 (photo)
1971 Boese, Weihplatten pp. 201–202 and pl. XXXI, 3 T 12 (study, drawing)
1975 Orthmann (ed.), Der alte Orient fig. 88 (photo)
1980 Amiet, Art fig. 327 (photo)
1982 André-Leicknam, Naissance de l'écriture p. 85 no. 42 (photo, study)
1982 Steible, ASBW 1 p. 266 Entemena 76 (edition)
1986 Cooper, SARI 1 pp. 67–68 La 5.28 (translation)
1991 Braun-Holzinger, Weihgaben p. 310 W 9 (edition, study)

TEXT

Inscription:	
1) ^{d}nin-g̃ír-sú 2) é-ninnu-ra	1–2) For the god Ning̃irsu of E-ninnu,
3) du-du 4) sag̃a-^{d}nin-g̃ír-sú-ka-ke$_4$	3–4) Dudu, the temple administrator of the god Ning̃irsu,
5) URU×A.A.KI-ta mu-na-ta-e$_{11}$	5) had (this stone) brought down from (the city of) URU×A,
6) kak-giš-ùr-šè 7) mu-na-dím	6) and had it made (to be fixed by) a peg beam.
Caption behind the standing man:	Caption behind the standing man:
1) [d]u-du 2) [sa]g̃a-maḫ- 3) ^{d}nin-g̃ír-sú-ka	1–3) [D]udu, the exalted [te]mple administrator of the god Ning̃irsu.

29

The inscription on a stone weight of unknown provenance mentions the temple administrator Dudu.

COMMENTARY

The weight stone was acquired by the Ashmolean Museum through purchase. It bears the museum number Ash 1921.870.

BIBLIOGRAPHY

1921 Langdon, JRAS pp. 575–77 (edition, study)
1956 Sollberger, CIRPL p. xiii Ent. 78 (study); p. 44 Ent. 78 (copy)
1982 Steible, ASBW 1 p. 267 Entemena 78 (study)
1986 Cooper, SARI 1 p. 68 La 5.29 (translation)

TEXT

1) ma-na síg-ba
2) du-du sag̃a

1) (One) mana (for measuring) wool rations.
2) Dudu (is) the temple-administrator.

30

A cone fragment from G̃irsu deals with Ning̃irsu's temple named Aḫuš.

COMMENTARY

The cone fragment, which measures 4.5 cm in length, with a head diameter of c. 8 cm and a shaft diameter of c. 4 cm, is in a private collection.

Aḫuš almost certainly corresponds to the Eḫuš mentioned in Gudea Cylinder A col. x line 19, and in the archival text de Genouillac, ITT 2 no. 4582 line 8. It likely ccrresponds to modern Ghaz, 6 km WSW of G̃irsu/ Tello.

BIBLIOGRAPHY

1984 Görg, Akkadica 39 pp. 8–9 (photo, edition, study)

TEXT

1) ^{d}nin-g̃ír-su
2) a-ḫuš-ra
3) en-TE.ME-na

ii 4–7) For the god Ning̃irsu of (the town) A-ḫuš ("Terrifying Water")
3–4) En-metena, ruler of Lagaš,

4) énsi-	
5) lagaš.KI	
6) šà-pa-da-	6–7) chosen in the heart by the goddess Nanše,
7) ^{d}nanše	
8) énsi-gal-	8–9) chief executive for the god Ningirsu,
9) ^{d}nin-g̃ír-su-ka	
10) dumu en-na-na-[túm]	10) son of En-anatum
Lacuna	Lacuna

En-anatum II

E1.9.6

En-metena was succeeded by his son En-anatum (II). The fact that there is only one known inscription for this ruler suggests that he had a relatively short reign. Indeed, Bauer (in Bauer, Englund and Krebernik [eds.], Mesopotamien p. 473) notes that no economic text can be securely dated to his reign.

Grégoire, Lagaš p. 11 has suggested that En-anatum II was killed as a result of an Elamite raid made on the territory of Lagaš; the incursion is alluded to in a late Presargonic Sumerian letter from G̃irsu (Thureau-Dangin, RA 6 [1907] p. 139). Bauer, (in Bauer, Englund and Krebernik [eds.], Mesopotamien p. 474) following Grégoire, Sollberger (Sollberger and Kupper IRSA p. 76), and Lambert (ArOr 23 [1955] pp. 566–67 note to DP 164) have suggested that the letter dates to the reign of En-anatum II. On the other hand, in a recent study of the text (Volk, Die sumerischen und akkadischen Briefe pp. 25–29) Volk suggests that the letter should dated on prosopographical grounds to years 4–6 of URU.KA-gi-na; if this be correct, the notation "year 5" at the end of the text almost would refer to year 5 of URU.KA-gi-na. This fact would preclude the claimed connection between the name of the temple functionary [E]n-etarzi of line 4 of the G̃irsu letter with the governor En-entarzi who succeeded En-anatum II.

1

An inscription found on four door sockets from de Sarzec's excavations in G̃irsu records En-anatum II's restoration of a brewery for the god Ning̃irsu. This was possibly a continuation of work begun by En-metena in the area of modern Tell K (see E1.9.5.12–13).

CATALOGUE

Ex.	Museum numbers	Dimensions (cm)	Sollberger CIRPL no.	cpn
1	MNB 1417	42×41×19.5	En. II 1	c
2	AO 249	—	En. II 2	n
3	EŞ 390	Height: 20 Dia.: 46	En. II 3	n
4	EŞ 1551	Height: 19 Dia.: 45	En. II 4	n

COMMENTARY

Ex. 2 could not be found in the storeroom of the Louvre.

BIBLIOGRAPHY

1884–1912 de Sarzec, Découvertes 2 pl. 6 no. 4 (ex. 1, photo)
1907 Thureau-Dangin, SAK pp. 40–42 En-an-na-tum II Türangelstein (ex. 1, edition)
1956 Sollberger, CIRPL pp. xiii En. II 1 (exs. 1–4, study); p. 45 En. II 1 (ex. 1, copy)
1982 Steible, ASBW 1 pp. 273–74 Enannatum II 1 (exs. 1–4, edition)
1986 Cooper, SARI 1 p. 68 (exs. 1–4, translation)

TEXT

1)	^{d}nin-g̃ír-su	1–2) For the god Ning̃irsu, warrior of the god Enlil,
2)	ur-sag̃-^{d}en-líl-ra	
3)	en-an-na-túm	3–4) En-anatum (II), ruler of Lagaš,
4)	énsi-	
5)	lagaš(NU$_{10}$.BUR.LA).KI	
6)	šà-pà-da-	6–7) chosen in her heart by the goddess Nanše,
7)	^{d}nanše	
8)	énsi-gal-	8–9) chief executive for the god Ning̃irsu,
9)	^{d}nin-g̃ír-su-ka	
10)	dumu-en-me-te-na	10–12) son of En-metena, ruler of Lagaš,
11)	énsi-	
12)	lagaš(NU$_{10}$.BUR.LA).KI-ka-ke$_4$	
13)	^{d}nin-g̃ír-su-ra	13–15) restored for the god Ning̃irsu his brewery.
14)	é-bàppirka-ni	
15)	ki-bé mu-na-gi$_4$	
16)	en-na-na-túm	16–21) En-anatum (II), is the one who restored the brewery of the god Ning̃irsu — his personal god is Šul-MUŠ×PA.
17)	lú-bàppir-	
18)	^{d}nin-g̃ír-su-ka	
19)	ki-bé gi$_4$-a	
20)	dig̃ir-ra-ni	
21)	^{d}šul-MUŠ×PA-am$_6$	

En-entarzi

E1.9.7

En-anatum II was succeeded by En-entarzi; according to Bauer (in Bauer, Englund, and Krebernik [eds.], Mesopotamien p. 474) he reigned only five full years. Despite this fact, we have a very large number of economic tablets from his reign. Surprisingly, however, we have only one royal inscription; it mentions his daughter.

A text dated to year 29 of En-metena (Thureau-Dangin RTC no. 16) mentions En-entarzi before his accession as ruler in the capacity of *sag̃a* priest. His wife dìm-tur is also attested while he was *sag̃a* priest; the text in question dates to year 17 of En-metena (Hackman, BIN 8 no. 352 lines 2–3 edited by Edzard in Rechtsurkunden no. 35). Her name is translated "kleine weibliche Statuette" by Bauer (in AWL p. 116 referring to Lambert, RA 47 [1953] p. 58). Cf. in this connection Lú = *ša* I 21–24, (Civil, MSL XII p. 165): $^{\text{di-li-ib}}$KA×ŠID = *a-mil-tú*, $^{\text{mu-rù-ub}}$SAL+LAGAR = *a-mil-tú*, dìm = *a-mil-tú*, ^{dàra}da-ra-sisi = *a-mil-tú*.

As noted in our discussion of En-anatum II (E1.9.6), the sometimes asserted connection between the name of the temple functionary [E]n-etarzi named in a late Presargonic letter from G̃irsu, with En-entarzi has not been universally accepted.

1

An inscription on a statuette fragment names Geme-Baba as daughter of En-entarzi.

COMMENTARY

The white stone statuette fragment, which consists of the upper left side of a male(?) torso, measures 9.5 cm in height. It was found in excavations of de Sarzec at Tello (see de Sarzec, Découvertes 1 pp. 336–37) but its precise findspot is not known. The piece bears the museum number AO 278.

BIBLIOGRAPHY

1884–1912 de Sarzec, Découvertes 1 pp. 336–37 (study); Découvertes 2 p. LIV ENLILTARZI (copy)
1956 Sollberger, CIRPL p. xiv Enz. 2 (study); p. 46 Enz. 2 (copy)
1971 Sollberger and Kupper, IRSA IC9b (translation)
1977 Braun-Holzinger, Beterstatuetten p. 73 (transliteration, study)
1981 Spycket, Statuaire p. 96 and n. 269 (study)
1982 Steible, ASBW 1 p. 275 Enentarzi 1 (edition)
1985 Asher-Grève, Frauen p. 202 no. 483 (study)
1986 Cooper, SARI 1 p. 68 La 7.1 (translation)

TEXT

1) gém[e]-^{d}ba-ba$_{6}$
2) dumu en-èn-ta[r]-⸢zi⸣
3) sag̃a-^{d}nin-g̃[í]r-⸢su⸣-k[a]

1–3) Gem[e]-Baba, daughter of En-entarzi, the temple administrator of Ning̃[i]rsu.

Lugal-Anda

E1.9.8

According to Bauer (in Bauer, Englund, and Kerbernik [eds.], Mesopotamien p. 475), En-entarzi was succeeded in the first month of his sixth year by his son Lugal-Anda. Lugal-Anda is the name found in the economic texts dated to his reign; his full name lugal-an-da-nu-ḫun-gá "king who never ceases in his efforts for the god An" is known from his seal inscription (see E1.9.8.1). He reigned six years, and a very large number of economic tablets from his reign are known. For the economic reforms instituted during his reign, see most recently "Lugalanda's Economic Reform in House of Lady in Girsu," Wu Yuhong, JAC 16 (2001) pp. 101–28. On the question of the date of his death, see Selz, "Wann starb Lugal-Anda?" NABU 1993 no. 107.

Lugal-anda's wife, Bara-namtara, is frequently attested in the G̃irsu archive (see Selz, Untersuchungen p. 18). Lugalanda's daughters are known to have been Geme-Nanše and Munus-saga (see Selz, NABU 1993 no. 107 p. 92).

1

A seal inscription of Lugal-Anda is known from four impressions on bullae.

CATALOGUE

Ex.	Museum number	DP number	cpn
1	AO 13219	11	n
2	AO 13220	12	n
3	AO 13221	13	n
4	Hermitage		n

COMMENTARY

Although exs. 1–3 are actually three different seal impressions, their texts are the same and their inscriptions are edited together here. The tablets with these impressions came from a large group of purchased tablets. Allotte de la Füye (RA 6 [1907] p. 105) notes:

> Dans son *Recueil de tablettes chaldéennes,* M. Thureau-Dangin fait mention d'une collection de tablettes trouvées à Tello par des indigènes, peu de temps après la mort de M. de Sarzec: ces tablettes, qu'il classe sous la rubrique de *tablettes de la deuxième série,* portent généralement le nom d'un patési de Lagash (Sirpourla), les unes celui de Lougal-an-da, les autres celui d'En-li-tar-zi, quelques-unes celui d'Ourou-ka-gi-na, qui prend tantôt le titre de patési, tantôt celui de roi.
>
> De mon côté, j'ai pu réunir plus de cinq cents documents de même provenance ...

BIBLIOGRAPHY

1907 Allotte de la Füye, DP I pls. V–VI, VIII (exs. 1–3, photo, drawing)
1907 Allotte de la Füye, RA 6 pp. 105–21 (exs. 1–3, study); pls. I–II (exs. 1–2, photo, drawing); p. 121 fig. 3 (ex. 3, drawing)
1907 Lichačev, DPBŠ pl. V and fig. 59 (ex. 4, copy, study)
1908 Nikol'skiy, DV 3/II no. 323 (ex. 4, copy)
1956 Sollberger, CIRPL p. xiv (exs. 1–4, study); p. 47 Lug. 1 (ex. 1, copy)
1980 Amiet, Glyptique p. 214 no. 1098 (ex. 2, edition [by Lambert]), p. 422 and pl. 83 no. 1098 (ex. 2, 4, drawing)
1971 Sollberger, IRSA IC10b (ex. 1, translation)
1982 Steible, ASBW 1 p. 276 Lugalanda 1–14 (study)
1986 Cooper, SARI 1 p. 69 La 8.1 (exs. 1–4, translation)

TEXT

1) lugal-an-da-nu-ḫun-gá
2) énsi-
3) lagaš.KI

1–3) Lugal-Anda-nuḫunga, ruler of Lagaš.

2

A brick inscription formerly attributed to URU-KA-gina, is now assigned to Lugal-Anda.

COMMENTARY

The brick, which measures 22.5×17.5×6 cm, comes from G̃irsu, and bears the museum number EŞ 6402. The inscription was not collated.

BIBLIOGRAPHY

1956 Lambert, RA 50 p. 106 (edition)
1956 Sollberger, CIRPL p. xiv Ukg. 9 (study); p. 55 Ukg. 9 (copy)
1958 Hallo, JNES 17 pp. 215–16 (study)
1971 Sollberger and Kupper, IRSA IC10a (translation)
1982 Steible, ASBW 1 pp. 276–77 Lugalanda 15 (=Uruʾinimgina9) (edition)
1986 Cooper, SARI 1 p. 69 La 8.2 (translation)

TEXT

Col. i′
Lacuna
1′) [la]gaš.KI
2′) [šà]-pà-da-
3′) ^{d}nanše
4′) gidri-maḫ-sum-ma-
5′) ^{d}nin-gír-su-ka
6′) [du]mu-tu-da-
7′) [^{d}]ba-ba$_{6}$
Lacuna
Col. ii′
Lacuna
1′) [laga]š.KI-ke$_{4}$
2′) [l]ugal-ki-an-na-áğ-ğá-ni
3′) ^{d}nin-gír-su-ra(Text: KE$_{4}$)

Lacuna
i′ 1′ [Lugal-Anda], ruler of Lag]aš,
i′ 2′–3′) chosen in her [heart] by Nanše,
i′ 4′–5′) granted the exalted sceptre by Ninğirsu,
i′ 6′–7′) [so]n born by Baba,
Lacuna

Lacuna
ii′ 1′) [son of En-entarzi, ruler of Laga]š,
ii′ 2′–3′) — for the master who loves him, Ninğirsu,

4′) na-rú-a
5′) mu-na-rú
6′) ^{d}nin-gír-su en nibru.KI-ta u_4-sù-šè ⸢maḫ⸣
7′) [mu mu-na-sa_4]
Lacuna
Col. iii′
Lacuna
1′) al[an-ni]
2′) mu-tu
3′) lugal-an-da-nu-ḫun-gá gí[r-nu]n-šè nu-[kúš]
4′) mu m[u-na-sa_4]
Lacuna
Col. iv′
Lacuna
1′) x [...]
2′) x [...] x [...]
Lacuna

ii′ 4′–5′) he erected a monument,

ii′ 6′–7′) and [named it] "Ningirsu Is the Lord Eternally Exalted in Nippur."
Lacuna

Lacuna
iii′ 1′–2′) He fashioned his (own) sta]tue

iii′ 3′–4′) and na[med it] "Lugal-Anda-nuḫunga Never [Ceases in His Efforts] for the G̃ir[nun]."
Lacuna

Lacuna
iv′ 1′–2′) Too broken for translation.

Lacuna

3

The impression of a seal of Bara-namtara, wife of Lugal-Anda is found on a clay bulla in the Louvre.

COMMENTARY

The bulla bears the museum number AO 13222. The inscription was collated.

BIBLIOGRAPHY

1907 Allotte de la Füye, DP pl. VII (photo, drawing)
1907 Allotte de la Füye, RA 6 pp. 121–23 (study); pl. III (photo, drawing)
1956 Sollberger, CIRPL p. xiv Lug. 5 (study); p. 47 Lug. 5 (copy)
1980 Amiet, Glyptique p. 215 no. 1102 (edition [by Lambert]), p. 422 and pl. 83 no. 1102 (drawing)
1971 Sollberger, IRSA IC10c (translation)
1986 Cooper, SARI 1 p. 69 La 8.3 (translation)

TEXT

1) bára-nam-tar-ra
2) dam lugal-an-da
3) énsi-
4) lagaš.KI

1–4) Bara-namtara, wife of Lugal-Anda, ruler of Lagaš.

URU-KA-gina

E1.9.9

Lugal-Anda was succeeded by URU-KA-gina as ruler of Lagaš.

Several features mark the reign of URU-KA-gina as being noteworthy, and a number of questions have been raised by scholars in connection with this ruler, namely: (1) the name of his father and his family ties, (2) the correct reading of the ruler's name, and (3) the legitimacy of his succession.

As for the first question, the fact that URU-KA-gina never mentions his father's name in any of his inscriptions almost certainly indicates that he was not the son of Lugal-Anda (or En-entarzi, for that matter). In his discussion of the family ties of URU-KA-gina, Powell (in Studies Hirsch p. 312) has suggested that he was the son of a certain Engilsa. In this connection he cites the evidence of Allote de la Füye DP 69, which records votive offerings made by Šaša, the wife of URU-KA-gina, to the goddess NinMAR.KI on behalf of herself and Engilsa.

It should be noted in this connection (as was pointed out to me by Selz in RIM readers' notes) that URU-KA-gina had served as GAL:UG̃ under Lugal-Anda (see Selz NABU 1994 no. 44). For the official UG̃-GAL, cf. Canonical lú = *ša* tablet II col. iii lines 14″–20″ (Civil, MSL XII p. 121): nun = *ru-bu-ú* "prince," gir_{14} = *ru-bú-u* "prince," egi = *ru-ba-tu* "princess," ug̃-gal = *šur-bu-ú* "very great (one), "lú = *be-e-lum* "lord," lugal = *be-e-lum* "lord," en = *be-e-lum* "lord." The word is also attested in lexical sources with the translation *šarratum* = "queen."

The second major question concerning URU-KA-gina is the correct reading of his name; this has been subject to considerable scholarly discussion. The debate has centred on the reading of the first two elements of his name, URU and KA. Edzard (in Studies Civil pp. 77–79) has argued that URU is to be read /iri/. W.G. Lambert (in AuOr 10 [1992] p. 257) gives a contrary opinion, and concludes "for the Lagaš ruler [URU-KA-gi-na] Uru- is more likely than Iri-." For the reading inim for the second element of the ruler's name see Hruška, ArOr 41 (1973) p. 11; Bauer, AWL p. 65; Lambert, Orientalia NS 39 (1970) p. 419; Edzard, ARET 5 p. 44; idem, AuOr 10 (1992) pp. 256–58; and Selz, NABU 1992 no. 44. Edzard indicates (in Studies Civil p. 79) that while a Sargonic period parallel to URU-KA-gi-na is attested in Akkadian *pù-su*-GI */pūšu-kīn/* there is no corresponding PN **/awāssu-kīn/* to match URU-inim-gi-na. Steinkeller (AuOr 9 [1991] p. 227), on the other hand, concludes that neither possibility can be excluded, citing the lexical entry inim-gi-n[a] = (*a-wa-tum*) [*ki-i-tum*] in Sag B 274 = Civil, Gurney and Kennedy, MSL SS1 p. 33. Selz (in NABU 1992 no. 44) suggests that the element URU may possibly be a writing for /er(e)/ "servant," a proposition the present author finds unlikely. The seemingly endless discussion of the reading of the ruler's name has been continued by Bauer, in Bauer, Englund, and Krebernik (eds.), Mesopotamien pp. 475–77 and Selz in the article entitled "u_{11}-ga-ni-mu-gi-na, aber steht die Lesung URU-KA-gi-na(-k) fest? Ein Beitrag zum Problem des göttlichen Wortes im sumerischen Personennamen," AoF 25 (1998) pp. 312–27. Rather than add to the long discussion, the author has purposefully given a broad (if vague) transcription, URU-KA-gina, in this edition.

The third major question about URU-KA-gina, namely the legitimacy of his succession, has also been the matter of some scholarly debate. The so-called Reform Texts of URU-KA-gina (edited as inscriptions E1.9.9.1–3 in this volume), which describe the rectifying of various alleged abuses that were said to have taken place before the accession of URU-KA-gina, has led some commentators to speculate that URU-KA-gina was a usurper. Commenting on this hypothesis most recently, Powell (in Studies Hirsch pp. 313–14) writes:

> ... in spite of many attempts, his [URU-KA-gina's] so-called "Reforms" have not been dated with certainty nor has anyone established their motivation. One thing, however, is clear: the assumption that he was an "usurper" rests upon no more evidence than the "empire" of Lugalzagesi. That Irikagina was related to the family of Enentarzi and Lugalanda is inherently likely from the fact that the ancestor cult is continued without a break.

Indeed, Sollberger (in Proceedings of the 22nd International Congress of Orientalists p. 29) notes:

> Et de fait, il s'en garde bien: Lugalanda et sa femme ne sont point mis à mort; ils restent, du moins en apparance, en bonnes termes avec leur successeur; et lorsque Baranamtara meurt, dans la deuxième année d'Urukagina roi, donc trois ans après sa décheance, on lui fait de véritables funérailles nationales auxquelles ne participions pas moins de 617 personnes en service commandé.

Further, Bauer (in Bauer, Englund and Kerbernik [eds.], Mesopotamien p. 477) notes that deliveries were made in the name of Bara-namtara, wife of Lugal-Anda, during year 1 of URU-KA-gina.

Of great utility for this particular discussion is the convenient list of texts for this crucial period given by Selz in Untersuchungen p. 307 and the discussion by Powell in Studies Hirsch p. 314 n. 31 where Powell cites the earlier studies by Selz, FAOS 15,1 (1989) p. 38 and FAOS 15,2 (1993) p. 59; see also Bauer, AWL p. 669; and Deimel, Orientalia 32 (1928) p. 17f. The text discussed in the last-cited article was copied by J. Marzahn as VS 25 (1991) no. 66; it is dated to the first month of URU-KA-gina as lugal.

Powell (in Studies Hirsch pp. 313–14) summarizes:

> ... the transfer of power from Lugalanda to Irikagina as ensi can be dated rather precisely to some point during the first month of Lugalanda's 7th year (or perhaps to the beginning of the 2nd month), and dating by Irikagina lugal begins with the first month of what would have been the 8th year of Lugalanda. [Powell here cites P. LaPlaca and M. Powell, BSAgr 5 (1990) p. 79.] None of this sounds like usurpation ...

Finally, Wu Yuhong in his article entitled "Lugalanda's Economic Reform in [the] House of [the] Lady in Girsu" (JHAC, 16 [2001) pp. 11–114) concludes that "Urukagina was the Legitimate Successor of Lugalanda." If URU-KA-gina were a usurper, which seems unlikely, then he would have probably come from the ranks of the military (as was pointed out to me by G. Selz, in RIM readers' notes).

Another notable feature of the reign of URU-KA-gina was the change of his title from ruler (énsi) to king (lugal) of Lagaš. One might be tempted to see a connection of this change in title with the apparent measures described in the so-called Reform Texts and postulate that URU-KA-gina issued a new edict or law-code when he adopted the new title. Evidence discussed below does indeed suggest that the first edition of the "Reforms" does date to an early period of the reign, but the exact time and the precise meaning of the "Reforms" are far from certain, so that the connection remains speculative. For the discussion, see F. Kraus, "Ein Edikt des Königs Samsu-iluna von Babylon," in Studies Landsberger pp. 225–31; J. Finkelstein, "Some New Mišarum Material and Its Implications," Studies Landsberger pp. 233–26; G. Komoróczy, "Zur Frage der Perioditát der altbabylonischen Mišarum-Erlässe," in Studies Diakonoff pp. 196–205; S. Lieberman, "Royal 'Reforms' of the Amurrite Dynasty," BiOr 46 (1989) pp. 241–359; R. Sweet, "Some Observations on the Edikt of Ammiṣaduqa prompted by Text C," in Studies Horn pp. 579–600; D. Charpin, "L'andurārum à Mari," MARI 6 (1990) pp. 253–70; and idem, "Les prêteurs et le palais: les édits de *mīšarum* des rois de Babylone et leurs traces dans les archivés privées," in A. Bongenaar (ed.), Interdependence of Institutions and Private Entrepreneurs. Proceedings of the Second MOS Symposium, PIHANS 88 pp. 185–211.

Of further note in URU-KA-gina's reign is the change of title of the ruler from "king of Lagaš" to "king of G̃irsu." This clearly was due to the diminished area controlled by the king as his city state was encroached upon by the forces of Lugal-zage-si of G̃iša (Umma).

Another intriguing question about URU-KA-gina is the possible validity of the hypothesis that the URU-KA-gina appearing in the Maništūšu Obelisk is in fact the same person as URU-KA-gina, ruler of Lagaš. The question has most recently been discussed by Powell in Studies Hirsch pp. 307–314; he supports the hypothesis of the identity and gives an extensive bibliography of the discussion of this question. Powell's conclusions have been considerably bolstered by the publication by Steinkeller ("An Ur III Manuscript of the Sumerian King List," in Studies Wilcke, pp. 267–92) of an apparent Ur III period manuscript of the Sumerian King List in which the name of King Maništūšu appears immediately after that of Sargon, not after Rīmuš, as had been found in previously published manuscripts of this text.

The reign of URU-KA-gina was marked by a series of assaults on Lagaš by Lugal-zage-si, the erstwhile ruler of G̃iša (Umma) and later king of Uruk. The destruction wrought by Lugal-zage-si on the territory of Lagaš is described in a unique document — whose form, but not content, resembles that of an economic tablet — which is edited as inscription E1.9.9.5 in this volume. Bauer (in Bauer, Englund, and Krebenik [eds.], Mesopotamien pp. 483–86) has also discussed the so-called "Muster Lists" which indicate a state of military preparedness early in the reign. These muster lists and other texts related to the war have been discussed in detail by Selz in Untersuchungen pp. 78–81 §§ 165–81. Indeed, M. Lambert has given us a very useful summary of the prelude to the fall of Lagaš in Iraq 25 [1963] pp. 192–93):

> (1) les noms de mois: "mois du vol du canal" daté de l'an I (D.P. 165).— "mois où il y eut deux désastres militaires (D.P. 99, daté de l'an 4 d'Urukagina). — "(Lorsque le chef d'Uruk assiégea la ville (D.P, 545 iii, de l'an 4 d'Urukagina).— "mois où Ning̃irsu entra dans son nouveau temple de l'Antasurra", ce qui suppose la perte d'un ancien antasurra, attesté hors les murs (D.P. 311, de l'an 4 d'Urukagina).— "mois où l'homme d'Uruk vint pour la troisième fois" (Nik. 227).—
>
> (2) l'arrêt du commerce extérieur;
>
> (3) la multiplication des ateliers de tissage pour les besoins de la guerre, probablement;

(4) la diminution, au début de l'an 6, des rations d'orge données aux ânes d'âttelage appartenant aux écuries de la princesse, rations qui passent journellement de 3/24 de gur (15 litres), à 2/24 (10 litres);

(5) Disparition des porcs de pâture au début de l'an 6 (Nik. 57); ils étaient mentionnés en fin de l'an 5 (T.S.A. 35);

(6) Repli des troupeaux de moutons de la princesse Shagshag et du prince A-enne-kiag; ces troupeaux apparaissent brusquement, au début de l'an 6, dans une série de documents où ils ne figuraient pas (Nik. 57, Vi-VII);

(7) déplacement de population (Nik. 19);

(8) Levées de troupes parmi le personnel ouvrier (Nik. 3; D.P. 135)

More recently, a detailed year-by-year account of the war, at whose conclusion Lugal-zage-si brought the independence of Lagaš to an end, has been given by Bauer in Bauer, Englund, and Krebernik (eds.), Mesopotamien pp. 479–93.

1

An inscription found on three clay cones gives the text of one recension of the so-called Reform Texts of URU-KA-gina. As noted, the text lists various reforms carried out by URU-KA-gina to correct abuses that apparently had been perpetrated by earlier rulers of Lagaš.

There were at least two, and possibly three, editions of the "Reform Texts." Differing dates can be proposed for at least two of them based on the extant titulary of the URU-KA-gina inscriptions. In E1.9.9.1. URU-KA-gina appears as "king of Lagaš." In E1.9.9.2, on the other hand, his title appears as "king of G̃irsu." As noted, the latter epithet likely refers to the diminished dominions of the kingdom of Lagaš after a first attack by Lugal-zage-si of G̃iša (Umma). While large pieces of the realm were apparently lost by URU-KA-gina, the king apparently managed to hold on to G̃irsu and its immediate environs (on this question see Cooper SANE 2/1 pp. 35–36).

The reference in col. xii line 33 to the canal work on the watercourse called "The God Ning̃irsu Received His Authority from Nippur" likely provides a terminus post quem for the redaction of E1.9.9.1, as was pointed out by Selz in Untersuchungen p. 244 n. 1177. He notes in this connection the archival text de Genouillac, TSA no. 23, which refers (col. xi line 1) to the digging of the canal "The God Ning̃irsu Received His Authority from Nippur" (i_7-al-dù-[^{d}n]in-g̃ír-su-[nib]ru.KI-[ta nir]-g̃ál); the archival text is dated to year 2 of URU-KA-gina and likely gives a more specific terminus post quem for the redaction of E1.9.9.1.

CATALOGUE

Exemplar	Museum Number	Dimensions (cm)	Lines preserved	cpn
1	AO 3278	Height: 28.2	i 1–11	c
		Dia. of base: 16.5 high	ii 1–14	
			iii 1–19	
			iv 1–22	
			v 1–23	
			vi 1–29	
			vii 1–30	
			viii 1–31	
			ix 1–35	
			x 1–38	
			xi 1–38	
			xii 1–44	
2	AO 3149	Height: 27	i 1–11	c
		Dia. of base: 14.2	ii 1–14	
			iii 1–19	
			iv 1–22	
			v 1–23	
			vi 1–29	
			vii 1–30	
			viii 1–31	
			ix 1–35	
			x 1–38	
			xi 1–38	
			xii 1–24	
3	Crozer Theological Seminary no. 5	—	v 1–7	n
			v 26 – vi 5	

COMMENTARY

The master text is ex. 1.

The cones, which almost certainly came from G̃irsu, were acquired through purchase and therefore no precise findspots are known. It may be noted, however, that one exemplar of a variant recension of the "Reforms Texts" (E1.9.9.2.1) was found on Tell H.

In col. ii line 1, the word bur-sag̃ is likely derived from the word bur "(stone) bowl" and sag̃ perhaps to be equated with Akkadian *reštû(m)* "foremost, first class." The compound has two meanings: either (1) "a servant" or (2) "a building" according to Sjöberg, PSD B p. 187. The context here makes it clear that the latter is meant. Perhaps the building was a storehouse where stone bowls with provisions for the temple were kept, following Cooper's translation "pantry(?)." Selz (Untersuchungen p. 28 n. 74 § 2) notes an archival text dated to year 6 of URU-KA-gina (VAT 4917 = Deimel, Orientalia 32 [1928] p. 78) which records a bursag̃ (building?) in connection with the é-EZEM-da "festival house(?)" of the "holy precinct" (uru-kù-ga) — this clearly was in G̃irsu — that provided emmer for the monthly regular provisions of the god Ning̃irsu (sá-du$_{11}$-itu-da-^{d}nin-g̃ír-su-ka). It is not impossible that this archival text refers to the same structure mentioned in the URU-KA-gina inscription.

According to Selz (Untersuchungen p. 28 n. 75) the G̃Á-udu-ur$_4$ "sheep-plucking shed" of col. ii line 4 is attested in various archival texts from G̃irsu.

In col. ii lines 12–13 for ab-šà-ga ... lá, see Sjöberg, TCS 3 p. 108, note to line 283.

In col. iii line 11 for the reading and translation of $^{\text{ù-mú}}$ú-mu$_{11}$(KA×SAR) see Alster, RA 85 (1991) pp. 5–6.

In col. iii line 16 the toponym AMBAR could have a number of readings. Civil, BiOr 40 (1983) col. 562, citing the evidence of an ED school exercise tablet from Lagaš (al-Hibā 29), indicates the reading aš-ti-(am$_6$) He further notes (p. 563):

> The geographical name ašte (spelled aš-ti, line 3) is not found in Proto-Ea, but is well documented in the syllabaries: Ea I 63 [see now Civil, MSL XIV p. 179 line 63: aš-te LAGAB×A MIN [*šá*] MIN [*la-gab-ba-ku*] MIN [*i-gub*] aš-te URU.KI], Aa I/2: 216 [see now Civil, MSL XIV p. 214, aš-te LAGAB×A ŠU-*ma* URU], Proto-Diri 533 [see for the present van der Meer, OEC 4 pl. XXXII no. 153 line 25: [AMBAR].KI aš-[(x)]-ti, Diri IV: 106 [see King, CT 11 pl. 14 K. 14396 line 5′ áš-te LAGAB×[A] [...]), Reiner and Civil, MSL XI 102:184 [LAGAB×Aaš-te.KI]].

However, the researches of the present author indicate that the GN ašte appearing in the Early Dynastic List of Geographical Names (Pettinato MEE 3 p. 231 line 48) clearly does not refer to a town in the province of Lagaš, but rather to a settlement near Kiš. Further, geographical evidence discussed in a forthcoming study by the author clearly indicates that in some cases the toponym AMBAR.KI in Lagaš province was to be read /ambar/. For general references to AMBAR.KI in the Presargonic texts from Lagaš see Edzard, Farber, and Sollberger, RGTC 1 pp. 11–12.

In col. iii line 14 for the reading of the logogram gudu$_4$ = UḪ.ME, see Renger, ZA 59 (1969) pp. 143–44, citing Ea V 114 (see now Civil, MSL XIV p. 400): gu-du ḪI×NUN.[ME = *pa*]-*ši-šu*). Similarly, a school text from Susa (van der Meer, MDP 27 no. 39 line 2) gives: UḪ.ME = gu-du. However, Krebernik (Beschwörung p. 124) suggests that the writing ga-da in an ED period incantation from Ebla may be a phonetic writing for gudu$_4$. The Akkadian equivalent is *pašīšu(m)* "anointed priest."

Jacobsen (PAPS 107 p. 477 n. 11) suggested that the anointing was for delousing purposes, and interpreted the sign gudu$_4$ as UḪ+IŠIB, a word picture denoting "lice-cleansed"; cf. Ea V 106 (Civil MSL XIV p. 400): [ú]-uḫ ḪI×NUN = *up-l*[*u*] "head-louse." The gudu$_4$ priest appears frequently in Presargonic administrative texts from Fara; see Visicato, Indices of Early Administrative Tablets of Šuruppak pp. 116–17 for the references. For references in the Presargonic texts from G̃irsu, see Selz, Untersuchungen pp. 20, 57, 62, 82, and 256.

In col. iv line 19 for the reading anše-bìr-ra one may refer to the comments of Sjöberg, PSD B p. 159:

> Although no preserved lexical text provides a sign value **bir$_3$** for **ERIN$_2$**, the occurrence of **ERIN$_2$-ra** in Presarg. econ. texts and royal inscri. indicates a sign value ending in **-r**. We therefore read **bir$_3$** based on the syllabic value in Akk. context; see von Soden Syllabar no. 226. Note, however, that in OB and Post-OB lex. indicate a reading **erin$_2$**.

For a discussion of the reading of ÉRIN in this context, see Steinkeller, WZKM 77 (1987) p. 192 and n. 19; JNES 46 (1987) pp. 58; and NABU 1990 pp. 9–10 no. 12. In the last cited article Steinkeller argues for a reading sur$_x$ based on a comparison with the toponyms e-ki-ÉREN-ra with the e-ki-sur-ra attested in royal inscriptions. However, in the text VAS 14 no. 156 col. v line 2 the GN e-ki-ÉREN-ka is almost certainly to be read e-ki-bìr-ra based on its likely correlation with the modern site of Ḫāfūr (to be demonstrated in a forthcoming article of the author). The reading of the sign is also discussed by Selz (in Amerikanischen Sammlungen p. 129). For anše-bìr "harnessed asses" see Maekawa, ASJ 1 (1979) p. 37.

In col. iv line 20 for gu$_4$-du$_7$ = *alpu*(*m*) *šuklulu*(*m*) "bull without defect," see Sjöberg and Bergmann, Temple Hymns p. 81 and Bauer, AWL p. 317.

Col. v lines 4ff. clearly deal with funerary goods; a comparison of various literary sources dealing with this type of goods is found in the chart below:

Funerary Items in Various Sumerian and Akkadian Literary Texts				
URU-KA-gina Reform Text 1 (cols. v and vi)	Adab Funerary text (Foxvog, in Alster [ed.], Death pp. 67–75)	Funeral of Enkidu from the Akkadian Gilgameš Epic, Tablet VIII (George, The Epic of Gilgamesh pp. 66–69)	Death of Ur-Nammu (Flückiger-Hawker, Urnamma pp. 92–142)	Neo-Assyrian Literary Royal Funerary text (McGinnis, SAAB 1 [1987] pp. 1–11)
col. v line 6: TÚG.ŠU.GABA.ÙR "draping which covers the hand and breast"	line 11: níg-lá-gaba-túg "chest-draping"	—	—	—
line 7 TÚG.níg-bar-ba "outer garment"	line 27: 1 níg-bar-3-túg "one triple outer garment"	—	—	—
line 11: sag̃-šu$_4$-zabar(=KA×UD.BAR) "bronze head-band"	line 30: níg-sag̃-kešda "head-band"	—	line 123: TÚG.sag̃šu "head-band"	col. ii line 4′: 16 SAG̃Š[U] "16 head-bands" col. ii line 15′: 4 SAG̃ŠU.BABBAR.M[EŠ]. "4 white head-bands"
line 12: URUDU.kak-zabar (=KA×UD.BAR) "bronze arrow"	—	—	line 88: G̃IŠ.kak-bán "wooden arrow"	—
line 13: RU.UR.RA zabar(=KA×UD.BAR) "bronze throw-stick/bow"(?)	—	viii 135: [*ta*?-*am*?-*ḫ*]i?-*ṣu* "[A *throw*]-*stick*"	—	—

Funerary Items in Various Sumerian and Akkadian Literary Texts				
URU-KA-gina Reform Text 1 (cols. v and vi)	Adab Funerary text (Foxvog, in Alster [ed.], Death pp. 67–75)	Funeral of Enkidu from the Akkadian Gilgameš Epic, Tablet VIII (George, The Babylonian Gilgamesh Epic)	Death of Ur-Nammu (Flückiger-Hawker, Urnamma pp. 92–142)	Neo-Assyrian Literary Royal Funerary text (McGinnis, SAAB 1 [1987] pp. 1–11)
line 14: kuš-zalag-ga "bright leather (bag) = (?) "quiver"(?)	—	viii 122 ⌈*iš-pat*⌉-*su* "its quiver"	line 88 é-mar-uru$_5$ "quiver"	—
line 18: maš-bar-dul$_5$ "a goat with its full fleece"	—	—	—	col. ii′ 13′: 4 BAR.DIB SU$_4$ "4 *kusītu*-garments" (see commentary)
col. vi line 4 GIŠ.ná "bed"	lines 15 and line 31: 1 G̃IŠ.taškarin-ná "one boxwood bed"	viii 84 "*uš-na-al-ka-a-ma ina ma-a-a-li* GAL-*i*] "[I shall lay you out on a magnificent bed]"	—	col. iii′ 17′: [1 G̃I]Š.ná URUDU šà G̃IR.II.MEŠ "[One] bronze [b]ed with feet"

In col. v line 4 for TÚG.GÉŠTU-^{d}nin-KILIM.$^{gi_4\text{-}lí\text{-}na}$ see Hruška (ArOr 14 [1973] p. 110); the significance of the literal translation "Gewand — Ohr des Mungo" in our text is very unclear. We may compare in this connection the TÚG.géštu-túg "ear muff"(?) found in Pohl, TMH NF I/II no. 230 line 10, an Ur III period list of garments from Nippur.

For the deity Ninkilim/Ningilin "mongoose" see most recently Krebenik, Beschwörungen pp. 287–97 and Heimpel, RLA 8 pp. 423–25.

In col. v line 6, for the reading TÚG.ŠU.GABA.ÙR see Krecher, ZA 63 (1973) p. 168 n. 48. The translation of the term is uncertain; perhaps it means "the cloth which wraps the hand to the chest." One may compare the TÚG.níg-lá-GABA "chest draping(?)" listed among the funerary goods of Bilala in the text edited by Foxvog in Alster (ed.), Death, p. 76 line 11.

In col. v line 7 TÚG.níg-bar-ba also occurs in E1.9.4.2 col. vi line 5 (En-anatum). One may compare the níg-bar-3-túg "triple outer garment," listed among the funerary goods of the wife of Bilala in the text edited by Foxvog in Alster, Death, p. 77 line 27; cf. Sjöberg, PSD p. 93 bar 1.1 "outside in contrast to inside."

In col. v line 8 gada-Ù.LÁ can be compared to the gada-dilmun-Ù.LÁ occurring in an archival text from Girsu dating to the reign of URU-KA-gina (see Bauer, AWL pp. 471–74 no. 167 col. ii line 3 and col. iii line 4); it apparently designated some apparel (perhaps a kind of draping) made of linen. Whether there is any connection with the túg-ù-gùn "multi-coloured U garment" mentioned in Waetzoldt, Textilindustrie p. 108 is unclear.

In col v line 9 for the translation gu-sù-ga, see Bauer, BiOr 46 (1989) col. 640:

> In gu-sù-ga gehört das sù-g wahrscheinlich zu "nackt sein". Der Ausdruck bezieht sich viel auch den sog. Schwingflachs. Vgl. A.L. Oppenheim, AOS 32 zu KK 24 wo es statt gu-su-ga -sù- heißen muß.

In col. v line 11 for sag-šu$_4$-zabar "bronze helmet" (literally "bronze head covering" = Akk. *kubšu*(*m*) see Wilcke, RLA 4 pp. 311–13 and Waetzoldt, RLA 6 pp. 200–201 § 8a sub *kubšu* = sagšu.

In col v line 12 for URUDU.kak-babbar, see Cooper, AnOr 52 p. 126.

In col. v line 13 for RU.UR.RA, we have tentatively assumed a connection with Sumerian GIŠ.RU = Akkadian *tilpānu*(*m*) as suggested by Cooper (SARI p. 71). The Akkadian term, according to von Soden (in AHw) is of unknown origin. The reading of GIŠ.RU in Sumerian texts is varied. Cooper (AnOr 52 pp. 127–28) notes /ilar/, /illuru/ and /g̃ešpa/. As to their meaning, he suggests:

> Although it is clear from Akk. references and late lexical equations that *tilpānu* (= GIŠ.RU) must, in the Post-OB period, be translated at times as "bow", there is no evidence in Sum. texts for assigning that meaning to GIŠ.RU.

Cooper follows by giving various references he interprets to show that GIŠ.RU means "throw-stick" in early Sumerian sources.

The discussion of this term was taken up again by Groneberg (RA 81 [1987] pp. 115–24) where she indicated that the word GIŠ.RU = tilpānu in most profane texts means the "bow" and not a javelin or lance.

Apparently in mythological contexts it stands for a magic staff, analogous to the biblical mattäh, which is some way — presumably as a shamanic tool — has connection to death and the underworld.

In a following article (RA 82 [1988] pp. 71–73) Groneberg, citing the evidence of an Ebla lexical text edited by Pettinato, in MEE 4 p. 245 line 413: GIŠ.RU = *ma*-DU-*um*/ *wa-ru*$_{12}$-*um*, suggests a connection of Eblaic ma-DU-um with Hebrew mṭh "twig, staff, stem." She notes:

Im Gilgameš-Epos wird GIŠ.RU = *tilpānu* unmittelbar vor GIŠ.MA.NU = *šabbiṭu* erwähnt. Das Paar *mṭh- šbṭ* ist im Buch Jesaja des AT wohlbekannt, ohne daß sich Klarheit gewinnen läßt darüber, wie die Gestalt beider Gegenstände tatsächlich ist.

In turn, Wilcke, NABU 1991 no. 17 indicated a translation "Reflexbogen," Alster, RA 85 (1991) "boomerang(?)" and Römer, AfO 40–41 (1993–94) perhaps "Wurfspeer." Whatever the correct meaning of GIŠ.RU, if connected with the RU.UR.RA of col. v line 13, its special connection with the underworld would well fit the context of the URU.KA-gina inscription. We may note lines 189–90 of the Sumerian composition, "Gilgameš, Enkidu and the Netherworld":

GIŠ.RU kur-ra nam-mu-e-sìg-ge
tilpāna ana erṣeti lā tanassuk
lú GIŠ.RU ra-a nam-mu-e-nigin-dè-eš
ša ina tilpānu mahṣu ilammûka

Do not throw/shoot a GIŠ.RU in the Netherworld
or
Those who were struck down by a GIŠ.RU will surround you.

The correlation of RU.UR.RA with Sumerian illuru would indicate the variation of l and r in the first consonant of the word. For this particular phenomenon, see Falkenstein, Das Sumerische p. 28; Cavigneaux, Zeichenliste p. 50; Civil, Orientalia NS 42 (1973) p. 29; ibid., JCS 25 (1973) pp. 173–74; Sjöberg, AfO 24 (1973) pp. 41 and 46; Thomsen, The Sumerian Language p. 45 § 28; Krebernik, Beschwörung p. 328 n. 149; Bauer, AoN 51 (1992); and Attinger, Eléments p. 143, note to Thomsen p. 45 § 28.

Also to be noted is Cooper's observation that the term G̃IŠ.RU.UR.KA appears in the archival text Allote de la Füye DP 421 line 1. This term was discussed most recently by Powell in BSA 6 (1992) p. 115 where he notes: "reading, order of signs and meaning uncertain." DP 421 was published by Deimel in Orientalia 16 (1925) pp. 14–15; the text contains a list of items made of ildag wood, perhaps "larch"; the traditional translation "poplar" seems to be ruled out by the poplar's identification with Sumerian GIŠ.ḫa-lu-ub; see Campbell Thompson DAB p. 291 where the cognates Arabic *ḫalāf* and Syriac *ḫelâphâ* = Populus euphratica are noted. In DP 421 RU.UR.KA is found in the following context: (1) 5 GIŠ.ildag-RU.UR.KA "Five RU.UR.KA objects made of ildag wood," (2) 10 GIŠ.ildag RU "10 RU objects made of ildag wood," (3) 6 GIŠ.ildag-á-apin "Six 'sides' of chariots made of ildag wood," (4) and 29 GIŠ.ildag ú-gibil "29 (sticks) of firewood made of ildag wood."

Quintana (NABU 1995 no. 27) has suggested that RU.UR.KA is to be related to the substantive RU.RU.MEŠ in Middle Elamite texts (there the meaning is obscure; perhaps a cult object is meant) and GIŠ.*ur-ir* in the Elamite version of Darius's inscription from Behistun where the Akkadian text gives *za-qi-pu* "arrow." Neither suggestion is particularly illuminating, or convincing, in my view.

In col. v, line 15 á-buru$_4$(NU$_{10}$.BUR)-GI.MUŠEN, according to Bauer (BiOr 46 [1989] p. 640), is to be read á-buru$_4$-sig$_7$.MUŠEN "wing(-feathers) of a yellow raven"; for GI with a reading sig$_7$ for "yellow" in ED texts, he notes the comments of Civil, OrAnt 22 (1983) p. 5. Cf. entries 21–22 in the ED bird list from Fāra and Ebla (Pettinato, OrAnt 17 [1978] p. 169: 21. buru$_4$.MUŠEN "raven" 22 buru$_4$.sig$_7$. MUŠEN "yellow raven." Cf. also Bird List B, Pettinato, MEE 3 p. 121 col. i lines 1–4: [b]uru$_4$.MUŠEN "raven," [b]uru$_4$-sig$_7$.MUŠEN "yellow raven," [buru$_4$]-nu$_{11}$(ŠIR) "'alabaster' = white raven" [bu]ru$_4$-ḪAR.MUŠEN "... raven." Cf. Ḫḫ XVIII 333 (Landsberger, MSL VIII/2 p. 151): ŠIR.BUR-GI = *na-ʾ-i-ri*. However, in this citation GI has been equated with Akkadian *naʾiru(m)* "shrieker." The URU-KA-gina text can be compared to the archival text VAT 4415 = Deimel Orientalia 9–13 (1924) pp. 243–44 = Marzahn, VS 25 no. 10 which records deliveries(?) of various fish (cols. i–iv and v–vi) by the fishermen of G̃irsu (col. v line 1) along with assorted birds (col. v). Among the birds (col. v line 2) are two buru$_4$-sig$_7$.MUŠEN "yellow ravens" as was pointed out by Selz, Untersuchungen p. 25, who noted the connection to the URU-KA-gina passage. It may be that denizens of the underworld were bedecked with feathers like birds; in this connection we may recall the remark of McGinnis in his article entitled "A Neo-Assyrian Text Describing a Royal Funeral," SAAB p. 9 n. 29:

We must not overlook the line *labšāma kīma iṣṣūrī ṣubāt kappi* "they were clothed like birds with wings as garments" in Gilgamesh VII.iv.38, the Descent of Ishtar and the epic of Nergal and Ereškigal ...

In col. v line 15 KU.MUL is apparently some kind of spice; see Bauer, BiOr 46 (1989) p. 640 referring to Pettinato, SVS 1/3 where Reisner, Tempelurkunden no. 121 obv. v line 2 is cited. KU-MUL is translated as "cumin" by Snell in ASJ 11 (1989) p. 220 without lexical equivalents. According to the evidence given by Snell it apparently was a material used by the brewer to prepare the king's drink: níg-dab$_5$ lú-ŠIM nag lugal. It may be a variant spelling of a medicinal plant, Akkadian *ka-mul-lu* found in Ḫḫ. XVII 122 (see Reiner, MSL X p. 87 line 122). In a potency incantation (Thompson, AMT 88 no. 3 lines 1–10 = Biggs, TCS 2 p. 52) the *kabulu(m)* plant (possibly a variant spelling for *kamullu[m]*) is one of a variety of ingredients to be ground up and put into the wine of a man to drink. After three days of this medicine his potency was supposed to be restored.

In col. v line 17 the translation of BÍL.GI.ŠUŠ$_x$ (ŠE+NÁM) is difficult. The first element BÍL.GI may possibly mean "shoot(s)." Sjöberg (in his discussion of the kinship terms pa$_4$-bíl-gi($_4$), pa-bíl-ga, pa-bìl-ga, bíl-gi$_4$, bìl, in Studies Falkenstein p. 217) writes:

Die Bedeutung bìl (in pa[$_4$]-bìl-ga) ist etwa "Spross" (= *pirʾu*) ... . Wörtlich ist also pabilga (pabilgi)" erster (ältester) Spross". Was -ga (gi$_4$) bedeutet, ist, unklar.

The second element, which consists of the signs ŠE+NÁM should be read šuš$_x$ according to the excellent summary of evidence given by Steinkeller in AuOr 2 (1984) pp. 139–41 § 2. Steinkeller notes:

These observations [concerning the reading of ŠE+NÁM] may have a bearing on the

> interpretation of ŠE+NÁM in the economic texts from Archaic Uruk [referring to the seminal study by Green in JNES 39 (1980) pp. 1–35], where ŠE+NÁM is used both as a technical operation involving animals and as an occupation or title.

Steinkeller's very tentative equation with su-si-(ig) "to flay (skins and hides)" and "flayer" is far from certain. The term is connected (according to B. Hruška, AoF 22 [1995] p. 80) with the Sumerian occupation conventionally read kurušda "fattener of small cattle (i.e., sheep and goats)." For an exhaustive study of the term LAK 535 = kurušda, see Deller, Bag. Mitt 16 (1985) pp. 358–61 and Selz, Amerikanischen Sammlungen pp. 91–92.

In summary, the translation of the compound BÍL.GI.ŠUŠ$_x$ remains unclear to this author.

In col. v line 18 we may compare the maš-bar-dul$_5$ with the garment TÚG.bar-dul$_5$ = Akkadian *kusītu(m)* translated in CAD K p. 585 as "an elaborate garment." Of interest is the appearance of 4 BAR.DIB SU$_4$ "4 red-brown *kusītu* garments" as grave goods in McGinnis, SAAB 1 (1987) p. 3 col. ii′ line 13. We have understood maš here as a variant for máš and seen the complex to refer to a goat with its full fleece; cf. B. Hruška AoF 22 (1995) p. 79: "bar-dul$_5$ 'junge oder ausgewachsenes Tiere mit vollem Vlies,' also vor der Schur."

In col. v line 20 the reading of ÍL (as a substantive) is not entirely certain. It should probably be read tubšig. The conventional reading has been dusu; see Edzard, Studies Falkenstein p. 50, von Soden, AHw p. 1371 sub *tupšikku(m)*, and A. Salonen, Ziegeleien pp. 78–86. The last-cited author gives some lexical citations and very extensive and interesting Sumerian and Akkadian text references for the term. The entry for GIŠ.ÍL had been missing from Landsberger's edition of Ḫḫ Tablet VII; it is now known to have lain in the gap between Landsberger, MSL VI p. 100 Landsberger, Tablet VII A line 206: giš-bar-dù-a = *bar-du-u* and Landsberger, MSLVI pp. 103 Tablet 7 A line 226: GIŠ.lid-daŠÀ.DIŠ = *li-ti-ik-tú*. The line was, however, available from the late commentary Ḫar-gud to Ḫḫ 7–9, but only from late (Kouyunjik sources) Landsberger MSL VII p. 69 line 32: gi.du-su-ÍL = *tup-šik-ku* = *ku-du-ru* "basket (to carry earth, bricks, etc. as a primary concern of corvée work)." It was also available from a gloss found in a very late commentary to Tablet 41 of á: A = *nâqu*, a tablet from Nippur likely dating from the reign of Artaxerxes I or II (see Hunger, Kolophon no. 120); for the entry, see now Civil MSL XIV pp. 506–507 line 22: [I d]u-si = ÍL *tup-šik-ku*: *ku-[dur-ru]*. It was also available from Diri Tablet IV (from a Kouyunjik source, K. 4174 = Thompson CT 11 pl. 47 rev. col. iii line 20): [x x] [gi]-ÍL gi-ga-tun-na-ku *tup-šik-[ku]*. Fortunately, we now have an earlier, albeit considerably post ED period, source, namely a Middle Babylonian tablet from ancient Emar (Arnaud, Emar VI. 4 p. 72 line 265′) which gives: tu-ub-ši-ig ÍL *tu-up-ši-ik-ku*.

In col. v line 21 the reading of the verb ÍL is not certain. Waetzoldt (NABU 1992 pp. 13–14 no. 16) has shown that the sign ÍL could be used to write two verbs in Sumerian with apparently similar meanings: (a) íl-l "to carry" ("tragen") and (b) ga$_6$(ÍL)-g, perhaps "to carry with difficulty, drag" ("schleppen"). For the latter, see SIG$_7$.ALAN = *nabnītu* tablet 17 line 138 (Finkel, MSL XVI p. 146): ga-aÍL = MIN (*na-šu-ú*).

In col. vi line 4 for the reading ad$_6$ see the comments of Steinkeller, ZA 71 (1981) p. 20:

> In addition TIL was inserted as a semantic indicator in the sign LU×TIL (or better LÚ×UŠ) = ad$_6$ or adda "human cadaver" (written UDU×TIL = àd or ádda when denoting an animal carcass) ...

The reading and translation of the first word of col. vi line 2 has been debated by scholars. Steible (ASBW 1 p. 284) read gi-lam and translated "Früchte." Bauer (AoN 21 [1985]), citing Landsberger, AfO Beiheft 17 p. 37, Ferrara, Nanna-Suen's Journey to Nippur p. 141 n. to line 290 and Berlin Enmerkar and Ensuḫkešdanna p. 67 n. to line 37, all take gi-lam to be connected to Ur III gìr-lam "a basket used for dates, other fruits, fish, eggs." On the other hand, Steinkeller, (NABU 1993 no. 10) writes:

> Since gi-LAM is a syllabic realization of the word for "bundle" — gilim(GIL) or kilib(LAGAB) in Sumerian and *kilibbu* or *kilimbu* in Akkadian — it follows that LAM had the variant pronunciations lìm and libx.

In col. vi line 13 for the translation "wailing woman" for umum see Selz, Untersuchungen p. 60 and n. 271

In col. v 36 for the translation of "old women" for AB$_x$ÁŠ.IGI see Bauer, WO 9 (1977) p. 8 n. 25 and AoN 21 (1985) p. 8. In the latter Bauer notes:

> Die Übersetzung mit "'alte Männer'" ist unrichtig, weil durch DP 159 bezeugt ist, daß die AB×ÁŠ.IGI ^{d}nanše in Lagas unter das weibliche Personal (géme) gerechnet wurden.

Cf. Selz, Untersuchungen p. 206 n. 957.

In col. vi line 11 for the possible reading */uruḫ/ for Presargonic UḪ.INANNA and its translation "undertaker," see Bauer, AoN 21 (1985) p. 8 and Civil, NABU 1987 no. 9. Civil notes a copy of Proto-Lu from Boghazköy:

> [ÙḪ-^{d}INAN]NA ú-⌈x-x⌉-[...] = OB Proto-Lu ÙH.^{d}INANNA

He comments:

> The two signs after ú- cannot be deciphered but one would a reading */uruḫ/ in view of ÙḪ.^{d}INANNA = *ú-ru-[uḫ-ḫu]* Antagal A 141 (Cavigneau, Güterbock and Roth, MSL XVII 186, revised).

This is supported by the occurrence of Sumerian SAG×ŠID in the following line of Antagal (A 142) which has a phonetic reading dilìb in Sumerian and an Akkadian translation *uruḫḫu(m)* "hair of the head" in Sb I 246 (see Civil in Studies Reiner p. 50). The line corresponding to OB Proto-Lu 255 ŠITA.^{d}INANNA occurs in a tablet from Emar; see Arnaud, Emar VI.4 p. 189 line 280′: [ù]-ru-uḫ ŠITA.^{d}INANNA = *[ú]-ru-uḫ-ḫu*.

As Civil points out, it is clear that there are two words *uruḫḫu*(*m*) in Akkadian: (A) "hair" and (B) "undertaker" or "priest performing funerary rites."

The occupation ÙḪ-INANNA occurs in two Presargonic texts from Lagaš, Allotte de la Füye DP 216 col. iii line 5 and DP 226 col. vi line 6.

In col. vi line 15 for parallels to the burial of the dead in reed thickets within the swamps, see Beaulieu, NABU 1988 no. 53. Beaulieu, citing McGinnis, notes the intriguing remark of Strabo (Geography XVI.1.11):

> [Strabo] adds (apud Aristobolus), that Alexander buried himself thus with the canals, and also thoroughly the tombs of the kings and potentates, most of which are situated among the lakes.

Beaulieu also points out a relevant passage from Arrian, History of Alexander VII.22.2:

> The great number of the tombs of the Assyrian kings were built in the lakes and marshlands ...

We may also note in this connection the new information revealed in the recent edition of "The Death of Gilgamesh" (Cavigneaux and Al-Rawi, Gilgameš el la mort. Textes de Tell Haddad VI avec un appendice sur les textes funéraires sumériens. Cuneiform Monographs 19) that Gilgamesh's tomb was surrounded by the waters of the Euphrates after the king was entombed in it.

In col. vi line 29 ninda-šu-íl-la is almost certainly to be translated "bread for the *šu-ila* rituals"; for these rituals, see in general Mayer, Untersuchungen zur Formensprache der Babylonischen Gebetsbeschwörungen (Studia Pohl SM 5). Selz (AoF 22 [1995] p. 203) notes Heidel's connection of the bread for the šu-íl-la rituals with burial rites for the dead (Heidel, The Gilgamesh Epic and Old Testament Parallels p. 151 and n. 42). This hypothesis is supported by a passage in the OB forerunner to Ḫḫ XX–XXIV (Landsberger, MSL XI p. 155) where we find the following entries:

> 212. ninda-šu-íl-la
> 213. ninda-ki-maḫ
> 214. ninda-ki-sì-ga
> 215. ninda-gizbun(KI.KAŠ.GAR)

In line 213 for ki-maḫ = Akkadian *kimaḫ*(*ḫ*)*u*(*m*) "grave" see von Soden, AHw p. 479 and CAD K p. 370. In line 214 for ki-sì-ga = Akkadian *kispu*(*m*) "funerary offering," see A. Tsukimoto Untersuchungen zur Totenplege (kispum) im alten Mesopotamien, AOAT 216. The term may mean "the silent place" (Lambert, Orientalia NS 56 [1987] p. 403). In line 215 for gizbun(KI.KAŠ.GAR), see Wilcke, Lugalbanda p. 136 commentary to line 12, Römer, SKIZ p. 197, and von Soden, AHw p. 1309 sub *tākultu*(*m*) "(cultic) meal"; in some cases this meal was likely for the dead. For the reading gizbun see BM 68366 (81-4-28) published in copy only by Pinches in JRAS 1905 pl. after p. 829 line 8: giš-bu-un = KI.KAŠ.GAR = MIN(ki-i)-MIN(ka-aš)-gá-ra-ku = *tak-kul-tum* (Diri V 201). Sumerian gizbun is conceivably a loan word from Akkadian *kispu*(*m*) "funerary offering or meal." For the term KI.KAŠ in Ur III texts, which is likely related to this word, see Waetzoldt NABU 1991 pp. 44–45 no. 71 and the literature cited there.

In col vi line 17 for the ŠUB-lugal designation of workers see the comments of Yamamoto (ASJ 3 [1981] p. 107):

> Among the lú-KUR$_6$-dab$_5$-ba people, there were anonymous persons titled as šub-lugal and àga-ús (referred to as "Militärkolonen" by Deimel) ... They always occur in teams under the strong control of their chiefs (ugula). Superiority of the chiefs (ugula) to their subordinate lú-KUR$_6$-dab$_5$-ba may be reflected in the texts of Urukagina's reforms.
>
> The soldiers/farmers (šub-lugal), however, owned asses, houses and gardens that could be sold. They were granted KUR$_6$-land, collectively at least, in compensation for their military duty and agricultural work, and were counted as lú-KUR-dab$_5$-ba."

Cf. Maekawa in Powell, (ed.), Labor pp. 55–58, who writes:

> The term RU-lugal, which occurs only in the pre-Sargonic archives of Girsu, is used as the collective designation of workers/soldiers in gangs and is similar in usage to the term erin2 in later [Ur III] periods. The men called RU-lugal usually come first in the list of rations to "those who get allottments," but the texts only refer to the members of each gang in the terms of the amount of barley to be supplied per capita, except that the lists mention the foreman by name. Etymologically, however, the traditional translation of RU-lugal as "subordinates of the king/the god Niĝirsu (or to their masters)" remains tentative [Deimel "Die Reformtexte Urukaginas," Orientalia 2 (1920) p. 28, ibid., Orientalia 6 (1923) p. 29, M. Lambert, "Les 'réforms' d'Urukagina," RA 50 (1961) p. 174, Diakonoff "Some remarks on the 'reforms' of Urukagina" RA 52 (1958) p. 8, and Selz, Ermitage p. 115.

For the term igi-nu-du$_8$ we may note the comments of Gelb in his article entitled "Prisoners of War in Early Mesopotamia," JNES 32 (1973) p. 87:

> The Sumerian term for "blind" is igi-nu-du$_8$, of the Pre-Sargonic texts written regularly with -du$_8$, never with -tuku or -gál, as in later periods. That igi-nu-du$_8$ means "blind" is certain from three Pre-Sargonic texts (VAS 14 66 and 195; Bab. 4 p. 247b), which list bulls and equids (ANŠE. BAR. AN) with two good eyes (igi silim), one good eye (igi 1), and completely blind (igi 2-na-bi nu-du$_8$). ... The igi-nu-du$_8$ personnel of the Pre-Sargonic texts work mainly in orchards, presumably in irrigation. Some of these blind individuals may have been naturally blind (partially or fully), others may represent blinded POWs. For the latter, see the Pre-Sargonic text DP 339, which deals with 12 igi-nu-du$_8$, dumu Uru-az.KI-ka-me "12 blind individuals of Uruaz" apparently representing captives from Uruaz (in Elam), who were

> blinded to inhibit their mobility. J. Bauer, Altsumerische Wirtschafttexte aus Lagasch, p. 611, translates igi-nu-du_8, without hesitation, as "Blinder."
>
> The custom of blinding (nuppulu) POWs is known best from the New Assyrian period.

For Akkadian words for "blind" see G. Farber, ZA 75 (1985) pp. 210–33.

Concerning addir in col. vii line 3, we may note that its Akkadian translation *nēberu(m)* (see CAD I/J pp. 145–47) can have a variety of meanings, namely: "ferry, ford, crossing-boat, ferry-boat man, ferrying." For a discussion of the Sumerian words addir and má-addir, see Salonen, Wasserfahrzeuge p. 24, Behrens, Enlil und Ninlil p. 199, Pomponio, Prosopografia p. 291, Civil, Studies Landsberger, p. 5 and nn. 18–20, Pomponio, "Notes on the Fara Texts § 2. The profession name addirx," Orientalia NS 53 (1984) pp. 7–10 and Selz, "Eine lexikalisch-kulturhistorishe Skizze zu den Bedeutungen von addir," AoF 22 (1995) pp. 197–209. Selz indicates on p. 198 that the element LAK 580 in this compound logogram, occasionally transliterated by some scholars by the signs BI.GIŠ, but more correctly as GISAL "oar," is the oldest integral part of the compound, that the element PAD is apparently a graphic element to indicate the nuance "supply provision" when addir had this meaning, and that the elements a and dir in the compound are likely indicators of the pronunciation of the complex. He further adds in the English abstract to the article (p. 197): "Like its Greek counterpart naulon and porqhmeion, addir has from its beginning very strong connotations with the 'Great Crossing', the passage of the dead to the netherworld."

In col. vii line 3, for the reading a-bul_5(ZAR)-la, here translated "great gate," see Steinkeller, "On the Reading and Meaning of a-ZAR-la," RA 72 (1978) pp. 73–76 and idem, "More Evidence for the Reading bul_x of Lagab×SUM," RA 73 (1979) pp. 91–92 no. 5. The "great gate" mentioned here may not necessarily have been the "city gate," as many commentators have indicated, but rather the "great gate" through which the dead passed on to the world beyond. The transit of the deceased to the other world is a complex concept in ancient Mesopotamian thought; in some cases it was conceived to take place in the west where the sun sets and in other case in the east where the sun rises. While the literature on this subject is extensive and cannot be quoted in the context of the present study, the reader is referred to important studies by Behrens, Tsukimoto, Hutter, Alster, Frymer-Kensky, Groneberg, and Bottéro cited by Selz in AoF 22 (1995) pp. 205–7 nn. 37–47. For a likely depiction of the "gate of judgment" in an Early Dynastic period seal, see Amiet, RA 54 (1960) p. 5 fig. 8. The seal depicts a boat approaching a "winged gate" from which two figures are issuing, one on the right and one on the left. A forthcoming study by the author will suggest an identification of this four-sided figure in astral terms with the great square of the constellation Auriga.

In col. vi line 22 for the a-muš-$ša_4$ "'Snake-water' (canal)" see Bauer, WO 8 (1975–76) p. 7. Cf. the "Snake Canal" (I_7.muš) mentioned in an Ur III letter order edited by Sollberger in TCS 1 p. 88 no. 360 line 8 and the reference in an Ur III period tablet from Umma to the I_7.A×MUŠ Canal (Falkenstein, Gerichtsurkunden 2 p. no. 215 line 14).

In col. vii line 11 the precise translation of zà ì-ús-ús-am_6 is not entirely certain. For the discussion see Deimel, Orientalia 26 (1927) p. 56 and Hruška ArOr 41 (1973) p. 10 n. 17. Pomponio (in JCS 36 [1984] pp. 96–100) noted a connection between the expression zà ... ús and the Ebla professional title zà-ús. He also noted the correspondence of Ebla zà-ús and Abū Ṣalābīḫ lú-gu-si in the Early Dynastic "Names and Professions List." There gú ... si can be connected with either Akkadian *napḫaru(m)* "total, sum" or the verb *šabāšu(m)* "to gather." The expression zà ... ús occurs in an archival text from Girsu from year 6 of URU-KA-gi-na cited by Selz in Untersuchungen p. 80 § 171 (Allote de la Füye DP 135 rev. 15): gú-an-šè 155 lú-ÉREN-kam lú-ÉREN-$suḫ_5$-ḫa-am_6 12 lú ama-ÉREN-kam lú-ú-rum-^{d}ba-ba_6 URU-KA-gi-na é-gal-la zà bí-ús "Total: 155 (men) are elite troops, 12 are ... troops. Men belonging to (the estate) of the goddess Baba. URU-KA-gina mustered them in the 'palace.'"

In col. vii 26 we have taken Sumerian be_6-lu_5-da (following recent scholarship) as a loan from Akkadian *bēlūt+a*. This term has recently been studied by Steible in connection with a passage from Gudea Statue E which deals with Gudea's asking for be_6-lu_5-da from the goddess Baba. Steible notes (in Studies Römer pp. 380–82):

> A. Falkenstein hatte für pi-lu_5-da ... die Übersetzung "die (göttlichen) Gebote" (AnOr 28 (1949) S. 29; 95 und 29 (1950) S. 231) und "die Riten" (AnOr 30 (1966) S. 66 mit Anm. 13) vorgeschlagen, während bei H. Steible, FAOS 9/1 (1991) S. 193 und S. 243 dieser Begriff mit "Kult" übersetzt ist. Dagegen verstand G. Farber-Flügge, Stud. Pohl. 10 (1973) S. 179 diesen Terminus als "(Kult-) Ordnungen (oder Vorschriften)". P. Steinkeller, JNES 46 (1987) S. 58 hat erstmals PI-lu_5-da als Lehnwort von *belūtu(m)* erkannt und auf dieser Grundlage die Übersetzung "power, rule, dominion, position of master" vorgeschlagen. Dem folgt auch das neue Verständnis von Ukg. 4 iii 2 - vii 28 = Ukg. 5 iii 3 - vii 11 bei H. Steible in der Festschrift für J. Oelsner, wo Ukg. 4 vii 26-28 = Ukg. 5 vii 9-11 be_6-lu_5-da / u_4-bi-ta / e-me-a (Var. in Ukg. 5: -am_6) mit "die Herrschaftsnormen, die seit fernen Tagen galten" wiedergegeben ist.

Steible further cites two passages from Šulgi hymns in which a translation "Herrschaftsanspruch" (claim to power) would seem to be appropriate.

We may also note that the etymology from *bēlūt+a* was accepted by Powell in ZA 62 (1972) p. 210 n. 128 where a translation "prevailing conditions" was given for our passage. It probably referred to the formerly existing relations between the lord and his subordinates as Selz indicates by his translation "Herrschaftsverhältnisse" (in RIM readers' notes). The term be_6-lu_5-da (more commonly transliterated pi-lu_5-da) is written logographically PA.AN in Sumerian, for which see Sjöberg, ZA 65 (1975) p. 230 note to line 108. It appears in the lexical list Proto-Diri; see M. Civil, Oriental Institute Annual Report 1978–79 p. 73 showing a copy of the rev. of CBS 1536, a fragment of Proto-Diri copied by I. Finkel; in rev. col. iii line 18 we read: bi-lu-da PA.AN *bi-il_5-lu-du-um*. The term was borrowed back from Sumerian to Akkadian as *pelludû(m)* for which see von Soden, AHw p. 853.

In col. viii line 9 for the translation of "restored" for e-šè-gar see Selz, Untersuchungen pp. 29–30 n. 84.

In col. x line 10 for NÍG.SAG.LÁ "cloth headress" see Edzard, Rechtsurkunden no. 70 commentary to i 11 and Waetzoldt, RLA 6 p. 200. A similar term, níg-lá-sag-túg, appears among the funerary goods of Bilala in a Presargonic text from Adab edited by Foxvog (in Alster [ed.] Death p. 67 line 10). Presargonic NÍG.SAG.LÁ may possibly be equivalent to later Sumerian balla; see Sjöberg PSD B p. 81 sub balla. Balla is written logographically TÚG.NÍG.SAG.ÍL.KÉŠ and appears in Diri V lines 122–23 (81-4-28 [from Rassam's excavations in Babylonia] = Pinches JRAS 1905 pl. after p. 829 rev. lines 26–27: ba-al-la-a NÍG.SAG.ÍL.KÉŠ) referring to both male and female "cloth headdresses." Cf. Ḫḫ XIX line 149 (Landsberger, Civil and Reiner, MSL X p. 132 lines 149–50) túg-balla (NÍG.SAG.ÍL.KÉŠ). It is translated by the Akkadian term *upru*(*m*) "a cloth headdress."

In col. x line 14 for ú-durun-durun see Deimel, Orientalia 5 (1922) p. 43:

> ú bedeutet häufig sicher Gras; so in dem Namen der Tiere: udu gu(d) ú d. h. "auf der Weide, durch Gras gemästet, im Gegensatz zu udu-še d. h. "mit Gerste gemästet". Gras kann aber getrocknet oder als Heu in Bündel gebunden und aufbewahrt werden. Dann hätte ú-durun-durun-na = "Heu" (Dauer-Gras) eine Bedeutung analog zu GAR-durun-durun-na "Dauerbrot, Zwieback."

In col. x line 16, according to Hruška, ArOr 41 (1973) pp. 112–13, ninda-NE is to be orthographically separated from ninda-gibil "fresh bread." For the reading kúm for NE, see Civil, MSL XIII p. 35 (Proto-Izi I Section A) line 5: ku-um NE *um*!-*šu*[*m*] "heat, summer." Cf. Landsberger, MSL VII p. 79 (Ḫḫ X) line 21: dug-a-kúm-ma *kar-pat me-e em-mu-ti* "pot of hot water." Cf. Civil MSL XIV p. 56 Proto-Ea line 615b [ku]-um NE.

In col. x line 17 for KA ... gub = Akkadian *naptānu*(*m*), see Civil, JNES 23 (1964) p. 9 note to line 46. The auslaut in our text in -b indicates that the compound is to be read KA ... gub not KA túm; cf. Gudea Cylinder A col. xix line 26: lú-níg-tur KA-a gub-ba-g̃im. For the reading zú in this line, see van Dijk in Studies Falkenstein p. 238 n. 20 where the gloss zu-gu-ub is given for KA-GUB. See also Alster, Dumuzi's Dream p. 106. For the translation "evening(?) meal" see the comments to col. xi line 3 below.

In col. x line 20 the lú-zi-ga is probably not "conscript" as Cooper suggests but rather, as Bauer, WO 89 (1977–78) p. 8 n. 24 indicates, is a helper of the gala "lamentation singer" and thus probably connected in some way with burials. The evidence comes from Allote de la Füye DP 220 col. iv line 5: 2 lú-zi-ga-gal[a]-e-⌈ne⌉; see Selz, Untersuchungen p. 56 n. 257.

In col. x line 21 for the reading and interpretation of the sign LAK 449 we may note that LAK 449 was later conceived by Mesopotamian scribes to consist of the component elements NUNUZ+ÁB. This is clear from the evolution of LAK 451 (which originally consisted of LAK 449 with inscribed LAK 346 = ašgab) into the ùsan sign (NUNUZ.ÁB.AŠGAB). A number of signs which ultimately derive from LAK 449 and its compounds appear in the lexical series Aa VIII/4; see Civil, MSL XIV p. 512, and among these it is generally assumed that the successor of LAK 449 is to be equated with Akkadian *ḫubūru*(*m*) "a large vat for beer." For a summary of the relevant lexical material see CAD Ḫ p. 220 sub *ḫubūru*. Two Sumerian readings are assigned to the signs equated to Akkadian *ḫubūru*(*m*). By far the most common is mu-ud; much rarer is ḫu-bur. Since the latter is clearly a loanword from Akkadian *ḫubūru*(*m*), we have, following Powell (RLA 7 pp. 507–8), read mud_x for LAK 449. He adds:

> mud (mud_x = LAK 449 = *ḫubūru*) = 50 kuli; Presargonic Girsu. Probably an amphora-like jar with a somewhat spindle-shaped body and a small round mouth, opening through a rather short neck with two handles attached. It was probably a container manufactured to a standard size rather than being a component of a separate metrological system. Its capacity seems to lie in the 30–60 liter range.
>
> Approximate size of both mud and kuli can be deduced from DP 159 (Allotte de la Fuye, RA 18, 105ff., collation results), where 350 persons each receive 1 bread (loaf or cake), some type of fish, and 1 kuli of beer; these 350 kuli are totaled as 7 mud.
>
> For the latest discussion of Sumerian mud_x and Akkadian *ḫubūru*(*m*) see Sallaberger, Töpfer pp. 56 and 112.

In col x line 21 for the *sadug* vessel see the comments of Powell, RLA 7 p. 506 § IVB.2.f:

> sá-dug_4. Liquid/dry measure attested in Presargonic-Akkad period texts from Girsu, probably of two distinct sizes. Literal meaning unclear; probably a non-finite ḫamṭu verbal noun (sá-di/dug_4) etymologically identical with sattukku, for which the closest parallel (ub not literal meaning) is "tithe." This suggests that sadug was a specific capacity associated with obligatory "offerings," something on the order of a tithe basket. As a term for a specific capacity it apparently does not survive the Akkad period; no sense of capacity is associated with *satukku* in OB and later usage.

In col xi line 1, the reading zár-ra-a for NI-ra-a given by Steible is uncertain. While a reading zár for NI is given in Ellermeier Sumerisches Glossar 1/I p. 376 sub zár, Proto Ea lines 90–96 (Civil MSL XIV p. 35) and Ea II lines 7–25 (Civil, MSL XIV p. 247) give no gloss za-ar for NI. On the other hand, Ea II line 93 (Civil, MSL XIV p. 251) does give a gloss za-ra for the complex BAD.AŠ, and we may conjecture (with all due reserve) that this may be the much later development of the NI-ra-a of the URU-KA-gina text. The Akkadian translation *nu-ku-du* given in Ea II line 93 is the D stem of *nakādu*(*m*); a meaning "to be very much concerned" is found in an OB letter cited in CAD N p. 154 sub *nukkudu*.

In col xi line 3 a passage from Izi = *išātu* Appendix to Tablet H (Civil MSL XIII p. 210) is suggestive of a translation "evening meal" for *patānu*. Lines 24–40 read:

[kiĝ]-⸢x⸣ = ⸢a⸣-k[a-lum] "meal" (literally "food")
[kiĝ-s]ig MIN *li-l[a-ti]* = "evening meal"
[kiĝ]-sig = MIN *mu-še-e* "meal at night"
[kiĝ]-sig = *nap-ta-nu* "evening(?) meal"
[ki]ĝ-sig = *ki-in-si-gu* "late afternoon meal"

In col. xi line 4 for gi$_6$-ba "middle of the night," "midnight" cf. Berlin, Enmerkar p. 69 line 43: buru$_5$-mušen gi$_6$-sa$_9$(BAR)-gin$_7$ gaba-ki zà-im-DU "Like a swarn at midnight, he fills the interior of the mountains" where a textual variant has gi$_6$-ba for to gi$_6$-sa$_9$. By analogy, if u$_4$-sa$_9$(BAR) is "midday" (see below) then gi$_6$-sa$_9$(BAR) should be "midnight." Cf. Civil, Farmer's Instructions p. 98 note to line 106:

> The expressions á-u$_4$-te-en and á-gi$_6$-ba, frequent in Ur III texts dealing with religious ceremonies, designate the time at which they were performed, "in the evening" and "at night."

Cf. Sigrist, Drehem pp. 124–128 á-gi-ba-a "durant la nuit."

In col. xi line 5 we have assumed (following the comment of Steible, ASBW 2 p. 155 n. 89) that u$_4$-sá corresponds to later u$_4$-sa$_9$(BAR) = *mi-šil* UD-*mu* "midday" of Ḫḫ 1 line 177 (Landsberger, MSL V p. 22). For a detailed discussion of u$_4$-sa$_9$ see Sjöberg and Bergmann, Temple Hymns p. 76 commentary to line 111.

In col. xi line 6 for ĝi$_6$-an-na cf. the comments of Hallo and van Dijk in Exaltation p. 76: ĝi$_6$-ù-na (ĝi$_6$-un$_x$ (BÀD)-na, cf. Gud. Cyl. A xi 26 ĝi$_6$-a-na = ĝi$_6$-an-na: mūšu "(mid)night." For ùn(BÀD)-na "height of heaven" see Sjöberg, Mondgott p. 66, Falkenstein ZA 56 (1964) p. 87 note to line 373, and George, House Most High p. 18 line 392: é-ùn(BÀD)-na referring to a temple of Inanna of Subartu.

In col. xi line 10 for lú-saĝ-bur, cf. Lú *ša* IV 183–85 (Civil MSL XI p. 134): pi-il-pi-li = *as-[sin-nu]*, saĝ-ur-saĝ = *as-sin-nu*, saĝ-bur-ra = KI.MIN (*as-sin-nu*). For Akkadian *assinnu* see CAD A p. 341, where a translation "a member of the cultic personnel of Ištar" is given. CAD notes: The *assinnu* seems to have functioned mainly in the cult of Ištar, to have sung specific songs and dressed in distinctive garments. Cf. von Soden, AHw p. 75 where a translation "etwa 'Buhlknabe (im Kult)" is given. For literature on the *assinnu*, see Römer, SKIZ pp. 157–58; Sjöberg ZA 65 (1975) pp. 233–36 note to line 81; ibid., JCS 40 (1988) pp. 170–71 note to col. iv line 10; Groneberg, WdO 17 (1986) pp. 34–36; idem, Lob der Ištar p. 47 n. 118.

For Sumerian saĝ-bur specifically, see most recently, Henshaw, Female and Male pp. 302-3 § App. 3.13. Steible, ASBW 2 p. 155 in connection with lú-saĝ-bur mentions OB lu-Series Tablet col. iv (Civil, MSL XII p. 182) line 33: lú saĝ-bur-⸢x x x⸣ = *mu-ḫa-mi-⸢šu-ri⸣-[ni]* and compares CAD M p. 172 *muḫammiṣu* (in *muḫamimiṣ/š šurinni*) "person who removes (the precious material from a divine emblem)." Taking this as a D-stem participle of *ḫamāṣu(m)* "to take off (clothing) by force," in a modification of a hypothesis given by Selz (in AoF 22 [1995] p. 203 n. 33), the author suggests that the reference might be related to the removal of the clothes of the deceased before the wrapping and dressing of the corpse for burial.

An anagraphic writing of the term saĝ-bur may be found in the writing bur-saĝ, as is suggested by two succeeding entries in OB Proto-Lu, 559a–560 (Civil MSL XII p. 53): s[aĝ]-bur, burúr-saĝ.

As for col xi line 17 we may note that there has been some scholarly debate on the correct translation for saĝa-ĜAR. Deimel (Orientalia 2 pp. 26–27) translated: "Vorsteher der Handwerker [director of craftsmen]." The term was briefly discussed by Bauer in AWL p. 343 note to col. ii line 6, where a reference to a dam-saĝa-ĜAR was noted. A full list of 11 saĝa-ĜAR's in Presargonic texts from Girsu was given by Selz in Untersuchungen p. 76 n. 316. Seventeen references in the Presargonic texts from Fara were given by Visicato in his Indices of the Early Dynastic Administrative Tablets of Šuruppak p. 126 sub sanga-GAR. Concerning the latter, Visicato (Power and Writing p. 3) writes:

> My analysis of the economic documents from Fara has identified the existence of a clearly defined hierarchy among the dignitaries and officials of the institution that governed and administered Šuruppak in the ED period. At the head of the hierarchy was the énsi, followed by the sanga-GAR, sa$_{12}$-du$_5$, dub-sar-maḫ, and then other officials of high rank. This hierarchy fits very well with the beginning sequence of the Names and Professions Lists.

Indeed, if we examine the first five entries of the Names and Professions List known from ED period copies from Abū Ṣalābīḫ and Ebla and an Ur III period copy of unknown provenance, we find the sequence énsi "city ruler" saĝa, sa$_{12}$-du$_5$ "cadaster official" dub-sar "scribe" and šagin(GÌR.NITA) "general." A connection between the two sequences would assume that saĝa and saĝa-ĜAR are related, a reasonable, if unproven, hypothesis.

Visicato further writes (Power and Writing p. 3):

> R.D. Biggs observes that the profession indicated by the sign SANGA should be understood as šid, "the accounting official," or as umbisag "administrator," contrary to Deimel, ŠL 314,28: "sanga-priest." Biggs notes that even if the profession of sanga appears to be distinct from that of dub-sar in the Fara period, the same anthroponyms that carry the title sanga in the colophon of lexical texts assume the title of dub-sar in certain administrative texts.

The significance of the element ĜAR in the term saĝa-ĜAR is uncertain. It may be compared to the title énsi-ĜAR also found in ED administrative texts; for the references in the Fara texts, see Viscato, Indices of the Early Dynastic Administrative Tablets of Šuruppak p. 114 sub énsi-<GAR-gal>. Perhaps the element ĝar simply means "appointed," recalling Renger's remarks regarding the priestly designation lukur-ĜAR [d]utu in OB administrative texts from Sippar: "Statt *nadītum šá* [d]Samaš ist auch eine Auflösung zu lukur-garax(GAR)-[d]Utu 'die eingesetze lukur des Utu,' zu erwägen." Likewise saĝa-ĜAR might simply mean "appointed saĝa"; this was the general interpretation given by Diakonoff in RA 52 (1958) p. 6.

Further, an extensive discussion of the term SAĜA has recently been given by Henshaw (Female and Male pp. 20–24 § 1.3). Henshaw writes:

He [the SAĜA] is variously understood as a "temple administrator" or "priest," but this function is unsure for the early [= ED lexical] texts.

In the URU-KA-gina text it is probable that the SAĜA-ĜAR referred to an administrator, but a cultic designation cannot be absolutely ruled out. The latter interpretation would be supported by the relative proximity of saĝa-ĜAR in col. xi line 17 and the lú-sag-búr-re in col. xi line 10. In a cultic commentary most recently published by Livingston (SAA 3 pp. 92–95) the *sangû* and *kurgaru*s (as noted, the latter often is connected with the lú-sag-búr-re in various texts) perform a ritual before the Assyrian king.

In col xi line 23 for the reading nu-mu-un-kúš (instead of traditional nu-mu-un-su), see Cavigneaux, RA 87 (1993) p. 111 note to line 137: "Les graphies nu-mu-un-kúš (Ma) et nu-mu-un-úkuš (Mb) prouvent définitivement que 'veuve, femme dépourvue de support familial' doit se lire nu-mu-un-kúš."

In col. xi line 30 for ÁB.ŠÀ-bi, see Proto-Diri 458–60, van der Meer, OEC 4 no. 153 pl. XXI lines 8–10: [ÁB].ŠÀ = *li-ib-bu-*[*um*] "heart (as the seal of emotions and intelligence," [ÁB].ŠA *ṣu-ur-*⸢*ru*⸣-[*um*] "heart (as the seat of emotions and intelligence," ÁB.ŠA = *uz-zu-ú-*[*um*] "(emotion of) anger." For an ED IIIb phonetic writing of this Sumerian word, see Krebernik, Beschwörungen p. 64 col. ii line 1–3:

> ša-gi li-bí-iš$_{11}$-gi mu-na-a to be compared with the normal logographic writing šà-gig lipiš-gig mu-na-ak. The writing in the Uru-KA-gina text with ÁB.ŠÀ follows the OB manner; post OB texts give ÁB×ŠÀ (see Cooper, ZA 61 [1971] p. 18 note to Reverse B 1.

For the semantic link between Sumerian libiš "middle" and "anger" cf. the comments of Edzard (ZA 73 [1983] p. 134):

> *qablu* A "center" und B "battle" sind — wie in AHw. — getrennt. Mann kann aber nicht umhin, an Zusammenhänge zu erinnern wie zwischen *libbu* "Inneres" und *libbātu* "Zorn" oder sum. libiš "Zentrum" und *libiš* "Zorn".

Krecher's reading (ASJ 9 [1987] p. 85 n. 4) ze$_x$ for ÁB.ŠÀ would not appear to be relevant here.

In col. xii line 4 šen = Akkadian *ruqqu*(*m*) is normally translated "kettle"; see Salonen Hausgeräte 2 pp. 253–63 ("Kessel"). More recently Steinkeller (OrAnt 20 [1981] pp. 243–49) has suggested a translation of the element šen in the compound *dub-šen as "chest." See also Krebernik, BiOr 41 (1984) col. 644. Selz (in RIM readers' notes) suggests "trunk."

For the translation of col. xii lines 13–22, see the excellent analysis of Steinkeller in Aula Orientalis 9 (1991) pp. 227–33. There he demonstrates that the Sumerian word é-ÉŠ, where the element ÉŠ likely is to be interpreted "rope," is to be translated "prison." For a grammatical analysis of lines 17–20, see Yoshikawa, ASJ 15 (1993) p. 166 where the elements -a in níg-zuḫ-a and sag-giš-ra-a are seen not as anticipatory genitives (as Steible indicated) but rather as examples of the completive participle suffix -a.

In col. xii line 28 for KA ... KEŠDA "to bind by an oral agreement" see Falkenstein, Neusumerischen Gerichtsurkunden 3 p. 126 sub KA-kešda. The reading of the second element KEŠDA(EZEN) is not absolutely certain; it may have been šìr, cf. CAD M p. 283 sub *markasu* (lexical section): [si-ir] [ŠÌR] ⸢šá KA⸣.[ŠÌR *mar-k*]*a-su* (A VIII/2: 5). Civil (MSL XIV p. 497) gives [si-ir EZEN [*ra-k*]*a-su* for the same entry; cf. Finkel, MSL XVI p. 310 (SIG$_4$.ALAN = *nabnītu* tablet W) who gives for col. ii lines 2′–3′: ka-kéš (*ri-ik-su*). Whatever the reading, it is clear that the KEŠDA element ended in the dr phoneme; see Bauer, AWL pp. 60–61 commentary to III 2. In col. xii line 35 we have given the verb e-šè-ĝar a translation "restored" following Selz in Untersuchungen p. 30 n. 84; Selz in turn was following Thureau-Dangin, SAKI p. 51 and Deimel, Orientalia 2 (1920) p. 9. In contrast, other scholars have given "set aside"; see Jacobsen, in Studies Landsberger p. 89 n. 14, Foster, JESHO 24 pp. 236 n. 37, and Cooper SARI 1 p. 73.

BIBLIOGRAPHY

1884–1912 de Sarzec, Découvertes 2 p. LI OUROU-KAGHINA 4 (ex. 1, copy); p. LII OUROU-KAGHINA 4bis (ex. 2, copy); pl. 32bis no. 4 (ex. 1, photo); pl. 32bis no. 5 (ex. 2, photo)
1907 Thureau-Dangin, SAK pp. 46–55 Uru-ka-gi-na h (exs. 1–2, edition)
1920 Deimel, Orientalia 2 pp. 1–31 (exs. 1–2, translation, study)
1931 Deimel, AnOr 2 pp. 75–78 (exs. 1–2, study)
1956 Kramer, FTS pp. 41 ff. (exs. 1–2, translation)
1956 Lambert, RA 50 pp. 169–84 (exs. 1–2, edition)
1956 Sollberger, CIRPL p. xiv Ukg. 4–5 (study); pp. 50–53 (exs. 1–2, conflated copy); p. 64 Ukg. 60 (ex. 3, study)
1958 Diakonoff, RA 52 pp. 1–15 (exs. 1–2, study)
1959 Rosengarten, RHR 156 pp. 75–78 (exs. 1–2, study)
1963 Kramer, Sumerians pp. 317–19 § C 24 (exs. 1–2, translation)
1964 Struve, "Istoričeskie Nadpisi Urukaginy i istorija ih interpretacii," Vestnik Dreveny Istorii no. 4 pp. 3–23 (study)
1965 Jacobsen in Studies Landsberger p. 89 (continuation of) n. 14 (study)
1973 Hruška, ArOr 41, pp. 4–13 (exs. 1–2, study)
1974 Edzard, "'Soziale Reformen'im Zeistromland bis ca. 1600 v. Chr.: Realität oder literarischer Topos," AAASH 12 pp. 147ff. (study)
1973–74 Maekawa, Mesopotamia 8–9 pp. 77–144 (study)
1974 Hruška, "Die Reformtexte Urukaginas: Der verspätete Versuch einer Konsolidierung des Stadtsstaates von Lagaš," CRRA 19 pp. 151–61 (study)
1981 Foster, JESHO 24 pp. 230–41 (study)
1982 Steible, ASBW 1 pp. 288–312 Ukg. 4–5 (exs. 1–3, edition) Ukg. 60 (study)
1982 Krispijn, in Veenhof (ed.), Schrijvend Verleden, pp. 126–30 (translation [into Dutch])
1986 Carroué, ASJ 8 pp. 16, 18–19, 24 (study)
1986 Cooper, SARI 1 pp. 70–74 (exs. 1–3, translation)
1986 Steiner, ASJ 8 pp. 219–300 (passim) (study)
1990 Lambert, ZA 80 pp. 42–43 (study)
1991 Alster, RA 85 pp. 5–6 no. 2 (study)
1994 Foxvog, JCS 46 pp. 11–15 (study)
1995 Selz, AoF 22 pp. 202–3 (study)

TEXT

Col. i
1) ^{d}nin-g̃ír-su
2) ur-sag-^{d}en-líl-lá-ra

i 1–2) For the god Ning̃irsu, warrior of the god Enlil,

3) URU-KA-gi-na
4) lugal-
5) lagaš(NU$_{10}$.LA.BUR).KI-ke$_{4}$

i 3–5) URU-KA-gina, king of Lagaš,

6) é-gal-ti-ra-áš
7) mu-na-dù

i 6–7) built the "palace" of (the city of) Tiraš,

8) an-ta-sur-ra
9) mu-na-dù

i 8–9) built the Antasur ("Northern[?] Boundary"),

10) é-^{d}ba-ba$_{6}$
11) mu-na-dù
Col. ii
1) bur-sag
2) é-sá-du$_{11}$-ka-ni
3) mu-na-dù

i 10 – ii 3) built the temple of the goddess Baba and built a pantry(?) for her, her building of regular provisions,

4) GÁ-udu-ur$_{4}$-
5) uru-kù-ga-ka-ni
6) mu-na-dù

ii 4–6) and built her sheep-plucking shed in the holy precinct for her.

7) ^{d}nanše
8) i$_{7}$-AB×ḪA.KI-du
9) i$_{7}$-ki-ág-ni
10) al mu-na-dù
11) kug̃-bi
12) ab-šà-ga
13) mu-na-ni-lá

ii 7–13) For the goddess Nanše, he dug the Nimin-DU canal, her beloved canal, and extended its outlet to the sea.

14) bàd-g̃ír-su.KI
Col. iii
1) mu-na-dù

ii 14 – iii 1) He built the wall of G̃irsu for him (the god Ning̃irsu).

2) u$_{4}$-ul-lí-a-ta
3) numun-è-a-ta

iii 2–3) Now, since time immemorial, since the seed (of life) came forth —

4) u$_{4}$-bi-a
5) lú-má-laḫ$_{5}$-ke$_{4}$
6) má e-dab$_{5}$

iii 4–6) In those days (before me), the head boatman appropriated boats,

7) anše ú-du-le
8) e-dab$_{5}$

iii 7–8) the livestock official appropriated asses,

9) udu ú-du-le
10) e-dab$_{5}$

iii 9–10) the livestock manager appropriated sheep,

11) $^{\text{ù-mú}}$ú-mu$_{11}$(KA×SAR)
12) enku-re$_{6}$
13) e-dab$_{5}$

iii 11–13) the fisheries inspector appropriated taxes,

14) gudu$_{4}$-ge-ne
15) še-gub-ba
16) AMBAR.KI-a
17) e-ág

iii 14–17) and the lustration priests measured out grain taxes (as payment) at (the town of) AMBAR.

18) sipa-udu-siki-ka-ke$_{4}$-ne
19) bar-udu-ḫád-ka
Col. iv
1) kù bi-gar-ré-éš

iii 18 – iv 1) The shepherds of wool-bearing sheep paid (a tax) in silver instead of (the correct practice of giving) a white sheep,

2) lú-éš-gíd
3) gala-maḫ
4) agrig
5) lú-bappìr

iv 2–8) and the surveyor, chief lamentation-singer, supervisor, brewer, and foremen paid (a tax) in silver instead of (the correct practice of giving) an offering lamb.

---

ii 9.2 i$_{7}$-ki-ág̃-g̃á-ni.
ii 14.2 g̃ír-sú.KI.

6) ugula-ugula-ne
7) bar-sila$_4$-GABA-ka-ka
8) kù bi-gar-ré-éš
9) gu$_4$-diĝir-ré-ne-ke$_4$
10) ki-sum-ma-
11) ensí-ka
12) ì-uru$_4$
13) GANÁ-sa$_6$-ga-
14) diĝir-ré-ne-ka
15) ki-sum-ma
16) ki-úkuš-
17) énsi-ka
18) e-gál-lam

iv 9–18) The oxen of the gods (i.e., of the temples) ploughed the garlic plot of the ruler, and the best fields of the gods (i.e., the temples) became the garlic and cucumber plots of the ruler.

19) anše-bìr-ra
20) gu$_4$-du$_7$-du$_7$
21) saĝa-saĝa-ne
22) e-ne-kéš-rá-am$_6$

iv 19–22) Teamed asses and unblemished oxen were yoked for the temple administrators,

Col. v
1) še-saĝa-saĝa-ne
2) éren-énsi-ka-ke$_4$
3) e-ba

v 1–3) and the grain of the temple administrators was divided up by the (work/military) crews of the ruler.

4) TÚG.GÉŠTU-^{d}nin-KILIM.$^{\text{gi}_4\text{-lí}}$-na
5) TÚG.Ù.ÁŠ
6) TÚG.ŠU.GABA.ÙR
7) TÚG.níg-bar-ba
8) gada-Ù.LÁ
9) gu-sù-ga
10) gu-sa-lá
11) sag-šu$_4$-zabar(=KA×UD.BAR)
12) URUDU.kak-zabar(=KA×UD.BAR)
13) ru-ur-ra-zabar(=KA×UD.BAR)
14) kuš-zalag-ga
15) á-buru$_4$(=NU$_{10}$.BUR)-sig$_7$.MUŠEN
16) ku-mul
17) BÍL.GI.ŠUŠx(ŠE+NÁM)
18) maš-bar-dul$_5$
19) sanga-sanga-ne
20) ÍL-šè
21) ì-ÍL-am$_6$

v 4–21) The temple administrators took (the following items as payments) instead of corvée duty: (woolen garments of the type) "Ear of the Mongoose," U.AŠ, and ŠU.GABA.UR, an outer woolen garment, a ... linen draping, naked flax, flax tied in bundles, a bronze helmet, a bronze arrow(?), a bronze throw-stick/bow(?), burnished leather, wing(-feathers) of a yellow raven, shoots (for) ... and a goat with its full fleece.

22) sanga-GAR-ke$_4$
23) kiri$_6$-ama-ukú-rá
Col. vi
1) giš na ba-ni-ri-ri
2) gi-lam
3) e-ta-kéš-rá

v 22 – vi 3) The ... temple administrators ripped out the orchards of the poor and tied up (the fruit) in bundles.

4) ad$_6$ ki-maḫ-šè DU
5) kas-ni 7 dug
6) ninda-né gešda-imin-nam
7) 2 (ul) še-ḫa-zi
8) 1 túg
9) 1 maš-sag-gá
10) 1 GIŠ.ná
11) uruḫ(ÙḪ.INANNA)-e
12) ba-DU

vi 4–12) When a corpse was brought to the grave, the undertaker took his seven jugs (140 l.) of beer, his 420 loaves of bread, 2 *gur* (72 l.) of *ḫazi*-grain, one woolen garment, one lead goat, and one bed.

---

v 7.2 Omits TÚG.
vi 4.1 ki-maḫ.KI DU.
vi 7.3 [še]-ḫa-zi-na.

13) 1 (gur) še lú-umum-ma-ke$_4$
14) ba-DU

vi 13–14) The wailing women took one *ul* (36 l.) of barley.

15) gi-^{d}en-ki-ka-ka
16) lú ù-DU

vi 15–16) When a man was brought (for burial) at the "reeds of Enki,"

17) kas-ni 7 dug
18) ninda 420-nam
19) 2 (ul) še
20) 1 túg
21) 1 GIŠ.ná
22) GIŠ.dúr-gar
23) uruḫ(ÙḪ.INANNA)-e
24) ba-DU

vi 17–24) the undertaker took his seven jugs (140 l.) of beer, his 420 loaves of bread, 2 *ul* (72 l.) of barley, one woolen garment, one bed, and one chair.

25) 1 (gur) še
26) lú-umum-ma-ke$_4$
27) ba-DU

vi 25–27) The old wailing women took one *gur* (72 l.) of barley.

28) giš-kin-ti
29) ninda-šu-íl-la
Col. vii
1) ì-tuku-am$_6$

vi 28 – vii 1) The craftsmen (took) the bread for the *šuila* rite,

2) guruš:min-me
3) addir$_x$(=PAD.DUG.GIŠ.SI)-a-bul$_5$(ZAR)-la
4) ì-tuku-am$_6$

vii 2–4) and the two "young men" received the safe passage toll for the"great gate" (to the world beyond).

5) é-énsi-ka
6) GANÁ-énsi-ka-ke$_4$
7) É-É.MÍ
8) GANÁ.É.MÍ-ke$_4$
9) é-nam-dumu
10) GANÁ-nam-dumu-ke$_4$
11) zà ì-ús-ús-am$_6$

vii 5–11) The estate and fields of the ruler, the estate and fields of the "Lady" (literally the "Woman") (i.e., the ruler's wife) and the estate and fields of the "Organization of the Children" (i.e., the ruler's children) were consolidated(?).

12) ki-sur-ra-
13) ^{d}nin-g̃ír-su-ka-ta
14) a-ab-šè
15) maškim-di
16) e-gál-lam

vii 12–16) Bailiffs (of the court) held jurisdiction from the boundary of the god Ning̃irsu to the sea.

17) ŠUB-lugal-ke$_4$
18) sag-GANÁ-ga-na-ka
19) pú-ni ì-dù

vii 17–19) When a subordinate to the king would build a well on the narrow edge of his field,

20) igi-nu-du$_8$
21) ba-dab$_5$

vii 20–21) the blind workers were appropriated (for the work),

22) a-muš-ša$_4$
23) ašax(GANÁ)-ga gál-la-a
24) igi-nu-du$_8$
25) ba-dab$_5$

vii 22–25) and the blind workers were also appropriated for (work on) the irrigation canals which were in the field.

26) be$_6$-lu$_5$-da-
27) u$_4$-bi-ta
28) e-me-a

vii 26–28) These were the proprietary rights of former days.

29) u$_4$ ^{d}nin-írg̃-su
30) ur-sag-^{d}en-líl-lá-ke$_4$

vii 29–30) When the god Ning̃irsu, warrior of the god Enlil,

Col. viii
1) URU-KA-gi-na-ra
2) nam-lugal-
3) lagaš.KI
4) e-na-sum-ma-a

viii 1–4) granted the kingship of Lagaš to URU-KA-gina,

5) šà-lú-36000-ta
6) šu-ni e-ma-ta-dab$_5$-ba-a

viii 5–6) selecting him from among the myriad people,

---

vii 28.2 e-me-am$_6$.

7) nam-tar-ra-
8) u$_4$-bi-ta
9) e-šè-gar
10) inim lugal-ni
11) ^{d}nin-g̃ír-su-ke$_4$
12) e-na-du$_{11}$-ga
13) ba-dab$_5$

viii 7–13) he restored the customs of former times, carrying out the command that the god Niñgirsu, his master, had given him.

14) má-ta
15) lú-má-laḫ$_5$
16) e-ta-šub

viii 14–16) He removed the head boatman from (control over) the boats,

17) anše-ta
18) udu-ta
19) ú-du-bi
20) e-ta-šub

viii 17–20) he removed the livestock official from (control over) asses and sheep,

21) ù-sar ú-mu$_{10}$-ta
22) enku
23) e-ta-šub

viii 21–23) he removed the fisheries inspector from (control over) taxes,

24) še-gub-ba-
25) gudu$_4$-ge-ne-ta
26) ka-gur$_7$
27) e-ta-šub

viii 24–27) he removed the silo supervisor from (control over) the grain taxes of the lustration-priests,

28) bar-udu-ḫád-ka
29) bar-sila$_4$-gaba-ka-ka
30) kù a-gá-gá-da
31) maškim-bi
Col. ix
1) e-ta-šub

viii 28 – ix 1) he removed the (court bailiff) (responsible) for the paying (of duties) in silver instead of white sheep and young lambs,

2) ÍL sanga-sanga-ne
3) é-gal-šè
4) mu-ÍL-a
5) maškim-bi
6) e-ta-šub

ix 2–6) and he removed the (responsibility) for the delivery of duties by the temple administrators to the palace.

7) é-énsi-ka
8) GANÁ-énsi-ka-ka
9) ^{d}nin-g̃ír-su
10) lugal-ba
11) ì-gub

ix 7–11) He installed Niñgirsu as proprietor over the ruler's estate and the king's fields;

12) é-É.MÍ
13) GANÁ.É.MÍ-ka
14) ^{d}ba-ba$_6$
15) nin-ba
16) ì-gub

ix 12–16) he installed Baba as proprietor of the estate of the woman's organization and the fields of the woman's establishment;

17) é-nam-dumu
18) GANÁ-nam-dumu-ka
19) ^{d}šul-šà-ga-na
20) lugal-ba
21) ì-gub

ix 17–21) and he installed Šulšagana as proprietor of the children's estate.

22) ki-sur-ra-
23) ^{d}nin-g̃ír-su-ka-ta
24) a-ab-šè
25) maškim lú nu-e

ix 22–25) From the boundary of the god Niñgirsu to the sea bailiffs ceased operations.

26) ad$_6$ ki-maḫ-šè DU
27) kas-ni 3 dug
28) ninda-ni 80-am$_6$
29) 1 GIŠ.ná
30) 1 maš-sag-gá
31) ÙḪ.INANNA-e
32) ba-tùm

ix 26–32) When a corpse is brought for burial, the undertaker takes his 3 jugs (60 l.) of beer, his 80 loaves of bread, one bed, and one "leading goat,"

33) 3 (bán) še lú-umum-ma-ke$_4$
34) ba-tùm
35) gi-^{d}en-ki-ka-ka

Col. x

1) lú ù-DU
2) kas-ni 4 dug
3) ninda-ni 420-am$_6$
4) 1 (gur) še
5) ÙḪ.INANNA-e
6) ba-tùm
7) 3 (bán) še
8) lú-umum-ma-ke$_4$
9) ba-tùm
10) 1 NÍG.SAG.LÁ MÍ
11) 1 silà ir-nun
12) ereš-di$\tilde{g}$ir-ré
13) ba-tùm
14) 420 ninda-durun-durun-na
15) ninda-gub-ba-am$_6$
16) 40 ninda-kúm
17) zú-gub-ba-am$_6$
18) 10 ninda-kúm
19) ninda-banšur-ra-kam
20) 5 ninda-lú-zi-ga-ka
21) 2 kas-LAK 449 1 sá-du$_{11}$
22) gala-
23) $\tilde{g}$ír-su.KI-kam
24) 490 ninda
25) 2 kas-LAK 449 1 sá-du$_{11}$
26) gala-
27) lagaš(NU$_{10}$.BUR.LA).KI-kam
28) 406 ninda
29) 1 kas-LAK 449 1 sá-du$_{11}$
30) gala-am$_6$
31) 250 ninda
32) 1 kas-LAK 449
33) nam-um-ma-am$_6$
34) 180 ninda
35) 1 kas-LAK 449
36) AB×ÁŠ.IGI
37) AB×ḪA.KI-na-me
38) igi-nu-du$_8$

Col. xi

1) zár-ra-a
2) gub-ba
3) ninda-zú-gub-ba-ni 1-am$_6$
4) 5 ninda-gi$_6$-ba-a-ka-ni
5) 1 ninda-u$_4$-sá-ka-ni
6) 6 ninda-gi$_6$-an-na-ka-ni
7) 60 ninda
8) 1 kas-LAK 449
9) 3 (bán) še

ix 33–34) and the wailing women takes 3 *ban* (18 1.) of barley.

ix 35 – x 1) When a man is brought for the "reed of Enki,"

x 2–6) then the undertaker takes his 4 jugs (80 1.) of beer, his 420 loaves of bread, and one *gur* (36 1.) of barley;

x 7–9) the wailing women take 3 *ban* (8 l.) of barley,

x 10–13) and the *ereš-di$\tilde{g}$ir*-priestess takes one lady's cloth headdress, and one *sila* (1 1.) of aromatic oil.

x 14–15) 420 loaves of dry bread are the bread duty,

x 16–17) 40 loaves of hot bread are for the meal,

x 18–19) and 10 loaves of hot bread are for the table bread;

x 20) 5 loaves of bread are for the *lu-ziga* attendants,

x 21–23) 2 *mud* vessels and 1 *sadug*-vessel of beer are for the lamentation singers of $\tilde{G}$irsu;

x 24–27) 490 loaves of bread, 2 mud vessels, and one *sadug*-vessel of beer are for the lamentation singers of Lagaš;

x 28–30) 406 loaves of bread, one *mud* vessel, and one *sadug*-vessel of beer are for the (other) lamentation singers;

x 31–33) 250 loaves of bread and one *mud* vessel of beer are for the old wailing women;

x 34–37) 180 loaves of bread and one *mud* vessel of beer are for the old women of Ni$\tilde{g}$in.

x 38 – xi 6) For the blind ones who wait anxiously — one loaf is their evening bread, five loaves are their bread for the middle of the night, one loaf is their bread for dawn, and six loaves are their bread for mid-day.

xi 7– 10) 60 loaves, one *mud* vessel of beer, and 3 *ban* (18 1.) of barley are for those who perform the role of *sa$\tilde{g}$bur*.

---

x 15.1 Has an erasure between -ba- and -am$_6$.
x 36.1 UNU(ABA$_4$).IGI.
xi 1.1 -a written over dù.
x i 5 . 2 u$_4$-sá--a-ka-ni

10) lú-sag-bur-ré ak-da-kam
11) addir$_x$ (=PAD.DUG.GIŠ.SI)-a-bul$_x$(ZAR)-la
12) guruš-MIN-ka
13) inim ì-gi$_4$
14) giš-kin-ti
15) ninda-šu-íl-la-ba
16) inim ì-gi$_4$
17) sanga-G̃AR
18) kiri$_6$-ama-ukú-rá
19) nu-laḫ$_5$
20) ŠUB-lugal-ra
21) anše-ša$_6$-ga
22) ù-na-tu
23) ugula-né ga-šè-sa$_{10}$
24) ù-na-du$_{11}$
25) u$_4$-da mu-šè-sa$_{10}$-sa$_1$
26) kù šà-gá a-ša$_6$-ga
27) lá-ma
28) ù-na-du$_{11}$
29) u$_4$-da nu-šè-sa$_{10}$-sa$_{10}$
30) ugula ÁB.ŠÀ-bi
31) na-na-tag-ge
32) é-lú-gu-la-ke$_4$
33) é-ŠUB-lugal-ka
34) ab-ús-sa
35) lú-gu-la-bi
36) ga-šè-sa$_{10}$
37) ù-na-du$_{11}$
38) u$_4$-da
Col. xii
1) mu-šè-sa$_{10}$-sa$_{10}$
2) kù šà-gá a-ša$_6$-ga
3) lá-ma
4) é-mu šen-nam
5) še si-ma-ni
6) ù-na-du$_{11}$
7) u$_4$-da nu-še-sa$_{10}$-sa$_{10}$
8) lú-gu-la-bi
9) ŠUB-lugal-ra
10) ÁB.ŠÀ-bi
11) na-na-tag-ge
12) ì-du$_{11}$
13) dumu-lagaš.KI
14) ur$_5$-ra ti-la
15) gur-gub-ba
16) še-si-ga
17) níg-zuḫ-a
18) sag-giš-ra-a
19) é-ÉŠ-bi
20) e-luḫ
21) ama-gi$_4$-bi

xi 11–13) He removed the safe passage toll of the great gate for the pair of workers,

xi 14–16) and lifted the (payment) of *šuila* bread for the craftsmen.

xi 17–19) The administrators no longer plunder the orchards of the poor.

xi 20–24) When a fine ass is born to a *šub-lugal*, and his foreman says to him, "I want to buy (it) from you";

xi 25–28) whether he lets him buy it from him and says to him, "Pay me the price I want!"

xi 29–31) or whether he does not let him buy (it) from him, the foreman must not strike at him in anger.

xi 32–34) When the house of a *šub-lugal* adjoins the house of a *šub-lugal*,

xi 35–37) and this ... says to him, "I want to buy it from you,"

xi 38 – xii 6) whether he lets him buy it from him, having said to him, "Pay me the price I want! My house is a large chest — fill it with barley for me!"

xii 7) Whether he does not let him buy it from him,
xii 8–11) that ... must not strike the *šub-lugal* in anger.

xii 12) (These things) he proclaimed.
xii 13–22) As for the citizens of Lagaš — the one living in debt, the one who had set up (a false) *gur* measure, the one who had (fraudulently) filled up the (legal) *gur* measure with barley, the thief, the murderer — he swept the prison clear (of them) and established their freedom.

---

xi 25.2 ù-da for u$_4$-da.
xi 29.2 u$_4$ nu-šè-sa$_{10}$-sa$_{10}$-a-a.
xi 34.1 A written over AB, then -ús-sa.
xi 38.2 ù-da fo u$_4$-da.
xii 7.2 ù-da for u$_4$-da.

22) e-gar
23) nu-siki nu-ma-kúš
24) lú-á-tuku
25) nu-na-gá-gá-a
26) ^{d}nin-g̃ír-su-da
27) URU-KA-gi-na-ke$_{4}$
28) inim-bi KA e-da-KÉŠDA

xii 23–28) URU-KA-gina made a binding oral agreement with the god Ning̃irsu that he would never subjugate the orphan (or) widow to the powerful.

29) šà-mu-ba-ka
30) i$_{7}$-TUR g̃ír-su.KI-
31) ì-tuku-a
32) ^{d}nin-g̃ír-su-ra
33) al mu-na-dù
34) mu-u$_{4}$-bi-ta-bi
35) e-šè-gar
36) i$_{7}$ ^{d}nin-g̃ír-su nibru.KI-ta nir-gál
37) URU-KA-gi-na-ke$_{4}$
38) mu mu-na-sa$_{4}$

xii 29–38) In that year URU-KA-gina dug for the god Ning̃irsu the "Little Canal which belongs to G̃irsu," and restored its former name, calling it "The God Ning̃irsu Received (His) Authority from Nippur."

39) i$_{7}$-AB×ḪA.KI-du-a
40) mu-na-ni-lá
41) i$_{7}$-kù-ga-am$_{6}$
42) šà-bi dadag-ga-am$_{6}$
43) ^{d}nanše
44) a-zal-le ḫé-na-tùm

xii 39–44) He extended it to the Nimin-DU-a canal. The canal is pure, its flood is bright — may it (ever) bring flowing water to the goddess Nanše!

2

A clay cone and jar fragments from G̃irsu bear an inscription of URU-KA-gina that gives a second recension of the ruler's "Reform Texts." It apparently dates to a later period than inscription E1.9.9.1, when URU-KA-gina had adopted the title "king of G̃irsu."

CATALOGUE

Exemplar	Museum Number	Dimensions (cm)	Lines preserved	cpn
1	MNB 1390	Frgms. A–C	i 2–11	c
		11.5×17.7	ii 2–18	
		Frgm. D	iii 1′–16′	n
		—	iv 8–20	
			v 2′–15′	
			vi 1′–9′	
			vii 1′–5′	
2	AO 12181	5×5×1.1	ii 15–16	c
			iii 8′–12′	
			iv 15–20	
			v	
3	AO 12782	5.2×5.7	v 11′–15′	c
			vi 4′–9′	
4	IM 5642	—	i 5–7	n
			ii 3–14	
			iii 1′–12′	

COMMENTARY

The master text is ex. 1; it was found (in four pieces) in Tell H at G̃irsu (see de Sarzec Découvertes 1 pp. 61 and 110–11).

The restriction of building activities of URU-KA-gina to G̃irsu, and Tiraš and Antasur (the latter two towns are likely to be located in the environs of G̃irsu) attests to the diminished territory controlled by URU-KA-gina at the time of the redaction of this inscription.

In col. ii line 4 for akkil, see Diri I 229–38 ak-kil GADA.KÍD.SI = *ik-ki-lum* "lamentation, clamour, uproar" = *rig-mu* "cry, noise" = *ši-si-tum* = "cry, clamour" *tan-nu-qa-tum* "battle cry." In addition to the é-akkil of our text, é-akkil is primarily attested as a temple of the deity Ninšubur of the town of Akkil, likely a small settlement in the neighbourhood of Pa-tibira; it is mentioned in the "Temple Hymns" of En-ḫedu-ana between Pa-tibira and G̃irsu. E-akkil is further attested as a temple of Ninšubur at Kiš and as a temple of the goddess Manungal = Nungal; see George, House Most High p. 66 nos. 49–52. For a hymn to Nungal see Sjöberg, AfO 24 (1973) pp. 19–46 with additional fragments cited by Attinger in Eléments p. 51.

In col. ii line 8 GIŠ.igi-tab "blinder," otherwise commonly attested as for blinkers for animals, as for example in the expression igi-tab-anše (Salonen Hippologica p. 131), likely refers in our text to the blinders which keep humans on the unerringly right path.

In col. ii line 15 the reading of the goddess Nin-SAR is not entirely certain; on this question see Selz, Untersuchungen p. 261 nn. 1263–67 where the appearance of the goddess in a Presargonic offering list is mentioned. The goddess's role as "butcher" is unequivocal. For the latest discussion of the deity, see Cavigneaux and Krebernik, RLA 9 pp. 484–86.

In col. iii line 12, for the canal name Pa-saman-KAŠ$_4$.DU, see Bauer, BiOr 46 (1989) col. 639. The writing KAŠ$_4$.DU probably indicates a phonetic complement ša$_4$, with KAŠ$_4$.DU interpreted as /kaša/. However, the precise nature of the sibilant in KAŠ$_4$ is by no means certain; the reading with -Š is conventional (see Attinger, Eléments p. 582 § 584). In favour of a reading /kas/, see Alster and Geller, CT 58 pl. 45 line 47 (an OB balag of Ninurta): ur-sag ki-bala KAŠ$_4$-a bí-in-du$_{11}$ compared with Delitsch, VS 2 no. 3 rev. col. i line 33 [ur-sag ki-ba]la-šè ka-sa mi-ni-du (cited by Attinger in Eléments p. 581 § 583 ex. 311). However, while a value ša$_4$ for DU is attested, the author is not aware of any value sa for DU. The element DU is certainly not to be seen as the auxilary element used to form compound verbs with kaš$_4$; it occurs only as du$_{11}$/e/di, never DU (see Attinger, Eléments p. 581).

In col. iv line 5 the GN is restored as G̃irsu based on the parallel in col. vii line 2′.

For the reading of col. v 6″, see Bauer, AoN 21 (1985) p. 8.

BIBLIOGRAPHY

1884–1912 de Sarzec, Découvertes 1 pp. 110–11 (ex. 1, study); Découvertes 2 pp. XXX–XXXI (ex. 1, translation); p. L OUROU-KAGHINA 3 (ex. 1, copy); pl. 32 (ex. 1, photo)

1888 Amiaud, in Sayce (ed.), RP NS 1 pp. 71–72 (ex. 1, partial translation)

1900 Radau, EBH pp. 53–54 (ex. 1, partial edition)

1907 Thureau-Dangin, SAK pp. 44–47 Uru-ka-gi-na g (ex. 1, edition)

1920 Deimel, Orientalia 2 pp. 1–31 (ex. 1, study)

1931 Deimel, AnOr 2 pp. 75–78 (ex. 1, study)

1936 de Genouillac, FT II pl. XLII (exs. 2–3, copy)

1959 Sollberger, CIRPL p. xiv Ukg. 1–3 (exs. 1–3, study); pp. 48–49 Ukg. 1–3 (exs. 1–3, copy)

1959 Sollberger, ZA 53 p. 6 Ukg. 62 and n. 11 (ex. 4, study)

1963 Kramer, Sumerians pp. 320–21 § C 25 (exs. 1–4, translation)

1973 Hruška, ArOr 41, pp. 4–13 and 104–32 (exs. 1–4, study)

1982 Steible, ASBW 1 pp. 278–97 Uruinimgina1 (exs. 1–4, edition)

1986 Cooper, SARI 1 pp. 74–76 La 9.2 (translation)

1986 Carroué, ASJ 8 p. 16 and n. 19 (study)

TEXT

Col. i	
1) [^{d}nin-ğír-su]	i 1–2) For the god [Ninğirsu, warrior of] the god En[lil],
2) [ur-sağ-^{d}]e[n-líl]-lá-ra	
3) URU-KA-gi-na	i 3–5) URU-KA-gina, king of G̃irsu,
4) lugal-	
5) ğír-su.!KI-ke$_4$	
6) an-ta-sur-ra	i 6–7) built (in) the (town of) Antasur (Northern[?] Boundary), his E-ḫegal-kalama "House — prosperity of the land"
7) é-ḫé-⸢ğál⸣-kalam-ma-[ka]-ni	
8) é-gal-ti-ra-áš-ka-ni	i 8–9) and his "palace" of (the city of) Tiraš;
9) mu-na-dù	
10) ⸢é⸣-^{d}ba-ba$_6$	i 10–11) [he] built the [te]mple of the goddess Baba (in G̃irsu).
11) [mu-n]a-dù	
(ca. 5 or 6 lines broken away)	(ca. 5 or 6 lines broken away)

Col. ii
1) [^{d}ig-alim-ma-ra]
2) [é-me-ḫuš]-gal-[an-ki]
3) m[u-na-dù]
4) ^{d}š[ul-šà]-ga-[na-ra]
5) ki-tu[š-akkil-lí-ni]
6) mu-[na-dù]
7) ^{d}[lama]-sa$_6$-[ga]
8) GIŠ.i[gi-tab]-⌜ba-ni⌝
9) é-ni mu-na-dù
10) šà-ba
11) ^{d}za-za-ru$_9$
12) ^{d}ní-pa-è
13) ^{d}úr-nun-ta-è-a
14) é mu-ne-ni-dù
15) ^{d}nin-SAR
16) [g̃í]r-lá-^{d}[nin-g̃]ír-su-[ka]-ra
17) [é-ni]
18) [mu-na-dù]
(ca. 4 or 5 lines broken away)
Col. iii
(ca. 3 or 4 lines broken away)
1′) [^{d}en-líl-l]a
2′) <é->[a]d-da-[i]m-sag-gá-ka-ni
3′) mu-na-dù
4′) ^{d}nanše
5′) i$_7$-ki-ág-gá-ni
6′) i$_7$-AB×ḪA.KI-du-a
7′) al mu-na-dù
8′) ka-ba é-ninnu
9′) ì-dù
10′) kug̃-ba é-sirarà.KI
11′) ì-dù
12′) ^{d}nin-g̃ír-s[u-ra]
13′) [i$_7$-ki-ág-gá-ni]
14′) [pa$_5$-^{d}sam]à[n-KAS$_4$.DU
15′) [al] mu-[n]a-dù
16′) [x]-ba an-[x(?)] ⌜x⌝-ra
(ca. 3 lines broken away)
Col. iv
1) [u$_4$ ^{d}nin-g̃ír-su]
2) [ur-sag-^{d}en-líl-lá-ke$_4$]
3) [URU-KA-gi-na-ra]
4) nam-lugal-
5) [g̃ír-su.KI]
6) [e-na-sum-ma-a]
7) [šà-lú-36000-ta]
8) [šu-ni e-ma-ta-da]b$_5$-⌜ba⌝-a
9) u$_4$-ba
10) lú-má-laḫ$_5$-da-ke$_4$
11) má e-dab$_5$-ba-a
12) anše ú-du-le
13) udu ú-du-le
14) e!(Text: MÀ)-dab$_5$-ba-a
15) ù-múú-mu$_{11}$(KA×SAR)
16) enku-re$_6$

ii 1–3) [For the god Igalim] he [built E-meḫuš]gal-[anki] "House of the Great, Fearsome Mes of Heaven and Earth" (in G̃irsu),
ii 4–6) for the god Š[ul-ša]ga[na] he built his Kit[uš-akkile] "Seat of Lamentations" (in G̃irsu),

ii 7–9) for [Lama]sa[ga], his (protective) b[linkers], he built her temple,

ii 10–14) and within it he built temples for the deities Zazari, Nipaʾe, and Urnuntaʾe.

ii 15–18) For the deity Nin-SAR, [Ning̃]irsu's [bu]tcher, [he built his/her temple (in G̃irsu)].

(ca. 4 or 5 lines broken away)

(ca. 3 or 4 lines broken away)
iii 1′–3′) F[or the god Enlil] he built his <E>-ada of [I]msag.

iii 4′–7′) For the goddess Nanše, he dug her beloved canal, the Nimen-DU-a canal,

iii 8′–11′) and built the E-ninnu at its beginning and the E-sirara at its end.

iii 12′–15′) [For] the god Ning̃irsu, he du[g his beloved canal, the Pa-saman-KAŠ].DU.

iii 16′) Too broken for translation
(ca. 3 lines broken away)

iv 1–2) [When the god Ning̃irsu, warrior of the god Enlil],
iv 3–6) [granted the kingship of G̃irsu to URU-KA-gina],

iv 7–8) [sele]cting him [from among the myriad people],
iv 9) at that time,
iv 10–11) because the head boatman appropriated Boats,
iv 12–14) because the livestock official appropriated asses and sheep,

iv 15–17) because the fisheries inspector appropriated taxes... ,

ii 10′.2 Written in two lines.

17) e-dab$_5$-ba-a
18) še-gub-ba
19) gudu$_4$-ge!(Text:NUN)-ne
20) AMBAR[.KI-a]
(4 lines broken away)
25) [lú-éš-gíd]
26) ⸢gala-ḫé⸣
27) ⸢lú-bappìr⸣-[ḫé⸣
28) agrig-ḫé
29) ugula-ḫé
30) bar-sila$_4$-gaba-ka-ka
31) kù a-gá-gá-a
32) ⸢dumu-lagaš.KI⸣
(ca. 2 or 3 lines broken away)
Col. v
(ca. 5 or 6 lines broken away)
1′) [sanga-GAR-ke$_4$]
2′) kiri$_6$-ama-ukú!(=GÀ.DU)-rá
3′) nu-laḫ$_5$
4′) giš na nu-ba-ni-ri-ri
5′) gi-lìm(LAM) nu-ta-kéš-DU
6′) ad$_x$ (=LÚ×BAD+BAD+A) ki-maḫ-šè D[U]
7′) kas-ni d[ug] 3
8′) ninda-ni 60[+20]
9′) 1 GIŠ.n[á]
10′) 1 maš-sag-[gá]
11′) uru[ḫ](UḪ.INAN[NA])-e
12′) ba-tùm
13′) 1 (gur) še-am$_6$
14′) lú-umum-ma-ke$_4$
15′) ba-tù[m]
(ca. 3 or 4 lines broken away)
1″) ⸢é⸣-[éns]i-k[e$_4$]
2″) níg-énsi-ke$_4$
3″) en-na tuku-a
4″) ^{d}nin-g̃ír-su
5″) [l]ugal-bi
6″) ⸢é⸣ É-MÍ
7″) [níg É.MÍ]
8″) [en-na tuku-a]
9″) [^{d}ba-ba$_6$]
10″) [nin-bi]
Col. vi
1) [é-nam-dumu]
2) [níg-é-nam-dumu]
3) [^{d}šul-šà-ga-na]
4) [lugal-bi]
5) [igi-nu-du$_8$]
6) [zár-ra-a]
7) [gub-ba]
8) [ninda-ka-gub-ba-ni 1-am$_6$]
9) [ninda-gi$_6$-ba-a-ka-ni 5-am$_6$]
10) [ninda-U$_4$.SÁ]-ka 1-a[m$_6$]
11) ninda-gi$_6$-a-na-ka-ni 6-am$_6$
12) 480 ninda-durun-durun-na
13) ninda-dub-ba-am$_6$

iv 18–20) [because] lustration priests [paid] grain taxes [at] AMBAR;

iv 25–29) and because, [whether he be a surveyor], or a lamentation singer, or a brewer, or a supervisor, or a foreman,

iv 30–31) (a person) paid (a duty) in silver instead of an offering lamb,
iv 32) a citizen of Lagaš
(ca. 2 or 3 lines broken away)

(ca. 5 or 6 lines broken away)
v 1′–3′) [The ... administrators] no longer plunder the orchards of the poor,

v 4′–5′) neither do they fell trees there nor tie up bundles/baskets.
v 6′) When a corpse is brought for burial,
v 7′–11′) the undertaker takes his 3 j[ugs] of beer, his ⸢80⸣ loaves of bread, one be[d], and one ...

v 12′–15′) The old (wailing) woman tak[es] one *gur* (72 l.) of barley.

(ca. 3 or 4 lines broken away)
v 1″–5″) [He installed] the god Niñgirsu as proprietor over the [rule]r's estate and the ruler's property, as much as he possessed,

v 6″–10″) [the goddess Baba as proprietor over] the estate of the woman's organization [and the property of the woman's establishment, as much as she possessed],

vi 1–4) [and the god Šulšagana as proprietor over the children's estate, as much as they possessed].

vi 5–9) [For the blind ones waiting anxiously one loaf is his dining bread, five are their loaves of bread at dawn(?)],

vi 10–17) one is [their loaf of bread at noon], six are their loaves of bread at night, 480 loaves of dry bread are the bread duty, 40 loaves of fresh bread are for dining, and 10 loaves of fresh bread are the table

v 13′.3 Omits -am$_6$.

14) 40 ninda-kúm	bread,
15) ninda-zú-gub-ba-am$_6$	
16) 10 ninda-kúm	
17) ninda-banšur-ra-kam	
18) ninda-lú-zi-ga-k[a] 3[+2]	vi 18) 5 loaves of bread [are] for the conscript;
19) [2 kas-LAK 449 1 sá-du$_{11}$]	vi 19–21) [5 ... vessels and 1 *sadug*-vessel of beer are for the lamentation singers of G̃irsu];
20) [gala-]	
21) [g̃ír-su.KI-kam]	
22) [490 ninda]	vi 22–25) [490 loaves of bread, 2 ... vessels and one *sadug*-vessel of beer are for the lamentation singers of Lagaš];
23) [2 kas-LAK 449 1 sá-du$_{11}$]	
24) [gala-]	
25) [lagaš.KI-kam]	
26) [406 ninda]	vi 26–28) [406 loaves of bread, one ... vessel, and one *sadug*-vessel of beer are for the (other) lamentation singers];
27) [1 kas-LAK 449 1 sá-du$_{11}$]	
28) [gala-am$_6$]	
29) [250 ninda]	vi 29–31) [250 loaves of bread and] one ... ves[sel of beer] are for the "old (wailing) women";
30) 1 ⌜LAK 449⌝-[kas]	
31) nam-um-m[a-am$_6$(?)]	
32) 180 ninda	vi 32–34) and 180 loaves of bread and one ... vessel of beer are for the "old woman" of Nig̃in.
33) 1 LAK 449-kas	
34) UNU =ABA$_4$).IGI. AB×ḪA.KI-kam	
35) add[ir$_X$](=PAD.DUG.[GIŠ.SI])-a-bu[l$_X$] (ZA[R])[-la]	vi 35) The tar[rif]/ wa[ge] of the city-gat[e]
(ca. 5 or 6 lines broken away)	ca. 5 or 6 lines broken away)
Col. vii	
(ca. 9 or 10 lines broken away)	(ca. 9 or 10 lines broken away)
1′) ⌜nam⌝-[lugal]-	vii 1′–3′) When [URU-KA-gina] received [the [kingship] in G̃irsu,
2′) g̃ír-su[.KI]	
3′) šu ba-ti-a	
4′) ama-gi$_4$-bi	vii 4′–5′) he cancelled their obligations.
5′) e-gar	

3

A clay plaque from G̃irsu is inscribed with a third recension of URU-KA-gina's "ReformTexts."

COMMENTARY

The plaque was found in excavations of de Sarzec and bears the museum number EŞ 1717.

The copy given by Sollberger in CIRPL has been superceded by that given by Donbaz in OrAt 15 (1976) pp. 6–7. While the divergences noted by Donbaz from Sollberger's copy have been included in this edition they are not listed as variants; a list is given in Steible, ASBW 1 pp. 322–24.

Col. ii lines 0′-1′ are restored on the basis of E1.9.9.1 col. iv lines 22–23.

In col. ii line 5′ the translation of addir$_x$ is uncertain; cf. Selz (AoF 22 [1995] p. 204) writes: "Die Frage, welche genaue Bedeutung /addir/ in diesem Kontext hat kann ich nicht beantworten ..."

In col. ii line 11′, for ur$_5$ SAG×ḪA, see first the comments of Civil, BiOr 40 (1983) cols. 565–56:

> The second example [of SAG×ḪA] has been known for a long time. It is one of the abuses that Urukagina seeks to remedy: dumu uku-rá-ke$_4$, ḪAR.SAG×HA-na ù-mu-ak ku$_6$-bi lú ba-da$_5$-kar-ré Ukg 6 ii 10′ff. "When a poor man made his ..., they took away the fish ... . ."
>
> There is general agreement on the translation: "laid out a fish pond" (Kramer, The Sumerians 322), "faisait un vivier" (M. Lambert, RA 50 175, "made a fishing-pond(??)" (Diakonov, RA 52 9), "sich einen Fischteich macht" (Hruska, ArOr 41 118), etc.
>
> The term ḪAR.SAG×ḪA ... consists of ḪAR,

> probably to be read ḫar or ur_5, in the meaning "hole," and of SAG×ḪA in a genitive construction: "he made his own hole of fish(?) (= to keep/breed fish)."

On this term see further Alster, RA 85 (1981) p. 6. Most recently this passage has been discussed in a detailed study by Steiner in Studies Römer pp. 397–413, and his basic understanding has been accepted for this edition.

In col. ii line 22′ the -NI- infix in the verb indicates a locative element in the sentence; we therefore understand sag as /sag̃a/ exhibiting the phenomenon called by Falkenstein as "überhangenden Vokal." A reading of the beginning of the line as lú-sag̃ would apparently be ruled out as this profession does not occur in ED administrative period texts from Fara (see Visicato, Indices of Early Administrative Tablets from Šuruppak p. 120), or apparently at G̃irsu (see Selz, Untersuchungen p. 402). For the LÚ.SAG.MEŠ "eunuchs" in Neo-Assyrian texts, see Parpola, Letters from Assyrian Scribes 2 pp. 20–21 and compare in this connection the extensive discussion given in Grayson, "Eunuchs in Power: Their Role in the Assyrian Bureaucracy,' in Dietrich and Loretz (eds.), Studies von Soden[2], pp. 85–98.

Concerning col. ii line 30′ we may note Sjöberg's comment on the writing of the term in this text (PSD A/2 p. 178):

> In Uruinimgina 6 ii 30′ and iii 4′ (see 1.2 above) NUN-ME.KA×ME and NUN.ME.KA×KAR_2 are prolonged by -l, therefore the readings $abgal_2$(NUN.ME.KA×KAR_2) and $abgal_3$(NUN.ME.KA×ME) are used. However, it should be noted that abgal (NUN.ME) occurs in ED Lu A 15 (Lexical 1.) and $abgal_2$ (NUN.ME.KA×KAR_2, NUN.ME. KA×$ŠE_3$-*tenû* in the same list line 52 (Lexical 2.). The reading $abgal_3$ might not exist; since wr. NUN. ME.KA×ME in Uruinimgina 6 ii 30′ is probably a scribal error; the reading of NUN.ME.KA×KA_2 as $abgal_2$ remains somewhat doubtful (in spite of the prolongation by -l). Based on the writing KA×KAR.NUN.ME in YOS 1, 12 iv 17 (ED Lu A 52, Lexical 2. above) a reading KA×KAR_2-abgal is a possibility.

According to the PSD abgal can have three basic meanings in Sumerian texts: 1) "a profession" (in Archaic and Presargonic texts — for examples in the the Fara texts see Visicato, Indices of Early Dynastic Administrative Tablets of Šuruppak p. 109) where 29 references to three abgals are given; 2) "a profession, a cultic functionary" (in Ur III, OB and Post OB texts); and 3) "a mythological sage." Similarly (according to CAD) the loan word *apkallu*(*m*) in Akkadian can have the three meanings: 1) "wise man, expert," 2) "a mythological sage," 3) "a priest or exorcist." In our text, meaning 3 is most likely meant; it apparently occurs here in the context of a funeral (so Sjöberg, PSD A/II p. 176). Of interest in this connection is the text Allote de la Füye, DP 187 in which an abgal priest of Nanše is mentioned with a gala-maḫ "chief lamentation singer"; the latter is clearly a figure connected with funerals. Also of note is the appearance of the abgal (NUN.ME) priest in an account dealing with the terminal illness of Gilgameš in the literary composition "The Death of Gilgameš"; see Cavigneaux and al-Rawi, Gilgameš et la Mort. Textes de Tell Haddad VI p. 14 line 2″. With the meaning of "expert," Akkadian *apkallu*(*m*) occurs in a text which relates how the gods Šamaš and Adad revealed the lore of *bārû* divination of the antediluvian king Enmeduranki of Sippar (see now Lambert, in Studies Borger pp. 141–58). Akkadian *apkallu*(*m*), in turn, was loaned into Aramaic; Kaufmann, Akkadian Influences p. 34, notes:

> apkallu, "a priest"—Palm., Nab., Hat. ʾpkl. The term occurs as well in E[pigraphic] S[outh] A[rabian] and appears to have been the name of a high religious functionary among early Arab peoples. If the Sumerian etymology is correct, it might have been an early loan into the Arabic cultural sphere and may represent an Arabic rather than an Aramaic title in the monumental texts.

While no absolutely certain English translation of abgal in the context of the URU-KA-gina inscriptions is certain, we have tentatively opted for "exorcist" following the suggestion of the PSD.

A possible idea of the role of the abgal priest can be gained from a much later Assyrian ritual text that gives a long description of the fabrication of *apkallu* figurines; the text was copied Ebeling as WVDOG 34 no. 298 and edited by Gurney, AAA 22 (1935) pp. 64–67 and Ritter, Assyrisch-babylonische Kleinplastik magischer Bedeutung vom 13.–6. Jh. v. Chr. pp. 151–54. For the corresponding figurines found in excavations and depicted in Neo-Assyrian art, see Rittig, Assyrisch-babylonische Kleinplastik magischer Bedeutung vom 13.–6. Jh. v. Chr. chapters 5 and 8, Green, Iraq 45 (1983) pp. 88–90 and pls. IX–X, and D. Kolbe, Die Reliefprogramme religiös-mythologischen Charakters in neu-assyrischen Palästen pp. 14–30 and pls. 3–4. These appear either as bird men or men cloaked with a fish-like garment.

In col. iii line 10′ for níg-zuḫ-a = *šurqu*(*m*) "stolen good," cf. Meissner, MAOG 1/2 (1925) pp. 10 and 48, line 173: níg-zuḫ-a = *šur-qu*; níg-zuḫ can also be equated with *šarrāqu*(*m*) "thief." Steinkeller, Sale Documents p. 331–32 note to lines 7–8, gives various lexical references proving a reading of ní-zuḫ instead of the im-zuḫ that had been given by Falkenstein in Gerichtsurkunden 1 p. 74 n. 6. Alternately, ní-zuḫ can also mean "thief."

In col. iii line 11′ for za-áš-da = Akkadian *kiššātu*(*m*) "indemnity payment, restitution," see Wilcke, AfO 25 (1974–77) p. 115, Steinkeller, RA 74 (1980) pp. 178–79, idem, Sale Documents p. 332 note to line 9, and Wilcke, NABU 1991 no. 16.

In col. iii line 12′ for níg-ú-gu_x(=PAD)-dé-a, cf. SIG_7.ALAN = nabnītu Tablet IV-IVa lines 283–84 (Finkel, MSL XVI p. 87): ú-gù-dé = *na-'a-bu-tum* "escaped," lú-ú-gù-dé = *mun-nab-tum* "fugitive." Cf. Erim-ḫuš V line 208 (Cavigneaux, et al., MSL XVII p. 77): ù-gù-dé *ḫa-la-qu* and Izi = *išātu* Tablet F line 314 (Civil, MSL XIII p. 194): ú-gù-dé-a *ḫa-la-a-qu* "to disappear, vanish." Cf. *Ana ittišu* VII col. iv lines 13–22 (Landsberger, MSL 1 pp. 103–104): [t]ukum-bi lú sag-gá-e lú-ḫun-gá-e-dè ba-úš ba-an-záḫ ugu bi-in-dé-e gà-la ba-an-dag ù tu-ra ba-ra-ak á-bi u_4-1-kám bán-še-ta-àm an-ág-ág "If a man hires a slave and then the slave either dies or vanishes or escapes or stops working or gets sick, that man will measure out 1 ban of grain (as payment)." The term may be connected with the Sumerian compound gù ... dé = Akkadian *šasû(m)*. The latter is attested with the meaning "to make an outcry against, to make a claim against" in reference to runaway slaves.

In col. iii line 15′ we read rib-ba for Steible's DAG-ba. For the translation, cf. Ea IV line 305 (Civil, MSL XIV p. 307): ri-ib KAL MIN (= gu-ru) *šu-tu-qu*; *šūtuqu*, according to CDA p. 84, can have the meaning "to trangress moral limits" as well as "to exceed in rank." Perhaps the term refers here to a woman who steps above her expected status or rank in society. For the clear differentiation between the rib and kal signs in ED texts, see Krebernik, ZA 76 (1986) p. 162 and n. 4.

In col. iii line 16′ the expression KA-KA-NI has engendered considerable discussion. Noting parallels in various early legal texts, van Dijk (ZA 55 [1962] p. 78 n. 17) transliterated ka-giri$_x$(KA) and translated "Gesicht und Nase(?)"; Edzard (Gerichtsurkunden p. 90) read ka kìri-na and translated "in ihren Mund (und) ihre Nase." Steible, ASBW 1 col. iii line 16′, on the other hand, read ka-ka-ni, citing the discussion of G. Farber-Flügge, in Inanna und Enki, pp. 48–49, and her reference to Landsberger and Civil's note in MSL IX p. 145: "the correctness [of the reading] ka-ka-na 'in its mouth' is proven by its frequent occurrence in the texts; A. i. VI ii 27 and often in literary debates and dialogues." In this reading she was followed by Krecher in ZA 63 (1973) pp. 188–92, Müller, AoF 6 (1979) p. 264 n. 10, Kienast in ZA 72 (1982) p. 41, Steible, ASBW 1 p. 318 line 16′ and Steinkeller, Sale Documents p. 55. A conceivable reading of KA-KA in some of the comparable early legal passages is zú-zú "teeth." Jestin, BiOr 26 (1969) pp. 355–56 suggested KA-KA-na could be read zú-zú-na "parmi ses dents" or zú-ka-na "parmis des dents de sa bouche." Further, Hackett and Huehnergard (Harvard Theological Review 77 [1984] pp. 259–75) have provided a very interesting study of a comparison of biblical and Akkadian parallels dealing with the "breaking of teeth" as a punishment; in the Biblical texts there is commonly found a reference to the breaking of teeth for "oral trespasses (lying, false accusations and tauntings). In the latter case, a punishment designed to inflict pain on the enemy's mouth is, of course, particularly fitting." If we read rib-ba in line 15′ and understand "speaking in a manner exceeding her status" or something similar to this, then the punishment may have been seen to fit the crime; admittedly, in view of the obscurity of the URU-KA-gina passage, this is far from certain. A very rough parallel would be found in the Ur-Nammu Lawcode § 22 (Finkelstein, JCS 22 [1969] p. 70 lines 45–52): tukum-bi géme-lú nin-a-ni-gin$_7$ dim-a-ar áš ì-ni-du$_{11}$ 1-sìla-mun-àm KA.KA-ni ì-sub$_6$(TAG)-bé "If someone's slave-woman, presuming her to be the equal of her mistress, has sworn at her, she shall scour out her mouth with one quart of salt."

For šuš, cf. Ea I 342–344: šú-ú ŠÚ bar-te-nu-u *e-re-bu šá* ᵈUD-*ši* "to set of the sun," MIN (= šú-ú) MIN (= bar-te-nu) *e-re-pu šá u$_4$-mi* "to grow dark of the storm," šú-uš ŠÚ MIN (= bar-te-nu) *sa-ḫa-pu* "to envelop, overwhelm." The passage would seem to describe the covering over of a women's mouth with a baked clay object.

The interpretation of col. iii lines 20′–24′ is particularly difficult. Edzard, Genava 8 p. 256, considered it as the abolishment of an earlier practice of fraternal polyandry "neben dem Mann, der zuerst mit einer Frau die Ehe eingeht ... auch dessen Bruder Zutritt zu der Frau." Von Soden, in Edzard, Fischer Weltgeschichte I p. 86 considered it to be a reform of earlier abuses connected with marriage and divorce. However, it may be (as Selz in RIM readers' notes suggests) that the verb tuku here refers not to marriage in a strictly formal legal sense but rather to the "taking" of two "wives" with the purpose of the second "wife" as being a kind of "insurance policy" for debt release. The fact that an allusion to idemnity (for debts) may have been abolished in the following line supports this hypothesis; relieved of potential debt servitude a man would no longer need to take two "wives."

In col. iii lines 25′–26′ the sequence ensi, igi-du$_8$, NÍG.ŠUB.ŠUB and nagar ki-a dù-dù is partially paralleled by ED Lu List C (unfortunately, an unduplicated text), col. iii lines 29–31 (Civil, MSL XII p. 14): nagar:KI (meaning unknown), x-igi-du$_8$ "seer," ME(?)⌉.EN.LI "dream interpreter." In the URU-KA-gina text, NÍG.ŠUB.ŠUB may possibly be related to the term giš-šub-šub cf. Ḫḫ I line 21: giš-šub-ba = *is-qu* "lot (a device to determine a selection)" and the line connected to a divinatory figure who determines omens by casting lots. The practice is paralleled by Hebrew *qesem* "divination by lot or sign"; see Henshaw, Female and Male pp. 171–72. The actual Sumerian term níg-šub-ba, with a variant reading níg-im-šub-ba, does appear in a bilingual incantation (Falkenstein, Haupttypen p. 95 line 16 and Kilmer and Landsberger, MSL IX p. 108 line 16) but níg-šub-ba is translated there into Akkadian as *ra-ʾa-ša-nu* and likely denotes a kind of illness of the head (see von Soden, AH2 p. 960 sub *rāšānu*). It is likely not relevant to understanding the URU-KA-gina passage.

Col. iii line 28′, in view of the three preceding lines, almost certainly refers to some kind of divination but the interpretation is uncertain. Diakonoff (VDI 1951 p. 28) suggests that it refers to a building oracle.

In col. iii line 29′, we have followed Struve (Trudy 25-ogo kongressa pp. 178–86) in interpreting the beginning of the line as urudu:ti(TI-URUDU) and seeing an example of belomancy (using arrows for divinatory purposes). This technique was practised by the Greeks and later by the Arabians, although its use was forbidden in the Koran. In the Bible (Ezekiel 21:21–22) the prophet Ezekiel narrates an incident in which king Nebuchadnezzar II of Babylon stood at the parting of two ways and used a threefold rite of divination — shaking arrows, consulting the household gods (teraphim), and inspecting the liver. The passage is elucidated by St Jerome:

> He will stop on the crossroads and will consult the oracles following the rites of his nation, placing arrows in a quiver and mixing them, after having inscribed them and marked them with the names of different adversaries to see which will come against him, and, as a result, what city he has to attack.

According to another source, labels were commonly attached to a given number of arrows, the archers let them fly, and the advice on the label of the arrow which flies farthest was accepted and acted on. For this practice in general in Mesopotamia, see Conetenau, La divination chez les assyriens et les babyloniens pp. 184–86.

In col. iv line 6′, as noted in our commentary on E1.9.3.1 col. ii line 25, šu-ur$_6$ is likely a syllabic writing for šúr = *ezzu* "angry"; see Bauer WO 8 (1975–76) p. 5 n. 29.

For the divinity ḪÉ-ĝír of v 16′, see Bauer, BiOr 46 (1989) col. 640 and Selz, Untersuchungen pp. 140–41. Selz notes:

[^{d}ḪÉ-g̃ír] Dies ist die bereits zur Fāra-Zeit bezeugtes und as. regelmässige Schreibung für späteres ^{d}ḪÉ-g̃ír-nun-na. Dabei steht g̃ír für g̃ír-nun, den "Hohen Weg" das ist die Prozessionstrasse in Girsu. Da ḪÉ mit der Lesung /gan/ als (alter) Allograph zu gemé bestimmt werden kann, bedeutet der Gottes-name "Magd (des 'Hohen) Weges'".

BIBLIOGRAPHY

1884–1912 de Sarzec, Découvertes 2 p. L ÉPOQUE D'OUROU-KAGHINA: PLAQUE OVALE DE TERRE CUITE (copy)
1907 Thureau-Dangin, SAK pp. 54–57 Uru-ka-gi-na i (edition)
1920 Deimel, Orientalia 2 pp. 9–10 (study)
1926 Poebel, in Studies Haupt pp. 238–39 (partial edition, study)
1929 Barton, RISA pp. 84–87 Urukagina 10 (edition)
1931 Deimel, AnOr 2 pp. 75–78 (study)
1956 Kramer, FTS pp. 41ff. (translation)
1956 Lambert, RA 50 p. 141 (study)
1956 Sollberger, CIRPL p. xiv Ukg. 6 study; pp. 53–55 Ukg. 6 (copy)
1958 Diakonoff, RA 52 pp. 1–15 (study)
1959 Rosengarten, RHR 156 pp. 129–60 (study)
1963 Kramer, Sumerians p. 321 § C 26 (translation)
1973 Hruška, ArOr 41 pp. 4–13 and 104–32 (study)
1976 Donbaz and Hallo, OrAnt 15 pp. 1–2 and 6–7 (copy, study)
1982 Steible, ASBW 1 pp. 312–24 Uru'inimgina 6 (edition)
1983 Cooper, SANE 2 pp. 15–16, 29, 33–51 no. 7 (translation)
1986 Cooper, SARI 1 pp. 76–78 La 9.3 (translation)
1986 Steible, Sumer 42 pp. 29–31 (study)
1990 Glassner, in Studies Moran pp. 79–83 (study [of lines iv 20′–24′])
1991 Alster, RA 85 p. 6 (study)
1994 Foxvog, JCS 46 pp. 11–15 (study)
1995 Selz, AoF 22 p. 204 (study)
1995 Quintana NABU p. 23 no. 27 (study)
1996 Westbrook, in Studies Moran pp. 450 and 455 (study)

TEXT

Col. i
Lacuna (about 15 cases broken)
0′) [...]
1′) kù ⸢ù⸣-ri-ri
2′) udu ù-sa$_{10}$
3′) udu-ba udu-sa$_{6}$-ga-bi
4′) lú ba-ta-túm-mu
5′) gudu$_{4}$-ge-ne
6′) še-gub-ba AMBAR.KI a e-ág
7′) gudu$_{4}$-bé-ne
8′) é-še-gub-ba-bi
9′) AMBAR.KI-a ì-dù-dù
10′) ⸢x x x⸣
11′) [agrig-ge-n]e
12′) ⸢ugula⸣-ne
13′) gala-e-ne
14′) engar-ré-ne
15′) lú-bappìr-ke$_{4}$-ne
16′) udu-siki ù-mu-DU
17′) é-gal-la ù-ur$_{4}$
18′) u$_{4}$-da udu e-ḫád
19′) siki-bi é-gal-la a-ba-DU
20′) kù gín-5-am$_{6}$
21′) e-gá-gá-ne
22′) gu$_{4}$-dig̃ir-ré-ne-ke$_{4}$
23′) [ki]-sum-ma-
24′) [é]nsi-ka
25′) ⸢ì⸣-uru$_{4}$
26′) [GANÁ-sa$_{6}$]-ga-
Lacuna (about 15 cases broken)

Lacuna (about 15 cases broken)
i 0′–1′) ... silver.

i 2′–4′) After he bought (some) sheep, one would take away the prime ones from those sheep.

i 5′–9′) The "anointed priests" (had to) measure out grain taxes at (the town of) AMBAR, and those "anointed priests" had (even) to build grain (store)-houses at (the town of) AMBAR for the grain taxes.

i 10′–21′) When the [...], stewards, foremen, lamentation singers, farm-bailiff, or brewers brought a full-fleeced sheep and had it sheared at the palace, (even) though the sheep was white (and therefore of highest value), after the wool was delivered at the palace, they had to pay (an additional payment of) five shekels of silver.

i 22′–26′) The oxen of the gods plowed the garlic [plot] of the [city r]uler, and [the bes]t [fields of the gods became the garlic and cucumber plots of the ruler]

Lacuna (about 15 cases broken)

Col. ii
Lacuna (about 15 cases broken)
0′) [a-muš-ša$_{4}$]
1′) [aša$_{5}$(GÁNA)-ga(?)-g]ál-[l]a-a
2′) igi-nu-du$_{8}$

Lacuna (about 15 cases broken)
ii 0′–7′) After blind workers were taken and set (to work) in the fields (by) [the "Snake Water (canal)"] the *šub-lugal*, for the period (a blind worker) was

3′) a-ba-dab$_5$
4′) ŠUB-lugal-ke$_4$
5′) addir$_X$ (=PAD.DUG.GIŠ.SI) en-na ak
6′) a-nag-nag
7′) nu-na-sum-mu

performing his "toll" service(?), gave him no water to drink.

8′) anše a-nag-nag
9′) nu-ba-sum-mu

ii 8′–9′) (The *šub-lug*al) (also) gave no water (to his) ass to drink.

10′) dumu-ukú-rá-ke$_4$
11′) ur$_5$ SAG×ḪA-na
12′) ù-mu-ak
13′) ku$_6$-bi lú ba-da$_5$-kar-ré
14′) lú-bi ì-^{d}utu ì-e

ii 10′–14′) If a poor man had an interest-accruing loan for his fish tank, (his creditor) could take away its fish (simply by) uttering a (simple) "O Sun god" complaint.

15′) lú dam ù-tag$_4$
16′) kù gín-5-am$_6$
17′) énsi-ke$_4$
18′) ba-DU
19′) kù gín-1-am$_6$
20′) sukkal-maḫ-e
21′) ba-DU

ii 15′–21′) After a man divorced his wife, the city ruler took five shekels of silver, the chief vizier took one shekel of silver,

22′) lú sag šembi ì-ni-dé
23′) kù gín-5-am$_6$
24′) énsi-ke$_4$
25′) ba-DU
26′) kù gín-1-am$_6$
27′) sukkal-maḫ-e
28′) ba-DU
29′) kù gín-1-am$_6$
30′) abgal$_x$ (=NUN.ME.KA×ME)-le
31′) ba-DU

ii 22′–31′) After a man rubbed antimony eye-paint on (his) face, the city ruler took five shekels of silver, the chief vizier took one shekel of silver, and the exorcist priest took one shekel of silver.

32′) lú GÌR-a DU
33′) TÚG GA ⌜x⌝ [...]

ii 32′–33′) [If?] a man ...

Lacuna (about 15 cases broken)

Lacuna (about 15 cases broken)

Col. iii

Lacuna (about 15 cases broken)

Lacuna (about 15 cases broken)

1′) ⌜kù x⌝ [...]
2′) énsi-ke$_4$
3′) sukkal-le
4′) abgal$_X$ (=NUN.ME.KA×KÁR)-le
5′) nu-ba-tùm

iii 1′–5′) The city ruler, the vizier, and the exorcist priest no longer take silver.

6′) dumu-ukú-rá-ke$_4$
7′) ur$_5$ SAG×ḪA-na
8′) ù-ak
9′) ku$_6$-bi lú nu-ba-da$_5$-kar-ré

ii 6′–9′) If a poor man had an interest accruing loan for his fish tank, (his creditor) can not take away his fish.

10′) níg-zuḫ-a
11′) za-áš-da-bi ì-šub
12′) níg-ú-gu$_X$(=PAD)-dé-a
13′) a-bul$_5$(ZAR)-la e-lá

iii 10′–13′) Indemnity payments for (possession) of stolen goods have been abolished; lost goods are (now) hung at the city gate.

14′) munus-e nita-ra
15′) ⌜x x x⌝ rib-ba ì-NI-du$_{11}$
16′) munus-ba KA-KA-NI
17′) BAḪÁR(=LAK 742) ì-šuš
18′) BAḪÁR(=LAK 742)-bi
19′) a-bul$_5$(ZAR)-la e-lá

iii 14′–19′) If a female speaks to a male (in a way) exceeding her rank (or position in society) one covers the mouth of that women with a baked clay "brick"(?), and that baked brick is hung (in display) at the city gate.

20′) munus u$_4$-bi-ta-ke$_4$-ne
21′) nita 2-ta
22′) ì-tuku-am$_6$
23′) munus-u$_4$-da-e-ne
24′) za-áš-da-bi ì-šub

iii 20′–24′) As for women of former times — a man (could) take two of them; but for women of today — idemnity payments (for debts?) have been removed (and the practice has been abolished).

25′) ensi(ME+EN.LI)
26′) igi-du$_8$
27′) NÍG.ŠUB.ŠUB
28′) nagar ki-a dù-dù
29′) inim-diĝir-ré-ne-ka
30′) urudu:ti(⸢TI⸣-URUDU)-bi ⸢DA(?)⸣

iii 25′–30′) The dream interpreter, the seer, the thrower of lots (?) the one who sets "pins" in the ground, in the word(s) of the gods, the belomancer(?) ...

Lacuna (about 15 cases broken)

Lacuna (about 15 cases broken)

Col. iv

Lacuna (about 15 cases broken)

Lacuna (about 15 cases broken)

1′) bar-še-ba-ka
2′) lú ḫé-ši-gi$_4$-gi$_4$-a-ka
3′) še-mu ḫa-mu-tùm
4′) ḫé-na-bé-a-ka

iv 1′–4′) Because of that barley, he (En-anatum I) sent envoys to him (Ur-LUM-ma), having them say to him: "You must deliver my barley!"

5′) ur-LUM-ma-ke$_4$
6′) šu-ur$_6$ e-ma-da-du$_{11}$
7′) an-ta-sur-ra
8′) gá-kam ki-sur-ra-mu
9′) bí-du$_{11}$

iv 5′–9′) Ur-LUM-ma spoke arrogantly with him: "Antasur is mine, it is my territory!" he said.

10′) ^{giš}KÚŠU.KI
11′) e-ma-zi
12′) kur-kur-ré šu e-ma-tag-tag

iv 10′–12′) He levied the people of G̃iša (Umma) and got a hold on foreigners for evil purposes.

13′) GANÁ-ù-gig-ga
14′) GANÁ-ki-ág-
15′) ^{d}nin-ĝír-su-ka-ka
16′) ^{d}nin-ĝír-su-ke$_4$
17′) ^{giš}KÚŠU.KI
18′) zi-ga-bi
19′) ì-ḫa-lam

iv 13′–19′) At the Ugiga-field, the beloved field of the god Ninĝirsu, Ninĝirsu destroyed the (troops) levied by G̃iša (Umma).

20′) ur-LUM-ma
21′) énsi-
22′) ^{giš}KÚŠU.KI-a
23′) gàr-dar-ra-ni
24′) SUḪUŠ-*gunû*-i$_7$-LUM-MA-ĝír-nun-ta-ka
25′) gaba-ni-šè ì-DU

iv 20′–25′) He overthrew Ur-LUM-ma, city ruler of G̃iša, at the ... of the LUM-ma-ĝirnunta canal and came right up against him.

26′) anše-ni erén-60-am$_6$
27′) e-šè-tag$_4$
28′) nam-l[ú!-ulù-ba]
29′) [ĝiri-PAD.DU-bi]
30′) [eden-da e-da-tag$_4$-tag$_4$]

iv 26′–30′) (Ur-LUM-ma's) asses — there were sixty teams(?) of them — he abandoned. [He left the bones of their dri]vers(?) [strewn over the Eden district].

Lacuna (about 12 cases broken)

Lacuna (about 12 cases broken)

Col. v

Lacuna (about 12 cases missing)

Lacuna (about 12 cases missing)

1′) mu-na-dù

v 1′) [(For the god Ninĝirsu)] he built [...]

2′) é-bappìr geštin-šita(SÌLA)-gal-gal
3′) lugal-bi-ra túm-ma
4′) mu-na-dù

v 2′–4′) He built the winery in which wine in great vats was brought for its master.

5′) i$_7$-ki-ág-ni
6′) pa$_5$-^{d}samàn-im-ša$_4$
7′) al mu-na-dù

v 5′–7′) He dug his beloved canal, the Pa-saman-imša;

8′) é-^{d}ba-ba$_6$
9′) mu-dù

v 8′–9′) he built the temple of the goddess Baba;

10′) ^{d}ig-alim-ma-ra
11′) é-me-ḫuš-gal-an-ki
12′) mu-na-dù

v 10′–12′) for the god Igalim, he built the E-meḫušgalanki;

13′) ^{d}šul-šà-ga-na-ra
14′) ki-tuš-akkil-lí-ni
15′) mu-na-dù

v 13′–15′) for Šulšagana he built his Kitušakkil;

16′) ^{d}GAŃ-ĝír
17′) lukur-ki-ág-

v 16′–19′) for ḪE-ĝir, beloved *lukur*-priestess of the god Ninĝirsu, he built her temple;

18′) ^{d}nin-g̃ír-su-ka-ra	
19′) é-ni mu-na-dù	
20′) ^{d}lama-sa$_{6}$-ga GIŠ.igi-tab-ba-ni	v 20′–21′) for Lamasaga, his guide, (?) he built her temple;
21′) é-ni mu-na-dù	
22′) ^{d}nin-SAR g̃ír-lá-	v 22′–24′) [for] Nin-SAR, Nin[g̃irsu's] butcher, [he built her temple].
23′) ⸢d⸣[n]i[n-g̃ír-su-ka-ra]	
24′) [é-ni mu-na-dù]	
Lacuna (ca. 10 cases broken)	Lacuna (ca. 10 cases broken)

4

A clay cone fragment from G̃irsu mentions (in a broken context) both URU-KA-gina and the wall of G̃irsu.

COMMENTARY

The cone fragment, which measures 9×11.5 cm, was found during excavations of Cros in 1904 at Tello near the Presargonic wall located near the "Porte-du Diable." It bears the museum number AO 4598. The inscription was collated.

The findspot of the piece is very likely significant and following from this we have interpreted the inscription to be connected with the construction of the (temenos) wall at G̃irsu. Part of the (temenos) wall, labelled as the "rempart pré-sargonique," appears in Cros, Tello, plan K after p. 312. It was partially excavated by Cros in the area of the "Porte-du Diable." The remaining sections were traced out by the French excavators by studying the differing colours appearing on the surface of the mound after the rain. In all, Cros was able to determine a seven-sided precinct. In the paper "Rebuilding E-ninnu" delivered before the 210th meeting of the American Oriental Society in Portland, Oregon March 2000, Frayne discussed the layout of this wall and attempted to show that a later reconstruction of the wall is to be identified as the é-ub-imin "House with Seven Corners" mentioned in Gudea Cylinder A. According to our understanding, a ground plan of the temenos wall is inscribed on the lap of Gudea Statue X following on a hypothesis put forth by Heimpel in JCS 48 (1996) pp. 17–29.

Col. i′ lines 0′–8′ find a parallel in E1.9.9.2 col. iii lines 4′–11′.

The reading of col. ii′ line 3′ has posed scholars some difficulty. Sollberger (Système verbal p. 242 § 132, and ZA 54 [1961] p. 23) read ba-ša$_{6}$-ša$_{6}$-ge$_{9}$-é, assigning NE a syllabic value ge$_{9}$; the reading was accepted by Falkenstein (ZA 55 [1962] p. 45) but questioned by Edzard (Rechtsurkunden p. 116 note to no. 61 col. i line 4, who analysed it as /ba-sasa-(e)d-eš/). Examples of the use of NE for writing g̃e were given by Krecher in Studies Falkenstein pp. 100–101, but in this case it was for the completely distinct phoneme g̃e not ge. We tentatively suggest that the text is to be emended to read ba-sa$_{6}$-sa$_{6}$-<ge>-dè-éš and that the -dè- marks the /ed/ verbal morpheme discussed by Edzard, Studies Falkenstein pp. 29–62 and Yoshikawa, JNES 27 (1968) pp. 251–61.

In col. 3′ line 3′ for da$_{5}$(URUDU) as a variant of dab$_{4}$ "to encircle, surround," see Poebel, AfO 9 (1933–34) pp. 283–87; Jacobsen in Moran (ed.), Tammuz p. 144 n. 49; Krecher, ZA 60 (1970) pp. 197–98; and Falkenstein, Bagh Mit 3 (1964) pp. 37–38, commentary to lines 94–95. Cf. also Dunham, RA 80 (1986) p. 53:

> Da$_{5}$ seems to have meanings similar to dub (*šapāku*, *lamû*) to which it is very close in form. The verb, which is equated with Akkadian *lawû*(*m*), can mean "to encircle" (a city), either by an enemy during a siege or by a city ruler with a city wall. For an example of the latter practice, see Frayne, RIME 4 p. 237 E4.2.13.18 line 19 (Kudur-mabuk): uru-ni ḫé-em-mi-da$_{5}$ "I surrounded his city (with a wall)."

In col. ii′ line 6′ for níg-á-zi ... AK see Civil and Biggs, RA 60 (1966) p. 3 n. 3; Sjöberg, ZA 65 (1975) p. 238 (with previous literature) and Attinger, Eléments pp. 628–29 §§ 681–86.

BIBLIOGRAPHY

1910 Cros, Tello p. 64 (findspot); pp. 213–15 (copy, edition [by Thureau-Dangin])
1952 Sollberger, Système verbal p. 92 n. 1 (partial edition)
1954 Lambert, RA 48 p. 92 (study)
1956 Sollberger, CIRPL p. xiv Ukg. 14 (study); p. 57 Ukg. 14 (copy)
1957 Sollberger, PICO 22 p. 23 (study)
1958 Struve, VDI pp. 8–12 (study)
1966 Lambert, RSO 47 pp. 1-22 (study)
1973 Hruška, ArOr 41 pp. 9 and 125–26 (study)

1974 Hruška, RAI 19 pp. 160–61 (study)
1982 Steible, ASBW 1 pp. 332–33 Uru'inimgian 14 (edition)
1983 Cooper, SANE 2 pp. 16, 35, and 52 no. 8 (translation, study)
1986 Carroué, ASJ 8 pp. 16 and 24 (study)
1986 Cooper, SARI 1 pp. 78–79 La 9.4 (translation, study)

TEXT

Col. i′
Lacuna
0′) [^{d}nanše]
0′ bis) [i$_7$-ki-ág-gá-ni]
1′) ⌜i$_7$⌝-A[B×ḪA].KI-du-a
2′) al mu-na-dù
3′) [k]a-ba
4′) ⌜é⌝-ninnu
5′) ⌜ì⌝-dù
6′) [ku]n-ba
7′) ⌜é⌝-sirarà.[KI]
8′) [ì]-dù
9′) [...]⌜x⌝
Lacuna
Col. ii′
Lacuna
1′) ul ù-⌜šu⌝-mú
2′) u$_4$-10-kam-ma-ka
3′) ba-sa$_6$-sa$_6$-<ge>-dè-éš
4′) gá-e a-na bí-tuk
5′) e-na-du$_{11}$
6′) níg-á-zi-šè nu-AK
7′) ur u$_4$-da
8′) [x u]ru(?)-mu [x (x)] ⌜x⌝
Lacuna
Col. iii′
Lacuna
1′) [...] ⌜x⌝ [...]
2′) ⌜g̃ír⌝-sú.KI
3′) [e]-ma-da$_5$
4′) URU-KA-gi-na-ke$_4$
5′) KU e-da-sìg
6′) bàd-bi ì-ni-mú
7′) ur-NI ì-ti
8′) uru-ni-šè ba-DU
9′) ⌜2⌝-kam-ma-ka
10′) [...]-⌜DU⌝
Lacuna

Lacuna
i 0′–2′) [For the goddess Nanše], (URU-KA-gina) dug [her beloved canal], the Nimin-DU canal.
i′ 3′–5′) At its uptake point he built the E-ninnu (temple).
i′ 6′–9′) At its mouth he buil[t] the E-sirara (temple).
Lacuna

Lacuna
ii′ 1′–3′) On the tenth day they rejoiced.
ii′ 4′–5′) (URU-KA-gina) said, "As for me, what do I have (to my name)?"
ii′ 6′) "I have not committed acts of violence.
ii′ 7′–8′) A man today ...
Lacuna

Lacuna
iii′ 1′–3′) He encircled G̃irsu (with a wall?).
iii′ 4′–5′) URU-KA-gina ...
iii 6′) He made its wall grow up ... .
iii 7′) ...
iii′ 8′) He approached his city.
iii′ 9′) A second time ...
iii 10′) ...
Lacuna

5

A royal inscription of URU-KA-gina preserved on a clay tablet records an attack against Lagaš by Lugal-zagesi of G̃iša (Umma).

COMMENTARY

The tablet, which measures 10.2×9.9×2.3 cm, was found during the first season of excavations of G. Cros at Tello (1903) in "Chantier 4" on Tell K ("Tell de la Maison des fruits") (see Cros RA 6 [1904] p. 17 Plan A and Parrot, Tello p. 25). It now bears the museum number AO 4162. The inscription was collated.

BIBLIOGRAPHY

1907 Thureau-Dangin, RA 6 pp. 26–32 (copy, edition, study)
1907 Thureau-Dangin, SAK pp. 56–59 Uru-ka-gi-na k (edition)
1910 Thureau-Dangin, in Cros, Tello pp. 45–51 (copy, edition, study)
1929 Barton, RISA pp. 88–91 Urukagina 18 (edition)
1956 Sollberger, CIRPL p. xiv Ukg. 16 (study); p. 58 Ukg. 16 (copy)
1957 Sollberger, PICO 22 pp. 29ff (study)
1963 Kramer, Sumerians pp. 322–24 § C 27 (translation)
1963 Lambert, Iraq 25 pp. 192–93 (study)
1965 Komoróczy, Az Ókori Mezopotámia Történetének Šumer és Akkád Nyelvíí Forrásai pp. 14ff. (study)
1966 Lambert, RSO 41 pp. 29ff (study)
1967 Hirsch, in Festschrift Eilers pp. 99–106 (study)
1971 Sollberger and Kupper, IRSA IC11m (translation)
1977 Westenholz, Iraq 39 p. 20 (study)
1982 Steible, ASBW 1 pp. 333–37 Uru'inimgina 16 (edition)
1984 Römer, in Borge et al., TUAT 1 pp. 313–15 (translation)
1986 Cooper, SANE 2 pp. 16, 35–37, and 52 no. 8 (translation, study)
1986 Cooper, SARI 1 pp. 78–79 La 9.5 (translation)
1996 Powell, in Studies Hirsch pp. 307–14 (study)

TEXT

Col. i	
1) lú-⌈^{giš}KÚŠU.KI -ke$_4$⌉	i 1–3) The leader of G̃iša (Umma) set fire to the Ekirbira.
2) e-ki-bìr-ra-ke$_4$	
3) izi ba-sum	
4) an-ta-sur-ra	i 4–5) He set fire to the Antasur
5) izi ba-sum	
6) kù-za-gìn-bi	i 6–7) and bundled off its precious metals and lapis-lazuli.
7) ba-ta-KÉŠ.KÉŠ	
8) é-gal-ti-ra-áš-ka	i 8–9) He plundered(?) the "palace" of Tiraš,
9) šu bi-TIL	
10) abzu-bàn-da-a	i 10–11) he plundered(?) the Abzu-banda,
11) šu bi-TIL	
12) bára-^{d}en-líl-lá	i 12 – ii 1) he plundered the chapels of the gods Enlil and Utu.
13) bára-^{d}utu-ka	
Col. ii	
1) šu bi-TIL	
2) a-ḫuš-a	ii 2–3) He plundered the Aḫuš
3) šu bi-TIL	
4) kù-za-gìn-bi	ii 4–5) and bundled off its precious metals and lapis lazuli;
5) ba-ta-KÉŠ.KÉŠ	
6) é-bábbar-ra	ii 6–7) he plundered the E-babbar
7) šu bi-TIL	
8) kù-za-gìn-bi	ii 8–9) and bundled off its precious metals and lapis lazuli;
9) ba-ta-kéš-kéš	
10) gi-gù-na-	ii 10–13) he plundered the *giguna* of Ninmaḫ of the sacred grove
11) ^{d}nin-maḫ-	
12) tir-kù-ga-ka-ka	
13) šu bi-TIL	
Col. iii	
1) kù-za-gìn-bi	iii 1–2) and bundled off its precious metals and lapis lazuli;
2) ba-ta-KÉŠ.KÉŠ	
3) ba-⌈gára⌉-a	iii 3–4) he plundered the Bagara
4) šu bi-TIL	

5) kù-za-gìn-bi	iii 5–6) and bundled off its precious metals and lapis lazuli;
6) ba-ta-kéš-kéš	
7) dug-ru	iii 7–8) he set fire to the Dugru
8) izi ba-sum	
9) kù-za-gìn-bi	ii 9–10) and bundled off its precious metals and lapis lazuli;
10) ba-ta-KÉŠ.KÉŠ	
11) abzu-e-ga-ka	iii 11–12) he plundered the Abzuʾeg;
12) šu bi-TIL	
13) é-^{d}g̃á-tùm-du$_{10}$-ke$_4$	iii 13–14) he set fire to the temple of G̃atumdu
14) izi ba-sum	
Col. iv	
1) kù-za-gìn-bi	iv 1–2) and bundled off its precious metals and lapis lazuli,
2) ba-ta-KÉŠ.KÉŠ	
3) alan-bi	iv 3–4) and destroyed its statuary;
4) ì-GUL.GUL	
5) ib-é-an-na-^{d}inanna-ka-ke$_4$	iv 5–6) he set fire to the shrine E-anna of Inanna,
6) izi ba-sum	
7) kù-za-gìn-bi	iv 7–8) bundled off its precious metals and lapis lazuli,
8) ba-ta-KÉŠ.KÉŠ	
9) alan-bi	iv 9–10) and destroyed its statuary;
10) ì-GUL.GUL	
11) šà-pà-da	iv 11–12) he plundered the Šapada
12) šu bi-TIL	
13) kù-za-gìn-b[i]	iv 13–14) and bundled off its precious metals and lapis lazuli.
14) ba-ta-KÉŠ.KÉŠ	
Col. v	
1) ḫe-en-da-ka	v 1–2) In Ḫenda, he overturned....
2) MUNSUB (= LAK 672) ì-BAL.BAL	
3) ki-èš.KI	v 3–5) in Kiʾeš, he plundered the temple of NinDARa
4) é-^{d}nin-dar-ka	
5) šu bi-TIL	
6) kù-za-gìn-bi	v 6–7) and bundled off its precious metals and lapis lazuli;
7) ba-ta-KÉŠ.KÉŠ	
8) ki-nu-NIR.KI	v 8–10) in KinuNIR he set fire to the temple of Dumuziabzu
9) é-^{d}dumu-zi-abzu-ka-ke$_4$	
10) izi [b]a-sum	
11) kù-za-gìn-bi	v 11 – vi 1) and bundled off its precious metals and lapis lazuli;
Col. vi	
1) ba-ta-KÉŠ.KÉŠ	
2) é-^{d}lugal-URU×KÁR.KI-ka-ke$_4$	vi 2–3) he set fire to the temple of Lugal-URU×KAR
3) izi ba-sum	
4) kù-za-gìn-bi	vi 4–5) and bundled off its precious metals and lapis lazuli;
5) ba-ta-KÉŠ.KÉŠ	
6) é-engur-ra-	vi 6–8) he plundered Nanše's E-engura
7) ^{d}nanše-ka	
8) šu bi-TIL	
9) kù-za-gìn-bi	vi 9–10) and bundled off its precious metals and lapis lazuli;
10) ba-⸢ta⸣-⸢KEŠ-KÉŠ⸣	
11) sag-⸢ubx⸣(⸢EZEN×BAD⸣)	vi 11) in Sag[ub]
Col. vii	
1) é-^{d}ama-geštin-na-ka	vii 1–2) he plundered (?) the temple of Ama-g̃eštin-Ana,
2) šu bi-TIL	
3) ^{d}ama-g̃eštin-ta	vii 3–5) bundled off precious metals and lapis lazuli (from the statue of) Ama-geštin-Ana,
4) kù-za-gìn-na-ni	
5) ba-ta-KÉŠ.KÉŠ	
6) ⸢pú⸣-ba ì-šub	vii 6) and threw them in a well.
7) GANÁ-^{d}nin-g̃ír-su-ka	vii 7–9) In the fields of Ning̃irsu, whichever were cultivated, he destroyed the barley.
8) en-na uru$_4$-a	
9) še-bi ì-⸢PAD⸣	

10) lú-^{g}[^{iš}]⸢KÚŠU⸣.⸢KI⸣-k[e$_4$]
11) ⸢eger⸣-⸢lagaš⸣(⸢ŠIR.BUR⸣.[LA].KI
12) ba-ḫul-a-ta

vii 10–12) The leader of G̃[iša] (Umma), hav[ing] sacked L[ag]aš,

Col. viii
1) nam-dag
2) ^{d}nin-g̃ír-su-da
3) e-da-ak-ka-am$_6$

viii 1–3) has committed a sin against the god Ning̃irsu.

4) šu in-ši-DU-a-am$_6$
5) e-ta-ku$_5$-ku$_5$

viii 4–5) The hand which he has raised against him will be cut off!

6) nam-dag-
7) URU-KA-gi-na
8) lugal-
9) g̃ír-su.KI-ka
10) nu-gál

viii 6–10) It is not a sin of URU-KA-gina, king of G̃irsu!

11) lugal-zà-ge-si
12) énsi-
13) ^{giš}KÚŠÚ.KI-ka
14) dig̃ir-ra-ni
Col. ix
1) ^{d}nissaba-ke$_4$
2) nam-dag-bi
3) gú-na ḫé-íl-íl

viii 11 – ix 3) May Nissaba, the god of Lugal-zage-si, ruler of G̃iša (Umma), make them (the people of G̃iša) bear this sin on their necks!

6

An inscription of URU-KA-gina on a stone tablet from G̃irsu records various building activities of the king.

COMMENTARY

The tablet, which was formerly in the Collection de Clercq, is now housed in the Louvre, museum number AO 22934. The inscription was collated.

As noted, the "coach-house" and brewery of Ning̃irsu are also mentioned together in inscription E1.9.5.4 of En-metena. The brewery, coach house, storehouse and wine cellar also occur together in Gudea Cylinder A xxviii 10–16 (see Edzard RIME 3/1 p. 87). The findspot of the former de Clercq piece is unknown; perhaps it came from the same general area as E1.9.5.4.

BIBLIOGRAPHY

1903 de Clercq, Collection 2 pl. VIII no. 1 (photo) and p. 72 (study)
1907 Thureau-Dangin, SAK pp. 42–43 Uru-ka-gi-na b (edition)
1929 Barton, RISA pp. 72–75 Urukagina 2 (edition)
1956 Sollberger, CIRPL p. xiv Ukg. 10 (study); p. 56 Ukg. 10 (copy)
1971 Sollberger and Kupper, IRSA IC11a (translation)
1982 Steible, ASBW 1 pp. 326–28 Uru'inimgina 10 (edition)
1986 Cooper, SARI 1 pp. 79–80 La 9.6 (translation)

TEXT

Col. i
1) ^{d}nin-g̃ír-sú
2) ur-sag-^{d}en-líl-lá-ra

i 1–2) For Ning̃irsu, warrior of the god Enlil,

3) URU-KA-gi-na
4) lugal-
5) lagaš.KI-ke$_4$

i 3–5) URU-KA-gina, king of Lagaš,

6) é-ni
7) [m]u-na-dù
8) é-gal-ti-ra-áš-ka-ni
9) mu-⸢na-dù⸣
Col. ii
1) an-ta-sur-erased RA-ra
2) mu-na-dù
3) é-GIŠ.gigir!(Text: NIGÍN)-ra
4) é-<me>-lám-bi-kur-kur-ra!(has extra vertical)-dul$_{5}$
5) mu-na-dù
6) é-bappìr-geštin!-šita$_{6}$-gal-[ga]l kur-ta DU-a
7) mu-na-dù
8) ^{d}šul-šà-ga-na-ra
9) ki-tuš(Text: TÚG)!-akkil!-⸢lí(?)-ni⸣
Col. iii
1) mu-na-dù
2) ^{d}ig-alim-ma-ra
3) é-me-ḫuš-gal-an-ki
4) mu-na-dù
5) é-^{d}ba-ba$_{6}$
6) mu-na-dù
7) ^{d}en-líl-la
8) é-ad-da-
9) im-sag-gá-ka-ni
Col. iv
1) mu-na-dù
2) bur-sag
3) é-sá-du$_{11}$-an-na-ta!(Text: BI)-ÍL-a-ni
4) mu-na-dù
5) URU-KA-gi-na
6) lugal-
7) lagaš.KI
8) lú é-ninnu
9) dù-a
10) diĝir-ra-ni
Col. v
1) ^{d}⸢nin⸣-šubur-ke$_{4}$
2) nam-ti-la-ni-šè
3) u$_{4}$-ul-la!-šè
4) ^{d}nin-ĝír-sú-ra
5) kìri šu ḫé-na-gál

i 6–7) built his temple,

i 8–9) built his "palace" of Tiraš,

ii 1–2) and built the Antasur.

ii 3–5) He built a coach-house for him, a building whose awesome splendour overwhelms all lands,

ii 6–7) and he built for him a winery, which provides (him with) great vats of wine from the mountains.

ii 8 – iii 1) For Šulšagana he built his Kitušakkile,

iii 2–4) and for Igalim he built the E-meḫušgalanki.

iii 5–6) He built the temple of Baba for her.

iii 7– iv 4) For the god Enlil he built his E-ada of Imsag, and built him a pantry, the room where his divine regular offerings are delivered.

iv 5–9) URU-KA-gina, king of Lagaš, who built the E-ninnu —

iv 10 – v 5) may his personal god, Ninšubur, forever pray for his life to Ninĝirsu!

7

A door socket inscription of URU-KA-gina records various temple constructions of the Lagaš ruler.

COMMENTARY

The door socket, which measures 40 cm across and 26 cm high, with the inscription having a diameter of 18 cm, was found in the plain west of the main mound of G̃irsu in the direction towards the Šaṭṭ al-Hai. It bears the museum number AO 120. The inscription was collated.

BIBLIOGRAPHY

1884–1912 de Sarzec, Découvertes 1 pl. 112 (study); Découvertes 2 p. XXX (translation); p. XLIX OUROU-KAGHINA 1 copy); pl. 5 no. 1 (photo)
1907 Thureau-Dangin, SAK pp. 42–45 Uru-ka-gi-na c (edition)
1929 Barton, RISA pp. 74–75 Urukagina 3 (edition)
1956 Sollberger, CIRPL p. xiv Ukg. 11 (study); p. 56 Ukg. 11 (copy)
1982 Steible, ASBW 1 pp. 328–30 Uru'inimgina 11 (edition)
1986 Cooper, SARI 1 p. 80 La 9.7 (translation)

TEXT

1) [^{d}nin-g̃ír-su]
2) [ur]-⌜sag̃-^{d}⌝[e]n-líl-lá-ra
3) [UR]U-KA-[g]i-na
4) [lu]gal-[lag]aš.KI-ke$_{4}$
5) [an]-ta-sur-ra
6) [é]-ḫé-gál-[kal]am-ma-[ka]-ni
7) [mu-n]a-dù
8) [é-gal]-ti-[ra-áš-k]a-ni
9) [mu-na]-dù
10) [...]
11) [...]
12) [^{d}i]g-alim-ma-ra
13) ⌜é⌝-[me-ḫuš-gal-an-ki]
14) [mu-na-dù]
15) [^{d}šul-šà-ga-na-ra]
16) [ki-tuš-akki]l-[lí]-ni
17) [mu-na-dù]
18) [...]
19) [...]
20) mu-na-dù
21) ⌜^{d}⌝nin-SAR
22) [g]ír-lá-
23) ⌜^{d}⌝nin-g̃ír-su!-ka-ra
24) é-ni
25) mu-na-dù
26) [^{d}]⌜ḪÉ⌝-g̃ír
27) [lukur]-⌜ki⌝-ág-
28) ⌜^{d}⌝nin-g̃ír-sú-ka-ra
29) ⌜é⌝-ni
30) [m]u-na-dù
31) bur-sag
32) é-sá-du$_{11}$-an-na-⌜ÍL⌝-a-ni
33) mu-na-dù
34) ^{d}en-líl-la
35) é-ad-da-
36) im-sag-gá-ka-ni
37) mu-na-dù
38) ^{d}nin-g̃ír-su-ra
39) é-GIŠ.gigir-ra
40) é-me-lám-<bi->[kur]-kur-ra-<dul$_{5}$>
41) mu-na-dù
42) ⌜é-x⌝-
43) ⌜^{d}nin-g̃ír-su⌝-ka
44) mu-⌜na⌝-dù
45) URU-KA-gi-na
46) lú é-⌜x⌝-
47) ^{d}nin-gí[r-su-ka-dù-a]

Lacuna

1–2) [For Ning̃irsu, wa]rrior of the god Enlil,

3–4) [UR]U-KA-gina, [ki]ng of [La]gaš,

5–7) [bu]ilt [An]tasura, his temple "Prosperity for the [La]nd";

8–9) [bu]ilt his "palace" of Tiraš;

10–11) [...]

12–14) For [I]galim [he built] the E-[meḫušgalanki]

15–17) and [for Šulšagana he built] his [Kitušakkile].

18–20) [For ...] he built [...].

21–25) For Nin-SAR, Ning̃irsu's butcher, he built her temple,

26–30) and for [Ḫ]E-g̃ir, [b]eloved [*lukur*-priestess] of Ning̃irsu, he built her temple,

31–33) and built her a pantry(?), the room where her divine regular offerings are delivered.

34–37) For the god Enlil he built his E-ada of Imsag.

38–41) For the god Ning̃irsu, he built a coach-house, a building whose awesome splendour <overwhelms> all lands,

42–44) and built the E-⌜x⌝ of the god Ning̃irsu for him.

45–47) URU-KA-gina, who [built] the E-⌜x⌝(?) of Ning̃irsu —

Lacuna

8

An inscription on a brick fragment from G̃irsu deals with URU-KA-gina's building of a cistern for the Nimin-DU canal.

COMMENTARY

The brick fragment, which measures 14×13.5×4 cm, was found in excavations of de Sarzec at G̃irsu; its precise findspot is unknown. It inscription, which bears the museum number AO 349, was collated.

The restoration of the first two columns of this text follows the suggestion given by Cooper in SARI 1 p. 80 La 9.8.

BIBLIOGRAPHY

1884–1912 de Sarzec, Découvertes 2 p. L OUROU-KAGHINA 2 (copy)
1907 Thureau-Dangin, SAK pp. 42–43 Uru-ka-gi-na a (edition)
1929 Barton, RISA pp. 72–73 Urukagina 1 (edition)
1956 Sollberger, CIRPL p. xiv Ukg. 7 (study); p. 55 Ukg. 7 (copy)
1973–74 Bauer, WO 7 pp. 10–11 (study)
1982 Steible, ASBW 1 pp. 324–25 Uru'inimgina 7 (edition)
1986 Cooper, SARI 1 pp. 80–81 La 9.8 (translation)
1986 Carroué, ASJ 8 pp. 17–18 (study)

TEXT

Col. i
1) [^{d}nin-ĝír-su]
2) [ur-sag-^{d}en-líl-lá-ra]
3) [URU-KA-gi-na]
4) [lugal-lagaš.KI-ke_4]
Lacuna(?)
Col. ii
1) [...]
2) [...]
3) [...]
4) [mu-na-dù]
5) [^{d}nanše]
6) [i_7-AB×ḪA.KI-du]
7) [i_7-ki-ág-ni]
Col. iii
1) [al m]u-[na]-dù
2) [URU-K]A-[gi]-na
3) [lu]gal-
4) [lag]aš.[KI]-ke_4
5) [^{d}n]in-ĝír-[su]-ra
6) [p]ú-pú-kù-[(x x)]-kù
Lacuna(?)
1′) [giš-kés-rá]-
Col. iv
1) i_7-AB×ḪA.KI-du
2) mu-na-dù
3) ⌜2 šár-gal⌝ sig_4-⌜BAḪÁR⌝-ra
4) 1820 gur-sag-gál ENGUR
5) mu-na-ni-dù

i 1–2) [For Ninĝirsu, warrior of the god Enlil],

i 3–4) [URU-KA-gina, king of Lagaš],

Lacuna(?)

ii 1–4) [built ...]

ii 5 – iii 1) [For Nanše he d]ug [her beloved canal, the AB×ḪA-DU-a-canal].

iii 2–4) [URU]-KA-[gi]na, [ki]ng of [Laga]š,

iii 5 –6) built for Ninĝirsu the holy cisterns(?) ...,

Lacuna(?)

iii 1′–iv 2) He built [the reservoir] of the Nimin-DU canal.

iv 3–5) He built it for him out of 432,000 fired bricks and 1820 standard *gur* (2649.6 hl.) of bitumen.

6) diĝir-ra-ni
7) ⌈^{d}nin⌉-[šubur-ke$_4$]
Col. v
1) u$_4$-⌈ul⌉-la-šè
2) ^{d}nin-ĝír-su-ra
3) é-ninnu-a
4) kirì šu ḫé-na-gál

iv 6 – v 4) May his personal god, Nin[šubur], forever pray [for his life] to Ninĝirsu in the E-ninnu!

9

A door socket from Ĝirsu records various temple constructions of URU-KA-gina.

COMMENTARY

The door socket was found at Ĝirsu but its precise findspot is not known. It AO number is unknown.

BIBLIOGRAPHY

1956 Sollberger, CIRPL p. 57 Ukg. 12 (copy)
1982 Steible, ASBW 1 pp. 330–31 Uru'inimgina 12 (edition)
1986 Cooper, SARI 1 p. 81 La 9.9 (translation)

TEXT

Lacuna
1′) [...]
2′) é-[gal-ti]-ra-[áš-k]a-ni
3′) [mu]-na-dù
4′) [x]-lugal-ka-ni
5′) [mu]-na-dù
6′) [^{d}b]a-ba$_6$
7′) [...]
8′) [mu-n]a-dù
9′) URU-<KA>-KA-gi-na
10′) lú é-PA-
11′) ^{d}nin-gí[r-su]-ka dù-[a]
12′) [diĝir]-r[a]-ni
13′) ⌈^{d}⌉šul-MUŠ×PA.
14′) u$_4$-ul-⌈la⌉-šè
15′) [^{d}nin-g]ír-sú-[ra]
16′) [nam-ti-la-ni-šè]
17′) [kirì šu ḫé-na-gál]

Lacuna
1′–3′) [For the god Ninĝirsu ... he] built his "pa[lace" of Ti]ra[š],

4′–5′) [and b]uilt his [...] of the master.

6′–8′) For [B]aba he built [her temple].

9′–11′) URU-<KA>-gina, who built the E-PA of the god Ninĝirsu.

12′–17′) [may] his [personal go]d, Šul-MUŠ×PA, forever [pray for his life to Nin]ĝirsu!

10

A brick fragment records URU-KA-gina's construction work on the wall of G̃irsu, the digging of a canal, and the building of various temples.

COMMENTARY

The brick, which measures 18.3×10.3 cm, was found at G̃irsu; its findspot is not known. The inscription, which was not collated, bears the museum number EŞ 6401.

BIBLIOGRAPHY

1956 Sollberger, CIRPL p. xiv Urk. 8 (study); p. 55 Urk. 8 (copy)
1982 Steible, ASBW 1 pp. 325–26 Uru'inimgina 8 (edition)
1986 Cooper, SARI 1 p. 81 La 9.10 (translation)

TEXT

Col. i′	
Lacuna	Lacuna
1′) [...]⸢x⸣	1′–2′) ...
2′) [...]⸢x⸣	
Lacuna	Lacuna
Col. ii′	
Lacuna	Lacuna
1′) [^{d}šul-šà-ga-na]-ra	ii′ 1′–5′) For [Šulšagana] he built his Kituš-akkile, and built a pantry for him, the room where his divine regular offerings are delivered.
2′) ki-tuš-akkil-lí	
3′) mu-na-dù!(Text: NI)	
4′) bur-sag é-sá-du$_{11}$-an-na-ta!(Text:ŠA)-ÍL-a-ni	
5′) mu-na-dù	
6′) bàd-g̃ír-su.KI-ke$_4$	ii 6′) ... the wall of G̃irsu
Lacuna	Lacuna
Col. iii′	
Lacuna	Lacuna
1′) im-[sag]-gá-k[a]-ni	iii′ 1′–2′) [For Enlil] he built his [E-ada] of Imsag̃.
2′) mu-na(Text: KI)-dù	
3′) ^{d}nin-g̃ír-su-ra	iii′ 3′–6′) For Ning̃irsu he dug his beloved canal, the Pasamanu-KAS.DU-canal.
4′) i$_7$-ki-ág-gá-ni	
5′) i$_7$-pa$_5$-^{d}samàn-KAS$_4$.DU	
6′) al mu-na-dù	
Lacuna	Lacuna
Col. iv′	
Lacuna	Lacuna
1′) [URU-KA-gi-na]	iv′ 1′–3′) [URU-KA-gina], ki[ng of] La[gaš]
2′) lu[gal]-	
3′) la[gaš.KI-...]	
Lacuna	Lacuna

11

A vase fragment from Sippar bears a dedicatory inscription of URU-KA-gina to the goddess Baba.

COMMENTARY

The vase fragment, which measures 11×7.5 cm, was found in excavations of H. Rassam at Sippar. The vase has been reconstructed from three pieces: BM 90902 (=12030) (+patch)+AH 82-9-18A+44+82-7-14,1018. The inscription was collated.

BIBLIOGRAPHY

1899 King, CT 7 pl. 3 BM 12030 (copy)
1929 Barton, RISA pp. 86–87 Urukagina 11 (edition)
1956 Sollberger, CIRPL p. xiv Ukg. 13; p. 57 Ukg. 13 (copy)
1980 Walker and Collon, in de Meyer (ed.) Tell ed-Dēr 3 p. 98 and pl. 27 no. 25 (copy, study)
1982 Steible, ASBW 1 pp. 331–32 Uru'inimgina 13 (edition)
1986 Cooper, SARI 1 p. 81 La 9.11 (translation)
1991 Braun-Holzinger, Weihgaben p. 118 G 13 (edition, study)

TEXT

1) [^{d}ba-ba$_{6}$]
2) [munus]-⌈sa$_{6}$⌉-ga-ra
3) ^{d}nin-g̃ír-sú-lú-mu sukkal
(patch)
4) [nam-ti-lugal]-ni
5) URU-KA-gi-na
6) lugal-
7) l[a]gaš.KI-[ka]-šè
Lacuna

1–2) For [the goddess Baba, the grac]ious [lady],

3) Ning̃ir-sulumu, the emissary,

4–7) for the l[if]e of his [master], URU-KA-gina, king of Lagaš,

Lacuna

12

A clay bulla from Girsu bears the impression of a seal of URU-KA-gina.

COMMENTARY

The clay bulla, which measures 16 ×7 cm, was found by Cros near a well that lay to the east of the so-called Porte du Diable; see Cros Tello p. 267 Plan G — the bulla was found at the point marked "g" on the plan. It now bears the museum number EŞ 4645.

BIBLIOGRAPHY

1910 Cros, Tello pp. 268–270 (translation, study, drawing)
1956 Sollberger, CIRPL p. xiv Ukg. 59 (study); p. 61 Ukg. 59 (copy)
1980 Amiet, Glyptique p. 422 no. 1098(bis) (study)
1982 Steible, ASBW 1 p. 357 Uru'inimgina 59 (study)
1986 Cooper, SARI 1 p. 82 La 9.12 (translation)

TEXT

1) URU-KA-gi-na
2) lugal
3) lagaš.KI

1–3) URU-KA-gina, king of Lagaš.

13

A weight stone from G̃irsu is inscribed with the name of URU-KA-gina.

COMMENTARY

The weight stone has not been located.

BIBLIOGRAPHY

1912 Scheil, CRAIB p. 479ff (study)
1956 Sollberger, CIRPL p. xiv Ukg. 58 (study); p. 61 Ukg. 58 (copy)
1982 Steible, ASBW 1 p. 357 Uruʾinimgina 58 (study)
1986 Cooper, SARI p. 82 La 9.13 (translation)

TEXT

1) 15 gín
2) ^{d}nin-g̃ír-su
3) URU-KA-gi-na
4) lugal-g̃ír-su-.KI

1–4) Fifteen shekels, for Ning̃irsu. URU-KA-gina, king of G̃irsu.

14

A large number of small clay ovoid tags from G̃irsu bear inscriptions naming URU-KA-gina. In view of the limited insight they provide, and the few if any changes that can be made to Steible's edition, they are not re-edited here.

CATALOGUE

Cooper, SARI 1 La 9. and RIME 1 E1.9. number	Steible, ASBW 1 Uru'inimgina number	Sollberger, CIRPL number
9.14a	Ukg. 34	Ukg. 34
9.14b	Ukg. 35	Ukg. 35
9.14c	Ukg. 36–37	Ukg. 36–37
9.14d	Ukg. 38	Ukg. 38
9.14e	Ukg. 39	Ukg. 39
9.14f	Ukg. 40	Ukg. 40
9.14g	Ukg. 41	Ukg. 41
9.14h	Ukg. 42	Ukg. 42
9.14i	Ukg. 43	Ukg. 43
9.14j	Ukg. 44	Ukg. 44
9.14k	Ukg. 45	Ukg. 45
9.14l	Ukg. 46	Ukg. 46
9.14m	Ukg. 47	Ukg. 47
9.14n	Ukg. 48	Ukg. 48
9.14o	Ukg. 49	Ukg. 49
9.14p	Ukg. 50	Ukg. 50
9.14q	Ukg. 51	Ukg. 51
9.14r	Ukg. 52	Ukg. 52
0.14s	Ukg. 53	Ukg. 53
9.14t	Ukg. 54–55	Ukg. 54–55
9.14u	Ukg. 56	Ukg. 56
9.14v	Ukg. 57	Ukg. 57
9.14w	Ukg. 61	Ukg. 61

COMMENTARY

Some of the clay tags came from the area east of the covered canal on the Tell V, the "Tell des tablettes"; see Cros, Tello p. 229 Plan F, Tranches G and G′. Cros (Tello p. 260) writes:

> Au milieu de quelques tablettes, on a rencontré trois grosses olives en terre cuite, perforées de bout en bout et portent des cases d'écriture, avec le nom d'Ourou-kaghina, qualifié sur quelques-unes du titre de roi. Deux jours après, un quatrième objet du même genre a été trouvé isolé, un peu plus loin.

The provenances of the "olives" purchased by the British Museum and the Vorderasiatische Museum are not known, but it is conceivable that they came from the same general area on Tell V.

Unnamed Rulers of Lagaš

E1.9.10

1

A clay cylinder fragment from G̃irsu gives part of an apparent royal inscription. Unfortunately, the name of the ruler of Lagaš who figured in this text is not preserved in the extant portion.

COMMENTARY

The inscription is found on AO 12779, a clay cylinder fragment from de Genouillac's excavations at G̃irsu which measures 12.7×12 cm. It bears the excavation number TG 2161. The inscription was collated.

BIBLIOGRAPHY

1936 de Genouillac, FT 2 pl. XLII (copy)
1956 Sollberger, CIRPL p. xvi N 10 (study); p. 63 N 10 (copy)
1963 Sollberger, PICO 22 pp. 23ff (study)
1983 Cooper, SANE 2 pp. 17 and 53 no. 11 (translation, study)
1985 Cooper, RA 79 p. 98 Table 1 no. 14 and pl. VII no. 14 (photo, study)
1986 Cooper, SARI I pp. 84–85 La 10.1 (translation)

TEXT

Transliteration	Translation
Unknown number of columns missing	
Col. i′	
Lacuna	Lacuna
1′) ⌈x⌉	i′ 1′–2′) ...
2′) [...] ⌈x⌉ [... D]U(?)	
Lacuna	Lacuna
Col. ii′	
Lacuna	Lacuna
1′) [...] a-šà a-mu	ii′ 1′–4′) [...] the field, he gave my water.
2′) saĝ-ĝe$_{26}$(GÁ)-šè mu-rig$_7$	Enlil ...
3′) ⌈^{d}en⌉-líl-[l]e	
4′) [...]-⌈šè⌉	
Lacuna	Lacuna
Col. iii′	
Lacuna	Lacuna
1′) [...]	iii′ 1′–7′) [...] which had escaped, in Umma, Ninĝirsu
2′) e-da-kar-ra-bi	... Nanše ...
3′) ^{ĝiš}KÚŠU.KI	

4′) ^{d}nin-g̃ír-su	
5′) x-mu-x-x	
6′) [^{d}]nanše	
7′) [...] ⸢x⸣	
Lacuna	Lacuna
Col. iv′	
Lacuna	Lacuna
1′) ⸢x⸣ (x) [g]i$_4$-gi$_4$	iv′ 1′) he *replied*:
2′) uru-zu gu[l]-gul-la-ba	iv′ 2′–4′ "Be it known that your city will be completely destroyed! Surrender!"
3′) ḫé-zu	
4′) gú ki-g̃ar ba-ni	
5′) ${}^{g̃iš}$KÚŠU.KI	iv′ 5′–9′) Be it kno[wn] that your city will be completely destroyed! Surrender! ...
6′) gul-gul-la-ba	
7′) ḫé-z[u]	
8′) gú ki-G̃[ar ba-ni]	
9′) ⸢x x⸣ [...]	
Lacuna	Lacuna
Col. v′	
Lacuna	Lacuna
1′) ⸢x⸣ [...]	v′ 1′) ...
Lacuna	Lacuna

2

A clay vessel fragment recounts a dispute between an unamed ruler of Lagaš and Lugal-TAR of Uruk.

COMMENTARY

The vessel fragment, which measures 13×6.5 cm was found in Genouillac's excavations at G̃irsu, Excavation number TG 2065. It bears the museum number IM 47456.

BIBLIOGRAPHY

1936 de Genouillac, FT 2 pl. XLII (copy)
1959 van Dijk, Sumer 15 pp. 5–8 and pl. I no. 1 (copy, edition, study)
1982 Steible, ASBW 2 pp. 337–39 Lugal-TAR 1 (edition)
1983 Cooper, SANE 2 pp. 17 and 53–54 (translation, study)
1986 Cooper, SARI 1 p. 85 La 10.2 (translation)
1989 Bauer, BiOr 46 col. 638 (study)

TEXT

Unknown number of columns missing	
Col. i′	
Traces	Traces
Col. ii′	
Lacuna	Lacuna
1′) [na]m-l[ú]-ùlu	ii′ 1′–3′) he bound the arms of [the per]so[n]nel abandoned there.
2′) ki-a-tag$_4$-a-ba	
3′) á ba-lá	

4′) kù-za-gìn-bi 5′) G̃iš-níg-ga-bi 6′) má-e ba-ÍL	ii′ 4′–6′) Their precious metal and lapis lazuli, their timber and treasure, he loaded on ships.
7′) 10-kam-ma-am$_6$ 8′) lugal-TAR 9′) énsi- 10′) unu.KI-ga⌜ke⌝ 11′) éren šu ì-mi-ús	ii′ 7′–11′) A tenth time, Lugal-TAR, ruler of Uruk, dispatched troops.
12′) še-muš 13′) š[e]-⌜x⌝-ra 14′) š[e]-⌜x x⌝	ii′ 12′–14′) "Bitter" grain, ... gra[in], ... gra[in]
Lacuna	Lacuna
Col. iii′	
Lacuna x′) [nam-dag-bi] x′) [gú-na] 1′) [ḫé-ÍL].ÍL	Lacuna iii′ 1′) [May the DN make him (Lugal-TAR) bear the sin!

3

A bowl fragment found at G̃irsu gives part of the titulary of a ruler of Lagaš.

COMMENTARY

The alabaster bowl fragment has a preserved height of 6 cm. It bears the museum number AO 194.

BIBLIOGRAPHY

1991 Braun-Holzinger, Weihgaben p. 121 G 31 (transliteration, study)

TEXT

Lacuna	Lacuna
1′ [éns]i 2′ lagaš.KI	1′–2′ [rul]er of Lagaš
Lacuna	Lacuna

Mari

E1.10

(a) Location

Ancient Mari is identified with the modern mound of Tell Ḥarīrī located on the Middle Euphrates just north of the present-day Iraqi-Syrian border (NLat 34° 33′ and ELong 40° 53′).

(b) Excavation History

The site has been unearthed by a long series of French expeditions during the years 1933–38, 1951–54, and 1961–74 (under the director A. Parrot), and 1979–82 (under the director J. Margueron); for the details of the publication of the preliminary reports of the campaigns, see G. Lehmann, BAFSL p. 334. For a popular account of the excavations in general, see Parrot, Mari capital fabuleuse, and for a general overview of the archaeology see Spycket, "Mari B" in RLA 7 pp. 390–403. For a survey of the finds of the third millennium in particular, see Parrot, Mari capital fabuleuse, chapter 2.

Objects of Presargonic date were found in the temples of Ishtar, Ishtarat and "Ninnizaza," Dagan, Shamash, and the Massif Rouge. Furthermore, after clearing the OB period levels of the palace of Zimrī-Līm the excavators uncovered part of the Presargonic palace beneath it (for a plan see Margueron, MARI 4 p. 498 and idem, AAAS 34 (1983) p. 205, and Spycket RLA 7 p. 397). Seven Presargonic administrative tablets were found in the palace (Charpin, MARI 4 pp. 76–80); they gave virtually no useful information on the history of the period except for telling us that Mari apparently controlled the city of Ṣarbat. The name Ṣarbat means "Euphrates poplar," and the settlement was an important cult city of the goddess Inanna. It is well known from the Ebla texts (see Pomponio and Xella, Les Dieux d'Ebla p. 65). Ancient Ṣarbat is likely to be located at modern Zalabīyah situated about 79 kms NW of Terqa. The same place is likely referred to by Isidore of Charax in his Parthian Mansions as "the temple of Artemis, founded by Darius, a small town; close by ... the canal of Semiramis, ... [where] the Euphrates is dammed with rocks, in order that by being thus checked it may overflow the fields" (edition W.H. Schoff); cf. Astour, in WGE p. 146 n. 47. A series of rapids on the Euphrates are found near Zalabīyah.

(c) Writing of the City Name

Mari's city name is written exclusively ma-rí.KI in ED texts. On the etymology of the city name we may note the remarks of Lambert (MARI 4 p. 535):

> If Mari were the original and major city cult centre of [the god] Mer, the question arises whether the name Mer is an alternative form of Mari. In inscriptions from the town itself the writing is ma-rí in third millennium texts, ma-ri in the Old Babylonian period ... The nearest

writing to Mer is me-ra in the Prologue to Hammurabi's laws (iv 30), but with variants má-ri(?) and me-ri^{ki}′ (R. Borger, BAL p. 10). A location is certainly meant where the šakkanakku Ilum-išar tells of bringing down the statue of Ḫubur to "the gate of Mer" (ká me-er^{ki}: RA 35 p. 177), and a letter of an official of Zimrī-Līm reports how two servants of the palace, apparently in an attempt to run away, "went out of the queen's quarters to the gate of Itūr-Mer" ([a-n]a ká ^{d}i-túr-me-er: ARM XIII 26 10). Thus, on present evidence it seems that the similiarly of Mer and Mari may be a coincidence, but the matter is not, perhaps, finally settled.

(d) Tutelary Deity

Mari's tutelary deity apparently was the god Itūr-Mēr. Concerning this god we may note the remarks of Lambert in MARI 4 pp. 534–35:

> Almost nothing is known of the character of Itur-Mer. Though the form of the name is such that this could in theory have served as a human name, it is characteristic of the religion of northern Mesopotamia and Syria of this time that both the simple divine name and compounds can be used of the gods, cf. Il and Il-aba. Thus the deity is properly Mer, and Itūr-Mer is presumably a particular (local) example of the god. Linguistically Mer probably belongs to some substrate language, because its first consonant does not obey normal phonetic rules. In Mari and district from the earliest occurence down to the late second millennium (in the royal name Tukulti-Mer) the name is consistently written Mer. In southern Mesopotamia from the beginning of the Third Dynasty of Ur to the end of the First Dynasty of Babylon, also in Assyria of the time of the Cappadocian merchants, the name is written Wer (we-er), but in Middle and Late Assyrian texts Ber (^{d}be-er). An = Anum deals only with Ilu-M/Wer and identifies him with Adad ... [Litke An: *Anum* p. 139] ... If these scraps of information are all reliable, Mer, Itūr-Mer and Ilu-Mer are names of an old storm god of northern Mesopotamia and Syria, for that reason one of the highest in the pantheon, and in this environment he could survive alongside Addu, though he was less popular after the middle of the second millennium, probably due to the decline of his main cult centres.

For Itūr-Mēr, see also Charpin, MARI 3 p. 42–44. On the god Mer/Wer, see most recently D. Schwemmer, Wettergottgestalten pp. 200–10.

(e) Studies on Mari

The following general (and not exhaustive) discussion lists some sources for several periods of Mari's history, not just the Presargonic, since this volume is meant to be an introduction to the RIME series as a whole.

For collections of studies on Mari, see A. Parrot (ed.) Studia Mariana, and Durand and Margueron (eds.) MARI, Annales de Recherches Interdisciplinaire 1–8 (1982–97).

For a bibliography of articles on Mari, see Spycket, "Bibliographie de Mari," in A. Parrot (ed.), Studiana 1 pp. 127–38; J.G. Heintz, Index documentaire des textes de Mari, fasicule 1 (=ARMT 17/1); idem, Bibliographie de Mari: Archéologie et Textes [1933–88]; and various supplements by Heintz, Bodi, and Millot in Akkadica 77 (1992) pp. 1–37; Akkadica 81 (1993) pp. 1–22; Akkadica 86 (1994) pp. 1–23; Akkadica 91 (1995) pp. 1–22; Akkadica 96 (1996) pp. 1–19; Akkadica 104 (1997) pp. 1–23; Akkadica 109 (1998) pp. 1–21; Akkadica 118 (2000) pp. 22–45.

Many subsequent articles about Mari's archaeology, history, and culture during all chronological periods have appeared in various Festschriften and symposia edited in large part by D. Charpin and J.-M. Durand, namely: Cahiers de NABU 1: J.-M. Durand et al., Tell Mohammed Diyab, campagnes 1987 et 1988; Mémoires de NABU 1: J.-M. Durand (ed.), Florilegium marianum I. Recueil d'études en l'honneur de Michel Fleury; Mémoires de NABU 2: J.-M. Durand et al., Recherches en Haute Mésopotamie. Tell Mohammed Diyab, campagnes 1990 et 1991; Mémoires de NABU 3: D. Charpin and J.-M. Durand (eds.), Florilegium marianum II. Recueil d'études à la mémoire de Maurice Birot; Mémoires de NABU 4: D. Charpin and J.-M. Durand (eds.), Florilegium marianum III. Recueil d'études à la mémoire de Marie-Thérèse Barrelet; Mémoires de NABU 5: N. Ziegler, Florilegium marianum IV. Le Harem de Zimrî-Lîm; Mémoires de NABU 6: D. Charpin and N. Ziegler, Florilegium marianum V. Mari et le Proche-Orient à l'époque amorrite: Essai d'histoire politique; Mémoires de NABU 7: D. Charpin and J.-M. Durand (eds.), Florilegium marianum VI. Recueil d'études à la mémoire d'André Parrot; Mémoires de NABU 8: J.-M. Durand, Florilegium marianum VII. Le Culte d'Addu d'Alep et l'affaire d'Alahtum.

One may also refer with profit to the symposium proceedings edited by G. Young, entitled Mari in Retrospect.

(f) Sources for the Political History of Mari in Presargonic Times

Five general sources give us the briefest outline of the political history of Mari in the ED period:

(i) Presargonic Mari in the Sumerian King List

According to an exemplar of the SKL from Tell Leilān (see C. Vincente ZA 85 [1995] pp. 234–70), the list of kings who ruled Mari during the early part of the Early Dynastic period runs as follows:

⸢ma⸣-ri.KI-a an-bu lug[al-àm] mu 90 in-ak	"In Mari, Anbu was ki[ng] and reigned 90 (variant: 30) years.
an-ba dumu an-bu-ke mu 7 in-ak	Anba, the son of Anbu, reigned 7 years.
dba-zi lú-ašgab mu 30 in-ak	Bazi, the leather-worker, reigned 30 years.
zi-zi lú-túg mu 20 in-ak	Zizi, the fuller, reigned 20 years.
[*l*]*i*(?)-*im-e r* gú-du mu 30 in-ak	[L]īm-ēr, the anointed priest, reigned 30 years.
LUGAL-*i-ter* mu 7 in-ak	Šarrum-īter reigned 7 years.
6 lugal mu-bi 120[+60+]⸢4⸣ in-⸢ak⸣	Six kings reigned 184 years."

(ii) The Enna-Dagān "Letter" or "Military Bulletin" from Ebla

One of the treasures of the Ebla archive is a tablet (TM.G.1975.2367) inscribed with what has been described as either a letter or military bulletin of King Enna-Dagān of Mari addressed to an unnamed king of Ebla, probably Irkab-Dāmu (on this last point, see Archi, CRRA 45 [2001] p. 1 and Pomponio, NABU 1995 no. 15). For a discussion of this important text there is an extensive bibliography: see Pettinato, Akkadica 2 (1977) pp. 24–25; idem., MEE 1 p. 171 no. 1806; a first edition in idem, OrAnt 19 (1980) pp. 231–45; Kienast, OrAnt 19 (1980) p. 256; a second edition in Edzard, Seb 4 (1981) pp. 89–97; Geller in Gordon, Rendsburg, and Winter (eds.), Eblaitica 1 p. 144 n. 11; Astour,

"An Outline of the History of Ebla (Part 1)" in Gordon (ed.), Eblaitica 3 pp. 26–51; 1988; Pomponio, AfO 35 p. 166; Pettinato, The Archives of Ebla: An Empire Inscribed in Clay pp. 103–8; Pettinato, Ebla: A New Look at History pp. 237–41; Bonechi, "Remarks on the III Millennium Geographical Names of the Syrian Upper Mesopotamia," in M. Lebeau (ed.), Subartu IV/1 pp. 224–27; and J.-W. Meyer, "Offene und geschlossene Siedlungen," AoF 23 (1996), in particular § 5 pp. 155–70; and finally, a third edition in Fronzaroli, ARET 13 pp. 35–76.

For photos of the tablet, see G. Pettinato, OrAnt 19 (1980) pls. xiv–xv; idem, Ebla: A New Look at History pl. xxxiiib; P. Matthaie, Ebla: Alle origini della civilità urbana p. 368; and Fronzaroli, ARET 13 pls. xxxvii–xxxviii. A copy is found in Fronzaroli, ARET 13 pls. vii–viii.

According to the letter, the Mari kings An(u)bu, Saʾūmu, Ištup-Šar, IB-LUL-il, and Enna-Dagān all waged war against the state of Ebla. We have assumed for the purposes of this study that they are listed in chronological order, although this is not absolutely certain, nor does the letter necessarily give a complete list of kings for this period. There are good reasons to believe that it does not. The various kings it mentions appear to date to the ED III period.

The zone of conflict between Mari and Ebla seems to have been the towns that lay on the banks of the Euphrates from the latitude of Carchemish down to the latitude of Emar (Eblaic Imar) and on both sides of the Euphrates SE from Emar. Episodes in the war between Ebla and Mari have been described in section 5 of M. Astour "An Outline of the History of Ebla (Part I)" in Gordon (ed.), Eblaitica 3 pp. 26–51. More recently the conflict between Ebla and Mari has been described by A. Archi and M. Biga, "A Victory Over Mari and the Fall of Ebla," JCS 55 (2003) pp. 1–44.

(iii) Presargonic Economic Documents of the Late ED III Period Royal Archive from Ebla Referring to Mari.

The political and economic relations between Ebla and Mari as attested in the Ebla documents have been discussed by A. Archi, "I rapporti tra Ebla e Mari," MARI 4 (1985) pp. 63–83; F. Pomponio, "Considerazioni sui rapporti tra Mari ed Ebla," VO 5 (1982) pp. 191–203; idem, "Funzionari di Ebla e di Mari in S. de Martino and F. Peechioli Daddi (eds.), Anatolia Antica. Studi in memoria di F. Imparati (Eothen 11: Florence, LoGisma, 2002) pp. 653–63. The older economic documents have been put in chronological order by L. Viganò, "Mari and Ebla: The Archives Reports," in L. Viganò, On Ebla. An Accounting of Third Millennium Syria (Aula Onientalis Supplementa 12; Sabadell: Editorial, AUSA, 1996), pp. 25-51. Other studies include those of Viganò in "Mari and Ebla: Of Times and Rulers," idem, pp. 3-24; P. Michalowski, "Mari: The View from Ebla," in C.D. Young (ed.), Mari in Retrospect. Fifty Years of Mari and Mari Studies (Winona Lake: Eisenbrauns, 1992), pp. 243-48, which could not use the corrections which A. Archi, "Le synchronisme entre les rois de Mari et les rois d'Ebla au IIIe millénnaire," MARI 4 (1985) 47-51 (especially p. 47, n. 4), introduced into his earlier list of the Mari kings. He had earlier indicated that the viziers Arennum/Arrukum, Ibrium, and Ibbi-Zikir were kings of Ebla. The personnages named in Archi's MARI 4 article, "Arennum" (likely to be read ar-ru$_{12}$-gúm "pale," see Pagan, ARES 3 p. 287), Ibrium, and Ibbi-Zikir, have subsequently been shown to be the names of viziers of the kings Igriš-Ḫalab, Irkab-Dāmu, and Išar-Dāmu respectively; see Biga and Pomponio, NABU 1987 no. 106, and note Archi's apologetic remark in CRRA 45 p. 1: "in these two articles [Archi, SEb 4 (1981) pp. 89–97 and idem, MARI 4 (1985) pp. 63–83] the minister Ibrium and Ibbi-Zikir are still considered to have been kings!" A complete study of the relations between Ebla and Mari is in preparation by Archi. Subsequently Biga and Pomponio in the article "Elements for a Chronological Division of the Administrative Documentation of Ebla," JCS 42 (1990) p. 198 have written:

> For the sychronism between the kings of Mari and Ebla, it seems probable that the reign of ibLUL-il, in its conclusive phase, and that of NIzi, which probably did not last longer than three years, were contemporaneous with that of Igriš-Ḫalam[Ḫalab] ... and the early years of Irkab-Damu.

Archi gives editions of many texts dealing with Mari in ARET 7. Finally, the latest treatment of the relations between Mari and Ebla is found in Archi and Biga's article in JCS 55 (2003) pp. 1–44.

(iv) Contemporary Presargonic Royal Inscriptions From Various Temples at Mari

The rulers Išgi-Mari, Ikū(n)-Šamagan, Ikūn-Mari, Ikūn-Šamaš, and IB-LUL-il are attested from various votive inscriptions (see editions below) largely found in temples at Mari.

(v) Presargonic Economic Texts Excavated from the Presargonic Palace at Mari

For the Presargonic economic texts from Mari, see Charpin, MARI 5 pp. 65–100 and idem, MARI 6 pp. 245–52. While of phonological and epigraphic interest, they shed virtually no light on the political history of this period.

Tentative List of ED Period Rulers of Mari

Sumerian King List	
RIM number	King
E1.10.1	An(u)bu
E1.10.2	Anba
E1.10.3	^{d}Bazi
E1.10.4	Zizi
E1.10.5	[L]īm-ēr
E1.10.6	Šarrum-īter
Gap	
(Order Uncertain)	
E1.10.7	Ikūn-Šamaš
E1.10.8	Saʾumu
E1.10.9	Išṭup-Šar
E1.10.10	Ikūn-Mari
E1.10.11	Ikūn-Šamagan
E1.10.12	IB-LUL-il
E1.10.13	NIzi
E1.10.14	Enna-Dagān
E1.10.15	Ikū(n)-išar
E1.10.16	ḪI-daʾar
E1.10.17	Išgi-Mari

An(u)bu

E1.10.1

1

A passage in the letter or military bulletin of Enna-Dagān deals with the conquests by King An(u)bu in the land of Belān.

The royal name An(u)bu has been connected with the AN.BU of the Sumerian King List by various scholars, for example, Alberti, NABU 1990 no. 124. Fronzaroli, on the other hand, suggests that it may be related to the onomastic type *i-nu-ub*-DN with a writing to be normalized as /yanūp-/ or /yinūp-/. Pagan, ARES 3 p. 282, translates the name as "He was exalted." Alternatively, An(u)bu could be seen as a theophoric element in a compound royal name. While it is more common to have the divine name in second position, personal names in which the divine name precedes are known, cf. *ʾà-da-hu* = Hadda-(ʿa)ḫu "Haddu is brother." A god Anubu occurs in the god list AN: *Anum* in tablet I: 204 (Litke, An: *Anum* p. 44) and tablet VI: 236 (Litke, An: *Anum* p. 217). In the former case he may be connected with the E-kur temple (according to Litke only the element é- is preserved). In this case he may have been a foreign king honoured at Nippur just as LUM-ma of G̃irsu and Ḫa-tá-ni-iš of Ḫamazi appear to have been (see Jacobsen, SKL p. 98 n. 168). In the latter An: *Anum* citation, he is equated with the god Martu. Since the Amorites were well attested in third millennium sources as being resident in the upper Euphrates valley (Archi "Mardu in the Ebla Texts," Orientalia NS 54 (1985) pp. 7–13), the appearance of a form of the god Martu at Mari would not be unexpected. Of interest is the equation of the god Martu two lines later in the second An: *Anum* citation with the god of equids, Šaḫan. Šaḫan forms part of the Mari Presargonic royal name Ikū(n)-Šamagan. The identification of Šaḫḫan with Šamagan is possible because of the large number of variant writings of the divine name (for a bibliography of the discussion see our edition of the inscription of king Ikū(n)-Šamagan in section E1.10.11 below). For the god Šamagan at Ebla, see most recently Pomponio and Xella, Les dieux d'Ebla pp. 324–26.

COMMENTARY

The relevant passage is found on obv. i 8 – ii 9 of TM.75.G.2367.

The proper name of obv. i 13 was first read as sá-ù-mu in Pettinato's editio princeps. Then, in 1986, it was changed by the same author to a verbal form a-nu-du$_{11}$. The almost certainly correct reading was established by Alberti in 1990 (see bibliography). Archi read the final sign (KA) as -bu$_{14}$; Bonechi gives -bu$_{16}$. Bonechi (in Lebeau [ed.], Subartu 4/1 p. 226) notes:

> King a-nu-bu$_{16}$ won a victory in a region that is probably located not far from Tuttul. This is because the four GN's quoted in this section are never attested elsewhere at Ebla, so they belong to the region immediately upstream

from Tuttul, where the political influence of Ebla never reached.

The GN *be-la-an*.KI is likely to be linked with the modern town of Tell Bellânê located about 55.5 km E of Old Meskeneh (Ebla Imar). It also occurs in E1.10.12.9. For a discussion of its location see also J.-W. Meyer AoF 23 (1996) p. 161.

The KUR.KI *la-ba-na-an*.KI of this text almost certainly does not refer to "the Lebanon," which is clearly much too far south to be considered in these inscriptions as an area conquered by Mari, but rather simply to mean "the white (mountain)," a common designation of oronyms. According to Bonechi the word is a *parsān* formation from the root l-b-n "white."

BIBLIOGRAPHY

For the bibliography of this text see the introduction to the Mari section sub (ii) The Enna-Dagān letter or military bulletin from Ebla.

TEXT

Obv. col. i
8) *a-bù-ru*$_{12}$.KI
9) *ù*
10) *íl-gi*.KI
11) KALAM-*tim* KALAM-*tim*
12) *be-la-an*.KI
13) *a-nu-bu*$_{14}$(KA)
Col. ii
1) EN
2) *ma-rí*.KI
3) GÍN.SÈ
4) DU$_6$.SAR
5) *in*
6) KUR.KI
7) *la-ba-na-an*.KI
8) G̃AR

i 8 – ii 8) An(u)bu, king of Mari, defeated the cities of Aburu and Ilgi in the lands of Belān and raised tumuli (honouring his dead) in the mountainous country of Labnān.

2

A mace-head from Ur bears an inscription of Anbu, the king; the text has been taken by some scholars to refer to King An(u)bu of Mari.

COMMENTARY

The mace-head was found by Woolley on the surface of the mound at Ur and given the excavation number U 11678. It bears the museum number IM 8997.

Steible (ASBW 1 p. 286 AnUr 13) assigned this piece as an anonymous inscription from Ur (cf. Bauer, BiOr 45 p. 638). If the piece does belong to King An(u)bu of Mari, its presence at Ur could be explained by assuming the mace-head was part of an exchange of royal gifts between Mari and Ur. The find of a bead of Mes-Ane-pada, king of Ur, at Mari (see E1.13.5.1) attests to this practice. However, the coincidence is certainly not enough evidence to prove a synchronism between Mes-Ane-pada and Anbu although we believe that the possibility is not out of the question.

The reading of the RN of line two as an-bu rather than the conceivable *ìl-śu* suggested by Gelb is based on the suggested identification of this ruler with the king of Mari.

BIBLIOGRAPHY

1934 Gadd, UE 2 pp. 322, 572, and pl. 183 a–c (photo, study)
1935 Frankfort in Studies Deimel pp. 114–16 and p. 117 fig. 13 (photo, study)
1960 Sollberger, Iraq 22 pp. 73-74 no. 71 (study)
1968 Solyman, Götterwaffen p. 132 and pl. XXXVII figs. 235–36 (photos, study)
1982 Steible, ASBW 1 p. 286 AnUr 13 (edition)
1985 Bauer, AoN 21 p. 12 (study)
1986 Cooper, SARI 1 p. 86 Ma 1.1 (translation)
1989 Bauer, BiOr 46 p. 638 (study)
1991 Braun-Holzinger, Weihgaben pp. 44–45 K 12 (edition, study)

TEXT

1) ^{d}utu	1–3) To the god Utu, An(u)bu, k[ing of Mari(?)],
2) *an-bu*	
3) l[ugal *ma-rí*.KI(?)]	
Lacuna	Lacuna

3

A stone cup was dedicated by a daughter(?) of Anbu; the latter may possibly refer to King An(u)bu of Mari, although this is very uncertain.

COMMENTARY

The cup, which measures 3.5 cm in height and 7.5 cm in diameter, was found in EH Square R8 at Ur and was given the excavation number U 6332. It bears the museum number CBS 16208.

Woolley (UE 2 pp. 321–22), Jacobsen (SKL p. 103 n. 189), Kupper and Sollberger (IRSA IG1a), and Cooper (SARI 1 p. 86 sub Ma 1.2) all connected the An(u)bu of this text with the king of Mari. The identification was rejected by Gelb (in Young [ed.], Mari in Retrospect p. 127) because the name is not followed by the expected title lugal "king." Gelb's reluctance to equate the two is understandable, but the example of inscription E1.8.3.1 in this volume in which untitled Enna-il (an almost certain reference to the same figure who is named as king in inscription E1.8.3.2) suggests that the identity should not be categorically ruled out.

In line 1 the divine name may refer to the deified physician (in Akkadian); cf. the OB PN *ì-lí-a-sí-i*, Meek AJSL 33 (1916–17) p. 233 RFH no. 22 line 2.

Although Cooper (SARI 1 p. 86 sub Ma 1.2) is correct that the dumu of line 3 could be translated as either "son" or "daughter," the fact the PN of line 2 is a "nin" name suggests that she was a daughter.

BIBLIOGRAPHY

1928 Gadd, UET 1 no. 12 (copy, edition)
1934 Woolley, UE 2 p. 321 (study)
1939 Jacobsen, SKL p. 103 n. 189 (study)
1960 Sollberger, Iraq 22 pp. 83–84 no. 70 (study)
1971 Sollberger and Kupper, IRSA, IG1a (translation)
1982 Steible, ASBW 1 pp. 285–86 AnUr 12 (edition)
1986 Cooper, SARI 1 p. 86 Ma 1.2 (translation)

TEXT

1) ^{d}*a-sum*	1) To the deity Asum
2) nin-me-te-bar-ré	2–4) Nin-mete-bare, daughter of ⌜An(u)bu⌝
3) dumu-	
4) ⌜an-bu⌝	
5) [a mu]-⌜ru⌝	5) [de]dicated (this cup).

Bazi and Zizi

E1.10.3–4

Although no royal inscriptions are as yet attested for the kings Bazi and Zizi named in the SKL, they do appear in a remarkable literary composition that is known from three OB period tablet copies from ancient Sippar, and several later manuscripts from ancient Emar and Ugarit. The text in question has been given various titles by modern scholars: "The Poem About Early Rulers," "The Ballad of Heroes of Former Times," and "A Life Without Joy." J. Nougayrol, who first identified the composition in three tablets from Ugarit, took it to be a collection of predominantly pessimistic sayings and found various parallels in Sumero-Akkadian wisdom literature. Subsequently, M. Civil, B. Alster, and U. Jeyes could see that the text published by Nougayrol was related to the Sumerian poem that they had entitled "The Poem About Early Rulers." Alster further edited another copy of the composition in Philadelphia (CBS 1208); the new piece seemed to indicate that the composition may have originally been a prayer composed for the OB king Abī-ešuḫ. C. Wilcke, in his study of the poem, radically turned away from previous interpretations; he considered the piece, in its impudence and cynicism, to be comparable to a student drinking song. Finally, Dietrich was able to provide us with a complete edition of all the known Emar and Ugarit exemplars.

Bazi and Zizi are mentioned in line 16 of the poem (Emar version)

(Sum.) me-e ^{m}ba-[z]i me-e [^{m}z]i-[zi]
(Akk.) *a-le-e* ^{m}*ba-zi a-le-e* ^{m}*zi-*[*zi*]

Where is Bazi? Where is Zizi?

The PNs Bazi and Zizi are attested in Presargonic economic tablets, cf. Steinkeller, "Observations on the Sumerian Personal Names in Ebla Sources and on the Onomasticon of Mari and Kish," in Studies Hallo, p. 238:

> Ba-zi. Attested also in MARI 4, p. 76 no. 84 where it identifies a man from Mari. This name, which is documented in Babylonia from the Fara (Pomponio, *Prosopografia*, p. 57; Names and Professions List line 132 = SEb 4, p. 184) through the Ur III period (Limet, Anthroponymie, p. 389), is very likely Sumerian. Cf. the name Zi-zi, borne by a man from Mari (ARET 1 7 rev. xi 1; MARI 4, p. 78 no. 125), which is also found in the Names and Professions List line 238 (SEb 4, p. 187) and in the sources from Babylonia (Pomponio *Prosopografia,* p. 279). Cf. also Zi-zi of Ḫamazi (Rivista Biblica 25 [1977] 240 iv 10, v 3).

BIBLIOGRAPHY

1963 Pinches, CT 44 no. 18 (partial copy)
1968 Nougayrol, Ugaritica 5 pp. 291–304 sub nos. 164–67 (partial edition, study)
1969 Civil, JNES 28 p. 72 (study)
1969 Civil, RA 63 p. 179 (study)
1972 Civil, Orientalia 41 p. 90 (study)
1986 Alster and Jeyes ASJ 8 pp. 1–9 (partial edition, study)
1987 Arnaud, "La Ballade des héros du temps jadis," in idem, Emar VI/4 pp. 359–65 (partial edition, study)
1988 Wilcke, "Die Sumerische Königsliste und erzählte Vergangenheit," in J.V. Ungern-Sternberg et al. (eds.), Vergangenheit in mündlicher Überlieferung, Colloquium Rauricum 1 pp. 137–39 (study)
1990 Alster, "The Sumerian Poem of Early Rulers and Related Poems," Orientalia Lovansiensia Periodica 21 pp. 5–25 (partial edition, study)
1992 Dietrich, "Eine Leben ohne Freude ...," UF 24 pp. 9–29 (edition)
1998 Kämmerer. šimâ milka pp. 208–13 (edition)
2005 Alster, Wisdom of Ancient Sumer pp. 288–322 (edition, study)

Ikū(n)-Šamaš

E1.10.7

1

A certain Ikū(n)-Šamaš, "The god Šamaš is firm," is known from an inscription on a stone statue from Sippar.

COMMENTARY

The limestone statue, which measures 34.5 cm in height and 21 cm across at the widest point, was probably found during Rassam's 1881 excavations at Sippar, and was given the museum number BM 90828 (formerly BM 12146). The inscription is found on the statue's right shoulder; its upper case measures 9×3.7 cm and its lower case 4.8×3.2 cm. The inscription was collated.

The god Šamaš played a very important role in the pantheon of Mari in Old Babylonian times as evidenced by the occurence of *Šamaš ša šamê* as the second entry in the so-called pantheon of Mari discussed by Lambert in MARI 4 pp. 525–39. Furthermore, as is well known, Iahdun-Līm of Mari built a temple to the god Šamaš in that city. For the ground plan of the temple see J. Margueron, "Le Temple de Shamash de Iahdun-Lim à Mari," in Studies Oates pp. 176–85. For the text, see Frayne RIME 4 E4.6.8.2, pp. 604–8.

The curved lower line of the lugal sign of line 2 as well as the broken vertical in the pa sign in line 3 suggest an early date for this inscription; palaeographic parallels suggest it dates to ED II times.

For ED Semitic names with the element ar-ra such as we find in line 5, see Krebernik, Personennamen p. 75. Cf. Archi, Biga, and Milano, ARES 2 p. 208 and n. 13. It is not certain whether the DIĜIR sign in line 5 is to be read /il/ or /ilum/; both writings *il* and *ì-lum* are attested in ED and Old Akkadian PNs.

BIBLIOGRAPHY

1898 King, CT 5 pl. 2 BM 12146 (copy)
1907 Thureau-Dangin, SAK pp. 170–71 § X. [...]-šamaš, König von Ma'er (edition)
1910 King, History pl. facing p. 102 (photo)
1929 Barton, RISA pp. 302–3 1. Irim-Shamash (edition)
1934 Thureau-Dangin, RA 31 p. 137 n. 5 (study)
1942 Jacobsen, Pre-Sargonid Temples p. 297 (study)
1961 Gelb, MAD 2² p. 2 (study)
1967 Gadd, in Parrot, Temples p. 310 (study)
1971 Sollberger and Kupper, IRSA IG3a (translation)
1974 Cooper, JNES 33 p. 416 (study)
1977 Braun-Holzinger, Beterstatuetten pp. 74–75 (edition)
1980 Walker and Collon in de Meyer, Tell ed-Dēr 3 p. 96 no. 1 (study)
1981 Spycket, Statuaire pp. 86–87 and n. 212 (study); p. 87 fig. 31 (drawing)
1984 Steinkeller, ArAnt 23 pp. 33–34 (edition, study)
1986 Cooper, SARI 1 p. 87 Ma 3 (translation)
1990 Gelb and Kienast, Königsinschriften p. 9 MP 8 (Ikūnšamagan 1 = "Ikūnšamaš") (edition)
1991 Braun-Holzinger, Weihgaben p. 250 St 55 (edition, study)

TEXT

1) *i-ku*-^{d}UTU
2) LUGAL *ma-rí*.KI
3) ÉNSI.GAL

1–4) Ikū(n)-Šamaš, king of Mari, chief ruler of the god Enlil:

4) ^{d}*en-líl*	
5) *ar-ra*-DIĜIR	5–6) Arra-Ilum, his courtier,
6) TUŠ IGI*me-śù*	
7) DÙL (Text: KA)-*śù*	7–9) presented a statue of him to the god Šamaš.
8) ^{d}UTU	
9) SAĜ.RIG$_9$	

Sa'ūmu

E1.10.8

Various passages in the letter or military bulletin of Enna-Dagān deal with campaigns of Sa'ūmu, king of Mari.

The king's name has been taken by some scholars to be derived from a root ś-y-m cognate with Akkadian *šâmu*(*m*) "to buy"; cf. Pagan, ARES 3 p. 362, who interprets it as *ša'ūmu*(?) "bought" taking the substantive as a *parūs* passive participial form.

1

The first inscription of Sa'ūmu deals with the defeat of cities likely along the left bank of the modern Euphrates east of Emar.

COMMENTARY

The passage is found on obv. ii 10 – iii 8 of TM.75.G.2367.

While *íl-wi-ì*.KI as such is not attested in the Ebla archive, it is probably to be connected to the GNs *íl-wu-ù*.KI and *íl-wu-um*.KI; the latter is fairly commonly attested in the archive. *Íl-wu-um*.KI is likely to be connected with modern Tell Bleïbis located 3.7 km NNE of modern Tell Bellâné located on the north shore of the Euphrates about 55.5 km E of Old Meskeneh (Eblaic Imar). *Íl-wu-um*.KI in turn is mentioned together with the important city of Ib'al (Biga and Milano, ARET 4 no. 12 § 35). Ib'al is likely to be identified with modern Tell ʿAbd ʿAli located 13 km ENE of modern Tell Bellâné. The site lies on the course of an ancient canal. *Ti-ba-la-at*.KI of obv. col. ii line 10 may be connected with the modern village of Mimlahat located 3.75 km east of Tell Bleïbis.

BIBLIOGRAPHY

For the bibliography of this text see the introduction to the Mari section sub. (ii) The Enna-Dagān letter or military bulletin from Ebla.

TEXT

Obv. col. ii
10) *ti-ba-la-at*.KI
11) *ù*
12) *íl-wi-ì*.KI
13) *sá-ù-mu*

ii 10 – iii 8) Sa'ūmu, king of Mari, defeated the cities of Tibalat and Ilwi, and raised tumuli (honouring his dead) in the mountainous country of Anga'i.

Obv. col. iii
1) EN
2) *ma-rí*.KI
3) GÍN.ŠÈ
4) *in*
5) KUR.KI
6) *an-ga-i*.[KI(?)]
7) DU_6.SAR
8) G̃AR

2

The second passage dealing with Sa'ūmu is found on obv. ii 9 – iv 12 of TM.75.G.2367.

BIBLIOGRAPHY

For the bibliography of this text see the introduction to the Mari section sub (ii) The Enna-Dagān "letter" or "military bulletin" from Ebla.

COMMENTARY

The ancient town of NIrum of line 12 is mentioned in the Ebla archive as being in close proximity to ancient Buzuga (see Sollberger, ARET 8 no. 533 § 61 col. xxi lines 8-11: NI-rúm.KI in bù-zu-ga.KI ŠU.BA_4.TI); the latter likely corresponds to modern Boujāq located some 23 km SSE of Tell Aḥmar. Eblean Buzuga, in turn, is to be correlated to the GN Buzqa attested in the MB tablets from Emar, cf. Arnaud, Emar VI/3 no. 370 line 56′ and Beckman, Texts from the Vicinity of Emar no. 84 line 6. A connection of NIrum with Ra'ak (confirming the evidence of the royal inscription) is found in Biga and Milano ARET 4 no. 3 § 59 lines 6–10: *'à-lum* NI-*rúm*.KI LÚ:TUŠ *in sal-ba-ù*.KI LÚ *ra-'à-ak*.KI "Alum of NIrum, resident in Salba'u of Ra'ak." The town of Salba'u likely corresponds to the modern village of Abou Safayeh located about 10 kms NE of modern Tell es-Sweyhat.

The town of Ra'ak may possibly be located at the modern town of Rimalah about 7 km NW of modern Tell es-Sweyhat (see Wilkinson et al., Excavations at Tell Es-Sweyhat, Syria, Volume 1: On the Margin of the Euphrates: Settlement and Land Use at Tell Es-Sweyhat and in the Upper Lake Assad Area, Syria, OIP 124 p. 4 fig. 112). This assumes that the writing Ra'ak lies behind an original GN *Ralak; ' often appears as a reflex of l in the Ebla orthography. Ra'ak occurs in the Ebla archives in connection with ancient Alagu; see Archi, Piacentini, and Pomponio, Luogo p. 142. Alagu could be connected with modern Tell Ali al-Haj, located between Rimalah and Tell es-Sweyhat.

The town of Ašaltu is likely to be connected with the large mound of Tell es-Sweyhat. For reports on the important site, see T. Holland, "An Inscribed Weight from Tell Sweyhat, Syria," Iraq 37 (1976) pp. 75–76; idem, "Preliminary Report on Excavations at Tell es-Sweyhat, Syria, 1973-74," Levant 8 (1977) pp. 36–70; idem, "Preliminary Report on Excavations at Tell es-Sweyhat, Syria, 1975," Levant 9 (1977) pp. 36–65; idem, "Tall as-Swēhat 1989–1992," AfO 40/41 (1993–94) pp. 275–85; T. Holland and R. Zettler, "Sweyhat" AJA 95 (1991) pp. 717–19; T. Holland, T. Wilkinson, and R. Zettler, "Sweyhat." AJA 98 (1994) pp. 39–42; and finally T. Wilkinson et al., Excavations at Tell Es-Sweyhat, Syria, Volume 1: On the Margin of the Euphrates: Settlement and Land Use at Tell Es-Sweyhat and in the Upper Lake Assad Area, Syria, OIP 124.

The town of Naḫal "Wadi" may be connected with modern Minnhal es Sallâl located about 10 km N of Tell Es-Sweyhat.

The reading ba-ul.KI of obv. col. iv line instead of the earlier ba-dul.KI given by Pettinato in the editio princeps results from a collation of the text by Fronzaroli communicated by Bonechi.

TEXT

Obv. col. Iii
9) KALAM-*tim* KALAM-*tim*
10) *ra-'à-ak*.KI
11) *ù*
12) NI-*rum*.KI
13) *ù*
14) *áš-al$_6$-tú*.KI
15) *ù*
Obv. col. iv
1) *ba-ul*.KI
2) [*sà*]-*ù-mu*
3) EN
4) *ma-rí*.KI
5) GÍN.ŠÈ
6) *in*
7) ZÀ
8) [x]-AN.KI
9) *in*
10) *na-ḫal*
11) DU$_6$.SAR
12) G̃AR

iii 9 – iv 12) Sa'ūmu, king of Mari, defeated the lands of Ra'ak, NIrum, Ašaltu, and Ba'ul and raised tumuli (honouring his dead) in the border region of x-an near the wadi.

Išṭup-Šar

E1.10.9

A king named Išṭup-Šar appears in one section of the military letter or bulletin of Enna-Dagān.

There has been some debate as to the correct reading of the royal name. Personal names with the divine element Šar are commonly attested at Ebla (see Pomponio and Xella, Les dieux d'Ebla pp. 501–2), and most commentators have read the name in TM.75.G.2367 as Išṭup-Šar. However, in their JCS 55 article, Archi and Biga read the royal name as Ištup-Išar. This is presumably based on the fact that a god Išar "Justice" is also well attested at Ebla (see Pomponio and Xella, Les dieux d'Ebla pp. 440–42, 501–2). Further, the god Išar appears as an important god at Mari in OB times (see Lambert, MARI 4 pp. 529–30).

We have opted for the more traditional reading in this volume.

1

A passage dealing with Išṭup-Šar is found in TM.75.G.2367.

COMMENTARY

The passage is found on obv. iv 13 – v 13 of TM.75.G.2367.

The phrase GA-*ni-um eb-la*.KI of v 1–2 has engendered some discussion by scholars. Pettinato (OrAnt 19 [1980] p. 239) translated it reasonably as "canneto di Ebla" "canebreak of Ebla." This is supported by the gloss [*ga*]-*nu-um* for GIŠ-gi in the Ebla vocabulary noted by Fronzaroli in ARET 13 p. 40. Kienast (OrAnt 19 [1980] p. 256) reiterated Pettinato's earlier (1978) improbable translation of GA-*ni-um* as "commercial colony." Geller in Gordon (ed.), Eblaitica 1 p. 144 n. 11 suggested an identification with Akkadian *qannu*(*m*) "border, environs" in which case a translation "on the border of (the state of) Ebla" would be in order. This seems unlikely to me. Fronzaroli (ARET 13 p. 40) suggested a connection with the Akkadian term *ganūnu*(*m*) "storehouse" which seems improbable.

The name Ebla here amost certainly does not refer to the great city of Ebla but rather a (small?) namesake, near Emar. The same town is probably referred to in a LB tablet from Tell Munbaqat (see Mayer, Tall Munbāqa-Ekalte-II: Die Texte [Saarbrücken: Saarbrücken Verlag, 2001], p. 105 no. 33 line 14), since the tablet refers to workers from the Euphrates river district around Emar. A connection with the modern village of Mallâh 5 km N of Meskeneh/Emar is conceivable.

The reading of the GN in iv 16 and v 11 is problematic. A noncommittal reading would be *la-la*-NI-*um*. Pettinato (OrAnt 19 [1990] p. 239), read *la-la-ni-um*.KI. Astour (in Gordon [ed.], Eblaitica 3 p. 29) transcribed the name as Lalayum and indicated that the town must have been located near Emar on the same (western) bank of the Euphrates. He suggested a connection with the town of *ša-la-la-la-im*.KI noted in Bardet, ARMT 23 no. 69 line 4; it was a town on the Euphrates in the district of Dūr-Iaḫdun-Līm. However, this is clearly much too far south to be connected with Emar. Archi, Piacentini, and Pomponio, Luogo p. 331, plausibly read the complex as *la-la-bu*$_{16}$-*um*. Bonechi in Rép. Géogr. 12/1, on the other hand, gave a noncommittal reading of *la-la*-NI-*um*.KI. Unfortunately, as far as can be determined, the GN is otherwise unattested in the Ebla archive. If read LA.LA-*bu*$_{16}$-*um*, a connection with the modern site of Ḥalāwa 12 km N of Meskeneh is conceivable. This is possible since thewriting la-la could stand, according to the Ebla writing system, for /alla/ (see Archi, Piacentini, and Pomponio, Luogo p. 17). This hypothesis is supported by the occurrence of a GN Bēt Ilu-abu in the LB tablets from Tell Ḥalāwa (Mayer, Tall Munbāqa-Ekalte-II: Die Texte [Saarbrücken: Saarbrücken Verlag, 2001], p. 117 no. 48 line 2), which may correspond to Eblaic LA.LA-*bu*$_{16}$-*um*. For the archaeological finds at Ḥalāwa, see W. Orthmann, AfO 26 (1978–79) pp. 157–59, AfO 28 (1981–82) pp. 223–26, and AfO 31 (1984) pp. 142–46. In the last article a spectacular EB limestone stele fragment from a temple is published attesting to the richness of the site in ED times.

Of further note is the appearance of the city of Emar in obv. col. iv line 14: *ì-mar*.KI. For ED text references to Emar in the Ebla archive, see Archi, "Imâr au IIIème Millénaire d'après les archives d'Ebla," MARI 6 pp. 21–38. For OB references see Durand, MARI 6 pp. 39–92.

For a general discussion of the excavations of Emar see the articles in D. Beyer (ed.), Meskéné-Emar: Dix ans de travaux 1972–1982, especially pp. 141–42 for a bibliography of relevant material up to 1982. For later articles see J. Margueron "Imar et Emar: Une recherche qui se prolonge ... (histoire d'une problématique)," MARI 6 pp. 103–6; B. Geyer, "Une ville aujord'hui engloutie: Emar contribution géomorphologique à la localisation de la cité," MARI 6 pp. 107–19 and the bibliographies cited there. See also Anastasio, 1 p. 215 sub. Meskené. For a survey of the later cuneiform sources (up to 1988) pertaining to the city, see H. Klengel "Die Keilschrifttexte von Meskene und die Geschichte von Aštata/Emar," OLZ 1988 cols. 645–53.

Until recently it was thought that no archaeological remains of the late ED and Old Akkadian periods had been found at Meskeneh; occupation was thought to have begun during the Middle Bronze period. However, the reopening of excavations at the site by a joint Syrian-German team (see U. Finkbeiner, Berytus 44 [1999–2000] pp. 534 and especially the contribution of Anja Rothmund on pp. 14–19) has yielded remains of the Early Bronze IV period. We can be reasonably certain that the site referred to as Imar in the Ebla texts corresponds to the early levels of the tell and is not to be placed at a neighbouring site as Margueron had previously suggested.

A large number of LB economic texts from Emar have been produced both from excavations of the French at the site (for the excavated texts see Arnaud, Emar VI/3) and by local inhabitants of the region after the flooding of the area by the Tabqa dam (for two recent bibliographies of the publications of the latter finds see J. Goodnik Westenholz, Cuneiform Inscriptions in the Collection of the Bible Lands Museum Jerusalem: The Emar Tablets pp. 99–107 and G. Beckman, Texts from the Vicinity of Emar in the collection of Jonathan Rosen pp. 141–43. For an extremely useful typologically organized catalogue of the texts, see G. Beckman, "Emar and Its Archives," in M. Chavalas (ed.), Emar: The History, Religion and Culture of a Syrian Town in the Late Bronze Age pp. 10–12. A very useful general bibliography on Emar (up to 1996) is found in Chavalas. ibid. pp. 165–72.

BIBLIOGRAPHY

For the bibliography of this text see the introduction to the Mari section sub. (ii) The Enna-Dagān letter or military bulletin from Ebla.

TEXT

Obv. col. iv
13) *ù*
14) *ì-mar*.KI
15) *ù*
16) LA.LA-*bu*$_{16}$ -*um*.KI
17) *ù*
Obv. col. v
1) *ga-ni-um*
2) *eb-la*.KI
3) *iš-ṭup*-LUGAL
4) LUGAL
5) *ma-rí*.KI
6) GÍN.ŠÈ
7) *in*
8) *ì-mar*.KI
9) *ù*

iv 13 – v 13) Now Išṭup-Šar, king of Mari, defeated Imar, LA.LA-bum at the reed thicket of Ebla and raised tumuli (honouring his dead) at Imar and LA.LA-bum.

10) *in*
11) LA.LA-*bu*$_{16}$ -*um*.KI
12) DU$_6$.SAR
13) G̃AR

Ikūn-Mari

E1.10.10

1

An inscription on a stone(?) jar names a certain ALma as wife of Ikūn-Mari, ("Mari is firm"), king of Mari.

COMMENTARY

The jar is housed in a private collection. Its script suggests that it dates to a period after the preceding inscription.

The straight lower line of the lugal sign of line 2 indicates a date later than the inscription of Ikū(n)-Šamaš. The relatively vertical second wedge of the –ma sign suggests a date before that of Išgi-Mari.

Of interest is the occurrence of a messenger of the city of u_9-*ra-na-a*.KI mentioned in Archi, ARET 5 no. 16 §23 line 9, especially since ALma herself appears in §17 line 3 of the same text. The text also mentions King NIzi of Mari as well as the future Mariote kings (then princes) Enna-Dagān and ḪI-da'ar. Prince Gulla appears in §13 line 6 of the same text (cf. E1.10.19 below).

The etymology of the PN ALma is unclear; Krebernik, Personenamen p. 139 does not attempt an interpretation, nor does Pagan, ARES 3, p. 286.

BIBLIOGRAPHY

1984 Fales, MARI 3 pp. 269–70 (photo, edition, study)

1990 Gelb and Kienast, Königsinschriften pp. 8–9 MP 7 (Ikūmari) (edition)

1991 Braun-Holzinger, Weihgaben pp. 126–27 G 68 (edition, study)

TEXT

1) AL_6-*ma* 2) DAM	1–2) ALma, wife of
3) *i-kùn-ma-rí*.KI 4) LUGAL *ma-rí*.KI	3–4) Ikūn-Mari, king of Mari,
5) ^{d}NIN.ZI WA-*ra-ne*.KI 6) $SAG.RIG_9$	5–6) dedicated (this jar) to the deity NIN.ZI of Warane.

Ikū(n)-Šamagan

E1.10.11

2001

A statue from Mari was dedicated for Ikū(n)-Šamagan "The god Šamagan is firm," king of Mari. His placement in the sequence of Mari kings is unknown. He is arbitrarily placed here.

COMMENTARY

The gypsum statue, which measures 114 cm in height with the socle and 92 cm in height without the socle, was found in room 13 of the temple of Inanna.ZA.ZA at Mari. The lower piece (bust and torso) was given the excavation number M 2300, and the upper piece (head) the number M 2323. The inscription was collated from the published photo. The statue is now housed in the museum in Damascus, with the museum number Š 2061.

Gelb and Kienast (Königsinschriften p. 10 sub MP 9) suggested that ^{d}*ša-ma-gan* was a phonetic writing for the Hurrian sun god, and thus identified this text as a second inscription of King *i-ku-*^{d}UTU (E1.10.2.1). However, according to Wilhelm (Hurrians p. 53), the name of the Hurrian son god was Šimike/a not Šamagan. It is clear that the divine component in the RN of line 1 is the equid god Šamagan, for which see Lambert, ASJ 3 (1981) pp. 31–36; Pomponio, Orientalia NS 53 (1984) pp. 1–7; Lambert, Orientalia NS 55 (1984) pp. 152–58; Lambert, in Durand and Kupper (eds.), Studies Birot p. 187; Pomponio, Prosopografia pp. 226 and 245; Alster, ASJ 9 (1987) p. 32 note to line 19; Krebernik, Personennamen p. 107; and Pomponio and Xella, Les dieux d'Ebla pp. 324–26.

BIBLIOGRAPHY

1953 Parrot, Syria 30 p. 211 and pls. XXI–XXII (photos, study)
1960 Parrot, Sumer pp. 116–17 and fig. 146; p. 380 (photo, study)
1967 Parrot, MAM 3 pp. 37–39 and figs. 31–35 (photos, study); pp. 309–10 and fig. 320 (copy, edition); pls. XII–XIII (photos)
1970 Lambert, RA 64 pp. 168 and 170 no. 1 (copy, edition)
1971 Sollberger and Kupper, IRSA IG5b (translation)
1977 Braun-Holzinger, Beterstatuetten pp. 51–52 sub Miss. Mari III no. 1 (study); pl. 23a and c (photos)
1981 Spycket, Statuaire pp. 86–88 and n. 213 (study); p. 87 fig. 31 (drawing)
1982 Cooper, SARI 1 pp. 86–87 Ma 2.1 (translation)
1990 Gelb and Kienast, Königsinschriften p. 10 MP 9 (Ikūnšamagan 2) (edition)
1991 Braun-Holzinger, Weihgaben p. 245 St 27 (edition, study)

TEXT

1) *i-ku-*^{d}*ša-ma-gán*	1–2) (For) Ikū(n)-Šamagan, king of Mari,
2) LUGAL *ma-rí*.KI	
3) AB×ÁŠ	3–4) Šēbum, the land registrar,
4) SA_{12}.SUG_5	

5) DÙL-*śù*
6) ^{d}INANNA×ZA.ZA
7) SAG.RIG$_{9}$

5–7) dedicated a statue of him (the king) to INANNA-ZA.ZA.

2002

A stone vessel from Mari bears a dedicatory inscription for King Ikū(n)-Šamagan.

COMMENTARY

The grey-green stone vessel, which measures 13 cm in height and 11.2 cm in width, was found in room 6 of the Aštarat temple at Mari and was given the excavation number M 2241 (present location unknown).

The regular script of this piece suggests that the date of the reign of Ikūn-Šamagan is to be placed after that of Ikūn-Mari.

BIBLIOGRAPHY

1967 Parrot, MAM 3 pp. 179–80, 229–330 fig. 346 and pl. LXX (photo, copy, edition)
1971 Sollberger and Kupper, IRSA, IG5a (translation)
1982 Cooper, SARI 1 p. 87 Ma 2.2 (translation)
1984 Krebernik, ZA 74 p. 165 (study)
1985 Lambert, in MARI 4 p. 535 (study)
1990 Gelb and Kienast, Königsinschriften pp. 10–11 MP 10 (Ikūnšamagan 3) (edition)
1991 Braun-Holzinger, Weihgaben p. 127 G 69 (edition, study)

TEXT

1) *i-ku-*^{d}*ša-ma-gan*
2) [LUGAL] *ma-rí*.KI
3) *śu-we-d*[*a*]
4) SÌLA.ŠU.DU$_{8}$
5) DUMU.NITA
6) BE*śù*-BÀD
7) GA.RAŠ(RAŠ:GA)
8) ^{d}ÍD
9) ^{d}*aš*$_{10}$(DIŠ)-*tár-at*
10) SAG.RIG$_{7}$

1–2) (For) Ikū(n)-Šamagan, [king] of Mari,

3–4) Šū-wēd[ā], the cup-bearer,

5–6) son of Beʾalśu-dūrum, the merchant,

7–10) dedicated (this vessel) to the river-god and Aštarat.

2003

A third statue fragment from Mari names Ikū(n)-Šamagan.

COMMENTARY

The alabaster statue fragment, which measures 11.4×6.2 cm, was found in room 13 of the Ninni-ZA.ZA temple at Mari, and was given the excavation number M 2385.

BIBLIOGRAPHY

1967 Parrot, MAM 3 pp. 39–40 no. 2 and fig. 37 (photo, study); pp. 310–11 and fig. 321 (copy, edition)
1977 Braun-Holzinger, Beterstatuetten p. 69 (transliteration, study)
1990 Gelb and Kienast, Königsinschriften p. 11 MP 11 (Ikūnšamagan 4) (edition)
1991 Braun-Holzinger, Weihgaben p. 245 St 28 (edition, study)

TEXT

1) *i-k*[*u*]-^{d}*ša-m*[*a*]-*ga*[*n*]
2) LUGA[L *ma-rí*.KI]
Lacuna

1–2) (For[?]) Ikū(n)-Šam[a]ga[n], ki[ng of Mari].

Lacuna

IB-LUL-il

E1.10.12

A variety of sources refer to a king of Mari whose name is consistently written IB-LUL-il. The RN has frequently been read Iplul-Il, but there has been some scholarly debate about its correct reading and interpretation. Krebernik (Personennamen p. 39) points out that, at least for the Ebla texts, a reading lul for LUL has not been firmly established. Further, if the verb were to be related to the Semitic root p-l-l "watch over," the "preterite" form (at least in normal Akkadian) would be *iplil* not *iplul*. A reading Iplu(s)-il for the RN has been suggested by some scholars; cf. Pagan, in his dissertation, Morphological and Lexical Study of Personal Names in the Ebla Texts p. 281:

> For /yiplus/, cf. [Krebernik, Die] P[ersonennamen der] E[bla] T[exte] pp. 39–40 s.v. B-L-S (Akk. palāsum or parāsum): [di Vito,] S[tudies in] T[hird] M[illennium] P[ersonal] N[ames] p. 194 24.6a: ip-lu$_5$-il/DINGIR, ip-lu$_5$/lu-sí-DINGIR, ip-lu-us-DINGIR "(The) god looked (graciously)."

However in Pagan's (later) publication of his dissertation (in ARES 3) he writes (p. 101):

> For /yiblul/, cf. *MAD 3,* p. 96 s.v. BLL /balālum/ "'to pour out' (or the like)": ib-lul-DINGIR, ib-lul-il (PSarg., Sarg. PN's); Westenholz, *ARES* 1, p. 111: i-pù-LUL-il (Šuruppak); p. 113: ib-lul-DINGIR (Northern Babylonia); p. 114: ib-lul-il (Nippur), etc. /yiblul-il/. For another view, cf Müller, *BaE*, p. 182: *ip-lul-il* (Edzard, ARET II, 107: "Il ist vorangegangen"); Müller, *Ebla 1975–1985,* p. 107: ip-lul-il "Il ging voran."

In view of these uncertainties a broad transcription IB-LUL-il is given in this volume.

IB-LUL-il seems to have been a particularly energetic campaigner in the wars Mari waged against Ebla; fully five passages from the Enna-Dagān letter or military bulletin deal with skirmishes with Ebla in the area of the Upper Euphrates river.

1

A statuette fragment from Mari bears an inscription indicating that it was dedicated to the goddess INANNA-ZA.ZA by a certain AMAR-AN for the life of King IB-LUL-il of Mari and his wife Paba.

COMMENTARY

The headless gypsum statue depicting a male figure is made up of three joined pieces, M 2620+2785+2853, and is now housed in the Aleppo museum. It measures 36.5 cm in height, with a width of 16.0 cm at the shoulders. It was found in the doorway between rooms 13 and 12 (M 2853) and in room 12 (M 2785) of the Ninni-ZA.ZA temple at Mari. The inscription appears in two columns on the back.

The form of the ma sign in line 2 of the text indicates a date for IB-LUL-il after that of Ikū(n)-Šamaš.

For the reading of the PN of line 3 as *pa*$_4$-*ba*$_4$ see Pomponio and Biga NABU 1989 no. 114. They write:

> On peut supposer que ses variantes, qui expliquent la lecture *Pa*$_4$-*ba*$_4$, soient: *Pa-a-ba*$_4$, nom de la personne qui, d'une part, reçoit de l'argent à porter à Mari (ARET 1, 44 r. I 7, v. II 3), d'autre part est "débitrice" (al$_6$) de 40 textiles pour les noces de Za'aše, fille de Ibbi-zikir (ARET 7, 132 r. I 4); et encore: *Ba-Ba*$_4$ (ARET 8, 533 r. VII 13), la femme de Hidar, un fonctionnaire de Nizi et de Enna-Dagan qui devint ensuite roi de Mari; et enfin (probablement): *Ba-ba*, nom d'un personnage de Mari qui s'occupe de métaux (ARET 2, p. 104) et d'un autre personnage de Tuttul "résidant" à Martu (ARET 8, 533 XVII 6; cf. aussi ARES I, p. 294).

They further note several records of gifts to queen Paba (of Mari), namely Archi, ARET 7 no. 3 obv. v lines 4–6 (received in the town of Zalagatum); Archi, ARET 7 no. rev. iv lines 6–7 (received in the town of Mane); Archi, ARET 7 no. 7 rev. i line 3 (presumably received in the town of Mane); and Archi, ARET 7 no. 12 obv. col. iii line 1 (locale of reception uncertain). As is noted below, Mane apparently lay near the border region between Ebla and Mari.

Sallaberger, in Lebeau (ed.) Subartu 4/2 p. 36, remarks in connection with the text from Tell Beydar published in copy by Van Leberghe and transliterated by Sallaberger and Talon as text no. 23 in Lebeau (ed.), Subartu 2: "Mit dem bisher dargelegten Befund vor Augen ist es wohl nicht zu gewagt, die, in i 1 genannte Person, Paba, mit der gleichnamigen Königin von Mari, der Gemahlin IbLUL-ils, zu identifizieren."

Four scholars (Bonechi, Catagnoti, Tonietti, and Sallaberger, see bibliography) have all proposed a tentative connection of AMAR-DIĜIR of line 5 with the *mar-ra*-DIĜIR EN *na-ĝàr* appearing in Archi, ARET 7 no. 16 § 19 lines 9–11. If this is true, it would provide an important synchronism between the reigns of NI-*zi* of Mari, *Ma-ra*-DIĜIR of Naĝar and IB-LUL-il of Mari. However, Catagnoti, in Lebeau (ed.), Subartu 4/2 p. 44, writes: " ... it is difficult to justify the writing AMAR- for mar-ra, especially as the meaning of the latter element is still unclear."

Further, Tonietti in the same volume p. 92 notes:

> As regards *ma-ra*-AN, the interpretation of the element *ma-ra-* is uncertain. ([Krebernik] PET 96 has /mar/- "'Mann'?"); Bonechi 1996a: [Bonechi, "Lexique et idéologie royale à l'époque proto-Syrien," in MARI 8 p. 519] §5.3 and n. 319 suggests considering it as a form of the divine element *mêrum*, comparing the name to the OAkk PNs *me-ra*-DINGIR and DINGIR-*me-ra* (ibid. n. 149), but the form *ma-ra-* is not otherwise attested. If *ma-ra*-AN and AMAR-AN were really two different spellings of the same PN, another possibility could be to interpret ma-ra-an as an unorthographic spelling of the Sumerian name amar-an, attested in normal writing in the Mari inscription.

For the PN of line 6 we may note the comments of Tonietti in Lebeau (ed.), Subartu 4/2 p. 93:

> The spelling with ŠA must indicate a Semitic reading of the name. In Sargonic PNs ^{d}UTU is often followed by the phonetic complement ši/si, always in PNs of the type DN-šamši "DN is my sun" ... In [Gelb and Kienast] FAOS 7: 12 a reading UR-^{d}*šamšā* is suggested, where *šamša* is interpreted as the *status determinatus* of the DN Šamaš (for which we can recall the presence of such pairs as Hadda/Hadad).

Tonietti, in Lebeau (ed.) Suabartu 4/2 pp. 93–94, suggests the element UR in the PN of line 6 could possibly be read kalab "dog."

The reading of line 8 is very problematic. Bonechi (in Lebeau [ed.] Subartu 4/1 p. 221 n. 20) writes:

> This writing A-PA-MAḪ is intriguing. Sollberger-Kupper 1971: 89, translate "le grand (?) ...", reading "LÚ A.PA MAḪ (?)"; Cooper 1986: 88, translates "the ..."; Gelb-Kienast 1990: 12, have a Semitic reading *a-bá-al*$_6$, and a translation "Būrilum, der Sohn des UR-UTU.ŠA der ... von Nagar, der 'Mann' des Abal", with a comparison with some Ebla PNs as *a-ba-lu* and *a-ba-la* (see also Kienast-Sommerfeld 1994: 29). I find it unlikely that "A-PA-MAḪ" is a PN, since AMAR-AN is clearly qualified as the son of Ur-^{d}UTU.ŠA; perhaps a qualification of nagar^{ki} is a better solution (even if it is difficult to accept the idea that this nagar^{ki} was different from Nagar -Tell Brak). The lacuna hampers any firm conclusion. However, a GN *a-bal*^{ki}, *a-ba*$_4$*-lu*^{ki} is well attested at Ebla, and it means "meadow"...

BIBLIOGRAPHY

1967 Parrot, MAM 3 pp. 51–52 no. 11 and figs. 57–60 (photos, translation); pp. 318–19 no. 11 (copy, edition, study); pl. XXV (photos)

1971 Sollberger and Kupper, IRSA IG4c (translation)

1977 Braun-Holzinger, Beterstatuetten p. 70 (transliteration, study)

1986 Cooper, SARI p. 88 Ma 5.1 (translation)

1989 Pomponio and Biga, "Pa$_4$-ba$_4$ épouse de Iblul-il, roi de Mari," NABU 1989 no. 114 (study)

1990 Gelb and Kienast, Königsinschriften p. 12 MP 12 (IpLULil 1) (edition)

1998 Bonechi, in Lebeau (ed.) Subartu 4 p. 221 n. 20 (study)

1998 Catagnoti, in Lebeau (ed.) Subartu 4 p. 44 sub AMAR-AN (study)

1998 Sallaberger, in Lebeau (ed.) Subartu 4 pp. 34–35 (study)

1998 Tonietti, in Lebeau (ed.) Subartu 4 pp. 92–95 (study)

TEXT

1) [IB-LUL]-*il*
2) LUGAL *ma-rí*.KI
3) *pa*$_4$*-ba*$_4$
4) NIN
5) AMAR-DIĜIR
6) DUMU UR-^{d}UTUša
7) [...] NAĜAR.KI
8) LÚ A PA AL$_6$
9) DÙL-*šù*
10) ^{d}INANNA×ZA.ZA
11) SAG.RIG$_7$

1–4) For [IB-LUL]-il, king of Mari, (and) Paba, the queen,

5–6) AMAR-DIĜIR, son of UR-Šamša

7) [...] of Nağar
8) of ...
9–11) dedicated a statue of himself to the goddess INANNA-ZA.ZA.

2

The inscription on a statue from Mari indicates that the sculpture was dedicated by a servant of IB-LUL-il.

COMMENTARY

The alabaster statue fragment, which measures 8.6×7.4 cm, was found in room 13 of the temple of Inanna-ZA.ZA. It is formed from the join of four pieces: M 2414, 2415, 2446, and 2450. The statue fragment may now be housed in Aleppo.

BIBLIOGRAPHY

1967 Parrot, MAM 3 pp. 55 no. 17 and fig. 66 (photo, study); p. 323 no. 17 and fig. 336 (copy)
1970 Lambert, RA 64 pp. 170–71 no. 17 (copy, edition)
1977 Braun-Holzinger, Beterstatuetten p. 71 sub Miss. Mari III no. 17 (study)
1986 Cooper, SARI 1 p. 88 Ma 5.3 (translation)
1990 Gelb and Kienast, Königsinschriften p. 13 MP 13 (IpLULil 2) (edition)
1991 Braun-Holzinger, Weihgaben p. 248 St 43 (edition, study)

TEXT

1) IB-LUL-⸢*il*⸣ 2) LUGAL *ma-rí*.KI	1–2) (For) IB-LUL-il, king of Mari,
3) *mín-ma-ḫir-šù* 4) ÌR-*šù* 5) UGULA GAL:É	3–5) Min-māḫiršu, his servant, the palace superintendant,
6) dINANNA×ZA.ZA 7) SAĜ.R[I]G$_9$	6–7) dedicated (this statue) to INANNA-ZA.ZA.

3

The inscription on a statuette fragment from Mari indicates that it was dedicated by Ur-Nanše to INANNA-ZA.ZA for IB-LUL-il.

COMMENTARY

The alabaster statuette fragment, which measures 12.8 cm in height and 12.2 cm in width, was found in room 13 of the temple of Ninni-ZA.ZA. It is formed from the join of three pieces: M 2272, 2376, and 2384.

The figure of Ur-Nanše can be compared to a certain Ur-Nanše who is named as a "junior singer" in two archival texts from Mari. On the possibility of the identify note Steinkeller in Studies Hallo p. 238:

Whether the same person is meant in both instances depends on the immensely complicated questions concerning the royal sequences of Ebla and Mari, which have not yet been definitively resolved.

If not identical, one could entertain the possibility of a family connection.

BIBLIOGRAPHY

1967 Parrot, MAM 3 pp. 93–96 no. 69 (study); p. 328 and fig. 345 (copy, edition); pl. 47 (photo)
1969 Sollberger, RA 63 p. 95 no. 7 (study)
1970 Lambert, RA 64 pp. 170–71 no. 17 (copy, edition)
1971 Sollberger and Kupper, IRSA, IG4a (translation)
1977 Braun-Holzinger, Beterstatuetten p. 71 sub Miss. Mari no. 69 (study)
1986 Cooper, SARI 1 pp. 88–89 Ma 5.2 (translation, conflated with E1.5.9.3)
1990 Gelb and Kienast, Königsinschriften p. 13 MP 14 (IpLULil 3) (edition)
1991 Braun-Holzinger, Weihgaben p. 249 St 52 (edition, study)

TEXT

1) IB-LUL-*il* 2) LUGAL *ma-rí*.KI	1–2) For IB-LUL-il, king of Mari,
3) ur-d[n]anše	3–4) Ur-Nanše, the chief-cantor,

4) NAR.MAḪ
5) ^{d}I[NANNA×ZA.Z]A
6) SAĞ.RIG$_{9}$

5–6) dedicated a statue of himself to INANNA-ZA.ZA.

4

A second statue of Ur-Nanše was found in the Ninni-ZA.ZA temple.

COMMENTARY

The gypsum statue, which measures 20×12.4 cm, was found in room 13 of the Inanna-ZA.ZA temple. It is formed from the join of two pieces: M 2416 and M 2365. It is now housed in the museum in Damascus, museum number Š 2071.

BIBLIOGRAPHY

1953 Parrot, Syria 30 p. 210 and pl. XXXIII (photo, study)
1960 Parrot, Sumer, fig. 155 (photo)
1962 Strommenger and Hirmer, Mesopotamien pls. 92–93 and pl. XXI (photos)
1967 Moortgat, Kunst pls. 68-69 (photos)
1967 Parrot, MAM 3 pp. 89–93 no. 68 and figs. 129–131 (photos, study); p. 327 and fig. 345 (copy, edition); pls. XLV-XLVI and frontispiece (photos)
1975 Orthmann (ed.), Der alte Orient fig. 24 (photo)
1977 Braun-Holzinger, Beterstatuetten p. 71 sub Miss. Mari no. 68 (transliteration, study)
1981 Spycket, Statuaire p. 92 and n. 246 (study); fig. 60 (photo)
1986 Cooper, SARI 1 pp. 88–89 Ma 5.2 (translation [conflation of E1.5.9.3 and 4])
1990 Gelb and Kienast, Königsinschriften p. 14 MP 15 (IpLULil 4) (edition)
1991 Braun-Holzinger, Weihgaben p. 249 St 51 (edition, study)

TEXT

1) [IB-LUL-*i*]*l*
2) [ur-^{d}n]anše
3) [N]AR.MAḪ
4) ^{d}INANNA×ZA.<ZA>
5) SAG.RIG$_{9}$

1) [IB-LUL-i]l
2–3) [Ur-N]anše, the chief-[mu]sician,
4–5) dedicated (this statue) to INANNA-ZA.ZA.

5

Various sections of the letter or military bulletin of Enna-Dagān deal with campaigns of IB-LUL-il, king of Mari. They are edited here as E1.10.13.5–9.

COMMENTARY

The first inscription is found in obv. v 14 – rev. vii 1 of TM.75.G.2367.

The reading of the toponym of obv. col. v line 15 is uncertain. As far as I can determine, it is only found in this royal inscription and in a variant form only in

Pettinato MEE 1 no. 1450 = TM .75.G.2012 = Mander MEE 10 no. 38 obv. iii line 9 *ga-la-la-bí-tù*^{ki} and Pettinato, MEE 1 no. 1451 = TM .75.G.2013 = Mander MEE 10 no. 39 obv. ii line 1 = *ga-la-la-bí-it*$_{x}$(NI).KI. Archi, Piacentini, and Pomponio, Luogo p. 228 read it as *ga-la-la*-NE-*ì*.KI. Bonechi (RGTC 12/2 p. 145) suggested a connection with *ga-la-la*-NE-NI.KI found in MEE X 39. Astour, in "The Geographical and Political Structure of the Ebla Empire," in WGE p. 146 n. 47, took it to be *ga-la-la-bí-ià*.KI and linked it to Galabatha in Isidore of Charax in his Parthian Mansions. This is almost certainly incorrect. Fronzaroli in ARET XIII pp. 36 and 41 read Ga-la-la-bí-ì^{ki} referring to Fronzarolii in Festschrift Leslau I p. 469 and Bonechi Rép Géogr. 12/1 p. 145. In MEE X no. 39 it is mentioned in connection with the cities of Arimu, Mane, and Emar suggesting a location on the west bank of the Euphrates north of Emar. A connection with modern Kheurbet Khaled 11.25 NE of modern Er Roumané (likely ancient Arimu) is conceivable.

The GN Abarsal mentioned in line obv. vi line 9 was apparently a very important city located on or near a navigable river. For a discussion of the city, see Archi, "La Ville d'Abarsal," in Lebeau and Tallon (eds.), Reflets des deux fleuves: volume de mélanges offerts à André Finet pp. 15–19. Archi, Piacentini, and Pomponio, Luogo p. 91 note: "Una localizzazione sulla riva sinistra dell'Eufrate risponde alla posizione geografica richiesta." Astour, in "The Geographical and Political Structure of the Ebla Empire," in WGE p. 147 n. 54, has plausibly located the city at or near modern Tell Aḥmar: "... very hypothetically Abarsil is located at Tell Aḥmar (Neo-Assyrian Til-Barsip) which has the right stratigraphy and whose position on a major Euphrates crossing seems to correspond to the indications of the text about the situation of Abarsil." Astour's hypothesis is very strongly supported by the evidence of the tablet published by Biga and Milano as ARET 4 no. 13 obv. i lines 5–11, which records the receipt of various textiles by the superintendent of the city of Abarsal in the villages of Zurigi and Abala. These clearly correspond to the modern villages of Zarqah and Billi, which both lie a mere 7 km NE of Tell Aḥmar. These identifications also agree with our tentative identification of ancient *ga-la-la-li*$_{9}$-*ì*.KI with Kalkali mentioned in this discussion, above.

A treaty between the city and Ebla is known from the Ebla archive; see Sollberger, "The So-Called Treaty Between Ebla and 'Ashur'," SEb 3 (1980) pp. 129–60; Edzard, "Der Vertrag von Ebla mit A-BAR-QA," in P. Fronzaroli (ed.), Literature and Literary Language at Ebla, QuSem 18 pp. 187–221; and Fronzaroli, ARET 13 pp. 43–76. The city apparently reappears in the form Apišal, written AB×ŠUŠ.KI, in an inscription of Narām-Sîn of Akkad; see Foster, ARRIM 8 (1990) pp. 25–44 for the inscription in general and pp. 40–42 § VI for the reading of the GN. See also Frayne, RIME 2 pp. 90–94, inscription E2.1.4.2. For the possible equation of Apišal appearing in an OB Mari letter and an economic text from Alalaḫ VII with Abarsal, see Tonietti, MARI 8 (1997) pp. 232–33 § 1.2.2. For the OB Mari letter itself, see Charpin and Ziegler, MARI 8 (1997) pp. 243–47.

The town of Zaḫiran could be linked to the modern Sirrîne ech Chimaâliye located on the modern Euphrates 18.75 km SE of modern Tell Aḥmar.

BIBLIOGRAPHY

For the bibliography of this text see the introduction to the Mari section sub (ii) The Enna-Dagān letter or military bulletin from Ebla.

TEXT

Obv. col. v	
14) *ù*	v 14 – vi 7) Now IB-LUL-il, king of Mari took possession of Galala-NE.NI and [GN] and ...,
15) *ga-la-la*-NE.NI.KI	
16) [*ù*]	
Col. vi	
1) [...].KI	
2) ⌜*ù*⌝	
3) *qá-nu-um*	
4) ŠU.DU$_{8}$	
5) IB-LUL-*il*	
6) EN	
7) *ma-rí*.KI	
8) *ù*	vi 8 – vii 1) defeated Abarsal near Zaḫiran and raised seven tumuli honouring his dead.
9) *a-bar-sal*$_{4}$.KI	
10) GÍN.ŠÈ	
11) *in*	
12) *za-ḫi-ra-an*.KI	

13) *ù*
14) ⌜7⌝ DU_6.SAR
15) [...]
Col. vii
1) G̃AR

6

The relevant passage is found in obv. vii 2 – obv. viii 4 of TM.75.G.2367.

BIBLIOGRAPHY

For the bibliography of this text see the introduction to the Mari section sub. (ii) The Enna-Dagān letter or military bulletin from Ebla.

COMMENTARY

The GN of viii 6 was read *ša-dab*$_6$ by Archi, Piacentini, and Pomponio (Luogo p. 435) and Bonechi (Rép. Géogr. 12/1 p. 121). However, Astour (in Chavalas [ed.], Emar p. 39) in noting the reading *ša-dab*$_6$ points out: "... da$_5$ is the only attested value of the sign in Old Akkadian, and it makes better sense in most, if not all, of its occurrences in Eblean personal and place names." Šada reappears as one of the cities along the Euphrates defeated by Tukultī-Ninurta I; see Weidner, TN p. 27 col. iii line 73. Ancient Šada is likely to be located at modern Jebel el Jaade on the west side of the Euphrates, a mere 7.5 km NE of modern Er Rommâne, possibly ancient Burman or Armiʾum (see below).

Šada is clearly to be separated from ancient GN Šatappa/Šatappi also attested in the Ebla texts; see Astour in Gordon (ed.), Eblaitica 3 p. 41 nn. 251–52 for a discussion of this place name. Šatappa almost certainly lay very close to Emar but clearly on the other side of the Euphrates, probably located at modern Jaibet just south of modern Muraybiṭ (the latter likely ancient Urim).

The GN in obv. vii line 8 was read *ad-da-bí-ì*.KI by Archi, Piacentini, and Pomponio, Luogo p. 147. In our view a preferred reading is *ad-da-ni-ì*.KI, since the name is likely to be connected with the modern site Tell Haoudâne located 10 km W of modern Er Rommâne, likely ancient Armiʾum.

The reading of the GN in obv. vii line 10 has been unclear since, according to Krebernik, ZA 72 (1982) p. 201, the sign SUM can have a value sum, zàr or sì in the Ebla texts. It was read *a-rí-sum*.KI in Archi, Piacentini, and Pomponio, Luogo p. 110; Bonechi Rép. Géogr. 12/1 p. 50; and Krecher, ARES 1 p. 185. The name is almost certainly to be connected with the modern ʿArūda Kabīra or Tell al-Ḥajj excavated by a team from the Schweizerische Geisteswissenschaftliche Gesellschaft in 1971–72 under the direction of R. Stuckey (see Anastasio, Lebeau, and Sauvage, Subartu 13 no. 106, Chalcolithic, EB, MB, Iron Age, Achaemenid, Hellenistic, Roman, Byzantine and medieval ceramics were found (see R. Stuckey, AAAS 25 [1975] pp. 165–81; a plan of the large site is found there on p. 171). In addition to a few scant remains of EB ceramics a fragment of a baked clay plaque showing parallels to the statuary found in the temples of Ištarat and Ninni-ZA.ZA at Mari was found. That a site in the vicinity bearing this name continued into LB times is indicated by the appearance of the name á-ra-s as entry 213 in the list of defeated cities in the account of the eighth campaign of Thutmoses III inscribed on the seventh pylon at Karnak. The name is found in the form Araziqi in inscriptions of Tiglath-pileser I (Grayson, RIMA 2 p. 25 A.0.87.1 col. vi line 64) and Aššur-bēl-kala (Grayson, RIMA 2 p. 103 A.0.89.7 col. iv 4); the texts refer to lion hunts in the area. It is also found in economic tablets from Alalaḫ (see Marín Rép. Géogr. 12/2 p. 3) among which the defeat of the city of Araziqi by King Niqmi-epuḫ of Aleppo is recorded in a year name. Not surprisingly, Araziqi also occurs in a tablet from nearby Emar (see D. Arnaud, AuOr 5 [1987] p. 233 no. 13 line 13). The city appears in the Peutinger Tables as Eragiza, Miller, Itineraria Romana, Stuttgart 1916 pp. 575–76 and in the work of Ptolemy A. Levi, Itineraria picta. Contributo allo studio della Tabula peutingeriana. Rome: L'erma di Bretschneider 1967 seg. 10).

The sites of ʿArūda Kabīra or Tell al-Ḥajj are not to be confused with the spectacular remains of Uruk date found at the nearby site of Jebel ʿArūda, a high spur on the western side of the Euphrates river, excavated by a Dutch team from Leiden University headed by G. van Driel. For the excavations at Jebel ʿArūda, see the notes of van Driel in AfO 26 (1978–79) p. 177; AfO 28 (1981–82) pp. 245–26; and AfO 31 (1984) pp. 134–37;

van Driel in Kohlmeyer and Strommenger (eds.), Land des Baal: Syrien – Forum der Völker und Kulturen Mainz am Rhein: P. Von Zabern, 1982 pp. 30–32; and van Driel in O. Rouault and M. Masetti-Rouault (eds.), L'Eufrate e il tempo: le civiltà del medio Eufrate e della Gezira siriana Milano: Electa, 1993 pp. 139–42. Cf. Anastasio, Lebeau, and Sauvage, Subartu 13 no. 28.

The GN Burman of line 12 is frequently attested in the Ebla texts (see Archi, Piacentini, and Pomponio, Luogo pp. 181–85). It is likely to be located at modern Oumm Mourhr on the western bank of the Euphrates about 5 km E of Jebel el Jaade. In the text published by Biga and Archi as ARET 3 no. 584, Burman occurs beside ra-ʾà-gú (likely modern Rammâlé on the east side of the Euphrates), gàr-mu (likely modern Tell Jerm on the west side of the Euphrates), and Lumnan — for the reading of the GN see Bonechi, NABU 1990 p. 22 no. 29 — (possibly modern Joubb el Hamâm on the west side of the Euphrates). All four cities occur in a more or less straight line within a distance of 10 km.

TEXT

Obv. col. vii
2) IB-LUL-*il*
3) EN
4) *ma-rí*.KI
5) *ù*
6) *ša-da*$_5$.KI
7) *ù*
8) *ad-da-ni-ì*.KI
9) *ù*
10) *a-rí-sum*.KI
11) KALAM-*tim*.KALAM-*tim*
12) *bur-ma-an*.KI
13) LÚ
14) *su-gú-rúm*.KI
15) IB-LUL-*il*
Col. viii
1) GÍN.ŠÈ
2) *ù*
3) DU$_6$.SAR
4) G̃AR

vii 2 – viii 4) IB-LUL-il, king of Mari, defeated Šada, Addani and Arisum in the lands of Burman (of the land of) Sugurum. He raised tumuli (honouring his dead).

7

The relevant passage is found in obv. viii lines 5–14 of TM.75.G.2367.

BIBLIOGRAPHY

For the bibliography of this text see the introduction to the Mari section sub. (ii) The Enna-Dagān letter or military bulletin from Ebla.

COMMENTARY

Šar-ra-an.KI of obv. col. viii line 8 clearly corresponds to the city of šu-ra-an.KI of the Ebla texts. Archi, Piacentini, and Pomponio, Luogo p. 44, have compared it with the URU.šu-ru-un.KI of the treaty between Šuppiluliuma of Hatti and Šattiwaza of Mitanni (see Klengel, Geschichte Syriens I pp. 51–52). It occurs there with the cities of Murmurik, Šipri, Mazuwati, and Aštata; the last of these almost certainly lay on the right bank of the Euphrates just south of Emar. *Ša/šu-ra-an*.KI may be compared to the GN Sure named in the

Peutinger Tables (see Miller, Itineraria Romana p. 758):

> Sure, Sura (N D — Garnison der Leg. XVI Flavia Firma — zu Augusta Eufratensisgerechnet), Suri (Ra[vennate Historian]) Zoura (Pt[olemy]) am Euphrat dagelegen ... Ruinen von Sûriah, gewöhnlich el Hammam genannt.

More precisely it is to be located at modern Sūrīyah just east of modern Qaraqol Ḥammâm.

The GN Dammium of obv. col. viii line 8 reappears in the writing *da-mi*-LUM.KI and *dam-mi-um*.KI in other Ebla texts; see Archi, Piacentini, and Pomponio, Luogo pp. 198–99. This is clear because of its association with the city of *šu-ra-an*.KI.

Ḫazuwan is attested as an important city in Ebla sources; see Bonechi and Catagnoti, NABU 1990 no. 30, Archi, Piacentini, and Pomponio, Luogo pp. 265–67, and Astour, UF 29 (1997) pp. 1–66. It has been equated by some scholars with OA, OB Ḫazu(m)/Ḫaššu(m) and Hittite Ḫašuwa. In OA sources Ḫazu occurs on the overland route to Kaniš at a point just west of Buruddum (see Nashef, Rekonstruktion der Reiserouten zur Zeit der altassyrischen Handelsniederlassungen p. 66). However, it is clear from the general geographical context of this inscription that a different Ḫazuwan is meant here. Ḫazuwan is occasionally mentioned in the triad of the cities of Kakmium, Ḫazuwan, and Irar (Archi, Piacentini, and Pomponio, Luogo p. 266). They can be linked in an east to west order with the modern sites of Qaraqol Hammâm, Sdeiyéné, and Abou Houreïra on the south shore of the Euphrates.

The reading of the GN NErat of obv. ix line 2 is uncertain. The fact that it occurs otherwise only once in the Ebla archive suggests it was a small town.

As for the GN Mane of rev. col. i line 3, we may note that three Manes are known from the Ebla archive: Mane of Gaduru, Mane of Imar, and Mane of Igdura (see Archi, Piacentini, and Pomponio, Luogo p. 380). Here we can be reasonably certain that the Mane of Imar is specified. The Mane of Imar was clearly an important city, apparently located in the border region between Ebla and Mari; there the kings of Mari received tribute from Ebla (see Archi, MARI 4 [1985] p. 65). Astour (in Gordon [ed.], Eblaitica 3 p. 38 and n. 233) has noted a possible connection with a place Mane named in a chronicle of Nabopolassar (see Grayson, Chronicles p. 91 line 7). This Mane, according to Astour, lay near a town Baliḫ situated at the mouth of the Balīḫ River. This seems unlikely in this case, because the town would seem to have been situated just to the east of ancient Imar. We would prefer a location at modern Nammâlé, 20.7 km east of Old Meskeneh (Imar).

TEXT

Obv. col. viii
5) *ù*
6) *ša-ra-an*.KI
7) *ù*
8) *dam-mi-um*.KI
9) IB-LUL-*il*
10) LUGAL
11) *ma-rí*.KI
12) GÍN.ŠÈ
13) 2 DU$_6$.SAR
14) G̃AR

viii 5 – 14) Now IB-LUL-il, king of Mari, defeated Šarān and Dammium, and raised two tumuli (honouring his dead).

Obv. col. ix
1) *in*
2) NE-*ra-at*.KI
3) *ù*
4) *in*
5) É.NA
6) *ḫa-zu-wa-an*.KI
7) È
8) IB-LUL-*il*
9) LUGAL
10) *ma-rí*.KI
11) *ù*
12) MU.TÚM
13) *eb-la*.KI

ix 1 – rev. i 3) IB-LUL-il, king of Mari, departed from NE-rat and the ... of Hazuwan and received the *tribute* of Ebla in the midst of Mane.

Reverse
Col. i
1) ŠÀ-*šù*
2) *má*:ne.KI
3) ŠU BA_4.TI
4) *ù*
5) *ì-mar*.KI
6) TUM×SAL
7) DU_6.SAR
8) G̃AR

rev. i 4 – ii 8) He (defeated) Imar and raised two tumuli (honouring his dead)

8

The relevant passage is found in rev. col. i 9 – ii 11 of TM.75.G.2367.

BIBLIOGRAPHY

For the bibliography of this text see the introduction to the Mari section sub. (ii) The Enna-Dagān letter or military bulletin from Ebla.

COMMENTARY

For the readings of the second sign in the GN in rev. ii line 5 (ḪI×MAŠ) see Steinkeller and Postgate, Texts Baghdad pp. 15–19 and Archi "The Sign-list from Ebla," in Gordon, Rendsburg, and Winter (eds.) Eblaitica 1 p. 96 entry 66: ḪI×MAŠ = *su-ru*$_{12}$*-um*. The reading -sùr is also proven by the variant spellings *ga-su-lu*.KI and *ga-su-ru*$_{12}$.KI noted by Bonechi in Rep. Geog. 12/1 p. 153 and Archi, Piacentini, and Pomponio, Luogo p. 234.

The town of Gasur was located on or near the Euphrates. For text references, see Pettinato, "Gasur nella Documentazione Epigrafica di Ebla," in Morrison and Owen (eds.), Studies in the Civilization of Nuzi and the Hurrians in Honor of Ernest R. Lacheman pp. 297–304, and Archi's notes about Gasur in Archi, "La ville d'Abarsal," in Lebeau and Talon (eds.), Reflets des deux fleuves: volume de mélanges offerts à André Finet pp. 15–19 and Archi, Piacentini, and Pomponio, Luogo pp. 233–36. It is clearly not to be identified with the Gasur located near Nuzi in the eastern trans-Tigridian lands as some commentators have earlier suggested. If this section deals with campaigns following IB-LUL-il's defeat of Imar then a possible connection might be made with the modern site of Kasra which lies on the west side of the Euphrates 33.7 km north of Old Meskeneh (Imar).

While Ganana, an apparent variant spelling of GanaNE, is attested in the Ebla archive — another spelling Gananum is also found — the texts give no indication as to its location. Ganane was the site of an important deity ^{d}BE *ga-na-na*.KI "Lord of Ganane." Pomponio and Xella (see Les dieux d'Ebla pp. 92–96) write:

> Archi (voir surtout ARES 2, p. 230), qui estime quant à lui que G[anana] doit être localisée près de l'Euphrate ... Une prise de position définitive sur cette question peut paraître encore prématurée, même si les indices dont on dispose invitent décidément à renoncer à l'idée suggestive [of Pettinato] de Canaan.

TEXT

Rev. col. i
9) IB-LUL-*il*
10) LUGAL
11) *ma-rí*.KI
12) *ù*

rev. i 9 – ii 11) IB-LUL-il, king of Mari, defeated Naḫal, Nubat, and Šada of the lands of Gasur, and raised seven tumuli (honouring his dead) in Ganane.

13) *na-ḫal*.KI
14) [*ù*]
Rev. col. ii
1) *nu-ba-at*.KI
2) *ù*
3) *ša-da$_5$*.KI
4) KALAM-*tim*.KALAM-*tim*
5) *ga-sùr*.KI
6) GÍN.ŠÈ
7) *in*
8) *ga-na-ne*.KI
9) *ù*
10) 7 DU$_6$.SAR
11) G̃AR

9

The relevant passage is found in rev. col. ii 12 – iii 10 of TM.75.G.2367. After this are five lines of uncertain interpretation.

BIBLIOGRAPHY

For the bibliography of this text see the introduction to the Mari section sub. (ii) The Enna-Dagān letter or military bulletin from Ebla.

COMMENTARY

For the location of Belān see the commentary section to inscription E1.10.1.1 where a connection with modern Tell Bellâné is proposed. Barama is likely to be located at modern Abou Barmil 15 km NW of Tell Bellâné.

TEXT

Rev. col. ii
12) IB-LUL-*il*
13) LUGAL
Rev. col. iii
1) *ma-rí*.KI
2) *ù*
3) *ba-ra-a-ma*.KI 2
4) *ù*
5) *a-bù-ru$_{12}$*.KI
6) *ù*
7) *ti-ba-la-at*.KI
8) KALAM-*tim* KALAM-*tim*
9) [*b*]*e-la-an*.KI
10) GÍN.ŠÈ

rev. ii 12 – iii 10) IB-LUL-il, king of Mari, defeated Barama twice and Aburu and Tibalat of the lands of [Be]lān.

NIzi

E1.10.13

IB-LUL-il of Mari was succeeded by King NIzi who reigned at least 3 years. For the few documents dating to his reign see Biga and Archi JCS 55 (2003) p. 4. Of interest to this study is the document TM.75.G.1953. Archi JCS 55 (2003) p. 2 writes:

> This document (TM.75.G.195) reveals to us the existence of a Mari king by the name of Nizi (*Ni-zi*), Iblul-Il's immediate successor, omitted in Enna-Dagan's letter, perhaps because nothing of great importance happened during his reign. Nizi received the same amount of silver as Enna-Dagan, but five more kilos of gold. In all probability this tablet was written on the death of Enna-Dagan and marks the start of a new phase, in which Ebla would exchange "gifts," níg-ba, with Mari on an equal footing within the context of ceremonial exchanges.

As yet no royal inscriptions of the king are known.

Enna-Dagān

E1.10.14

NIzi was succeeded by King Enna-Dagān /ḫinna-dagān/ "(Have) mercy, oh god Dagān." About this king, Archi (JCS 55 [2003] pp. 4–5) writes:

> Enna-Dagan, who succeeded him [Nizi] already appears in some of his predecessor's documents as the receiver of gifts. ARET VII 17 relates to the first year of Enna-Dagan's reign, rev. vi 1–3: áš-du En-na-^{d}Da-gan lugal 1 mu "since Enna-Dagan has been king: one year."
>
> [...]
>
> The text MEE II 35 rev. x 3–5 shows that Enna-Dagan was king for more than two years: dub-gar-nig-ba En-na-[^{d}]Da-gan [1/2+]2 mu "document of the gifts (for) Enna-Dagan (for) 3/4 years." This text, which refers to a number of years, must have been drawn up immediately after the death of king Irkab-damu, rev. viii 9–XI: 1: in ud níg-ba en šu-mu-"tag$_4$"ÉxPAP "(silver as gift for PN) on the occasion of the gift (which) the king (of Ebla) has brought (to his own?) funeral ceremony."
>
> Apart from the famous letter which allows us to reconstruct the expansion of the Mari state, the archives of Ebla also include another document from Enna-Dagan, TM.75.G.1913+, which deals with events of his reign [Fronzaroli ARET XIII 1].

The document, brilliantly edited by Fronzaroli in ARET XIII, is of major interest for the history of religion but cannot be discussed in this corpus of royal inscriptions.

1

A passage dealing with Enna-Dagān is found in rev. col. iii 11 – iv 11 of TM.75.G.2367. For the bibliography of this text see the introduction to the Mari section sub. (ii) The Enna-Dagān letter or military bulletin from Ebla.

COMMENTARY

In rev. col. iv, line 4, ma-da-a was taken by Astour (in his "History of Ebla") to be related to Akk. ma(d)dattu(m) "payment, obligation, tribute." Fronzaroli, on the other hand, in ARET XIII (p. 42), takes the form to be a dual of the word mātum "land" and writes:

> Lo scriba, che usa sempre altrove il sumerogramma kalam-*tim*, sembra avere preferito qui la grafia fonetica per esprimere il numero. Il duale /māt-ay(n)/ "i due paesi" può indicare l'area di influenza mariota e l'area di influenza eblaita (cf. *mātum elîtum* "il Paese Superiore" nei testi marioti di età paleobabilonese). Per le forme del duale nominale nei testi eblaiti, Fronzaroli, *Fs Segert*, pp. 112-119. Per l'interpretazione di questo passo proposta da Pettinato (*OA* 19 [1980], p. 242 e p. 244; così anche in *AuOr* 13 [1995], p. 83), si veda quanto osservato da Edzard, *SEb* 4 (1981), p. 95.

In line 5 of the same column, Ì.GIŠ apparently designated "una cerimonia con la quale Ebla si legava a città importanti" (Archi, Piacentini, and Pomponio, Luogo p. 235). Fronzaroli in ARET XIII p. 42 writes in connection with this word:

> Per l'occasione rituale cui si riferisce questa formula, si veda in questo stesso volume il testo 18 (r. I 3-6) [TM 75G.1477]. Al giuramento di alleanza si riferiscono anche i testi 19 [TM 75G.2561] (r. VI 15-v. I 1), 20 (r. I 1-5) e 21 (v. IV 7-9).

BIBLIOGRAPHY

For the bibliography of this text see the introduction to the Mari section sub. (ii) The Enna-Dagān letter or military bulletin from Ebla.

TEXT

Rev. col. iii
11) *en-na-da-gan*
12) EN
13) *ma-rí*.KI
Rev. col. iv
1) [N DU_6.SAR]
2) ĜAR
3) *ma-da-a*
4) *in*
5) Ì.GIŠ
6) KALAM-*tim* KALAM-*tim*
7) ŠU.DU_8

rev. iii 11–iv 2) Enna-Dagān, king of Mari raised [N tumuli (honouring his dead)].

rev. iv 3 – 7 and on the occasion of (the offerings) of the oil of the lands took possession of the two lands.

Ikū(n)-išar

E1.10.15

Concerning Ikūn-išar, Enna-Dagan's successor, Archi and Biga (JCS 55 [2003] p. 5) comment:

> Iku(n)-išar is mentioned in an AAM from the first year of minister Ibrium (in the first months of the same year in which king Irkab-damu died): TM.75.G.1705 (Ibr. 1.b) rev. vi 4–10: tar kù-gi *I-ku-i-šar* en *Ma-rí*[ki] *Du-tum Ma-rí*[ki] šu-mu-"tag" "30 (shekels) of gold for Iku-išar, king of Mari, Dutum of Mari has brought." The only other reference to this king is in ARET I 11 (17): *I-ku-šar* en *Ma-rí*[ki] *I-ga-iš-ru*$_{12}$ šu-mu-"tag$_4$" "(garments for) Iku(n)-(i)šar, king of Mari, Iga-išru has brought." This MAT registers in section (41) the gifts for Taḫir-malik, daughter of minister Ibrium, on the occasion of her marriage. It has to be dated to the same year as the AAM Ibr. 1.b, which mentions "the marriage of Ibrium's daughter" in rev. XI 18–21: in ud níg-mu-sá dumu-mí *Ib-rí-um* and has other parallel sections.

A broken seal impression found at Mari in 2000 mentions a certain *i-ku-*[..]. We suggest (as does Charpin) that the name is to be restored as Ikū[(n)-išar].

1

COMMENTARY

The impression is found on TH.00.161, a clay door sealing. On its discovery, see Beyer "Les sceaux de Mari au IIIe millénaire: observations sur la documentation ancienne et les données nouvelles des Villes I et II" (forthcoming). He notes:

> Une précision chronologique pourrait être éventuellement fournie par le scellement TH. 00. 161 (fig. 21): sur ce document, qui porte une empreinte lacunaire du sceau d'Iddin-Eshtar, figurent également les vestiges très fragmentaires d'un autre sceau dont seul le début du cartouche inscrit est visible. Il est naturellement tentant d'y retrouver le nom d'Ikun-Ishar, avant-dernier souverain de Mari cité dans les textes d'Ebla, plutôt que les rois de Mari Ikun-Shamaganou encore Ikun-Shamash, connus par leurs statue, à placer sans doute plus tôt dans la chronologie. Mais on ne peut actuellement rien exclure, y compris le nom d'un nouveau souverain, au service duquel aurait été le Shakkanakku Iddin-Eshtar.

BIBLIOGRAPHY

Beyer "Les sceaux d'Ishqi-Mari et l'idéologie royale à Mari au IIIè millénaire" (forthcoming).

Beyer "Les sceaux de Mari au IIIe millénaire: observations sur la documentation ancienne et les données nouvelles des Villes I et II" (forthcoming)

I am very grateful to Professor Beyer for providing me with copies of his articles before their publication.

TEXT

1) *i-ku-*[*i-šar*]
2) LUGAL [*ma*]-*r*[*í*]

1-2) Ikū[(n)-išar], king of [Ma]r[i].

Ḫl-da᾿ar

E1.10.16

A king of Mari named Ḫl-da'ar is mentioned during the time of Išar-Damu of Ebla (Archi and Biga, JCS 55 [2003] p. 5). Although Archi believed that a seal impression of this king was found at Mari, a re-examination of the piece by Beyer indicates that this is no longer tenable (Beyer "Les sceaux d' Ishqi-Mari et l'idéologie royale à Mari au IIIè millénaire"). Charpin, JCS 55 (2005) no. 1, suggests that Ḫl-da'ar followed after Ikun-išar, possibly as his immediate successor. According to Charpin, the tablets of Chantier B which date to years 18–35 date to King Ḫl-da᾿ar and his reign was roughly contemporaneous with that of Išar-Damu of Ebla. As yet no royal inscriptions of Ḫl-da᾿ar have appeared.

Išgi-Mari

E1.10.17

According to Archi and Biga, as well as Charpin, the reign of Išgi-Mari followed upon that of ḪI-da'ar and likely lasted eight years before the destruction of the city by Sargon. According to Charpin, the tablets of groups C and D from level P-1 date to the time of Išgi-Mari.

For the reading and interpretation of the RN, see Müller, "Das eblaitische Verbalsystem nach den bisher veröffentlichen Personennamen," in Cagni (ed.), La lingua di Ebla p. 229.

A small statue from Mari which supposedly had the name iš-gi$_4$ in the first line was taken by some to be a second inscription of Išgi-Mari based on the assumption that the element Mari was not written. The piece was found in the Presargonic palace at Mari; it was given the museum number M 4380 and was published in Parrot, Syria 42 (1965) p. 214 and n. 2 and pl. 13 no. 1 (photo, study); Braun-Holzinger, Beterstatuetten p. 72 (study); and Gelb and Kienast, Königsinschriften p. 15 MP 18 (Išqīmari 2 = "Lamgimari") (edition). However, as we were kindly informed by G. Marchesi (oral communication, 02-07-2005), in Marguernon's recently published book on Mari there is a photo of the inscription which shows a clear BE sign after the element Išgi. Consequently the inscription is likely not a royal inscription at all, but simply a votive of a certain Išgi-Bēlum.

A handful of royal inscriptions of Išgi-Mari are known.

1

A small statue of a standing figure from Mari bears the inscription of Išgi-Mari "(The god) Mari is great." For the reading and interpretation of the RN see Müller, "Das eblaitische Verbalsystem nach den bisher veröffentlichen Personennamen," in Cagni (ed.), La lingua di Ebla p. 229.

COMMENTARY

The white limestone statue, which measures 27.2 cm in height and 10.2 cm in width, was found in courtyard 20 of the Ištar temple at Mari. It was given the excavation number M 174; the statue is now housed in the Aleppo Museum, no. 1486. The inscription is on the right upper-arm and back of the statue.

The straight lower line of the lugal sign of line 2 as well as the unbroken pa element in the word énsi clearly indicates a date later than the inscription of Ikū(n)-Šamaš.

For the deity ^{d}INANNA.NITA, probably a reference to the male form of Aštar, cf. Ugaritic and South Arabian ʿṯtr, see Edzard, CRRAI 15 pp. 53–54; Cooper, JNES 33 (1974) p. 416; Lambert, MARI 4 (1985) p. 537; and Heimpel "A Catalogue of Near Eastern Venus Deities," SMS 4/3 (1982) pp. 13–15.

BIBLIOGRAPHY

1934 Thureau-Dangin, RA 31 pp. 140–41 (photo, edition)
1935 Parrot, Syria 16 pp. 23–24 and pls. VI–VII (photo, study)
19xx Mari, une ville perdue pp. 102–4 and figs. 8–9 (...)
1953 Parrot, Mari pls. 8–10 (photo)
1956 Parrot, MAM 1 pp. 68–70 no. 1, fig. 46 and pls. 25–26 (photo, study, edition)
1961 Gelb, MAD 2 p. 2 no. 2 (study)
1967 Moortgat, Kunst fig. 84 (photo)
1971 Sollberger and Kupper, IRSA IG2a (translation)
1974 Parrot, Mari pl. 4 no. 1 (photo)
1975 Orthmann (ed.), Der alte Orient pl. 30 (photo)
1977 Braun-Holzinger, Beterstauetten pp. 57–58, 69 and pls. 28 c–e (photo, transliteration, study)
1981 Spycket, Statuaire pp. 88–89 and n. 222 (study)
1984 Krebernik, ZA 74 p. 164 (study)
1986 Cooper, SARI 1 p. 89 Ma 6 (translation)
1990 Gelb and Kienast, Königsinschriften p. 15 MP 17 (Išqīmari 1 = "Lamgimari") (edition)
1991 Braun-Holzinger, Weihgaben p. 244 St 24 (edition, study)

TEXT

1) *iš*$_{11}$(LAM)-*gi*$_4$-*ma-rí* 2) LUGAL *ma-rí* 3) ÉNSI GAL 4) ^{d}*en-líl*	1–4) Išgi-Mari, king of Mari, chief ruler for the god Enlil,
5) DÙL-*šu* 6) *a-na* 7) ^{d}INANNA.NITA 8) SAG.RIG$_9$	5–8) dedicated a statue of himself to the male Aštar.

2

A seal inscription known from several clay impressions found in the year 2000 in Mari mentions Išgi-Mari as king of Mari.

COMMENTARY

Object numbers for the seal impressions include TH.00.1621–42 found in III P 10 NE 25 and TH.00.152 found in IIIQ 10 SO 13.

BIBLIOGRAPHY

Beyer, "Les sceaux d'Ishqi-Mari et l'idéologie royale à Mari au IIIe millenaire (forthcoming).

TEXT

1) *iš*$_{11}$-*gi*$_4$-*ma-rí*	1) Išgi-Mari,
2) LUGAL *ma-rí*	2) king of Mari.

3

A second seal inscription known from 15 clay impressions found in the year 2000 in Mari gives a fuller version of Išgi-Mari's titulary.

COMMENTARY

Object numbers for the seal impressions are TH.00.151.1–15 found in III P 10 NE 28.

BIBLIOGRAPHY

Beyer, "Les sceaux d'Ishqi-Mari et l'idéologie royale à Mari au IIIe millenaire (forthcoming).

TEXT

1) *iš*$_{11}$-*gi*$_4$-*ma-rí*	1) Išgi-Mari,
2) LUGAL *ma-rí*	2–3) king of Mari,
3) *ma-rí*	
4) ÉNSI GAL	4–5) chief ruler for the god Enlil.
5) ^{d}*en-líl*	

Inscriptions of Members of the Royal Family

Kūn-durī

E1.10.18

Kūn-durī is attested as the brother of a king of Mari.

1

A statue fragment from Mari bears the inscription of Kūn-durī.

COMMENTARY

The limestone statue fragment, consisting of the shoulder and right arm of a presumably male figure, measures 6 cm in height and 11.6 cm in width. It was found in courtyard 6 of the temple of Ištarat, and was given the excavation number M 2239. It may be housed in Aleppo.

The reading of the PN of line 1 is not entirely certain. The first sign, KUM, is commonly found in PNs at Ebla. Krebernik (ZA 74 [1984] pp. 164–65) suggested a reading of the first element as *qūm* "stand up!" and the second as tur_x (BÀD) "return!" Gelb and Kienast, (Königsinschriften p. 7) following Sollberger (ARET 8 [1986] p. 29) read the KUM sign as *kùn*, taking it to be derived from the root KŪN "to be firm." As for the second element, Gelb and Kienast (Königsinschriften p. 7) note the interesting parallel *kùn*-URU.KI to *kùn*-BÀD. They thus interpret the second element of the PN as *dūrī* "my wall." The whole name, then, can be tentatively translated "Be Firm, My Wall."

BIBLIOGRAPHY

1967 Parrot, MAM 3 p. 56 no. 21 (translation, study); p. 57 fig. 68 (photo); p. 325 no. 21 (copy, edition [by Dossin])
1977 Braun-Holzinger, Beterstatuetten p. 71 (transliteration, study)
1984 Krebernik, ZA 74 pp. 164–65 (study)
1986 Cooper, SARI 1 pp. 87-88 Ma 4.1 (translation)
1990 Gelb and Kienast, Köngisinschriften pp. 16 MP 20 (Kūn-durī = "KUM.BAD3") (edition)
1991 Braun-Holzinger, Weihgaben pp. 249–50 St 47 (edition, study)

TEXT

1) *kùn*-BÀD
2) ŠEŠ LUGAL

1–2) Kūn-durī, brother of the king,

3) DÙL-⌈*šù*⌉
4) [^{d}DN]
5) [SAG.RIG$_{9}$]

3–5) [presented] a statue of himself [to the deity DN]

Gullā

E1.10.19

Gullā is attested as the nephew of an unnamed king of Mari.

1

A statue fragment from Mari bears the inscription of Gullā.

COMMENTARY

The alabaster statue fragment, the upper torso of a male figure, consists of the join of four smaller pieces (M 2240+2278+2247+2334). Altogether, the joined pieces measure 15.9 cm in height and 11.0 cm in width. The statue fragment was found in room 13 of the temple of Inanna-ZA.ZA.

A certain gul-la is attested as brother of Enna-Dagān of Mari (see Archi, MARI 4 [1985] p. 71 and idem., ARET 7 no. 16 § 13 line 6 and idem. no. 17 § 2 obv. iv line 4).

The reading of the DN dINANNA as Aštar follows the writing d*aš-tár za-àr-ba-at* which Oliva has pointed out is likely to be found in Archi, ARET 7 no. 9 rev. ix § 17. The term GIŠ.TIR appears in an Ebla vocabulary list (see Pettinato MEE 4 p. 244 line 400): GIŠ.TIR = *qá-sa-tum*, cf. Akkadian *qīštu*(*m*).

Steinkeller (OrAnt 23 [1984] pp. 34–35 § b) suggested that dINANNA GIŠ.TIR was a mistake or defective writing for dINANNA GIŠ.ASAL.

BIBLIOGRAPHY

1967 Parrot, MAM 3 p. 53 no. 12 and figs. 61–62 (photo, study); pp. 319–20 no. 12 and fig. 331 (copy, edition [by Dossin])

1970 Lambert, RA 64 pp. 169–70 no. 12 (copy, study)

1977 Braun-Holzinger, Beterstatuetten pp. 70–71 (transliteration, study)

1984 Krebernik, ZA 74 p. 165 (study)

1984 Steinkeller, OA 23 pp. 34–35 § b (edition, study)

1986 Cooper, SARI 1 p. 88 Ma 4.2 (translation)

1986 Edzard, MARI 4 p. 61 (study)

1990 Gelb and Kienast, Köngisinschriften pp. 6–7 MP 4 (Gullā = "Dubla") (edition)

1993 Oliva, NABU no. 42 (study)

TEXT

1) *gul-la*	1) Gullā,
2) DUMU	2–4) son of Kūn-dūrī, brother of the king,
3) *kùn*-BÀD	
4) ŠEŠ LUGAL	
5) DÙL-*śù*	5–8) set up a statue of himself before the goddess Aštar of the forest.
6) IGI*me*	
7) dINANNA GIŠ.TIR	
8) Ì.GUB	

Nippur

E1.11

(a) Location

Ancient Nippur is identified with the modern mound named Nuffar (NLat 32° 08′ and ELong 45° 15′).

(b) Excavation History

The site was excavated by a joint expedition of the University of Pennsylvania and the Babylonian Exploration Fund from 1889 to 1900, and by a joint expedition of the Oriental Institute of the University of Chicago and the University Museum of the University of Pennsylvania in the years following 1948.

(c) Writing of the City Name

The city name Nippur (Sumerian Nibru, Akkadian Nippur) is written EN.LÍL.KI in post Ur III sources; for earlier writings, see the discussion below. The logogram is, according to Michalowski's understanding, is to be translated as "Enlil Place." The reading of the toponym as nibru is determined from later lexical sources.

(d) Patron Deities

The chief god of the city in ED times was the effective head of the Sumerian pantheon; his name has commonly been read as Enlil (see discussion below). The logogram for the city name is EN.LÍL.KI. His shrine in Nippur was called the E-kur ("Mountain House").

The chief god's wife, commonly read as Ninlil, was honoured in her own shrine in the E-kur complex named E-Kiur ("House — Levelled Place").

Enlil's second-in-command at Nippur was the god Ninurta, commonly named in inscriptions as the "eldest son of Enlil" (dumu-sag̃-^{d}en-líl-lá). Of interest is Steinkeller's observation that in Sargonic texts from Nippur it is the god Ninurta, not Enlil, who is commonly invoked in oaths (Steinkeller, Texts Baghdad p. 6).

Recently, Steinkeller has suggested a new understanding of the etymology and reading of the divine name conventionally read by scholars as Enlil. While his views are provocative, and likely not shared by all Assyriologists, it was thought important to briefly outline his hypothesis in the context of the present work. It has recently been summarized by Steinkeller in his article "On Rulers, Priests, and Sacred Marriage: Tracing the Evolution of Early Sumerian Kingship," in K. Watanabe (ed.), Priests and Officials in the Ancient Near East, p. 114 n. 36. He writes:

> ... throughout the third millennium Enlil's name is consistently written with the signs ^{d}EN.É, and not ^{d}EN.LÍL, as commonly believed ... . This suggests that Enlil's name is a logogram, whose literal sense is "master of the house, paterfamilias" ... there are various indications

> that Enlil may have been a foreign (Semitic?) name: (1) the earliest attested spelling of the name, preserved in Ebla sources, is I-li-lu, suggesting a possible etymology *il-ilī, "god of (all) the gods" …

The present author would prefer to see this as a loan from Sumerian Enlil exhibiting an assimilation of n to l (/enlil/ > /illil/) and a "Semiticization" of the word by the addition of a -u case ending; for the latter phenomenon see Civil and Rubio, Orientalia 68 (1999) pp. 263–66.

Steinkeller continues (p. 114, n. 36):

> (2) Enlil was a typical universal god, lacking any clear individual traits and without any specific domain ...; (3) his wife ᵈNIN.LÍL was but a female reflection of Enlil; the only certain pronunciation of her name is Mulliltu ...

Whether Steinkeller is correct is a matter to be determined by scholarly debate. Whatever the outcome of this discussion it was thought to be prudent to retain for the time being the conventional readings ᵈen-líl and ᵈnin-líl for the divine pair of Nippur in this edition, even if they turn out to be incorrect.

(e) Nippur in ED history

Although we have virtually no evidence that Nippur held political power in its own right in ED times (one exception may be an ED year name recording a seige of the city of Šarrākum by the ruler (énsi) of Nippur; see Westenholz, OSP 1 p. 116 year date 20), evidence suggests that rulers who claimed to exercise hegemony in the land (Sumerian: kalam) sought to have these claims legitimized by the (religious?) authorities in Nippur. Westenholz, as noted, indicates that an inscription of King Lugal-zage-si found on a large number of vessel fragments from Nippur seems to deal with Nippur's blessing of the Uruk king's claim to exercise kingship in the land.

The question of whether in ED times an assembly of Sumerian city rulers convened in Nippur is discussed in the general introduction to this volume.

(f) Additional Note

A ruler of Nippur named Nammaḫ-abzu was considered by Steible (ASBW 1 p. 225) to be an ED ruler of Nippur. However, as I have shown in RIME 2, Sargonic and Gutian periods pp. 245–46, he is almost certainly to be assigned to Sargonic times.

Nammaḫ

E1.11.1

1

A bowl found at Nippur names the Nippur ruler Nam-maḫ.

COMMENTARY

The broken, translucent gypsum bowl measures 7.0 cm in height; the diameter of the rim measures 16.5 cm in width and the diameter of the base 9.8 cm with a thickness of 0.9 cm. It was found at Nippur in locus IT 205, Level VII A, on top of the horizontal drain in the west wall of the room. The piece was given the excavation number 8 N 4; it now bears the museum number IM 66994.

This Nippur ruler Nammaḫ is to be kept distinct from the Sargonic period governor Nammaḫ-abzu whose inscription is edited in RIME 2 p. 245 as E2.6.3.2001. Cooper had edited it in SARI 1 p. 91 as Ni 4.

For the divine name ^{d}RU-kalam-ma of line 1, see Bauer, BiOr 46 (1989) p. 639.

BIBLIOGRAPHY

1969 Buccellati and Biggs, AS 17 pp. 56 and 21 no. 5 (copy, transliteration, study)
1970 Goetze, JCS 23 pp. 46–47 8N 4 (edition)
1975 Westenholz, BibMes 1 p. 97 (study)
1982 Steible, ASBW 2 p. 224 Nammaḫ 1 (edition)
1986 Cooper, SARI 1 Ni 1 (translation)
1991 Braun-Holzinger, Weihgaben p. 128 G 75 (edition, study)

TEXT

1) ^{d}RU-kalam-ma
2) pa$_{4}$-UN
3) dam-
4) nam-maḫ
5) énsi-
6) nibru.KI
7) a mu-ru

1) To the deity RU-kalama,
2–6) Pa-UN, wife of Nammaḫ, ruler of Nippur,
7) dedicated (this bowl).

Ur-Enlil

E1.11.2

1

An inscription found on a brown limestone bowl indicates that it was dedicated for the life of the Nippur ruler Ur-Enlil.

COMMENTARY

The bowl fragments were found on the southeast side of the ziqqurrat in the E-kur complex. The joined piece measures 7.2 cm in height and 12 cm in width, with a bowl thickness of 1.1 cm. The bowl bears the museum numbers CBS 9621+9617. The inscription was collated.

BIBLIOGRAPHY

1896 Hilprecht, BE 1/2 no. 96 (copy)
1907 Thureau-Dangin, SAK pp. 158–59 Patesis und sonstige Beamte von Nippur 6 (edition)
1929 Barton, RISA pp. 6–7 1. Ur-Enlil 2 (edition)
1982 Steible, ASBW 2 pp. 225–26 Urenlil 1 (edition)
1986 Cooper, SARI 1 p. 90 Ni 1 (translation)
1991 Braun-Holzinger, Weihgaben p. 128 G 76 (edition, study)

TEXT

1) ^{d}nin-líl	1) To the goddess Ninlil,
2) a-ba-^{d}en-líl	2–4) Aba-Enlil, son of Lugal-[ni]-BE-du, the merchant,
3) dumu-lugal-[nì]-BE-du$_{10}$	
4) ⸢dam⸣-gàr-ke$_{4}$	
5) nam-ti	5–7) for the life of Ur-Enlil, ruler of Nippur,
6) ur-^{d}en-líl	
7) énsi-nibru.KI-da	
8) nam-ti	8–10) [and] for the life of .... [dedicated (this bowl)].
9) [...] ⸢x⸣-da	
10) [...] x	
Lacuna	Lacuna

2

A calcite vessel from Nippur is incised with the dedicatory inscription of the Nippur ruler Ur-Enlil.

COMMENTARY

The calcite vessel measures 4.5×4.5 cm, with a vessel thickness of 1 cm. It was found on the southeast side of the ziqqurrat in the E-kur complex. It now bears the museum number CBS 9932.

BIBLIOGRAPHY

1896 Hilprecht, BE 1/2 no. 97 (copy)
1907 Thureau-Dangin, SAK pp. 158–59 Patesis und sonstige Beamte von Nippur 7 (edition)
1929 Barton, RISA pp. 6–7 1. Ur-Enlil 3 (edition)
1982 Steible, ASBW 2 p. 226 Urenlil 2 (edition)
1986 Cooper, SARI 1 p. 90 Ni 2.1 (translation)
1991 Braun-Holzinger, Weihgaben p. 128 G 77 (edition, study)

TEXT

1) [^{d}e]n-lí[l]	1) To [the god E]nli[l]
2) [ur]-^{d}en-l[íl]	2–3) [Ur]-Enl[il], [r]uler of Nipp[ur],
3) [é]nsi nibr[u.KI]	
4) [nam-t]i-l[a-šè]	4) [for his (own) l]if[e]
Lacuna	Lacuna

Abzu-kidu

E1.11.3

1

An inscription found on two joined bowl fragments from Nippur names Abzu-kidu as ruler of Nippur.

COMMENTARY

The stone bowl fragments measure 20×10.8 and 13.5×10.5 cm respectively. They were found in fill of Level VII B of the Inanna Temple, and were given the excavation number 7 N–128. The inscription appears on the smooth inside of the bowl just below the rim. The joined fragments bear the museum number IM 66123.

BIBLIOGRAPHY

1970 Goetze, JCS 23 pp. 43 and 50 (edition, copy)
1982 Steible, ASBW 2 p. 223 Abzukidu 1 (edition)
1986 Cooper, SARI 1 p. 91 Ni 3 (translation [conflated with E1.6.3.2])
1991 Braun-Holzinger, Weihgaben p. 127 and pl. 6 G 73 (photo, edition, study)

TEXT

1) [d]inanna	1) To the goddess Inanna,
2) a-kalam	2–5) A-kalam, wife of Abzu-kidu, ruler of Nippur,
3) dam-abzu-ki-du$_{10}$	
4) énsi	
5) nibru.KI	
6) a mu-ru	6) dedicated (this bowl).

2

An inscription on a bowl fragment from Nippur refers to the wife of Abzu-kidu. If this is the same Abzu-kidu who appears in the previous inscription, then we would have two inscriptions of his wife.

COMMENTARY

The stone bowl fragment measures 9 cm in height and 10 cm in width. It was found in fill of Level VII of the Inanna temple, and given the excavation number 7 N-147. The inscription appears about 1.5 cm below the rim of the bowl.

BIBLIOGRAPHY

1970 Goetze, JCS 23 pp. 43 and 51 (edition, copy)
1982 Steible, ASBW 2 pp. 223–24 Abzukidu 2 (edition)
1986 Cooper, SARI 1 p. 91 Ni 3 (translation [conflated with E1.6.3.1])
1991 Braun-Holzinger, Weihgaben p. 128 G 74 (edition, study)

TEXT

Lacuna
1′) dum[u]
2′) amar-^{d}iškur
3′) dam
4′) abzu-ki-du$_{10}$
5′) a mu-ru

Lacuna
1′–4′) daught[er] of Amar-Iškur, wife of Abzu-kidu,
5′) dedicated (this bowl).

G̃iša and Umma

E1.12

(a) Notes on the Cities of G̃iša and Umma

Although they are not mentioned in the SKL, the neighbouring cities of G̃iša and Umma were important players on the stage of late Presargonic history.

Complicating our understanding of the royal inscriptions of the rulers of these two cities is the fact that it now seems reasonably clear that two distinct GNs have been subsumed by modern scholars under the one name Umma; this was because of lexical glosses in Proto-Diri and Diri which (erroneously) indicated that $^{\text{g̃iš}}$KÚŠU.KI is to be read: um-me-en, um-ma, um-me, or um-mi.

As is pointed out in W. Lambert's study of the names of Umma (Lambert JNES 49 [1990] pp. 75–80), the city name is consistently written $^{\text{g̃iš}}$KÚŠU.KI in inscriptions of the ED kings of Lagaš, but most commonly ŠÁR×DIŠ (but never with the KI determinative) in contemporaneous inscriptions of the native rulers of Umma. Based on the assumption that the lexical tradition has arbitrarily(?) assigned one of these two GNs as a "Sumerian" word and the other as an "Akkadian" word, we may reexamine the data collected by Lambert:

Reference	G̃iša	Umma
zà-mì Hymns	$^{\text{g̃iš}}$kúšu	ŠÁR×DIŠ
cf. RN at Umma	g̃i$_x$(G̃IŠ)-šà-ki-du$_{10}$	—
Sargonic inscriptions	$^{\text{g̃iš}}$kúšu	ub-mì
Proto-Diri	$^{\text{g̃iš}}$kúšu *gi$_5$-iš-[ša]*	um-me-en
Diri III 74	$^{\text{g̃iš}}$kúšu *gi$_5$-is-[sa]*	um-ma um-mi
Late Balag hymn	$^{\text{g̃iš!}}$kúšu *gi$_5$-sa*	—

As for the meaning of *kúšu*, CAD 8 p. 602b notes:

> ... kušú, with det. ku$_6$, is described as a terrifying animal living in the marshes; the mythological contexts do not allow for any closer identification than some kind of aquatic monster.

If the kúšu denotes "some kind of aquatic monster," parallels in toponymy may be seen in the GN Adamšaḫ in Elam, possibly "crocodile" or "hippopotamus" town (see introductory section to E1.3 in this volume) and Greek Crocodopolis in Egypt.

Since the translation "wooden *kušû* beast" makes no sense, the GN $^{\text{g̃iš}}$KÚŠU.KI may possibly be interpreted as a logogram kúšu with the element

G̃IŠ added as a phonetic indicator to distinguish it from Sumerian KÚŠU /uḫ/ "spittle." A reading /g̃iša/ or the like is virtually certain in view of Lambert's observation that the city name ^{giš}kúšu.KI is related to the first element in the PN g̃i$_x$(G̃IŠ)-šà-ki-du$_{10}$ "G̃iša is a good place" attested as the name of an ED ruler of this area; we have normalized the city name as G̃iša in this volume. This view is also shared by G. Selz in his article "Aka, König von G̃iš(š)a: zur Historizität eines Königs und seiner möglichen Identität mit Aka, König von Kiš(i)," in Kienast Festschrift, p. 508. He notes:

> ... die sumerische Lesung des Logogramms KÚŠU, also /kušu/ mit der sumerischen Aussprache des Ortsnamen g̃iš(š)a phonetisch verbunden wurde, bleibt gleichwohl möglich. ... Wir besitzen somit zwei Ortsnamen G̃iš(š)a (> Kiš(š)a, Kis(s)a, vielleicht auch Ku/üš(š)a) und Ubme (oder Umme/i/a), die vermutlich zwei verschiedene Toponyme im Bereich des ummäischen Gebietes repräsentieren.

Whatever the original form of G̃iša, it is clear that it was the forerunner of the modern GN Jōḫa, where modern ḫ, the velar spirant, corresponds to ancient š.

While a reading umma for ŠÁR×DIŠ is not lexically attested as far as can be determined, Steinkeller suggests the value /umma/ in view of its occurrences in the ED royal inscriptions (Steinkeller and Postgate, Texts Baghdad p. 16 no. 22).

Further light on the cities in the region of Umma is provided by the evidence of the archaic zà-mì hymns and the literary text IAS no. 282. Five cities in the G̃iša/Umma region can be discerned in these texts.

Cities in the Area of G̃iša

Source	(1) Zabala(m)	(2) Dulum	(3) G̃iša	(4) Ki'an	(5) Umma
zà-mì Hymn	AN.INANNA.KUR.(KI) ll. 46–51	NAGAR.GÍD (=dulum).(KI) ll. 92–97	^{giš}KÚŠU.(KI) ll. 104–105	ki-an.(KI) ll. 106–107 ki-a-an.(KI) ll. 212–14	ŠÁR×DIŠ ll. 205–206 ll. 215-20
Tutelary deities in zà-mì hymns	^{d}inanna ḪU UD (?) line 50 (f) ^{d}nin-um (?) line 51	^{d}nin-duluma (NAGAR.GÍD) (m) line 97	^{d}nin-ur$_4$ (f) line 105 (f)	^{d}šára l. 107 (m) ^{d}tu-da line 214 (f)	en (^{d})bu-lú-lu$_x$(NU) line 206 (f) ^{d}ama-ušum-gal l. 220 (m)
IAS 282	AB.INANNA.KI	NAGAR.GÍD.(KI)	^{giš}KÚŠU.KI	ki-an.KI	—
Modern name	Tell Ibzēḫ	(Tell) Salbuḫ (site no. 036 in Adams, Uruk Countryside)	Tell Jōḫa	= ? Khayta (site no. 170 in Adams, Uruk Countryside)	Umm al-ʿAqārib

Ancient G̃iša, as noted, is located at modern Tell Jōḫa (NLat 31° 40′ ELong 45° 53′). This is clear from Scheil's comment (RT 19 [1897] p. 63) that he brought inscribed material with the GN ^{giš}KÚŠU.KI from Tell Jōḫa. On the other hand, an inscription (E1.12.4.2) from Umm al-ʿAqārib, about 6 km SSE of Tell Jōḫa, gives the GN ŠÁR×DIŠ "Umma."

Also to be noted in the above chart is ancient Zabala (with tutelary deity Inanna of Zabala, Akkadian *Ištar supalītum*) which corresponds to modern Tell Ibzēḫ (NLat 31° 45′ ELong 45° 52′). Ancient Dulum$_x$(NAGAR.GÍD) with tutelary deity Nin-Duluma (for the reading see Powell, OrNS 45 [1976] p. 102

n. 15) apparently lay close to it, probably at modern Salbuḫ, which maycontain a reflex of the ancient name. Ancient ki-an or ki-a-an (the latter writing indicates a reading ki-an rather than ki-dig̃ir) apparently lay in the same general region; it may possibly be located at modern Khayta.

In addition to the evidence of the royal inscriptions from Umma itself, names of various rulers of Umma are known (always as enemies) in inscriptions of the rulers of Lagaš. The data is set out in tabular form below.

Early Dynastic Rulers of Umma Attested in the Lagaš Inscriptions

Ruler of Umma	Lagaš source inscription	Contemporary Lagaš ruler alluded to in text	RIM reference number
Pabilga-tuk	Ur-Nanše	Ur-Nanše	E1.9.1.6b rev. col. iv lines 5–7
Uš	En-metena	(not named)	E1.9.5.1 col. i lines 13–15
En-akale	En-metena	E-anatum	E1.9.5.1 col. i lines 39–41
Ur-LUM-ma (son of En-akale)	En-anatum I	En-anatum I	E1.9.4.2 col. vii lines 7–9
Il (grandson of En-akale)	En-metena	En-metena	E1.9.5.1 col. iii lines 34–37; col. iv lines 19–21

Early Dynastic Rulers of Umma Attested in the Umma Inscriptions

Ruler of Umma	Umma source inscription	RIM reference number
Eanda-mua (father of Il, not actually attested as ruler of Umma)	Il (U)	E1.12.5.1
Il	Il (U)	E1.12.4.1
Il	Il (U)	E1.12.4.2
G̃iša-kidu (son of Il)	G̃iša-kidu (U)	E1.12.6.1
Bubu, father of Lugal-zage-si	Lugal-zage-si (U)	E1.12.7.1
Lugal-zage-si	Lugal-zage-si (U)	E1.12.7.1

Pa-bilga ...

E1.12.1

1

A duplicate set of statuettes, said to have come "from Umma," depict a ruler of the Early Dynastic II period; on one of them the inscription has survived. Unfortunately due to the apparently random arrangement of the signs within the case (which is typical of ED II period texts), the interpretation of the statuette inscription is most uncertain.

COMMENTARY

A greenish alabaster fragment of a statuette was said to have been found at "Umma," but we don't know precisely which site it came from (Umm al ʿAqārib or Jōḫa). The piece was exhibited (as part of a private collection) in the Iraq Museum in the late 1920s and published in a photo by H. Frankfort in 1939 (statue 1). In 1945 a companion piece was found at "Umma" and purchased by the Iraq Museum (IM 51023) (statue 2). Both statuettes originally (in antiquity) contained a short inscription on their right shoulders, but unfortunately it has been erased "with a precision that could be deliberate" on the piece that was found in 1945. Statue 1 measures 12.41 cm in height. The statues are ithyphallic.

It is unclear whether the whole inscription is to be read as a single RN, a dedicatory inscription to a king, or a royal inscription with a verb form gi_4 "return" at the end. Also, it is uncertain whether the inscription is to be read from top to bottom or from bottom to top (see bibliography). Edzard, (Sumer 15 [1959] p. 21) writes:

> Das Verhältnis der drei oben aufgestellten Gruppen ^{d}en-líl-gi_4, pa-GIŠ.BIL-ga, lugal-ŠÁR×DIŠ zueinander ist nicht eindeutig zu bestimmen. Wir nehmen Enlilgi und Pabil-ga als Përsonennamen und lugal-ŠÁR×DIŠ als Titel an, der sich auf eine der beiden Personen bezieht. "Enlilgil (für) Pabilga, den König von ŠÁR×DIŠ". Wir lesen dabei die drei Gruppen hintereinander, ohne zu springen. Oder: "(Für) Enlilgi, Pabilga, König vor Š.". Da sich der Titel auf die Respektsperson, der die Statue geweiht ist, beziehen dürfte, ziehen wir die erste Deutung vor. Nicht ausgeschlossen ist aber auch, dass ^{d}en-líl:gi_4:pa-GIŠ.BIL-ga nur ein einziger Name ist mit nicht sicher zu bestimmender Anordnung der drei Glieder.

Despite their appearance in different spaces, pa and GIŠ.bíl-ga are most likely to be linked together. For the kinship term pa_4-bíl-gi/gi_4, pa-bíl-ga, pa-bìl-ga, bíl-ga, bìl-gi_4, bìl "grandfather" see Sjöberg, Studies Falkenstein pp. 212–19. The names with pa_4-bíl-gi/gi_4 and variants are common in texts of the Fāra period; see also Deimel, Wirtschaftstexte aus Fara p. 46* and Jacobsen, SKL p. 187. See also Krebernik, "Zur Struktur und Geschichte des älteren sumerischen Onomastikons" in M. Streck und S. Weninger (eds.), Altorientalische und semitische Onomastik, Münster 2002, pp. 15-16, and Marchesi, Orientalia NS 73 pp. 196–97.

BIBLIOGRAPHY

1939 Frankfort, Sculpture pp. 12, 41, and 78, and pl. 115 no. 206 (statue 1, photo, study)

1946 Lloyd, Sumer 2 pp. 2–5 and pl. m (statues 1–2, study, photo, copy published upside down and in mirror image of inscription on statue 1)

1947 Lambert, Sumer 3 pp. 131–32 (statue 1, copy [correctly oriented] study)

1959 Edzard, Sumer 15 p. 21 (statue 1, study)

1960 Edzard, CRRAI 8 p. 250 n. 73 (statue 1, study)
1960 Strommenger, Bagh. Mitt. 1 p. 32 n. 255a (statue 1, study)
1964 Nagel, in Festschrift Moortgat p. 183 n. 12 (statue 1, study)
1975–76 Basmachi, Treasures pp. 173 and 398 no. 67 (statue 2, photo)
1977 Braun-Holzinger, Beterstatuetten pp. 44, 64, and 80 (statues 1–2, study)
1982 Steible, ASBW 2 pp. 265–66 Enlilpabilgagi 1 (inscription on statue 1, edition)
1991 Braun-Holzinger, Weihgaben p. 252 St 68 (transliteration, study)
2002 Krebernik in Streck and Weninger, Onomastic, pp. 15-16 (study)
2004 Marchesi Orientalia NS 73 pp. 196–97.

TEXT

lugal	King
pa umma(ŠÁR×DIŠ)	Pa- Umma
GIŠ.bíl-ga	bilga
^{d}en-líl	Enlil-
gi$_4$	gi$_4$

Aka

E1.12.2

1

A lapis lazuli bead of unknown provenance names a certain Aka as king of G̃iša.

COMMENTARY

The lapis-lazuli bead has four facets; each measures 2.4×1.3 cm. The piece is no. 4 in the collection of J. Mariaud de Serres, Paris. It was not collated. The direction of the writing is parallel to the long axis of bead.

As Cooper, SARI 1 p. 92 Um 2, points out, it is possible that this inscription might belong to Aka, son of EN.ME-barage-si of Kiš, known from Sumerian literary tradition. He notes that palaeography suits such a date. If so, the title adopted by Aka would be an honourific title, and not a designation of his dynastic affiliation.

For further discussion of this hypothesis, see Selz, "Aka, König von G̃iš(š)a: zur Historizität eines Königs und seiner möglichen Identität mit Aka, König von Kiš(i)," in Selz (ed.), Kienast Festschrift pp. 499–518. Selz suggests that the name Aka is derived from the verb ak+a meaning "Product (of the deity DN)." See also Krebernik, "Zur Struktur und Geschichte des älteren sumerischen Onomastikons" in M. Streck und S. Weninger (eds.) Altorientalische und semitische Onomastik, Münster 2002, p. 12.

A tentative identification with the ak gal-ug̃kin "Ak, chief of the assembly" of the "Ušumgal Stele" (for which see Gelb, Land Tenure p. 44), is suggested by Selz in Kienast Festschrift, p. 510. The "Ušumgal Stele" is thought to have likely come from Umma. If this equation be true, it would suggest, in the view of the present author, that this Aka was a local ruler of Umma and not a title of Aka of Kiš.

BIBLIOGRAPHY

1981 Grégoire MVN 10 no. 1 (copy)
1982 Steible, ASBW 2 p. 266 Aka 1 (edition)
1986 Cooper, SARI 1 p. 92 Um 2 (translation)
1991 Braun-Holzinger, Weihgaben p. 365 P 1 (edition, study)
2002 Selz in Streck and Weninger, Onomastic, pp. 499–518 (study).

TEXT

1) ^{d}inanna
2) aka
3) lugal
4) ^{giš}KÚŠU.KI

1) To the goddess Inanna,
2) Aka,
3–4) king of G̃iša (dedicated this bead).

E-abzu

E1.12.3

1

An inscription found on three stone statuette fragments names E-abzu as ruler of Umma.

COMMENTARY

The limestone statuette fragments, which come from the shoulder of a male figure, measure 11 cm in height and 6.5 cm in width. They were purchased by de Sarzec at Shaṭra, and are said to have come from the site Moulagareb. Cooper (SARI 1 p. 92) indicates that this is almost certainly a reference to Umm-al-ʿAqārīb, site 198 of Adam's Warka survey. It bears the museum number AO 22937. The inscription was not collated.

The placement of the statue fragments is uncertain. De Sarzec's copy shows traces of a sign before the pa_4 sign. Steible, ASBW 2 p. 270 notes:

> ... es ist unsicher, ob dieser Strich zu einem Zeichen gehört oder nicht.

If the piece copied by de Sarzec at the bottom of his copy did, in fact, belong to the top of the inscription, we could possibly restore line 1 as the divine name $^{d}pa_4$-bil-sag̃ "To the god Pabilsag̃," but this is very uncertain.

BIBLIOGRAPHY

1884–1912 de Sarzec, Découvertes 1 pp. 74 and 108–109 (study, findspot); Découvertes 2 p. LVI and pl. 5 no. 3 (copy, photo)
1902 Heuzey, Catalogue Louvre pp. 222–23 no. 84 (study)
1907 Thureau-Dangin, SAK pp. 150–51 Könige und Patesis von Giš-ḪU 1 E-abzu (edition)
1908 Toscanne, RT 30 pp. 121–22 texte B (partial copy, edition)
1929 Barton, RISA pp. 92–93 1. Eabsu (edition)
1977 Braun-Holzinger, Beterstatuetten p. 73 (transliteration, study)
1982 Steible, ASBW 2 pp. 269–70 Eʾabzu 1 (edition)
1986 Cooper, SARI 1 p. 92 Um 3 (translation)
1991 Braun-Holzinger, Weihgaben p. 252 St 69 (edition, study)

TEXT

1) d⌜x⌝ [...]
2) é-ab-zu
3) lugal-gišKÚŠU.KI
4) m[u-x]
Lacuna
1′) [G̃I]Š.pa_4-bil-s[ag̃]
Lacuna

1) To DN,
2–4) E-abzu, king of G̃iša, ...
Lacuna
1′) [G̃I]Š.pa_4-bil-s[ag̃]
Lacuna

Ur-LUM-ma

E1.12.4

1

A lapis lazuli tablet is incised with a building inscription of Ur-LUM-ma, king of Umma.

COMMENTARY

The provenance of the tablet, which measures 4.5×3.1 cm, is unknown. Formerly in the Collection de Clercq, it now bears the museum number AO 22246. Lines 1–5 appear on the obverse, line 6 on the reverse. The inscription was collated.

BIBLIOGRAPHY

1903 de Clercq, Collection 2 pp. 92ff. and pl. X no. 6 (photo)
1907 Thureau-Dangin, SAK pp. 150–51 Könige und Patesis von Giš-ḪU 2 Ur-LUM-ma (edition)
1929 Barton, RISA pp. 92–93 2. Urlumma (edition)
1971 Sollberger and Kupper, IRSA ID3a (translation)
1982 Steible, ASBW 2 p. 267 Urluma 1 (edition)
1986 Cooper, SARI 1 p. 93 Um 4.1 (translation)
1995 Tallon, Pierres, pp. 71 and 74 no. 98 (photo [of obverse only], study)

TEXT

1) [d]en-ki-gal
2) ur-[d]LUM-ma
3) lugal-umma(ŠÁR×DIŠ)
4) dumu-en-á-kal-le
5) lugal-umma(ŠÁR×DIŠ)
6) é mu-na-dù

1) For the god Enkigal,
2–3) Ur-LUM-ma, king of Umma
4–5) son of En-akale, king of Umma,
6) built (his) temple for him.

2

A silver tablet is incised with a second building inscription of Ur-LUM-ma, king of Umma.

COMMENTARY

The tablet, which measures 6.6×4.6×0.5, was found at Umm-al-ʿAqārib and subsequently purchased by the Iraq Museum; it bears the museum number IM 62510. Only the convex (obverse) side is inscribed.

BIBLIOGRAPHY

1980 Braun, RO 41/2 pp. 13–14 and pl. facing p. 13 (photo, edition, study)

1986 Cooper, SARI 1 p. 93 Um 4.2 (translation)

TEXT

1) ^{d}nagar-pa-è	1) For the god Nagar-paʾe,
2) ur-^{d}LUM-ma	2–3) Ur-LUM-ma, king of Umma,
3) lugal-umma(ŠÁR×DIŠ)	
4) dumu en-á-kal-le	4–5) son of En-akale, king of Umma,
5) lugal-umma(ŠÁR×DIŠ)	
6) é mu-na-dù	6) built (his) temple for him.

Il

E1.12.5

1

An alabaster foundation tablet records the construction of the temple of the deity TAG.NUN (reading uncertain) by Il, king of Umma.

COMMENTARY

The stone tablet, which measures 8.6×5.5×1.9 cm, was acquired by purchase in November 1933. Its provenance is unknown. Only the convex side (obverse) is inscribed. The tablet bears the museum number NBC 6067 and its inscription was collated.

For a tentative identification of ^{d}TAG.NUN with ^{d}TAG.TÚG = ^{d}uttu, the goddess of weaving, see Sjöberg, in Edzard (ed.), Studies Falkenstein p. 209. Cf. Steinkeller and Postgate, Texts Baghdad pp. 65–66 (where a reading uttuk is suggested) and Krebernik, ZA 76 (1986) pp. 202–203. In this connection we may note the following lexical entries ut-tu : TAG×KU = ^{d}TAG×KU (Aa V/1 266 [Civil, MSL XIV, 414]); [ut-tu] : [TAGKU] = [^{d}]TAG×KU (Civil, Ea V 68 [Civil, MSL XIV, 399]); ut-tu : TAG×TÚG = ^{d}TAG×TÚG (Reciprocal Ea Tablet A 237 [MSL14, 529]); [ut-tu] : [uttu (TAG×KU)] = [ut]-tum (Secondary Proto-Ea/Aa no. 22 i 23′ [Civil, MSL XIV, 144]); ^{d}TAG.TÚG = ut-⸢tu⸣ (OB Diri Nippur Section 11 12) ^{d}TAG.TÚG (OB Diri "Oxford" 658).

BIBLIOGRAPHY

1937 Stephens, YOS 9 no. 6 (copy, study)
1938 Thureau-Dangin, RA 38 p. 90 (edition, study)
1967 Sjöberg in Edzard, HSAO pp. 209–10 (edition, study)
1971 Sollberger and Kupper, IRSA ID4a (translation)
1982 Steible, ASBW 2 pp. 267–68 Il 1 (edition)
1986 Cooper, SARI 1 p. 93 Um 5 (translation)

TEXT

1) ^{d}TAG.NUN-ra	1) For the deity TAG.NUN,
2) íl lugal-umma(ŠÁR×DIŠ)	2) Il, king of Umma,
3) dumu é-an-da-mú	3) son of E-anda-mua,
4) dumu-KA	4–6) grandson of En-akale, king of Umma,
5) en-á-kal-le	
6) lugal-umma(ŠÁR×DIŠ)-ka-ke$_4$	
7) é-ni mu-na-dù	7) built her temple for her.

G̃iša-kidu

E1.12.6

Il was succeeded by his son G̃iša-kidu on the throne of Lagaš.

1

A gold plaque bears the inscription of Bara-irnun, wife of Giša-kidu, king of Umma.

COMMENTARY

The gold plaque, which measures 8.5×6.7×0.2 cm, is perforated by five holes; perhaps (as Braun-Holzinger, Weihgaben p. 378 suggests) it was once attached to a wooden object. The plaque was acquired by the Louvre through purchase and given the museum number AO 19225; it is said to have come from Tell Jōḫa. The inscription was collated.

BIBLIOGRAPHY

1937 Thureau-Dangin, RA 34 pp. 177–82 (photo, edition, study)
1967 Sjöberg, in Edzard, HSAO p. 210 (edition, study)
1971 Sollberger and Kupper, IRSA ID5a (translation)
1982 André-Leicknam, Naissance de l'écriture p. 86 no. 44 (photo, translation, study)
1982 Steible, ASBW pp. 268–69 Giššakidu 1 (edition)
1983 Cooper, SANE 2 pp. 16, 33–36, and 52 (translation, study)
1986 Cooper, SARI 1 pp. 93–94 Um 6 (translation)
1991 Braun-Holzinger, Weihgaben p. 378 Varia 9 (edition, study)

TEXT

1)	^{d}šára lugal-é-maḫ-ra	1) For the god Šara, lord of the E-maḫ,
2)	bára-ir-nun dam gi$_{x}$(GIŠ)-šà-ki-du$_{10}$ lugal-umma(ŠÁR×DIŠ)-ka-ke$_{4}$	2) Bara-irnun, wife of G̃iša-kidu, king of Umma,
3)	dumu ur-^{d}LUM-ma lugal-ŠÁR×DIŠ-ka-ke$_{4}$	3) daughter of Ur-LUM-ma, king of Umma,
4)	dumu-KA en-á-kal-le lugal-umma(ŠÁR×DIŠ)-ka-ke$_{4}$	4) granddaughter of En-akale, king of Umma,
5)	é-gi$_{4}$-a íl lugal-umma(ŠÁR×DIŠ)-ka-ke$_{4}$	5) daughter-in-law of Il, king of Umma —
6)	u$_{4}$ ^{d}šára pa mu-è-a	6–7) when she made the god Šara resplendent and built for him a shining dais,
7)	bára-kù mu-na-dù-a	
8)	nam-ti-la-ni-da	8–9) she presented (this plaque) to the god Šara in the E-maḫ.
9)	^{d}šára é-maḫ-šè sag-šè mu-ni-rig$_{9}$(DU.KAB)	

2

An inscription found on a terracotta vase, stone tablet fragment, and a limestone cone deals with G̃iša-kidu's demarcation of the "Boundary of Šara."

CATALOGUE

Ex.	Museum number	Provenance	Object	Dimensions (cm)	Lines preserved	cpn
1	Was in the Erlenmeyer collection	—	Terracotta vase	Max. dia.: 13.5 Dia. at lip: 6.2	8–32 38–69 77–93	p
2	YBC 2139	—	Stone tablet	10.3 ×8.0 3.25 thick	9–17 38–52	c
3	Schøyen Collection MS 2426	—	Limestone cone fragment	11.9 long 5.7–7.3m dia.	1–18	c*

*Ex. 3 was kindly collated and communicated to the author by P. Steinkeller.

COMMENTARY

Ex. 3 was apparently in the collection of a British soldier who was on active duty during the Second World War and it was in England from 1945 to 1996. It is now in the Schøyen Collection in Oslo and notes on it can be viewed at the web page www.nb.no/baser/schoyen/. According to the web source it is to be published by Mark Wilson.

The Schøyen source allows for the proper identification of the inscription, hitherto erroneously assigned to Lugal-zage-si.

For the measure NINDA.DU found in line 27 and passim, see Powell, ZA 62 (1972) pp. 199–201.

The author intends to identify (in a separate communication) several of the place names appearing in this text on the "Border of Šara" with sites depicted as lying on the canal flowing south from modern Imrebia in the map published by Jacobsen in Sumer 25 (1969), p. 109.

BIBLIOGRAPHY

1958 Sollberger, Orientalia NS 28 pp. 336–350 and pls. LXI–LXII (ex. 1, photo, copy, edition)

1971 Sollberger and Kupper, IRSA 1H2a (ex. 1, edition)

1982 Cooper, Reconstructing History pp. 16–17, 52–53 (exs. 1–2, translation, study)

1982 Steible, ASBW 2 pp. 325–336 and pl. 5 Lugalzagesi 2 (exs. 1–2, edition, ex. 2, photo)

1983 Cooper, SANE 2 pp. 16–17, and 52–53 (exs. 1–2, translation, study)

1985 Cooper, RA 79 p. 98 "Frontier of Shara" (study)

1986 Cooper, SARI 1 pp. 95–96 (translation)

1987 Christie's London Auction Catalogue: Ancient Near Eastern Texts from the Erlenmeyer Collection p. 31 no. 60 (ex. 1, photo, study)

TEXT

Col. i

1) u$_4$ ^{d}šára	1–4) When the god Šara spoke to the god Enlil the prayers gathered together in (his) heart,
2) ^{d}en-líl-ra	
3) ara$_x$(DU)-⸢zu⸣ ur$_4$-šà/-ga	
4) e-na-du$_{11}$-ga	
5) e-na-gin-na	5) and proceeded to him,
6) g̃i$_x$(G̃IŠ)-šà-ki-du$_{10}$ sipa ki-ág̃-g̃á	6) (then) G̃iša-kidu,
7) ^{d}šára	7) shepherd beloved of the god Šara,
8) a ⸢x x⸣-šè/ ⸢tu-da⸣	8) [b]orn to ...,

9) nir-gál/ sag-ḫuš-ki-en-gi-ke$_4$
10) gaba-gál nu-gi$_4$ kur-kur-ra-ke$_4$
11) en-zà-kešda-^{d}nin-ur$_4$-ke$_4$
12) ama-šà-kúš-^{d}en-ki-ka-ke$_4$
13) ku-li-ki-ág̃-
14) ^{d}ištaran(KA.DI)-ke$_4$
15) énsi-kala-ga-
16) ^{d}en-líl-lá-ke$_4$
17) lugal mu-pà-^{d}inanna-ke$_4$
18) ég-bi mu-ak
19) na-bi mu-rú
20) im-dub-ba-bi
21) pa e-mi-è
22) na-rú-a-bi
23) ki-bé bi-gi$_4$
24) [x] ⸢x⸣ [(x)] ⸢x⸣
25) ⸢x x⸣ [...]
26) zà-na-rú-[a]-^{d}šára-[kam]
27) i$_7$-A[L-(x)]-t[a]
28) i$_7$(Text: A)-DU$_8$-a-[šè]
29) 45 NINDA.D[U]
30) zà-na-rú-[a]-^{d}šár[a-kam]
31) ⸢i$_7$⸣-[DU$_8$-a-ta]
32) K[A(?)-...-šè]
33) [x NINDA.DU]
34) [zà-na-rú-a-^{d}šára-kam]
35) [KA(?)-...-ta]
36) [ḪAR-AL-šè]
37) [x NINDA.DU]
38) ⸢zà⸣-na-rú-a-⸢d⸣[šára-kam]
39) ḪAR.AL-t[a]
40) bàd(Text: EZEN×U)-⸢da⸣
41) ANŠE.du$_{24}$(DUN)-ùr-gá-ra-š[è]
42) 390 NINDA.[DU]
43) ⸢zà⸣-na-rú-a-^{d}šára-kam
44) 10 bàd-⸢da⸣
45) ANŠE.du$_{24}$(DUN)-ùr-gá-ra-⸢ta⸣
46) nag-^{d}nanše-šè
47) 636 NINDA.⸣DU⸣
48) zà-na-rú-⸢a⸣-šára-kam
49) nag-^{d}nanše-ta
50) i$_7$-gibil-šè
51) 1200-lá-20 NINDA.DU
52) zà-na-rú-a-^{d}šára-kam
53) i$_7$-gibil-ta
54) é-^{d}dimgal(GAL:DIM)-abzu-ka-šè
55) 960 NINDA.⸣DU⸣
56) z[à-na-rú-a-^{d}šára-kam]
57) é-[^{d}di]mgal-abz[u]-ka-ta
58) mur-⸢gu$_4$⸣-^{d}⸢šára⸣-šè
59) 790 NINDA.DU
60) [z]à-na-rú-a-⸢d⸣-šára-kam
61) [mur]-gu$_4$-<^{d}šára>-ta
62) [...] -⸢x⸣^{d}ištaran-šè

9) preeminent one, fearsome head of the land of Sumer,
10) who has no rival in all the lands,
11) en-*priest* attached to the side of the goddess Nin-ur,
12) who is counselled in a motherly fashion by Enki,
13–14) the beloved friend of the god Ištarān,

15–16) the mighty ruler for the god Enlil,

17) the king chosen by the goddess Inanna,
18) constructed its (the boundary's) dyke,
19) erected its monument,
20–21) made its levee preeminent,

22–25) and restored its monuments.

26–29) This is the frontier according to the monument of the god Šara: fr[om] the Al-... -canal [to] the Dua-canal is 45 *nind*[*an*] (270 m).

30–33) This is the frontier according to the monum[ent of] the god Šara: [from the Dua]-cana[l to ... is x *nindan*].

34–37) [This is the frontier according to the monument of the god Šara: from ... to Ḫaral is x *nindan*].

38–42) This is the frontier according to the monumen[t of the god Šara]: fr[om] Ḫaral to the fortress Dur-gara is 21,630 *nind*[*an*] (129.78 km).

43–47) This is the frontier according to the monument of the god Šara: from the fortress Dur-gara to Nag-nanše is 636 *nindan* (3.816 km).

48–51) This is the frontier according to the monument of the god Šara: from Nag-Nanše to the Gibil-canal is 1180 *nindan* (7.08 km).

52–55) This is the frontier according to the monument of the god Šara: from the Gibil canal to E-dimgalabzu is 960 *ninda*[*n*] (5.76 km).

56–59) [This is the] f[rontier according to the monument of the god Šara]: from E-[di]mgalabz[u] to Murgu-Šara is 790 *nindan* (4.74 km).

60–63) This is the [f]rontier according to the monument of the god Šara: from [Mur]gu-<Šara> to [...]-Ištarān is [x *n*]*indan*.

44.2 bàd! = EZEN×U.

63) [x NI]NDA.⸢DU⸣
64) [zà-n]a-rú-a-⸢^{d}⸣šára-kam
65) [...]^{d}ištaran(KA.DI)-[t]a
66) [an-za]-gàr-šè
67) [6000(?)+6]80 NINDA.DU
68) [zà-n]a-rú-a-⸢^{d}⸣šára-kam
69) [an-za]-gàr-ta
70) [GN-šè]
71) [x NINDA.DU]
Lacuna of five lines.
77) ⸢im-dub⸣-[ba]-bé
78) nu-ni-⸢dib⸣
79) na-rú-a-bi
80) ki-bé bi-gi$_4$
81) inim-^{d}ištaran(KA.DI)-ta
82) ki-ba na bi-rú
83) lú-kur-ra
84) ki-bé al(?)-gul-la
85) ⸢šu ba⸣-ta-⸢ti⸣-a
86) ab-záḫ-a
87) ur[u(?-né(?)]
88) ki-muš-ḫul-a-⸢gin$_7$⸣
89) sag-⸢íl⸣ na-du$_{12}$-du$_{12}$
90) é-gal-ḫul-a-na
91) énsi-bi
92) zú-gig
93) ḫa-ma-dù(Text: NI)-⸢e⸣

64–67) This is the [frontier] according to the [mo]nument of the god Šara: [f]rom [...]-Ištarān to [Anza]gar 12]80(?) *nindan* (7.68 km).

68–71) This is [the frontier] according to [the m]onument of the god Šara: from [Anza]gar [to ... is x *nindan*].

Lacuna of five lines.
77–78) He did not go beyo[nd] its levee.

79–82) He restored its (former) monuments and, at the god Ištarān's command, erected a (new) monument on that spot.

83–84) If another leader destroys it there,

85–86) or takes it away and makes off (with it),

87–89) may [his] cit[y], like a place (infested) with harmful snakes, not allow him to hold his head erect!

90–93) May poisonous fangs bite that ruler in his ruined palace!

Lugal-zage-si

E1.12.7

While it is clear that the reigns of Bubu and Lugal-zage-si at Umma are to be placed after G̃iša-kidu's tenure of office, it is not clear if they were his immediate successors.

In his inscriptions Lugal-zage-si names Bubu, *lumaḫ* priest of the goddess Nissaba, as his father, and he himself served in the same priestly role before his accession to the throne of G̃iša. For notes on the origins of Lugal-zage-si see the article by P. Steinkeller entitled "The Question of Lugalzagesi's Origins" in Kienast Festschrift, pp. 621–37. A new inscription of Lugal-zage-si edited below now makes it clear that Bubu had also served as ruler of Umma. This fact was previously unknown.

In the aforementioned article P. Steinkeller discusses the location of the city of Ereš and notes that evidence points to a location of the city either in the area of Nippur or Umma.

The conclusions of Steinkeller's article are fully supported by this author's own research, which suggests that there were two ancient cities called Ereš, one near Nippur (appearing in five Nippur texts listed by Westenholz in OSP 1 p. 112), to be located at modern Tulūl Werriš, about 10 km NE of Nippur, site 983 in Adams Heartland of Cities, and the other modern Abū Ruwaysh, to be located at (Abū) Ruwayš, site no. 208 in Adams, Uruk Countryside, 6 km west of Umma (Umm al-ʿAqārib).

After serving as ruler of Umma, Lugal-zage-si united into one state much of the land of Sumer, including the city-states of G̃iša and Umma, Uruk, Eridu, Larsa, and Adab (or Šarrākum) as evidenced by the deities appearing in the king's titulary. At this time Lugal-zage-si adopted the title "king of Uruk" and his inscriptions dating to this period of his reign are edited in section E1.14.20 in this volume.

1

An inscription on a foundation tablet of unknown provenance deals with the construction of a temple for the god Dumuzi by Lugal-zage-si, ruler of G̃iša.

COMMENTARY

The foundation tablet, numbered BLMJ 3937 (Bible Lands Museum Jerusalem), is made of white calcite and measures 9×8×1.4 cm. It was purchased at Christie's and appears in the London auction catalogue for 11 June 1997, as item no. 5. It was inscribed in two columns on the top edge, obverse, and bottom edge. A transliteration and study of this inscription was very kindly provided by Dr J. Westenholz, who graciously allowed an edition to appear in this RIM volume in advance of her own publication of the piece.

For the town e_{11}.KI, see Sallaberger, Kalender 1 pp. 260–61, where Ur III texts referring to the temples of the goddess ^{d}nin and the god ^{d}dumuzi of e_{11}.KI are noted. Almost certainly, e_{11}.KI was a small town in the neighbourhood of G̃iša and Kiʾan.

TEXT

Col. i	
Upper edge	
1) ^{d}dumu-zi	1–2) For the god Dumuzi of (the town) E,
Obv.	
2) lugal-e$_{11}$-ra	
3) lugal-zà-ge-si	3–5) Lugal-zage-si, ruler of G̃iša, *lumaḫ* priest of the goddess Nissaba,
4) énsi-^{giš}KÚŠU.KI	
5) lú-maḫ-^{d}nissaba-ke$_{4}$	
6) dumu bu$_{11}$-bu$_{11}$	6–8) son of Bubu, ruler of G̃iša, *lumaḫ* priest of the goddess Nissaba,
7) énsi-^{giš}KÚŠU.KI	
8) lú-maḫ-^{d}nissaba-ke$_{4}$	
Lower edge	
9) ^{d}dumu-zi	9–12) for the god Dumuzi of (the town) E, (and) for his (Lugal-zage-si's) life, built his (Dumuzi's) temple.
Col. ii	
10) lugal-e$_{11}$-ra	
11) nam-ti-la-ni-šè	
12) é-ni mu-na-dù	
13) temen-bi ki-a mi-ni-si-si	13) He drove its foundation (pegs) into the ground.
14) me-bi si ì-mi-sá-sá	14) He perfectly executed its *mes*.
15) é-^{d}li$_{9}$-si mu-dù	15) He built the temple of the god Lisi.
16) é-^{d}nissaba mu-dù	16) He built the temple of the goddess Nissaba.
17) é-PA- ^{giš}KÚŠU.KI mu-dù	17) He built the E-PA of G̃iša.
Lower edge	
18) [é]-PA-ki-an.KI mu-dù	18) He built the [E]-PA of Ki-an.

UR

E1.13

(a) Location

Ancient Ur (Sumerian and Akkadian Urim) has long been identified with the modern mound al-Muqayyar (NLat 30° 57.5′, ELong 46° 6.5′). The modern site name, meaning "provider of pitch," clearly refers to the layers of pitch which were used in the construction of the ancient ziqqurrat.

(b) Excavation History

The site has been examined and/or excavated by a large number of researchers, including: J.B. Fraser in 1835, W.K. Loftus in 1850, J.E. Taylor in 1853–55, W.H. Ward in 1885, the British Museum in 1888, the University Museum of the University of Pennsylvania and the Babylonian Exploration Fund Philadelphia in 1890, J.H. Haynes in 1891, R.C. Thomsen in 1918, H.R. Hall in 1919, Sir C.L. Woolley in 1922–34, A. Mahdi and S.Md.-A. al Siwani in 1960–61, S.Md.-A. al Siwani in 1961–62, H.M. al-Najafi in 1963–64, and W. al-Ruba'i in 1967–68. Ur is notable in Early Dynastic times for the spectacular "royal graves" excavated by Sir C.L. Woolley in the 1920s.

(c) Writing of the City Name

The city name Ur is written ŠES.AB(uri$_5$).KI in early texts; in later periods we find the orthography ŠEŠ.UNUG(úri).KI.

(d) Patron Deities

The patron deity of Ur was the moon god Nanna-Suen; his consort was the moon goddess Ningal. The ziqqurrat terrace of Nanna's temple was called the E-temen-ni-guru ("Foundation Platform Clad in Terror") and the main temple the E-kišnugal "Alabaster House."

(e) Appearance in the Sumerian King List

The SKL assigns four kings to its Ur I dynasty: Mes-Ane-pada, Mes-kiag̃-nun, Elulu, and Balulu. In addition, Mes-Ane-pada and Mes-kiag̃-nun appear in the "Tummal Chronicle"; Mes-Ane-pada is named there as the builder of the Bur-šušua temple in Nippur (for this temple, see George, House Most High p. 73 no. 130).

Two kings, Mes-KALAM-du and A-KALAM-du, although not appearing in the SKL, are known from other sources from Ur to have ruled before Mes-Ane-pada at Ur. The dynastic relationship between Mes-Ane-pada of the SKL and the earlier kings of Ur named Mes-KALAM-du and A-KALAM-du had long been unclear. However, the evidence of a bead excavated at Mari led J. Böse (ZA 68 [1978] pp. 6–33) to demonstrate (in my view convincingly — for reservations, see Charvat "Early Ur — War Chiefs and Kings of Ur Dynastic III," AoF 9 (1982) p. 54: "... I am afraid that the traces of the signs on the bead do not permit safe interpretation of the sign group in question") that Mes-Ane-pada was the son of Mes-KALAM-du. Thus we have, starting with Mes-KALAM-du, evidence of a native dynasty at Ur which seems to have exerted considerable influence over Sumer. Seals of various personages, A-Anzu,

Ur-Pabilsag̃, and Gan-kug̃-sig, were found in the "royal tombs" at Ur; they likely predate the dynasty which may have begun with Mes-KALAM-du. However, we do not know whether or not they were native rulers of Ur. Indeed, there is some evidence to suggest they were not. We know that Lagaš may have exercised influence over Ur for a short period during Early Dynastic times. P. Charvát, "Early Ur — War Chiefs and Kings of Ur Dynastic III," AoF 9 (1982) pp. 55–56 notes:

> A still unresolved problem is presented by the find of a stele of Urnanše of Lagaš at Ur in secondary position in a Neo-Babylonian building. The interesting thing is that the name of the father of Urnanše and that of Lagaš are hewn away. Of course, there is always the possibility that the stele was brought from some other spot. However, the piece is of so little value that it is difficult to imagine the purpose of carrying it to Ur if it was not cut up for stone ... It is possible that the Ur stele was defaced ... because it commemorated a conquest of Ur by Lagaš or at least a military victory of Lagaš over Ur. It is a question how far the "barren stratum" dividing layers of burials from different periods at the "Royal cemetery" and containing occupational debris might be brought into connection with the destruction of buildings on that level. Military activities of Urnanše of Lagaš are documented [in the Ur inscriptions]: he built a city wall of Lagaš and a text of his mentions booty (nam-ra-ak). The possibility that Urnanše conquered — or at least exercised decisive influence at — Lagaš is illustrated by the fact that a "subordinate of the ensi of Lagaš" (ir_{11}-ensí-lagaš) received rations together with other Ur people.

Charvat notes in an addendum to that article that an inscription published by Crawford indicates that Ur-Nanše did in fact conquer Ur. The text is treated as inscription E1.9.1.6b in this volume.

It is also worth noting that a certain A-Anzu appears with the title "king of Kiš" in an inscription of Enna-il, edited as E1.8.3.1 in this volume. It is uncertain whether he might be the same figure who appears in the seal inscription from Ur. The fact that his successor Mes-Ane-pada also appears with the title "king of Kish" would support this identification; details will have to be examined in a different study.

A-Anzu

E1.13.1

1

A cylinder seal found in the largest of the stone-built tombs of the early royal tombs at Ur bears the name of a certain A-Anzu. Reade (JNES 60 [2001] p. 18) suggests he was a king of Ur.

The element A- in the personal name apparently means "[the] father," not son, as has commonly been believed. See Marchesi, Orientalia 73 (2004) p. 183 n. 173 and the extensive literature (including important articles by Krebernik) cited there for the details.

Reade (JNES 60 [2001] p. 19) points out that a battle scene is found in the lower register of the seal He notes that this motif seems to be a "diagnostic of the royal seals in the earliest phase of the cemetery." Reade's hypothesis is strongly supported by the similarities of this cylinder seal to the royal seals of Išgi-Mari published by Beyer (see E1.10.17.2–3).

COMMENTARY

The shell cylinder seal measures 44 cm in length and 2.6 cm in diameter. It was found in PG/1236 and given the excavation number U12461. It now bears the museum number BM 122538. The inscription was collated from the published photo.

BIBLIOGRAPHY

1934 Woolley in Woolley, UE 2 (text) p. 113 (findspot); Burrows in Woolley, UE 2 (text) p. 316 (transliteration, translation); Burrows in Woolley, UE 2 (plates) pl. 191 U 12461 (copy)

1960 Sollberger, Iraq 22 p. 71 no. 28 (study)

2001 Reade, JNES 60 pp. 18–20 and fig. 3 (study, drawing [of seal design])

TEXT

1) A-AN.IM.DUGUD.MUŠEN	1) A-Anzu.

Ur-Pabilsag̃

E1.13.2

1

A bowl fragment found at Ur bears the inscription of King Ur-Pabilsag̃. It is not certain that he was a native king of Ur.

Marchesi (Orientalia 73 [2004] p. 170 n. 100) has shown that the element Pabilsag̃ should strictly speaking be read Pabilsag̃a. However, the introduction of so-called overhanging vowels in the normalization of proper names in this volume would have likely led to confusion of the readers. A more general transcription was decided upon.

COMMENTARY

The inscription is incised on a fragment of a stalagmitic calcite bowl formed by the join of two pieces. One was found in the layer of burnt brick rubbish below the Ur-Nammu filling by the Boat shrine, and the other to the southeast, c. 0.30 m above the archaic floor level, just below the sand. The joined fragments measure 8 cm in height, with a rim diameter of 20 cm, and a base diameter of 12 cm. The bowl fragment was given the excavation number U 18232, the registration number 1933-10-13, 1, and the museum number BM 124348. The inscription was collated.

The king of line 3 has often been assumed to be a native king of Ur, although there is no compelling evidence that this is the case.

The findspot of one of the pieces was c. 30 cm above the Dynasty 1 (= Mes-Ane-pada) level. However since this was in a disturbed context we believe that it cannot be used to conclusively date Ur-Pabilsag̃.

Reade, JNES 60 (2001) p. 29, suggests that tomb PG 779 at Ur, which he dates to the period around A-Anzu, may have belonged to Ur-Pabilsag̃.

Nissen points out (from a communication from Sollberger) that the form of the lugal sign in the text indicates a date to the period of Ur-Nanše or later, likely ruling out an assignment to pre-Ur I times. He cannot be assigned to the so-called Second Dynasty of Ur proposed by Jacobsen (Jacobsen, SKL pp. 175–76) since duplicates of the SKL published since Jacobsen's editio princeps clearly indicate that so-called Second Dynasty of Ur is a phantom and is not recorded in the SKL. So Nissen argued for a date at the very end of the ED period.

The late date proposed by Nissen is rejected by Marchesi in Orientalia NS 73 (2004) pp. 171–72 n. 121. Marchesi suggests that the writing GIŠ.BIL (found in the seal inscription edited in this volume immediately after this text) likely dates to the ED IIIb period. On the other hand, this inscription, with its writing ᵈpa-bil$_x$(NE×PAP)-sag̃, he suggests likely dates to the ED IIIa period.

The divine name of line 1, ᵈLAK 566 (DUG×KAS), occurs in the great god list from Fāra published in copy by Deimel in SF 1, col. ix line 2; see also Krebernik, ZA 76 (1986) p. 176. ᵈLAK 566 (DUG×KAS) also appears in the great god list from Abū Ṣalābīḫ, found in copies given in Biggs, Abū Ṣalābīkh nos. 82–89; see Mander, Pantheon p. 28 no. 183 for ᵈLAK 566 (DUG×KAS). As far as the author can determine the reading is unknown.

As is noted by Sollberger (UET 8 p. 1) ᵈLAK 566 (DUG×KAS) is followed two lines later in the great Fāra god list by the god Pabilsag̃ (ᵈpa-bìl(GIŠ.NE.PAP)-sag̃). He notes that the appearance of King Ur-Pabilsag̃ in this inscription is unlikely to be coincidental. The name Ur-Pabilsag̃ appears in an economic tablet from Lagaš from the time of URU-KA-gina (Sollberger, CT 50 no. 36 col. xi line 1′).

In the great Fāra god list ᵈLAK 566 (DUG×KAS) appears in a section (col. viii 29 – ix 14) dealing with several deities of the Lagaš region, namely: (a) ᵈšul-LAK 442 (Ur-Nanše's personal god, see Selz, Untersuchungen pp. 279ff.); (b) Pabilsag̃ (see Selz, Untersuchungen p. 272 where a reference is noted to the "Riddles of Lagaš" text edited by Biggs in JNES 32 (1973) and in particular p. 31 col. ix line 3′: dig̃ir-bi ᵈpa-bìl-sag̃ ur-sag̃-ᵈen-líl-lá "Its deity is Pabilsag̃, warrior of Enlil"; the line likely indicates that, in addition to other cult centres at Isin and Nippur, the god

Pabilsağ was a deity of a town in the Lagaš region); (c) the divine Kiki bird (chief deity of the town of AB×ÁŠ, likely ancient Ašabu, a settlement near Umma and Lagaš, see the archaic zà-mì hymns edited by Biggs, Abū Ṣalābīkh p. 49 lines 100–101); (d) Nanše; (e) Niminta-e; and (f) Ğatumdu, "mother of Lagaš." It may be that ᵈLAK 566 (DUG×KAS) was originally a deity of a town in the Lagaš region.

The sign after lugal in line 3 is broken; a possible reading of Š[EŠ.AB.KI] would be only guess.

We must note that no ruler Ur-Pabilsağ is extant in ED royal inscriptions of Lagaš or in the so-called Lagaš King List edited by Sollberger in JCS 21 (1967) pp. 279–91.

BIBLIOGRAPHY

1965 Sollberger, UET 8 no. 3 (copy, study)
1982 Steible, ASBW 2 p. 279 Urpabilsag 1 (edition)
1968 Biggs, JNES 27 p. 145 (study)
1986 Cooper, SARI 1 p. 97 Ur 1 (translation)
1991 Braun-Holzinger, Weihgaben pp. 140–41 G 154 (edition, study)
2001 Reade, JNES 60 p. 20 (note to PG 779) (study)

TEXT

1) ᵈLAK 566(DUG×KASKAL)
2) ur-ᵈpa-bíl-sağ
3) lugal-⌈x⌉
Lacuna

1) To the deity... ,
2–3) Ur-Pabilsağ, king of ...

Lacuna

Gan-kuĝ-sig

E1.13.2.1001

1

The seal of a certain Gan-kuĝ-sig *ereš-diĝir* priestess of the god Pabilsaĝ was found in a royal tomb at Ur. The findspot of the seal suggests she may have been a member of a royal family at Ur.

COMMENTARY

This exquisite seal of lapis lazuli, which measures 3.9 cm in length, was found near the entrance of PG. 580 (see Woolley, UE 2 p. 50 where it is marked in fig. 4 with the number 1), a royal tomb in which no human body was recoverable. The seal was given the excavation number U 9315; it is now housed in Iraq with the museum number IM 4294.

According to Nissen Königsfriedhof (p. 111) the relative date of the PG. 580 to the other royal tombs cannot be determined. In his chart on p. 117 Nissen indicates a general date to the Mes-KALAM-du-Lugal-anda period.

There may be some connection between this royal lady's priestly title and the name of the ruler of the preceding inscription. If she had served as queen, we might conjecture that Ur-Pabilsaĝ was her son. This idea is supported by the fact that the tombs Reade suggests should be attributed to Ur-Pabilsag (PG 779) and Pabilsaĝ's wife (PG 777) lie immediately beside PG 580 where the seal of Gan-kuĝ-sig was found. A full investigation of the problem is outside the scope of this volume.

For the reading gan as an old allograph for géme "young women, servant" cf. Selz, Untersuchungen, p. 142 n. 582:

> Dagegen vermutete bereits A. Deimel, Or 34/35, 122, eine Entsprechung von ḪÉ und gemé. In ZA 61 (1971) erwog J. Bauer eine Deutung als "Dienerin, Zuständige" und wies in AoN 9 darauf hin, dass das Element ḪÉ-/GAN- nur in weiblichen PN und GN vorkomme. — Andernots zu diskutierende Belege erweisen ... Namen als alte Schreibung des Wortes gemé "Magd"; vgl.a. W.G. Lambert apud P. Mander, PAS S. 59.

One may also note the comments of Krebernik in Streck and Weninger (eds.), Altorientalische und semitische Onomastik (AOAT 296, Münster 2002, p. 12):

> Im präsargonischen Lagaš läßt sich jedoch beobachten, daß der Name derselben Frau zunächst gan-tilla und später géme-tilla geschrieben wird. Auch in zwei altakkadischen Texten aus Nippur variieren gan- und géme- im ... freilich erst später bezeugte - Emesalform /gin/ von géme anführen. Allerdings ist die Identifikation nicht ganz unproblematisch: (a) neben gan-kommt wohl schon Fāra-zeitlich auch géme- vor; (b) analog gebildete männliche Namen mit dem Element ir- oder ir_{11}- "Diener" fehlen in kontemporären Quellen. Ich möchte daher nicht ausschließen, daß der Ersatz von gan durch géme auf der Umdeutung eines von géme ursprünglich verschiedenen, nicht mehr gebräuchlichen bzw. verstandenen Wortes beruht.

The reading and meaning of kuĝ-sig is not clear to me. Marchesi in Orientalia NS 73 (2004) p. 172 notes:

> The *hapax legomenon* kun-sig may denote a cultic place or installation as is the case with kun-saĝ in the comparable PN géme-kun-saĝ (DP 230 vii 14; FAOS 15/1, Nik 21 ii 7; etc.); cf. kun-saĝ(-ĝá) = Akk. *muḫru*, a chapel marking the turning point of a processional circuit, according to CAD M/2, 177.

Concerning line two Steinkeller (in Watanabe [ed.], Priests and Officials in the Ancient Near East, p. 121) reads NIN-diĝir as ereš-diĝir. There he cites notes of Moran, NABU 1988 no. 36 and Fleming, NABU 1990 no. 8 referring to an Emar copy of Ḫḫ 19 which gives a gloss i-ri-iš-ti-gi-ra for Sumerian NIN-diĝir-ra. The issue is taken up in considerably more detail by Marchesi in Orientalia NS 73 (2004) pp. 186–89. In his summary Marchesi notes that NIN has a reading ereš or eriš when it corresponds to Akkadian *bēltu* "lady" and *šarratu* "queen" and nin when it means "sister" (more specifically nin_9) or "mistress/proprietress."

BIBLIOGRAPHY

1934 Woolley in Woolley, UE 2 (text) p. 49 (findspot); Burrows in Woolley, UE 2 (text) p. 316 (transliteration, translation); Burrows in Woolley, UE 2 (plates); pl. 191 U 9351 (copy); pl. 200 no. 98 (photo)

1966 Nissen, Königsfriedhofe pp. 14, 111, 172 (findspot)

1999 Steinkeller in Watanabe (ed.), Priests and Officials in the Ancient Near East, p. 121 (study)

TEXT

1) gan-kuĝ-sig
2) ereš-diĝir
3) ^{d}pa-bìl-saĝ

1) Gan-kuĝ-sig
2) *Ereš-diĝir* priestess
3) of the god Pabilsaĝ

Mes-KALAM-du

E1.13.3

1

A seal of King Mes-KALAM-du was found in a royal tomb at Ur. The king appears with the prestigious title lugal kiš "king of Kiš" in an inscription of his son Mes-Ane-pada, but is not actually attested in the SKL. However, Mes-Ane-pada does appear as a member of the "First Dynasty of Ur" in the SKL.

CATALOGUE

Ex.	Museum number	Excavation number	Ur provenance	Object	Dimensions (cm)	Lines preserved
1	BM 122536	U 11751	In a box containing a man with two gold daggers; ascribed to Grave PG. 1054 by Woolley (see discussion below)	Shell cylinder seal; the ends are inlaid with pierced disks of lapis-lazuli	Length: 4.9 cm Dia.: 0.3 cm	1–2

COMMENTARY

Following Woolley, scholars have generally considered the grave PG. 1054 to be the tomb of King Mes-KALAM-du. However, recently M. Müller-Karpe has argued, in an article entitled "Meskalamdug and the Ziggurat of Ur," Proceedings of the International Conference on the Tower of Babylon and the Ziggurat at Borsippa, Baghdad Sept. 15–20, 1998, that its chief occupant was a woman. He writes:

> The main person of tomb 1054 lay in a stone chamber at the bottom of a deep shaft. She was equipped with typical female ornaments and surrounded by four men with daggers.

Müller-Karpe suggests that Woolley's cross-sectional drawing of PG 779 and PG 1054 may be in error, and that tomb PG 779 may have actually contained the wooden chest in which the man with Mes-KALAM-du's seal was found. He further suggests that PG 1054 was the tomb of Mes-KALAM-du's wife — unfortunately her name is unknown — and PG 779 was Mes-KALAM-du's tomb. According to his correction of Woolley's plan, PG 1054 and PG 779 were aligned so precisely that a direct relationship between the two was highly likely.

The reading of the king's name has been the matter of some debate by scholars. It was first read mes-kalam-dùg by Burrows in his publication of the inscriptions of the royal tombs of Ur (UE 2 [text] p. 316). In his comments (p. 318 n. 2) Burrows writes:

> DÙG in mes-kalam-DÙG may also be read ŠÁR (all), and Mr. Gadd has adopted this reading.

However, the reading of the third element of the name is almost certainly -du_{10} (= LAK 359) not šár. The reading šár (= LAK 809) was suggested by Gadd because the signs LAK 359 and 809 coalesce in later cuneiform script. However, as has been pointed out by Krebernik (in Bauer, Englund and Krebernik [eds.], Mesopotamien p. 277), LAK 359 and LAK 890 were distinct in ED period script. The name is almost certainly not to be translated as "hero of the good land" as Burrows, in Woolley UE 2 (text) p. 318 n. 2 suggested, since that would have been mes-kalam-du_{10}-ga, but rather the name could mean "Hero who provides well-being for the land," understanding du_{10} as a reduplicated non-finite verbal form.

The reading of the second sign, however, has been less straightforward; both the values kalam and uĝ have been proposed. Edzard, RLA 5 p. 553 fig. 25 and p. 554b, maintained that the signs RÉC 420 = LAK 729

= kalam (with one vertical wedge in the middle of the first element of the sign possibly a "DAG" sign, in contrast to RÉC 421 = LAK 730 = uĝ with three vertical wedges in the middle of the "DAG" part of the sign) were differentiated at Fāra in ED times and to some degree in later periods. He noted that the distinction between the two was clearly made in royal inscriptions of Ḫammu-rāpi of Babylon. For a discussion of this problem, see also Limet, RA 72 (1978) pp. 6–7. However, as pointed out to me by Steinkeller in RIM readers' notes, the situation does not seem to be as simple as Edzard indicates. The differentiation is apparently found in Gudea Statue B col. vii, where line 16 has: uĝ(RÉC 421)-ĝá gù ù-na-dé-a "(the god Ningirsu) had addressed him (Gudea) from the crowd" and line 64: nimĝir-kalam(RÉC 420)-ma-ke$_4$ "herald of the land" and the distinction was emphasized by Steible in ASBW 2 pp. 271–72 in his edition of this king's inscriptions. However in texts from Lagaš (Rosengarten Répertoire p. 28 sub no. 136) RÉC 420 is apparently found with both values; Rosengarten points to Allote de la Füye DP 573 iv 6: GÁNA kalam-ma and Allote de la Füye DP 136 xii 10: gal:uĝ, as was noted by Bauer in AoN 21 (1985) p. 10 and by Selz in FAOS 15, 1 pp. 85–86 note to col. iii line 4. However, Steible (ASBW 2 p. 272) writes: "Soweit ich sehe, werden die beiden Zeichenformen in der Überlieferung von Lagaš/Girsu deutlich auseinandergehalten, während sie in Nippur schon früh alternieren ..." Krebernik, ZA 76 (1986) p. 162 n. 5, indicates that in the great god list from Fāra only LAK 729 appears and "die in AB zu beobachtende Verteilung KALAM für ùĝ und kalam kann ich in Fāra nicht belegen." Steinkeller (in RIM readers' notes) points out that a reading kalam is more probable because the adjective du$_{10}$ normally describes loci in ED PNs.

On this question Marchesi (Orientalia NS 73 [2004] pp. 190–92) has written most recently. He notes that the PN mes-KALAM-du$_{10}$ has been variously interpreted as "Hero/Herald of the good land," (Burrows; M. Lambert) "the hero who is good for the country," (Roux), "le heros (est) bon (pour le) pays," (Sollberger) "le héraut, le bon pays ..." (M. Lambert, abbreviated), "the mes-tree beneficial to the Land" (Parpola). He notes that substantial agreement so far on reading this name as mes-kalam-du$_{10}$/dùg. He suggests that the name is to be read as a defective spelling for the PN Mes-uĝe-idu(g), meaning "the mes is pleasing to the people" and provides the details to support this understanding.

A more detailed discussion and definitive resolution of this question is beyond the scope of this volume, and for the present a broad transliteration, mes-KALAM-du$_{10}$, has (conservatively) been given.

BIBLIOGRAPHY

1934 Woolley in Woolley, UE 2 (text), p. 98 (findspot); Burrows in Woolley, UE 2 (text), p. 316 (transliteration, translation), Burrows in Woolley, UE 2 (plates), pl. 191 U 11751 (copy), pl. 196 no. 55 (photo)
1960 Sollberger, Iraq 22 p. 71 no. 6 (study)
1971 Sollberger and Kupper, IRSA IIB2a (conflated translation)
1978 Boese, ZA 68 p. 16 fig. 2 (copy)
1986 Cooper, SARI 1 pp. 97–98 Ur 3 (conflated translation)
1998 Müller-Karpe, "Untersuchungen zur Genese und Struktur von Eliten in vor- und frühgeschichtlichen Gesellschaften," Jahrbuch des Römisch-Germanischen Zentralmuseums, Mainz 44 1997 (1998) pp. 673–77 (findspot)
2002 Müller-Karpe, "Meskalamdug and the Ziggurat of Ur," Proceedings of the International Conference on the Tower of Babylon and the Ziggurat at Borsippa, Baghdad Sept. 15–20, 1998 (findspot, study)

TEXT

1) mes-KALAM-du$_{10}$	1) Mes-KALAM-du
2) lugal	2) the king

2

Two spear points from Ur bear an inscription of Mes-KALAM-[du] likely dedicated to the god Sîn.

CATALOGUE

Ex.	Museum number	Excavation number	Ur provenance	Object	Lines preserved
1	IM 45086	U 17659	Ziqqurat 1931 floor of the I Archaic level	Bronze spear point	1–2
2	IM 32684	U 17608	Ziqqurat 1931, ED level	Copper spear point	

COMMENTARY

The existence of these texts was kindly pointed out to me by G. Frame; M. Müller-Karpe very kindly provided me with a draft copy of his presentation in Baghdad in advance of its publication.

The restoration of the DN in line 1 is uncertain. In view of the spear points' provenance a restoration of the name of the god Sîn is likely.

BIBLIOGRAPHY

1994 Müller-Karpe, Jahrbuch des Römisch-Germanischen Zentralmuseums, Mainz 41 1994 (1996) pp. 638–39 and fig. 79 (exs. 1–2, study, photo)

2000 Müller-Karpe, Abstracts of 2nd International Congress on the Archaeology of the Ancient Near East, Copenhagen May 22–26 p. 35 (exs. 1–2, study)

Müller-Karpe, Proceedings of the International Conference on the Ziggurats and Temples of Babylon and Borsippa Sept. 15–20, 1998 (exs. 1–2, study) (forthcoming)

TEXT

1) ᵈEN.[ZU]
2) mes-KALAM-[du_{10}]
3) [...]
4) [...]

1) (To) the god [S]în
2) Mes-KALAM-du
3) [...]
4) [...]

3

A cylinder seal found at Ur bears the inscription of Pū-abum, "the queen." The fact that her seal was found in the tomb beside that of Mes-KALAM-du almost certainly means that she was a (second) wife of that king.

COMMENTARY

The lapis-lazuli seal, which measures 4.8 cm in length and 2.5 cm in diameter, was found in the grave PG. 800 at Ur, and given the excavation number U 10939.

The PN of line 1 has for a long time been read in Akkadian as Pû-abī rather than Sumerian šùd-ad, following Gelb, MAD 3, p. 12 who compared this name to ŠÙD(*pù*)-*a-bí* on an Old Akkadian period tablet from Susa published by Legrain in MDP 14. More recently Marchesi (Orientalia 73 [2004] pp. 193–94) has discussed the reading and meaning of the PN pù-AD and concluded that a reading Pū-abum is possible.

It is reasonably clear that the spouse of Pū-abum was interred in the tomb PG 789 which lay immediately beside PG 800. Woolley (UE 2 [text] pp. 72–73) writes:

> ... a king has been buried [in tomb PG 789], and some years after his death a queen [Pū-abum] has to be buried in turn. ... The obvious explanation is that Shub-ad [=Pū-abum] was the widow of the king and wished to be buried next to him for that reason. If that is so, a close time relation is established between the two graves.

Unfortunately, there were no objects found in tomb PG 789 which gave the name of its male occupant. According to Nissen (Königsfriedhof p. 111) PG 789 and PG 800 date roughly to the time of PG 1054; as noted the latter yielded the seal with the name of Mes-KALAM-du, the king.

PG 789 almost certainly does not belong to King A-KALAM-du. He likely was buried in the tomb PG 1050. Although this structure was ultimately classed by Woolley as one tomb, he originally thought it was two; we are inclined to believe that the compartments of the structure served as the resting places of both A-KALAM-du and his wife A-šu-sikilam.

BIBLIOGRAPHY

1934 Woolley, UE 2 (text) pp. 312 n. 3, 316, 564 (transliteration, study); (plates) pl. 191 (copy)
1957 Gelb, MAD 3 p. 12 sub *abum* (study)
1960 Sollberger, Iraq 22 pp. 71–72, 79 no. 1 (study)
1971 Sollberger and Kupper, IRSA IB1a (translation)
1980 Amiet, Glyptique, p. 215 no. 1182 (study)
1986 Cooper, SARI 1 p. 97 Ur 2 (translation)
2004 Marchesi, Orientalia NS 73 pp. 193–94 (study)

TEXT

1) *pù*-AD	1) Pu-abum,
2) nin	2) the queen.

A-KALAM-du

E1.13.4

1

Mes-KALAM-du was apparently succeeded by his son A-KALAM-du as king of Ur. While no inscription of the king himself is as yet extant, a seal inscription from a royal tomb at Ur mentions his wife A-šu-šikilam.

COMMENTARY

The lapis-lazuli seal with this inscription measures 3.5 cm in length and 1.9 cm in diameter. It was found in the Royal Grave PG. 1050 B, and was given the excavation number U 11825. The seal is housed in Philadelphia, museum number UM 30–12-1.

According to Nissen (Königfriedhof p. 111) tomb PG. 1050 dates to a period very slightly later than PG. 1054 (that is, the tomb that yielded the inscription of King Mes-KALAM-du).

The PN of line 4 may possibly be translated (as Selz in RIM readers' notes suggested) "The father (has) pure hands" or "the father is a purifier"; for the latter translation of šu-sikil, see van Dijk, in Studies Böhl p. 113. Marchesi in Orientalia NS 73 (2004) pp. 179–80 n. 152 translates "the Father is the pure hand of An."

BIBLIOGRAPHY

1934 Woolley, UE 2 (text) p. 316 (transliteration); p. 574 (study); (plates) pl. 191 (copy)

1980 Amiet, Glyptique, p. 213 and pl. 78 no. 1039 (copy, study)

1971 Sollberger and Kupper, IRSA IB3a (translation)

1986 Cooper, SARI 1 p. 98 Ur 4 (translation)

TEXT

1) a-KALAM-du_{10}	1–3) A-KALAM-du, king of Ur,
2) lugal	
3) uri_5	
4) a-šu-sikil-àm	4–5) A-šu-sikilam (is) his wife.
5) dam-ni	

Mes-Ane-pada

E1.13.5

1

A bead found at Mari names Mes-Ane-pada as the son of Mes-KALAM-du.

COMMENTARY

The lapis-lazuli bead, which measures 11.9 cm in length and 1.9 cm in width, was found in a jar in room XXVII of the Presargonic palace at Mari. It was assigned the excavation number M 4439.

The jar with the bead contained a number of precious objects; among them were a small figure of a lion-headed eagle, various statuettes of nude goddesses and women, bracelets, stars, toggle pins, a pendant, necklaces, amulets, and cylinder seals. The whole lot was considered by Parrot to be homogeneous and to represent a royal gift. He notes (Parrot, MAM 4 p. 48):

> Les objets du "trésor" proviennent donc d'Ur. Deux hypothèses sont possibles entre lesquelles on ne saurait choisir: ou bien le roi Mesannipadda envoya ce cadeau, ou bien il l'apporta lui-même. Quelle que soit la réponse que l'on fournisse, la conclusion demeure la même: au IIIe millénaire, Mari avait une importance tout aussi grande qu'au IIe. Qu'un souverain, comme Mesannipadda ait éprouvé le besoin, soit de rendre visite, soit d'envoyer au roi de Mari, un pareil présent, montre assez que dans sa pensée, le souverain du Moyen-Euphrate était une puissance dont il y avait tout lieu de s'assurer les bonnes grâces.

Unfortunately, we do not know to which king of Mari the gift was presented.

In connection with the Mari find, the discovery at Ur of an inscription of King Anbu, possibly the king of Mari, is an interesting and even tantalizing datum. However, as noted earlier in this volume, the existence of the Mari bead and the Ur bowl are hardly definitive evidence for establishing a synchronism between Mes-Ane-pada and Anbu.

The former reading of the RN as Gansud-ansud given by Parrot, following Dossin, is erroneous. The correct reading follows the interpretation of Boese refined by the the collations provided by Renger RA 78 (1984) pp. 175–76. Boese had read the last sign of line 1 as KALAM but Renger indicated there was insufficient space, and suggested instead a broken –ni, a reading we have adopted here.

As noted, in addition to showing the links between Ur and Mari, the text is important because it established the fact that Mes-Ane-pada was the son of Mes-KALAM-du.

Of further importance is Mes-Ane-pada's adoption of the title "king of Kiš." While the precise historical significance of this cannot be discussed at detail in the present study, a military victory over Kiš is not inconceivable in view of the ED period destruction level attested there, although Mes-Ane-pada would hardly be the only candidate for causing damage.

BIBLIOGRAPHY

1968 Dossin in Parrot, Trésor p. 44 and fig. 35 (photo [one side only], translation); pp. 53–56 and figs. 36–37 (photo, copy, edition); pls. XXI–XXII (photo)
1969 Sollberger, RA 63 pp. 169–70 (edition, study)
1970 Dossin, RA 64 pp. 163–68 (study)
1971 Sollberger and Kupper, IRSA IB4c (translation)
1978 Boese, ZA 68 pp. 6–33 (copy, edition, study)
1979 Westenholz in Larsen, Power p. 119 (edition)
1982 Steible, ASBW 2 pp. 272–73 Mesannepada 1 (edition)
1984 Renger, RA 78 pp. 175–76 (study)
1986 Cooper, SARI 1 p. 98 Ur 5.1 (translation)
1991 Braun-Holzinger, Weihgaben p. 365 P 2 (edition, study)

TEXT

1)	an lugal-⌈ni⌉	1) To the god An, his lord,
2)	mes-an-né-pà-da	2–3) Mes-Ane-pada, king of Ur,
3)	lugal-uri$_5$.KI	
4)	dumu	4–6) son of Mes-KALAM-du, king of Kiš,
5)	mes-⌈KALAM⌉-du$_{10}$	
6)	lugal-kiš.KI	
7)	a mu-na-ru	7) dedicated (this bead) to him.

2

A clay sealing from Ur names Mes-Ane-pada as husband of the *nugig* priestess.

COMMENTARY

The clay sealing, which was found in two pieces, has a diameter of c. 1.3 cm. It was found loose in the soil of the Royal Cemetery (stratum SIS 1) and was given the excavation number U 13607.

For Sumerian nu-gig = Akkadian *qadištum, ištarītum*, a type of priestess, see most recently recently Henshaw, Female and Male pp. 206–13 §§ 4.11-4.12 and cf. the earlier literature of Renger, ZA 58 (1967) pp. 179–84 referring to the *qadištu* priestess in OB times. Cf. also Lambert, in "Prostitution," in Haas (ed.), Außenseiter und Randgruppen, Xenia 32 (1992) pp. 140–44. Lambert notes that the Sumerian term nu-gig contains the element nu = lú "person" and gig; the latter likely means "(cultically) set apart," as in Sumerian níg-gig = Akkadian *ikkibu*(*m*) "taboo thing" both in the positive and negative sense of "sacred" and "forbidden" respectively. Cooper's suggestion (SARI p. 98 n. 1 to § 5.1) that nugig might simply be a personal name appears less likely to this author than a translation as "*nugig* priestess." The question of the possible role of the nu-gig in the "New Year's Festival" mentioned by Cooper will not be taken up in this volume.

BIBLIOGRAPHY

1934 Woolley, UE 2 (text) p. 312 (transliteration); p. 588 sub U. 13607 (study); (plates) pl. 191 (copy); pl. 207 (photo)
1971 Sollberger and Kupper, IRSA IB4a (translation)
1980 Amiet, Glyptique p. 213 and pl. 80 no. 1063 (edition, copy)
1986 Cooper, SARI 1 p. 98 Ur 5.2 (translation)

TEXT

1)	mes-an-né-pà-da	1) Mes-Ane-pada,
2)	lugal-kiš.KI	2) king of Kiš,
3)	dam nu-gig	3) spouse of the *nugig* priestess.

3

A cylinder seal found at Ur names Nin-TUR as the wife of Mes-Ane-pada.

COMMENTARY

The lapis-lazuli seal, which measures 4 cm in length, was found "loose in the soil at a depth of 1.40 m. from the modern surface, i.e., on the level of the higher Sargonid graves and in or a little above the stratum of the 1st Dynasty rubbish which covers the older cemetery." (Ur Notebooks). It was given the excavation number U 8981 and the museum number CBS 16852.

In line 1 the first sign is clearly nin_1 (MUNUS+TÚG) "lady" not nin_9 (MUNUS+KU) "sister"; for the distinction, see Borger, HKL p. 409.

For the RN nin-TUR, see Bauer, AoF 21 (1985) p. 12 and cf. the Ur III RN nin-TUR.TUR-g̃u (Frayne, RIME 3/2 p. 168 no. 16). The reading of nin-TUR is very likely nin-bànda analogous to lugal-bànda, but this is not absolutely certain. One may compare the term dam-bàn-da "Nebenfrau" (= "junior wife") noted by Neumann in CRRA 33 p. 135 where Sjöberg, PSD B p. 86 lexical section 2 is noted (giving dam-bàn-da = *še-ʾ-i-tum*).

BIBLIOGRAPHY

1928 Gadd, UET 1 no. 268 (copy, edition)
1934 Woolley, UE 2 (text) p. 312 (edition, study); p. 540 sub U. 8981 (study); (plates) pl. 207 no. 216 (photo)
1971 Sollberger and Kupper, IRSA IB4b (translation)
1980 Amiet, Glyptique p. 213 and pl. 80 no. 1064 (edition, copy)
1986 Cooper, SARI 1 p. 98 Ur 5.3 (edition)

TEXT

1) nin-TUR nin
2) dam mes-an-né-pà-da

1–2) Nin-TUR, the queen, spouse of Mes-Ane-pada.

4

An inscription known from a copper bowl and two seal impressions gives the name Nin-TUR; very likely she was the lady mentioned in the previous inscription.

CATALOGUE

Ex.	Museum number	Excavation number	Ur provenance	Object	Dimensions (cm)	Lines preserved	cpn
1	BM 121663b	U 10081b	Royal Grave, PG. 755 (the tomb of prince Mes-KALAM-du) from the mass of copper vessels found corroded together.	Copper bowl	—	1	n
2	—	U 13678	Loose in the soil of stratum SIS 1–2	Clay sealing		1	
3	—	U 13686 A, B	Loose in the soil of stratum SIS 1–2	Clay sealing	Dia.: c. 3.5 cm	1	

COMMENTARY

The line division follows ex. 1. Exs. 2–3 give: 1) nin- 2) TUR nin.

BIBLIOGRAPHY

1934 Woolley, UE 2 (text) p. 316 sub U. 10081 (ex. 1, transliteration); pp. 553–54 (ex. 1, study); p. 588 (ex. 3, study) (plates); pl. 190a (ex. 1, photo); pl. 191 (ex. 3, copy); pl. 207 no. 215 (ex. 3, photo)
1936 Legrain, UE 3 p. 44 no. 516 (exs. 2–3, study); pl. 57 no. 516 (ex. 3, photo)
1980 Amiet, Glyptique p. 214 and pl. 80 no. 1067 (exs. 2–3, study, ex. 3, copy)
1986 Cooper, SARI 1 p. 99 Ur 5.4 (exs. 1–3, translation)

TEXT

1) nin-TUR nin	1) Nin-TUR, the queen.

A-Ane-pada

E1.13.6

1

A gold bead found in excavations at Tell al-ʿUbaid (almost certainly ancient Nu-BANDA) is inscribed with the royal name A-Ane-pada.

COMMENTARY

The hollow gold bead of scaraboid form measures 1.5×1.2×1.0 cm. It was found near the front face of the Ninḫursaĝ temple about 1.5 m SW of the stone stairs (see Hall, UE 1 pl. 2 no. 39). It was given the excavation number TO 286; its IM number is not known. The inscription appears on the convex side of the bead, with the direction of writing parallel to the long axis.

For the identification of modern al-ʿUbaid with ancient nu-BANDA, see Frayne, RIME 3/2 p. 102, Sallaberger, Kalender 1 p. 59 n. 246, and Steinkeller, ASJ 17 (1995) p. 280. If the name were read nu-banda it may have served as the precursor of the modern name (Tell al) ʿUbaid.

BIBLIOGRAPHY

1927 Hall and Woolley, UE 1 pp. 79–80 (study); p. 127 (edition [by Gadd]); pl. XXXV no. 2 (photo); pl. XL (copy [by Gadd])

1929 Barton, RISA pp. 2–3 Aanipadda 2 (edition)

1960 Sollberger, Iraq 22 pp. 73–74 no. 42 (study)

1982 Steible, ASBW 2 p. 273 Aʾanepada 1 (edition)

1986 Cooper, SARI 1 p. 99 ur 6.1 (translation)

1991 Braun-Holzinger, Weihgaben p. 365 P 3 (transliteration, study)

TEXT

1) a-an-né-pà-da
2) lugal-uri$_5$.KI

1–2) A-Ane-pada, king of Ur.

2

An inscription incised on a bowl fragment from Ur gives the beginning part of A-Ane-pada's name.

COMMENTARY

The calcite bowl fragment, which measures 8×8 cm, was found under the pavement of rooms 16–17 of the E-nun-maḫ and was given the excavation number U 266. It bears the museum number BCM 1103′ 52.

BIBLIOGRAPHY

1965 Sollberger, UET 8 no. 1 (copy, study)
1982 Steible, ASBW 2 pp. 276–77 A'annepada 6 (edition)
1986 Cooper, SARI 1 p. 99 Ur 6.2 (translation)
1991 Braun-Holzinger, Weihgaben p. 140 G 152 (edition, study)

TEXT

1) d˹x˺-[...]
2) a-an-[né-pà-da]
3) lugal-[uri$_5$.KI]
Lacuna

1) To the deity [DN],
2–3) A-An[e-pada], king [of Ur, dedicated (this bowl)].
Lacuna

3

An inscription found on a foundation tablet and a copper bull figurine records A-Ane-pada's construction of Ninḫursag̃'s temple.

CATALOGUE

Ex.	Museum number	Excavation number	Tell al-ʿUbaid provenance	Object	Dimensions (cm)	Lines preserved	cpn
1	BM 116982 (reg. no.) 1924-9-20, 245)	TO 160	"Found near the south corner of the ramp of the main stairs well above floor level and in grey brickwork of the Second Period." See Hall and Woolley pl. 2 no. 40	White marble foundation tablet in the shape of a plano-convex brick	9.2×5.8 cm	1–7	c
2	BM –	U –	Found near the face of the Ninḫursaga temple about 7 m NE of the stone stairs	Fragment of a copper bull	22.8×10.1	1–7 (traces only)	n

BIBLIOGRAPHY

1924 Legrain, MJ p. 152 no. 1 (ex. 1, study)
1929 Barton, RISA pp. 2–3 Aanipadda 1 (ex. 1, edition)
1927 Hall and Woolley, UE 1 p. 80 (ex. 1, study); p. 126 (ex. 1, edition [by Gadd]); pl. XXXV no. 5 (ex. 1, photo [obverse only]); pl. XL (ex. 1 copy [by Gadd])
1929–30 Gadd, BMQ 4 p. 107 and pl. 56a (study)

1930 Hall, Season's Work pp. 241–42 and fig. 216 (ex. 2, copy, study)
1960 Sollberger, Iraq 22 pp. 73–74 no. 43 (study)
1963 Kramer, Sumerians p. 308 § C 1 (ex. 1, translation)
1971 Sollberger and Kupper, IRSA IB5a (ex. 1, translation)
1982 Steible, ASBW 2 pp. 273–74 A'anepada 2 (exs. 1–2, edition)
1986 Cooper, SARI 1 p. 99 Ur 6.3 (translation)
1991 Braun-Holzinger, Weihgaben p. 326 T 11 (ex. 2, edition, study)

TEXT

1)	^{d}nin-ḫur-sag̃	1) For the goddess Ninḫursag̃,
2)	a-an-né-pà-da	2–3) A-Ane-pada, king of Ur,
3)	lugal-uri$_5$.KI	
4)	dumu-mes-an-né-pà-da	4–5) son of Mes-Ane-pada, king of Ur,
5)	lugal-ur[i$_5$](ŠEŠ.A[B]).[KI]	
6)	^{d}nin-ḫur-sag̃-ra	6–7) built the temple for Ninḫursag̃.
7)	é mu-na-dù	

4

A dedicatory inscription for King A-Ane-pada is found on a bowl fragment from Tell al-ʿUbaid.

COMMENTARY

The inscription appears on a rim fragment of large black diorite bowl; it measures 13.9×9.5 cm. The piece was found in the area of the Ninḫursag̃ temple and was given the excavation number TO 287. It is now housed in Philadelphia, museum number CBS 15106.

The text is restored in large measure following Sollberger, Iraq 22 (1960) p. 82.

BIBLIOGRAPHY

1927 Hall and Woolley, UE 1 p. 80 (study); p. 126 (edition [by Gadd]); pl. XXXVI no. 1 (photo); pl. XL (copy [by Gadd])
1960 Sollberger, Iraq 22 pp. 73–74 no. 44 and p. 82 (transliteration, study)
1971 Sollberger and Kupper, IRSA, IB5c (translation)
1982 Steible, ASBW 2 pp. 274–75 A'annepada 3 (edition)
1986 Cooper, SARI 1 pp. 99–100 Ur 6.4 (translation)
1991 Braun-Holzinger, Weihgaben p. 140 G 150 (edition, study)

TEXT

1)	[^{d}nin-ḫur-sag̃-ra]	1) [For the goddess Ninḫursag̃]
2)	[a-an-né-pà-da]	2–6) [when A-Ane-pada, king of Ur, son of Mes-Ane-pada, [b]uilt [the temple of the goddess Ninḫursag̃],
3)	[lugal-uri$_5$.KI]	
4)	[dumu-mes-an-né-pà-da]	
5)	[u$_4$ é-^{d}nin-ḫur-sag̃]	
6)	[i]n-dù-a	
7)	x-kù	7–8) offered(?) a shining ... (vessel) to her (Ninḫursag̃).
8)	[m]u-na-ÍL	
9)	[nam-ti]-⸢a⸣-an-né-pà-da-šè	9–11) For [the life] of A-Ane-pada, Inimzi and Nanna-ursag̃ dedicated (this vessel) to her (Ninḫursag̃).
10)	[ini]m-[z]i ^{d}nanna-ur-sag(ur:^{d}nanna:sag)	
11)	[a] mu-na-šè-ru	

5

A bowl fragment found in excavations at Tell al-ʿUbaid bears an inscription very similar to the previously edited inscription. In all likelihood it was a dedicatory inscription on behalf of A-Ane-pada.

COMMENTARY

The inscription appears on a fragment near the rim of an alabaster bowl; it measures 8.3×6.5 cm. The piece was found near the south corner of the main stairs of the Ninḫursaĝ temple, and was given the excavation number TO 159. Its IM number is unknown.

The text restoration follows in part Sollberger, Iraq 22 (1960) p. 82.

In line 7, for Sumerian gan = Akkadian *kannu*(*m*) "a small container, usually of stone or precious metal" see CAD M p. 156.

In line 8 we have taken the verb ⸢Í⸣L to be equivalent to Akkadian *šūlû*(*m*) "to offer or dedicate (something) to a deity."

BIBLIOGRAPHY

1927 Hall and Woolley, UE 1 p. 80 (study); p. 126 (edition [by Gadd]); pl. XL (copy [by Gadd])
1960 Sollberger, Iraq 22 pp. 73–74 no. 45 and p. 82 (transliteration, study)
1971 Sollberger and Kupper, IRSA IB5c n. b (study)
1982 Steible, ASBW 2 pp. 275–76 Aʾannepada 4 (edition)
1986 Cooper, SARI 1 p. 100 Ur 6.5 (translation)
1991 Braun-Holzinger, Weihgaben p. 140 G 151 (edition, study)

TEXT

1) [^{d}nin-ḫur-saĝ]
2) [u$_4$ a-an-né-pà-da]
3) [lugal-uri$_5$.KI]
4) d[umu] m[es-an-né-pà-da]
5) é ^{d}nin-ḫ[ur-saĝ]
6) in-dù-a
7) gan-kù
8) mu-na-Í[L]
9) [inim-z]i ^{d}[nanna-ur-sag(ur:^{d}nanna:sag)]
10) [nam-ti-a-an-né-pà-da-šè]
11) [a mu-na-šè-ru]

1) [For the goddess Ninḫursaĝ
2–6) [when A-Ane-pada, king of Ur], so[n of] M[es-Ane-pada], built the temple of the goddess Ninḫ[ursag],

7–8) he offered(?) to her a shining *kannu* vessel.

9–11) [Inim]-zi and N[anna-ursag dedicated (this vessel) for her (the goddess Nin-ḫursaĝ) for the life of A-Ane-pada].

6

A clay tablet from Ur bears a dedicatory inscription for A-Ane-pada.

COMMENTARY

The small baked clay tablet was found in a trial trench "between 150 and 200 levels," at Ur and was given the excavation number U 26. The present whereabouts of the tablet are unknown.

BIBLIOGRAPHY

1927 Hall and Woolley, UE 1 p. 128 (study); pl. XL copy [by Gadd]; pl. XLI no. 2 (photo)
1960 Sollberger, Iraq 22 pp. 73–74 no. 46 (study)
1965 Sollberger, UET 8 p. 1, note to no. 1 (study)
1971 Sollberger and Kupper, IRSA IB5b (translation)
1982 Steible, ASBW 2 p. 276 Aʾanepada 5 (edition)
1986 Cooper, SARI 1 p. 100 Ur 6.5 (translation)

TEXT

1) ⸢dnin⸣-a-zu_5
2) lú-du_{10}-[ga]
3) nam-ti-
4) a-an-né-pà-da-šè
5) a mu-na-šè-ru

1) For the god Ninazu,
2–5) Lu-du[ga] dedicated (this tablet) for the life of A-Ane-pada.

Mes-KALAM-du (the prince)

E1.13.7

An inscription found on one copper and three golden objects excavated from "Royal Grave" PG 55 at Ur (clearly the tomb of a high personage, likely a prince) names a certain Mes-KALAM-du.

1

CATALOGUE

Ex.	Museum number	Excavation number	Ur provenance	Object	Dimensions (cm)	Lines preserved	cpn
1	IM 8270	U 10001	Grave PG 755, inside the coffin	Gold vessel	Height: 7 Length: 22 Width: 12	1	n
2	IM 8271	U 10002	Grave PG 755, inside the coffin	Gold vessel	Height: 7 Dia.: 13.5	1	n
3	IM 8273	U 10004	Grave PG 755, inside the coffin	Gold lamp	Max. length: 16.9 Max. width: 8.5 Length of body: 14.5	1	n
4	BM 121663a (reg. no.) 1928-10-10, 392A).	U 10081a	Grave PG 755	Copper vessel	Height: 5.9 Dia: 9.4	1(?)	c

COMMENTARY

According to Nissen, Königsfriedhofes p. 97: "stammte PG. 755 aus der Zeit des RT. 1054 [the tomb which yielded the inscription naming Mes-KALAM-du, the king] oder kurz danach." For a description of the extremely rich tomb goods of PG. 755, see Woolley, UE 2 (text) pp. 155–60.

Scholars have debated whether or not this Mes-KALAM-du is the same figure as the Mes-KALAM-du who appears as king of Ur in the previously edited inscriptions. Woolley originally argued for the identity (in UE 2 [text] p. 340), but in an erratum deemed important enough to be included in a separate insert at this point in the book he wrote: "Mes-kalam-dug the king is not the same person as the Mes-kalam-dug buried in Grave PG. 755." Further, the identity of the two figures was rejected by Nagel, Orientalia NS 28 (1959) p. 150 n. 34. On the other hand, the identity was supported by Pallis, Chronology p. 204, Hallo, Royal Titles pp. 13–14 and 31, and Sollberger, Iraq 22 (1960) p. 80.

Boese, ZA 68 (1978) p. 24, suggested that this Mes-KALAM-du was probably the oldest son of Mes-Ane-pada, who apparently died prematurely; Keith (in Woolley UE 2 [text] pp. 402–3) notes that the skeletal remains indicated a young man less than 30 years old. Whether he was unceremoniously deposed by his royal mother as Boese suggests is possible, but hardly certain.

BIBLIOGRAPHY

1934 Woolley, UE 2 (text) p. 316 (transliteration)
1960 Sollberger, Iraq 22 p. 71 nos. 6–10 (exs. 1–4, study)
1971 Sollberger and Kupper, IRSA IB2a (exs. 1–4, conflated translation)
1978 Boese, ZA 68 p. 16 fig. 2 (exs. 1–3, 5, copy)
1982 Steible, ASBW 2 pp. 271–72 Meskalamdu 1 (exs. 1–4, edition)
1986 Cooper, SARI 1 pp. 97–98 Ur 3 (exs. 1–4, translation)

TEXT

1) mes-KALAM-du_{10}	1) Mes-KALAM-du

Mes-kiag̃-nun

E1.13.8

1

A bowl fragment found in excavations at Ur bears a dedicatory inscription of a wife of a king of Ur; his name is plausibly to be restored Mes-kiag̃-nun.

COMMENTARY

The calcite bowl fragment measures 11.7×11.2 cm; the inscription case that is preserved measures 4.8 cm wide and 9.3 cm high. It was found in the Royal Cemetery area "loose in the upper soil" (Woolley, UE 2 p. 572); "above the level of the graves" (Woolley, UE 4 p. 222 n. 1 [wrong reference]), "in the rubbish above the Royal Cemetery" (Woolley, UE 4 p. 40). It was given the excavation number U 11675, the registration number 1929-10-17, 61 and the museum number BM 122255. The inscription was collated.

I have followed Sollberger's copy in the reading of line 1′ although I was unable to ascertain any trace of the ág̃ sign when I collated the inscription.

The name occurs in the writing mes-ki-ág̃-nun-na in the Tummal Chronicle, Mes-kiág-Nanna in the SKL. We have normalized it following the Ur inscription.

In line 3′ the element gan is likely an old allograph for géme "young women, servant." Cf. Selz, Untersuchungen, p. 142 n. 582:

> Dagegen vermute bereits A. Deimel, Or 34/35, 122, eine Entsprechung von ḪÉ und gemé. In ZA 61 (1971) erwog J. Bauer eine Deutung als, "Dienerin, Zuständige" und wies in AoN 9 darauf hin, dass das Element HÉ-/GAN- nur in weiblichen PN und GN vorkomme. — Andernots zu diskutierende Belege erweisen Namen als alte Schreibung des Wortes gemé "Magd"; vgl.a. W.G. Lambert apud P. Mander, PAS S. 59.

In the same line ŠE.NUN.ŠÈ.BU is to be read sàman = Akkadian *šumannu*(*m*); the vocable is attested both as a common noun meaning "lead-rope" as well as a deity (for the deity, see Selz, Untersuchungen p. 274 and Krebernik ZA 76 [1986] p. 202). The extra -NU at the end of the PN is difficult to account for. Bauer (AoN 38 [1987] p. 12) indicates that taking -nu as gan-DN-ak (genitive) is problematic. Krebernik (ZA 76 [1986] p. 202) indicates that a writing NU.NUN for NUN is commonly found in the tablets from Abū Ṣalābīḫ. The expected genitive ending in -na is found in the PN Ur-Samana (Owen, MVN 3 no. 361) written ur-[d]saman$_4$(ŠAGAN)-na in rev. 2 of the text and ur-ŠE.ŠÈ.NUN.BU in the seal impression.

BIBLIOGRAPHY

1934 Wooley, UE 2 p. 321 n. 10 (study)
1956 Woolley, UE 4 p. 40 (study)
1965 Sollberger, UET 8 no. 2 (copy, study)
1967 Pettinato, Orientalia NS 36 pp. 450–51 (study)
1968 Biggs, JNES 27 p. 145 (study)
1968 Lambert, RA 62 p. 171 no. 2 (study)
1971 Sollberger and Kupper, IRSA IC6a (translation)
1970–71 Bauer, WO 6 p. 150 (study)
1982 Steible, ASBW 2 pp. 277–78 Meskiʾagnun 1 (edition)
1986 Cooper, SARI 1 p. 100 Ur 7 (translation)
1991 Braun-Holzinger, Weihgaben p. 140 G 153 (edition, study)

TEXT

Lacuna
1′) [mes-ki-á]g̃-nun
2′) LUGAL URI_5.KI
3′) gan-$saman_x$(ŠE.NUN.ŠÈ.BU.NU)
4′) DAM-*śù*
5′) A MU.RU

Lacuna
1′–2′) [for the life of Mes-kia]g̃-nun, king of Ur,

3′–5′) Gan-samana, his wife, dedicated (this bowl).

Elili

E1.13.9

1

According to the SKL Mes-kiağ-nun was succeeded by King Elili, to whom a reign of 25 years is ascribed. An inscription found on two clay cones deals with a certain Elili's construction of Enki's Abzu almost certainly in Eridu. Scholars have universally equated this king of Ur with the Elulu of the king list.

CATALOGUE

Ex.	Museum number	Registration number	Dimensions (cm)	Lines preserved	cpn
1	BM 121343	1931-2-13, 1	Cone length: 6.2 Cone dia: 3.3 Case width: 3.9	1–7	c
2	Private collection in Göttingen	—	Length: 10.7 Dia.: 3.6	1–6	n

COMMENTARY

The precise provenance of neither cone is known; presumably they both came from Eridu. Ex. 1 was presented by S. Smith.

BIBLIOGRAPHY

1932 Smith, JRAS pp. 306–8 (ex. 1, copy, edition, study)
1971 Sollberger and Kupper, IRSA IB7a (translation)
1973–74 Schramm, WO 7 pp. 16–17 (ex. 2, copy, edition, study)
1982 Steible, ASBW 2 p. 278 Elili 1 (exs. 1–2, edition)
1986 Cooper, SARI 1 p. 101 Ur 8 (exs. 1–2, translation)

TEXT

1) ^{d}en-ki
2) lugal-
3) eridu.KI-ra
4) é-li(over)-li
5) lugal-uri$_5$.KI-ma-ke$_4$
6) abzu-ni
7) mu-na-dù

1–3) For the god Enki, king of Eridu,

4–7) Elili, king of Ur, built his (Enki's) Abzu (temple).

Balulu

E1.13.9

1

According to the Sumerian King List, Elulu was succeeded by King Balulu, to whom a reign of 36 years is ascribed. As yet no inscriptions of this ruler are known.

Uruk

E1.14

(a) Location

Ancient Uruk is identified with the modern mound named Warkāʾ (NLat 31° 19′ and ELong 45° 40′).

(b) Excavation History

The city was scientifically excavated by teams of archaeologists from the Deutsche Orient-Gesellschaft, Berlin, 1912–13 and 1925–1939, and the Deutsches Archäologische Institut, Berlin and the Deutsche Orient-Gesellschaft, Berlin from 1954.

While the ED period levels of this E-anna temple at Uruk are now completely covered by the massive rebuilding of the ziqqurrat undertaken by Ur-Nammu of the Ur III dynasty, traces of ED architecture employing plano-convex bricks were found in probe trenches dug by H. Lenzen into the core of the ziqqurrat (see Lenzen, Entwicklung pl. 12, where the ED period levels under the Ur-Nammu structure are shaded in blue). Further, various scholars have recently indicated that the so-called Stampflehmgebäude marks the site of an ED period palace; see U. Finkbeiner in U. Finkbeiner and W. Röllig (eds.), Ǧamdat Nasr: Period or Regional style pp. 44, 49; R. Eichmann, Uruk: Die Stratigraphie, Ausgrabungen in Uruk-Warka, Endberichte 3 pp. 60–62; J. Postgate, Early Mesopotamia: Society and Economy at the Dawn of History p. 140; and R. Boehmer, Bagh. Mitt. 22 (1991) pp. 165–74.

(c) Writing of the City Name

The city name Uruk is written with the Sumerian logogram unug; the sign originally depicted a temple tower, in this case apparently the temple tower of the goddess Inanna in the E-anna precinct.

Three hymns glorifying Uruk and its deities are found in the ED period collection of zà-mí hymns edited by R. Biggs.

The first zà-mí hymn (lines 15–17) praises the goddess Nin-unug "Lady of Uruk" in her cult centre of Unug (Uruk). The hymn relates that Unug was the "twin" (maš) of Kulab.

The second zà-mì hymn glorifies Kulab and its tutelary goddess Inanna. Kulab is well attested as being a city quarter or suburb of Uruk. In ED times a northern Kulab (see Steinkeller, Vicino Oriente 6 [1986] p. 4) and later a district of Babylon (see A. George, Babylonian Topographical Texts pp. 322–23) also bore this name. In addition, a city called Kulab appears in NA and NB documents; see Edzard, RLA 6 p. 305 § 2 and Beaulieu, NABU 1993 no. 22. This late Kulab may have lain at modern Ḫalāwi, a small site about 10 km SE of Uruk.

A third zà-mì hymn (lines 41–43) praises the sky god An.

(d) Paucity of Sources for an ED History of Uruk

Despite the fact that Uruk was undoubtedly one of the major political powers in the land of Sumer during much of the ED period, relatively few inscriptions belonging to its rulers are known. Most of these come from

Nippur; very few come from Uruk itself. This may be due to the fact that the temple precinct in Uruk was apparently levelled by Sargon of Akkad when he attacked the city; what he did not destroy may have been removed by the Ur III kings when they rebuilt the E-anna precinct.

No royal inscriptions are known for the twelve kings of the Uruk I dynasty of the SKL. However, epic texts dealing with Enmerkar, Lugal-banda, and Gilgameš, likely composed in Ur III times and known to us from OB tablet copies, are extant. Furthermore, Gilgameš and his son Ur-lugal are mentioned in the Tummal Chronicle. The latter also likely appears in the literary composition entitled "The Death of Gilgameš"; see Veldhuis, JCS 31 (2001) p. 139 in this connection.

Uruk Dynasty I was apparently followed by four kings (here 13–16) for whom we have inscriptions but no mention in the SKL.

Inscriptions of only one king of the Uruk II dynasty (En-šakuš-Ana) are known .

The names of kings for whom we have royal inscriptions are displayed in bold font in the chart below.

ED Kings of Uruk

King number	King	No. of years of reign in SKL	Transcription in Greek sources	RIM number
Uruk I				
1	Mes-kiag-gašer	324	—	E1.14.1
2	En-mer-kar	420	Ευηχορος	E1.14.2
3	Lugal-banda	1,200	—	E1.14.3
4	Dumu-zi	100	Δαωνος	E1.14.4
5	Gilgameš	126	Γιλγαμος	E1.14.5
6	Ur-Nungala	30	—	E1.14.6
7	Utul-kalama	15	—	E1.14.7
8	Labaḫ	9	—	E1.14.8
9	En-nun-dara-ana	8	—	E1.14.9
10	Mes-ḫé	36	—	E1.14.10
11	Melam-ana	6	—	E1.14.11
12	Lugal-kitun	36	—	E1.14.12
Other kings post Uruk I				
13	**Lugal-SILA-si**	—	—	E1.14.13
14	**Lugal-kiĝine-dudu**	—	—	E1.14.14
15	**Lugal-KISAL-si**	—	—	E1.14.15
16	**Ur-zage**	—	—	E1.14.16
Uruk II				
17	**En-šakuš-Ana**	60	—	E1.14.17
18	Lugal-ure	120	—	E1.14.18
19	Ar-gandea	7	—	E1.14.19
Uruk III				
20	**Lugal-zage-si**	25	—	E1.14.20
Other				
21	**Lugal-[SILA]**	—	—	E1.14.21

Lugal-SILA-si

E1.14.13

1

A plano-convex lapis lazuli foundation tablet, which on the basis of its registration number can be determined to have come from Uruk, bears an inscription of a ruler named Lugal-SILA-si. His epithet "king of Kiš" (lugal KIŠ.KI) is apparently an honourific title, since the tablet's provenance and content suggest that Lugal-SILA-si was a king of Uruk. He may be connected to the Lugal-SILA who appears as "ruler" (énsi) of Uruk in an inscription on a clay vessel from G̃irsu (see E1.9.10.2). The chronological relationship of Lugal-SILA-si to Lugal-kig̃ine-dudu and Lugal-KISAL-si is unclear.

COMMENTARY

The tablet, which measures 5.5×3.1 cm, bears the museum number BM 910130 (formerly BM 12155), registration number 92–12–13, 9 and, as noted is, from Uruk. The inscription was collated.

The reading of line 3 is uncertain. Wilcke, RLA 5 p. 75 § 2.1 took NIN.dINANNA to be a mistake for nin-an-na "Himmelsherrin." In this he generally followed Cooper, JNES 33 (1974) p. 415 note to IA4a, who translates "mistress of Eanna(?)." On the other hand, Sollberger and Kupper, IRSA IA4a, n. 1 understood it to be "reine des déesses." Alternatively, the elements dINANNA could conceivably be read an-mùš. Mùs, in turn, corresponds to Akkadian *zīmu*(*m*) "lustre, glow." If so, a translation of nin an-mùš as "lady of bright heaven" would be conceivable in view of the goddess's identification with the planet Venus. Certainly Akkadian *zīmu*(*m*) is linked with other heavenly lights, namely Šamaš and Ningal (see CAD z p. 120).

In line 4 the reading of the element SILA is uncertain. Steible (ASBW 2 p. 219) points out that Nissen's comment that the sign is actually kur is mistaken; however collation by Walker reveals it is a clear TAR/SILA. But which of the two possible readings for this sign is correct is not entirely clear. For various compounds with SILA, see the comments of Selz, Untersuchungen p. 26 n. 73.

In line 6 the first sign is clearly to be read bàd; the sign is so small that it was not possible to see the expected bad sign within it.

BIBLIOGRAPHY

1898 King, CT 3 pl. 1 (BM) 12155 (copy)
1907 Thureau-Dangin, SAK pp. 160–61 VIII. Patesis und Könige von Kiš. 3. Lugal-TAR-si (edition)
1971 Sollberger and Kupper, IRSA pp. 40–41 IA4a (translation)
1974 Cooper, JNES 33 p. 415 (edition)
1982 Steible, ASBW 2 pp. 218–20 Lugal-TAR-si (edition)
1986 Cooper, SARI 1 pp. 21–22 Ki 8 (translation)

TEXT

1) an lugal-kur-kur-ra
2) dinanna
3) NIN dINANNA-ra

1) For the god An, king of all lands,
2-3) and Inanna, lady of ...,

4) lugal-SILA-si 5) lugal kiš	4–5) Lugal-SILA-si, king of Kiš,
6) bàd-kisal 7) mu-na-dù	6–7) built the courtyard wall.

Lugal-kiĝine-dudu

E1.14.14

The king's name apparently appears in two different spellings: (a) lugal-ki-DU-ni-du$_7$-du$_7$ (in [northern] inscriptions from Nippur), and (b) lugal-ki-ni-ŠÈ-du$_7$-du$_7$-(d) (in [southern] inscriptions from Ĝirsu); see Edzard, RLA 7 1/2 (1989) p. 146; Bauer, AoN 21 (1985) pp. 12–13; and Cooper, Iraq 46 (1984) p. 92.

1

A seventeen-line dedicatory inscription of Lugal-kiĝine-dudu is found on numerous stone vessel fragments from Nippur.

CATALOGUE

Ex.	Museum number	Excavation number	Object	Dimensions (cm)	BE 1/2 number	Lines preserved	cpn
1	CBS 9464	—	White limestone	Height: 12 Width: 11 Thickness: 0.5–2.6	—	1–3	c
2	CBS 9465	—	—	—	—	15–17	c
3	CBS 9466	—	—	—	—	16	c
4	CBS 9581+9463	—	White calcite	Height: 9 Width: 13	—	1–11	c
5	CBS 9591+9608+9679+9990	—	Grey-white limestone	Height: 7.4 Original rim dia.: c. 15	pl. XVIIII no. 47	4–16	c
6	CBS 9593	—	—	5.5×3	—	10–15	c
7	CBS 9599	—	—	—	—	—	n
8	CBS 9605	—	—	Width: 7 Rim dia.: 4	pl. XVIIII no. 44	6–14	c
9	CBS 9607 +9609 +9657	—	Calcite	Height: 4.5 Original rim dia.: c. 18	pl. XVIII no. 41 pl. XVIII no. 43 pl. XVIII no. 42	1–10, 19	c
10	CBS 9632	—	—	Height: 5.5 Width: 4 Thickness: 0.7	—	3–5	c
11	CBS 9633	—	White calcite	7.5×2	—	9–15	c
12	CBS 9634	—	—	5×4	—	18–19	c
13	CBS 9680	—	—	—	—	7–12	c
14	CBS 9703	—	—	—	—	—	n
15	CBS 9825	—	Dark grey stone	Height: 9.5 Width: 17 Thickness: 2.4	—	1–15	c
16	CBS 9901	—	Cylindrical vessel	—	—	1–4	n
17	CBS 9902	—	Cylindrical vessel	7×4	—	2–5	c
18	CBS 9904	—	Cylindrical vessel	3×4	—	15–16	c
19	CBS 9917	—	Red-brown veined stone	Height: 6.3 Width: 9.4 Tm dia.: 3.2	—	16–18	c
20	CBS 9988	—	Rim fragment of bowl	Height: 8.5 Width: 4.5	—	2–4	c
21	CBS 9989	—	—	—	—	—	n

Ex.	Museum number	Excavation number	Object	Dimensions (cm)	BE 1/2 number	Lines preserved	cpn
22	CBS 9991	—	—	—	—	—	n
23	CBS 10001	—	Conical vessel	—	pl. XVIII no. 48	13–17	c
24	CBS 10124	—	—	—	—	7–8	c
25	HS 1959	—	—	—	—	12–19	c
26	—	4N–T73	—	—	—	—	n
27	IM 70315	9N–48	—	—	—	—	n

COMMENTARY

The fragments excavated by Hilprecht came from the area southeast of the Ekur ziqqurrat.

BIBLIOGRAPHY

1896 Hilprecht, BE 1/2 no. 86 (exs. 4–5, 7–11, 14, 16–18, 23, composite copy); pl. XVIII nos. 40–48 (exs. 5, 8, 9, 23, photo); pp. 57–58 (translation)
1906 Thureau-Dangin, SAK pp. 156–57 3. Lugal-ki-gub-ni-du-du b (edition)
1929 Barton, RISA pp. 94–95 1. Lugalkigubnidudu 1.1 (edition)
1963 Kramer, Sumerians p. 308 § C 2 (translation)
1969 Buccellati and Biggs, AS 17, no. 36 (exemplar 27, copy)
1969 Oelsner, WZJ 18 p. 51 no. 1 (ex. 25, study)
1971 Sollberger and Kuper, IRSA IE1c (translation)
1978 McCown, Haynes, and Biggs, Nippur II p. 91, no. 46 (exemplar 26, copy)
1980 Cooper, JCS 32 pp. 116–17 (exs. 1–11, 12–18, 20–27, (translation)
1982 Steible, ASBW 2 pp. 299–301 Lugalkiginnedudu 2 (exs. 1–8, 20–27, edition)
1986 Cooper, SARI 1 p. 101 Uk 1.1 (exs. 1–18, 20–27, translation)
1988 Römer, in Delsman et al., TUAT 2 pp. 461–62 (translation)
1991 Braun-Holzinger, Weihgaben p. 146 G 174–75 (exs. 1–2, edition, study)

TEXT

1) ^{d}en-líl
2) lugal-kur-kur-ra-ke$_4$
3) lugal-ki-ĝin-né-du$_7$-du$_7$-ra
4) u$_4$ ^{d}en-líl
5) gù-zi e-na-dé-a
6) nam-en
7) nam-lugal-da
8) e-na-da-tab-ba-a
9) unu.KI-ga
10) nam-en
11) mu-ak-ke$_4$
12) uri$_5$.KI-m[a]
13) nam-lugal
14) mu-ak-ke$_4$
15) lugal-ki-ĝin-né-du$_7$-du$_7$-dè
16) nam-gal-ḫúl-la-da
17) ^{d}en-líl lugal-ki-ág-ni
18) nam-ti-la-ni-šè
19) a mu-na-ru

1–2) Enlil, king of all lands,

3) for Lugal-kiĝine-dudu —
4–5) when the god Enlil truly summoned him,

6–8) and (Enlil) combined (both) lordship and kingship for him,

9–11) he (Lugal-kiĝine-dudu) exercised lordship in Uruk

12–14) and exercised kingship in Ur.

15–16) Lugal-kiĝine-dudu, in his great joy,

17–19) dedicated (this vessel) for his life to the god Enlil, his beloved lord.

2

A dedicatory inscription of Lugal-kiĝine-dudu to the goddess Inanna is found on two stone vessels from Nippur.

CATALOGUE

Ex.	Museum number	Excavation number	Nippur provenance	Object	Dimensions (cm)	Lines preserved	cpn
1	IM —	5-N 274	Inanna Temple IV (Ur III) locus 4 floor 2	Cylindrical vessel	Height: 13	1–16, 19–22	n
2	IM 70315	9N -48	Area III, dump	White stone bowl	3.7×3	8–10	n

BIBLIOGRAPHY

1956 Haines, ILN p. 268 fig. 8 (ex. 1, photo)
1961 Goetze, JCS 15 pp. 105–107 (ex. 1, edition, copy, study)
1969 Buccellati and Biggs, AS 17 no. 36 (ex. 2, copy, study)
1971 Sollberger and Kupper, IRSA IE1d (ex. 1, translation)
1982 Steible, ASBW pp. 302–303 Lugalkiginnedudu 4 (exs. 1–2, edition)
1986 Cooper, SARI 1 p. 102 Uk 1.2 (exs. 1–2, translation)
1991 Braun-Holzinger, Weihgaben p. 145 G 172 (ex. 1, edition, study); p. 146 G 175 (ex. 2, transliteration, study)

TEXT

1) an lugal-kur-kur-ra	1) For the god An, king of all lands,
2) ^{d}inanna nin-é-an-na-ra	2) and Inanna, queen of E-anna,
3) lugal-ki-ĝin-né-du$_7$-du$_7$	3–4) Lugal-kiĝine-dudu, king of Kiš —
4) lugal-kiš.KI	
5) u$_4$ ^{d}inanna-ke$_4$	5–9) when the goddess Inanna combined lordship with kingship for Lugal-kiĝine-dudu,
6) lugal-ki-ĝin-né-du$_7$-du$_7$-šè	
7) nam-en	
8) nam-lugal-da	
9) e-na-da-tab-ba-a	
10) unu.KI-ga	10–14) he exercised lordship in Uruk and kingship in Ur.
11) nam-en mu-ak-k[e$_4$]	
12) uri$_5$.K[I]-ma	
13) nam-lugal	
14) mu-ak-[ke$_4$]	
15) u$_4$ ^{d}inann[a-ke$_4$]	15–17) When Inan[na truly summoned] Lugal-k[iĝi]ne-du[du],
16) lugal-k[i-ĝin]-né-du$_7$-[du$_7$-ra]	
17) [gù-zi e-na-dé-a]	
18) [u$_4$-ba]	18–21) [then(?) Lugal-kiĝine-dud]u dedicated (this vase) for his l[i]fe to Inanna, his mistress.
19) [lugal-ki-gi]n-[né-du$_7$-d]u$_7$-dè	
20) ^{d}inanna nin-né	
21) a mu-na-ru	

3a

A dedicatory inscription of Lugal-kiĝine-dudu for the god Enlil is found on three large unhewn stone blocks and a door socket from Nippur.

CATALOGUE

Ex.	Museum number	Object	Dimensions (cm)	Hilprecht, BE 1 no.	Lines preserved	cpn
1	CBS 10050	Stone block	29×21×19.5 Inscription: 6×5.3	23	1–3	p
2	—	Stone block	Inscription: 7×6.2	24	1–3	n
3	—	Stone block	Inscription: 6.5×7.7	25	1–3	n
4	CBS 8751	Diorite door socket	33×28×5.35	21	—	n

COMMENTARY

The blocks were found southeast of the E-kur ziqqurrat. Ex. 4 was re-cut to add an inscription of the Ur III king Amar-Suena; for the Amar-Suena inscription, see Hilprecht, BE 1/1 no. 21.

BIBLIOGRAPHY

1893 Hilprecht, BE 1/1 nos. 23–25 (exs. 1–3, copy); pp. 28–30, 46 and n. 3 (exs. 1–3, study)
1896 Hilprecht, BE 1/2 p. 46 (ex. 4, study)
1906 Thureau-Dangin, SAK pp. 156–57 Lugal-ki-gub-ni-du-du a (exs. 1–3, edition)
1963 Kramer, Sumerians p. 308 § C 3 (exs. 1–3, translation)
1971 Sollberger and Kupper, IRSA IE1a (exs. 1–3, translation)
1982 Steible, ASBW 2 pp. 298–99 Lugalkiginnedudu 1 (exs. 1–4, edition)
1986 Cooper, SARI 1 pp. 102 Uk 1.3 (exs. 1–3, translation)

TEXT

1) ^{d}en-líl-la
2) lugal-ki-ĝin-né-du$_7$-du$_7$-dè
3) a mu-na-ru

1–3) For Enlil, Lugal-kiĝine-dudu dedicated (this block).

3b

A dedicatory inscription of Lugal-kiĝine-dudu for the god Enlil is found on a limestone disk from Nippur.

COMMENTARY

The limestone disk, CBS 263, measures 25.5 cm in diameter with a thickness of 6.5 cm.

BIBLIOGRAPHY

1991 Braun-Holzinger, Weihgaben p. 375 Varia 4 (transliteration, study)

1.2, 3 Omit -la.
2 2,3 Omit -dè.

TEXT

1) ^{d}en-líl-la
2) lugal-ki-ĝin-né-du$_7$-du$_7$-dè
3) a mu-na-ru

1–3) For Enlil, Lugal-kiĝine-dudu dedicated (this block).

4

A fragment of a vessel from Nippur bears an inscription of Lugal-kiĝine-dudu.

COMMENTARY

The white calcite vessel, which measures 10.2 cm in height, 4 cm in width, and 2 cm in thickness, was found in the area southeast of the ziqqurrat. It was given the museum number CBS 9900.

BIBLIOGRAPHY

1896 Hilprecht, BE 1/2 no. 88 (copy)
1929 Barton, RISA pp. 96–97 Lugalkigubnidudu 6 (edition)
1982 Steible, ASBW 2 p. 305 Lugalkiginnedudu 7 (edition)
1986 Cooper, SARI 1 p. 102 Uk 1.4 (translation)
1991 Braun-Holzinger, Weihgaben p. 147 G 179 (study)

TEXT

Col. i
1) ⸢d⸣en-líl
Lacuna
Col. ii
Lacuna
1′) ⸢d⸣[en-líl(?)]
2′) nun-⸢an-ki⸣-ra
3′) ⸢lugal⸣-ki-[gi]n-[né-du$_7$-du$_7$]
Lacuna
Col. iii
Lacuna
1′) ŠÈ ⸢x x⸣ [...]
2′) gù-zi e-na-dé-⸢a⸣(?)
Lacuna

i 1) For Enlil,
Lacuna

Lacuna
ii 1′–3′) For [Enlil(?)], sovereign of heaven and earth, Lugal-ki[ĝi]n[e-dudu]

Lacuna

Lacuna
iii 1′–2′) ... truly summoned him

Lacuna

5

A small fragment of a stone object from Nippur names Lugal-kiĝine-dudu.

COMMENTARY

The inscription is found on HS 1961, a fragment of a stone object.

BIBLIOGRAPHY

1969 Oelsner, WZJ 18 p. 51 no. 2 (transliteration, study)
1982 Steible, ASBW 2 p. 304 Lugalkiĝinnedudu 6 (edition)
1986 Cooper, SARI 1 p. 102 Uk 1.5 (translation)

TEXT

Lacuna	Lacuna
1′) x x	1′–4′) ... scribe, Lugal-kiĝine-dudu, the deity N[in ...]
2′) dub-sar	
3′) lugal-ki-ĝin-né-du$_7$-du$_7$-dè	
4′) ^{d}n[in(?) ...]	
Lacuna	Lacuna

6

A dedicatory inscription found in excavations at Ur names Lugal-kiĝine-dudu, his apparent son Lugal-KISAL-si, and apparent wife Nin-banda.

COMMENTARY

The inscription is incised on two fragments of a white calcite vessel which were found in the Enunmaḫ under the Kurigalzu level and given the excavation numbers U 258 A and B. The joined pieces measure 13 cm in height and 5.5 cm in width, with a reconstructed upper diameter of 9 cm. The vessel was given the museum number BM 116439. The inscription was not collated.

Line 3 is important for the reading dam-gàr-ra which suggests a reading dam-gàra for the conventionally read dam-gàr.

The correct reading of line 6 as lugal-⸢kiš⸣.KI-a "king of Kiš" was pointed out by Cooper in Iraq 46 (1984) p. 92. Previously it had been read lugal-ŠÁR×DIŠ.KI-a "king of Umma."

For the reading of the PN in line 10, see the intoductory comments to E1.14.15. It may refer to the prince.

BIBLIOGRAPHY

1928 Gadd, UET 1 no. 3 (copy, study)
1956 Woolley, UE 4 p. (study)
1960 Sollberger, Iraq 22 pp. 75–76 and pp. 84–85 no. 76 (transliteration, study)
1964 Nagel, in Festschrift Moortgat p. 202 § d) (study)
1971 Sollberger and Kupper, IRSA IE1b (translation)
1974 Woolley, UE 6 p. 168 (study)
1982 Steible, ASBW 2 pp. 301–302 Lugalkiginnedudu 3 (edition)
1984 Cooper, Iraq 46 p. 92 and pl. V b (photo, study)
1986 Cooper, SARI 1 p. 103 Uk 1.6 (translation)
1991 Braun-Holzinger, Weihgaben p. 146 and pl. 9 G 173 (edition, study)

TEXT

1) ^{d}nanna	1) For the god Nanna,
2) a-nu-zu	2–3) Anuzu, the commercial agent,
3) ⸢dam⸣-gàr-ra	

4) [nam-ti]
5) [lugal]-⸢ki⸣-[ĝin-né]-éš-du$_7$-du$_7$
6) lugal-⸢kiš⸣.KI-a
7) nam-ti-
8) nin-bànda-šè
9) nam-ti-
10) lugal-KISAL-[si-šè]
11) a m[u-na-ru]

4–6) [for the life] of [Lugal]-ki-[ĝin]eš-dudu, king of Kiš,

7–8) for the life of Nin-banda,

9–10) for the life of Lugal-KISAL-[si],

11) he de[dicated (this vessel)].

Lugal-KISAL-si

E1.14.15

Lugal-kiĝine-dudu was likely succeeded by his son Lugal-KISAL-si.

For the reading of the royal name as lugal-KISAL-si as lugal-ĝipar$_x$-si, see the comments of Steinkeller, ZA 75 (1985) p. 46; Krebernik, ZA 76 (1986) pp. 194 and 204; Bauer, JAOS 107 (1987) p. 327 note to p. 27b. 34–36; idem, AfO 36–37 (1989–90) p. 80 note to 1 I 15; and Steinkeller, in Watanabe (ed.), Priests and Officials in the Ancient Near East p. 109 and nn. 18 and 23. However, Selz, in his Amerikanischen Sammlungen 1 p. 174 note to 2:4, has given writings which suggest that we should not categorically rule out the traditional reading of kisal. In view of these differences of scholarly opinion, we have (conservatively) transcribed the sign in question as KISAL in this volume.

1

Various vessel fragments found at Nippur bear an inscription indicating they were dedicated by Lugal-KISAL-si to the god Enlil.

CATALOGUE

Ex.	Museum number	Object	Dimensions (cm)	Lines preserved	cpn
1	CBS 9604	High cylindrical vessel fragment	Rim width: 5.5 Inner dia.: c. 8.5	8–14	c
2	CBS 9606	Light coloured limestone	Dia. width: 3.5 Fragment width: 6	7–10	c
3	CBS 9620	Rim fragment of a bowl	6×4	5–6	c
4	CBS 9627	Rim fragment of a bowl	6×4	7–9	c
5	CBS 9630	Rim fragment of a bowl	7×3.5	9–10	c
6	CBS 9631	Rim fragment of a bowl	7×4	10–11	c
7	CBS 9635	Fragment of a wide straight vessel rim	6×3.5	4–7	c
8	CBS 9639	Rim fragment of a bowl	Height: 2 Width: 6	10–12	c
9	CBS 9644	Fragment of a limestone vessel	9.5×5 Thickness: 0.9–1.5	11–14	c
10	CBS 9322	Vessel fragment of a dark stone	5×7	10–13	c
11	CBS 9648a+b	Two joined vessel fragments of white calcite	4.85×4.9×2	1–4	c
12	CBS 9632	Vessel fragment	5.2×3.7	7–8	c
13	CBS 9917	Vessel fragment	9.24×6.67	10–13	c

COMMENTARY

Ex. 11 was treated as a separate inscription by Steible (ASBW 2 p. 309 Lugalkisalsi 4; cf. Bauer BiOr 46 [1989] p. 638). A photo of ex. 1 is found in Hilprecht, BE 1/2 pl. XVIII no. 45.

BIBLIOGRAPHY

1896 Hilprecht, BE 1/2 pl. 37 no. 86 (b) (exs. 1–10, conflated copy); no. 89 (ex. 11, copy); p. 58 (study)
1906 Thureau-Dangin, SAK pp. 156–57 3. Lugal-ki-gub-ni-du-du c) (exs. 1–10, edition); d) (ex. 11, edition)
1957 Jacobsen, ZA 52 p. 128 n. 82 (study)
1964 Nagel, in Moortgat Festschrift p. 202 Lugalkisalesi a) 1. (study)
1971 Sollberger and Kupper, IRSA IE2a (ex. 1–11, translation)
1980 Cooper, JCS 32 p. 117 (exs. 1–11, transliteration, study)
1982 Steible, ASBW 2 pp. 305–307 Lugalkisalsi 1 (exs. 1–10, edition); p. 309 Lugal-kisal-si 4 (ex. 11, edition)
1986 Cooper, SARI 1 p. 103 Uk 2.1 (exs. 1–11, translation)
1991 Braun-Holzinger, Weihgaben p. 147 G 180 (ex. 1–13, edition, study)

TEXT

1) ^{d}en-⸢líl⸣
2) lugal-kur-kur-r[a]
3) [l]ugal-KISAL-s[i]
4) d[umu-sa]g
5) lugal-ki-g̃in-né-du$_7$-du$_7$
6) lugal-unu.KI-ga-ke$_4$
7) lugal-uri$_5$.KI-ma-ka-ke$_4$
8) lugal-KISAL-si
9) lugal-unu.KI-ga-ke$_4$
10) lugal-uri$_5$.KI-ma-ke$_4$
11) nam-ti-la-šè
12) ^{d}en-líl
13) lugal-ni
14) a mu-na-ru

1–2) For Enlil, king of all lands,

3–7) [L]ugal-KISAL-s[i], el[dest](?) so[n] of Lugal-kig̃ine-dudu, king of Uruk and king of Ur —

8–14) Lugal-KISAL-si, king of Uruk and king of Ur, dedicated (this vessel) for his life to the god Enlil, his lord.

2

A stone foundation peg acquired through purchase by the Vorderasiastische Museum Berlin is incised with an inscription of King Lugal-KISAL-si of Uruk. Two figurines, ex. 2 from Uruk, and ex. 3 of unknown provenance, are virtually identical in their modelling. Unfortunately, the parts of figurines 2 and 3 that were once inscribed are now broken away. In all likelihood all three figurines came from Uruk.

CATALOGUE

Ex.	Museum number	Excavation number	Provenance	Object	Dimensions (cm)	Lines preserved	cpn
1	VA 4855	—	Unknown; purchased piece	Limestone foundation peg	Length: 23.8	1–7	c
2	VA 10936	W 13923	Uruk, PaXVI2, between the ziqqurrat and the Ur-Nammu casement wall, 5 m from the edge of the baked brick pavement, 0.5 m below the Old Babylonian baked brick mantle of the ziqqurrat	Light-brown limestone foundation peg	Preserved length: 12.5	Inscription not preserved	c
3	AO 10921	—	Unknown, aquired through purchase	Limestone foundation peg	Length: 12.5 Width: 11.0	Inscription not preserved	p

COMMENTARY

For the reading of the DN of line 1 see most recently, E. Flückiger-Hawker, Urnamma of Ur in Sumerian Literary Tradition pp. 8–9. She writes:

... The reading of the second element LAGAB×HAL (ENGUR) is complex because attested spellings in both lexical texts and texts in non-standard orthography contradict each other. The conventional reading is nammu, but more recently M. Civil [Orientalia NS 54 (1985) p. 27 n. 1] has argued for a reading namma. ...

For LAGAB×ḪAL (ENGUR) the Old Babylonian lexical list Proto Ea 53 (= *MSL* 14 33) gives the readings na-am-ma (1×), na-ma (1×), and five manuscripts have -mu as final sign. The lexical list Ea 1 71 (= *MSL 14* 180) has na-am-ma (1×) and nam-mu (2×) (cf. also Aa 1/2 235, nam-mu). Thus, the lexical evidence makes it difficult to decide if nam-mu or nam-ma is the original reading. In view of the non-standard writing ur-^{d}na-na-ma-ke (for ur-^{d}namma-ke_4) in source B (= *TCL 15 38* = AO 6316) of Urnamma B 53; 56; 60; 64; 68 and the Akkadian *ur-na-am-ma* in the bilingual Ur C 1 = Šulgi 54 6 the reading /namma/ in the name UR.^{d}NAMMU is preferred here over /n ammu/.

Besides the non-standard writing of the name in source B of Umamma B ur-^{d}na-na-ma-ke, there is another non-standard writing in the bilingual Ur C I = Šulgi 54 4 ⸢*il*⸣-*na-am-na-am -mi*, the Sumerian version's equivalent of the Akkadian version's *ur-na-am-ma*, mentioned above. na-na-ma can be explained as < na(m)-nama and na-am-na-am-mi as <nam-nam(i). This looks like {namma+namma}, an original reduplicated lexeme */nammanamma/ which developed into > */namnamma/ and finally > /nanama/ according to the pattern /barbar/ > /babbar/. In the last stage, the m either assimilated to the following n or dropped out.

This shows that we may have to postulate for the sign LAGAB×ḪAL (ENGUR) both a single and a reduplicated lexeme. In summary, the reading of the name UR.^{d}NAMMU cannot be established with certainty, but the comments made above argue for / urnanama/ or /urnamma/ rather than /urnammu/ or /surnammu/. The reading /namma/ instead of /nanama/ is maintained in this study because it is a conventional reading.

BIBLIOGRAPHY

1915 Weber, Amtl. Ber. 36 pp. 73ff and figs. 28, 30, 31 (ex. 1, study)
1926 Unger, RLV IV p. 565 (ex. 1, study)
1926 Unger, SuAK p. 71 fig. 3 (ex. 1, photo)
1931 Contenau, Manuel 2 pp. 569–73 figs. 379–81 (exs. 1, 3, photo, study)
1930–31 Opitz, AfO 6 p. 21 n. 1 (ex. 1, study)
1931 Van Buren, Foundation Figurines pp. 9–10 and pl. V Fig. 9 (ex. 1, photo, study)
1935 Zervos, Encyclopédie p. 204 A (ex. 3, photo)
1935 Zervos, L'art pp. 86–88 (ex. 2, photo); p. 89 (ex. 1, photo)
1960 Lenzen, UVB 16 pp. 41–42 and pl. 20 a–c (ex. 2, photo, study)
1960 Strommenger, Bagh. Mitt. 1 p. 34 (exs. 1–3, study)
1962 Garbini, Stauaria pl. XXVIII (ex. 3, study)
1964 Nagel, in Festschrift Moortgat p. 202 Lugalkisalesi § a) 2 (study)
1966 Rost, Sumerische Kunst pl. 24 (ex. 1, photo)
1967 Moortgat, Kunst p. 45 (exs. 1–3, study); fig. 83 (ex. 1, photo); fig. 81 (ex. 3, photo); fig. 82 (ex. 2, photo)
1968 Ellis, Foundation Deposits pp. 49–50 (exs. 1–3, study)
1968 Spycket, Statues pp. 38–39 (edition, study)
1970 Meyer, Altorientalische Denkmäler fig. 34 (ex. 1, photo)
1975 Catalogue Göttingen Exhibition (p. 68 no. 110 and figs. p. 115, ex. 2)
1975 Orthmann (ed.), Der alte Orient p. 168 and fig. 33b (ex. 1, photo, study)
1977 Braun-Holzinger, Beterstatuetten pp. 54, 57, and pl. 31 c (ex. 1, study, photo); pl. 30 c (ex. 2, photo); pl. 30 d (ex. 3 photo)
1983 Rashid, Gründungsfiguren p. 10 nos. 70–72 (exs. 1–3, study); pl. 8 no. 70 (ex. 1, drawing)

TEXT

1) ⸢d⸣namma
2) dam-an-ra
3) lugal-KISAL-si
4) lugal-unu.KI-ga
5) lugal-uri_5.KI-ma
6) ⸢é⸣-^{d}namma
7) mu-dù(Text: NI)

1–2) For the ⸢goddess⸣ Namma, the wife of the god An,
3–5) Lugal-KISAL-si, king of Uruk and king of Ur,
6–7) built the temple of the goddess Namma.

3

An inscription on a stone bowl gives the name of Me-g̃irimta, daughter of Lugal-KISAL-si.

COMMENTARY

The bowl is composed of a translucent greenish variety of calcite or aragonite. It measures 10 cm in height with a diameter of 16.4 cm at the top, tapering to a base of 5.4 cm in diameter. The piece was purchased by Banks and is said to have come from Uruk. The bowl subsequently entered the Morgan Library Collection where it was given the museum number MLC 2630. The inscription was collated.

I could find no traces of the "obliterated" inscription (purportedly containing the signs lugal kiš) referred to by Banks in AJSL 21 pp. 62–63.

The reading of the DN in line 1 is uncertain. What was copied by Clay as a conceivable wedge (read $EŠ_4$ by Steible) is simply a damaged fleck in the stone (see Krebernik, BiOr 41 [1984] p. 646).

Since the PN Lugal-KISAL-si in this inscription appears without title, it is not entirely certain that he was the king of Uruk. However, Porada (bibliography item for 1976) notes:

> Lugal-kisal-si's daughter, whatever her father's position, must have been highly placed herself because the stone vessel which she dedicated belongs to a type of object valued and preserved over many centuries.

BIBLIOGRAPHY

1904–1905 Banks, AJSL 21 pp. 62–63 (copy, edition, study)
1923 Clay, BRM 4 no. 45 (copy, translation, study)
1929 Barton, RISA pp. 96–97 Lugalkigubnidudu and Lugalkisalsi 8 (edition)
1964 Nagel, in Festschrift Moortgat p. 202 § b) 3 (study)
1971 Sollberger and Kupper, IRSA IE2b (translation)
1976 Schlossman, Ancient Mesopotamian Art pp. 26–28 (photo, edition, study)
1982 Steible, ASBW 2 pp. 308–9 Lugalkisalsi 3 (edition)
1984 Krebernik, BiOr 41 p. 646 (study)
1986 Cooper, SARI 1 p. 104 Uk 2.3 (translation)
1991 Braun-Holzinger, Weihgaben p. 147 G 181 (edition, study)

TEXT

1) ᵈNE.DAG!	1) For the deity DN,
2) me-g̃ìrim-ta	2–4) Me-g̃irimta, offspring (daughter[?]) begotten by Lugal-KISAL-si,
3) dumu lugal-KISAL-si	
4) ⸢tu⸣-da	
5) dam-	5–6) spouse of Muni-ḫursag̃,
6) mu-ni-ḫur-sag̃	
7) a mu-ru	7) dedicated (this bowl).

4

An inscription incised on a stone statue fragment gives the name of Lugal-KISAL-si's grandson, Silim-Utu.

COMMENTARY

The stone statue, the upper portion of a male figure, was acquired through purchase; it is said to have come from Uruk. It measures 27 cm in height, 15 cm in width, and 8.7 cm in thickness. The piece bears the museum number AO 5681. The inscription was collated from the published photo.

For the reading of the PN of lines 1 and 7 see Steinkeller in Studies Hallo p. 239 note to no. 25.

BIBLIOGRAPHY

1923 Thureau-Dangin, RA 20 pp. 3–5 (copy, edition, study)
1931 Contenau, Manuel 2 pp. 556–57 and figs. 365–66 (photo, study)
1934 Contenau, Monuments pp. 6–7 and pl. II (photo, study)
1935 Zervos, L'art p. 90 (photo)
1940 Christian, Altertumskunde pl. 260 no. 1 (photo)
1962 Strommenger and Hirmer, Mesopotamien pl. 104 (photo)
1964 Nagel in Moortgat Festschrift p. 202 § c) 4 (study)
1968 Nagel and Strommenger, BJV 8 p. 150 (study)
1971 Sollberger and Kupper, IRSA IE3a (translation)
1977 Amiet, L'art pl. 3 (photo)
1977 Braun-Holzinger, Beterstatuetten p. 75 (transliteration, study); pl. 27c (photo)
1981 Spycket, Statuaire p. 86 and pl. 56 (photo, study)
1982 André-Leicknam, Naissance de l'écriture p. 82 no. 38 (photo)
1982 Steible, ASBW 2 pp. 307–8 Lugalkisalsi 2 (edition)
1984 Cooper, OrAnt 23 pp. 160–61 (translation, study)
1986 Cooper, SARI 1 p. 104 Uk 2.4 (translation)
1991 Braun-Holzinger, Weihgaben p. 253 St 74 (edition, study)

TEXT

1) DI-UD
2) dumu-
3) lú-bára-si
4) dumu-
5) lugal-KISAL-si
6) lugal-unu.KI
7) DI-UD
8) ir_{11}
9) gìrim(A.BU.ḪA.DU)-si
10) énsi:G̃AR(Text: PA.GAR.TE.SI)
11) unu.KI

1–3) Silim-Utu, son of Lu-bara-si,

4–6) son of Lugal-KISAL-si, king of Uruk —

7–11) Silim-Utu (is) servant of G̃irim-si, ensi-G̃AR of Uruk.

Ur-zage

E1.14.16

An inscription found on three vase fragments from Nippur names Ur-zage as "king of Kiš" (lugal kiš.KI). According to the evidence of a juridical document published by Lambert (RA 73 [1979] pp. 2–22 col. i lines 14–15) he was a king of Uruk.

1

As noted, three vase fragments from Nippur name Ur-zage as "king of Kiš" (lugal-kiš.KI).

CATALOGUE

Ex.	Museum number	Object	Dimensions (cm)	Lines preserved	(cpn)
1	CBS 9616+9931	Rim fragment of calcite vessel, perhaps a conical bowl	Height: 8.5 Width: 12.5	2–9	c
2	CBS 9622	—	—	4–6	c
3	CBS 9594	—	—	1–3	c

COMMENTARY

The reading of line 5 is difficult. Steinkeller, in RIM readers' notes, points out:

> The sequence of the signs is TÙR ŠE NI NA. The reading niga-na-ni proposed by Jacobsen, is impossible, because niga does not end in /g/. Read, therefore, TÙR ŠE ì-na, which can be interpreted as tùr še ì-na, "the cattle pen of his (Enlil's) grain (and) fat," or šilam/immal niga ì-na, "the grain-fed cow of his fat." Here note that value šilam (and, therefore, also immal, both meaning *littu*) is assigned to TÙR already in the Ebla Syllabary; the logogram TÙR×SAL (Proto-Ea 399–400), with values šilam and immal, is clearly an OB development.

BIBLIOGRAPHY

1896 Hilprecht, BE 1/2 no. 93 (ex. 1, copy); p. 61 (ex. 2, study)

1906 Thureau-Dangin, SAK pp. 160–61 VIII. Patesis und Könige von Kiš. 4. Ur-zag-e (ex. 1, edition)

1957 Jacobsen, ZA 52 p. 125 n. 76 (ex. 1, edition, study)

1982 Steible, ASBW 2 pp. 220–21 Urzage 1 (exs. 1–3, edition)

1985 Bauer, OLZ 80 col. 150 (study)

1986 Cooper, SARI 1 p. 104 Uk 3 (exs. 1–3, translation)

1991 Braun-Holzinger, Weihgaben p. 126 G 65 (ex. 1, edition); G 66–67 (exs. 2–3, transliteration, study)

TEXT

1) ⸢^{d}en⸣-[líl]
2) lugal-kur-[kur]-ra
3) ^{d}nin-líl
4) nin-an-ki-ra
5) TÙR ŠE ì-na
6) dam-^{d}en-líl-ra
7) ur-⸢zag⸣-è
8) lugal-kiš.KI
9) ⸢lugal⸣-[unu.KI]
Lacuna

1–2) For the god En[lil], king of all lands,

3–6) and the goddess Ninlil, queen of heaven and earth, the grain-fed cow of his (Enlil's) fat, the wife of Enlil,

7–9) Ur-zage, king of Kiš, and king [of Uruk]

Lacuna

En-šakuš-Ana

E1.14.17

The SKL assigns three kings to its "Uruk II dynasty" with a total dynastic length of rule of 187 years. The first of the "Uruk II" kings was a certain En-šakuš-Ana, to whom an improbably long (although not impossible) reign of 60 years is given. Four inscriptions are known for this king. Likely his most notable achievement was a siege and victory over the city of Kiš. For the year names of the king see Westenholz, OSP 1 p. 115, where we may note:

(1a) mu en-šà-kúš-an-<na> kiš.KI-da ab-da-tuš-a "The year En-šakuš-Ana beseiged Kiš."

(1b) (a variant of year [a]) mu lú-unu.KI kiš.KI-da ì-da-tuš-a "The year 'the man of Uruk' beseiged Kiš."

(2) mu en-š[à-kúš-AN-na] ag-[g]a-dè.+KI⌉ GÍN×KÁR bí-⌈sì-ga⌉ "The year En-s[akuš-Ana] was victorious over Ag[a]de."

1

An inscription of En-šakuš-Ana known from stone vessels from Nippur commemorates his victory over King Enbi-Ištar of Kiš.

CATALOGUE

Ex.	Museum number	Object	Dimensions (cm)	Copy	Lines preserved	cpn
1	CBS 9930	Fragment of a straight-walled cylindrical vessel of calcite	5.8×7.8×1.8	BE 1/2 no. 90	1–5	c
2	CBS 9578	Fragment of a dark stone vessel with a broad rim	Width: 7 Rim width: 2.5	PBS 5 no. 29	4–11	c
3	CBS 9974	—	—	PBS 5 no. 28	5–8	c
4	CBS 9924+9954	Two rim fragments of a large open bowl of sandstone	7.6×4.3×1.3	BE 1/2 no. 103	5–9	c
5	CBS 9951	Bowl fragment of dark brown tuff (a fragmentary volcanic rock composed of material varying in size from fine sand to coarse gravel)	Height: 7.4 Width: 7.3 Thickness: 1	BE 1/2 no. 104	6–11	c
6	CBS 9675+9691	Fragment of a large vessel of white limestone	Height: 4 Width: 8	PBS 15 no. 15	10–15	c
7	CBS 9614	Fragment of a large conical bowl of white calcite	8.5×9.5×2.7	BE 1/2 no. 102	12–18	c
8	CBS 9297+9298	Sandstone fragment	—	—	12–16	c
9	CBS 9547+9575 +9579	Fragment of a large sandstone bowl with slightly conical walls	16.7×11×1.5	BE 1/2 no. 110	1′–8′	c
10	CBS 9570	Fragment of a large sandstone bowl with slightly conical walls	Height: 11.4 Width: 9 Thickness: 0.7	—	6′–8′	n
11	CBS 9612	Rim fragment of a white limestone vessel	Height: 10.5 Width: 6.5 Thickness: 1.5	—	1–2	n

COMMENTARY

The text, following Cooper, is a conflation of Steible, ASBW 2 pp. 293–96 Enšakušanna 2 and 3.

BIBLIOGRAPHY

1896 Hilprecht, BE 1/2 nos. 90, 103, 104, 102, 110 (exs. 1, 4, 5, 7, 9 [respectively], copy)
1906 Thureau-Dangin, SAK pp. 152–53 VI Könige des "Landes" (Sumer) I. a (exs. 4, 10, edition); b (ex. 5, edition); c (ex. 7, edition); pp. 156–57 4. En-ša(g)-kuš-an-na a (ex. 1, edition)
1914 Poebel, PBS 4/1 pp. 151–56 (edition, study)
1929 Barton, RISA pp. 6–7 1. Enshagkushanna 1 (edition)
1957 Jacobsen, ZA 52 p. 134 and nn. 95–97 (study)
1963 Kramer, Sumerians p. 308 §C 4 (translation)
1971 Sollberger and Kupper, IRSA IHb (translation)
1980 Cooper, JCS 32 pp. 115–16 (exs. 1–9, conflated transliteration, study)
1982 Steible, ASBW 2 pp. 293–95 Enšakušanna 1 (exs. 1–9, edition)
1986 Cooper, SARI 1 p. 105 Uk 4.1 (exs. 1–9, edition)
1991 Braun-Holzinger, Weihgaben pp. 143–44 G 168 (exs. 1–11, edition, study)

TEXT

1) ^{d}en-líl
2) lugal-kur-kur-ra
3) en-šà-kúš-an-n[a]
4) en ki-en-⸢gi⸣
5) lugal-kalam-⸢ma⸣
6) u$_{4}$ diğir-re-ne
7) e-na-né-eš-a
8) kiš.KI
9) mu-ḫul
10) *en-bí-eš$_{18}$-tár*
11) lugal-KIŠ.KI
12) mu-dab$_{5}$
13) lú-akšak.KI-ka-ke$_{4}$
14) lú.KIŠ.KI-ke$_{4}$
15) uru na-ga-ḫul-e
16) ⸢x⸣-ga
17) [x] ⸢x⸣-ne
18) [...] ⸢x x x⸣ [...]
Lacuna
1′) [...-n]e-a
2′) mu-né-gi$_{4}$
3′) alan-bi
4′) kù-za-gìn-bi
5′) ⸢giš⸣-níg-ga-bi
6′) ^{d}en-líl-la
7′) [n]ibru.KI-šè
8′) ⸢a⸣ [m]u-na-ru

1–2) For Enlil, king of all lands,

3–5) En-šakuš-Ana, lord of the land of Sumer and king of the nation —

6–7) when the gods commanded him,

8–9) he sacked Kiš

10–12) (and) captured Enbi-Ištar, the king of Kiš.

13–18) The leader of Kiš and the leader of Akšak, (when) both their cities were destroyed ...

Lacuna
1′–2′) in(?) [..] he returned to them,

3′–8′) but [he] dedicated their statues, their precious metals and lapis lazuli, their timber and treasure, to the god Enlil at [N]ippur.

2

Three stone vessel fragments from Nippur bear an inscription indicating they were booty of Kiš dedicated to the god Enlil.

CATALOGUE

Ex.	Museum number	Object	Dimensions (cm)	Copy	Lines preserved	cpn
1	CBS 9590+9963+9998	Fragments of a bowl with outward flaring rim	4.8×5.5×1.2	BE 1/2 no. 90	1–5	c
2	CBS 9618	Rim fragment of a bowl of white calcite	Preserved height: 9 Width: 4.5 Thickness: 1.6	BE 1/2 no. 92	3–5	c
3	CBS 9964	Vessel fragment of white limestone	3×2.5	—	3	c

BIBLIOGRAPHY

1896 Hilprecht, BE 1/2 nos. 91–92 (exs. 1–2, copy); p. 50 n. 1 (exs. 1–2, edition)
1897 Winckler, AoF I p. 372 1b (exs. 1–2, translation)
1900 Radau, EBH pp. 45 (ex. 1, edition); pp. 45–46 (exs. 2, edition)
1906 Thureau-Dangin, SAK pp. 156–57 4. En-ša(g)-kuš-an-na b) (exs. 1–2, edition)
1914 Poebel, PBS 4/1 pp. 151–52 (study)
1982 Steible, ASBW 2 p. 295 Enšakušanna 2 (exs. 1–3, edition)
1986 Cooper, SARI 1 p. 105 Uk 4.2 (exs. 1–3, translation)
1991 Braun-Holzinger, Weihgaben p. 144 G 169 (ex. 1–3, edition, study)

TEXT

1) [^{d}e]n-líl-⸢la⸣
2) [e]n-šà-kúš-an-n[a]
3) níg-GA-kiš.KI
4) ḫul-a-kam
5) a nu-na-⸢ru⸣

1) For [the god E]nlil,
2) En-šakuš-Ana,
3–5) dedicated the treasure of sacked Kiš.

3

A foundation tablet in the Hermitage, St Petersburg, is inscribed with a building inscription of En-šakuš-Ana.

COMMENTARY

The tablet is said to have come from Uruk.

The reading of the DN of line 1 is uncertain. Sollberger and Kupper, IRSA IH1a, read it as ^{d}ug$_{x}$-gu-ra, apparently following from Landsberger, MSL 2 p. 78, who reads line 633 as ug = lú-*šeššig*. In this he was followed by von Weiher, Nergal p. 41, who notes that de Genouillac, TCL 15 no. 10 line 354 gives ^{d}u-gur = sukkal ^{d}nergal "Ugur is the 'vizier' of Nergal." Lambert (BiOr 30 [1973] p. 356) explains this as likely being a loanword from Akkadian *uqur* "destroy" (the imperative of *naq̄aru*[*m*]) as the name of the sword of Nergal. However, in his re-edition of Proto-Ea in MSL XIV, Civil (p. 56) indicates that line 633 is missing. However, Civil in the same volume (p. 462) for Aa VII/2, p. 462 reads line 55 as [ad-da] LÚ-šeššig = *šá-lam-*[*tu*] "corpse."

In line 5 Elili(n) is generally taken by scholars to be the same person as the king of Ur whose inscription likely came from Eridu (see E1.13.9.1).

BIBLIOGRAPHY

1915 Shileiko, VN p. 11 no. V and pl. III no. 3 (photo, copy, edition, study)
1971 Sollberger and Kupper, IRSA IH1a (translation)
1982 Steible, ASBW 2 pp. 297–98 Enšakušanna 5 (edition)
1986 Cooper, SARI 1 p. 105 Uk 4.3 (translation)

TEXT

1) ᵈRÉC 290(LÚ-šeššig)-KU-ra
2) en-šà-kúš-an-na
3) en ki-en-gi
4) lugal-kalam-ma
5) dumu é-li-li-n[a]
6) é-ni mu-na-dù

1) For the god DN,
2) En-šakuš-Ana,
3–4) lord of the land of Sumer and king of the land,
5) son of Elili,
6) built his temple.

4

A dedicatory inscription on a tablet in Brussels mentions En-šakuš-Ana.

COMMENTARY

The limestone tablet, of unknown provenance, measures 7×7.5 cm. It bears the museum number O 173.

The reading of the DN of line 1 is uncertain.

BIBLIOGRAPHY

1925 Speleers, Receuil no. 14 (copy, edition)
1957 Jacobsen, ZA 52 p. 134 n. 95
1971 Sollberger and Kupper, IRSA IH1c (translation)
1982 Steible, ASBW 2 pp. 296–97 Enšakušanna 4 (edition)
1986 Cooper, SARI 1 p. 106 Uk 4.4 (translation)

TEXT

1) ᵈ⸢x⸣-si
2) šu-na-mu-gi₄
3) [sukkal-m]aḫ-e
4) [nam]-ti-
5) en-šà-kúš-an-na-ka-šè
6) n[a]m-ti-la-ni-šè
7) nam-ti-
8) dam-dum[u-na--šè]
9) é-ni m[u]-dù

1) For the deity DN,
2–3) Šuna-mugi, the [chancel]lor,
4–5) for the [li]fe of En-šakuš-Ana,
6) for his (own) life,
7–8) (and) for the lives of [his] wife and children,
9) built his (the deity's) temple.

Lugal-zage-si

E1.14.20

1

An inscription found on numerous stone bowl fragments from Nippur celebrates Lugal-zage-si's reign of peace and stability in Sumer.

CATALOGUE

Ex.	Museum number	Lines preserved	cpn
1	6982a*	i 8–18; i 46–ii 8	c
2	8614	i 1–5, i 33–35, i 36–42, ii 35–39, ii 40–46, iii 34–35	c
3	8615	i 2–9, ii 10–12	c
4	9284*	iii 31–40	c
5	9291*	i 25–29	c
6	9292*	i 21–25	c
7	9293*	i 1, ii 7–9, iii 8–9	n
8	9294	iii 24–25	c
9	9300	i 26–33, ii 17–28	c
10	9301	i 26–38	c
11	9304 + 10287* (= PBS 15,14)	i 37–43, iii 5–10	c
12	9305 + 9601	ii 15–22, iii 26–27, iii 28–40	c
13	9306	i 33–42	c
14	9307 (+) 9668	i 29–32, ii 18–21, 28–40, iii 15–18, iii 31–37	c
15	9308	ii 20–22, iii 10–20	c
16	9309 + 9311 + 9314 + 9316 + 9916 + 9924	(cannot be found)	n
17	9310 (+) 9646	i 1–2, i 39–41, i 42–43, ii 43, ii 44–46, iii 37–40	c
18	9312 (= BE 12 pl. XIX: 59)	ii 37–39, iii 31–32	c
19	9313 + 9921	i 1–3, ii 2–3, ii 4–9, iii 10–12	c
20a	9315 + 9584	i 26–32, ii 25–31	c
20b	9584	i 26–31	c
21	9317	i 19–30, ii 28–36	c
22	9318 (+) 9645	i 15–26, i 46–ii 3, ii 6	c
23	9319 + 9659 + 9660	i 17–31, ii 23–42, iii 28–40	c
24	9320 + 9910 + 9913 + 9914 + 9915 (= BE I2 pl. XIX: 49)	i 1–6, i 40–46, ii 1–8, ii 38–46, iii 1–6, iii 39–40	n
25	9325*	i 31–32, ii 25–31	c
26	9583	i 13–17	c
27	9585*	i 16–19	c
28	9587*	i 4–8	c
29	9589*	i 22–24	c
30	9595	i 39–40	c
31	9598	i unplaceable traces, ii 7–10	c
32	9602	iii 35–40	c
33	9610 (+) 9611 (= BE 12 pl. XIX: 50f)	i 1–2, i 6–9, ii 7–8, ii 9–14, ii 17–22, iii 26–28	c
34	9619	i 42–46, ii unplaceable traces	n
35	9624	ii 16–18 (in col. i), iii 27–29	c
36	9625	i 39–42, ii 40–41	c
37	9623(= BE I2 pl, XIX:53)	i 23–25	c
38	9637 + 9696 (= BE 12 pl. XIX: 52)	i 11–13	c
39	9638	i 39–41, ii 38	c
40	9640* (PBS 15, 25)	i 32–33	c
41	9642	i 10–20, ii 8–13	c
42	9651 + 9911	i 19–22, ii 20–23, iii 15f.	c
43	9654	i 13–17, ii 32–37	c

Ex.	Museum number	Lines preserved	cpn
44	9656 + 9685 (= BE I2 pl. XIX: 58)	i 15–16, ii 20–24	c
45	9658 + 9912	i 17–19, ii 3–6	c
46	9662 + 9665	i 3–5, i 43–ii 1, ii 37–42, iii 29–34	c
47	9663	ii 35–38, iii 28–33	c
48	9666	iii 19–25	n
49	9667	i 45–ii 5, ii 38–40	c
50	9670	ii 31–32, iii 21–25	c
51	9671	ii 14–16, iii 21–25	c
52	9673	ii 2–5, ii 44	c
53	9674	i 2–6, ii 10–13	c
54	9680*	text of Lugal-kiğine-dudu	c
55	9683 (= BE I2 pl. XIX: 60)	ii 9–13	c
56	9687 (= BE I2 pl. XIX: 61)	ii 13–15	c
57	9688*	ii 4–5, ii 45–46	c
58	9689	i 12–16	n
59	9692 (= BE I2 pl. XIX: 56)	i 12–13	c
60	9694	ii 7, iii 1	c
61	9695 (= BE I2 pl. XIX: 57)	i 36–39	c
62	9697 + 9927	iii 11–13	c
63	9698	iii 30	c
64	9700 (= BE I2 pl. XIX: 55)	i 22–23	c
65	9701	i 43–44	c
66	9702	i 19–20	c
67	9903	i 46–ii 6, iii 1–7	c
68	9905	ii 9–16	n
69	9906	i 13–20	c
70	9907	i 33–37, ii 33–36	c
71	9909 + 10286	i 1–5, 45, ii 46–ii 39–44	c
72	9921	i 1–2	c
73	9922	i 44–46, ii 39–44	c
74	9923	i 1–2	c
75	9925	i 6–9	c
76	9926	iii 4–7	c
77	9927	ii 16–17, iii 18–21	c
78	9928	ii 36–iii 8	n
79	9929	iii 19–21	c
80	9933	iii 17–29	c
81	9983*	i 3–4, i 28–29	c
82	9985* + 9986*	i 40–42	n
83	9994*	i 17–20, ii 18–20	c
84	9995*	ii 31–32, ii 38–40, iii 24–30	c
85	9997*	i 29–31, ii 38–39	c
86	10125	i 34–37	n
87	13155	i 14–18	n
88	13156	iii 37–40	n
89	HS 1952	i 31–38, i 42–43, ii 37–38, ii 42–43	n
90	HS 2000	ii 1–14, ii 46, iii 1–12	n
91	HS 2006	i 36–41, ii 39–42	n
92	A 28943 (Chicago)	iii 11–12	n
93	IM 57882	—	n
94	IM 70312	i 31–33	n
95	A 32781 (Chicago)	i 1–2	n
Possible fragments			
96	CBS 9987	—	n
97	CBS 13228	—	n
98	CBS 13229		n

For the divisions into columns, line/case divisions, and line omissions, see Steible, in ASBW 2 pp. 313–14. The differing attested line numbers given here results from collations of the fragments by the author.

COMMENTARY

Precise findspots are not available for the vessel fragments found by the Hilprecht expedition. Hilprecht indicates (in only general terms) that they came from the area southeast of the ziqqurrat. Ex. 92 (2 N 372) came from the courtyard of the E-kur; ex. 93 (2N-T 227) from Tablet Hill, from a house dating to the first millennium BC., and ex. 95 (9 N 242) from the Area I dump. Ex. 94 has the excavation number 9 N 34.

As noted earlier in this volume, the vessels may be connected with a feast for the coronation of Lugal-zage-si as king of the land.

As noted previously, the reading of the name of Lugal-zage-si's father, broadly transliterated here as Ú-Ú, is uncertain. See the commentary at E1.12.7.

In i 30, for the god ᵈmes-sağa-unu.KI see the detailed discussion of Krebernik, RLA 8 pp. 94–95. The name has sometimes been read (incorrectly) as pisan-sağa-unu.KI (see Lambert, AfO 23 [1970] p. 13 line 15). The cult place of this god probably lay in the greater vicinity of Uruk. In the archaic zami hymns it is mentioned (lines 78–79) just before a mention of the ancient city of Eneg̃ir. A location at modern Tell al Waznīyah on the ancient Iturungal canal about 4 km SW of Larsa will be suggested elsewhere by the author. The site lies about halfway between Uruk and modern Tell Mašar, the latter being a possible candidate for the city of Eneg̃ir.

In connection with i 32, for the various writings of the incantation goddess Nin-g̃irim see Krebernik, Beschwörungen pp. 233–42. For further discussion of the goddess, see Krebernik, RLA 9 pp. 363–67.

BIBLIOGRAPHY

1896 Hilprecht, BE 1/2 pp. 52–53 (partial translation); pls. 38–42 no. 87 (conflated copy [ex. 24 restored by duplicates]); pl. XIX (exs. 18, 24, 33, 37–38, 44–45, 55–56, 59, 61, 64) (photo)
1897 Thureau-Dangin, RS pp. 263 ff
1907 Thureau-Dangin, SAK pp. 152–57 2. Lugal-zag-gi-si edition [based on BE 1/2 no. 87])
1929 Barton, RISA pp. 96–101 (edition [based on BE 1/2 no. 87])
1926 Legrain, PBS 15 no. 14 (part of ex. 11 [CBS 10287], copy)
1963 Kramer, Sumerians pp. 323–24 C 28 (translation [based on BE 1/2 no. 87 and PBS 15 no. 14])
1964 Nagel, in Festschrift Moortgat p. 202 Lugalzagesi a) 1 (study)
1971 Sollberger and Kupper, IRSA 1H2b (translation [based on BE 1/2 no. 87 and PBS 15 no. 14)
1982 Steible, ASBW 2 pp. 310–25 Lugalzagesi 1 (exs. 1–98, edition)
1986 Cooper, SARI 1 pp. 94–95 Um 7.1 (translation)
1989 Westenholz, RLA 7 1/2 pp. 155–56 (study)
1990 Ludwig, Išme-Dagan p. 209 (study)
1990 Wilcke, in Studies Moran pp. 455–505 (study)
1991 Braun-Holzinger, Weihgaben p. 148–49 G 183 (edition, study)
2002 Steinkeller, in Kienast Festschrift p. 621 (study)

TEXT

Col. i

1) ^{d}en-líl	i 1–2) For the god Enlil, king of all lands—
2) lugal-kur-kur-ra	
3) lugal-zà-ge-si	i 3–5) to Lugal-zage-si, king of Uruk (and) king of the land,
4) lugal-unu.KI-ga	
5) lugal-kalam-ma	
6) išib-an-na	i 6) *išib*-priest of the god An,
7) lú-maḫ-	i 7–8) *lumaḫ*-priest of the goddess Nissaba,
8) ^{d}nissaba	
9) dumu-Ú-Ú	i 9–12) son of U-U, [rul]er of G̃iša (Umma) and [*l*]*umaḫ*-priest of the goddess Nissaba,
10) [én]si-^{giš}KÚŠU.KI	
11) [l]ú-maḫ	
12) ^{d}nissaba	
13) igi-zi-bar-ra-	i 13–14) looked upon approvingly by An, king of all lands,
14) an-lugal-kur-kur-ra-ka	
15) énsi-gal-	i 15–16) chief ruler for Enlil,
16) ^{d}en-líl	
17) géštu-sum-ma-	i 17–18) granted wisdom by the god Enki,
18) ^{d}en-ki	
19) mu-pà-da	i 19–20) chosen by the god Utu,
20) ^{d}utu	
21) sukkal-maḫ	i 21–22) vizier of the god Sîn,
22) ^{d}EN.ZU	
23) GÌR.NÍTA	i 23–24) military governor for the god Utu,
24) ^{d}utu	
25) ú-a-^{d}inanna	i 25) who sustains the goddess Inanna,
26) dumu-tu-da	i 26–27) son born by the goddess Nissaba,
27) ^{d}nissaba	
28) ga-zu-kú-a	i 28–29) nourished by wholesome milk by the goddess Ninḫursag̃,
29) ^{d}nin-ḫur-sag̃	
30) lú-^{d}písan-sag̃-unu.KI-ga	i 30) "servant" of the god Mes-sag̃-Unug,
31) sag-á-è-a-	i 31–32) who was brought up by the goddess Ning̃irim,
32) ^{d}nin-gìrim(A.BU.ḪA.DU)	
33) nin-unu.KI-ga-ka	i 33) the mistress of Uruk,
34) agrig-maḫ-	i 34–35) chief steward of the gods —

35) diĝir-re-ne-ra	
36) u$_4$ en-líl	i 36–37) When the god Enlil, king of all lands,
37) lugal-kur-kur-ra-ke$_4$	
38) lugal-zà-ge-si	i 38–41) gave to Lugal-zage-si the kingship of the land,
39) nam-lugal-	
40) kalam-ma	
41) e-na-sum-ma-a	
42) igi-kalam-ma-ke$_4$	i 42–43) directed (all) the eyes of the land (obediently) toward him,
43) si e-na-sá-a	
44) kur-kur gìr-na	i 44–45) put all the lands at his feet,
45) e-ni-sè-ga-a	
46) utu-è-ta	i 46 – ii 2) and from east to west made them subject to him
Col. ii	
1) ^{d}utu-šú-šè	
2) gú e-na-gar-ra-a	
3) u$_4$-ba	ii 3–11) then, from the Lower Sea, (along) the Tigris and Euphrates to the Upper Sea, he (Enlil) put their roads in good order for him.
4) a-ab-ba-	
5) SIG.TA-ta	
6) idigna-	
7) buranun(U$_4$.KIB.NUN.KI)-bi	
8) a-ab-ba-	
9) IGI.NIM-ma-šè	
10) gìr-bi	
11) si e-na-sá	
12) utu-è-ta	ii 12–16) From east to west, Enlil permitted him no [ri]val;
13) utu-šé-šè	
14) [^{d}e]n-líl-le	
15) [gaba-š]u-gar	
16) [n]u-mu-ni-tuku	
17) kur-kur ú-sal-la	ii 17–18) under him the lands rested contentedly,
18) mu-da-ná	
19) kalam-e	ii 19–20) the people made merry.
20) a-<ne> ḫúl-la mu-da-e	
21) bára-bára-ki-en-gi-	ii 21–22) The suzerains of the land of Sumer and rulers of other lands
22) énsi-kur-kur-ra	
23) ki-unu.KI-ge	ii 23–25) at the land of Uruk determine for him the princely *me*s.
24) me nam-NUN-šè	
25) mu-na-TAR-e-ne	
26) u$_4$-ba	ii 26–29) Then under him, Uruk spent its time rejoicing.
27) unu.KI-ge	
28) giri$_{17}$(KA)-zal-a	
29) u$_4$ mu-da-zal-zal-le	
30) úri.KI-e	ii 30–32) Ur, like a bull, raised high its head;
31) gu$_4$-ĝim saĝ an-šè	
32) mu-da$_5$(URUDU)-íl-	
33) larsa.KI	ii 33–37) Larsa, the beloved city of the god Utu, made merry;
34) uru-ki-ág-	
35) ^{d}utu-ke$_4$	
36) a-ne-ḫúl-la	
37) mu-da-e	
38) ^{giš}KÚŠU.KI	ii 38–42) Ĝiša (Umma), the beloved city of Šara, lifted its huge horns;
39) uru-ki-ág-	
40) ^{d}šára-ke$_4$	
41) á-maḫ	
42) mu-da$_5$-íl	
43) ki-zabala.KI-e	ii 43–45) the region of Zabala cried out like a ewe reunited with its lamb;
44) u$_8$-sila$_4$-gur$_5$-a-ĝim	
45) sig$_4$ mu-da-gi$_4$-gi$_4$	
46) KI.DIĜIR.KI-ke$_4$	ii 46 – iii 2) and Kiʾan raised high its neck.

Col. iii
1) gú an-šè
2) mu-da$_5$-z[i]
3) lugal-zà-[g]e-si
4) lugal-unu.[KI-ga]
5) lugal-kalam-ma
6) KIN.KIN-ma
7) ^{d}en-líl
8) lugal-ni
9) nibru.KI-a
10) nidba-gal-gal
11) e-na-su$_{13}$-dè
12) a-du$_{10}$ e-na-dé-e
13) tukunx(ŠU.TUR)
14) ^{d}en-líl
15) lugal-kur-kur-ra-ke$_4$
16) an an-ki-ág-ni
17) nam-šita$_6$-mu
18) ḫé-na-bé
19) nam-ti-mu
20) nam-ti
21) ḫa-ba-daḫ-he
22) kur ú-sal-la
23) ḫa-mu-da-né
24) nam-lú-ùlu
25) ú-šim-g̃im
26) šu-dagal ḫa-mu-da$_5$-du$_{11}$
27) ubur-an-na-ke$_4$
28) si ḫu-mu-da$_5$-sá
29) kalam-e
30) ki-sa$_6$-ga
31) igi ḫa-ma-da-du$_8$
32) nam-sa$_6$-ga
33) mu-tar-re-éš-a
34) šu na-mu-da-ni-bal-e-ne
35) sipa sag GU$_4$ gál
36) da-rí ḫé-me
37) nam-ti-la-ni-šè
38) ^{d}en-líl
39) lugal-ki-ág-ni
40) a mu-na-ru

iii 3–5) Lugal-zage-si, king of Uruk, and king of the land,

iii 6–12) solicitously provides plentiful food offerings and libates sweet water for his master the god Enlil in Nippur.

iii 13–18) "If the god Enlil, king of the gods, supplicates on my behalf to the god An, his beloved father,

iii 19–21) may he add (additional) life to my life!

iii 22–23) Under me, may the lands rest contentedly,

iii 24–26) may the populace become as widespread as the grass,

iii 27–28) may the nipples of heaven function properly,
iii 29–31) and the people experience prosperity!

iii 32–34) May they (the gods An and Enlil) never alter the propitious destiny they have determined for me!
iii 35–36) May I always be the leading shepherd.

iii 37–40) For his life, he dedicated this to the god Enlil, his beloved master.

2

A limestone plaque bears a Sumerian inscription which, on the basis of its titulary, can be assigned to Lugal-zage-si.

COMMENTARY

The plaque, which measures 9.0×10.1×2.8 cm, was found at Uruk and given the excavation number W 17891. It bears the museum number IM 45446.

BIBLIOGRAPHY

1959 Edzard, Sumer 15 pp. 24–25 and pl. 3 no. 7 (edition, photo)
1982 Steible, ASBW 2 pp. 336–37 Lugalzagesi 3 (edition)
1986 Cooper, SARI 1 pp. 96–97 Um 7.3 (translation)

TEXT

Col. i′

Lacuna
1′) [lugal]-⌜unu.KI⌝
2′) ú-a-^{d}inanna
3′) lú-^{d}písan-sag̃-⌜unu⌝.KI
4′) dumu-tu-[d]a-
5′) ⌜^{d}⌝niss[aba]
Lacuna

Col. ii′

Lacuna
1′) ⌜x⌝
2′) ^{d}ina[nna]
3′) ⌜géštu⌝-su[m-ma]
4′) ^{d}[en-ki]
5′) s[ag-á-è-a-^{d}nin-g̀irim(A.BU.ḪA.DU)]
Lacuna

Lacuna
i 1′–5′) [king] of Uruk, who sustains Inanna, “man” of the god Mes-sag̃-⌜Unug⌝, son born by the goddess Niss[aba ...]
Lacuna

Lacuna
ii′ 1–5) [...] of the goddess Ina[nna], [grant]ed wisdom by the god [Enki, who was brought] up [by the goddess Nin-girim(?)]
Lacuna

Lugal-[SILA]

E1.14.21

1

An alabaster bowl fragment from Tell al-ʿUbaid bears the inscription of a ruler (énsi) named lugal-[...]. According Sollberger's understanding of the text it may have referred to Lugal-[SILA], ruler of Uruk.

COMMENTARY

The vase fragment was found in front of the bottom tread of the stairs of the temple of Ninḫursaĝa t Tell al-ʿUbaid and was given the excavation number TO 220. It is now housed in the Iraq Museum; its IM number is not known.

Sollberger (Iraq 22 [1960] p. 83) connected the text with Lugal-SILA of Uruk, based on the hypothesis that the sign in line 3 read kiš(?) by Gadd (UE 1 p. 126) might instead be a damaged UNUG sign. Certainly, the title *ensi* of Kiš would be totally unexpected for a piece from such a southerly site. Unfortunately, the text is not available for collation.

BIBLIOGRAPHY

1927 Hall, UE 1 pp. 80 and 126 (provenance, transliteration, study)
1960 Sollberger, Iraq 22 p. 83 (study)
1982 Steible, ASBW 2 p. 283 AnUr 10 (edition)
1986 Cooper, SARI 1 p. 20 Ki 4.2 (translation)
1989 Bauer, BiOr 46 p. 638 (study)

TEXT

1) lugal-[SILA]	1–3) Lugal-[SILA], ruler of Uruk(?)
2) énsi	
3) ⌈unug⌉(?)	
Lacuna	Lacuna

Unattributed

E1.15

Unknown "Vanquisher of Ḫamazi"

E1.15.1

1

A vase fragment from Nippur names the son(?) of a certain [P]ussussu (for the name type, see Römer Orientalia NS 57 [1988] pp. 224–25, note to Ki 6) as "vanquisher of Ḫamazi." Since epithets celebrating military victories are normally reserved for city rulers, it is likely that this piece is part of a royal inscription. Hilprecht thought that the fragment joined the "Uḫub" inscription copied as BE 1/2 no. 108 (and edited here as E1.7.42), but collation by J. Cooper (Iraq 46 pp. 92–93 and pl. V) reveals that the two pieces cannot belong to the same vessel, hence it is edited separately here.

COMMENTARY

The vase fragment, formerly CBS 9571+CBS 9577, is now numbered BM 129402. For the reason for the transferal of the fragment from Philadelphia to London, see Cooper, Iraq 46 (1984) p. 29 and n. 19.

BIBLIOGRAPHY

1896 Hilprecht BE 1/2 no. 109 (copy)

1906 Thureau-Dangin, SAK pp. 160–61 VIII Patesis und Könige von Kiš 1. U-tug (edition [conflated with E1.7.42.1])

1929 Barton, RISA pp. 2–3 KISH 1. Utug (edition [conflated with E1.7.42.1])

1972 Sollberger and Kupper, IRSA IA2a (translation [conflated with E1.7.42.1])

1982 Steible, NSBW 2 pp. 214–15 Uḫub 1 (edition [conflated with E1.7.42.1])

1984 Cooper, Iraq 46 pp. 92–93 and pl. V a (photo, study)

1986 Cooper, SARI 1 p. 21 Ki 6 n. 2 (study)

1991 Braun-Holzinger, Weihgaben p. 125 GB 61 (edition, study)

TEXT

Lacuna
1) [p]ù-sú-sú
2) TÙN.ŠÈ
3) ḫa-ma-zi.KI
4) sag-ri[g₉(KAB.[D]U)

Lacuna
1′–4′) [To the deity DN P]ussussu, vanquisher of Ḫamazi, dedi[cated] (this vessel).

Lugal-[...]

E1.15.2

1

An alabaster bowl fragment from Tell al-ʿUbaid bears the inscription a ruler (énsi) named lugal-[...]. It is unclear how this PN should be restored.

COMMENTARY

The vase fragment was found in front of the bottom tread of the stairs of the temple of Ninḫursag̃ at Tell al-ʿUbaid (ancient Nutur) and was given the excavation number TO 220. It is now housed in the Iraq Museum; its IM number is not known. Sollberger (Iraq 22 [1960] p. 83) connected the text with Lugal-SILA-si (E1.14.13) based on the hypothesis that the sign in line 3 read kiš(?) by Gadd (UE 1 p. 126) might be a damaged UNUG sign.

BIBLIOGRAPHY

1927 Hall, UE 1 pp. 80 and 126 (provenance, transliteration, study)
1960 Sollberger, Iraq 22 p. 83 (study)
1982 Steible, ASBW 2 p. 283 AnUr 10 (edition)
1986 Cooper, SARI 1 p. 20 Ki 4.2 (translation)
1991 Braun-Holzinger, Weihgaben p. 141 G 159 (edition, study)

TEXT

1) lugal-[...]
2) énsi-
3) x [...]
Lacuna

1–3) Lugal-[...], ruler [of ...]
Lacuna

Supposed Unnamed King of Kiš

E1.15.3

1

A female statuette found in Area P of the plano-convex building at Kiš was said by Langdon (Kiš 1 p. 36) to bear an inscription of a "king of Kiš" (lugal-kiš.KI). However, a collation of the statuette (Ash. 1924.258) indicates that the reading lugal-kiš.KI is highly unlikely.

Unknown Ruler

E1.15.4

1

A fragment of a votive plaque of unknown provenance in the Yale Babylonian Collection deals with a ruler who is named as "builder of the temple of the god Marduk."

COMMENTARY

The plaque fragment, which was acquired through purchase, is made of a yellowish limestone; its preserved dimensions are 8.5×8.7×5.8 cm. The piece bears the museum number YBC 2305.

BIBLIOGRAPHY

1937 Stephens, YOS 9 no. 2 (copy)
1961 Gelb, MAD 22 p. 208 (study)
1982 Sommerfeldt, Aufstieg pp. 19–21 (transliteration, study)
1990 Gelb and Kienast, Königsinschriften pp. 34–35 VP 17 (edition)
1991 Braun-Holzinger, Weihgaben p. 312 W18 (edition, study)

TEXT

Lacuna	Lacuna
1′) ⸢énsi⸣	1′–2′) ruler of BAR,
2′) BAR.KI <<BAR>>	
3′) DUMU *a-ḫu-ì-lum*	3′) son of Aḫu-ilum, the "man" of Ilum-BE, the "man" of Urkubi,
4′) LÚ *ì-lum*-BE!	
5′) LÚ ur-kù-bi	
6′) DÍM É	6′–7′) builder of the temple of the god Marduk,
7′) ^{d}AMAR.UTU	
8′) MU.DU.AN	8′) ...
9′) ⸢SAG.RIG$_9$⸣	9) dedicated (this object).

Index of Museum Numbers

Aleppo, Aleppo Museum

Allard Pierson Museum

Athens, National Museum

Baghdad, Iraq Museum

Baghdad, Private Collection

Banks Collection

Berkeley, University of California, R.H. Lowie Museum of Anthropology

No.	El	No.	El	No.	El
UCLM 9-1766	9.5.5.3	UCLM 9-1767	9.5.5.4	UCLM 9-1972	9.5.3.30

Berlin, Vorderasiatisches Museum

No.	El	No.	El	No.	El
VA 2088	9.3.12	VA 3112	9.3.9.7	VA 5355	9.9.14c
VA 2100	9.4.8	VA 3143	9.9.14e	VA 5356	9.9.14o
VA 2201	9.4.7	VA 3311	9.5.10.3	VA 5357	9.9.14q
VA 2202	9.4.14.2	VA 4855	14.15.2.1	VA 5358	9.9.14r
VA 2599	9.3.8.4	VA 5350	9.9.14a	VA 5359	9.9.14c
VA 3057	9.4.14.5	VA 5351	9.9.14s	VA 7248	9.5.25
VA 3058	9.4.14.3	VA 5352	9.9.14n	VA 10936	14.15.2.2
VA 3059	9.4.14.4	VA 5353	9.9.14p		
VA 3095	9.5.12.3a-b	VA 5354	9.9.14t		

Berlin, Private Collection

No.	El
—	9.5.3.29

Birmingham City Museum

No.	El
1103'52	13.6.2

Brussels, Musée du Cinquantenenaire

No.	El
O 23	9.1.7.2a-b
O 173	14.17.4
O 868	9.5.3.6

Cambridge, Massachusetts, Harvard Semitic Museum

No.	El
HSM 7495	9.1.7.1
HSM 7497	9.3.2.2
HSM 8668	9.5.5.1

Chester, Pennsylvania, Crozer Theological Seminary

No.	El
5	9.9.1.3

Chicago, University of Chicago, Oriental Institute

No.	El	No.	El	No.	El
A—	11.3.2	A 192	8.1.3	A 208	1.5.2

A 211	8.1.2.1	A 543	1.7.2.2a	A 3604	9.4.17
A 212	1.2.1	A 1159	1.7.2.4	A 4106	9.4.14.8
A 217	1.5.1A 227 1.3.1	A 1160	1.7.2.5	A 7121	9.5.4.2
A 228	8.1.2.2	A 1161	1.7.2.6	A 7122	9.5.4.3
A 541a	1.7.2.1b	A 1162	1.7.2.7	A 7447	1.3.2001
A 541b	1.7.2.1a	A 1164	1.2.1.2	A 28943	14.20.1.92
A 542	1.7.2.2b	A 1399	9.3.9.28	A 32781	14.20.1.95

de Clerq Collection

No.	El
—	9.9.6
—	12.4,1

Cros Collection

No.	El
—	9.3.8.5

Damascus, Damascus National Museum

No.	El
Š 2061	10.11.2001
Š2071	10.12.4

Erlenmeyer Collection

No.	El
—	9.4.5.2
—	9.4.5.3
—	

Geneva, Bodmer Collection

No.	El
—	9.4.11
—	9.5.3.27

Greene Collection

No.	El
—	9.5.3.23

Göttingen, Private Collection

No.	El
—	13.9.1.2

Istanbul, Arkeoloji Müzel

No.	El	No.	El	No.	El

Jena, Friedrich-Schiller Universität, Hilprect Collection of Babylonian Antiquities

Leiden, Netherlands Institute for the Near East, de Liagre Böhl Collection

London, British Museum

Milwaukee, Milwaukee Public Museum

Munich, Private Collection

No.	EI
—	9.3.9.37
—	9.3.9.38

New Haven, Yale University, Yale Babylonian Collection

No.	EI
YBC 1944	9.9.14t
YBC 2139	12.6.2.2
YBC 2183	9.5.27
YBC 2184	9.5.2
YBC 2316	9.5.3.15
YBC 2317	9.5.3.16
YBC 2318	9.5.3.17
YBC 2319	9.5.3.18
YBC 2320	9.5.3.19
YBC 2321	9.5.3.20
YBC 2322	9.5.3.21
YBC 2323	9.5.3.22
YBC 2400	9.3.16
YBC 2408	9.3.2.3
YBC 2520	9.4.12
YBC 3020	9.9.14w

New Haven, Yale University Library, James B. Nies Collection

No.	EI
NBC 2501	9.5.1.2
NBC 2520	9.4.12
NBC 6067	12.5.1

New Haven, Yale University Library, J. Pierpont Morgan Collection

No.	EI
MCL 2325	9.9.14b
MCL 2498	9.9.14h
MCL 2499	9.9.14i
MCL 2500	9.9.14j
MCL 2501	9.9.14k
MCL 2502	9.9.14l
MCL 2503	9.9.14u
MCL 2630	14.15.3

New York, New York Public Library

No.	EI
RR-3	9.5.3.33

Oxford, Ashmolean Museum

No.	EI
Ash 1921.870	9.5.28
Ash 1967.1502	9.5.3.37

Paris, Musée du Louvre, Département des Antiquités Orientales

No.	EI
AO —	9.3.7.1
AO —	9.1.20
AO —	9.1.21
AO —	9.3.8.8
AO —	9.7.1
AO —	9.9.9
AO 50+	9.1.3
AO 120	9.9.7
AO 233	9.1.24b
AO 249	9.6.1.2
AO 252	9.1.22
AO 253	9.1.13
AO 255	9.3.6.2
AO 256	9.5.12.1a-b
AO 294	9.1.7.6a-b
AO 314	9.1.7.7a-b
AO 315	9.1.14
AO 349	9.9.8
AO 350	9.1.7.10
AO 351	9.3.8.2
AO 352	9.3.8.7
AO 353	9.3.9.9
AO 354	9.3.9.10
AO 355	9.5.11.2
AO 402	9.9.14d
AO 2344	9.1.2
AO 2345	9.1.3
AO 2349	8.1.1
AO 2351	9.1.7.5a-b
AO 2353a	9.5.13.6

No.	EI
AO 2353b	9.5.12.2a-b
AO 2354	9.5.28
AO 2436+	9.1.3
AO 2437+	9.1.3
A0 2438+	9.1.3
AO 2674	9.5.7
AO 2675	8.2.1
AO 2677	9.5.7
AO 2783	9.1.26
AO 2784	9.1.15
AO 3004	9.5.1.1
AO 3149	9.9.1.2
AO 3177	9.1.9
AO 3179	9.1.11
AO 3180	9.1.12
AO 3278	9.9.1.1
AO 3281	9.1.24a
AO 3294	9.4.3.1
AO 3295	9.2.1
AO 3297	9.5.14
AO 3604	9.4.17
AO 3867	9.1.10
AO 4109	9.1.1
AO 4162	9.9.5
AO 4195	9.9.14f
AO 4442	9.3.3.1
AO 4443	9.5.1.3
AO 4597	9.3.3.2
AO 4598	9.9.4
AO 4644	9.3.8.1
AO 4645	9.3.8.6
AO 5681	14.15.4
AO 10921	14.15.2.3
AO 11945+	9.4.3.4
AO 12181	9.9.2.2
AO 12480	9.5.3.2
AO 12746+	9.4.3.4
AO 12778	9.9.14g
AO 12779	9.10.1
AO 12782	9.9.2.3
AO 13219	9.8.1.1
AO 13220	9.8.1.2
AO 13221	9.8.1.3
AO 13222	9.8.3
AO 16109	9.3.1
AO 19225	12.6.1
AO 20146	5.1.1
AO 22246	12.4.1
AO 22934	9.9.6
AO 22937	12.3.1
AO 24414	9.5.4.1

Paris, Musée du Louvre, Musées Nationaux Collection

No.	EI
MNB 1390	9.9.2.1
MNB 1415	9.1.8
MNB 1417	9.6.1.1
MNB 1418	9.5.21

Philadelphia, University of Pennsylvannia, University Museum, Babylonian Section

No.	EI
CBS—	13.2.1
CBS 1217	1.1.1.2
CBS 6982a	14.20.1.1
CBS 8614	14.20.1.2
CBS 8615	14.20.1.3
CBS 9084	9.3.7.3
CBS 9222	1.4.1
CBS 9284	14.20.1.4
CBS 9291	14.20.1.5
CBS 9292	14.20.1.6
CBS 9293	14.20.1.7
CBS 9294	14.20.1.8
CBS 9297+	14.17.1.8
CBS 9298+	14.17.1.8
CBS 9300	14.20.1.9
CBS 9301	14.20.1.10
CBS 9304+	14.20.1.11
CBS 9305+	14.20.1.12
CBS 9306	14.20.1.13
CBS 9307+	14.20.1.14
CBS 9308	14.20.1.15
CBS 9309+	14.20.1.16
CBS 9310+	14.20.1.17
CBS 9311+	14.20.1.16
CBS 9312	14.20.1.18
CBS 9313+	14.20.1.19
CBS 9314+	14.20.1.16
CBS 9315+	14.20.1.20
CBS 9316+	14.20.1.16
CBS 9317	14.20.1.21
CBS 9318+	14.20.1.22
CBS 9319+	14.20.1.23
CBS 9320+	14.20.1.24
CBS 9322	14.15.1.10
CBS 9324+	14.20.1.16
CBS 9325	14.20.1.25
CBS 9328	9.5.18
CBS 9463	14.14.1.4
CBS 9463+	9.5.18
CBS 9464	14.14.1.1
CBS 9465	14.14.1.2
CBS 9466	14.14.1.3
CBS 9547+	14.17.1.9
CBS 9570	14.17.1.10
CBS 9571+	15.1
CBS 9572	7.42.1
CBS 9547+	14.17.1.9
CBS 9577+	15.1
CBS 9578	14.17.1.2
CBS 9579+	14.17.1.9
CBS 9581	14.14.1.4
CBS 9583	14.20.1.26
CBS 9584+	14.20.1.20
CBS 9585	14.20.1.27
CBS 9587	14.20.1.28
CBS 9589	14.20.1.29
CBS 9590+	14.17.2.1
CBS 9591+	14.14.1.5
CBS 9593	14.14.1.6
CBS 9594	14.15.1.3
CBS 9595	14.20.1.30
CBS 9598	14.20.1.31
CBS 9599	14.14.1.7
CBS 9601+	14.20.1.12
CBS 9602	14.20.1.33
CBS 9604	14.15.11
CBS 9605	14.14.18
CBS 9606	14.15.12
CBS 9607+	14.14.1.9
CBS 9608+	14.14.1.5
CBS 9609+	14.14.1.9
CBS 9610+	14.20.1.33
CBS 9611+	14.20.1.33
CBS 9612	14.17.1.11
CBS 9614	14.17.1.7
CBS 9616+	14.16.1.1
CBS 9617+	11.2.1
CBS 9618	14.17.2.2
CBS 9619	14.20.1.34
CBS 9620	14.15.1.3
CBS 9621+	11.2.1
CBS 9622	14.16.1.2
CBS 9623	14.20.1.37
CBS 9624	14.20.1.35
CBS 9625	14.20.1.36
CBS 9627	14.15.14
CBS 9628	14.20.1.37
CBS 9630	14.15.1.5
CBS 9631	14.15.1.6
CBS 9632	14.14.1.10
CBS 9633	14.14.1.11
CBS 9634	14.14.1.12
CBS 9635	14.15.1.7
CBS 9637+	14.20.1.38
CBS 9638	14.20.1.39
CBS 9639	14.15.1.8
CBS 9640	14.20.1.40
CBS 9642	14.20.1.41
CBS 9643+	14.14.1.4
CBS 9644	14.15.1.9
CBS 9645+	14.20.1.22
CBS 9646+	14.20.1.17
CBS 9648a+b	14.15.1.11
CBS 9651+	14.20.1.42
CBS 9654	14.20.1.43
CBS 9656+	14.20.1.44
CBS 9657	14.14.1.9
CBS 9658+	14.20.1.45
CBS 9659+	14.20.1.23
CBS 9660+	14.20.1.23
CBS 9662+	9.5.18
CBS 9662+	14.20.1.46
CBS 9663	14.20.1.47
CBS 9665+	9.5.18
CBS 9666	14.20.1.48
CBS 9667	14.20.1.49
CBS 9668	14.20.1.15
CBS 9669+	9.5.8
CBS 9670	14.20.1.50
CBS 9671	14.20.1.51

Paris, J. Mariaud de Serres Collection

Princeton, Art Museum

Samhery Collection

San José, Rosicrucian Egyptian Museum

New Brunswick Museum, St. John

St Petersburg, Russia, Hermitage

No.	EI	No.	EI	No.	EI
—	1.7.2.8	—	9.4.14.1	—	9.9.14w
—	9.3.9.8	—	9.8.1.4	—	14.17.3

Stockholm, Haldar Collection

No.	EI
—	9.5.3.26

Stockholm, National Museum Stockholm

No.	EI
NMS 2089	9.5.3.25

Toronto, Royal Ontario Museun of Archaeology

No.	EI
D 1297	9.5.3.35

Tournay Collection

No.	EI
—	9.5.3.24

Index of Excavation Numbers

Uruk (Warka)

Concordances of Selected Publications

Barton, RISA

P.	No.	EI
2-3	Utug	7.42.1
2-3	Mesilim	8.1.1
2-3	Aanipadda 1	13.6.3
	Aanipadda 2	13.6.1
6-7	Ur-Enlil 2	11.2.1
	Ur-Enlil 3	11.2.2
6-7	Enshagkushanna 1	14.17.1
14ff.	Ur-Nina 1	9.1.17
	Ur-Nina 2	9.1.11
	Ur-Nina 3	9.1.9
	Ur-Nina 4	9.1.12
	Ur-Nina 5	9.1.10
	Ur-Nina 6	9.1.27
	Ur-Nina 7	9.1.8
	Ur-Nina 8	9.1.21
	Ur-Nina 9	9.1.2
	Ur-Nina 10	9.1.3
	Ur-Nina 11	9.1.4
	Ur-Nina 12	9.1.22
	Ur-Nina 13	9.1.1
	Ur-Nina 14	9.1.20
22ff.	Eannatum 1	9.3.1
	Eannatum 2	9.3.5
	Eannatum 3	9.3.6
	Eannantum 4 and 5	9.3.7
	Eannatum 6 and 7	9.3.2
	Eannatum 8	9.3.4
	Eannatum 9	9.3.8
	Eannatum 10-14	9.3.9
46ff.	Enannatum I 1	9.4.4
	Enannatum I 2	9.4.3
	Enannatum I 3	9.4.19
	Enannatum I 4	9.4.10
50ff.	Entemena 3	9.5.21
	Entemena 4	9.5.14
	Entemena 6	9.5.16
	Entemena 7	9.5.27
	Entemena 8	9.5.7
	Entemena 9	9.5.18
	Entemena 10	9.5.28
	Entemena 11	9.5.26
	Entemena 15	9.5.1
	Entemena 17	9.5.17
72ff.	Urukagina 1	9.9.8
	Urukagina 2	9.9.6
	Urukagina 3	9.9.7
	Urukagina 10	9.9.3
	Urukagina 11	9.9.11
	Urukagina 18	9.9.5
	Lugaldalu	1.1.4
92-93	Eabsu	12.3.1
92-93	Urlumma	12.4.1
94ff.	Lugalkigubnidudu 1	14.14.1
	Lugalkigubnidudu 6	14.14.4
	Lugalkigubnidudu and Lugalkisalsi 8	14.15.3
96-101	Lugalzaggesi	14.20.1
302-303	Ikū(n)-Shamash	10.7.1

Braun-Holzinger, Weihgaben

P.	No.	EI
42	K 1	9.4.19
44	K 9	8.1.1
44–45	K 12	10.1.2
115	G 1	9.1.27
	G 2	9.1.28
	G 3	9.1.33
	G 4	9.3.7b
	G 5	9.3.13
116	G 6	9.3.11
	G 7	9.4.4
116–17	G 8	9.5.18
117	G 10	9.5.25
117–18	G 11	9.5.7
118	G 12	9.5.24
	G 13	9.9.11
119	G 16	9.3.19
121	G 32–33	1.2.1
	G 34	1.5.1
	G 35	1.5.2
123	G 46	1.3.1
	G 50	7.40.1
125	G 60	7.22.2
	G 61	7.42.1
	G 62	8.1.2
126	G 64	8.1.3
	G 65–67	14.16.1
126–27	G 68	10.10.1
127	G 69	10.11.2002
	G 73	11.3.1
128	G 74	11.3.2
	G 75	11.1.1
	G 76	11.2.1
	G 77	11.2.2140
	G 150	13.6.4

	G 151	13.6.5	250	St 6	8.3.2
	G 152	13.6.2		St 55	10.7.1
	G 153	13.8.1	252	St 68	12.1.1
140–41	G 154	13.2.1		St 69	12.3.1
143–44	G 168	14.17.1	253	St 74	14.15.4
144	G 169	14.17.2	255	St 88	1.9.2001
144–45	G 171	14.14.1	265	P 1	12.2.1
146	G 173	14.14.6	308	W 2	9.1.3
	G 174–75	14.14.2	309	W 3	9.1.4
147	G 179	14.14.4		W 4	9.1.5
	G 180	14.15.1	310	W 8	9.4.1
	G 181	14.15.3		W 9	9.5.28
148–49	G 183	14.20.1	324	T 1	9.1.24a
240	St 2	9.4.15		T 2	9.1.24b
240–41	St 3	9.5.17		T 3	9.1.25
241	St 6	5.1.1		T 4	9.2.1
242	St 9	1.3.2001	326	T 11	13.6.3
242	St 10	1.4.1	334	St 3	9.1.8
244	St 24	10.17.1	334–35	St 4	9.1.31
245	St 27	10.11.2001	335	St 5	9.1.6a
	St 28	10.11.2003		St 6	9.1.6b
248	St 43	10.12.2	336	St 8	7.43.1
249	St 52	10.12.3	365	P 2	13.5.1
	St 51	10.12.4		P 3	13.6.1
249–50	St 47	10.18.1	378	Varia 9	12.6.1

Cooper, SARI 1

P.	No.	El	P.	No.	El
15	Ad 1	1.2.1		La 1.17	9.1.17
	Ad 2	1.5.1–2		La 1.18	9.1.18
16	Ad 3.1	1.7.1		La 1.19	9.1.19
	Ad 3.2	1.7.2		La 1.20	9.1.20
16f.	Ad 4.1	1.3.1		La 1.21	9.1.21
	Ad 4.2	1.3.2001		La 1.22	9.1.22
17	Ad 5	1.4.1		La 1.23	9.1.23
17	Ad 6	1.9.2001		La 1.24	9.1.24a
17-18	Ee 1	5.1.1		La 1.24	9.1.24b
18	Ki 1	7.22.1–2		La 1.25	9.1.25
18f.	Ki 2	7.40.1		La 1.26	9.1.26a
19f.	Ki 3.1	8.1.1		La 1.27	9.1.27
	Ki 3.2	8.1.2		La 1.28	9.1.28
	Ki 3.3	8.1.3		La 1.29	9.1.29
20	Ki 4.1	8.2.1		La 1.30	9.1.30a
20	Ki 5	7.41.1		La 1.31	9.1.31
21	Ki 6	7.42.1	33	La 2.1	9.2.1
	Ki 7	8.3.1		La 2.1	9.2.2a
	Ki 8	14.13.1	33ff.	La 3.1	9.3.1
22ff.	La 1.1	9.1.1		La 3.2	9.3.2
	La 1.2	9.1.2		La 3.3	9.3.3
	La 1.3	9.1.3		La 3.4	9.3.4
	La 1.4	9.1.4		La 3.5	9.3.5
	La 1.5	9.1.5		La 3.6	9.3.6
	La 1.6	9.1.6		La 3.7	9.3.7
	La 1.7	9.1.7		La 3.8	9.3.8
	La 1.8	9.1.8		La 3.9	9.3.9
	La 1.9	9.1.9		La 3.10	9.3.10
	La 1.10	9.1.10		La 3.11	9.3.11
	La. 1.11	9.1.11		La 3.12	9.3.12
	La 1.12	9.1.12		La 3.13	9.3.13
	La 1.13	9.1.13		La 3.14	9.3.14
	La 1.14	9.1.14		La 3.15	9.3.15
	La 1.15	9.1.15			
	La 1.16	9.1.16			

	La 3.16	9.3.16
	La 3.17	9.3.17
47 ff.	La 4.1	9.4.1
	La 4.2	9.4.2
	La 4.3	9.4.3
	La 4.4	9.4.4
	La 4.5	9.4.5
	La 4.6	9.4.6
	La 4.7	9.4.7
	La 4.8	9.4.8
	La 4.9	9.4.9
	La 4.10	9.4.10
	La 4.11	9.4.11
	La 4.12	9.4.12
	La 4.13	9.4.13
	La 4.14	9.4.14
	La 4.15	9.4.15
	La 4.16	9.4.16
	La 4.17	9.4.17
	La 4.18	9.4.18
	La 4.19	9.4.19
	La 4.20	9.4.20
54ff.	La 5.1	9.5.1
	La 5.2	9.5.2
	La 5.3	9.5.3
	La 5.4	9.5.4
	La 5.5	9.5.5
	La 5.5a	9.5.5a
	La 5.6	9.5.6
	La 5.7	9.5.7
	La 5.8	9.5.8
	La 5.9	9.5.9
	La 5.10	9.5.10
	La 5.11	9.5.11
	La 5.12	9.5.12
	La 5.13	9.5.13
	La 5.14	9.5.14
	La 5.15	9.5.15
	La 5.16	9.5.16
	La 5.17	9.5.17
	La 5.18	9.5.18
	La 5.19	9.5.19
	La 5.20	9.5.20
	La 5.21	9.5.21
	La 5.22	9.5.22
	La 5.23	9.5.23
	La 5.24	9.5.24
	La 5.25	9.5.25
	La 5.26	9.5.26
	La 5.27	9.5.27
	La 5.28	9.5.28
	La 5.29	9.5.29
68	La 6	9.6.1
68	La 7	9.7.1
69	La 8.1	9.8.1
	La 8.2	9.8.2
	La 8.3	9.8.3
70ff.	La 9.1	9.9.1
	La 9.2	9.9.2
	La 9.3	9.9.3
	La 9.4	9.9.4
	La 9.5	9.9.5
	La 9.6	9.9.6
	La 9.7	9.9.7
	La 9.8	9.9.8
	La 9.9	9.9.9
	La 9.10	9.9.10
	La 9.11	9.9.11
	La 9.12	9.9.12
	La 9.13	9.9.13
	La 9.14a	9.9.14a
	La 9.14b	9.9.14b
	La 9.14c	9.9.14c
	La 9.14d	9.9.14d
	La 9.14e	9.9.14e
	La 9.14f	9.9.14f
	La 9.14g	9.9.14g
	La 9.14h	9.9.14h
	La 9.14i	9.9.14i
	La 9.14j	9.9.14j
	La 9.14k	9.9.14k
	La 9.14l	9.9.14l
	La 9.14m	9.9.14m
	La 9.14n	9.9.14n
	La 9.14o	9.9.14o
	La 9.14p	9.9.14p
	La 9.14q	9.9.14q
	La 9.14r	9.9.14r
	La 9.14s	9.9.14s
	La 9.14t	9.9.14t
	La 9.14u	9.9.14u
	La 9.14v	9.9.14v
	La 9.14w	9.9.14w
84f.	La 10.1	9.10.1
	La 10.2	9.10.2
86	Ma 1.1	10.1.2
	Ma 1.2	10.1.3
86f.	Ma 2.1	10.11.2001
87	Ma 3	10.7.1
87f.	Ma 4.1	10.18.2001
	Ma 4.2	10.18.2002
88f.	Ma 5.1	10.12.1
	Ma 5.2	10.12.3–4
	Ma 5.3	10.12.2
89	Ma 6	10.17.1
90	Ni 1	11.1.1
90	Ni 2.1	11.2.1
	Ni 2.2	11.2.2
91	Ni 3	11.3.1–2
91f.	Um 1	12.1.1
92	Um 2	12.2.1
92	Um 3	12.3.1
93	Um 4.1	12.4.1
	Um 4.2	12.4.2
93	Um 5	12.5.1
93ff.	Um 6	12.6.1
94ff.	Um 7.1	14.20.1
	Um 7.2	14.20.2
	Um 7.2	12.6.2
97	Ur 1	13.1.1
97	Ur 2	13.3.3
97f.	Ur 3	13.3.1
98	Ur 4	13.4.1
98f.	Ur 5.1	13.5.1
	Ur 5.2	13.5.2
	Ur 5.3	13.5.3
	Ur 5.4	13.5.4
99f.	Ur 6.1	13.6.1
	Ur 6.2	13.6.2
	Ur 6.3	13.6.3
	Ur 6.4	13.6.4
	Ur 6.5	13.6.5

	Ur 6.6	13.6.6	103f.	Uk 2.1	14.15.1
100	Ur 7	13.8.1		Uk 2.2	14.15.2
101	Ur 8	13.9.1		Uk 2.3	14.15.3
101ff.	Uk 1.1	14.14.1		Uk. 2.4	14.15.4
	Uk 1.2	14.14.3a?	104	Uk 3	14.16.1
	Uk 1.3	14.14.3b?	105	Uk 4.1	14.17.1
	Uk 1.4	14.14.4		Uk 4.2	14.17.2
	Uk 1.5	14.14.5		Uk 4.3	14.17.3
	Uk 1.6	14.14.6		Uk 4.4	14.14.4

Gelb and Kienast, Königsinschriften

P.	No.	EI	P.	No.	EI
6f.	MP 4 Gullā	10.18.1	12ff.	MP 12 IpLULil 1	10.12.1
8f.	MP 7 Ikūnmari	10.10.1		MP 13 IpLULil 2	10.12.2
9–10	MP 8 Ikūnšamaš	10.7.1		MP 14 IpLULil 3	10.12.3
10	MP 9 Ikūnšamagan 1	10.11.2001		MP 15 IpLULil 4	10.12.4
10–11	MP 10 Ikūnšamagan 2	10.11.2002	15	MP 17 Išqīmari 1	10.17.1
11	MP 11 Ikūnšamagan 3	10.11.2003			

Rashid, Gründungsfiguren

P.	No.	EI	P.	No.	EI
7f.	41-48	9.1.7	10	70-72	14.15.2
9f.	62	9.5.13	13	Bismayah	1.7.2
	69	9.5.4			

Sollberger and Kupper, IRSA

P.	No.	EI	P.	No.	EI
39	IA1a	7.22.1		IC6b	9.4.14
	IA1a	7.22.2		IC6c	9.4.8
39–40	IA2a	7.42.1		IC6d	9.4.5
40	IA3a	8.1.1		IC6e	9.4.10
	IA3b	8.1.2		IC6f	9.4.15
	IA3c	8.1.3	66ff.	IC7a	9.5.17
40–41	IA4a	14.13.1		IC7b	9.5.27
	IB1a	13.3.3		IC7c	9.5.13
	IB2a	13.3.1		IC7d	9.5.26
	IB3a	13.4.1		IC7e	9.5.7
41f.	IB4a	13.5.2		IC7f	9.5.20
	IB4b	13.5.3		IC7f	9.5.20a
	IB4c	13.5.1		IC7g	9.5.23
42f.	IB5a	13.6.3		IC7h	9.5.3
	IB5b	13.6.6		IC7i	9.5.1
	IB5c	13.6.4	77	IC9b	9.7.1
	IB5c	13.6.5	77f.	IC10a	9.8.2
43f.	IB7a	13.8.1		IC10b	9.8.1
44f.	IC3c	9.1.2		IC10c	9.6.3
44f.	IC3a	9.1.6b	78ff.	IC11a	9.9.6
	IC3b	9.1.19		IC11e	9.9.14c
	IC3c	9.1.2		IC11f	9.9.14g
	IC3d	9.1.17		IC11g	9.9.14h
	IC3f	9.1.27		IC11i	9.9.14p
47	IC4a	9.2.1		IC11k	9.9.14s
47ff.	IC5a	9.3.1		IC11l	9.9.14u
	IC5b	9.3.5		IC11m	9.9.5
	IC5c	9.3.9	83	ID3a	12.4.1
	IC5d	9.3.4	83	ID4a	12.5.1
62ff.	IC6a	9.4.3	83	ID5a	12.6.1

84f.	IE1a	14.14.3		IG2a	10.4.1
	IE1b	14.14.6	88	IG3a	10.7.1
	IE1c	14.14.1	88f.	IG4a	10.12.3
	IE1d	14.14.2		IG4c	10.12.1
85f.	IE2a	14.15.1		IG5a	10.11.2002
	IE3a	14.15.4	90	IG5b	10.11.2001
87	IF1	1.1.1	90f.	IH1a	14.17.3
	IF2a	1.2.1		IH1b	14.17.1
	IF3a	1.4.1		IH1c	14.17.4
	IF4a	1.7.2	91ff.	IH2a	12.6.2
	1G1a	10.1.3	93f.	IH2b	14.20.1

Sollberger, CIRPL

P.	No.	El	P.	No.	El
1ff.	Urn. 1	9.1.1		En. I 17	9.4.7
	Urn. 2-7, 9-17	9.1.7		En. I 18	9.4.4
	Urn. 8	9.1.19		En. I 19	9.4.19
	Urn. 19	9.1.29		En. I 21-22	9.4.5
	Urn. 20	9.1.2		En. I 23	9.4.12
	Urn. 22	9.1.4	32ff.	Ent. 1	9.5.17
	Urn. 23	9.1.5		Ent, 2-7	9.5.13
	Urn. 24	9.3.9		Ent. 8-14	9.5.12
	Urn. 25	9.1.11		Ent. 15	9.5.4
	Urn. 26	9.1.9		Ent. 16	9.5.27
	Urn. 27	9.1.12		Ent. 17	9.5.9
	Urn. 28	9.1.10		Ent. 18-21	9.5.10
	Urn. 29	9.1.13		Ent. 22	9.5.14
	Urn. 30	9.1.14		Ent. 23	9.5.16
	Urn. 31	9.1.15		Ent. 24	9.5.21
	Urn. 32	9.1.18		Ent. 25	9.5.22
	Urn. 33	9.1.16		Ent. 26	9.4.23
	Urn. 34	9.1.17		Ent. 27	9.5.20
	Urn. 34	9.1.20		Ent. 28-29, 31	9.5.1
	Urn. 35	9.1.21		Ent. 32	9.5.18
	Urn. 35	9.1.22		Ent. 33	9.5.25
	Urn. 37	9.1.23		Ent. 34	9.5.7
	Urn. 39	9.1.8		Ent. 35	9.5.26
	Urn. 40	9.1.31		Ent. 36-40	9.5.11
	Urn. 41	9.1.26a		Ent. 41	9.5.2
	Urn. 44	9.1.24a		Ent. 42	9.5.15
	Urn. 45	9.1.24b		Ent. 43	9.5.8
	Urn. 46	9.1.25		Ent. 44	9.5.19
	Urn. 47	9.1.27		Ent. 45-73	9.5.3
	Urn. 48	9.1.28		Ent. 74-75	9.5.5
8	Akg. 1	9.2.1		Ent. 76	9.5.28
	Akg. 2	9.2.2a		Ent. 78	9.5.29
	Akg. 3-6	9.2.2b	45	En. II 1	9.6.1
9ff.	Ean. 1	9.3.1	46	Enz. 2	9.7.1
	Ean. 2	9.3.5	47	Lug. 1	9.8.1
	Ean. 3	9.3.6		Lug. 5	9.8.3
	Ean. 5	9.3.7	48ff.	Ukg. 1-3	9.9.2
	Ean 6-7	9.3.2		Ukg. 4-5	9.9.1
	Ean. 11	9.3.8		Ukg. 6	9.9.3
	Ean. 60	9.3.4		Ukg. 7	9.9.8
	Ean. 62	9.3.11		Ukg. 8	9.9.10
	Ean. 63	9.3.3		Ukg. 9	9.8.2
	Ean. 64	9.3.12		Ukg. 10	9.9.6
	Ean. 64	9.3.13		Ukg. 11	9.9.7
27ff.	En. I 1	9.4.1		Ukg. 12	9.9.9
	En. I 3-8	9.4.3		Ukg. 13	9.9.11
	En. I 9	9.4.8		Ukg. 14	9.9.4
	En. I 10-15	9.4.14		Ukg. 16	9.9.5
	En. I 16	9.4.6		Ukg. 34	9.9.14a

P.	No.	EI
	Ukg. 35	9.9.14b
	Ukg. 36-37	9.9.14c
	Ukg. 38	9.9.14d
	Ukg. 39	9.9.14e
	Ukg. 40	9.9.14f
	Ukg. 41	9.9.14g
	Ukg. 42	9.9.14h
	Ukg. 43	9.9.14i
	Ukg. 44	9.9.14j
	Ukg. 45	9.9.14k
	Ukg. 46	9.9.14l
	Ukg. 47	9.9.14m
	Ukg. 48	9.9.14n
	Ukg. 49	9.9.14o
	Ukg. 50	9.9.14p
	Ukg. 51	9.9.14q
	Ukg. 52	9.9.14r
	Ukg. 53	9.9.14s
	Ukg. 54-55	9.9.14t
	Ukg. 55	9.9.14u
	Ukg. 57	9.9.14v
	Ukg. 58	9.9.13
	Ukg. 59	9.9.12
	Ukg. 60	9.9.1
	Ukg. 61	9.9.14w
	Ukg. 62	9.9.2
64	N15	9.3.16

Steible, ASBW 1

P.	No.	El
79ff.	Urnanše 1	9.1.1
	Urnanše 2	9.1.7
	Urnanše 8	9.1.19
	Urnanše 19	9.1.29
	Urnanše 20	9.1.2
	Urnanše 21	9.1.3
	Urnanše 22	9.1.4
	Urnanše 23	9.1.5
	Urnanše 24	9.1.17
	Urnanše 25	9.1.11
	Urnanše 26	9.1.9
	Urnanše 27	9.1.12
	Urnanše 28	9.1.10
	Urnanše 29	9.1.13
	Urnanše 30	9.1.14
	Urnanše 31	9.1.15
	Urnanše 32	9.1.18
	Urnanše 33	9.1.16
	Urnanše 34	9.1.20
	Urnanše 35	9.1.21
	Urnanše 36	9.1.22
	Urnanše 37	9.1.23
	Urnanše 39	9.1.8
	Urnanše 40	9.1.31
	Urnanše 41	9.1.26a
	Urnanše 44	9.1.24a
	Urnanše 45	9.1.24b
	Urnanše 46	9.1.25
	Urnanše 47	9.1.27
	Urnanše 48	9.1.28
	Urnanše 49	9.1.31
	Urnanše 50	9.1.6a
	Urnanše 51	9.1.6b
118f.	Akurgal 1	9.2.1
	Akurgal 2	9.2.2a
	Akurgal 4-6	9.2.2.b
	Akurgal 7	9.2.3
	Akurgal 7	9.4.13
120ff.	E'annatum 1	9.3.1
	E'annatum 2	9.3.5
	E'annatum 3-4	9.3.6
	E'annatum 5, 8	9.3.7
	E'annatum 6-7	9.3.2
	E'annatum 11	9.3.8
	E'annatum 22	9.3.9
	E'annatum 60	9.3.4
	E'annatum 62	9.3.11
	E'annatum 63	9.3.3
	E'annatum 64	9.3.12
	E'annatum 64	9.3.13
	E'annatum 67	9.3.14
	E'annatum 69	9.3.10
182ff.	Enanatum I 1	9.4.1
	Enanatum I 2	9.4.3
	Enanatum I 9	9.4.8
	Enanatum I 10	9.4.14
	Enanatum I 16	9.4.6
	Enanatum I 17	9.4.7
	Enanatum I 18	9.4.4
	Enanatum I 19	9.4.19
	Enanatum I 20	9.4.10
	Enanatum I 21	9.4.11
	Enanatum I 22	9.4.12
	Enanatum I 26	9.4.15
	Enanatum I 28	9.4.17
	Enanatum I 29	9.4.2
	Enanatum I 30	9.4.18
	Enanatum I 32	9.4.20
	Enanatum I 33	9.4.9
	Enanatum I 34	9.4.16
	Enanatum I 35	9.4.5
211ff.	Entemena 1	9.5.17
	Entemena 2	9.5. 3
	Entemena 2	9.5.13
	Entemena 8	9.5.12
	Entemena 16	9.5.27
	Entemena 17	9.5.9
	Entemena 18	9.5.10
	Entemena 22	9.5.14
	Entemena 23	9.5.16
	Entemena 24	9.5.21
	Entemena 25	9.5.22
	Entemena 26	9.5.23
	Entemena 27	9.5.20
	Entemena 28-29, 31	9.5.1
	Entemena 32	9.5.18
	Entemena 33	9.5.25
	Entemena 34	9.5.7
	Entemena 35	9.5.26
	Entemena 36	9.5.11
	Entemena 41	9.5.2
	Entemena 42	9.5.15

	Entemena 43	9.5.8
	Entemena 44	9.5.19
	Entemena 74	9.5.5
	Entemena 76	9.5.28
	Entemena 78	9.5.29
	Entemena 79	9.5.4
	Entemena 80	9.5.6
	Entemena 96	9.5.24
273	Enannatum II 1	9.6.1
275	Enentarzi 1	9.7.1
276	Lugalanda 1-14	9.8.1
	Lugalanda 15	9.8.2
288ff.	Uruʾinimgina 1	9.9.2
	Uruʾinimgina 4-5	9.9.1
	Uruʾinimgina 6	9.9.3
	Uruʾinimgina 7	9.9.8
	Uruʾimingina 8	9.9.10
	Uruʾinimgina 10	9.9.6
	Uruʾinimgina 11	9.9.7
	Uruʾimingina 12	9.9.9
	Uruʾimingina 13	9.9.11
	Uruʾinimgina 14	9.9.4
	Uruʾinimgina 16	9.9.5
	Uruʾimingina 34	9.9.14a
	Uruʾimingina 35	9.9.14b
	Uruʾimingina 36-37	9.9.14c
	Uruʾimingina 38	9.9.14d
	Uruʾimingina 39	9.9.14e
	Uruʾimingina 40	9.9.14f
	Uruʾimingina 41	9.9.14g
	Uruʾimingina 42	9.9.14h
	Uruʾimingina 43	9.9.14i
	Uruʾimingina 44	9.9.14j
	Uruʾimingina 45	9.9.14k
	Uruʾimingina 46	9.9.14l
	Uruʾimingina 47	9.9.14m
	Uruʾimingina 48	9.9.14n
	Uruʾimingina 49	9.9.14o
	Uruʾimingina 50	9.9.14p
	Uruʾimingina 51	9.9.14q
	Uruʾimingina 52	9.9.14r
	Uruʾimingina 53	9.9.14s
	Uruʾimingina 54-55	9.9.14t
	Uruʾimingina 56	9.9.14u
	Uruʾimingina 57	9.9.14v
	Uruʾimingina 58	9.9.13
	Uruʾimingina 59	9.9.12
	Uruʾimingina 61	9.9.14w
363f	AnLag. 11	9.3.16
364	AnLag. 12	5.1.1

Steible, ASBW 2

P.	No.	El
187	Medurba 1	1.2.1
187–88	Barahe-NI-du 1	1.3.2001
189–90	Eʾiginimpaʾe 1	1.7.2
190–91	Eʾiginimpaʾe 2	1.7.1
191	Lugaldalu 1	1.4.1
191–92	Lumma 1	1.5.1
192–3	Lumma 2	1.5.2
197	AnAdab 9	1.3.1
199–200	AnAgr. 2	7.40.1
213	Mebarasi 1	7.22.1
	Mebarasi 2	7.22.2
214–15	Uḫub 1	7.42.1
215–16	Mesalim 1	8.1.1
216–217	Mesalim 2	8.1.2
217	Mesalim 3	8.1.3
218	Ennaʾil A1	8.3.1
218–20	Lugal-TAR-si 1	14.13.1
220	Lugal-UD 1	7.41.1
220–21	Urzage 1	14.16.1
221–22	AnKiš 1	8.2.1
223	Abzukidu 1	11.3.1
223–24	Abzukidu 2	11.3.2
224	Nammaḫ 1	11.1.1
225–26	Urenlil 1	11.2.1
226	Urenlil 2	11.2.2
265–66	Enlilpabilgagi 1	12.1.1
266	Aka 1	12.2.1
267	Urluma 1	12.4.1
267–68	Il 1	12.5.1
268–69	Giššakidu 1	12.6.1
269–70	Eʾabzu 1	12.3.1
271–72	Meskalamdu 1	13.7.1
272–73	Mesannepada 1	13.5.1
273	Aʾannepada 1	13.6.1
273–74	Aʾannepada 2	13.6.3
274–75	Aʾannepada 3	13.6.4
275–76	Aʾannepada 4	13.6.5
276	Aʾannepada 5	13.6.6
276–77	Aʾannepada 6	13.6.2
277–78	Meskiʾagnun 1	13.8.1
278	Elili 1	13.9.1
279	Urpabilsaga 1	13.2.1
283	AnUr 10	14.21.1
285–86	AnUr 12	10.1.3
286	AnUr 13	10.1.2
293–95	Enšakušana 1	14.17.1
295	Enšakušana 2	14.17.2
296–97	Enšakušana 4	14.17.4
297–98	Enšakušana 5	14.17.3
298–99	Lugalkiginnedudu 1	14.14.3a
299-301	Lugalkiginnedudu 2	14.14.1
301–2	Lugalkiginnedudu 3	14.14.6
302–3	Lugalkiginnedudu 4	14.14.2
304	Lugalkiginnedudu 6	14.14.5
305	Lugalkiginnedudu 7	14.14.4
305–7	Lugalkisalsi 1	14.15.1
307–8	Lugalkisalsi 2	14.15.4
308–309	Lugalkisalsi 3	14.15.3
310–25	Lugalzagesi 1	14.20.1
325-36	Lugalzagesi 2	12.6.2
336–37	Lugalzagesi 3	14.20.2
337	Lugal-TAR 1	9.10.2

Thureau-Dangin, SAK

P.	No.	EI
2ff.	Ur-ninâ a	9.1.17
	Ur-ninâ b	9.1.11
	Ur-ninâ c	9.1.9
	Ur-ninâ d	9.1.12
	Ur-ninâ e	9.1.10
	Ur-ninâ f	9.1.20
	Ur-ninâ g	9.1.8
	Ur-ninâ h	9.1.32
	Ur-ninâ i	9.1.7
	Ur-ninâ k	9.1.21
	Ur-ninâ l	9.1.22
	Ur-ninâ m	9.1.2
	Ur-ninâ n	9.1.3
	Ur-ninâ o	9.1.4
	Ur-ninâ p	9.1.27
10ff.	E-an-na-tum a	9.3.1
	E-an-na-tum b	9.3.5
	E-an-na-tum c	9.3.6
	E-an-na-tum d	9.3.7
	E-an-na-tum f	9.3.2
	E-an-na-tum g	9.3.4
	E-an-na-tum h	9.3.8
	E-an-na-tum i	9.3.9
	E-an-na-tum k	9.3.11
28ff.	En-an-na-tum I a	9.4.4
	En-an-na-tum I b	9.4.3
	En-an-na-tum I c	9.4.19
30ff.	En-te-me-na a	9.5.12
	En-te-me-na b	9.5.10
	En-te-me-na c	9.5.20
	En-te-me-na d	9.5.14
	En-te-me-na e	9.5.9
	En-te-me-na f	9.5.16
	En-te-me-na g	9.5.18
	En-te-me-na h	9.5.7
	En-te-me-na i	9.5.28
	En-te-me-na k	9.5.26
	En-te-me-na l	9.5.11
	En-te-me-na n	9.5.1
40ff.	En-an-na-tum II Türanglestein	9.6.1
42ff.	Uru-ki-gi-na a	9.9.8
	Uru-ki-gi-na b	9.9.6
	Uru-ki-gi-na c	9.9.7
	Uru-ki-gi-na g	9.9.2
	Uru-ki-gi-na h	9.9.1
	Uru-ki-gi-na i	9.9.3
	Uru-ki-gi-na k	9.9.5
150f.	E-abzu	12.3.1
150f.	Ur-LUM-ma	12.4.1
152f.	E-sar	1.4.1
152f.	Unbekannt a	14.17.1
152f.	Unbekannt b	14.17.1
152f.	Unbekannt c	14.17.1
152f.	Unbekannt d	14.17.1
152ff.	Lugal-zag-ge-si	14.20.1
156f.	Lugal-kigubnidudu a	14.14.3
	Lugal-kigubnidudu b	14.14.1
	Lugal-kigubnidudu c	14.15.1
	Lugal-kigubnidudu d	14.15.1
156f.	En-ša(g)-kuš-an-na a	14.17.1
	En-ša(g)-kuš-an-na b	14.17.2
158f.	Nippur 6 vase E	11.2.1
	Nippur 7 vase F	11.2.2
160f.	U-tug	7.42.1
160f.	U-tug	15.1.1
160f.	Me-salim	8.1.1
160f.	Ur-zag-ge	14.16.1
160f.	Lugal-TAR-si	14.13.1
170f.	[...]-šamaš	10.7.1

www.ingramcontent.com/pod-product-compliance
Lightning Source LLC
Chambersburg PA
CBHW080751200725
29844CB00005B/82

9781487545130